SOCIAL FACTS
Introductory Readings

James L. Price

ASSOCIATE PROFESSOR OF SOCIOLOGY / THE UNIVERSITY OF IOWA

The Macmillan Company
Collier-Macmillan Limited, London

To My Mother and Father

Library of Congress catalog card number: 69–10181

THE MACMILLAN COMPANY
COLLIER-MACMILLAN CANADA, LTD., TORONTO, ONTARIO

Printed in the United States of America

PREFACE

STATEMENT OF PURPOSE

During eleven years of teaching introductory sociology courses, one of my biggest difficulties has been finding a convenient source of factual information[1] that is at the same time comprehensive within a society, comparative between societies, and historical. This reader is intended to help solve the problem. The better introductory sociology textbooks provide systematic treatment of the basic sociological concepts and propositions;[2] however, most of the factual information in these textbooks refers to the contemporary United States. The better introductory sociology anthologies also emphasize basic sociological concepts and propositions: the factual information in the anthologies is mostly found in case studies. Although case studies are valuable, they are inherently noncomprehensive, noncomparative, and nonhistorical.[3]

The lack of comprehensive, comparative, and historical factual information in introductory sociology textbooks and anthologies obscures the real strength and weaknesses of contemporary sociology. Sociology lacks a common set of concepts,[4] has very few verified propositions, and is totally devoid of systematically tested theory.[5] However, sociology has a large amount of comprehensive, comparative, and historical factual information. The feature of contemporary sociology that is perhaps its point of greatest strength—its relatively solid factual base—is underrepresented in introductory sociology textbooks and anthologies, whereas the features of relative weakness—its concepts, propositions, and theory—are overrepresented.

The introductory sociology textbooks and anthologies may not contain the type of factual information that this anthology seeks to supply, because the

[1] Factual information will be defined and illustrated in the section "A Case for Social Facts."

[2] The following sources contain discussions of concepts and propositions: Hans L. Zetterberg, *On Theory and Verification in Sociology* (Totowa, N.J.: The Bedminster Press, 1965), pp. 9–86; Talcott Parsons, *The Structure of Social Action* (New York: The Free Press, 1949), pp. 3–42; Robert K. Merton, *Social Theory and Social Structure* (New York: The Free Press, 1957), pp. 85–101; and George C. Homans, "Contemporary Theory in Sociology," in Robert E. L. Faris (ed.), *Handbook of Modern Sociology* (Chicago: Rand McNally and Company, 1964), pp. 951–977.

[3] The comments about the better introductory sociology textbooks and anthologies are also applicable to the Bobbs-Merrill reprint series and the introductory sociology paperbacks published by Prentice-Hall and Random House.

[4] Sociology is not, of course, devoid of conceptual agreement. For a discussion of some areas of agreement, see Alex Inkeles, *What Is Sociology?* (Englewood Cliffs, N.J.: Prentice-Hall, Inc., 1964), p. 12.

[5] This is, of course, using *theory* in its most rigorous sense, as a set of interrelated propositions. Discussions of theory are listed in note 2.

purpose of introductory sociology courses is generally to acquaint the student with the *sociological perspective,* and this perspective is perhaps best taught by emphasizing concepts and propositions. The editor does not disagree with an emphasis on concepts and propositions for introductory sociology courses; this is clearly the most efficient means to teach the sociological perspective, and is the means that the editor has always used. If the teacher uses this means, then, in a sense any facts will serve an illustrative purpose. However, when factual information is used in introductory sociology courses to illustrate the concepts and propositions, the factual information should be comprehensive, comparative, and historical, because it is this type of information that must ultimately be collected if there is ever to be a "science of society" rather than a "science of selected segments of the United States in the midtwentieth century." Constant use of this type of factual information shows the students and reminds the teachers of the preferred type of information.

This anthology is not intended to de-emphasize the importance of concepts and propositions in introductory sociology courses; rather it is intended to provide the teacher with the best possible types of factual information with which to illustrate the concepts and propositions. Teachers who use the anthology will probably want to use it as a supplement to a textbook which emphasizes basic concepts and propositions.

A CASE FOR SOCIAL FACTS

This anthology primarily contains factual information, yet the editor knows that introductory sociology students are not particularly enthusiastic about this type of information. Before presenting a case for social facts, the term will be defined and illustrated.

Facts are empirically verifiable statements about phenomena.[6] For example, it is a fact that the suicide rate in the United States in 1962 was 10.8 per 100,000 population.[7] The term *social fact* comes from Émile Durkheim (1858–1917), a French sociologist who is well known for his description and explanation of suicide rates.[8] As Durkheim, this anthology views social facts to be empirically verifiable statements about group phenomena.[9] Because sociologists study group phenomena, social facts are the kind of facts that are of special interest to them.

Social facts—and this is the first argument—cannot be avoided because they are necessary to *understand* the basic concepts and propositions that are

---

[6] Parsons, *op. cit.,* pp. 41–42.

[7] Jack Gibbs, "Suicide," in Robert K. Merton and Robert A. Nisbet (eds.), *Contemporary Social Problems* (New York: Harcourt, Brace, & World, Inc., 1966), p. 297.

[8] Social facts are discussed in Émile Durkheim, *The Rules of Sociological Method,* trans. Sarah A. Solovay and John H. Mueller (New York: The Free Press, 1938). Suicide is described and explained in Émile Durkheim, *Suicide,* trans. John A. Spaulding and George Simpson (New York: The Free Press, 1951).

[9] This is Durkheim's meaning of social fact, not his exact definition.

emphasized in introductory sociology courses. It is impossible, for example, for a teacher to get across to students the concept of "class" without at some point referring to a specific class, and once specific classes are referred to, the teacher has begun to make factual statements. If social facts cannot be avoided, and this seems to be the case, then the question becomes one of selecting which facts to use for illustrative purposes.

The type of factual information that is most helpful for introductory sociology students—and this is the second argument—is what might be termed the "bench-mark" type. Bench-mark factual information refers to very comprehensive types of data and is helpful because it facilitates the *interpretation* of large amounts of commonly encountered factual information. Consider, for example, the results of a study of religious groups in New York City.[10] This study found the following distribution among the three major religious groups: Roman Catholics, 44 per cent; Protestants, 22 per cent; and Jews, 28 per cent. How is the reader to interpret this factual information? Is there anything unusual about the distribution of the three major religious groups in New York City? The factual information in this study—and this is a commonly encountered type of factual information—can be interpreted if the reader has learned that the distribution of the three major religious groups in the United States is the following: Roman Catholics, 26 per cent; Protestants, 66 per cent; and Jews, 3 per cent.[11] In New York City, Roman Catholics and Jews are statistically overrepresented—New York City Roman Catholics, 44 per cent, and United States Roman Catholics, 26 per cent; New York City Jews, 28 per cent, and United States Jews, 3 per cent. New York City Protestants, on the other hand, are statistically underrepresented—New York City Protestants, 22 per cent, United States Protestants, 66 per cent. The factual information about the distribution of the three religious groups *in the United States* is a bench-mark type of factual information, and is the type which should be emphasized in introductory sociology courses.[12]

OUTLINE OF THE ANTHOLOGY

The outline of the anthology reflects its emphasis on factual information in four ways.

First, the anthology excludes some of the traditional units for classifying sociological information. There are four parts of the anthology: Part I, "The Individual and the Group"; Part II, "The Social Structure of the Group"; Part III, "Types of Groups"; and Part IV, "Population and Ecology." The

---

[10] Seymour M. Lipset, Martin A. Trow, and James A. Coleman, *Union Democracy* (New York: The Free Press, 1956), p. 114.

[11] Donald J. Bogue, *The Population of the United States* (New York: The Free Press, 1959), p. 689.

[12] Factual generalizations may also serve as bench-marks. An example is the statement that members of white-collar occupations vote Republican relatively more often than members of blue-collar occupations. For a discussion of factual generalizations, see Merton, *op. cit.*, pp. 95–96. Merton refers, not to *factual* generalizations, but to *empirical* generalizations.

exact wording will vary, but units of classification similar in meaning to these four will be found in most introductory sociology textbooks and anthologies. Two traditional units are not included in this anthology:"The Nature of Sociology" and "Social Change." The information which would be discussed under "The Nature of Sociology"—or some other similar heading—is primarily conceptual, because it generally defines science and indicates why sociology should be viewed as a science. This type of conceptual analysis is inappropriate in an anthology which emphasizes factual information; the type of textbook that this anthology is intended to supplement will discuss the nature of sociology. There is no unit on social change because the historical information presented throughout the anthology reports information about this subject. Any textbook will contain conceptual and propositional material about the nature, types, determinants, and consequences of social change.

The exclusion of some of the traditional units for classifying sociological information is also apparent in the sections within each of the four parts of the anthology. Part II, "The Social Structure of the Group," for example, contains six traditional units: "Economy," "Polity," "Kinship," "Religion," "Education," and "Stratification." However, neither Part II nor any of the other three parts has a section on social control. There is no section on social control because some of the material that is traditionally discussed under this heading is found in Part II under four sections: "Kinship," "Religion," "Education," and "Stratification." The standard introductory textbook will, of course, contain conceptual and propositional material about the nature, types, and determinants of social control.

Second, the introductions found in each part primarily summarize the factual information contained in the selections, and indicate its significance for basic sociological concepts and propositions. The introductions do not contain expositions of the basic concepts and propositions; these will be contained in the type of textbook that the anthology is designed to supplement.

Third, the Additional Readings at the end of the parts or the sections within the parts provide further readings for interested individuals. These readings are some of the many excellent selections of factual information which could not be included in the anthology.

Fourth, "A Note for Researchers," immediately following the Preface, contains the editor's suggestions about some of the topics which require factual information. No attempt has been made to make the list of topics exhaustive; the list merely contains a few topics about which the editor unsuccessfully sought to locate information.

ACKNOWLEDGMENTS

Anyone who compiles an anthology for a discipline like sociology must rely on the assistance of his colleagues, because the discipline is so complex that no single individual can master it completely. My colleagues at the University of Iowa have been extremely generous in the assistance they have given me, and it is to them that I owe the deepest debt of gratitude. I have especially benefited from the assistance of Ira Reiss, John Stratton, and Bob Terry.

Ted Jitodai, Benton Johnson, and Hans Zetterberg graciously consented to read the entire manuscript and I profited immensely from the valuable suggestions that they made. The flaws which remain in the anthology are not there because of any lack of effort by these sociologists.

Very few sociologists share my enthusiasm for the codification of social facts. One notable exception is the eminent theorist Hans Zetterberg, by whose example I have been very much encouraged. The sociological almanac which he coedited with Murray Gendell has been especially helpful in teaching introductory sociological courses.[13]

When I began work on this anthology I asked several colleagues at other universities for suggestions. I received very helpful suggestions from Robert Blumstock, Roy Bowles, Douglas Card, Kenneth Cunningham, Ted Jitodai, Benton Johnson, John Scanzoni, Donald Spence, Lee Spray, and Curt Tausky.

A Macmillan Company grant made it possible for me to hire a research assistant, Renée Hoffman. Her intelligent and diligent labor greatly speeded the compilation of the anthology.

J. L. P.

---

[13] Murray Gendell and Hans L. Zetterberg, *A Sociological Almanac for the United States* (New York: The Bedminster Press, 1961). The following publication by one of Zetterberg's students has also been helpful: Murray Hausknecht, *The Joiners* (New York: The Bedminster Press, 1962).

A NOTE FOR RESEARCHERS

This note, which indicates areas that seem to require factual information, could be made very brief by simply stating that the scope of all the selections should be expanded. Case studies within a country should be broadened to random samples; comparative studies between two countries should be broadened to include the world; historical studies of recent periods should be broadened to cover all recorded history. However, such a broad observation produces little specific information for researchers. Consequently, this note will indicate specific types of information that were sought but were unavailable or could not be located.

PART I, THE INDIVIDUAL AND THE GROUP

Role. The editor could not locate direct, systematic data about sex roles for adolescents, adults, and older persons. Barry, Bacon, and Child, in "A Cross-Cultural Survey of Some Sex Differences in Socialization," focus on "infancy" and "childhood." Parsons argues that the adult male role is anchored in the occupational world, whereas the adult female role is anchored in the family.[1] However, Parsons' data, although systematic, do not consist of direct measurement of sex role content. This lack of data is surprising in view of the long tradition of research on sex differences.

Two types of information about "minorities" ("racial and ethnic relations") could not be found: first, information about "discrimination" toward Jews in the United States; and second, information about "prejudice" and discrimination toward Jews in Europe. The selection by Stember, "Attitudes Toward Jews," contains information only about prejudice toward Jews in the United States. There is some data about discrimination toward Jews—an example is Baltzell's *The Protestant Establishment*.[2] However, this information is not as systematic as Stember's material. The European data should be especially interesting, because of the long history of anti-Semitism in Europe.

Culture. Systematic data about upper-class norms could not be located. The selections by Cohen, "The Middle-Class Norms," and Miller-Riessman, "The Working-Class Norms," although not as firmly based as preferred— especially the selection by Cohen—at least contain systematic data about two important classes. There are some good studies of upper-class life from which

[1] Talcott Parsons, "The American Family: Its Relations to Personality and to the Social Structure," in Talcott Parsons and Robert F. Bales (eds.), *Family, Socialization and Interaction Process* (New York: The Free Press, 1955), pp. 3–34.
[2] E. Digby Baltzell, *The Protestant Establishment* (New York: Random House, 1964).

information about norms can be abstracted—again the work of Baltzell comes most readily to mind[3]—but such studies, although quite helpful, are no substitute for systematic data.

The "information explosion" has now taken its place alongside the "population explosion" as a topic of major importance to scientists and nonscientists. There is an abundance of compact and systematic studies documenting the "population explosion"; however, comparable studies could not be located to document the "information explosion." A massive amount of data is contained in Machlup's work; however, this material is too long for an anthology.[4] The work of Price comes the nearest to supplying the type of required information.[5] However, Price's focus is too narrow, because he mostly presents information about the natural sciences.

Deviant Behavior. It is now a common practice to include topics such as the following within the area of deviant behavior: delinquency, crime, drug addiction, alcoholism, mental disorders, suicide, family disintegration, discrimination, and prejudice.[6] Selections could be found for the separate types of deviant behavior, such as Kohn's "On the Social Epidemiology of Schizophrenia" and Sykes' "The Characteristics of Criminals," but no selection could be found which encompasses all the specific types of deviant behavior, and which might have been entitled "On the Social Epidemiology of Deviant Behavior."

PART II, THE SOCIAL STRUCTURE OF THE GROUP

Economy. The selection by Folger and Nam, "Trends in Education in Relation to the Occupational Structure," presents information about the occupational structure in the United States for 1900 and 1960. However, no selection could be found which presented information encompassing the total history of the United States. Profound changes occurred in the United States before 1900—the most important example is the industrial growth between 1860 and 1900—and it would be very helpful to have information about the earlier period to compare with the information about the later period.

Blauner's selection, "Work Satisfaction in Modern Society," summarizes information about work "orientation" rather than work "behavior." The editor could not find systematic data about such behavioral variables as rates of turnover and absenteeism. For example, no studies could be found which indicated average rates of turnover and absenteeism for the typical organization

---

[3] Baltzell, *op. cit.*; and E. Digby Baltzell, *Philadelphia Gentleman* (New York: The Free Press, 1958).

[4] Fritz Machlup, *The Production and Distribution of Knowledge in the United States* (Princeton, N.J.: Princeton University Press, 1962).

[5] Derek J. de Solla Price, *Science Since Babylon* (New Haven, Conn.: Yale University Press, 1961), and Derek J. de Solla Price, *Little Science, Big Science* (New York: Columbia University Press, 1963).

[6] These topics came from Marshall B. Clinard, *Sociology of Deviant Behavior* (New York: Holt, Rinehart and Winston, Inc., 1963).

or for different kinds of organizations. This apparent gap in the data is surprising, because there is an immense literature about turnover and absenteeism.

Polity. Information about the distribution of democracy could not be located for areas other than the European and English-speaking nations and the Latin American nations, the two areas which Lipset treats in his "The Distribution of Democracy." There are democracies in areas which Lipset does not treat—such as Japan, the Philippine Islands, and India—and it would be helpful to have systematic data about the distribution of democracy in these areas.

Kinship. It is generally believed that individuals who marry are generally similar in terms of race, age, religion, ethnicity, and class. This hypothesized pattern—which is a highly probable factual generalization—is referred to as "marital endogamy." Hollingshead's classic paper "Cultural Factors in the Selection of Marriage Mates" is frequently cited to support the idea of marital endogamy.[7] Hollingshead's paper, however, only reports data about a single study of a single community—New Haven, Connecticut. There are other studies which contain relevant data, but the editor could not locate any single selection which summarized the existing literature.

Religion. The selection by Lazerwitz, "Some Factors Associated with Variations in Church Attendance," reported information which indicated a positive relationship between class and church attendance: the higher the class, the higher the rate of church attendance. However, neither Lazerwitz nor any of the other authors reported any information about class and religious "beliefs." The upper classes may be more religious than the lower classes when religiosity is measured by "practices" such as church attendance; however, the same pattern may not exist when religiosity is measured by beliefs.

Mass Media. Sociologists have only recently evidenced an interest in the mass media. The newness of the field may, therefore, account for the paucity of factual information. So little information could be located that the anthology has no section on the mass media.

PART III, TYPES OF GROUPS

Community. It is frequently pointed out that a disproportionate amount of deviant behavior is found in urban communities. However, some scholars have also pointed out that urban communities also contain a disproportionate amount of significant conformity, such as high degrees of achievement in business, the arts, sciences, and professions.[8] It is relatively easy to locate systematic factual information to support the point about deviant behavior in

[7] August B. Hollingshead, "Cultural Factors in the Selection of Marriage Mates," in Robert F. Winch and Robert McGinnis, *Marriage and the Family* (New York: Holt, Rinehart and Winston, 1953), pp. 399–412.

[8] An example is Robert K. Merton, "Anomie, Anomia, and Social Interaction: Contexts of Deviant Behavior," in Marshall B. Clinard (ed.), *Anomie and Deviant Behavior* (New York: The Free Press, 1964), pp. 222–223.

urban communities;[9] however, no corresponding information could be located to support the point about conformity.

Organization. The importance of large organizations for society is primarily documented with statistics based on economic organizations. An example of this emphasis is Means' "A Contemporary View of Industrial Concentration." There is, however, a sizable literature documenting the importance of large organizations in the areas of the polity and social control. However, the editor could not locate any selections which summarized this literature. What is needed is a single selection which indicates the importance of large size for economic, political, and control organizations.

The Berle and Means thesis—whose replication was reported by Larner in "Ownership and Control in the 200 Largest Nonfinancial Corporations, 1929 and 1963"—basically suggests that control in the large business corporation rests with the managers rather than with the boards of directors, who are supposed to represent the owners. An interesting question arises as to whether the same type of relationship which exists between the managers and the boards of directors in large business corporations also exists between managers and governing board members in other areas. (Boards of directors are usually viewed as one type of governing board; other examples are school boards, city councils, university regents, hospital trustees, and church elders.) There is an immense literature about the relationship between managers and governing boards, especially in the areas of government and schools, but factual information relating to this question has not been compactly summarized.

---

[9] Clinard, *Sociology of Deviant Behavior, op. cit.* This selection by Clinard was not used in the anthology because of the limitations of space.

CONTENTS

PART I *The Individual and the Group*

Introduction 2

ROLE

HERBERT BARRY III, MARGARET K. BACON, AND IRVIN L. CHILD, *A Cross-Cultural Survey of Some Sex Differences in Socialization* 5
CHARLES H. STEMBER, *Attitudes Toward Jews* 9
PAUL B. SHEATSLEY, *White Attitudes Toward the Negro* 17

CULTURE

ALBERT K. COHEN, *The Middle-Class Norms* 27
S. M. MILLER AND FRANK RIESSMAN, *The Working-Class Norms* 31

PERSONALITY FORMATION

THOMAS F. PETTIGREW, *Negro American Intelligence: A New Look at an Old Controversy* 42

DEVIANT BEHAVIOR

NEGLEY K. TEETERS AND DAVID MATZA, *The Extent of Delinquency in the United States* 56
GRESHAM M. SYKES, *The Characteristics of Criminals* 67
MELVIN L. KOHN, *On the Social Epidemiology of Schizophrenia* 78

Additional Readings 83

PART II *The Social Structure of the Group*

ECONOMY

Introduction 86
SURENDRA J. PATEL, *Rates of Industrial Growth in the Last Century, 1860-1958* 88
ABDELMEGID M. FARRAG, *The Occupational Structure of the Labour Force: Patterns and Trends in Selected Countries* 100

HAROLD L. WILENSKY, *Trends in the Amount of Time Worked*   114
ROBERT BLAUNER, *Work Satisfaction in Modern Society*   119
Additional Readings   125

POLITY

Introduction   126

SEYMOUR M. LIPSET, *The Distribution of Democracy*   128
SEYMOUR M. LIPSET, *Economic Development and Democracy*   130
LESTER W. MILBRAITH, *Political Participation as a Function of Social Position*   136
Additional Readings   153

KINSHIP

Introduction   154

IRA L. REISS, *The Universality of the Family*   156
ALEXANDER A. PLATERIS, *The National Divorce Trend*   169
GEORGE P. MURDOCK, *Family Stability in Non-European Cultures*   174
MARVIN B. SUSSMAN AND LEE BURCHINAL, *Kin Family Network: Unheralded Structure in Current Conceptualizations of Family Functioning*   181
FRANK F. FURSTENBERG, JR., *Industrialization and the American Family: A Look Backward*   189
Additional Readings   206

RELIGION

Introduction   207

DONALD J. BOGUE, *Religious Affiliation*   210
NORVAL D. GLENN AND RUTH HYLAND, *Religious Preference and Worldly Success: Some Evidence from National Surveys*   236
JEFFREY K. HADDEN, *Theological Belief and Political Ideology Among Protestant Clergy*   244
BERNARD LAZERWITZ, *Some Factors Associated with Variations in Church Attendance*   256
SEYMOUR M. LIPSET, *All-Pervasiveness, a Consistent Characteristic of American Religion*   266
Additional Readings   273

EDUCATION

Introduction   274

JOHN K. FOLGER AND CHARLES B. NAM, *Trends in Education in Relation to the Occupational Structure*   276

HERMAN P. MILLER, *Annual Income in Relation to Education*, 1939-1959   280

CHARLES H. STEMBER, *Education and Attitude Change*   287

DAVID E. LAVIN, *Demographic and Ecological Determinants of Academic Performance*   299

Additional Readings   308

STRATIFICATION

Introduction   310

HERMAN P. MILLER, *The Distribution of Income*   313

HERMAN P. MILLER, *Trends in the Distribution of Income*   321

ROBERT W. HODGE, PAUL M. SIEGEL, AND PETER H. ROSSI, *Occupational Prestige in the United States*, 1925-63   330

ALEX INKELES AND PETER H. ROSSI, *National Comparisons of Occupational Prestige*   338

URIE BRONFENBRENNER, *Socialization and Social Class Through Time and Space*   346

ROBERT R. ALFORD, *Class Voting in Anglo-American Countries*   370

WILLIAM J. GOODE, *A Cross-Cultural Analysis of Class Differentials in Divorce Rates*   375

ELTON F. JACKSON AND HARRY J. CROCKETT, JR., *Occupational Mobility in the United States: A Point Estimate and Trend Comparison*   384

BERNARD BARBER, *A Comparison of the Amount of Social Mobility in the Contemporary United States and Europe*   398

Additional Readings   404

PART III   *Types of Groups*

Introduction   406

COMMUNITY

PHILIP M. HAUSER, *The Growth of Metropolitan Areas in the United States*   409

KINGSLEY DAVIS, *The Urbanization of the World*   427

WILLIAM SPINRAD, *Power in Local Communities*   432

ORGANIZATION

GARDINER C. MEANS, *A Contemporary View of Industrial Concentration*   443

REINHARD BENDIX, *The Growth of Bureaucracy*   457

ROBERT J. LARNER, *Ownership and Control in the 200 Largest Nonfinancial Corporations, 1929 and 1963*   460

COLLECTIVE BEHAVIOR

MAURICE PINARD, *Poverty and Political Movements*   470

Additional Readings   477

PART IV   *Population and Ecology*

Introduction   480

POPULATION

PHILIP M. HAUSER, *Population Growth in the United States*   483
HAROLD F. DORN, *World Population Growth: An International Dilemma*   490
RONALD FREEDMAN, *American Studies of Family Planning*   502
HAROLD F. DORN, *Differential Mortality*   516

ECOLOGY

DONALD J. BOGUE, *Internal Migration and Residential Mobility*   520
KARL TAEUBER, *Trends in Negro Residential Segregation*   538

Additional Readings   543

PART I

The Individual and the Group

Introduction

Part I, "The Individual and the Group," contains four sections: "Role," "Culture," "Personality Formation," and "Deviant Behavior."

ROLE. Data about the "sex role" is often used to illustrate the concept of *role*.[1] In their survey of five aspects of *socialization* in 110 societies, "A Cross-cultural Survey of Some Sex Differences in Socialization," Barry, Bacon, and Child point out that sex role differentiation is unimportant in infancy but that in childhood girls are expected to be more nurturant, obedient, and responsible, whereas boys are expected to be more self-reliant and achievement-oriented. In short, the authors have indicated that there are no sex roles in infancy and have documented the content of sex roles in childhood.[2]

Role is usually distinguished from "stereotype." The selections by Stember, "Attitudes Toward Jews," and Sheatsley, "White Attitudes Toward the Negro," present information about two categories of persons who have long been the objects of stereotypes, Jews and Negroes. Stember's selection indicates that prejudice toward Jews has declined in the United States between the end of World War II and the early 1960's; Sheatsley's selection indicates that prejudice toward Negroes has declined in the United States between 1942 and 1963 (and probably 1966). The reader should remember that Stember and Sheatsley's information refers to "atti-

[1] Role is italicized because it is a basic sociological concept. Each basic concept is italicized the first time it is used. As previously indicated in the "Outline of the Anthology," the basic concepts will not be defined in the Introductions.

[2] There is no section on "Socialization" in Part I; however, if there were, the information summarized by Barry, Bacon, and Child could also be discussed under this type of section. The survey by Barry, Bacon, and Child is also relevant to the material on "Kinship" in Part II, "The Social Structure of the Group."

tudes" (prejudice) and not to "behavior" (discrimination). Prejudice toward Jews and Negroes may decline without a corresponding decline in discrimination; similarly, discrimination may decline without a corresponding decline in prejudice. In short, because they can vary independently, prejudice and discrimination must be distinguished. Prejudice may also assume very subtle forms; the reader is referred to Stember's selection on "Education and Attitude Change" in the section on "Education" in Part II, "The Social Structure of the Group," for a discussion of some of the subtle forms of prejudice.[3]

CULTURE. *Norms* are a frequently used example of *culture*. The selections by Cohen, "The Middle-Class Norms," and Miller and Riessman, "The Working-Class Norms," present information about two important sets of norms. Middle-class norms emphasize ambition, individual responsibility, achievement, worldly asceticism, rationality, personability, control of violence, wholesome recreation, and respect for property. On the other hand, working-class norms are more security-oriented, traditional, intense, person-centered, pragmatic, and excitement-oriented. A shorthand way to characterize the middle-class norms would be to state that they are universalistic, affectively neutral, achievement-oriented, diffuse, and self-oriented, whereas working-class norms are particularistic, affective, ascriptive, specific, and collectivity-oriented.[4] The norms which Cohen describes are most clearly exemplified by middle-class individuals; however, it should be noted that these norms are often exemplified by upper-class individuals and lower-class individuals. It should also be noted that not every middle-class individual embodies all the middle-class norms. The norms which Miller and Riessman describe—and this is their definition of the working-class—characterize the "regular members of the nonagricultural labor force in manual occupations." Miller and Riessman exclude irregular working people, whom they term the "lower class," from their definition of working-class.

PERSONALITY FORMATION. Sociology advances the proposition that the social environment is the major determinant of personality formation. The factual information cited to support this proposition commonly relates to performance on intelligence tests. The selection by Pettigrew, "Negro American Intelligence: A New Look at an Old Controversy," contains a statement of the proposition and factual information about the performance of Negroes on intelligence tests. The following quotation is typical: ". . . the overwhelming opinion of modern psychology concludes that *the mean differences* [on intelligence tests] often observed between Negro and white children are largely the result of *environmental, rather than genetic, factors.* (Emphasis supplied.) The material about "environmental and genetic factors" (sometimes "heredity" is substituted for "genetic") relates to the proposition, whereas the material about "the mean differences" which are observed on intelligence tests relates to the factual information. The editor, in keeping with the anthology's emphasis on factual information, preferred a selection which either did not present the proposition about personality formation or which clearly separated the proposition from the factual information. Such a selection, however, could not be located. The student should remember that Pettigrew reports both statements of propositions and statements of fact.[5]

---

[3] The selections by Stember and Sheatsley present information which is often discussed not in connection with role, but in connection with "minorities" (or, as it is often termed, "racial and ethnic relations").

[4] These shorthand ways to describe middle-class and working-class norms are Talcott Parsons' "pattern variables." For a good discussion of the pattern variables, see Harry M. Johnson, *Sociology* (New York: Harcourt, Brace & World, 1960), pp. 135–141.

[5] The selection by Pettigrew presents information which is often discussed not in connection with the determinants of personality formation, but in connection with "minorities" ("racial and ethnic relations").

DEVIANT BEHAVIOR. Juvenile delinquency and crime are commonly used examples of *deviant behavior*. The selections by Teeters and Matza, "The Extent of Delinquency in the United States," and Sykes, "The Characteristics of Criminals," present factual information about, respectively, juvenile delinquency and crime. Teeters and Matza believe that although the official statistics they use (Juvenile Court cases and the Uniform Crime Reports) perhaps overstate the increase in the delinquency rates, there has, nevertheless, been some real increase between 1940 and 1957. Teeters' and Matza's position is somewhere between the "alarmists," who are greatly disturbed by the "rising tide" of delinquency, and the "skeptics," who are not ready to take seriously the increase in delinquency indicated by the official statistics.

Sykes' selection indicates that males, younger persons, Negroes, and lower-class individuals have higher rates of crime than females, older persons, whites, and higher-class individuals. Sykes also believes that nobody has ever been able to show convincingly that the criminal is mentally any less normal than the rest of the population. Like the preceding selection by Pettigrew, the selection by Sykes contains both factual information and propositions. One of Sykes' propositions is contained in his discussion of crime and race: "The idea that skin color, the shape of the head, the structure of the nose, or a similar racial trait is a cause of differences in behavior has been thoroughly discredited. Instead, the more promising line of research appears to be *the social position* of whites and Negroes and the consequent differences in the *sociocultural environment*." (Emphasis supplied.) However, like Pettigrew, Sykes is clearly aware of the difference between factual information and propositions; so the reader should not have too much difficulty picking out the factual information from Sykes' selection.

Crime and juvenile delinquency are the most commonly used examples of deviant behavior. Less often used examples are mental illness, drug addiction, alcoholism, suicide, divorce, and discrimination.[6] The selection by Kohn, "On the Social Epidemiology of Schizophrenia," summarizes factual information about the most prevalent type of mental illness, schizophrenia.[7] Kohn's summary of the literature indicates that, for the larger cities, the rates of schizophrenia are the highest in the central areas of the city and in the lowest-prestige occupations.

[6] See, for example, Marshall B. Clinard, *Sociology of Deviant Behavior* (New York: Holt, Rinehart & Winston, Inc., 1963).

[7] Kohn uses "epidemiology" as a synonym for "distribution."

A Cross-cultural Survey of Some Sex Differences in Socialization[1]

HERBERT BARRY III, MARGARET K. BACON, AND IRVIN L. CHILD

In our society, certain differences may be observed between the typical person-ality characteristics of the two sexes. These sex differences in personality are generally believed to result in part from differences in the way boys and girls are reared. To the extent that personality differences between the sexes are thus of cultural rather than biological origin, they seem potentially suceptible to change. But how readily susceptible to change? In the differential rearing of the sexes does our society make an arbitrary imposition on an infinitely plastic biological base, or is this cultural imposition found uniformly in all societies as an adjustment to the real biological differences between the sexes? This paper reports one attempt to deal with this problem.

DATA AND PROCEDURES

The data used were ethnographic reports, available in the anthropological literature, about socialization practices of various cultures. One hundred and ten cultures, mostly nonliterate, were studied. They were selected primarily in terms of the existence of adequate ethnographic reports of socialization prac-tices and secondarily so as to obtain a wide and reasonably balanced geographical distribution. Various aspects of socialization of infants and children were rated on a 7-point scale by two judges (Mrs. Bacon and Mr. Barry). Where the ethnographic reports permitted, separate ratings were made for the socialization of boys and girls. Each rating was indicated as either confident or doubtful; with still greater uncertainty, or with complete lack of evidence, the particular rating was of course not made at all. We shall restrict the report of sex difference ratings to cases in which both judges made a confident rating. Also omitted is the one instance where the two judges reported a sex difference in opposite

Reprinted from the *Journal of Abnormal and Social Psychology*, **55** (November, 1957), pp. 327–332, by permission of the authors and the publisher.

[1] This research is part of a project for which financial support was provided by the Social Science Research Council and the Ford Foundation. We are greatly indebted to G. P. Murdock for supplying us with certain data, as indicated below, and to him and Thomas W. Maretzki for suggestions that have been used in this paper.

directions, as it demonstrates only unreliability of judgement. The number of cultures that meet these criteria is much smaller than the total of 110; for the several variables to be considered, the number varies from 31 to 84.

The aspects of socialization on which ratings were made included:

1. Several criteria of attention and indulgence toward infants.

2. Strength of socialization from age 4 or 5 years until shortly before puberty, with respect to five systems of behavior; strength of socialization was defined as the combination of positive pressure (rewards for the behavior) plus negative pressure (punishments for lack of behavior). The variables were:

(*a*) Responsibility or dutifulness training. (The data were such that training in the performance of chores in the productive or domestic economy was necessarily the principal source of information here; however, training in the performance of other duties was also taken into account when information was available.)

(*b*) Nurturance training, i.e., training the child to be nurturant or helpful toward younger siblings and other dependent people.

(*c*) Obedience training.

(*d*) Self-reliance training.

(*e*) Achievement training, i.e., training the child to orient his behavior toward standards of excellence in performance, and to seek to achieve as excellent a performance as possible.

Where the term "no sex difference" is used here, it may mean any of three things: (*a*) the judge found separate evidence about the training of boys and girls on this particular variable, and judged it to be identical; (*b*) the judge found a difference between the training of boys and girls, but not great enough for the sexes to be rated a whole point apart on a 7-point scale; (*c*) the judge found evidence only about the training of "children" on this variable, the ethnographer not reporting separately about boys and girls.

SEX DIFFERENCES IN SOCIALIZATION

On the various aspects of attention and indulgence toward infants, the judges almost always agreed in finding no sex difference. Out of 96 cultures for which the ratings included the infancy period, 88 (92%) were rated with no sex difference by either judge for any of those variables. This result is consistent with the point sometimes made by anthropologists that "baby" generally is a single status undifferentiated by sex, even though "boy" and "girl" are distinct statuses.

On the variables of childhood socialization, on the other hand, a rating of no sex difference by both judges was much less common. This finding of no sex difference varied in frequency from 10% of the cultures for the achievement variable up to 62% of the cultures for the obedience variable, as shown in the last column of Table I. Where a sex difference is reported, by either one or both judges, the difference tends strongly to be in a particular direction, as shown in the earlier columns of the same table. Pressure toward nurturance,

TABLE I. RATINGS OF CULTURES FOR SEX DIFFERENCES ON FIVE VARIABLES OF CHILDHOOD
SOCIALIZATION PRESSURE

Variable	Number of Cultures	Both Judges Agree in Rating the Variable Higher in		One Judge Rates No Difference, One Rates the Variable Higher in		Percentage of Cultures with Evidence of Sex Difference in Direction of		
		Girls	Boys	Girls	Boys	Girls	Boys	Neither
Nurturance	33	17	0	10	0	82%	0%	18%
Obedience	69	6	0	18	2	35%	3%	62%
Responsibility	84	25	2	26	7	61%	11%	28%
Achievement	31	0	17	1	10	3%	87%	10%
Self-reliance	82	0	64	0	6	0%	85%	15%

obedience, and responsibility is most often stronger for girls, whereas pressure toward achievement and self-reliance is most often stronger for boys.

For nuturance and for self-reliance, all the sex differences are in the same direction. For achievement there is only one exception to the usual direction of difference, and for obedience only two; but for responsibility there are nine. What do these exceptions mean? We have re-examined all these cases. In most of them, only one judge had rated the sexes as differently treated (sometimes one judge, sometimes the other), and in the majority of these cases both judges were now inclined to agree that there was no convincing evidence of a real difference. There were exceptions, however, especially in cases where a more formal or systematic training of boys seemed to imply greater pressure on them toward responsibility. The most convincing cases were the Masai and Swazi, where both judges had originally agreed in rating responsibility pressures greater in boys than in girls. In comparing the five aspects of socialization we may conclude that responsibility shows by far the strongest evidence of real variation in the direction of sex difference, and obedience much the most frequently shows evidence of no sex difference at all.

In subsequent discussion we shall be assuming that the obtained sex differences in the socialization ratings reflect true sex differences in the cultural practices. We should consider here, two other possible sources of these rated differences.

1. The ethnographers could have been biased in favor of seeing the same pattern of sex differences as in our culture. However, most anthropologists readily perceive and eagerly report novel and startling cultural features, so we may expect them to have reported unusual sex differences where they existed. The distinction between matrilineal and patrilineal, and between matrilocal and patrilocal cultures, given prominence in many ethnographic reports, shows an awareness of possible variations in the significance of sex differences from culture to culture.

2. The two judges could have expected to find in other cultures the sex roles which are familiar in our culture and inferred them from the material on the cultures. However, we have reported only confident ratings, and such a bias seems less likely here than for doubtful ratings. It might be argued, moreover, that bias has more opportunity in the cases ambiguous enough so that only one judge reported a sex difference, and less opportunity in the cases where

the evidence is so clear that both judges agree. Yet in general, as may be seen in Table I, the deviant cases are somewhat more frequent among the cultures where only one judge reported a sex difference.

The observed differences in the socialization of boys and girls are consistent with certain universal tendencies in the differentiation of adult sex role. In the economic sphere, men are more frequently allotted tasks that involve leaving home and engaging in activities where a high level of skill yields important returns; hunting is a prime example. Emphasis on training in self-reliance and achievement for boys would function as preparation for such an economic role. Women, on the other hand, are more frequently allotted tasks at or near home that minister most immediately to the needs of others (such as cooking and water carrying); these activities have a nurturant character, and in their pursuit a responsible carrying out of established routines is likely to be more important than the development of an especially high order of skill. Thus training in nurturance, responsibility, and, less clearly, obedience, may contribute to preparation for this economic role. These consistencies with adult role go beyond the economic sphere, of course. Participation in warfare, as a male prerogative, calls for self-reliance and a high order of skill where survival or death is the immediate issue. The childbearing which is biologically assigned to women, and the child care which is socially assigned primarily to them, lead to nurturant behavior and often call for a more continuous responsibility than do the tasks carried out by men. Most of these distinctions in adult role are not inevitable, but the biological differences between the sexes strongly predispose the distinction of role, if made, to be in a uniform direction.[2]

The relevant biological sex differences are conspicuous in adulthood but generally not in childhood. If each generation were left entirely to its own devices, therefore, without even an older generation to copy, sex differences in role would presumably be almost absent in childhood and would have to be developed after puberty at the expense of considerable relearning on the part of one or both sexes. Hence, a pattern of child training which foreshadows adult differences can serve the useful function of minimizing what Benedict termed "discontinuities in cultural conditioning".

The differences in socialization between the sexes in our society, then, are no arbitrary custom of our society, but a very widespread adaptation of culture to the biological substratum of human life . . . .

References

MEAD, MARGARET. *Male and female.* (New York: Morrow, 1949).
MURDOCK, G. P. Comparative data on the division of labor by sex. *Social Forces,* 1937, 15, 551–553.
SCHEINFELD, A. *Women and men.* (New York: Harcourt, Brace, 1944).

[2] For data and interpretations supporting various arguments of this paragraph, see Mead, Murdock, and Scheinfeld.

"Attitudes Toward Jews"

CHARLES H. STEMBER

The public-opinion studies on which our analyses are based measure a broad assortment of public attitudes in all their dimensions: the affective, cognitive and conative. Taken together, they constitute what we believe to be a reasonably comprehensive representation of Americans' feelings toward their Jewish fellow citizens over the years. We are therefore in a position to assess the trend of attitudes during the last quarter-century with some degree of assurance.

THE TREND OF ATTITUDES

One fact consistently emerges from our analyses: Anti-Semitism in all its forms massively declined in the United States between the prewar or war years and the early 1960s. This conclusion is strikingly illustrated by (though by no means exclusively drawn from) under those issues for which we have data spanning all or most of the period under study. Each of these measures registers a substantial diminution of anti-Semitism or of ignorance or stereotypy with respect to Jews, no matter whether it is the affective, cognitive or conative aspect that is gauged (Figure 1). Thus, as of 1962, significantly fewer people than formerly believed that Jews as a group had distinctive undesirable traits or considered them a "race." Fewer thought Jews were clannish, dishonest, unscrupulous or excessively powerful in business and finance. Fewer believed colleges should limit the number of Jewish students. Much fewer objected to Jewish neighbors or employees. And fewer opposed marriage between Jews and others than had done so as late as 1950.

At the outset, each of the 12 measures used to explore these issues drew anti-Semitic responses from at least 10 per cent of the population, and all but four from more than 25 per cent. In 1962, only five of the 12 measures obtained such responses from as much as 10 per cent, and only one from more than 25 per cent. Of the remaining seven, four did not attain even the 5 per cent mark: the ideas that Jews are clannish, have too much financial power, are undesirable neighbors and should be denied unrestricted acceptance by colleges. Even with the most careful evaluation of the facts, we are bound to conclude that at least these four issues have ceased to function significantly as focuses of anti-Semitic feeling.

Though anti-Semitism was much less prevalent at the end of the quarter-century studied than at its outset, the trend during the intervening years was by no means uniformly downward. According to our evidence, hostility against Jews actually increased from the beginning of the period until the final phase of the war, turned down sharply toward the later 1940s and has consistently ebbed since.

That a steep drop in anti-Semitism should have occurred in the decade after the war is perhaps surprising. The early years of the Cold War, particularly the period of the inconclusive struggle in Korea, were a time of frustration and anxiety, comparable in some ways to 1944, the year in which anti-Semitism had reached a peak. In this climate, a number of emerging issues seemed more than likely to worsen the public's attitude toward Jews. One was the birth of Israel, which according to some observers was sure to cast doubts on the loyalty of American Jewry. Another was America's growing concern about Communist espionage and subversion, culminating in the trial and conviction of several Soviet spies, some of whom bore Jewish names. A third was the Negro's mounting demand for equality—a development which heightened social tensions all over the United States.

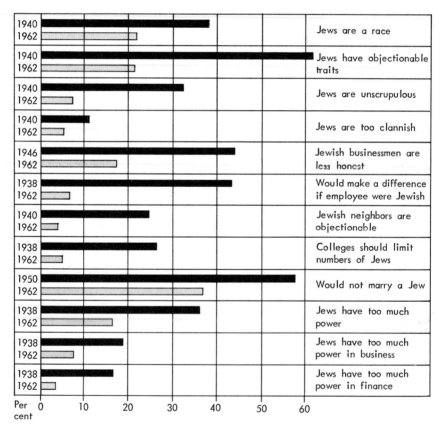

FIGURE 1. Long-term decreases in anti-Semitism, according to 12 measures (1938–62).

As it happened, none of these developments produced the expected anti-Semitic reaction. The creation of Israel (1948) does not seem to have altered the public's perception of American Jews as Americans; neither did Israel's subsequent invasion of Egyptian territory (1956), an act which directly challenged policies of the United States Government. Longstanding fears that American Jewry might be linked in the public mind with political radicalism proved equally groundless; even at the time of the spy trials (1950–51), the nation showed little disposition to associate Jews as a group with radicalism, espionage or loyalty to the Soviet Union.

As for the civil-rights issue, which came increasingly to the fore following the U.S. Supreme Court's outlawing of segregated public schools (1954), Jews appear to have been objects of widespread ignorance. Large segments of the public remained unaware of how strongly Jews supported the Negro cause. Lacking this knowledge, integrationists and segregationists alike frequently based their appraisals of the Jews' position on their own attitudes: Persons reasonably free from anti-Semitism tended to view Jews as allies while, to a less marked degree, anti-Semites seemed inclined to think of them as taking a position opposed to their own. In any event, toward the end of the period under study the question became increasingly academic; leadership of the movement was so rapidly passing into the Negroes' own hands that what Negroes were doing became much more significant than what Jews or other whites were thinking. In sum, whatever forces caused anti-Semitism to wane during the postwar years remained virtually unaffected by this as by other seemingly ominous developments.

CHANGES IN IMAGERY

In two distinct ways, traditional images of the Jew lost ground during the period we have studied. First, some particular prejudices very nearly disappeared. Thus, notions of "Jewish clannishness," "Jewish power" and "Jewish domination of finance" are no longer widespread; and many more individuals today state they would support a hypothetical Jewish candidate for the Presidency of the United States than said so two or three decades ago. Second and perhaps more important, far fewer persons than formerly think of Jews as having any distinctive traits or characteristics at all, whether good or bad. Jews, it would appear, are being perceived more and more as individuals, rather than as a special kind of people with fixed qualities.

Of the changes in the prevalence of particular stereotypes, perhaps the most significant is the waning of the "Shylock" image—the notion that Jews as a group are "greedy," "dishonest" or "unscrupulous." This image has long served as a nucleus around which other permanent and ephemeral prejudices (for example, "aggressiveness," "lack of refinement," "warmongering") have organized themselves. The "Shylock" image has not altogether disappeared, but has become both less prevalent and less extreme: Fewer persons today think

Jews are merely "shrewd" or "tricky" than considered them downright dishonest a generation ago.

Though the currency of anti-Jewish stereotypes has been much reduced, their content—except in the case just cited—has undergone no marked change. Among persons who continue to see Jews as a group in an unfavorable light, the perennial accusations still hold sway, centering as always on the Jews' supposed economic preoccupations, their alleged aggressiveness in business and their success in that field. Certain accusations connected with the war ("lack of patriotism," "warmongering," "draft dodging" and "avoidance of frontline action") probably were mere variants of traditional stereotypes, adapted to the conditions of the moment. Since such adaptations require a reasonably well-structured pre-existing image, the recent weakening of the central "Shylock" concept should go far toward inhibiting their growth in the future.

That the various specific perceptions which make up the dominant stereotype of the Jew have all declined simultaneously is heartening indeed but not especially surprising in the light of our observations. As we have seen, ideas about a given group of people reinforce one another; each separate component attains its full significance only in conjunction with the rest. For example, the idea that Jews have certain unchangeable group characteristics undoubtedly depends to a considerable extent on the belief that they are a "race." Therefore, the recent weakening of the latter concept probably has helped to undermine the former. Similarly, the Jews' supposed aggressiveness presumably is linked with their "clannishness" and "dishonesty," being viewed as one of the means by which they are thought to pursue their allegedly selfish goals. Therefore, if Jews are less widely perceived as clannish or dishonest than formerly, we may count on them to appear less aggressive as well.[1]

Consistent with this observation, we note that new ideas about groups find acceptance only if they fit into whatever well-developed stereotypes may exist. It will be recalled that neither the actual participation of a number of Jews in left-wing movements nor the publicity surrounding accused Soviet spies with Jewish names gave added circulation to the notion that Jews generally tend to be Communists. The reason, we believe, is that in the context of the American culture this notion conflicted with the dominant image of the Jew as rich, not poor; as economically rather than politically oriented; as preoccupied with advancing his own group, not the working class or society as a whole.[2] Only among a relatively sophisticated segment of the public, which no longer believed the old stereotype, did the image of the Jew as a leftist hold any meaning, and even within this segment only a small minority embraced the idea during the 1950s.

If the future should bring a further weakening of the central stereotype, the image of the Jew as an "economic man," certain beliefs that contradict this

---

[1] The decline in the perception of Jews as "clannish" may also explain why they were not widely viewed as primarily loyal to Israel.

[2] These beliefs probably also account for the fact that Jews were not especially closely associated with the Negro cause in the public's mind.

image might gain readier acceptance. Thus, prejudices now of limited currency—such as the association between Communism and Jews as a group—theoretically could become the prevailing view. But of course this reasoning applies as much to "good" as to "bad" images. Favorable ideas about Jews will also enjoy increasing chances of public acceptance as the fabric of older prejudices crumbles.

ASSOCIATION WITH JEWS

Unwillingness to associate with Jews has shown a marked decline in recent decades. The available data, for the most part, do not reach back to the 1930s; but as far as the postwar years are concerned, the general downward trend of anti-Semitism finds unmistakable expression in a growing willingness to mingle with Jews in a variety of situations. As early as 1947, nearly the entire public declared itself willing to work next to Jews. When respondents were invited, about the same time, to consider employment of Jews from an imagined employer's standpoint, acceptance was less general; but by 1962 even this rather hypothetical form of resistance had virtually disappeared.

The longstanding desire of many Americans to restrict Jews to segregated neighborhoods has similarly ebbed. By the early 1960s, an overwhelming majority appeared ready to accept individual Jews as next-door neighbors. As might be expected, however, fears of Jewish newcomers in massive numbers were somewhat stronger; as of 1959, a sizable minority still held that such "invasions" made neighborhoods undesirable.

Judging by what some rather sketchy but intriguing figures, the reasons for whatever resistance to Jewish neighbors persists have undergone a change during recent decades. True, the belief that the presence of Jews lowers property values was rarely voiced even in the earlier years covered by our data; but while two decades ago alleged undesirable qualities of Jews still loomed large, the emphasis apparently has now changed to their supposedly strange or "different" ways. Possibly, this shift reflects the growing suburbanization of the country; for in the suburbs the neighborhood is much more definitely the arena of middle-class social life than in the city, where well-developed public transportation and a relative absence of localized community life combine to spread social associations over larger areas.

It must be noted that declared willingness to mix socially with Jews undoubtedly remains theoretical in most cases. In the past, actual social relations between Jews and non-Jews appear to have been relatively rare. Our figures do not tell us whether the picture changed during recent years, but they do suggest that many more people were ready to enter friendships with Jews than actually did so. The small number of Jews in the population may well have been the main reason though reluctance on their part was probably a contributing factor.

Where institutionalized social settings, such as vacation resorts, were involved, the picture was not the same as when purely individual friendship was considered. In recent as in earlier data, Jews appeared more willing to fraternize with non-Jews in such settings than vice versa. But at least part of the reason, we believe, is simply that Jews are relatively well acquainted with the customs of the surrounding non-Jewish majority culture, while non-Jews are likely to be unfamiliar with what they imagine to be the peculiar ways of Jews.

Association of one's own offspring with persons of other backgrounds affords a crucial index of intergroup attitudes. Unfortunately, the data we have illuminate only a few of the numerous facets of this issue. Respondents generally expressed themselves as willing to let their children associate with Jews, but we do not know how many were thinking of young children in this context, and how many of adolescent or adult sons and daughters. Nor do the findings concerning college admission shed much light on the topic. Quotas to restrict the admission of Jews to colleges, still widely approved by adults (though not by students) in the 1940s, had almost completely fallen out of favor by the 1960s; but whether this change signals greater approval of social contact between young people of Jewish and other backgrounds remains an open question.

On the other hand, the data leave no doubt that sentiment against marriage with Jews has waned. Of course, rejection remains much more frequent here than in other contexts; as of 1962 intermarriage was the only issue covered in polls on which a majority of respondents expressed some degree of reservation. But this is hardly cause for surprise, inasmuch as intermarriage is not only the most intimate form of association, but one in which attitudes derive from a variety of ideological and practical considerations—obscured as often as illuminated by the belief that "love conquers all," and hedged about with expectations and theories concerning the chances of success. It is more noteworthy that between 1950 and 1962 acceptance of Jews as marriage partners increased at about the same rate as did acceptance of Jewish employees, fellow students and neighbors.

ATTITUDE COMPONENTS AND THEIR INTERRELATIONS

In the polls which form the basis of this study, attitudes toward Jews are measured in all of their components: affective, cognitive and conative. We therefore may confidently conclude that we have indeed measured the attitudes themselves, not some incidental factors; and this conclusion is confirmed by the fact that the trends in all three components exhibit a high degree of consistency. Thus, over the years, the tendency to invest Jews with distinctive objectionable traits (affective) runs parallel with the prevalence of particular hostile stereotypes (cognitive) and with attitudes toward Jews in specific situations (conative).

Our data do not identify the particular component in which a change first occurred, but the parallelism among all three is such as to suggest that a major change in any one is bound ultimately to affect the other two. Even deeply embedded and rigidly held attitudes or beliefs—for example, opposition to mixed marriages or to the idea of a Jew's running for President—have lost ground as the acceptance of Jews in other fields has made conspicuous progress.

Components of a given attitude are occasionally at variance over short periods of time, but in the long run they tend to revert to a common configuration.[3]

ACTIVE HOSTILITY TOWARD JEWS

Our information about the potential support for organized anti-Semitism in the United States extends only from the prewar to the early postwar years. Before the war and during most of it, the idea of a large-scale anti-Jewish campaign drew a substantial response; at one time, perhaps as much as a third of the population felt ready to join or at least approve such an undertaking. This sentiment seems to have reached a peak in 1944, together with other kinds of anti-Semitic feelings; it had dropped rather sharply by 1946, at which point our data end.

At least during the war years, willingness to take organized action against Jews was in no sense an isolated phenomenon; it was part of a general anti-minority sentiment. When hostility toward Jews showed an increase in the opinion polls, so did hostility toward other minorities. This finding throws considerable doubt on the theory that ethnic prejudices necessarily displace one another—that when public resentment is centered on one group, others may expect to feel it less. On the contrary, our evidence suggests that hostile attitudes arising out of general social tensions like those of war are likely to encompass a variety of target groups, rather than to focus on one.

Whether such a comprehensive anti-minority climate develops and what groups become its objects would seem to depend also on the presence or absence of cognitive similarities among possible target groups. Thus, during the postwar years, hostility against political radicals increased drastically, while anti-Jewish feeling declined. Apparently the public does not, or did not then, react uniformly to minorities *qua* minorities; in the case just mentioned, a political minority evoked a response quite different from that to an ethnic one.

Another conclusion suggested by our analyses is that the degree of potential public support for anti-Semitic movements is not significantly related to public awareness of anti-Semitism. Such awareness appears to be much more closely linked to the circulation of anti-Jewish stereotypes.

THE EFFECT OF THE WAR

The findings of opinion polls make plain how deeply the Second World War affected the American public's attitudes toward Jews. Anti-Semitism

---

[3] This is one theoretical justification for the policy, followed by intergroup relations agencies, of concentrating on whatever attitudinal component may be most open to change at the moment—for example, to work chiefly for acceptance of minority group members in employment, on the assumption that this will ultimately cause them to be differently perceived and less disliked. It must be noted that this theory is predicated on change in the components of attitudes, not merely in social relationships *per se*.

during those years evidently served as one outlet for the mounting aggressive feelings fostered by the tensions and deprivations of wartime. Other groups were similarly pressed into service as targets for this hostility—among them big business, organized labor and ethnic groups other than Jews.

Certain alleged reactions of Jews to the war crisis furnished a rationale to the growing numbers of persons willing to support whatever organized anti-Semitic action seemed likely to materialize. Between 1938 and 1942, over a quarter of the population described Jews as less patriotic than other citizens. During the months just before Pearl Harbor, a sizable minority of Americans accused Jews of seeking to involve the United States in the conflict. In the years that followed, Jews were more often charged than any other ethnic group with shirking their share of the war effort, with draft dodging and, once drafted, with avoiding front-line combat. As noted earlier, these widely accepted if transient images—held by well over a third of the population throughout the war—all were consonant with, and presumably derived from, the more general stereotypes current at the time.

Wartime antagonism against Jews, it must be noted, did not as a rule express itself in openly aggressive attitudes. Though widespread, it appears to have had little salience, remaining latent rather than becoming active. Still, it is paradoxical that such hostility should have existed at all in the midst of a conflict with the Jews' archenemy. Propaganda by the Axis powers does not seem to have played more than a minimal role in its formation. A more likely explanation is that Americans, by and large, interpreted the war against Germany, Italy and Japan not so much in ideological as in conventionally nationalistic terms. In any event, the wartime prejudices against Jews disappeared quickly at the end of hostilities, and so did most of the potential support for anti-Semitic movements.

The persecution and ultimate destruction of European Jewry by the Hitler regime exerted surprisingly little effect upon American attitudes toward Jews. While Hitler was in power, Americans for the most part remained ignorant of the dawning truth about the nature and extent of the annihilation program; and even the revelations of the early postwar years, which laid bare the crime in its whole enormity, do not seem to have increased whatever sympathy may have existed for the Jews as a people or affected public attitudes toward American Jewry. Whether the renewed and enlarged recital of the horror at the trial of Adolf Eichmann, in 1961, made any more of an impression on the American people is a question the opinion polls do not answer.

The plight of Hitler's victims and the obvious need to resettle hundreds of thousands of survivors failed to shake the nation's longstanding opposition to increased immigration. Indeed, the fact that most of the potential immigrants were Jewish seems to have strengthened the public's determination to keep the gates closed. Whatever sympathy existed for the refugees from the Nazi regime expressed itself, rather, in widespread approval of plans to settle the victims in other countries. Specifically, it may have strengthened opinion favoring Jewish immigration into Palestine and creation of a Jewish state there, even against the wishes of America's ally, Great Britain. . . .

CONCLUDING OBSERVATIONS

Anti-Jewish prejudice obviously is not yet a thing of the past, any more than anti-Jewish discrimination is, but both are unmistakably in a state of decline. As we have seen, hostile attitudes toward Jews are finding less widespread support in the 1960s than at any other time since the systematic study of public attitudes began. Actual discriminatory practices also have lessened to a marked degree during that period, so that we probably are safe in asserting that prejudice and discrimination today are not prevalent enough to reinforce or perpetuate each other significantly, as they formerly did. In both feeling and behavior toward Jews, our society has undergone a profound change within the span of one generation.

What of the future? Having come this far, American society may look foward to opportunities for even more fundamental rapprochements between gentile and Jew—opportunities which scarcely could have been forseen two short decades ago, when it seemed conceivable that anti-Semitism might engulf a majority of the American people. Today, practitioners in the field of intergroup relations may reasonably strive to do more than help assure that hostility remains at the low levels to which it has fallen. Beyond the existing, largely accidental, relationships of Jews and non-Jews, more meaningful encounters—religious dialogue, friendship, shared civic enterprises—await increasingly intense cultivation.

Plans and hopes like these hinge, of course, on the assumption that the tendencies we have observed will continue in years to come. To take this for granted would be reckless as well as presumptuous, for throughout the long history of the Jews, periods of acceptance and security have alternated with periods of rejection and oppression. But we may confidently state that the current trend toward more and more complete acceptance of the Jew—both individually and in the abstract—appears unlikely to be reversed by anything short of a catastrophic crisis in American society. The longer such a crisis is averted, the more firmly will recognition of Jews as equal and respected fellow citizens become grounded in the mores of the American people.

White Attitudes Toward the Negro

PAUL B. SHEATSLEY

Any attempt to describe white attitudes toward Negroes in the 1870's or the 1890's, or immediately before or after World War I, must necessarily rely on impressionistic or anecdotal evidence, or on secondary studies of contemporary newspapers, letters, diaries, and similar materials. Only since the advent of public opinion research in the mid-nineteen thirties has it been possible to

Reprinted from *Daedalus*, **95** (Winter, 1966), pp. 217–238, by permission of the author and the publisher, the American Academy of Arts and Sciences, Boston, Massachusetts.

address a series of standard questions to representative samples of the general population by means of personal interviews, and to cross-tabulate the results by such factors as age, sex, race, and geographical region.

It tells much about white attitudes toward the Negro that, during the seven years from 1935 to 1942, only four questions bearing even indirectly on the subject seem to have been asked by the national public opinion polls of that time.[1] Three of these questions, dealing with opinions about the "lynching bill" then before Congress in 1937, are practically irrelevant because the results simply show that most Americans thought people should not be lynched and the question itself said nothing about race. The fourth question was asked in 1939 and reveals that two-thirds of the American public approved of Mrs. Franklin D. Roosevelt's resignation from the Daughters of the American Revolution in protest against the refusal of that organization to permit a "well-known Negro singer" to give a concert in a D.A.R. hall. The polls, for obvious reasons, tend to ask their questions about the issues that are hot, and it is clear that, during the decade preceding World War II, race relations did not qualify on this basis. Negroes had their place, and it was a rare American white who became exercised over this fact of life.

Today, of course, the situation is entirely different. Since mid-summer 1963, the question of race relations has been consistently cited by Americans as "the most important problem facing the United States," except when it has been temporarily displaced by some international crisis such as Vietnam.[2] As in 1935–42, public opinion polls have responded to the times, but today they are doing so by asking every question they can think of which will reveal more clearly the white American's response to the Negro protest movement. The results of these polls are widely publicized, but quite often are contradictory and confusing. A recent Gallup report, for example, tells us that "Today, white Americans seem more sympathetic to Negro rights than they have ever been";[3] a recent Harris report, on the other hand, warns that "At least for now, the dominant mood of white America is to put a brake on the pace of civil rights progress."[4] Actually, surveys such as these tell us much more than the quotations suggest, and one poll does not differ from others so much as it differs from itself, depending upon the questions asked. Hardly any white Americans have attitudes toward Negroes which are clearly thought out and rigidly maintained; and even those who do may have sudden qualms when they read about racial

[1] Hadley Cantril, *Public Opinion, 1935–1946* (Princeton, N.J., 1951). This volume is a compendium of published poll results during the first dozen years of systematic opinion research. All twenty-seven questions listed under "Negroes" are dated 1942 or later; thirty-two of thirty-three questions listed under "U.S. Race Relations" are dated 1942 or later. The three questions on lynching referred to below were found under "Crime and Criminals."

[2] Gallup Poll releases, July 21, 1963, October 2, 1963, *et passim*. The question, "What do you regard as the most vital issue before the American people today?" was first asked in September 1935 (the answer was "Unemployment") and has been repeated by the Gallup Poll at regular intervals, with slight changes of wording, since that time. "Racial problems" was not mentioned frequently enough to receive a separate code until 1944–45.

[3] "America's Mood Today," *Look*, June 29, 1965.

[4] Harris Survey news release, May 17, 1965.

murders in the South or Negro violence on Northern streets. The problem is one of interpreting what the polls and surveys tell us so we can understand what it all means.

Proper interpretation of survey data requires some baseline or norm against which a particular finding can be evaluated. While it is of interest to know, for instance, that "eight in ten white Americans said they would not move" if a Negro family moved next door, or that 41 per cent feel that the pace of civil rights progress is too fast,[5] the numbers have little meaning unless we can anchor them somehow. One means of anchoring is to compare findings over the course of time. The figures take on added significance if we can determine whether they are increasing or decreasing in response to events. A second means is to compare subgroup differences (for example, North *vs.* South, the well-educated *vs.* those with little formal education) against the national norm. We propose to examine past and current survey findings with a view to clarifying and interpreting their meaning. In the course of this examination we shall rely mainly, though not exclusively, on data gathered by the National Opinion Research Center of the University of Chicago. The NORC data are particularly suitable for two reasons. First, the earliest national survey of white attitudes toward Negroes was conducted by NORC on behalf of the Office of War Information in 1942, and a number of the same questions have been periodically repeated in subsequent surveys. Second, in December 1963, NORC devoted an entire interview schedule to questions on race relations, administered to a national sample of white Americans. The possibilities of fruitful analysis of such a study are more promising than the examination of scattered poll results from a great number of separate surveys.

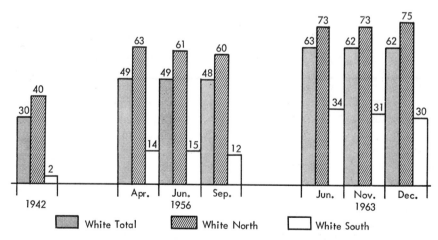

FIGURE 1. Twenty-year trends on school integration.[6]

[5] *Look* and Harris survey, *op. cit.*

[6] Much of the material in this section has previously been presented in Herbert H. Hyman and Paul B. Sheatsley, "Attitudes Toward Desegregation," *Scientific American*, Vol. 211 (July 1964), pp. 16–23.

Figure 1 shows for each of three years—1942, 1952, and 1963— the proportion of American whites who expressed approval of integration when asked the question, "Do you think white students and Negro students should go to the same schools or to separate schools?"[7] The most striking message of the chart is the revolutionary change in white attitudes, both North and South,[8] which has taken place on this explosive issue in less than a generation. In 1942, not one American white in three approved of integrated schools. Even in the North, majority sentiment was strongly opposed, while in the South only two whites in one hundred could be found to support the proposition. By 1956, two years after the historic Supreme Court decision which abolished the "separate but equal" doctrine, white attitudes had shifted markedly. Nationwide, support for integration was now characteristic of about half the white population, while in the North it had clearly become the majority view. In the South, where only one white person in fifty had favored integration fourteen years earlier, the proportion by 1956 had risen to approximately one in seven.

The continuation of the trend from 1956 to 1963 is especially noteworthy, since the years between were marked by agitation and occasional violence which might easily have led one to suspect a reversal of attitudes and a white revulsion against integration. Desegregation of Southern schools in accordance with the Supreme Court decision had sparked physical conflict not only in Little Rock in 1957 but in dozens of smaller communities during these years. The start of the "sit-in" movement in 1960, the freedom rides of 1961, the Oxford riots of 1962 might well have hardened white attitudes and halted the trend toward acceptance of integration. But repetition of the same question to three different national samples in 1963 showed that this massive trend was still intact. By that year, almost two-thirds of all American whites expressed approval of integrated schools; among white persons in the North, the proportion was close to three in four. And in the South, which was then bearing the brunt of the Negro protest movement, sentiment for integration had climbed even faster, so that almost a third of all white Southerners agreed that white students and Negro students should attend the same schools.

The strength of the long-term trend was further attested by its immunity to short-run events. In both 1956 and 1963, it was possible to ask the question on three separate surveys at different times of the year, and it is evident that all three surveys in each year produced essentially identical results.[9] One would not necessarily have expected such short-term stability. Though largely forgotten

---

[7] The question was asked also in 1944 and 1946. Results for those years, while consistent with the trend, are not shown for reasons of space. Absence of financial support precluded asking the question on any other occasions, so we cannot conclude that the trend lines are uniformly smooth.

[8] "South" refers to the South Atlantic, East South Central, and West South Central regions, as defined by the Bureau of the Census. "North" refers to the rest of the country, except Alaska and Hawaii, where no interviews were conducted.

[9] Sample sizes ranged from 1,250 to 1,500. The minor changes from one 1956 or 1963 survey to another are well within the range of normal sampling error.

now, there appeared between the June and September 1956 surveys the first banner headlines of racial conflict as the long slow task of Southern school desegregation began in Clay, Kentucky, Clinton, Tennessee, and other small towns in border states across the country. Between June and November 1963, there occurred the march on Washington and the September school openings, while between the November and December surveys there intervened the shocking assassination of President Kennedy in a Southern metropolis. But even so dramatic an event, with all its implications for the civil rights movement, failed to disturb, in either North or South, the attitudes which had been expressed a month earlier.

The figures shown on the chart for the South represent, of course, a geographical composite of Deep South states like Mississippi and Alabama, border states such as West Virginia and Kentucky, and southwestern states such as Arkansas and Oklahoma. We shall indicate certain regional differences later. It is possible, however, to sort the Southern respondents to the 1963 surveys into three groups, according to the amount of school integration in their communities. When this is done, it is found that a solid majority of Southern whites (58 per cent), in those few places where there had been (as of 1963) considerable integration of schools, declared that they approved of school integration. In Southern communities which had accepted only some token desegregation, 38 per cent approved; while in the hard-core segregationist communities, only 28 per cent were in favor of integration. Though the sample sizes are small, particularly in the desegregated areas, the correlation is clear: Where integration exists in the South, more whites support it.[10]

It is dangerous to try to unravel cause and effect from mere statistical correlation, yet a close analysis of the data indicates that official action to desegregate Southern schools did not wait for majority opinion to demand it, but rather preceded a change in community attitudes. In the 1956 surveys, only 31 per cent of Southern whites in those few areas which had begun at least token desegregation expressed approval of integrated schools. Clearly there was no public demand for integration in those areas then. Furthermore, by 1963 the integrated areas included not only those communities which had pioneered in integration in 1956, but also many additional communities where anti-integration sentiment had in 1956 been even stronger. Yet by 1963 the majority of Southern whites in such communities had accepted the integration of their schools. It may be noted that even in the most segregationist parts of the South, approval of integration has continued to climb. In 1956, only 4 per cent of Southern whites residing in segregated school areas approved of integration, but by 1963 the proportion in communities which had not by then introduced even token integration—the essential "hard-core" areas—had nevertheless risen to 28 per cent.

---

[10] The same holds true for the North. Northern whites living in segregated school areas were 65 per cent for integration, but in areas where there had been considerable integration, 83 per cent favored the policy.

TRENDS ON OTHER RACIAL ISSUES

School integration is one of the most basic and explosive of the civil rights issues, and it has provided perhaps the most apt illustration of the dramatic shift in white attitudes over the past two decades. Additional evidence from the same surveys is available, however, to show that the increasing accommodation of whites to equal rights has not been restricted to the schools, but extends to other spheres as well. Table I shows the trends in attitudes with respect to

TABLE I. PER CENT WHO APPROVE RESIDENTIAL AND PUBLIC TRANSPORTATION INTEGRATION
IN 1942, 1956, JUNE AND DECEMBER, 1963

	Surveys in			
Approval of	*1942*	*1956*	*June 1963*	*Dec. 1963*
Residential Integration				
National white total	35	51	61	64
Northern whites only	42	58	68	70
Southern whites only	12	38	44	51
Public Transportation Integration				
National white total	44	60	79	78
Northern whites only	57	73	89	88
Southern whites only	4	27	52	51

residential integration and the integration of public transportation. The three later surveys used exactly the same questions that were employed in 1942. These were: "If a Negro with the same income and education as you have moved into your block, would it make any difference to you?"[11] and "Generally speaking, do you think there should be separate sections for Negroes on streetcars and buses?" Nationwide, in 1942 only 35 per cent of American whites would not have objected to a Negro neighbor of their own social class; by 1963 almost two out of three would accept such a neighbor. Nationwide, in 1942 fewer than half of all American whites approved of integrated transportation facilities; by 1963 almost four out of five had adopted this view. The changes are especially dramatic among Southern whites, for in 1942 only one out of eight of them would have accepted a Negro neighbor and but one in twenty-five the idea of sharing transportation facilities on an integrated basis. By the end of 1963, both forms of integration had achieved majority approval.

Though not shown in the data thus far presented, it should be noted that throughout this twenty-one-year period the proportion of persons having "No opinion" on any of these questions rarely exceeded 3 or 4 per cent. This finding is in sharp contrast to the public's answers on most other national issues, where

[11] In the 1956 and 1963 surveys, a special category was added for the response, "Yes, I would welcome it," and persons giving this reply were combined with the "No Difference" group.

it is common to find upwards of 10 per cent expressing ignorance or indecision. The fact that almost everybody has been aware of the civil rights issue and has had an opinion on it during all this time has implications for the significance of the trends we have observed. There have been no masses of apathetic or undecided people, swayed this way and that by events, and drifting from segregationist to doubtful, from doubtful to integrationist, and perhaps back again. Rather, support for civil rights today comes from a younger generation that, during the last two decades, has come of age and has replaced an older, more segregationist generation in our population; and from former segregationists whose senses and consciences have been touched by the Negro protest, or who have simply changed their opinions as segregation appears increasingly to be a lost cause.

On four occasions, starting in July 1957, the Gallup Poll has asked the question: "Do you think the day will ever come in the South when whites and Negroes will be going to the same schools, eating in the same restaurants, and generally sharing the same public accommodations?" In 1957 and 1958, only a small majority of white people answered "Yes" to that question; in 1961, the proportion had grown to three-fourths, and by 1963, to five-sixths. Conversely, the proportion who answered "No" (or "Never") had dropped by by 1963 to 13 per cent. As the Civil Rights Act of 1964 hastens the day when whites and Negroes actually are sharing the same restaurants and public accommodations and as the pace of Southern school desegregation quickens, it is difficult to foresee any reversal in the massive trends we have shown.

An important shift in white beliefs on one further issue helps explain the trends we have observed and underlines the solid base on which they rest. In 1942, a national sample of whites was asked, "In general, do you think that Negroes are as intelligent as white people—that is, can they learn things just as well if they are given the same education and training?" At that time only about half the Northern whites and one Southern white in five answered "Yes." Today, four-fifths of the white population in the North and a substantial majority in the South (57 per cent) believe that Negroes are as intelligent as white people. The implications of this revolutionary change in attitudes toward Negro educability are far-reaching. It has undermined one of the most stubborn arguments formerly offered by whites for segregated schools and has made the case for segregation much more difficult to defend.

SINCE DECEMBER 1963

We are aware that many readers will question the relevance of public opinion poll findings from December 1963 to the situation today. After all, the year 1964 alone saw the nomination of Barry Goldwater, the Presidential election campaign, general elections in every state, Congressional passage of a comprehensive Civil Rights Act, Negro rioting in several Northern cities, the murder of three civil rights workers in Mississippi—to mention only some of the most striking events which might have affected the attitudes we have described. And the pace the civil rights movement in 1965 has shown no signs of slackening. We urge such readers, however, to regain their perspective by looking again at the twenty-year trend shown in Chart 1, and especially at the absence of short-run change over the three separate surveys conducted in 1956 and 1963, when racial tensions were also high. It cannot be doubted that people do respond to short-run events and often have very strong opinions about them. But all the evidence we know of indicates that attitudes toward the basic issues included in the Pro-Integration Scale*—such as school and residential integration, social mixing, the use by Negroes of public accommodations—are not subject to sudden and dramatic shifts. If all the events in the months and years preceding December 1963 did not halt the rising trend toward acceptance of integration, it may be doubted that more recent events have produced any major change in the attitudes we have examined.

Indeed, the 1964 Presidential election itself provided a very important test of civil rights sentiment in the United States, for there, "in the privacy of the voting booth," the widely heralded "white backlash" failed to materialize in the North, while President Johnson carried the South in spite of his forthright stand on civil rights for Negroes. The result could hardly be construed as other than a rejection by the American people of the views of those who would try to stem the progress of the Negro protest movement. Yet, both the Gallup Poll and the Harris Survey, during 1964 and 1965, reported seeming inconsistencies in the attitudes of the white public. Each has found, just as we saw in the 1963 NORC study, that whites generally disapprove of direct action by Negroes and would welcome relief from racial tensions. Thus, Harris reported (August 17, 1964) that "Fully 87 per cent of the American people feel that the recent riots in New York, Rochester and Jersey City have hurt the Negro cause," and (May 17, 1965) that there existed an "... apparent uneasiness of the American people over the current pace of civil rights progress. Six months ago, the public tended to feel that steady and sound progress was being registered. After recent events, the number who feel things are moving 'too fast' has risen rather sharply." (The increase was from 32 per cent in November to 41 per cent in May, shortly after the events in Selma, Alabama.) Only six days earlier (May 11, 1965) Gallup had also warned that "Criticism of integration speed has grown among Northern whites. . . . The number who believe the Johnson Administration is pushing integration 'too fast' has grown considerably over the last few weeks." Gallup had also been reporting such results as (June 7, 1964) "Eight in ten say demonstrations more likely to hurt than to help Negro. . . . Opposition among both races has grown," and (November 12, 1964) "Six in ten favor a gradual approach" to enforcement of the new Civil Rights Law rather than "strict enforcement right from the beginning." In that same release, Gallup reported that 73 per cent of his sample "think Negroes should stop demonstrating, now that they have made their point."

But both of these polling agencies have also reported a steady support for civil rights measures. Harris found a large and increasing majority for the 1964

*[The material referred to is not included—Editor.]

Civil Rights bill between November 1963 and April 1964, with 70 per cent of the public favoring it by the latter date. Both polls reported public approval of the 1965 voting rights bill, though their figures differed considerably. Gallup (April 14, 1965) found 76 per cent in favor, Harris (May 10, 1965) only 53 per cent, the difference apparently tracing to a reference in the Harris question that "opponents feel this is an invasion of the rights of states to control their own elections." The Gallup question made no mention of states' rights. Gallup also found (March 19, 1965) that 56 per cent of the public believe that people who cannot read or write should nevertheless have the right to vote and that 63 per cent disagree with the proposition that only persons who have had at least five years of schooling should be allowed to vote.

Opportunity to apply a more rigorous test of the hypothesis that the long-term trends are still intact finally occurred in June 1965, when NORC was able to append a few of the 1942–1963 questions to a current national survey. It was not possible to ask all of the items included in the December 1963 survey, but the measures which were obtained strongly confirmed the inexorability of the trend. The proportion of white Americans who favor school integration rose from 62 per cent to 67 per cent during this eighteen-month period, and the proportion who would not object to a Negro neighbor of the same social class rose from 64 per cent to 68 per cent. Perhaps the most striking finding was that the increases were accounted for entirely by the South. While the figures for the North held steady or showed small and insignificant fluctuations, Southern attitudes were undergoing revolutionary change. The proportion of Southern whites who favor integrated schools almost doubled within this eighteen-month period, moving from 30 per cent at the end of 1963 to 55 per cent—a clear majority—in mid-1965. The proportion of Southern whites who would not object to a Negro neighbor rose from 51 per cent to 66 per cent during this same period. Again it was found that exposure to integration fosters pro-integrationist attitudes. Of Southern whites whose children had attended school with Negroes, 74 per cent said Negroes and whites should attend the same schools; of Southern whites whose children had not attended school with Negroes, only 48 per cent held that view.

There will, of course, be those who now ask, "But what about Los Angeles? Surely that violence must have produced a white revulsion against civil rights"— but if the past is any guide, the answer can be predicted with considerable assurance. Certainly large majorities of American whites, and especially the dwindling ranks of segregationists, will say that the Los Angeles rioting has "hurt the Negro's cause," that "they have made their point," and that nothing is settled by violence, but not even Los Angeles will halt the massive attitudinal changes we have demonstrated over the last generation. Furthermore, it should be noted that the rioting in Watts took scarcely anyone by surprise. The June 1965 NORC survey asked, "As you probably recall, there were race riots in several Northern cities last summer. The way it looks now, do you expect that this summer there will be many race riots around the country, some, hardly any, or none at all?" Only 2 per cent said they expected no Negro rioting during the summer, and almost a quarter of the white population expected many riots.

Thus, the unprecedentedly high level of support expressed for integration in this survey actually seems to have discounted Los Angeles in advance. With the full expectation of at least some riots in Northern cities, American whites nevertheless (or perhaps for that reason?) actually increased their support of integration.

A recent (but pre-Los Angeles) Gallup Poll release confirms the remarkable change in white Southern attitudes between 1963 and 1965. In May 1963, Gallup asked a representative sample of white parents, "Would you yourself have any objection to sending your children to a school where a few of the children are colored?" and 61 per cent of those in the South said, "Yes, I would object." When he repeated the same question two years later, the proportion of Southern parents who would object had dropped abruptly to 37 per cent. Similar, though less dramatic, changes were found in the attitudes of Northern parents. The millennium has scarcely arrived. Gallup went on to ask whether the parents would object to sending their children to a school where half, and then where more than half, of the children were colored. A majority of white parents in the North and almost four out of five of those in the South said they would object to the latter situation.

Certainly there is no evidence that the majority of American whites eagerly look forward to integration. Most are more comfortable in a segregated society, and they would prefer that the demonstrators slow down or go away while things are worked out more gradually. But most of them know also that racial discrimination is morally wrong and recognize the legitimacy of the Negro protest. Our survey data persuasively argue that where there is little or no protest against segregation and discrimination, or where these have the sanction of law, racial attitudes conform to the existing situation. But when attention is kept focused on racial injustice and when acts of discrimination become contrary to the law of the land, racial attitudes change. Conversely, there is no persuasive evidence thus far that either demonstrations and other forms of direct action, or legal sanctions applied by government, create a backlash effect and foster segregationist sentiment. On the contrary, they may simply demonstrate, ever more conclusively, that it is more costly to oppose integration than to bring it about. The mass of white Americans have shown in many ways that they do not want a racist government and that they will not follow racist leaders. Rather, they are engaged in the painful task of adjusting to an integrated society. It will not be easy for most, but one cannot at this late date doubt the basic commitment. In their hearts they know that the American Negro is right.

CULTURE

The Middle-Class Norms

ALBERT K. COHEN

. . . These norms are, in effect, a tempered version of the Protestant ethic[1] which has played such an important part in the shaping of American character and American society. In brief summary, this middle-class ethic prescribes an obligation to strive, by dint of rational, ascetic, self-disciplined and independent activity, to achieve in worldly affairs. A not irrebuttable but common corollary is the presumption that "success" is itself a sign of the exercise of these moral qualities.

From another point of view, these middle-class standards may be regarded as the positive evaluation in children of those characteristics which facilitate and lay the ground for the achievement of respectable social class status in adulthood. From this point of view, there is an important continuity and integration of the legitimate expectations attaching to childhood and adult roles, in the sense that indoctrination with this morality prepares the child for the easy assumption of, or success in, the adult roles.

One more observation is here in order. The requisites for the achievement of social class status in the adult role are not quite the same for men and for women. The social class status of both men and women is that of their family. The status of the family, in turn, depends, more than it does on any other one thing, on the occupational achievement of the male "head." The social class status of women depends primarily upon marriage to an occupationally successful male. The road to vertical mobility for men, much more than for women, then, is through independent occupational achievement. To the extent that middle-class standards for the evaluation of children are continuous with adult roles, we should expect these standards to be different, at least in emphasis, for boys and girls. The following summary description[2] of these middle-class standards is primarily applicable to the male role.

Reprinted with permission of The Macmillan Company from *Delinquent Boys* by Albert K. Cohen. © The Free Press, a Corporation, 1959.

[1] See Max Weber, *The Protestant Ethic and the Spirit of Capitalism*, tr. by Talcott Parsons (London: George Allen and Unwin, 1930).

[2] We will attempt no point by point documentation of this description. It is based on induction from a voluminous literature on social class and socialization in America, and almost every source we refer to in this chapter is relevant to this description. Two items which merit special mention, however, are Kingsley Davis, "Mental Hygiene and the Class Structure," *Psychiatry*, I (February, 1938), 55–65 and Margaret Mead, *And Keep Your Powder Dry* (New York: William Morrow and Company, 1942).

1. Ambition is a virtue; its absence is a defect and a sign of maladjustment. Ambition means a high level of aspiration, aspiration for goals difficult of achievement. It means also an orientation to long-run goals and long-deferred rewards. It means an early determination to "get ahead." It is incumbent upon the good parent to encourage in his children those habits and goals which will help them to be "better off" than himself, and his first duty is to make his child *want* to "be somebody."

2. The middle-class ethic is an ethic of individual responsibility. It applauds resourcefulness and self-reliance, a reluctance to turn to others for help. In Margaret Mead's words:

> Parenthood in America has become a very special thing and parents see themselves not as giving their children final status and place, rooting them firmly for life in a dependable social structure, but merely as training them for a race which they will run alone.[3]

Although it recognizes, as does the ethic of every society, a certain virtue in generosity, it minimizes the obligation to share with others, even with one's own kin, especially insofar as this obligation is likely to interfere with the achievement of one's own goals. If one's first obligation is to help, spontaneously and unstintingly, friends and kinsmen in distress, a kind of minimum security is provided for all, but nobody is likely to get very far ahead of the game.

3. Middle-class norms place a high evaluation on the cultivation and possession of skills and on the tangible achievements which are presumed to witness to the possession of skills and the application of effort. Outstanding performance of almost any kind is applauded, e.g., athletic achievement, but there is special emphasis on academic achievement and the acquisition of skills of potential economic and occupational value.

4. Middle-class norms place great value on "worldly asceticism," a readiness and an ability to postpone and to subordinate the temptations of immediate satisfactions and self-indulgence in the interest of the achievement of long-run goals. Industry and thrift, even divorced from any conscious utilitarian objectives, are admirable in themselves.

5. Rationality is highly valued, in the sense of the exercise of forethought, conscious planning, the budgeting of time, and the allocation of resources in the most economic and technologically most efficient way. This involves a disinclination to trust to the irrational workings of chance and moral suspiciousness of gambling despite the fact that gambling enjoys a certain shady popularity among many middle-class adults and children.

6. The middle-class value system rewards and encourages the rational cultivation of manners, courtesy and personality. In the middle-class world, mastery of certain conventions of speech and gesture carry prestige and are instrumental to success. Furthermore, and more importantly, the middle-class

[3] Mead, *op. cit.*, p. 75.

adult, especially the male, circulates in a world of numerous transient and segmental but highly important secondary-group relationships. A facility in such relationships, an ability to "make friends and influence people," or at least to avoid antagonizing them is vital. A pamphlet published by the National Association of Manufacturers for free distribution to school children and significantly entitled *Your Future Is What You Make It* neatly expresses this theme:

> Here's an item for your personal rule book: *Don't let your courtesy get rusty.* You'll have to get along with all the people around you, so treat them as you wish to be treated. In any organization, there's a certain amount of friction. No wonder we prize those persons who make life happier by helping to reduce it! *Getting along with people is one of the most important requirements for those who want to get ahead on the job—or off.*[4]

The achievement of these skills necessarily implies the cultivation of patience, self-control and the inhibition of spontaneity.

7. The middle-class ethic emphasizes the control of physical aggression and violence, which are subversive, on the one hand, of good personal relations with as many people as possible and, on the other hand, of an impersonal competitive order in which intellectual, technical and social skills may realize their maximum value.

8. Recreation should be "wholesome." That is, one should not "waste" time but spend his leisure "constructively." Play is necessary and desirable, but play gains in merit to the degree that it involves some measure of foresight, study, practice and sustained endeavor toward the development of a collection, a skill or a fund of specialized knowledge. Hence the pride and pleasure of the middle-class parent in his children's pursuit of a "hobby."

9. Lastly, middle-class values emphasize "respect for property." This does not mean a desire for material goods nor does it mean simple "honesty." It means a particular cluster of attitudes regarding the nature of property rights and the significance of property.

It includes an emphasis on the *right* of the owner to do as he wishes with his belongings *versus* an emphasis on the *claims* of others who may stand in primary-group relationships to the owner. It includes an emphasis on the explicit consent of the owner prior to the use or conversion of his articles of property *versus* "helping yourself" with the understanding that the willingness and the obligation to share is implicit in your relationship to the owner. It includes a quasi-sacred attitude toward things, whether others' or one's own or collective property. Things are to be husbanded, treated carefully, not wantonly wasted, carelessly abused or destroyed.

The orderly functioning of the middle-class economic world depends upon a system of strict property accounting, the clear and precise allocation of

---

[4] *Your Future Is What You Make It* (New York: National Association of Manufacturers, 1947), pp. 23–24.

property rights to individuals or the incumbents of certain offices, and the transfer of rights to access, control and usufruct in accordance with fixed and formal procedures, either an explicit act of giving, a decree or order by a duly authorized official or an act of contract. Casualness and imprecision in the allocation and delimitation of property rights and failure to signalize changes in these rights by written instrument or explicit verbal understandings are a source of confusion and conflict in the world of commerce and large-scale organization. Children, it is felt, should get into the habit of thinking in these terms.

Another source of this stress on respect for property lies in the ethic of individual responsibility. This means that a person should make his own way in the world by dint of his own efforts. His claims on the resources accumulated by others and their claims on his resources are minimized. Such claims still exist, particularly between close kin and friends, but they are more severely limited than in most cultures. Insofar as giving and sharing are approved ("Don't be selfish; let your little brother play with your toys!") the emphasis tends to be placed on the merit of the giver rather than on the right of the recipient.

Property, furthermore, is not only of utilitarian or esthetic value, but it is extraordinarily ego-involved, for it is the most conspicuous sign of achievement, the most universally legible symbol of worth. All property, including cash, is, in this sense, of purely sentimental value. But it is of little value in this symbolic respect if it may be easily dissipated by either oneself or others. The ability of property to perform this function is not incompatible with sharing, provided that the claims of the other are not pressed as a matter of legitimate expectation. If things are explicitly given without being asked for or in response to a properly respectful request, the whole transaction becomes a minor ritual dramatizing the ownership and the act of supererogation. Daddy solemnly requests a loan of Johnny. Sister is justly angry because somebody used her stationery without asking, although sister would have been delighted to share it if the other "had only asked." The visitor to the middle-class home is careful to write his bread-and-butter letter.

Lastly, a middle-class home is, to a great extent, a carefully ordered museum of artifacts for display, representing a great deal of "congealed labor." Their function for conspicuous consumption depends upon the preservation of their original state and upon ready recognition of their value, and middle-class children are trained to respect such objects and the order in which they have been lovingly arranged.

The Working-Class Norms

S. M. MILLER AND FRANK RIESSMAN

A decade and a half ago the working class was depicted by Allison Davis and Robert J. Havighurst[1] as permissive and indulgent toward their children and free of the emotional strain of impulse-inhibition which characterized the middle class in the United States. Indeed, it was felt by many that the middle class had much to envy and imitate in the working class.[2] This romantic view of the working class has faded. It is now asserted that the working class (usually termed the "lower class") is incapable of deferring gratification[3] and consequently unable to make major strides in improving their conditions. Frequently accompanying this view is the belief that this lower class is "immoral," "uncivilized," "promiscuous," "lazy," "obscene," "dirty," and "loud."[4] With the rising plane and standard of living of workers has come the argument that workers are middle class in their outlook and desires;[5] the difficulties in attaining full middle-class status lead to juvenile delinquency on the part of those youth who fall back into the working and lower classes[6] and to authoritarianism on the part of those who rise into the middle class.[7] Recently, a further vigorous blow has

Reprinted from *Social Problems*, **9** (Summer, 1961), pp. 86–97, by permission of the authors and the publisher, The Society for the Study of Social Problems. Presented at Annual Meetings of the American Sociological Association, New York, August 30, 1960.

[1] Allison Davis and Robert J. Havighurst, "Social Class and Color Differences in Child Rearing," *American Sociological Review*, 11 (December, 1946), pp. 698–710.

[2] Cf. David Riesman in his introduction to Ely Chinoy's *American Workers and Their Dreams* (New York: Doubleday & Company, 1955).

[3] Louis Schneider and Sverre Lysgaard, "The Deferred Gratification Pattern: A Preliminary Study," *American Sociological Review*, 18 (April, 1953), pp. 142–9.

[4] These adjectives are taken from Rodman who then goes on to declare: "Lantz, Centers, Warner *et al.*, Hollingshead, Drake and Cayton, West, and David, Gardner and Gardner make it clear that this is the way the lower class is viewed within the United States, the Henriques and Braithwaite studies make it clear that this is the way the lower class is viewed within the West Indies." Hyman Rodman, "On Understanding Lower-Class Behaviour," *Social and Economic Studies*, 8 (December, 1959). Other authors state: "One of the most venerable stereotypes has been that applied by middle-class people to lower-class people. The qualities have from time to time included lack of thrift, intellectual inferiority, habitual dirtyness, licentiousness, and many that have derogatory implications." Robert R. Sears, Eleanor E. Maccoby, and Harry Levin, *Patterns of Child Rearing* (Evanston: Row, Peterson and Company, 1957), p. 442. We have isolated five types of stereotypes of workers—anomic, depraved, incapable of deferring gratification, class conscious and middle-class oriented; these are discussed in S. M. Miller and Frank Riessman, "Images of Workers," a paper presented to the Eastern Sociological Society, New York, 1957.

[5] Daniel Bell, *The End of Ideology* (Glencoe: Free Press, 1959), and in various issues of *Fortune* magazine. On the other hand, see his path-breaking article, "The Subversion of Collective Bargaining," *Commentary*, March, 1960.

[6] Albert Cohen, *Delinquent Boys: The Culture of the Gang* (Glencoe: Free Press, 1955).

[7] Joseph Greenblum and Leonard I. Pearlin, "Vertical Mobility and Prejudice: A Socio-Psychological Analysis," in Reinhard Bendix and Seymour Martin Lipset, eds., *Class, Status and Power* (Glencoe: Free Press, 1953).

felled any notions of desirable characteristics of workers: their economic liberalism is not paralleled by political liberalism for workers are said to be more authoritarian in outlook than are members of the middle class.[8] The free, spontaneous worker is now seen as an aggressive, authoritarian, yet fettered person. . . .

In this paper, we can only present a few elements of what we believe is a more realistic picture of workers. This analysis is severely compressed and truncated in this presentation and it might be helpful therefore to indicate at the outset an important element of our general orientation. Our stress is much more on cognitive and structural factors than on the more commonly cited affectual and motivational ones. The nature of the conditions of working-class lives (jobs, opportunities, family structure) affects behavior more than has been frequently realized; similarly, modes of understanding the environment can be more important than deep-seated personality factors in behavioral patterns. (For example, workers' low estimates of opportunities and high expectations of risk and loss may be more crucial in the unwillingness to undertake certain long-term actions than personality inadequacies involved in a presumed inability to defer gratification.) This is not to argue that motivational-psychological-affectual variables are unimportant but that they have been over-stressed while cognitive and structural variables have been underemphasized. The recognition of the importance of the internal life of man has sometimes overshadowed the significance of the more manifest aspects of his existence.

Our definition of working class is simple: regular members of the non-agricultural labor force in manual occupations. Thus, we exclude the "lower class," irregular working people, although the analysis has some relevance to the lower class as will be mentioned below. One of the greatest sources of difficulties in understanding non-upper and non-middle class behaviour is that social scientists have frequently used the omnibus category of "lower class" to encompass the stable, and frequently mobile, fairly high income skilled workers, the semi-skilled factory worker, the worker in varied service trades, the unskilled worker and the irregular worker. This collection is probably more a congeries of fairly disparate groups than a category with similar life chances and circumstances. It is especially important to distinguish the segment which has irregular employment (and "voluntary" withdrawals from the labor force), unskilled jobs in service occupations (and is largely Negro and Puerto Rican now) from the other groupings, which are larger and have more of a commonness to them.

This latter group of regular workmen we call "working class" despite the reluctance of many social scientists today to use this historic term; the opprobrious term "lower class" might be applied to the irregular segment although it would probably be better all around if a less invidious term (perhaps "the unskilled") were employed.

The reluctance to make the distinction between "working class" and "lower

---

[8] Seymour Martin Lipset, *Political Man: The Social Bases of Politics* (Garden City: Doubleday & Company, 1960), Chapter IV.

class," despite useful discussions by Kahl[9] and others, not only is a topic worthy of independent study, but leads to error. For example, Hollingshead and Redlich in their important study have been interpreted as finding that the lower the class, the higher the rate of mental illness. Close examination of their data reveal, however, that the working class, Class IV, is closer to the upper and middle classes, Classes I, II and III, than to the lower class, Class V. Classes I through IV are similar, while Class V is quite dissimilar from all the other classes, including the working class.[10]

Within the working class, we are primarily interested in the *stable* working-class subculture. We believe there is considerable variation within the working class,[11] but the differences probably are variations upon the theme of the stable working-class pattern. While we think in terms of working-class subcultures, and, to some extent, lower-class subcultures, a key to understanding them, we believe, is likely to be the *stable* working-class subculture.

Our analysis is aimed at developing *themes* in working-class life. Thus, we are interpreting the *meaning* of findings rather than reporting new findings. We have utilized the published materials commonly employed plus our own interviews and observations of working-class people. . . .

BASIC THEMES

Before discussing a few of the themes which we think are basic in working-class life, we present a brief overall picture of what we believe are the essential characteristics of the stable American worker today.

He is traditional, "old fashioned," somewhat religious, and patriarchal.[12] The worker likes discipline, structure, order, organization and directive, definite

[9] Joseph A. Kahl, *The American Class Structure* (New York: Rinehart and Company, 1959), pp. 205 ff.

[10] For the original report, see A. B. Hollingshead and Frederick C. Redlich, *Social Class and Mental Illness* (New York: John Wiley and Sons, 1958). The point above is taken from S. M. Miller and Elliot G. Mishler, "Social Class, Mental Illness, and American Psychiatry," *Milbank Memorial Fund Quarterly*, XXXVII (April, 1959), pp. 174–99.

[11] Robert Blauner, in his thoughtful paper, "Industrial Differences in Work Attitudes and Work Institutions," points out important differences among workers in different industries. Bennett Berger, *Working Class Suburb* (Berkeley: University of California Press, 1960) believes there are differences in attitudes among workers of "Arkie" and "Okie" backgrounds, and workers of a non-rural background. A variety of studies show the importance of educational differences among workers, a factor with which we are very concerned. See Frank Riessman, *Workers' Attitudes Towards Participation and Leadership*, unpublished Ph.D. dissertation in social psychology, Columbia University, 1955.

[12] The cross-class F-scale studies uniformly show that workers are more likely than middle-class individuals to support the statement that "the most important thing a child should learn is obedience to his parents." Maccoby and Gibbs have pointed out that workers strongly demand respect and obedience from their children. Eleanor E. Maccoby, Patricia K. Gibbs, *et al.*, "Methods of Child Rearing in Two Social Classes," in William E. Martin and Celia Burns Stendler, eds., *Readings in Child Development* (New York: Harcourt Brace and Company, 1954), pp. 380–96. Riessman's data indicate that not only parents but older people in general are to be obeyed and respected. See Frank Riessman, *op. cit.*, Evelyn Millis Duvall, "Conceptions of Parenthood," *American Journal of Sociology*, LII (November, 1946), pp. 193–203.

(strong) leadership, although he does not see such strong leadership in opposition to human, warm, informal, personal qualities.[13] Despite the inadequacy of his education, he is able to build abstractions, but he does so in a slow, physical fashion.[14] He reads ineffectively, is poorly informed in many areas, and is often quite suggestible, although interestingly enough he is frequently suspicious of "talk" and "new fangled ideas."

He is family centered; most of his relationships take place around the large extended, fairly cooperative family.[15] Cooperation and mutual aid are among his most important characteristics.[16]

While desiring a good standard of living, he is not attracted to the middle-class style of life with its accompanying concern for status and prestige.[17]

He is not class conscious although aware of class differences. While he is somewhat radical on certain economic issues, he is quite illiberal on numerous matters, particularly civil liberties and foreign policiy.[18]

The outstanding weakness of the worker is lack of education. Strongly desiring education for his children, he shows considerable concern about their school work, although he feels estranged and alienated from the teacher and the school, as he similarly feels alienated from many institutions in our society.[19] This alienation is expressed in a ready willingness to believe in the corruptness of leaders and a general negative feeling toward "big shots."

He is stubborn in his ways, concerned with strength and ruggedness, interested in mechanics, materialistic, superstitious, holds an "eye for an eye" psychology, and is largely uninterested in politics.

STABILITY AND SECURITY

We suspect that one of the central determinants in working-class life is the striving for stability and security.[20] External and internal factors promote

[13] Frank Riessman, *op. cit., passim.*

[14] For a review of the relevant literature, see Frank Riessman, *Education and the Culturally Deprived Child* (New York: Harper and Brothers, 1961).

[15] Floyd Dotson, "Patterns of Voluntary Association Among Urban Working Class Families," *American Sociological Review,* **16** (October, 1951), pp. 687–93. "In at least 15 of the 50 families, leisure time activities of the husbands and wives were completely dominated by the kin group. In another 28 families, regular visiting patterns with relatives constituted a major, although not exclusive, form of social activity." (p. 691) Also see p. 693.

[16] August B. Hollingshead, "Class Differences in Family Stability," in Bendix and Lipset, *op. cit.,* p. 290. A similar point is made by Allison Davis, Burleigh B. Gardner and Mary R. Gardner, *Deep South* (Chicago: University of Chicago Press, 1941), p. 111. Also see John Useem, Pierre Tangent, and Ruth Useem, "Stratification in a Prairie Town," *American Sociological Review,* **7** (June, 1942), p. 334.

[17] S. M. Miller and Frank Riessman, "Are Workers Middle Class?" *Dissent,* **8** (Autumn, 1961), pp. 507–516.

[18] The Centers' findings can be interposed to support the first sentence of the paragraph despite Centers' mode of analysis. Richard Centers, *The Psychology of Social Classes* (Princeton: Princeton University Press, 1949). Cf. Ralf Dahrendorf, *Class and Class Conflict in Industrial Society* (Stanford: Stanford University Press, 1959), pp. 288–289. On civil liberties and foreign policy, see Lipset, *op. cit.*

[19] Riessman, *Education and the Culturally Deprived Child,* has a discussion of some of the relevant literature.

[20] Hollingshead, *op. cit.,* pp. 290–1.

instability and insecurity. Chief among the external factors is unemployment and layoff. Prosperity has of course barred the anguish of the prolonged depression of the 1930's, but the danger of occasional layoffs of some duration are not remote during the usually shaky prosperity conditions which are interlarded with episodes of recession, plant relocation, industry decline and strikes.[21]

Chief among the internal factors promoting instability are family discord, including divorce and desertion, intergenerational conflict, and the desire for excitement.

Coping with the instability threats becomes a dominant activity within the working-class family. Many practices, such as mutual aid and cooperation, extended family perspectives, are important as adjustive mechanisms. "Getting by" rather than "getting ahead" in the middle-class self-realization and advancement sense is likely to be dominant.[22]

For example, the limited desire to become foremen is partly a result of the economic insecurity resulting from the loss of job seniority in case of a layoff.[23]

Part of the ambivalence toward obtaining a college education reflects the same emphasis on security. Even a highly talented working-class youth is not sure what he can do with a college diploma, and he may fear the disruption of his familial, community and peer group security.[24]

The poll data indicating the unwillingness of workers to take economic risks and their greater concern for jobs with security, is part of the same pattern of a striving for stability.[25]

TRADITIONALISM

The American working class is primarily a migrant group; not only have people come from European farms and rural settlements to American factories but they also have migrated from America's rural life to the industrial scene.[26] Traditional practices, once thought to be infrequent in urbanized, industrialized, nuclear-oriented families, are very strong in working-class families.[27] The pattern

[21] Charles H. Hession, S. M. Miller and Curwen Stoddart, *The Dynamics of the American Economy* (New York: Alfred A. Knopf, 1956), Chapter 11.

[22] Joseph A. Kahl, *op. cit.*, pp. 205–210.

[23] Ely Chinoy, *op. cit.*, and Charles R. Walker, *Steeltown* (New York: Harper and Brothers, 1950), have data showing the considerable reluctance of workers to become foremen.

[24] The initial attraction of many working-class youth to engineering is partly due to the apparently concrete and clear nature of the work and the presumed definiteness of the education for a particular type of job. Motivating working-class youth to go to college may require an expansion and sharpening of working-class children's interpretation of the job market.

[25] Centers, *op. cit.*, p. 62.

[26] Lloyd Reynolds, *Labor Economics and Labor Relations* (New York: Prentice-Hall, Inc., 1949), pp. 7–23.

[27] Recent literature, particularly Weinstein and Axelrod, have pointed out that traditional practices are more widespread than previously thought in the middle class. The lack of differences between middle-class and working class respondents reported in the studies may be due to the lack of sensitive instruments. While our analysis is not necessarily based on the notion of greater traditional and extended practices in working-class than in middle-class families, we believe that these practices assume a greater importance in the overall activities of the former.

is patriarchal, extended (with many relevant cousins, grandparents, and aunts and uncles) and delineated by sharply separated sex roles. The family is not child-centered (or child-dominant or dominating), but parent-centered and controlled. Traditional values of automatic obedience by children are expected to be the norm even if not always observed in practice.[28]

One probable consequence of this is that workers seem to be more authoritarian than they probably are. For a while on the F-scale type of test, they tend to be "conventional," a characteristic of the authoritarian according to Adorno et al., it is doubtful, as we have tried to argue elsewhere,[29] that this conventionalism means the same in both the middle and working class.

The worker also has a traditional attitude toward discipline which again may be confused with authoritarianism. All the child-rearing data indicate that workers utilize physical punishment as a basic discipline technique. In the eyes of the worker punishment discourages people from wrong-doing whether the punishment is inflicted upon them or upon others who serve as "examples." There is also a "rightness" about punishment for a misdeed, for punishment is the other side of responsibility for one's actions. Thus, for example, acceptance of the death penalty may not be the result of a sado-maschistic character structure but the product of a belief in the efficacy of punishment in deterring others from misdeeds and in the value of attaching responsibility to people's actions.[30] Workers consequently do not easily accept the notion that an individual is not responsible for his crimes because of his emotional state at the time of their occurrence.

INTENSITY

We believe that one of the most neglected themes in working-class life and one of the most difficult to understand and interpret is that of intensity. This intensity is expressed in a number of different ways. It is found in the areas in which workers have belief and emotional involvement. While there are numerous areas about which workers are confused, and lacking in opinion (e.g., the high percentage of "no answer" and "don't know" on public opinion polls), there are important spheres in which they have definite convictions, and indeed, are highly stubborn. Their beliefs about religion, morality, superstition, diet, punishment, custom, traditional education, the role of women, intellectuals, are illustrative here. Many of these attitudes are related to their traditional orientation and they are held unquestioningly in the usual traditional manner. They are not readily open to reason and they are not flexible opinions.

[28] Duvall, *op. cit.*

[29] S. M. Miller and Frank Riessman, "'Working-Class Authoritarianism': A Critique of Lipset," *British Journal of Sociology*, forthcoming. Also, our "Social Class, Education and Authoritarianism," a paper presented to the American Sociological Society, Washington, 1957.

[30] David Joseph Bordua, *Authoritarianism and Intolerance: A Study of High School Students*, unpublished Ph.D. thesis, Department of Social Relations, Harvard University, 1956.

Other possible sources of this intensity may be their physical (less symbolic) relation to life,[31] their person centeredness (to be discussed below), and their lack of education.

PERSON-CENTERED

Threaded through much of working-class life is a person-centered theme. On one level this theme has an informal, human quality, of easy, comfortable relationship to people where the affectionate bite of humor is appreciated. The factory "horse-play," the ritualistic kidding, is part of this although by no means all of it. It is an expressive component of life.[32]

At another level, it is the importance of personal qualities. One learns more from people than from books, it is said. At a political level, the candidate as a decent, human person is more important than the platform.[33]

In the bureaucratic situation, the worker still tends to think of himself as relating to people not to roles and invisible organizational structure. This orientation is an aspect of particularism, the reaction to persons and situations in terms of their personal qualities and relations to oneself rather than in terms of some universal characteristics of their social position. The neighbor or workmate who gets ahead is expected "not to put on airs"; he should like the "old gang" and accept them despite his new position. An individual is expected to transcend his office. A foreman is a s.o.b. not because he has stresses and demands on the job which force him to act forcibly and harshly, but because of his personal qualities. Contrariwise, one of the top executives is frequently regarded as one who would help the rank-and-file workers if he had the chance, because *he* is a "nice guy"; putting him in the stresses of a new position would not force him to act as others in that position have acted.[34] It is the man not the job that makes for behavior; this attitude is not a class-conscious one, far from it. Another example of particularism is the juvenile delinquent who reacts positively to the social worker or therapist who seems to be interested in him beyond the call of professional duty.

PRAGMATISM AND ANTI-INTELLECTUALISM

With workers, it is the end-result of action rather than the planning of action or the preoccupation with means that counts. An action that goes astray is not liked for itself; it has to achieve the goal intended to be satisfactory.[35] It is results that pay off. While this orientation has an anti-intellectual

---

[31] The discussion by Miller and Swanson on the "motoric" orientation of workers is one of the most suggestive in the literature. Daniel R. Miller and Guy E. Swanson, *Inner Conflict and Defense* (New York: Henry Holt and Company, 1960).

[32] *Ibid.*

[33] Cf. Lipset, *op. cit.*, pp. 285–86.

[34] S. M. Miller, *Union Structure and Industrial Relations: A Case Study of a Local Labour Union*, unpublished Ph.D. thesis, Princeton University, 1951.

[35] Melvin L. Kohn, "Social Class and the Exercise of Parental Authority," *American Sociological Review*, **24** (June, 1959), pp. 364–65.

dimension, it does somewhat reduce the reliance on personality (person-centered theme) by its emphasis on results. Workers like the specific action, the clear action, the understood result. What can be seen and felt is more likely to be real and true in the workers' perspectives, which are therefore likely to be limited. The pragmatic orientation of workers does not encourage them to see abstract ideas as useful. Education, for what it does for one in terms of opportunities, may be desirable but abstract intellectual speculation, ideas which are not rooted in the realities of the present, are not useful, indeed may be harmful.

On the other hand, workers often have an exaggerated respect for the ability of the learned. A person with intellectual competence in one field is frequently thought to be a "brain" with ability in all fields; partly this is due to the general abstract nature of ideas regardless of field. If a real obstacle comes up, they may expect "the brain" to have a ready solution for it, even if they may not be willing to adopt it.

At first glance, the anti-words orientation may appear to be incompatible with the possible appeal of the charismatic. But it is not. For the charismatic are charismatic because they can be emotional and expressive, qualities not usually associated with abstract ideas. Also, the charismatic leader may promise "pie in the sky" but it is a very concrete, specific set of ingredients with a clear distribution of the pie.

EXCITEMENT

Another component in workers' lives is the appreciation of excitement, of moving out of the humdrum. News, gossip, new gadgets, sports, are consequently very attractive to workers. To some extent, the consumership of workers—the desire to have new goods, whether television sets or cars—is part of this excitement dimension. The excitement theme is often in contradiction with the traditional orientation.

It is worth noting that different subgroups within the working class may favor one theme rather than another. Thus younger groups and, especially juvenile delinquents, are probably much more attracted to the excitement theme, are more alienated and less traditional. On the other hand, workers with a more middle-class orientation are probably less alienated, more traditional and pragmatic.

PARSIMONY AND VARIATION

In the preceding remarks we have touched only very fleetingly on a few themes of working-class life and ignored other important themes, like cooperation and a physical orientation, almost completely. While we can sum up our analysis in a relatively few descriptive adjectives, such as person centered, traditional, pragmatic, etc., we have been unable to develop a parsimonious conceptualization, such as a non-deferred gratification pattern which attempts to explain by this single formulation or theme a vast array of behavior. Perhaps the simplest shorthand, if one wishes to use it, would be Parsons'; employing his criteria, we could say that workers are particularistic rather than universalistic, affective rather than neutral, ascriptive rather than achievement-minded, diffuse in definition of role rather than specific. But this summary may obscure more than it reveals.

Indeed, our analysis contains a number of themes which may, in part, be in opposition to each other. For example, traditionalism and alienation have certain conflicting features, as do pragmatism and person centeredness, and the resulting strains and adjustive mechanisms are important to analyze.

Let us make just two points to indicate the general value of the orientation that we have only sketchily presented here: (1) It may be possible to understand other working-class and lower-class styles by looking for sources of variation from the stable working-class pattern. (2) The development of the stable working-class style among lower-class and working-class youth might be the goal of educational and other socializing and remedial forces rather than instilling the middle-class value structure.

VARIATIONS OF WORKING-CLASS CULTURE

By stating that we are describing the *stable* worker we imply that there are other worker subultures. We feel that the stable worker has been relatively ignored in the emphasis on the "underprivileged," "lower class," unskilled, irregular worker and the middle-class oriented worker. By understanding the stable worker, important leads are provided for understanding other subcultural variations.

The unskilled, irregular (read "lower class") worker lacks the disciplined, structured and traditional approach of the stable worker and stresses the excitement theme. He does less to cope with insecurity and instability. In the large industrial and commercial centers today the lower-class style of life (as distinct from the stable working-class style) is found particularly among peoples relatively new to industrial and urban life: Negroes, Puerto Ricans, transplanted Southern whites. They have not been able so far to make the kind of adjustment that stable workers have. Frequently, they have special problems not only of discrimination but of fairly menial (service) jobs at low pay, extremely poor housing and considerable overcrowding. Some children of stable workers do not develop the stable pattern and assume the lower-class style. A few children of middle-class parents become lower class: they have unskilled jobs and adopt the lower-class style of life. But the bulk of individuals with the lower-class style come from those who are children of unskilled workers and of farmers, thus including many of the ethnic people of whom we spoke earlier.[36]

---

[36] The data to support this assertion can be computed from the two American studies detailed in the appendix to S. M. Miller, "Comparative Social Mobility," *Current Sociology*, 1961.

Another deviant group from the main working-class pattern are those workers who are very much concerned with achievement of success for children and for the symbols of success in consumership. In many cases the families are secure and stable and have been able to make a workable accommodation to the stresses of their lives. But this is not enough for the middle-class orientation; in many cases there is a vague opportunity and motivational factor present.

Those of working-class origins who do move into the middle class and into the middle-class style of life are likely to have a middle-class cross-pressure in that they have more frequently than other working-class children have relatives who were or are middle class. Their grandparents may have been middle class; their parents though in working-class occupations are more likely to have more education than is typical in the working class and to have other attributes of middle-class life.[37] If we may give a literary example, in *Sons and Lovers*, the hero, brought up in a mining community, had a working-class father but his mother was a teacher and came from a middle-class community. Undoubtedly, the hero, whose life follows that of D. H. Lawrence, received motivation from her to move into literary activities and probably also some early direct help in reading and school. The motivational factor is important but it is likely linked to the background and experiential factor of grandparental and paternal activities.

We have discussed these two styles in different ways. The lower-class style is considered to be the inability to develop an adequate measure of coping with the environment so that some degree of security and stability ensues. The origin of the middle-class style would seem to emerge from the stable pattern. A working-class family would likely first go through a stable period of accommodation before it or the children developed middle-class orientations. *It is not intrinsic in the stable pattern that a middle-class orientation emerge but the stable stage would seem to be a necessary step in most cases for the development of a middle-class orientation.*

Other variations in the subculture of workers exist. Religious, ethnic, educational, and regional factors are important in producing deviations from the pattern we have described.

THE STABLE STYLE AS GOAL

Explicitly as well as implicitly, many agents of educational and other institutions that deal with working-class and lower-class youth attempt to "middle-classize" them. When any effort is extended toward the juvenile delinquent, it usually with this orientation. Such endeavors are largely a failure because the middle-class outlook is alien to the experiences, prospects and values of these youth. Possibly there is a better chance of emphasizing working-class values; for example cooperation—as happens in group therapy—rather than vocational success in middle-class terms. We recognize that it is not easy to develop some

[37] Cf. the remarks of Kaare Svalastoga in "Report of the Fifth Working Conference on Social Stratification and Social Mobility," International Sociological Association, 1960.

of the working-class values but they are probably much easier to develop than the middle-class ones. In addition, emphasis on the former may develop a more favorable attitude on the part of the youth to both the institution and its agents than does the insistence on the middle-class values.

A basic value question is involved here: Do we attempt to make the middle-class style a model for all to follow? Or do we adopt a rigid cultural relativity position that the lower class has a right to its way of life regardless of the social effects? Or do we attempt to develop what appear to be the most positive elements, from the point of view of society and the individuals involved, of the styles of life closest to them? While we have some doubts about the answer, the possibility of the stable working-class style as the goal adds a new dimension to a deep problem that deserves more forthright scrutiny than it has received.

Our attempts at interpreting working-class life will undoubtedly prove inadequate. But we are certain that without an attempt at analyzing the contexts and the genotypes of working-class behavior and attitude, the *description* (and there is faulty description) and interpretation of working-class life will remain a reflex of social scientists' changing attitudes toward the middle class.

PERSONALITY FORMATION

Negro American Intelligence: A New Look at an Old Controversy

THOMAS F. PETTIGREW

INTRODUCTION

Following the Supreme Court's school desegregation decision in 1954, white supremacists mounted a major revival of racist doctrines. These claims, centering on the alleged genetic intellectual inferiority of Negro Americans, have received considerable publicity in the mass media. But American public opinion is far less receptive to such reasoning now than it was a generation ago. Public opinion poll data reveal that, while only two out of five white Americans regarded Negroes their intellectual equals in 1942, almost four out of five did by 1956— including a substantial majority of white Southerners. Much of this change is due to the thorough repudiation of racist assertions by the vast majority of modern psychologists and other behavioral scientists. Indeed, the latest research in this area lends the strongest evidence yet available for this repudiation. The present paper takes a new look at this old controversy and presents a summary of the relevant research. . . .

THE MEDIATORS OF INTELLECTUAL UNDERDEVELOPMENT

Within this new perspective* on intelligence as a relatively plastic quality, a series of environmental mediators of the individual Negro child's intellectual undervelopment has been determined. In fact, these mediators exert their effects upon even the Negro fetus. One study found that dietary supplementation by vitamins supplied during the last half of pregnancy had directly beneficial effects on later I.Q. scores of the children. In a sample of mothers from the

Reprinted from the *Journal of Negro Education,* **33** (Winter, 1964), pp. 6–25, by permission of the author and the publisher. Thorough documentation for this article will be found in: Thomas F. Pettigrew, *A Profile of the Negro American*, Princeton, New Jersey: Van Nostrand, 1964. The author wishes to acknowledge with appreciation the considerable aid provided him by Professor Gordon W. Allport, Dr. Irving I. Gottesman, Dr. Ronald Nuttall, and his physician wife, Dr. Ann Hallman Pettigrew.

* [The material referred to is not included—Editor.]

lowest socio-economic level, 80 per cent of whom was Negro, the group fortified with iron and vitamin B complex had children whose mean I.Q. at three years of age averaged five full points above the children of the unfortified control group, 103.4 to 98.4. One year later, the mean difference had enlarged to eight points, 101.7 to 93.6. The same researchers failed to find a similar effect among white mothers and their children from a mountain area. Presumably, the largely Negro sample was even poorer and more malnourished than the white mountain sample. Dire poverty, through the mediation of *the mother's meager diet*, can thus begin acting to impair intelligence before the lower-class Negro child is born.

Economic problems also hamper intelligence through the mediation of *premature births*. Premature children of all races reveal not only a heightened incidence of neurologic abnormalities and greater susceptibility to disease, but also a considerably larger percentage of mental defectives. A further organic factor in intelligence is *brain injury* in the newborn. And both of these conditions have higher incidences among Negroes because of their greater frequency in the most economically depressed sectors of the population.

Later complications are introduced by the impoverished environments in which most Negro children grow up. At the youngest, pre-school ages, race differences in I.Q. means are minimal. Repeated research shows that in the first two years of life there are no significant racial differences in either psycho-motor development or intelligence. Racist theorists deny the importance of these findings on two conflicting grounds. They either claim that infant tests have no predictive value whatsoever for later I.Q. scores, or cite an older study by McGraw that found Negro infants retarded in comparison with white infants. Neither argument is adequate. Two recent investigations provide convincing evidence that properly administered infant tests *do* predict later scores. And the 1931 McGraw study is no longer regarded as a critical experiment. It was a pioneer effort that compared white infants with Negro infants of markedly smaller stature on an unvalidated adaptation of a European test. Furthermore, later Northern investigations show little or no Negro lag in intellectual development through kindergarten and five years of age when thorough socio-economic controls are applied.

It is only after a few years of inferior schooling have passed that many Negro children begin to drop noticeably in measured I.Q. Part of this drop is due to the heavier reliance placed by intelligence tests at these ages upon verbal skills, skills that are particularly influenced by a constricted environment. Thus, one Southern study of *"verbal destitution"* discovered that those Negro college students most retarded in a reading clinic came from small, segregated high schools and exhibited language patterns typical of the only adult models they had encountered—poorly educated parents, teachers, and ministers.

Another factor in the declining test averages over the school years is simply *the nature of the schools* themselves. Deutsch gives the example of an assignment to "write a page on 'The Trip I took'" given to lower-class youngsters in a ghetto school who had never been more than 25 city blocks from home. Deutsch maintains: "The school represents a foreign outpost in an encapsulated community which is surrounded by what, for the child, is unknown and foreign."

This tendency of the measured I.Q.'s of Negro children to diminish with increasing age is interpreted by racists not as evidence of the eroding effects of ghetto living but as proof that Negroes mature rapidly and begin to decline earlier than whites. Such an idea, based on the belief that Negroes as a "race" are less evolved, is seriously embarrassed by the often demonstrated fact that environmentally-deprived Caucasian groups reveal precisely the same phenomenon—mountain and other rural children in America and the canal-boat and gypsy children of England. Furthermore, the positive relationship between socio-economic status and tested I.Q. among Negroes increases with age, again suggesting that environmental factors become evermore vital as the child matures.

The nature of the *disrupted family life* of many lower-status Negro youths adds to the slum's lack of environmental stimulation. Most of these youngsters are reared in large families, with reduced parental contact. In addition, many of them are in fatherless homes. And Deutsch and Stetler have each demonstrated that Negro children raised in such broken homes score significantly below comparable Negro children from intact homes on intelligence measures.

Other research pinpoints which tasks tested by intelligence tests are most impaired by this restriction of stimulation. Woods and Toal matched two groups of Negro and white adolescents on I.Q. and noted sub-test differences. While superior to the whites on some tests, the Negroes were noticeably deficient on tasks such as detection of errors and drawing pictorial completions which required ability to visualize spatially. A series of similar studies reached the same conclusion; one demonstrated that this difficulty with perceptual and spatial relations was considerably more marked in a southern-reared Negro sample than in an I.Q.-matched northern-reared Negro sample. This *breakdown of spatial performance* among otherwise intelligent Negro children, especially in the more restrictive South, offers a suggestive parallel with the comparable spatial breakdown noted in the sensory deprivation research. In any event, two additional studies provide evidence that this disability is correctable. Both studies gave groups of Negro and white children special training in spatial perception and found that the Negro subjects benefited more from the practice. I.Q. test scores were markedly higher for the Negro subjects five months after the training. Anastasi believes this work supports the idea that the Negroes tested suffered from an unusually barren perceptual experience in early life.

Organic complications and environmental impoverishment are not the only mediators depressing Negro American intelligence. Both the "functioning intelligence" and the measured I.Q. of an individual are inseparably intertwined with his personality. Weisskopf has given case evidence of the great variety of ways *personality problems* can deter normal intellectual development. A child may do poorly in learning situations in a conscious or unconscious desire to punish his parents, to inflict self-punishment, or to avoid self-evaluation. And Roen has demonstrated that such personality problems are more highly related to intelligence test scores among Negroes than among whites. He equated two racial groups of soldiers on a wide range of social variables and found that a series of personality measures were more closely correlated with intelligence for the Negroes than for the whites. In particular, he noted that Negro soldiers who scored low on a self-confidence questionnaire had unusually low intelligence scores.

Racist claims of Caucasian superiority contributes to the Negro's lack of intellectual self-confidence. This insecurity is especially provoked by any direct comparison with white performance. One investigation administered a task to Negro Southern college students with two different sets of instructions. One set told how other students at their college did on the task, while the second told how whites throughout the nation did. Those subjects who anticipated white comparison performed significantly poorer on the task and indicated stronger concern and anxiety about their performance.

The *role of "Negro"* is also a critical factor. Put simply, the Negro is not expected to be bright. To reveal high intelligence is to risk seeming "uppity" to a white racist. And soon a self-fulfilling prophesy begins to operate, for the Negro who assumes a facade of stupidity as a defense mechanism against oppression is very likely to grow into the role. He will not be eager to learn, and he will not strive to do well in the testing situation. After all, an intelligence test is a middle-class white man's instrument; it is a device whites use to prove their capacities and get ahead in the white world. Achieving a high test score does not have the same meaning for a lower-status Negro child, and it may even carry a definite connotation of personal threat. In this sense, scoring low on intelligence measures may for some talented Negro children be a rational response to perceived danger.

In addition to stupidity, the role of "Negro" prescribes both passivity and lack of ambition as central traits. And these traits have been found to be crucial personality correlates of I.Q. changes in white children. The Fels Research Institute found that aggressiveness and high need for achievement differentiate those children whose scores rise between six and ten years of age from those whose scores recede.

Another protective device is slowness. This trait assumes major importance in the speed instruments typically employed to estimate intelligence. In the Negro lower class there is no premium on speed, for work is generally paid by the hour and there are realistically few goals that fast, hard endeavor can attain. Consequently, a number of experimenters have noted that differences in speed of response are primarily responsible for racial differences in I.Q. estimated by timed performance tests.

Playing "Negro" is made especially critical when the examiner is white. Even two-year-old Negroes seem verbally inhibited when *tested by a white*. In fact, this verbal inhibition may be the principal factor underlying the common observation that Negro children generally evidence verbal comprehension quite superior to their verbal communication. One investigation had students of both races tested alternately by Negro and white examiners. For both groups, the mean I.Q. was approximately six points higher when the test was administered by an examiner of their own race. Similarly, adult Negroes in North Carolina were significantly more accurate in rendering the names of the candidates for governor in a recent election to a Negro poll interviewer than to a white interviewer.

VARYING OPPORTUNITIES AND RESULTS

If all of these mechanisms are operating to mediate the influence of a lean, hostile, and constricted environment upon the individual Negro's tested intelligence, certain group trends under conditions of varying opportunities can be predicted. These testable hypotheses are: (a) in environments which approach being equally restrictive for children of both races, the intelligence test means of both will be low and will approach equality; (b) in environments which approach being equally stimulating for children of both races, the intelligence test means of both will be high and will approach equality; and (c) when any racial group moves from a restrictive to a comparatively stimulating environment, its measured I.Q. mean will rise.

The first of these hypotheses was tested on an isolated Caribbean Island, offering little stimulation to its youth. It had "no regular steamship service, no railroad, motion picture theatre, or newspaper. There were very few automobiles and very few telephones. The roads were generally poor. There were no government schools above the elementary level and no private schools above the secondary level. . . . People of all colors, then, were restricted to a rather narrow range of occupational opportunity."

Even here, however, complete equality of status between whites and Negroes was not achieved. White skin was "highly respected," whites typically held the better jobs, and, while almost half of the white students attended private schools nine-tenths of the Negroes attended government schools. Nevertheless, there were no significant color differences on nine of the 14 intelligence measures. The Negroes did best on tests which were less class-linked, less threatening, and less dependent on uncommon words. Thus, socio-economic status was a more important factor than race on four of the five instruments which did yield racial discrepancies, and "lack of confidence," as rated independently by teachers, was highly related to three of them. In general, the island youngsters scored rather low on the tests, with race a relatively insignificant consideration. And the selective migration possibility that the brighter whites were leaving the island is not an explanation for these findings, since there was apparently little out- or in-migration. These data, gathered in a locality which approached being equally restrictive for both races, do "not lend support to the conclusion that colored inferiority in intelligence tests has a racial basis."

The second hypothesis has also received support from a number of studies. Three investigations testing young children in Minneapolis, grade school students in a Nevada city, and adolescents in the Boston area revealed that once social class factors are rigorously controlled there are only minor black-white mean I.Q. differences. In these relatively stimulating, educationally desegregated urban communities, both racial groups secured test averages equal to the national norms.

An additional study was conducted in West Germany. A representative sample of 51 "neger-mischlingskinder"—the mulatto children of Negro American soldiers and German women—was administered a number of intelligence tests and its performance contrasted with a comparable group of 25 white German children. There were no significant differences. Two counterbalancing factors complicate the interpretation of this research. The Negro fathers of these children are undoubtedly an intelligent, highly selected group, selected not only in terms of being chosen to serve in the United States Army in Germany but also in terms of acculturating enough to establish an intimate relationship with a German woman. But this factor is balanced by the fact that the children are mostly illegitimate and viewed as such in the German culture almost by virtue of their color. Furthermore, most of their mothers are probably of lower-status backgrounds and have not been able to provide them with the cultural enrichment of the typical German home. And, finally, German culture, even in this post-Hitler era, can hardly be described as totally free of racist thinking. All in all, the satisfactory test performance of these mulatto Germans appears quite remarkable.

Thus, I.Q. means of groups are retarded when there are constrictive environmental conditions and elevated when there are at least average conditions. Three ecological projects provide further evidence for this generalization. One project correlated home rentals with the I.Q. average of the school children in 300 New York City neighborhoods. Moderately high and positive relationships were found; the more expensive the neighborhood, the higher the test scores. Another noted very close and positive associations between such variables as per capita income and the mean I.Q. level of sixth-grade pupils in 30 American cities. The third project discovered that these ecological correlations tend to be higher for intelligence scores than for scholastic achievement, demonstrating again the extreme sensitivity of the measured I.Q. to the total social environment.

This research is confirmed by additional investigations conducted exclusively on Negroes. Especially since World War II and its attendant expansion of social class differentiation among Negro Americans, socio-economic variables correlate highly and positively with I.Q. in Negro samples. For example, the I.Q. means of groups of Negro third-graders in Washington, D.C. tended to be highest in areas where radios were most often present in the homes and rents most expensive.

These results suggest the third hypothesis: when any group moves from a restrictive to a comparatively stimulating environment, its measured I.Q. mean will rise. Dramatic evidence for this proposition comes from the unique situation of the Osage Indians. Like many other Indian groups, the Osage were ceded land that they did not choose for the establishment of a reservation. But oil was later discovered on their land, and the Osage became relatively prosperous. Since the Osage did not choose their land, the oil discovery was not an indication of native ingenuity beyond that of Indian groups in general. But now they could afford living standards vastly superior to other Indians and on both performance and language tests were found to meet the national norms and be the equal of comparable whites in the area. This finding is all the more impressive when it is remembered that Indian children generally have measured I.Q.'s considerably below that of Negroes.

Similar improvements are recorded from white mountain children in East Tennessee, public school students in Honolulu, and white enlisted men in World War II. Wheeler gave tests to over 3,000 mountain children in 1940, and compared their performance to that of children in the same areas from virtually the same families in 1930. This ten-year span had witnessed broad economic, social, and educational changes in East Tennessee, and the median I.Q.'s reflected these changes in an increment of 11 points, from 82 to 93. Equally remarkable gains are reported for children of many racial groups in Honolulu after a 14-year period of steady improvement in the city's schools. And, finally, 768 soldiers, representative of white enlisted men in World War II, took the old Army Alpha verbal test of World War I and provided striking evidence of the nation's rising intelligence between the two wars. Tuddenham shows that the typical white World War II enlisted man did better than 83 per cent of the enlisted men of the first war.

This last study, incidentally, refutes reasoning put forward by McGurk concerning the intelligence test performances of Negroes in the two world wars. He has argued that if environmental factors are responsible for racial differences in intelligence scores then Negro scores should have steadily approached the white scores between the two wars; yet "the various differences in socioeconomic environments of the Negroes, between 1918 and 1950, have not altered the Negro-white test score relationship." Such "logic" assumes that the socio-economic standards of whites have not changed over these same years. But in fact the prosperity of whites throughout the nation has been improving in many ways faster than that of Negro Americans. If the old Alpha test had been administered to World War II Negroes, they would have most certainly done significantly better than World War I Negroes. "The Negro-white test score relationship," McGurk refers to, has only remained constant because Negroes have made giant strides in intellectual growth when environmental improvements allowed it. Meanwhile, as the Tuddenham data demonstrate, the white median intelligence has also been climbing with environmental improvements. Intelligence, like longevity, is not a fixed capacity for either Negroes or whites.

Another curious assumption made by racist theory arises from interpreting regional as well as racial results on the World War I Alpha. A number of social scientists noted that Negro recruits in such states as Ohio and Illinois had higher median scores than white recruits from such states as Arkansas and Mississippi. These extreme comparisons provided an example of where the environmental deprivations of Southern whites clearly exceeded even those of some Northern Negroes. Garrett hesitated to apply his usual explanation for low scores and concludes that whites in these Southern states were innately inferior intellectually. Instead, he emphasized that Negroes scored below whites within each state; he argued that the low white scores in the South were environmentally induced, but that the even lower Negro scores in the South were a combination of environmental factors and genetic inferiority. To make this argument, Garrett had to assume that Negroes and whites in the South were *equally* deprived—even before World War I. This assumption, of course, is absurd. The period 1890 to the First World War was the lowest ebb of Negro fortunes since slavery. Today the remnants of that era ensure that Negro Southerners as a group are the most environmentally impoverished of all Southerners. And while there were often no public schools for Negroes whatsoever in some rural areas of the South before World War I, the belatedly improved facilities of today still lag behind those of the whites.

Once the Negro American escapes these inferior conditions, however, his improved performance parallels that of the Osage Indians and East Tennessee mountain children. Service in the Armed Forces is one of the most important sources of wider experience and opportunities for Negroes, including those who are illiterate. The Army in the Second World War operated Special Training Units and provided a basic fourth-grade education in eight weeks for 254,000 previously illiterate soldiers—roughly half of them Negroes and the great majority Southerners. A slightly higher percentage of the Negroes than whites successfully completed the intensive course, though how this bears on larger questions of Negro intelligence is a matter of debate because the men given this special training were selected. There is no debate, however, that the success of these units proves the educability of many apparently retarded men of both races.

Another mode of improvement for many Negroes is to migrate North. Negro Northerners routinely achieve higher test medians than comparable Negro Southerners; and Negro children born in the North achieve higher medians than those who come to the North from the South. But do the Negro children who migrate improve their group performance as they remain in the North? This was the central question Klineberg set out to answer in 1935 with perhaps the best known research in the field of race differences. Over 3,000 ten-to-12-year-old Harlem Negroes took an array of individual and group intelligence instruments. These data clearly indicate that the longer the Southern-born children had resided in New York City, the higher their intelligence scores. Those who had been in the North for a number of years approached the levels attained by the native-born Negroes. Smaller studies with less elaborate designs obtained parallel results in Cleveland and Washington, D.C.

More recently, Lee replicated these findings in Philadelphia with the most rigorous research on the topic to date. Employing large samples in a variety of different schools, Lee analyzed the test scores of the *same* children as they progressed through the city's school system. Though never quite catching up with the Philadelphia-born Negro students, the Southern Negro migrants as a group systematically gained in I.Q. with each grade completed in Northern schools. And the earlier they began in the Philadelphia system, the greater their mean increase and final I.Q. The effects of the more stimulating and somewhat less discriminatory North, then, are directly reflected in the measured intelligence of the youngest of Negro migrants.

The major complication in interpreting the Klineberg and Lee work is again introduced by possible selection biases. Those Negro Southerners who migrate North in search of a better life may be selectively brighter and rear brighter children. Such a possibility is emphasized by the "scientific racists," though Shuey concedes this factor could reasonably account for only one-third to one-half of the I.Q. increases observed. But other possibilities also exist. Many of the more intelligent Negroes in the South gain some measure of success and establish roots that are more difficult to break than those of the less intelligent. This phenomenon would operate to make the Klineberg and Lee data all the more impressive. Or, perhaps, intelligence has little or nothing to do with the decision to migrate; personality traits, such as aggressiveness or inability to control hostility over racial frustrations, may be more decisive. Klineberg found the Southern school grades of 562 Negro youths who had since gone North were typical of the entire Negro school populations from which they migrated. More research is needed, but it seems that selective migration cannot begin to account for the dramatic improvement in test performance demonstrated by Negro children who move to the North.

Further evidence that Negro ability goes up when environmental opportunities expand derives from the great diversity of educational enrichment programs current in many major cities. The best known of these is New York City's "Higher Horizons" project. This effort has provided a selected and largely Negro student body with an expensive saturation of skilled specialists—remedial reading teachers, guidance counselors, psychologists, social workers. Its results have been striking; in the first year, the program cut third graders' retardation in reading from six months to a single month. Backed by major foundation grants, other cities have also begun to experiment. Detroit and Philadelphia tried sending "school-community agents" into ghetto schools in an attempt to win parental support for education. Kansas City's Central High School and Tucson's Pueblo High School initiated imaginative new programs. And Washington D.C. launched in 1959 a "talent search" project for 200 deprived seventh graders, 92 per cent of whom were Negro. Similar to Higher Horizons in its concentration of staff and exposure of students to new cultural experiences, "talent search" was soon declared a success. Contrasted with a matched control group, the students of the program evidenced a sharply reduced scholastic failure rate and notable instances of I.Q. increments.

Perhaps the most remarkable demonstration of all is Dr. Samuel Shepard's "Banneker group" work in St. Louis. Shepard, a large, forceful educator, has performed his "miracles" on the most underprivileged school children in the city without the vast expenditures of other efforts. The Banneker group consists of 23 elementary schools with over 16,000 slum and public housing children, more than 95 per cent of them Negro. A Negro who overcame serious economic disadvantages himself, Shepard adamantly rejected the old dogma that sub-standard school work is all you can realistically expect from ghetto children.

He bluntly challenged the pupils, parents, principals, and teachers of the district to perform up to national standards; he appealed to race pride and resorted to continuous exhortations, rallies, contests, posters, and meeting with teachers and parents. Students who made good grades were asked to stand in assemblies for the applause of their class-mates. Teachers were asked to visit the homes of their charges. And parents were asked to provide their offspring with encouragement, study space, a library card, and a dictionary, and to give them books as gifts. For a concrete incentive, Shepard pointed out the new and better jobs now open to Negroes in St. Louis and the lack of qualified Negroes to fill them.

The results of the Banneker effort speak for themselves. Despite an unending stream of poorly educated migrants feeding the area from the South, all test indicators have risen. In the first four years of the program, the median I.Q. increased from the middle 80's to the 90's; median reading, language, and arithmetic levels all climbed; and the percentage of Banneker graduates accepted for the top ability program in St. Louis's desegregated high schools tripled.

The striking results of these imaginative demonstrations may not be directly due to the exact procedures introduced. Given their vast variety of techniques and their uniform success, the demonstrations probably achieve most of their gains because of the sheer fact of intervention—any kind of thoughtful intervention. Often the rate of initial progress slows once the beginning enthusiasm cools. But this is irrelevant to the larger issue of Negro American intelligence. Dramatic improvement in Negro performance for whatever reason is evidence of the underlying potential for learning heretofore stifled by lack of opportunity and attention. This potential for learning is also evident in the findings of a recent experiment at the University of Texas. Negro children learned series of paired material as rapidly and well as white children, even though they came from lower socio-economic backgrounds and had significantly poorer I.Q.'s.

Such demonstrations arouse speculation concerning the effects of desegregation of public school systems. Segregationists have long voiced the unsubstantiated opinion that "school mixing" would mean educational chaos, with the Negroes dragging down the higher white standards. But the experience of a great diversity of communities indicates that these fears are unjustified. Administrators of 17 desegregated school systems appeared before the U.S. Civil Rights Commission in March of 1959 and candidly discussed their problems. Twelve of the educators dealt with the question of academic standards. Ranging from Logan County, Kentucky and Muskogee, Oklahoma to Baltimore and Nashville, all twelve reported unequivocally that their academic standards had not been lowered—in fact, many maintained that their standards had improved for both races.

Washington provided the acid test. It embarked upon a sweeping process of educational desegregation in 1954 with Negroes comprising three-fifths of the students, many of them with limited Southern backgrounds. The *U.S. News and World Report* soon published articles claiming that the District of Columbia's public school system was well on its way to ruin, and these tracts were widely quoted by segregationists. But such dire consequences never materialized. A four-track system of ability grouping and other fresh innovations were adopted. Five years later, in 1959, a factual assessment of the changes was made. Though Negro students, swelled by migrants, now comprised three-fourths of the student body, achievement test scores had risen significantly for each grade level sampled and each subject area tested approached or equalled national norms. Furthermore, both Negro and white students shared in these increments. Such results are not unique to Washington. Louisville reported substantial gains in Negro performance and slight gains in white performance after only one year of desegregation.

Clearly, desegregation *per se* does not accomplish these feats. The Banneker demonstration in St. Louis took place in virtually all-Negro schools; Washington and Louisville witnessed sharply improved test medians among their Negro students, whether in biracial or uniracial schools. The principal factor seems to be the new and healthier self-image Negroes acquire in the process. The act of community desegregation operates to bolster and encourage Negro pupils, parents, and teachers alike. Also important is the sudden interest Negro education finally wins from the whole community. As long as it is a separate system, dominant white interests can and do forget it. But once desegregation forces the community to handle the education of its youth in one package, to consider Negro education as an integral part of the whole process, new attention is attracted. Indeed, the increase in white scores suggests that public education as a whole benefits from the greater public interest.

Washington offers an illustration. Prior to desegregation, survey testing was only done with the white pupils; Negroes were ignored. But immediately after desegregation, testing throughout the system was instituted and the same standards applied at last to both races. Certainly, desegregation is no panacea for the immense problems faced by public school systems with large percentages of environmentally impoverished children. But it does prepare the path for tackling these *real* problems of modern education.

Thus, an array of stimulating circumstances—service in the armed forces, migration to the North, and participation in revitalized schools systems—all act to lift substantially the intelligence and achievement levels of Negroes. Often these improvements still do not bring the average Negro performance completely up to white norms, but this is no evidence for genetic racial differences until *all* racial discrimination is abolished.

THE INDIVIDUAL VERSUS THE GROUP

The discussion so far has concentrated on group results, yet many of the most important considerations involving Negro American intelligence concern the individual. Not even racists deny the existence of outstanding Negro Americans. Usually, however, the same individuals are cited—Marian Anderson, Ralph Bunche, George Washington Carver—and are considered "exceptions" and special "credits to their race." The truth is that a surprising number of such "exceptional" Negroes have somehow managed to overcome the formidable obstacles of discrimination. Many have naturally entered the struggle for equal rights. But others achieve such stature in non-stereotyped work that they are no longer thought of as Negro. For instance, the originator of the Hinton test for syphilis, the late Professor William A. Hinton, was well-known as a bacteriologist and immunologist at Harvard Medical School but not as a Negro.

Superior intelligence comes in all skin colors. While the intelligence test means of the two races are still divergent, the range of performance—from the most retarded idiot to the most brilliant genius—is much the same in the two groups. Some Negro children achieve I.Q.'s into the gifted range (130 plus) and right up to the testable limit of 200. To be sure, the frequency of such bright Negroes is smaller than that of whites, but this, too, can be explained by differential environmental factors. The great majority of these superior Negroes are located in biracial schools in the urban North and West, which suggests that many potentially gifted Negroes go either undiscovered or undeveloped in the segregated schools of the South. Proof that such children do exist in the South comes from programs which intensively seek talented Negro Southerners. Once found, they receive scholarships and attend a variety of desegregated high schools and colleges in the North, and the great majority of them accommodate well to their new and challenging situations.

A further embarrassment to racist theories is created by the fact that the degree of white ancestry does not relate to Negro I.Q. scores. Among intellectually superior Negroes, for example, the proportions of those with varying degrees of white ancestry correspond closely with those of the total Negro American population. Indeed, the brightest Negro child yet reported—with a tested I.Q. of 200—had no traceable Caucasian heritage whatsoever. "Race *per se*," concludes Martin Jenkins, "is not a limiting factor in psychometric intelligence."

There exists, then, a considerable overlap in the I.Q. distributions of the two groups. A few Negroes will score higher than almost all Caucasians, and many Negroes will score higher than most Caucasians. Figure 1 shows two

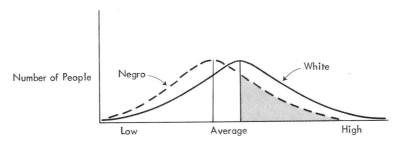

FIGURE 1. Typical test distributions with 25 per cent overlap.

typical intelligence test distributions with an overlap of 25 per cent, that is, 25 per cent of the Negroes tested (shaded area) surpass the performance of half the whites tested. Notice how the ranges of the two distributions are virtually the same, even though the means are somewhat different. This figure illustrates one of the most important facts about "race" and measured intelligence: individual differences in I.Q. *within* any one race greatly exceed differences between races.

There are two practical consequences of this phenomenon for desegregated education. First, when a school system institutes a track program of ability grouping, there will be Negroes and whites at all levels. Second, some gifted Negroes will actually lead their biracial classes even during the initial stages of desegregation. Thus, Janice Bell, a 17-year-old Negro girl, led the first graduating class of track 1-A superior students at Beaumont High in St. Louis; Julius Chambers, a 24-year-old Negro Southerner, became the 1961–62 editor of the University of North Carolina's *Law Review* in recognition of his leadership of his law school class; and Charles Christian, a 37-year-old Negro Virginian, academically led his Medical College of Virginia senior class in 1962. "In the study of individuals," summarizes Anastasi, "the only proper unit is the individual."

THE CURRENT CONCLUSION

Intelligence is a plastic product of inherited structure developed by environmental stimulation and opportunity, an alloy of endowment and experience. It can be measured and studied only by inference, through observing behavior defined as "intelligent" in terms of particular cultural content and values. Thus, the severely deprived surroundings of the average Negro child can lower his measured I.Q. in two basic ways. First, it can act to deter his actual intellectual development by presenting him with such a constricted encounter with the world that his innate potential is barely tapped. And, second, it can act to mask his actual functioning intelligence in the test situation by not preparing him culturally and motivationally for such a middle-class task. "Only a very uncritical psychologist would offer sweeping generalizations about the intellectual superiority or inferiority of particular racial or ethnic groups," comments Tuddenham, "despite the not very surprising fact that members of the dominant racial and cultural group in our society ordinarily score higher than others on tests of socially relevant accomplishments invented by and for members of that group."

The principal mechanisms for mediating these environmental effects vary from the poor nutrition of the pregnant mother to meeting the expectations of the social role of "Negro." Some of these mechanisms, like fetal brain injuries, can leave permanent intellectual impairments. Consequently, the permanency and irreversibility of these effects are not, as some claim, certain indicators of genetically low capacity. Fortunately, many of these effects are correctable. Moving North to better schools, taking part in special programs of environmental enrichment, and benefiting from challenging new situations of educational desegregation have all been shown to stimulate Negro children to raise their I.Q. levels dramatically.

From this array of data, the overwhelming opinion of modern psychology concludes that the mean differences often observed between Negro and white children are largely the result of environmental, rather than genetic, factors. This is *not* to assert that psychologists deny altogether the possibility of inherited racial differences in intellectual structure. There may be a *small* residual mean difference—small not only because of the demonstrably sweeping influence of experience but also because the two "races" are by no means genetically "pure" and separate. . . .

DEVIANT BEHAVIOR

The Extent of Delinquency in the United States

NEGLEY K. TEETERS AND DAVID MATZA

During this year when preparations are being made for the Sixth White House Conference on Children and Youth, it is not out of place, in assaying the extent of delinquency, to quote from the third conference held in 1930: "There exists no accurate statement as to the amount of delinquency in this country, nor whether it is increasing or decreasing." And again: "There is no accurate conception as to what actually constitutes delinquency."[1] These same words might well be stated at the White House Conference in 1960.

The term "juvenile delinquency" does not appear in the literature until 1823 when a New York philanthropic society changed its name from the *Society for the Prevention of Pauperism* to the *Society for the Reformation of Juvenile Delinquents.* But there can be little doubt that there have always been juvenile delinquents. But as to "how many" we cannot know. They were referred to through the years as "wayward," "depraved," "unfortunate," "wild," "headstrong," "wilfull," or "handicapped." The first special institutions for delinquents in this country were the early Houses of Refuge established in New York in 1824, in Boston, in 1826, and in Philadelphia in 1828. The first institution in the world for the treatment of delinquent youth was the *Hospice of San Michael* in Rome in 1704.

It has always been difficult—even impossible—to compute the extent of delinquency. It has always been popular for each generation to believe its children were the worst, the most lawless, and the most unruly. Sir Walter Scott, writing in 1812, deplored the insecurity of Edinburgh where groups of boys between 12 and 20 scoured the streets at night and knocked down and robbed all who came in their way. In an article in the *Atlantic Monthly* for December, 1926 and bearing the intriguing title "The Habit of Going to the Devil," Archer Butler Hulbert presents an array of diatribes against youth, as culled from the press during the early part of the nineteenth century. He found that in 1827 "a glance at our country and its moral conditions fills the mind with alarming apprehension; the moral desolation and flood tides of wickedness threaten to sweep away not only the blessings of religion, but the boasted freedom of our republican

Reprinted from the *Journal of Negro Education*, **28** (Summer, 1959), pp. 200–213, by permission of the authors and the publisher.

[1] *The Delinquent Child*, New York: Century, 1932, p. 23.

institutions as well." In 1828 he found: "No virtuous public sentiment frowns down upon the criminal to shame him into secrecy" and a year later, "And what of our youth? The lamentable extent of dishonesty, fraud, and other wickedness among our boys and girls shocks the nation." He found that in 1831, "Half the number of persons actually convicted of crime are youths who have not yet reached the age of discretion (how familiar that sounds in 1959)." He further finds that in 1830 "The army of youthful criminals from the slums are augmented by children abandoned by the shiftless of the working classes, by families wrecked by living beyond their means, and by wayward unfortunates from reputable families. Large numbers of these youngsters belong to organized gangs of thieves and cut-throats . . . Of 256 convicts in the Massachusetts State Prison, forty-five were thieves at 16 and 127 had, at that age, become habitual drinkers." [2]

A century later, in 1930, we find the oft-quoted statement of the Wickersham Commission of the prison population of that year—54.8 per cent had been less than 21 years of age when convicted. In 1938 Harrison & Grant, in their startling study of young offenders in New York City, stated that of those persons arrested for lesser offenses, minors were responsible for only 4.5 per cent of the total, whereas of the more serious crimes, the arrest rates of those under 21 were many times higher. [3]

It was the startling data presented in this work that galvanized into motion the American Law Institute to draw up the Youth Correction Authority Model Act of 1940 which subsequently was adopted in modified form in California and a few other states. Almost twenty years ago we found the following sober analysis of youthful delinquency and crime to substantiate the findings of Harrison & Grant; it could well have been written in 1959:

> Youthful offenders are an especially serious factor in the crime problem. Young people between 15 and 21 constitute only 13 per cent of the population above 15, but their share in the total amount of serious crime committed far exceeds their proportionate representation. They are responsible for approximately 26 per cent of the robberies and thefts; they constitute some 40 per cent of our apprehended burglars and nearly half of our automobile thieves. Boys from 17 to 21 are arrested for major crimes in greater numbers than persons of any other four year group. They come into court, not for petty offenses but for serious crimes, twice as often as adults of 35 and 39; three times as often as those of 45 and 49; five times as often as men of 50 to 59. Nineteen year olds offend more frequently than persons of any other age, with 18 year olds next. Moreover, the proportion of youths less than 21 in the whole number arrested, has increased 15 per cent during the past three years; 108,857 not yet old enough to vote were arrested and fingerprinted last year. [4]

Such was the situation as reported in 1940.

[2] The *Atlantic Monthly*, 138: 804–6, December, 1926.

[3] Leonard V. Harrison & Pryor M. Grant, *Youth In the Toils*. New York: Macmillan, 1939, pp. 44–45.

[4] Digested in the *Prison Journal*, April-July, 1940, pp. 57–8, from a pamphlet *The American Law Institute*. See also, Thorsten Sellin, "The Criminality of Youth," Philadelphia: *The American Law Institute*, October, 1940.

Before analyzing the exent of delinquency, let us set down some data from the Uniform Crime Reports for 1957. Taking the serious categories of crime we find that arrests for all crimes reported (by the police in 1,473 cities of over 2,500 representing a population of 40,176,369 based on the 1950 census) 19.3 per cent were of persons under 21 years of age. Of the arrests for the serious categories, 14.5 per cent of all for homicides were of those under 21; 44.7 per cent of the robberies; 16.9 per cent for all aggravated assaults; 44.1 per cent for the rapes; 68.0 per cent of all the burglaries; 62.4 per cent of all larcenies; and 80.6 per cent of all auto thefts.

At first glance and without interpretation this is indeed an alarming picture. But like all statistics, they do need considerable interpretation. We quote in this connection, the former F.B.I. affiliate and presently operating Director of the Chicago Crime Commission, Mr. Virgil Peterson:

A few years ago the Attorney General of the United States . . . informed the people: "I have been asked to bring you the facts and the figures, the tragic evidence of juvenile crime . . . Here are some . . . of the figures chargeable to some of our youth . . . 51 per cent of all burglaries, over half of them; 36 per cent of all robberies. . . ." Naturally; these figures given by the highest law enforcement official of the land were widely quoted in the press, over the radio, from speakers' platforms, and by crime prevention groups. Actually, the figures were based only on the available fingerprint cards of persons arrested and charged with burglary and robbery—a small sample from a huge army of burglars and robbers.[5]

Mr. Peterson points out that of all burglaries reported, only 31.3 per cent were cleared by arrest; and that of each ten burglaries reported no one knows who committed seven of them; and of the vast number arrested, the majority were youth. He continues:

Their youthful recklessness and inexperience in crime make it relatively easy to apprehend them. The professional criminal is more difficult to detect and apprehend. And it is reasonable to assume that he is responsible for a large percentage of our unsolved crimes. At any rate, the Attorney General's flat statement that over half of the burglaries were attributable to youth was little more than an opinion—an opinion that may be far from the truth.

Further along in his article Mr. Peterson adds this startling remark: "During the five year period from 1947 through 1951 over a million burglaries were reported to the police in about 2,200 cities . . . No one knows who commited over 800,000 of them." But the bulk of those arrested were youth under 21 years of age. The same can be stated of practically all categories. The monetary value of articles stolen by youth is generally quite small. Lumped into these "burglaries" are thefts of hub caps or tire gauges from filling stations, or other objects of trifling value. It is important to note that the Federal Bureau of Investigation's definitions of robbery and burglary include "attempts" as well as the actual commission of these acts. The arrest rate also includes many instances of mistaken identity at the scene of the crime.

[5] *Atlantic Monthly*, "Crime Does Pay." pp. 38–42, Feb. 1953.

In order to present a picture of national delinquency trends between 1940 and 1957 it is necessary to use a number of different sources of information.[6] The reason for this is that prior to 1952 it is not possible to convert Uniform Crime Report data into rates since there is no base population reported. Therefore, we shall infer the trends between 1940 and 1952 from the Juvenile Court Statistics. While this may be questioned, there seems to be good reason to believe there is considerable similarity between the direction or changes indicated by both collecting systems. As I. Richard Perlman of the Children's Bureau, states:

> We find that despite the fact that neither of these series (Juvenile Court Cases and Police Arrest data from the Uniform Crime Reports between 1938 and 1947) represents a completely accurate measurement of juvenile delinquency and despite the differences in the unit of count, the extent of coverage and geographical representation, nevertheless there is remarkable similarity between the direction of changes indicated by the two lines. Both increased sharply from 1942 to 1943, both decreased between 1943 and 1944, both increased again in 1945 to the ten year peak and both showed sharp decreases in 1946 and 1947.[7]

If Perlman is right we are able to increase greatly the length of time subsumed by our descriptive series. Table I below shows the increase in juvenile delinquency rates between 1940 and 1952 as indicated by the Juvenile Court Statistics. Table II shows the increase in juvenile delinquency rates between 1952 and 1956 as supplied by the Uniform Crime Reports.

TABLE I. JUVENILE DELINQUENCY CASES (AGES 10–17) 1940–1952 JUVENILE COURT STATISTICS*

Year	Per Cent (1940 as 100)	Child Population of United States Per Cent (1940 as 100)
1940	100	100
1941	112	99
1942	125	98
1943	172	97
1944	165	96
1945	172	95
1946	148	94
1947	131	93
1948	128	93
1949	135	92
1950	141	91
1951	149	93
1952	165	95

* Herbert A. Block and Frank T. Flynn, *Delinquency, The Juvenile Offender in America Today.* New York: Random House, 1956, p. 27.

[6] Figures for 1958 will not be available until autumn, 1959.
[7] "The Meaning of Juvenile Delinquency Statistics," *Federal Probation*, pp. 63–67.

TABLE II. INCREASE IN DELINQUENCY RATES
BETWEEN 1952 AND 1956*

Year	Per Cent (1952 as 100)
1952	100.0
1953	107.7
1954	111.6
1955	121.3
1956	147.9

* Rates computed from Uniform Crime Report data using estimated number of children (0–18) in reporting areas as base population.

We may infer from Tables I and II the following tendencies: A gradual increase between 1940 and 1942, a marked increase in delinquency beginning in 1943 and lasting through 1945 with a slight dip in 1944, a gradual decreas beginning in 1946 and continuing through 1948, a gradual increase from 1949 to 1951, a more marked increase between 1951 and 1952, a continuing gradual increase from 1952 to 1954, and finally another marked increase beginning in 1955 and lasting at least until 1957. Except for the period 1946 to 1948 and except for a slight dip in a high plateau in 1944, the picture revealed by official national statistics is one of continuous increase, sometimes gradual, sometimes rather rapid.

For the years between 1952 and 1957, we have computed delinquency rates by specific offense categories in order to obtain a more concise understanding of trends during this period. In Table III we present the delinquency rates per 100,000 persons using the number of persons in the Populations represented in the Uniform Crime Reports as the base population. In Table IV we present the delinquency rates per 100,000 children (0–18) using the estimated number of children in the Populations represented in the Uniform Crime Reports as a base population.[8] We see in Tables III and IV that there is considerable variation by offense in the shifting delinquency rates experienced during this period. In a few offenses, Embezzlement and Fraud, Prostitution and Offenses Against the Family, we observe decreasing rates of delinquency. These, however, are the exceptions. In all other offense categories we see varying degrees of increase in the delinquency rates. In Table V, we have classified the offenses according to the magnitude of the increase.

This series of tables represents the basis upon which we shall continue in this paper. The problem is obviously one of interpretation. What do the figures tell us?

[8] The base population in Table III is the number of persons residing in the cities included in the Uniform Crime Reports as of the 1950 Census. The base populations for Table IV were computed by first correcting the total populations for increases that had taken place since 1950, and then applying the proportion of children for each year to the corrected total population. We are indebted to the Population Reference Bureau for the estimates of total population (1950–1958) and the estimates of youthful population (1950–1956).

TABLE III.* DELINQUENCY RATES PER 100,000: USING THE UNIFORM CRIME REPORTS ESTIMATES OF REPRESENTED POPULATION AS THE BASE POPULATION 1952–1957

Offense	1952	1953	1954	1955	1956	1957	Per cent of 56–52	Per cent of 57–52
Criminal Homicide	.37	.36	.35	.39	.52	.52	141	141
a) Murder and Nonnegligent Manslaughter	.22	.24	.20	.23	.34	.33	155	150
b) Manslaughter by Negligence	.15	.12	.15	.16	.18	.19	120	127
Robbery	5.45	5.68	5.91	6.56	6.53	7.78	120	143
Aggravated Assault	2.75	3.43	3.37	4.14	4.78	5.20	174	189
Other Assault	6.91	9.63	10.48	12.02	13.49	15.06	195	218
Burglary (B & E)	46.56	48.77	50.61	56.02	60.72	70.14	130	151
Larceny-Theft	62.95	73.46	83.09	92.72	112.76	130.80	179	208
Auto-Theft	27.05	29.36	30.22	34.99	45.18	48.99	167	181
Embezzlement and Fraud	.83	1.16	.78	.72	.75	1.13	90	136
Stolen Property: buying, receiving, etc.	1.41	1.83	2.10	2.13	6.10	3.11	433	221
Forgery and Counterfeiting	1.04	1.27	1.18	1.20	1.41	1.64	136	158
Rape	1.27	1.75	1.51	1.99	2.04	2.32	161	183
Prostitution and Commercialized Vice	.63	.63	.48	.53	.37	.30	59	48
Other Sex Offenses	5.22	6.16	7.56	6.64	7.37	8.50	141	163
Narcotic Drug Laws	.41	.63	.41	.60	.71	.55	173	134
Weapons: carrying, possessing, etc.	3.07	4.15	4.60	5.74	6.82	7.46	222	243
Offenses Against Family and Children	2.95	3.30	4.10	2.40	.62	.72	21	24
Liquor Laws	4.62	7.71	9.45	10.06	13.90	17.73	301	384
Driving While Intoxicated	.92	1.04	.93	1.21	1.53	1.66	166	180
Disorderly Conduct	43.26	42.93	42.67	47.57	61.73	64.79	143	150
Drunkenness	11.71	12.33	12.00	13.33	15.69	16.87	134	144
Vagrancy	7.25	8.32	6.99	6.56	8.97	11.71	124	162
Gambling	1.12	1.22	.92	.96	1.25	1.53	112	137
Suspicion	24.41	31.08	23.60	27.78	38.47	39.75	158	163
All Other Offenses	106.78	105.91	120.26	131.79	157.15	173.49	147	163
Total	368.95	402.10	423.54	468.09	568.85	631.76	154	171

* These rates have been computed from data appearing in the Uniform Crime Reports, 1952–1957.

The fundamental question is whether this increase in delinquency is apparent or real. There are three positions that may be taken in attempting to come to any conclusion: First, that the data accurately reflect a real increase; second, that the increases are due to artifacts of data-collecting methods; and finally that the official statistics overrate the increase but that there has been some real increase.

The official description of delinquency trends is not readily accepted by the academician. The point of departure for the theoretical criminologists has been the insistence that the official increase represents, not a reflection of real increases, but rather they are due to a number of diverse artifacts inherent in the subtle processes involved in the collection of the data.

TABLE IV. DELINQUENCY RATES PER 100,000: USING THE ESTIMATED POPULATION OF CHILDREN (0–18) IN THE POPULATION REPRESENTED IN THE UNIFORM CRIME REPORTS: 1952–1956

Offense	1952	1953	1954	1955	1956	% of 56–52
Criminal Homicide	1.11	1.08	1.01	1.10	1.48	133
a) Murder and Nonnegligent Manslaughter	.66	.71	.58	.64	.97	147
b) Manslaughter by Negligence	.45	.37	.43	.46	.51	113
Robbery	16.26	16.77	17.16	18.74	18.71	115
Aggravated Assault	8.20	10.12	9.78	11.81	13.70	167
Other Assaults	20.63	28.42	30.42	34.32	38.64	187
Burglary	139.02	144.01	146.93	159.96	173.95	125
Larceny-Theft	187.96	216.91	241.25	264.77	323.01	172
Auto-Theft	80.76	86.69	87.74	99.90	129.42	160
Embezzlement and Fraud	2.48	3.42	2.27	2.04	2.16	87
Stolen Property: buying, receiving, etc.	4.21	5.40	6.09	6.09	17.46	415
Forgery and Counterfeiting	3.11	3.75	3.43	3.44	4.04	130
Rape	3.80	5.17	4.39	5.68	5.84	154
Prostitution and Commercialized Vice	1.89	1.86	1.41	1.52	1.05	56
Other Sex Offenses	15.59	18.20	21.95	18.95	21.11	135
Narcotic Drug Laws	1.23	1.86	1.20	1.70	2.03	165
Weapons: carrying, possessing, etc.	9.17	12.25	13.34	16.40	19.55	213
Offenses Against Family and Children	8.81	9.74	11.92	6.85	1.79	20
Liquor Laws	13.80	22.76	24.73	28.72	39.81	288
Driving While Intoxicated	2.75	3.08	2.69	3.46	4.39	160
Disorderly Conduct	129.18	126.77	123.85	135.83	176.83	137
Drunkenness	34.97	36.42	34.85	38.06	44.96	129
Vagrancy	21.66	24.56	20.29	18.72	25.69	119
Gambling	3.34	3.59	2.66	2.75	3.58	107
Suspicion	72.88	91.76	68.51	79.53	110.19	151
All Other Offenses	318.84	312.74	349.16	376.33	450.17	141
Total	1101.66	1187.33	1229.72	1336.67	1629.55	148

The academicians—who may be referred to here as skeptics—possess an antipathy to "alarmist" tendencies in the interpretation of delinquency statistics; furthermore, they are concerned with distortions and error usually inherent in any system of collecting information.

The strength of the "alarmist" point of view exists, for the most part, outside the university. It is found most frequently among spokesmen of mass media, law-enforcement officials, serious citizens, and practitioners who are face to face with the delinquent, especially juvenile court jurists. The public has aligned itself with this "alarmist" point of view, especially since its "common-sense" impression of the problem supports it. Thus, it is not surprising that many informed and most uninformed Americans are disturbed by the "rising tide" of juvenile delinquency during the past twenty years.

TABLE V. CLASSIFICATION OF OFFENSES BY AMOUNT OF
INCREASE: 1952–1956 (ESTIMATED YOUTHFUL POPULATION
USED AS BASE POPULATION) RATIO OF 1956 RATES
TO 1952 RATES

High Increase Offenses	*(160 and above)*
Receiving Stolen Property	415
Liquor Laws	288
Weapons	213
Other Assaults	187
Larceny	172
Aggravated Assault	167
Narcotics	165

Medium Increase Offenses	*(Between 136 & 160)*
Auto-Theft	160
Driving While Intoxicated	160
Rape	154
Suspicion	151
Murder and Manslaughter	147
All Other Offenses	141
Disorderly Conduct	137

Low Increase Offenses	*(Between 100 & 139)*
Other Sex Offenses	135
Forgery and Counterfeiting	130
Drunkenness	129
Burglary	125
Vagrancy	119
Robbery	115
Murder by Negligence	113
Gambling	107

Decrease Offenses	*(Below 100)*
Embezzlement and Fraud	87
Prostitution and Vice	56
Offenses Against Family	20

The academic intellectual finds it impossible to accept the obviousness of the "common-sense" approach. His skepticism sometimes manifests itself in a rather charming—even if irritating—"hide-bound conservatism." Yet, the reluctance to accept new ideas is simply a form of skepticism that is necessary in any scientific endeavor. Scholars or academicians are, by definition, endowed, rightly or wrongly, with a near-monopoly of expertness. Thus they are in the intellectually impossible situation of being the judges and the judged. Therefore, we must bend over backward to be certain that we consider carefully the the "alarmist" point of view, precisely because our first impulse is to dismiss it. More important, we must sometimes supply the opposition point of view with the sophistication that it, unfortunately, so often lacks. In reality, the "alarmists" are not the best spokesmen for their own position. They often lack the technical skills necessary to support their position and thus become vulnerable to those trained in the arts of logic, argumentation and scientific methodology.

There are a number of methods used by the "skeptics" in minimizing the apparent increases in delinquency. One is the thesis of the "expanding denominator" which contends that the growth of child population offsets the increase in delinquency rates. Empirically this argument has some validity but not too much. Thus, if we compare Table III with Table IV we see that the delinquency rate of 1956 was 54 per cent higher than that of 1952 if we *do not* take into consideration the expanding youthful population for that period; but if we *do* take the growth into consideration we find the increase in delinquency about 48 per cent. Thus, while we may contend that the "expanding denominator" may reduce the cause for alarm, it by no means completely disarms the vocal proponents of common sense.

The second argument of the skeptics is more sophisticated. It may well be asserted that the legal definition of delinquency throughout the nation has become less precise, more confused and vague. Stated another way, there is more delinquency because more and more overt acts—as well as covert—are being defined or considered delinquent. In addition, too, more and more minors are being counted for the same act, e.g., "57 youths charged with homicide" with one murder tabulated; "20 youths charged with carrying firearms" when only one of the group possessed a pistol. The skeptics contend that it is official policy in administering justice that has changed rather than the actual content and substance of juvenile behavior. We should also add that quite frequently it is the same child who is arrested over and over again and thus increases the delinquency rate.

This argument is often coupled with the assertion that norms in urban communities become increasingly formalized. This results in certain types of youthful behavior being officially dealt with rather than being handled through unofficial or informal forces of control such as parents, storekeepers, and neighbors. In many cities, the agents of formal control usually have a penchant for "recording" and "bookkeeping" and "referring" which usually results in an almost insatiable hoarding of a wide variety of records and statistics. The norms of bureaucratic management therefore impel the recording of many trivial deviant acts rather than of disposing of such cases on a personal and informal level. Thus, in many of our large cities, we find records of cases labeled with the vague nomenclature, "adjusted" or "unofficially handled."

What empirical evidence is there that the changes in methods of law-enforcement are responsible for the alleged increase in delinquency? The available evidence leads us to believe that some, but by no means all, can be explained by these changes. For instance, if we examine the data between 1952 and 1956, there is little evidence that the bulk of the increase can be attributed to vague and diffuse definitions. This is admittedly a short period of time but it is a period within which the data seem roughly comparable and it is, furthermore, a period during which a significant increase in delinquency rates took place.

In Table V above, we divided the various offense categories into (a) High Increase Offenses; (b) Medium Increase Offenses; (c) Low Increase Offenses, and (d) Decrease Offenses. The four best examples of vaguely defined offenses which appear in the Uniform Crime Reports are "Suspicion," "Disorderly Conduct," "Vagrancy" and "All Other Offenses." Three of these are "Medium Increase" offenses. This means that the rates of increase for these offense categories was about the same as that for total delinquency. The fourth, "Vagrancy," was a "Low Increase" offense. The vaguely defined offenses, therefore, contributed *slightly less* than their share to the increases that had taken place in delinquency within this five year period.

TABLE VI.   PERCENTAGE INCREASE IN DELIN-
QUENCY RATES BETWEEN 1952 AND 1956 (TOTAL
DELINQUENCY VS. DIFFUSELY DEFINED OFFENSE
CATEGORIES)

Total Delinquency	48%
Suspicion	51%
All Other Offenses	41%
Disorderly Conduct	37%
Vagrancy	19%

Another factor involves wider definitions of delinquency related to techno-logical innovations. Traffic violations and the casual sale and use of guns are examples of anti-social behavior which parents and grandparents of modern youth could not have easily committed. Therefore, in some states—Utah for example—traffic offenses comprise more than half of all delinquencies. In the period between 1954 and 1956, traffic violations in Utah constituted 58.4 per cent of all delinquencies. In that state traffic violations rose from 1 per 1,000 of school age children in 1935 to 40 per 1,000 in 1955. It must be pointed out, however, that in Utah, conventional delinquency followed the national pattern. For example, out of each 1,000 school age children, there were 12 delinquents in 1935, 18 in 1940, 41 in 1943, 27 in 1945, 16 in 1950 and 30 in 1955.[9]

A final argument used by the skeptics pertains to the improvements in techniques of apprehending and recording delinquents. We have more delin-quents simply because we are better able to capture and count them. Such im-provements have taken place but it is doubtful that a significant proportion of increased rates can be attributed to these improvements.

[9] Biennial Report of the Director, Bureau of Services for Children, State Department of Public Welfare, Utah, Juvenile Courts, Jan. 1, 1954 to June 30, 1956.

In discussing improved methods of collecting statistics, it must be remembered that every additional reporting area brings with it not only an additional number of recorded delinquents (the numerator) but also an increase in the base population (the denominator). With each increase in the numerator, there is an increase in the denominator. The question is whether the increase in the denominator is proportionate or disproportionate to increases in the numerator.

Let us assume that City X reports for the first time in 1954. If its rate of delinquency has been higher through the years than the average of cities reporting prior to 1954, then all previous rates were underestimated because City X, a high delinquency city, was not included in previous compilations. On the other hand if City X has traditionally been a low delinquency area then all previous rates have been overestimated because it was not included in previous compilations. The answer to our question, therefore, depends on whether or not the cities that have only recently begun to report are relatively high or low delinquency areas. One may suggest that generally the larger cities tend to report first and smaller communities later. If delinquency is more concentrated in the large cities, as sociologists have traditionally held, then it may well be that we have *overestimated* the national rates of delinquency in the past and therefore *underrated* the differences between the rates of from 1940 to 1956.

While all of the above is quite conjectural, it can be stated that a major innovation in reporting that took place in 1953 was coupled with an increase that was rather "average" in all respects. We see in Table VII below that the

TABLE VII. POPULATION REPRESENTED IN UNIFORM
CRIME REPORTS 1952–57

1952	23,344,305	(232 cities over 25,000)
1953	37,255,808	(1,174 cities over 2,500)
1954	38,642,183	(1,389 cities over 2,500)
1955	41,792,800	(1,477 cities over 2,500)
1956	41,219,052	(1,551 cities over 2,500)
1957	40,176,369	(1,473 cities over 2,500)

Uniform Crime Reports in 1952 were based on data compiled from 232 cities with population over 25,000. Starting in 1953, there are a great many cities reporting, ranging from 1,174 in 1953 to a maximum of 1,551 in 1956 (all over 2,500). The increase in delinquency rates between 1952 and 1953, the year of the major innovation in the number and type of cities included in the compilation, was 7.7 per cent. Between 1953 and 1954 the increase was 3.9 per cent. Between 1954 and 1955 there was a 9.7 per cent increase. Between 1955 and 1956 there was a 26.6 per cent increase. Thus it would seem that there is no striking relationship between major changes in the system of data-gathering and the official increases in delinquency.

There remains the question of improved methods of apprehension. Once again our belief is that we cannot attribute much of the increase to this, important though it may be. If we did make this contention, we would be obliged to answer some knotty questions as, for example, how account for the decreased rates between 1946 and 1948? Was there a decrease in police effectiveness during those years? If there are any years during which a realistic decrease in police effectiveness might be assumed, it would be the wartime period 1942 through 1945 when there was a critical manpower shortage; yet in this period we find an extremely high rate of delinquency. The inescapable fact is that delinquency rates are highly fluctuating in character, whereas there is every reason to assume that methods of apprehension and police efficiency have constantly improved. We do not intend to dismiss completely the role played by increasing police effectiveness in artificially raising the official rates. We merely wish to point out that its importance can, like all other phases of the problem, be overemphasized.

Thus far our position has been somewhere between that of the "alarmist" and the "skeptic." For the years between 1940 and 1957 our belief is that although the official statistics perhaps overrate the increase in the delinquency rates, there has, nevertheless, been some real increase. . . .

The Characteristics of Criminals

GRESHAM M. SYKES

Ever since men have been punishing the criminal in their midst they have found it comforting to believe that somehow the offender must be different, alien, or tainted. To think that a normal, fully accepted member of the community could murder, steal, or commit serious improprieties confounds our expectations about human behavior; and if the criminal is not a scoundrel or a madman, marked by an inward badness to match the badness of his outward actions, the supposed reassuring link between virtue and conformity becomes questionable.

If popular theories of criminality have viewed the offender as a person set apart from ordinary men, many scientific theories of crime have also tended to see the criminal as abnormal. Cesare Lombroso claimed that the individual who violated the laws of society was a throwback to an earlier form of more primitive life;[1] Johannes Lange, with his studies of identical and fraternal twins, came to the conclusion that criminology was a matter of defective biological inheritance;[2] E. A. Hooton followed a similar vein and argued that the criminal is biologically inferior.[3] These theories of physical inadequacies find a

[1] Cesare Lombroso, *Crime, Its Causes and Remedies* (Boston: Little, Brown, 1911).

[2] Johannes Lange, *Crime As Destiny* (New York: Boni, 1930).

[3] E. A. Hooton, *The American Criminal* (Cambridge, Mass.: Harvard University Press, 1939).

counterpart in the field of psychology in the assertion that the criminal is generally mentally defective or psychotic. And some writers have claimed that the criminal's psychological defect is an emotional one and that the psychopathic personality (in which right and wrong are intellectually distinguished but remain a matter of emotional indifference) typically lies behind much criminal behavior.

All of these theories have been sharply criticized for their paucity of evidence and lack of precision in the use of concepts; but the fault most commonly cited is that representative samples of criminals and noncriminals have never been obtained. Offenders who are detected, arrested, and convicted may differ sharply from the more successful criminals who elude the law. When we consider those who run afoul of the police, the slightest probing reveals that official records contain but a small part of the individual's criminal behavior. Moreover, study after study indicates that presumed noncriminals often exhibit a startling amount of criminal behavior that has gone undetected.[4] These are only a few of the biases that confuse the comparison of criminals and noncriminals, and they must make us cautious. However, an examination of some of the major apparent differences between those who break the law and those who hold to the law is necessary if we are to develop a theory of crime causation. We must use such data as we have, remembering again to remain always a trifle skeptical.

CRIME AND SEX

One of the outstanding features of the criminal-victim relationship is that the criminal side of the picture is so frequently male. In 1966, for example, 88 per cent of the individuals arrested were men.[5] We are probably fairly safe in assuming that the sex ratios of those accounted criminal and noncriminal differ markedly. Here, certainly, is a biological factor that cannot be ignored. But before we leap to the conclusion that man's physical nature is a source of criminality, let us note two things: (1) although most detected crimes are committed by males, most males do not commit detected crimes; and (2) differences in the behavior of men and women in our society far transcend the biological differences between the sexes—the physical characteristics of males and females form the basis for the ascription of diverse social roles, which influence behavior extensively. A minor but pointed example can be found in the fact that the incidence of being struck by lightning is far greater for men than for women, not because of biological differences per se but because men are

---

[4] See, for example, James S. Wallerstein and Clement J. Wyle, "Our Law-Abiding Law-Breakers," National Probation (March–April, 1947), pp. 107–112. The authors report that in their study of 1,698 individuals, supposedly noncriminal, 91 per cent had committed offenses sufficiently serious to draw a maximum sentence of not less than one year. The average number of offenses was 18 for men and 11 for women.

[5] U.S. Department of Justice, Uniform Crime Reports—1966 (Washington, D.C.: U.S. Government Printing Office, 1967).

more frequently in situations where the chances of being struck by lightning are high.

When we examine the variation in crime rates of men and women, the assumption that the social positions held by the sexes account for their relative criminality makes a good deal more sense than the assumption that crime springs from some physical characteristic linked to sex. If the first assumption is valid, it would follow that as the social status of men and women became more nearly alike, their crime rates would become more nearly alike. And, in fact, a number of comparisons bear out this line of reasoning. During the years of World War II, women in the United States came to hold a social position more nearly like that of men's, and the difference between their crime rates decreased accordingly. There is good evidence to indicate that in certain ethnic subgroups, such as Negroes in the United States, equality between the sexes is much increased; and among Negroes the difference between the crime rates of males and of females is less than in the case of whites. It has long been argued that in large cities women play a less subordinate role than they do in small towns; and it is true that the crime rates of men and women are more alike in the former than in the latter.[6]

It is difficult to explain these and similar variations in the sex ratio of criminals on strictly biological grounds—we would have to construct a complex set of assumptions about fluctuations in the link between physical differences and criminality, with physical factors varying by nation, historical period, place of residence, and so on. But a social-psychological explanation, based on the individual's socially defined role, has much to recommend it in terms of both existing theory and empirical data.

Otto Pollak has claimed that the idea that women are less criminal than men is largely erroneous, because women conceal their crimes more frequently than do men.[7] He agrees, apparently, with the cry of the dramatist Thomas Otway: "Destructive, damnable, deceitful woman!" Mabel Elliott notes with some asperity that Pollak's conclusions are less than scientific, pointing out, for example, that he is convinced of woman's essential criminality by the fact that women are arrested and convicted for child abandonment more frequently than men.[8] Elliott certainly has the better argument, and she outlines the different cultural demands imposed on men and women in our society, such as the private world of marriage and the family versus the public world of economic struggle and striving for achievement.[9] Undoubtedly women do commit crimes that go undetected, but so do men; and it can hardly be convincingly argued that the amount of undetected crime among women is so great that it can compensate for the large, persistently reported excess of criminality among males.

6 E. H. Sutherland, *Principles of Criminology*, revised by D. R. Cressey (Philadelphia: Lippincott, 1955), pp. 111–115.

7 Otto Pollak, *The Criminality of Women* (Philadelphia: University of Pennsylvania Press, 1950).

8 Mabel Elliott, *Crime in Modern Society* (New York: Harper & Row, 1952), Chapter 8.

9 *Ibid.*, pp. 201–203.

CRIME AND AGE

As the individual passes through his life cycle, in effect he moves through a sequence of subcultures, each with its pattern of approved and disapproved conduct. Some of these subcultures are, perhaps, more difficult to live in than others; our society makes much of the *Sturm und Drang* of adolescence, the waning powers of middle age, and the discomforts of old age, with its "evils that do not mend but every day get worse." In any case, an individual's age is an important sociological characteristic, carrying in its train particular values, attitudes, goals, and so on.

Many criminologists have argued that the younger age levels are more conducive to criminal behavior than the later-years levels; it is frequently pointed out the majority of persons arrested are under the age of thirty-five and that the peak age for arrests lies somewhere between eighteen and twenty-four. Ruth Cavan, for example, has asserted that "criminal activity begins in childhood, reaches full flower in late adolescence or early adulthood, and declines with age." [10] Certainly those who deal with criminals first-hand in reformatories, prisons, probation work and other areas of crime control have often noted that many offenders seem to "burn out." With the passage of years, many lawbreakers appear to lose their energy and their interest in crime and its excitements. Other observers, more sanguine perhaps, have spoken of a "maturation" process in which the individual settles willingly into the routines of orderly life and criminality diminishes. "Most juvenile delinquents outgrow their delinquencies. Relatively few become adult offenders. They grow up, come to terms with their world, find a job or enter the armed forces, get married and indulge in . . . only an occasional spree." [11]

We must be cautious, however, in interpreting the general youthfulness of the offender as a sign that the forces leading to criminal behavior are more strongly at work in the earlier phases of the life cycle than in the later phases. It must be remembered that about 40 per cent of the population in the United States is nineteen years old or less and the majority is under the age of thirty-five; statistics indicate that the proportion of offenses contributed by the younger age groups is only slightly in excess of their representation in society as a whole. [12] Furthermore, although crime in general may be a young man's game, there are a number of crimes that are typically committed by persons who are older. Thus, for example, if we use the arrest statistics of the Department of Justice for 1966, we find that for auto theft, larceny, and burglary the percentage of those arrested who are under eighteen is 63 per cent, 56 per cent, and 54 per cent respectively.

[10] Ruth S. Cavan, *Criminology* (New York: Crowell, 1952), p. 285.

[11] Jessie Bernard, *Social Problems at Midcentury* (New York: Dryden Press, 1957), pp. 421, 444; cited in David Matza, *Delinquency and Drift* (New York: Wiley, 1964), p. 22. Matza, in a deeply thoughtful analysis of juvenile delinquency, discusses the problems posed by the fact of "maturation" or "burning out," whatever it may be called, for theories of delinquency. He notes that apparently anywhere from 60 per cent to 85 per cent of delinquents do not become adult violators; moreover, this reform seems to occur without regard to the intervention of correctional agencies or the quality of correctional services.

[12] T. Sellin, *Criminality of Youth* (Philadelphia: American Law Institute, 1940), pp. 67–68.

In the case of criminal homicide, rape, robbery, and aggravated assault, however, the percentage—again in order—is 9 per cent, 19 per cent, 31 per cent, and 17 per cent. Similarly, the average age of those who are arrested for arson, vandalism, and violations of liquor laws turns out to be relatively low, as we might expect. But in embezzlement, gambling, and drunkenness, the age at arrest is a good deal higher.[13]

Incidentally, in American criminology, arrest data are frequently used to provide information on the characteristics of criminals. The number of persons arrested, however, is only a small proprotion of offenses known to the police—23 per cent in 1966. And of those arrested, only 26 per cent were in fact found guilty of the offenses with which they were charged.[14] The possibilities for distortion in our picture of the criminal population are obvious; and it is a prime example of the need for skepticism mentioned earlier.

In any event, any easy attempt to find the roots of crime in the hot blood of youth is bound to be somewhat misleading. Even if it is true that most criminal behavior is engaged in by younger individuals, we still must ask why this should be so. It seems reasonable to suppose that the subcultures of different age groups may well involve different patterns of motivation and social controls that influence the likelihood of various types of criminal behavior. Family ties, economic pressures, social participation, orientation toward one's peers, success or failure in social mobility, willingness to take risks—these are not constants but factors that take on different values in the individual's passage through the course of social development. Although there is a growing body of research on these and similar factors, the precise nature of their operation is yet to be determined.

CRIME AND RACE

If sex and age are characteristics dividing the members of society into broad social groups exhibiting different amounts of criminal behavior, the individual's racial status is no less important. The most significant categories here are Negro and white; and as suggested earlier, the former is marked by a higher crime rate than the latter. The meaning to be attached to this difference is our present concern.

The devastating attacks on race as an explanation of social conduct preclude reliance on superficial physical differences for theoretical purposes. The most recent attempts in this direction, Hooton's *Crime and the Man* and *The American Criminal*, have suffered much the same fate at the hands of informed critics as the works of Lombroso, Lange, and others.[15] The idea that skin color, the shape of the head, the structure of the nose, or a similar racial trait is a cause of differences in behavior has been thoroughly discredited. Instead, the more

[13] *Uniform Crime Reports—1966, op. cit.*, p. 116.

[14] *Ibid.*, p. 104.

[15] See Hooton, *op. cit.* and *Crime and the Man* (Cambridge, Mass.: Harvard University Press, 1939); and Robert K. Merton and M. F. Ashley Montagu, "Crime and the Anthropologist," *American Anthropologist*, 42, No. 3 (July–September, 1940), 384–408.

promising line of research appears to be the social position of whites and Negroes and the consequent differences in the sociocultural environment.

Although statistics on arrests by race are notoriously subject to large errors, perhaps worse than in the case of sex and age, they provide the only society-wide measure of criminal behavior on the part of Negroes and whites that we possess; and, such as they are, they indicate not only that Negroes commit relatively more crimes than do whites but that the offenses of Negroes are more heavily concentrated in the category of crimes against the person. To a large extent the differences between the two groups appear to be attributable to the subordinate socioeconomic position of the Negro in American society, with its bitter implications of economic deprivation, overcrowded housing, inadequate education, shattered families, and so on. And yet at least one study has indicated that when the socioeconomic differences between Negroes and whites are held constant, the crime rates of the former still exceed those of the latter, although the difference is much less.[16]

Clearly, the meaning of minority-group status goes far beyond poverty and its attendant problems; to be treated as an inferior species creates a psychological burden that can never be cast aside completely, as Abram Kardiner and Lionel Ovesey have indicated in their book fittingly entitled *The Mark of Oppression*.[17] In addition, patterns of migration, the disorganization of the Negro community, and the breakdown of the Negro family structure, weakened first by slavery and then by the impact of urbanization, have all created a situation of ineffective social controls that cannot be traced simply to lower socioeconomic status. The environment of the Negro, then, so largely a compound of discrimination, need, and defective mechanisms of social restraint, offers a prolific breeding ground for violations of the criminal law. No one of these factors can be singled out as the primary source of criminality, but acting in conjunction they exert a powerful force.

In the middle of the 1960's, a wave of riots swept many Negro ghettoes in the large cities of the United States: Los Angeles, New York, Philadelphia, Chicago, Pittsburgh—all erupted in wild disorder. The exact nature and causes of the riots are still being studied, and some attempts to remedy the immediately obvious sources of the problem have been undertaken, although many critics argue that these efforts are patently inadequate. It seems likely, however, that the stage was set by increasing levels of frustration and hostility, engendered by rising unemployment, sharpening irritations of prejudice and its concomitants, a greater awareness of inequalities, and changing patterns of leadership. The initial blow-up was, in some cases, followed by a brief, frantic carnival spirit; as one seventeen-year-old Negro boy said in an interview conducted by the

[16] Earl R. Moses, "Differentials in Crime Rates Between Negroes and Whites, Based on Comparisons of Four Socio-economically Equated Areas," *American Sociological Review*, 12, No. 4 (August, 1947), 411–420. For an excellent summary of recent theory and research in this area, see Thomas F. Pettigrew, *A Profile of the American Negro* (Princeton, N.J.: Van Nostrand, 1964), particularly Chapter 6.

[17] Abram Kardiner and Lionel Ovesey, *The Mark of Oppression* (New York: Norton, 1951).

Institute of Government and Public Affairs of UCLA, "Man, it was just like Christmas. You could walk right through the front window and pick that stuff right off the racks." But a number of these riots have become defined in the language of ideology and are viewed by members of both the Negro and the white community not as riots but as war in which Negro protest speaks in a voice the white man cannot ignore.[18]

The important point, as far as our present analysis is concerned, is that criminal behavior is not necessarily a deviant response to deprivation, frustration, and so on, within a structure of power accepted as more or less legitimate, but may become a "politicized" act, in terms of both its meaning for the actor and society's reactions to it. Criminal behaviour becomes part of a more general attack on the structure of power itself and is viewed by society as especially threatening for that reason. "We won," said one unemployed Negro youth after the Watts outbreak in August, 1965, "because we made the whole world pay attention to us. The police chief never came here before; the mayor always stayed uptown. We made them come."[19]

One further matter should be mentioned in our discussion of crime and race: Some criminologists heavily discount the apparent excess of criminal behavior among Negroes as compared to whites on the grounds that the administration of criminal law is biased against minority-group members. It is asserted that Negroes, along with other targets of discrimination, are more defenseless in the hands of the police and the courts and that the Negro is punished where the white man would go free.[20] Unquestionably there is truth in this, but all the evidence suggests that it is insufficient to explain the observed differences. It is the easier task of tolerance and the liberal point of view to dismiss the relatively higher crime rates of Negroes as a chimera; the far more difficult problem is to determine precisely the causes and consequences of discrimination, in terms of criminal behavior, and carry out the social changes needed to eradicate the problem.

CRIME AND SOCIOECONOMIC STATUS

Of all the variables with which the sociologist deals, few are so powerfully predictive as socioeconomic status. Income, education, and occupation form a set of closely interrelated factors highly correlated with human conduct in a

---

[18] See Andrew Kopkind, "Watts—Waiting for D-Day," *The New Republic*, June 11, 1966, pp. 15–17; and Bayard Rustin, "The Watts 'Manifesto' and the McCone Report," *Commentary*, March, 1966, pp. 29–35. The artist is sometimes spoken of as prophet, but it must be accounted a coincidence that the German artist Kurt Schwitters entitled a collage in 1947 "Watt's the Use of Living?" See Harriet Janis and Rudi Blesh, *Collage* (Philadelphia: Chilton, 1962), p. 77. The title expresses the essence of the issue.

[19] Quoted in Rustin, *op. cit.*, p. 30. The role of delinquent gangs in political movements outside the United States is discussed in Roul Tunley, *Kids, Crime, and Chaos* (New York: Harper & Row, 1962).

[20] Robert K. Merton and Robert A. Nisbet, eds., *Contemporary Social Problems* (New York: Harcourt, Brace & World, 1966), pp. 151–153.

variety of areas, and the field of criminal behavior is no exception. In the preceding pages we have touched on the relationship between crime and socioeconomic status, but now we must explore the matter in more detail.

One fact seems clear: Individuals who are committing the so-called major crimes are drawn predominantly from the ranks of those who have had little education, who work at jobs that stand low in the hierarchy of occupations, who have relatively low incomes. The criminality of the higher reaches of the stratification system is largely directed elsewhere. However, as every student of scientific method is repeatedly told, a correlation between two factors cannot be taken as proof of cause and effect; and indeed there is good reason to believe that low socioeconomic status is not per se a cause of criminal behavior. Rather, it is the accompaniments of low socioeconomic status that probably serve as a source of crime, and these conditions may well be reciprocally influenced by offenses against the criminal law.

Let us divide socioeconomic status into its components and first consider the question of income. If money is a claim on the goods and services produced by society, it is obvious that the poor will live poorly. One of the more important aspects of this is the area of the community in which the individual lives and the quality of his housing. Clifford Shaw and Henry McKay have carefully documented the fact that low-rent neighborhoods near the center of the city have relatively high crime rates.[21] Furthermore, poor areas of the city have high crime rates over a long period of time without regard to changes in national, racial, or cultural composition of the population. There is some confusion over whether "high crime areas" are parts of the city where crimes are likely to be committed or where criminals are likely to live,[22] but the greatest difficulty is that the reason why poor areas have high crime rates is not entirely clear. Is it the characteristics of the people who live there, characteristics that go beyond crude demographic factors? Or is it the characteristics of the area itself? It seems reasonable to suppose, of course, that individuals living in deteriorating portions of the community are more exposed to criminal attitudes and criminal techniques for committing crimes. The physical layout of poor areas with unsupervised and unwatched spaces surrounding low-income, high-rise apartment buildings is an invitation to crime, according to Jane Jacobs.[23] On the other hand, the poor area may draw to it individuals already inclined in a criminal direction, and they in turn may inculcate their taste for crime in their children.

Residence in blighted neighborhoods is not, however, the only implication of low income. The structure of families in the lower portion of the economic scale is often marred by periods of unemployment for the male wage earner;

[21] Clifford R. Shaw and Henry D. McKay, *Juvenile Delinquency and Urban Areas* (Chicago: University of Chicago Press, 1942).

[22] See El-Saat, "Juvenile Delinquency in Egypt" (unpublished doctoral thesis, Faculty of Arts, University of London, 1946), cited in Terrence Morris, *The Criminal Area* (London: Routledge, 1957), Chapter 2. The latter provides one of the best treatments of the variation in crime by geographical area.

[23] Jane Jacobs, *The Death and Life of Great American Cities* (New York: Random House, 1961).

for the male in our society, to be without a job is to be left feeling useless, undeserving of respect, and disorganized, his role as a father and husband seriously undermined.[24] In addition, in families with low income the wife may enter the labor market through necessity, in exhausting jobs with long hours, rather than in a more leisurely pattern supplementing the family income. Both of these factors may serve to weaken parental control and impair the process of socialization, which leads to normative conformity, as far as adolescents are concerned; and for adults the sudden economic stress caused by unemployment may well contribute more acutely to the sense of deprivation than low but continual wages. For parents and their children alike, to live in poverty or on its fringes is to live where the injunction to work, save, and get ahead is apt to take on the air of a pious sham.

And yet, as has been pointed out, immediate economic want is not sufficient by itself to explain criminal behavior. The second component of socioeconomic status—education—must also be taken into account. Low levels of schooling carry one crucial consequence that cannot be ignored: education and social mobility in American society are closely related, and the individual who has not finished high school faces the strong possibility that his present and future position in the stratification system may hardly differ at all. With the hope of later improvement removed, the ability to endure existing frustration is likely to decrease. It is this view that dominates the work of Richard Cloward and Lloyd Ohlin in their investigation of delinquency; as they phrase it, ". . . pressures toward the formation of delinquent subcultures originate in marked discrepancies between culturally induced aspirations among lower-class youth and the possibilities of achieving them by legitimate means."[25] Presumably, the same forces are operative in a good deal of adult crime. The situation has become particularly acute in the 1960's as the children of the so-called baby boom, born during and immediately after World War II, have scrambled to find a place in a labor market where the jobs open to those with few skills and little education are rapidly disappearing.[26] It is not simply the high school drop-out who is affected but the high school graduate as well; and the pessimistic outlook for young people out of school and with marginal jobs or no jobs as all has created what some writers refer to as social dynamite.

There are, in addition, several other correlates of low education that appear likely to play a role in producing criminality. The early withdrawal from school leaves a gap in the individual's life in terms of agencies of social control. Not yet integrated into the circle of demands and expectations posed by marriage, home, and work, the adolescent is often momentarily adrift in a youth culture characterized by high levels of conspicuous consumption, few responsibilities,

[24] Mirra Komarovsky, *The Unemployed Man and His Family* (New York: Dryden Press, 1940), pp. 74–77.

[25] Richard A. Cloward and Lloyd E. Ohlin, *Delinquency and Opportunity* (New York: Free Press, 1960), p. 78.

[26] See U.S. Department of Labor, *Manpower Report of the President and a Report on Manpower Requirements, Resources, Utilization, and Training* (Washington, D.C.: U.S. Government Printing Office, 1965).

a search for excitement, and constant pressure to prove oneself in the eyes of peers.[27] If these are coupled with personality problems, in what David Riesman has called the agenda of emancipation from parental domination, the impulses to criminal behavior that may arise find few barriers.

It is not so much that education provides immunity against motives leading to crime, although this too may happen; rather, a lack of education and the absence of controls by educational institutions thrust the individual into a social situation where little may be lost but much may be gained by resorting to criminal means. The potential reaction of the individual's primary groups plays a major part in determining whether or not the individual will engage in deviant behavior; and if the individual lacks primary groups that support adherence to the norms and at the same time identifies himself with others who place a positive value on violating the laws of society, the likelihood of crime increases. This principle forms the backbone of Sutherland's theory of differential association—a theory that has exerted so large an influence in the field of criminology. By seeing how a lack of education may entail a loss of association with law-abiding groups, we can better understand the relationship between socio-economic status and crime.

When we come to the question of occupation, we are confronted with a hard problem. Is there anything about certain types of jobs that is conducive to criminality and is not a reflection of the factors already mentioned? If laborers are apt to commit crimes more frequently than clerks, is this due to the nature of their work or the associated characteristics of required education, wages, steadiness of employment, and so on? We have no definitive answer, although hypotheses could be constructed about frustration and work satisfaction, personality types and occupational recruitment, jobs that bring the individual into contact with the underworld, or occupations and the formation of loyalties to particular primary groups. An exploration of this issue is best delayed until we examine theories of crime causation more completely in the next chapter.* In the meantime, we must be satisfied with the observation that the lower portion of the occupational hierarchy is disproportionately represented in official statistics on criminal behavior.

CRIME AND MENTAL ABNORMALITY

Scientific explanations are to some extent, like women's dresses, subject to the vagaries of fashion. Several decades ago much was made of defective intelligence as the cause of crime; the electrifying theories of Freud next dominated the scene; and today the extremists of the sociological position concentrate on the social structure and deride their opponents for "psychologizing." The phenomenon of crime, however, shows an odd reluctance to confine itself to the

---

[27] Matza, *op. cit.* For a discussion of these "subterranean" themes in a wider behavioral context, see, by the same author, "Subterranean Traditions of Youth," *The Annals of the American Academy of Political and Social Science,* 338 (November, 1961), 102–118.

* [The material referred to is not included—Editor.]

compartments of academic disciplines; the body simply will not fit neatly into the box that has been prepared for it.

The fundamental issue that underlies a good deal of this theoretical conflict is whether the criminal is generally mentally abnormal. Since crimes by definition can be committed only by individuals who are legally sane, the grosser forms of psychosis are supposedly eliminated from the picture, although this is not always true in practice. Dr. Fredric Wertham, for example, gives an account of a man named Albert Fish, a sadomasochistic murderer of children who dismembered his victims, cooked portions of the bodies, and ate them. Fish was declared legally sane (a psychiatrist testifying for the prosecution asserted with a macabre and extremely unfortunate choice of words that "a man might for nine days eat that human flesh and still not have a psychosis. There is no accounting for taste") and was executed by the State of New York.[28] The major debates, however, have centred on less obvious psychological defects and personality traits.

Mental abnormality is, of course, a wide category, but in general five major types can be distinguished that are relevant to the etiology of criminal behavior. First, inferior intelligence may be linked to crime because the feeble-minded individual is easily led into illegal paths or is unaware of the risks that attach to his actions. Second, a variety of internal conflicts may erupt into deviant behavior that the individual recognizes as reprehensible but cannot control. Third, the individual may be characterized by a "moral apathy" or indifference; the criminal act is intellectually known to be counter to the normative dictates of society, but the commission of the act evokes little or no emotional effect. Fourth, the individual may be "normal" in intelligence, appear to control his behavior, and hold the moral values of the society, but he has become divorced from reality. Acting under the sway of delusions, the individual strikes back at his persecutors in a paranoid fantasy or plays the part of avenger for an imaginary wrong. And fifth, the individual may suffer from an altered state of consciousness and be quite unaware of his actions, as in an epileptic fugue.

There is little doubt that one or more of these types of mental abnormality appear in *some* criminals and are directly tied to the behaviour that has brought them into conflict with the law. The crucial question, however, is whether it can be shown that criminals in general, or even a large share of criminals, differ significantly in the incidence of psychic illness or psychic defects causally related to crime. At the present time, the evidence is far from complete; but known facts strongly suggest that we cannot use mental abnormality as a general explanation of criminal behavior. Independent psychiatric diagnosis does not support the claim that the known criminal population differs markedly from the members of conforming society in terms of mental disorders or other personality deviations.[29] Emotional stability or maturity, personality disturbances as measured by

[28] Fredric Wertham, *The Show of Violence* (Garden City, N.Y.: Doubleday, 1949), Chapter 4.

[29] K. F. Schuessler and D. R. Cressey, "Personality Characteristics of Criminals," *American Journal of Sociology*, LV, No. 5 (March, 1950), 476–484.

the Minnesota Multiphasic Personality Inventory or the Rorschach Test, traits of temperament such as carelessness or dependability, traits of character such as honesty, personal adjustment in terms of introversion-extroversion, and so on—none has been shown to be correlated with criminality in any consistent or significant fashion.

At this point we must be very cautious indeed. Techniques of psychiatric classification may be inadequate; measures of criminal behavior are known to be inaccurate; the wrong set of psychological characteristics may have been selected for investigation; and gross groupings, both of crimes and psychiatric disorders, may obscure finer relationships that actually exist. It cannot be asserted with finality that the criminal does not differ psychologically from the noncriminal; rather, we can only hold that at the present time such a difference has not been demonstrated in any general sense. Nobody has ever been able to show convincingly that the criminal is any less normal—or abnormal—than the rest of the population.

Probably the best thing to do on the question of the psychic disorder of the criminal is to say "not proven," a suspended judgment between "guilty" and "not guilty" allowed by Scottish law. . . .

On the Social Epidemiology of Schizophrenia

MELVIN L. KOHN

My intent in this paper is to review a rather large and all-too-inexact body of research on the epidemiology of mental illness, to see what it adds up to and what problems it poses for further research. I shall be highly selective, and I shall be highly summary. Instead of reviewing the studies one by one, I shall talk of general issues and bring in whatever studies are most relevant. It hardly need be stressed that my way of selecting these issues and my evaluation of the studies represent only one person's view of the field and would not necessarily be agreed to by others. . . .

I

It seems to me that most of the important epidemiological studies of schizophrenia can be viewed as attempts to resolve problems of interpretation posed by the pioneer studies, Faris & Dunham's ecological study of Chicago[1] and

From Melvin L. Kohn, "On the Social Epidemiology of Schizophrenia," *Acta Sociologica*, 9 (1966), pp. 209–221. By permission of the author and publisher.

[1] Robert E. L. Faris and H. Warren Dunham: *Mental Disorders in Urban Areas: An Ecological Study of Schizophrenia and Other Psychoses*, Chicago: University of Chicago Press, 1939.

Clark's analysis of occupational rates.[2] Their findings were essentially as follows:

Faris and Dunham: The highest rates of first hospital admission for schizophrenia are in the central area of the city, with diminishing rates as you move toward the periphery.

Clark: The highest rates are for the lowest status occupations, with diminishing rates as you go to higher status occupations.

Let us consider the issues that arise in trying to interpet these findings.

1. The first issue, the simplest but nevertheless a strangely perplexing issue, is whether or not the findings are somehow peculiar to Chicago. This much we can say with certainty: the findings are not unique to Chicago. The essential finding of the Faris and Dunham investigation, on the ecological distribution, has been replicated or partially replicated in a number of American cities—Providence, Rhode Island; Peoria, Illinois; Kansas City; St. Louis; Milwaukee; Omaha, Nebraska[3]—and in Oslo, Norway.[4] The essential finding of the Clark investigation, on the occupational distribution, has been confirmed again and again, in these same investigations, in Hollingshead and Redlich's study of New Haven,[5] in the research by Srole and his associates in midtown, New York City,[6] and in several other investigations.[7] Svalastoga's re-analysis of Strömgren's data for northern Denmark is consistent,[8] as is Leighton's for "Stirling County," Nova Scotia. Ødegaard has presented some partial data for Norway that seem to lead to the same conclusion.[9]

But there are some exceptions. Clausen and I[10] happened across the first, when we discovered that for Hagerstown, Maryland, there was no discernible relationship between either ecological area or occupation and rates of schizophrenia. On a re-examination of past studies, we discovered a curious thing: the larger the city, the stronger the correlation between rates of schizophrenia

[2] Robert E. Clark: *Psychoses, Income, and Occupational Prestige*, American Journal of Sociology, LIV (March, 1949), pp. 433–440.

[3] The findings for Providence are reported in Faris and Dunham, *op. cit.* All the others are reported in Clarence W. Schroeder: *Mental Disorders in Cities*, American Journal of Sociology, 48 (July, 1942), pp. 40–48.

[4] Per Sundby and Per Nyhus: *Major and Minor Psychiatric Disorders in Males in Oslo: An Epidemiological Study*, Acta Psychiatrica Scandinavica, 39 (1963), pp. 519–547.

[5] A. B. Hollingshead and F. C. Redlich: *Social Class and Mental Illness*, New York: John Wiley, 1957.

[6] Leo Srole with Thomas S. Langner, Stanley T. Michael, Marvin K. Opler and Thomas A. C. Rennie: *Mental Health in the Metropolis: The Midtown Manhattan Study.* Volume I. New York: McGraw-Hill, 1962.

[7] See, for example, Robert M. Frumkin: *Occupation and Major Mental Disorders*, in Arnold Rose, ed., Mental Health and Mental Disorder, New York: W. W. Norton, 1955.

[8] Kaare Svalastoga: *Social Differentiation*, in press.

[9] Ørnulv Ødegaard: *The Incidence of Psychosis in Various Occupations*, International Journal of Social Psychiatry, II (Autumn, 1956), pp. 85–104; "Psychiatric Epidemiology," Proceedings of the Royal Society of Medicine, 55 (October, 1962), pp. 831–837; and "Occupational Incidence of Mental Disease in Single Women," Living Conditions and Health, 1 (1957), pp. 169–180.

[10] John A. Clausen and Melvin L. Kohn: *Relation of Schizophrenia to the Social Structure of a Small City*, in Passamanick, B. (ed.): Epidemiology of Mental Disorder, D.C. Washington: American Association for the Advancement of Science, 1959.

and these indices of social structure. In the metropolis of Chicago, the correlation is large, and the relationship is linear: the lower the social status, the higher the rates. In the cities of 100,000 to half a million (including Oslo, as Sundby and Nyhus showed), the correlation is smaller and not so linear: it is more a matter of a pile-up of cases in the lowest socio-economic strata, with not so much variation among higher strata. When you get down to a city as small as Hagerstown—36,000—the correlation disappears. This proved to be the case not only for Hagerstown, but for the tiny city of " Bristol," Nova Scotia, in the Leightons' investigation,[11] and for the rural area of Scania, in Sweden, that Hagnell and and Essen-Möller have been investigating.[12] So one must conclude that although there is overwhelming evidence for a correlation of both ecological area and occupation to rates of schizophrenia, it has been demonstrated only for larger cities. We are dealing then with the social structure of the larger urban environment.

2. The second issue is, depending on how you look at it, either a trivial technical issue or a substantive issue of great importance. As a technical issue, it is generally referred to as the "drift hypothesis"; as a substantive issue, it is the issue of mobility.

The drift hypothesis was first raised as an attempt to explain away the Faris and Dunham findings. The argument is that in the course of their developing illness, schizophrenics tend to drift down into lower status occupations and lower status areas of the city. It is not that more cases of schizophrenia are produced in these strata of society, but that schizophrenics who are "produced" elsewhere end up at the bottom of the heap by the time they are hospitalized, and thus are counted as having come from the bottom of the heap.

There have been odds and ends of evidence for and against the drift hypothesis,[13] none of it definitive, but the best-designed studies seem to indicate that schizophrenics have been no more downwardly mobile than other people coming from the same social backgrounds.[14] The really critical evidence in the controversy, it seems to me, is the recent finding of Srole and associates that

[11] Dorothea C. Leighton, *et al.*: *Psychiatric Findings of the Stirling County Study*, American Journal of Psychiatry, 119 (May, 1963), pp. 1021–1026.

[12] Olle Hagnell: *A 10-year followup of a psychiatric field study*, mimeographed, 1963; E. Essen-Möller: *Individual Traits and Morbidity in a Swedish Rural Population*, Acta Psychiatrica et Neurologica Scandinavia (1956), Suppl. 100, pp. 1–160; Erik Essen-Möller: *A Current Field Study in the Mental Disorders in Sweden*, in Paul H. Hoch and Joseph Zubin (ed.): Comparative Epidemiology of the Mental Disorders, New York: Grune and Stratton, 1961.

[13] See, for example, Mary Bess Owen: *Alternative Hypotheses for the Explanation of Some of Faris and Dinham's Results*, American Journal of Sociology, 47 (July, 1941), pp. 48–52; Mary H. Lystad: *Social Mobility Among Selected Groups of Schizophrenic Patients*, American Sociological Review, 22 (June, 1957), pp. 288–292; Morris S. Schwartz: *The Economic and Spatial Mobility of Paranoid Schizophrenics and Manic Depressives*, Unpublished M. A. Thesis: University of Chicago, 1946; Donald L. Gerard and Lester G. Houston: *Family Setting and the Social Ecology of Schizophrenia*, Psychiatric Quarterly, XXVII (January, 1953), pp. 90–101; SROLE, *et al., op. cit.*; Clausen and Kohn, *op. cit.* August B. Hollingshead and Frederick C. Redlich: *Social Stratification and Schizophrenia*, American Sociological Review, 19 (June, 1954), pp. 302–306.

[14] This conclusion may be premature: I have belatedly learned of an important Study that supports the drift hypothesis. See: E. M. Goldberg and S. L. Morrison: *Schizophrenia and Social Class*, British Journal of Psychiatry, 109 (November, 1963), pp. 785–802.

rates of mental disorder correlate nearly as well with their *parents'* socio-economic status as with patients' own socio-economic status. Certainly the parents didn't drift downward because of the patient's disease, and so the simple drift hypothesis does not hold. (More complicated formulations, that include genetic factors, may still have some merit.)

The mobility issue as a substantive issue is another thing again. Ever since Ødegaard's classic study of rates of mental disorder among Norwegian migrants to the United States,[15] we have known that mobility is a matter of considerable consequence for mental illness. We have not known *how* and *why* it is a matter of consequence—whether it is a question of who migrates or of the stresses of migration—and unfortunately subsequent research has failed to clarify this issue. This question is one of considerable importance, but since it takes me afield from the main theme of my discussion I shall not pursue it here. My concern for the moment is not with mobility but with social structure.

3. The third issue in interpreting the Faris and Dunham and the Clark investigations is the most serious of all: the question of the adequacy of hospital admission rates as a measure to the incidence of mental disorder. Faris and Dunham tried to solve the problem by including patients admitted to private as well as to public mental hospitals. This was insufficient because, as several subsequent studies have shown, many people who become seriously mentally ill never enter a mental hospital. Subsequent studies have attempted to do better than Faris and Dunham by including more and more social agencies in their search for cases; Hollingshead and Redlich in New Haven, and Jaco in Texas,[16] for example, have extended their coverage to include everyone who falls into any sort of treatment facility—Jaco going so far as to question all the physicians in the state of Texas. This is better, but clearly the same objections hold in principle. And Srole has demonstrated that there are considerable social differences between people who have been treated, somewhere, for mental illness, and severely impaired people, some large proportion of them schizophrenic, who have never been to any sort of treatment facility. So we must conclude that using treatment—*any* sort of treatment—as an index of mental disorder is suspect.

The alternative is to go out into the community and diagnose everyone—or a representative sample of everyone—yourself. This has been done by a number of investigators, for example Essen-Möller in Sweden, Srole and his associates in New York, Leighton in Nova Scotia. They have solved one problem, but they have run into two others, perhaps equally serious.

One problem is finding a reliable and valid criterion of mental illness.[17] For

[15] Ørnulv Ødegaard: *Emigration and Mental Health*, Mental Hygiene, 20 (1936), pp. 546–553. See also: Christian Astrup and Ørnulv Ødegaard: *Internal Migration and Disease in Norway*, Psychiatric Quarterly Supplement, 34 (1960), pp. 116–130.

[16] E. Gartley Jaco: *The Social Epidemiology of Mental Disorders*, New York: Russell Sage Foundation, 1960.

[17] See: Bruce P. Dohrenwend and Barbara Snell Dohrenwend: *The Problem of Validity in Field Studies of Psychological Disorder*, Journal of Abnormal Psychology, 70 (February, 1965), pp. 52–69.

all its inadequacies, hospitalization is at least a reliable index, and you can be fairly certain that the people who are hospitalized are really ill. But can one really be certain that the Leightons' estimate that approximately 48% of their population suffer at least 10% impairment,[18] or Srole's that 23.4% of his are impaired are meaningful? Psychiatric diagnoses, even of hospitalized patients, are notoriously unreliable. Psychiatric diagnoses of people in the community, usually based on second-hand reports, are likely to be even more unreliable.

Personal examination by a single psychiatrist using presumably consistent standards is one potential solution, but applicable only to relatively small populations. Another is the further development of objective rating scales, such as the Neuropsychiatric Screening Adjunct first developed by social scientists in the Research Branch of the U.S. Army in World War II[19] and later used in both the Leighton's and Srole's investigations, but not developed to anything like its full potential in either study. Meantime, we have to recognise that the community studies done so far have been based on indices whose reliability and validity are at any rate suspect.

The other problem with community studies is even more serious. In most of these studies we are no longer dealing with the *incidence* of mental disturbance, but with its prevalence.[20] That is, we are no longer measuring the number of new cases arising in various population groups during some period of time, but the number of people currently ill at the time of the survey. This reflects not only incidence but duration of illness. And, as Hollingshead and Redlich have convincingly shown, duration of illness is highly correlated with social class. Various approximations to incidence have been tried, and various new—and often fantastic—statistical devices invented, to get around this problem, but without any real success. Clearly, what is needed is *repeated* studies of the population, to pick up new cases as they arise and thus to establish true incidence figures. (This is what Hagnell and Essen-Möller are attempting in Scania, and it is a very brave effort indeed.) The crucial problem, of course, is to develop a reliable measure of mental disorder, for without that our repeated surveys will measure nothing but the errors of our instruments. Meantime, we have to recognize that the many prevalence studies of communities—including all the recent large studies in the United States—are using an inappropriate measure that exaggerates the relationship of socio-economic status to mental disorder.

So the results are hardly definitive. It may even all wash out—one more example of inadequate methods leading to premature, false conclusions. I cannot prove otherwise. Yet I think the most parsimonious interpretation of all these findings is that they point to something real. Granted that there isn't a

---

[18] Dorothea Leighton: *The Distribution of Psychiatric Symptoms in a Small Town*, American Journal of Psychiatry, 112 (March, 1956), pp. 716–723.

[19] Shirley Star: *The Screening of Psychoneurotics in the Army*, in S. A. Stouffer with L. Guttman, E. A. Suchman, P. F. Lazarsfeld, Shirley A. Star, and J. A. Clausen (ed.): *Measurement and Prediction*, N.J. Princeton: Princeton University Press, 1950.

[20] See: Morton Kramer: *A Discussion of the Concepts of Incidence and Prevalence as Related to Epidemiologic Studies of Mental Disorders*, American Journal of Public Health, 47 (July, 1957), pp. 826–840.

single definitive study in the lot, the weaknesses of one are compensated for by the strengths of some other, and the total edifice is probably much stronger than you would conclude from knowing only how frail are its component parts. A large number of complementary studies all seem to point to the same conclusion: that rates of mental disorder, particularly of schizophrenia, are correlated with various measures of socio-economic status, at least in large cities, and this probably isn't just a matter of drift or duration of illness or who gets hospitalized or some other artifact of the methods we use. In all probability, more schizophrenia is actually produced at lower socio-economic levels.

Additional Readings

ROLE

HERBERT H. HYMAN and PAUL B. SHEATSLEY, "Attitudes Toward Desegregation," *Scientific American*, 195 (December, 1956), pp. 35–39.

HERBERT H. HYMAN and PAUL B. SHEATSLEY, "Attitudes Toward Desegregation," *Scientific American*, 211 (July, 1964), pp. 16–23.

THOMAS F. PETTIGREW, *A Profile of the Negro American* (Princeton, N.J.: D. Van Nostrand Company, Inc., 1964).

CHARLES H. STEMBER, *Jews in the Mind of America* (New York: Basic Books, Inc., 1966), pp. 219–230.

CULTURE

HERBERT H. HYMAN, "The Value Systems of Different Classes: A Social Psychological Contribution to the Analysis of Stratification," in Reinhard Bendix and Seymour Martin Lipset (eds.), *Class, Status and Power* (New York: The Free Press, 1953), pp. 426–442.

DEREK J. DE SOLLA PRICE, *Science Since Babylon* (New Haven: Yale University Press, 1961), pp. 92–124.

DEREK J. DE SOLLA PRICE, "The Exponential Curve of Science," *Discovery*, 17 (1956), pp. 240–243.

DEVIANT BEHAVIOR

JACK GIBBS, "Suicide," in Robert K. Merton and Robert A. Nisbet (eds.), *Contemporary Social Problems* (New York: Harcourt, Brace & World, Inc., 1966), pp. 296–308.

HERBERT GOLDHAMER and ANDREW W. MARSHALL, *Psychosis and Civilization* (New York: The Free Press, 1949).

S. M. MILLER and ELLIOT G. MISHLER, "Social Class, Mental Illness and American Psychiatry," *Milbank Memorial Fund Quarterly*, 37 (April, 1959), pp. 174–199.

Task Force Report: Crime and Its Impact—An Assessment, The President's Commission on Law Enforcement and Administration of Justice (Washington, D.C.: U.S. Government Printing Office, 1967), pp. 14–41.

PART II

*The Social Structure
of the Group*

ECONOMY

Introduction

Part II, "The Social Structure of the Group," contains six sections: "Economy," "Polity," "Kinship," "Religion," "Education," and "Stratification." Unlike the sections in Part I, which were preceded by a single introduction, there will be a separate introduction for each of the sections in Part II.

Industrialism is commonly discussed as a type of *economic* system. The growth of industrialism is often measured by the growth of industrial output, that is, production in factories. The selection by Patel, "Rates of Industrial Growth in the Last Century, 1860–1958," presents factual information about the growth of industrial output. Patel emphasizes four main points. First, the world industrial output has expanded by about 3.6 per cent per year over the last one hundred years. Second, the rate at which industrial output has taken place in each of the newly industrializing countries over the last century has progressively continued to rise—from 2 to 3 per cent in the early nineteenth century, to 4 to 5 per cent in the period before World War I, and finally to 8 to 10 per cent in the last few decades. Third, the rate of growth of the producer goods sector (raw materials, semimanufactured articles, and capital goods) was throughout this period higher than the rate of growth of the consumer goods sector (finished and semifinished goods that are largely bought by the public primarily for consumption in the home). Fourth, the industrial output of the centrally planned economies (e.g., the Soviet Union) is increasing at a faster rate than that of the private enterprise economies (e.g., the United States).

The occupational system of a society, although not equivalent to the economy of a society (there are occupational roles in the economy, polity, and control structures of a society), is frequently discussed in connection with the economy. The next three selections provide factual information about occupational systems.

The selection by Farrag, "The Occupational Structure of the Labour Force:

Patterns and Trends in Selected Countries," distinguishes four types of occupations: white-collar, blue-collar, farm, and service. The percentage of white-collar workers in the labor force has been increasing, whereas the percentage of farmers in the labor force has been decreasing. No definite trend exists for the blue-collar and service occupations. It should be noted that Farrag's information primarily pertains to Australia, Canada, England-Wales, and the United States. There is information about other countries, such as the U.S.S.R. and India, but this information is not as systematic as the information about these four countries.[1]

Wilensky, in "Trends in Amount of Time Worked," presents information about the amount of time devoted to occupational performance. It generally has been the impression that there has been a widespread decline in the amount of time worked. Wilensky's information corrects this general impression in three ways. First, the perspective of a longer time span reveals that time at work increased before it decreased. As Wilensky dramatically states: "The burden of labor in our century, of course, has lessened; today annual hours are down in the range of 1,900–2,500— *a return to the work schedules of medieval guildsmen.*" (Emphasis supplied.) Second, recent increases in leisure have been unequally distributed by industry and occupational category. Most of the real gain in leisure in the United States has come to private nonagricultural industries, and to agriculture in the last fifty years. White-collar occupations have experienced little real gain in leisure, and some occupations have lost. Third, despite an increase in the age of entry into the labor force and a decrease in the age of retirement from the labor force, men today work more years over the life cycle than they did in 1900. Wilensky's information does, however, confirm the general impression of a widespread decline in the amount of time worked in one respect: the trend for women by occupation is away from long-hour jobs, such as those in domestic service and farm labor, and toward shorter-hour jobs, such as those in sales and clerical work.[2]

A general impression exists that most workers are dissatisfied with their occupations. The selection by Blauner, "Work Satisfaction in Modern Society," indicates that, contrary to this general impression, most workers—more than 80 per cent—are satisfied with their occupations. Blauner's selection also indicates that occupational prestige and occupational satisfaction are positively related: the higher the prestige of an occupation, the higher the level of satisfaction of its members. It should be noted that the work satisfaction deals with the "internal orientation" of workers and does not encompass such significant and much studied "behavior" as turnover and absenteeism. Workers may be relatively dissatisfied with their jobs and yet not be characterized by high rates of turnover and absenteeism; similarly, workers may be relatively dissatisfied with their jobs and be characterized by high rates of turnover and absenteeism. Because work satisfaction may vary independently of turnover and absenteeism, it is well to remember these distinctions.[3]

---

[1] Farrag's information is also relevant to the section on "Organization" in Part III, "Types of Groups," especially the selection by Bendix, "The Growth of Bureaucracy."

[2] The selection by Wilensky is also relevant to discussions of "leisure." The title of the original selection was "The Uneven Distribution of Leisure."

[3] The selection by Blauner is also relevant to discussions of "morale," a common topic in the study of organizations.

Rates of Industrial Growth in the Last Century, 1860–1958

SURENDRA J. PATEL

Nearly two centuries have elapsed since the start of the industrial revolution. But in the first of these two centuries the revolution was essentially an experimental and small-scale affair. Although many inventions had been made by the middle of the nineteenth century, the adoption of advanced technique was limited to Great Britain and even there, except for the textile industry, only on a small scale. The world of the first quarter of the nineteenth century had little experience with the steam locomotive and the railways which were to revolutionize transportation; even by 1850, the total length of the railway network in the three most developed countries—the United Kingdom, France and Germany —was not quite 20,000 kilometres, i.e. less than a sixth of the network that these countries had by the end of the century. The output of pig iron in the whole world was only 4.6 million tons in 1850, half of which was in Great Britain. The technique of producing steel had hardly gone beyond the handicraft stage. Even the most advanced countries in the world were still in the last days of the iron age. Cast iron could be used in rails, pillars, bridges, engine cylinders and even wheels, but it had its limits; it was not suited for the working parts of engines and machines. The steel age was about to begin. The Bessemer converter was invented in 1856 and even with the advance made by the Martin-Siemens process (1864–67) the total output of steel in the world was no more than 700,000 tons in 1870, or less than one-half of India's output in 1958.

Hence only the last hundred years can be regarded as a century of the machine age and industrial expansion. This study attempts to measure the scale and the speed of this growth and the relationship between the major sectors of industrial output in various countries; it also sets out to indicate the rates of growth at which the gaps in the volume of industrial output among the major industrial countries were closed in the past in order to suggest the rates of growth that may be necessary to close the present gap between the industrial and the pre-industrial countries.

The limitations of index number series stretching over a hundred years should not be overlooked. The availability and accuracy of the figures cannot be expected to be uniform over so long a period of such rapid change. Moreover, since they were prepared in part by different individuals or institutions, linking the various series introduces a number of distortions in the continuity. In consequence, and in order to avoid repeating words of caution every time these figures are mentioned, it should be emphasized right at the beginning that they represent no more than an order of magnitude—adequate for indicating the broad sweep of movement over the century, but not precise enough to measure accurately each succeeding stage.

Reprinted from *Economic Development and Cultural Change*, 9 (April, 1961), pp. 316–330, by permission of the author and the publisher.

I. THE RATES OF GROWTH OF INDUSTRIAL OUTPUT

Over the last century industrial output[1] in the world as a whole rose some thirty-to-forty fold (see Table 1). World population, on the other hand, slightly more than doubled. Hence industrial output per capita is now some 15 to 20

TABLE 1. GROWTH OF INDUSTRIAL OUTPUT AND POPULATION IN WORLD AND SELECTED COUNTRIES, 1860–1958

Period	World[a]	United Kingdom	France	Ger-many[b]	United States	Italy	Sweden	Japan	U.S.S.R.
Index Numbers of Industrial Output, 1953 = 100									
1860	4	15	15	6	2	–	–	–	–
1870	5	19	20	8	3	5	2	–	(1)
1880	8	23	24	10	5	7	3	–	(1)
1890	12	28	31	18	8	12	7	–	1
1900	16	33	40	29	12	17	16	10[c]	3
1910	24	36	56	42	20	30	23	12	4
1913	28	43	66	51	23	35	26	16	5
1920	26	43	45	30	30	32	25	28	1
1925–29	38	45	80	53	39	50	33	44	5
1932	30	45	67	35	24	41	34	49	12
1938	51	64	74	77	36	61	59	88	31
1950	–	94	87	72	84	79	97	55	69
1953	100	100	100	100	100	100	100	100	100
1958	133	114	150	151	102	142	118	168	172
1959	–	120	159	162	115	158	121	208	191
Population in Millions									
1850	1200	28	36	36	23	24	3.5	–	60
1900	1600	42	39	56	76	33	5.1	47	111
1950	2400	51	42	(50)	152	47	7.0	83	–
1958	2800	52	45	(54)	174	49	7.4	92	(206)

SOURCES: Industrial output: 1860 from Rolf Wagenführ, *Die Industriewirtschaft, Entwicklungstendenzen der deutschen und internationalen Industrieproduktion, 1860 bis 1932*, Institut für Konjunkturforschung (Berlin, 1932): 1870–1900 from League of Nations, *Industrialization and Foreign Trade* (Geneva, 1945), except for Sweden and Russia up to 1910, Japan up to 1932 and the world up to 1938; 1910 to recent years from O.E.E.C., *Industrial Statistics 1900–1957* (Paris, 1958), and United Nations, *Statistical Yearbook* and *Monthly Bulletin of Statistics*; also United States, *Historical Statistics: 1789–1945*, U.S.S.R., *Narodnoye Khozyaistvo* (Moscow, 1956); I. Svennilson, *Growth and Stagnation in the European Economy* (Geneva, 1954) and Y. Kotkovsky, *International Affairs*, No. 2 (1959). For population, W. S. Woytinsky and E. S. Woytinsky, *World Population and Production* (New York, 1953).

NOTE ON METHODS: World index of industrial output (excluding mining up to 1938 and handicraft production throughout the period) based on League of Nations figures up to 1938; figures based on the "net value added" concept, except for the U.S.S.R. where they refer to the gross value of output and may over-estimate the trend between 1925–29 and 1938; for post-war years, United Nations index linked to these and adjusted, in a very rough and ready way, for the inclusion of the output in the U.S.S.R., eastern Europe and China, thus: 1953 adjusted world-weights were derived by taking U.S.S.R. output as one-third of that of the United States, eastern European as one-half of U.S.S.R. and Chinese output as one and a half to two times that of India; 1925–29 index (base period of League of Nations index) linked with 1953 index by deflating the weights of U.S. industrial output in the world total for 1925–29 and 1953 by the movement of the U.S. index in this period.
[a]Including U.S.S.R., eastern Europe and China.
[b]Western Germany only for post-war years.
[c]1905.

[1] Throughout the study, industrial output refers to the production in factories and excludes that of the handicraft and cottage industries sector.

times higher than a hundred years ago. The absolute growth in per capita indus-trial output in the last 100 years was thus a number of times higher than that attained in the entire preceding period of man's existence; and the per capita rate of growth (2.6 percent per year in contrast to less than 0.1 percent in preceding centuries) was much higher still.[2]

Considerable interest attaches to an analysis of the rates of growth of indus-trial output for the world as a whole and for the major industrial countries. As can be seen from Table 2, world industrial output has expanded by about 3.6 percent per year over these hundred years. Whatever the period chosen, the rate has varied little, except during the inter-war period (1918–1938) of stagnation and the great depression, when the rate fell to 2.4 percent per annum. But these years of inhibited growth seem to have piled up such a vast backlog of demand for capital and consumer goods that under its pressure the recent post-war decade was a period of very rapid industrial growth. Consequently, if the whole period from 1913 to 1958 is considered, the rate of 3.5 percent per year is not

TABLE 2. ANNUAL RATES OF GROWTH IN INDUSTRIAL OUTPUT IN SELECTED COUNTRIES, 1860–1958, PERCENT (COMPOUNDED)

Period	World[a]	United Kingdom	France	Ger-many[b]	United States	Italy	Sweden	Japan	U.S.S.R.
1860 to 1880	3.2	2.4	2.4	2.7	4.3	–	–	–	–
1880 to 1900	4.0	1.7	2.4	5.3	4.5	4.5	8.1	–	6.4
1900 to 1913	4.2	2.2	3.7	4.4	5.2	5.6	3.5	3.8[c]	4.8
1913 to 1925–29	2.2	0.3	1.4	0.3	3.7	2.6	1.6	7.5	1.1
1925–29 to 1938	2.8	3.1	−0.7	3.5	−0.9	1.7	5.4	6.5	17.2
1913 to 1938	2.4	1.4	0.4	1.7	1.7	2.2	3.3	7.1	7.8
1938 to 1958	4.9	2.9	3.6	3.5	5.3	4.3	3.5	3.4	8.9
1860 to 1913	3.7	2.1	2.8	4.1	4.6	–	–	–	–
1880 to 1913	4.1	1.9	3.1	4.9	4.8	4.9	6.3	–	5.7
1880 to 1958	3.8	2.1	2.3	3.5	3.9	3.9	4.6	–	7.2
1900 to 1958	3.7	2.2	2.3	2.9	3.7	3.7	3.5	5.0[c]	7.5
1913 to 1958	3.5	2.2	1.9	2.4	3.3	3.1	3.4	5.4[d]	8.3
1925–29 to 1958	4.1	3.0	2.1	3.5	3.1	3.4	4.2	4.4	11.8

SOURCES: Same as Table 1.
[a]Including U.S.S.R., eastern Europe and China.
[b]Western Germany only for post-World-War II years.
[c]1905–58.
[d]1938 level reached only in 1952. If these 14 years are excluded, the rate would be 8.2 percent.

[2] See J. M. Keynes, *Essays in Persuasion* (London, 1931), p. 360.

substantially different from the rate of 3.6 percent per year for the century as a whole.

The relative constancy of the rate of growth of industrial output for the world as a whole does not imply that all countries expanded their output at the same rate. The factors responsible for different rates of economic growth are complex and beyond the scope of this study. Broadly speaking, industrial output grew rather slowly in the countries where industrialization started earlier. Thus, for instance, the lowest growth rates are found in the United Kingdom and France. On the other hand, the rate of growth of industrial output attained by each new entrant in the field of industrialization has tended to be successively higher. As can be seen in Table 2, where the countries are arranged from left to right in the approximate chronological order in which they began industrializing, this trend is maintained in the period before as well as after the first world war.

For the period of 33 years (1880 to 1913) the rate of growth of industrial output rises from about 2 percent per year in the United Kingdom, to 3 percent for France, 5 percent for Germany, the United States and Italy, and to about 6 percent for Sweden and Russia. For the 45-year period from 1913 to 1958 the rates rise from about 2 percent for the United Kingdom and France to 2.4 percent for Germany, over 3 percent for the United States, Italy and Sweden, 5.4 percent for Japan and over 8 percent for the U.S.S.R.—and in these crowded 45 years there were two world wars and an international depression! The list of countries is not, of course, complete; but it does include nearly all the major countries, which accounted throughout the period for eighty to ninety percent of the world's industrial output.

One explanation for this rise in the rate of industrial growth for each successive new entrant into the industrial field might be the fact that the volume of its industrial output in the initial stage was so small that relatively limited additions to it would appear large in percentage terms. But this seems an inadequate explanation, for two reasons. First, the high rates would continue for the initial years only; they would not be almost consistently maintained, as they were, for a rather long period. Second, it would then be reasonable to expect that in some early phase of industrial development in the advanced industrial countries the rate of growth was also very high and that it declined subsequently as the volume of their industrial output rose. But the available evidence does not seem to support this. In the early stage of industrial expansion in Great Britain—the forty years (1820 to 1860) following the Napoleonic wars—the rate of growth of industrial output was a little over 3 percent per year, which was very close to the rate of 3 percent for the 31 years (1925–29 to 1958) following the first World War. Examination of the long-term development suggests that there was a fair amount of almost monotonous continuation of nearly the same per capita rate of growth in the United Kingdom, France, Germany and the United States; disregarding a few years of slow growth—due to either a war or a depression—even the older industrial countries do not seem to have suffered from what Keynes called "the rheumatics of old age." Although rates of growth after the first World War were in most countries somewhat lower than those before it, with the notable exception of Japan and the U.S.S.R., this is—as shown below—almost entirely explained by changes in the rate of population growth—not to speak of the influence of the years spent in war and the depression.

Perhaps a more valid explanation of the progressively higher rates of growth of industrial output for each new entrant to the process of industrialization lies in the opportunity of benefiting from accumulated technological advance—a factor which was so emphatically stressed by Veblen. It is reasonable to suppose that the rate of growth in the United Kingdom and France was determined in the main by the pace of technological advance. These countries could only apply new techniques as they evolved; whereas for each new entrant there was already an accumulated body of technological progress to assimilate. The newly industrializing countries did not have to follow religiously the slow and necessarily step-by-step developments in techniques common to the countries which set out early on the road to industrialization. Nor did they have to bear the costs and delays of evolving and industrially trying out the new techniques; the countries which were ahead continued doing most of this. The later a country entered the field of industrialization, the larger was the fund of technological advance upon which it could draw, and hence the faster its possible rate of growth. So long as the technological gap between the pioneering countries and the newcomers was not bridged, the high rate of growth in the latter could be maintained.

It would follow that, in technological terms, the rates of industrial growth could not have been much higher in the pioneering countries. For the same reason—and again technologically speaking—the rates of growth in the countries just starting industrialization in the second half of the twentieth century can be higher (depending upon the ability to assimilate and spread advanced technology) than the rates attained by the countries industrializing in the first half of the twentieth century, and substantially higher than the rate of growth attained by countries which began industrializing earlier.

As to growth in per capita output—during the last century, population increased by less than 1 percent per year in the older industrial countries (and much less in France) or at about the same rate as the population of the world as a whole. The increase was in general faster in the first half than in the second half of the century. Only in the United States, where Europeans migrated in larger numbers in this period, was the rate of growth of population for the century as a whole as high as about 2 percent per year. As in the other countries, in the United States the rate of growth during the first half of this period—nearly 3 percent per year—was more than twice as high as that during the second period.

As shown in Table 2, the rate of growth of industrial output in the older industrial countries in the period 1913 to 1958 was somewhat lower than in the period 1860 to 1913. This decline has often been attributed to two causes: the expectation of a slowing down in the rate of growth as the industrial base became larger; and the disturbances caused by the two wars and the great depression. However, when the rate of growth of industrial output is deflated by changes in the rate of population growth, there is relatively little difference in the per capita annual rate of growth for both the periods, before and after the first World War. This is strikingly borne out by the experience in the United States, where the growth of industrial output was 4.6 percent in the period of 1860–1913 and 3.3 percent in the period 1913 to 1958; but the rate of growth of population was about 3 percent a year in the first period and 1.3 percent in the second period. Per capita industrial output thus grew at roughly the same rate—in fact slightly faster in the second period—despite the fact that the volume in output of the period after 1913 was substantially higher than in 1860 and that there was a decade of depression.[3] Analysis of per capita rates of growth of industrial output in the United Kingdom, Germany and France shows that in each country the rate was not significantly different in either of the two periods.

Viewed over this long period, the differences in the rates of growth of population and industrial output bring out forcibly the immense power of compound growth at higher rates. The differences in rates of growth of 1 to 2 percent (population) and 3 to 7 or more percent (industrial output) are indeed large. But they may not appear spectacular. Only when these rates are compounded over a long period—say a century—can one see the full impact of the staggering force of compound growth at higher rates. Over a century, a given quantity (population or output) will increase 2.7 times at 1 percent, 7.2 times at 2 percent, 19 times at 3 percent, 50 times at 4 percent, and 130 times at 5 percent. The extent of the growth during a hundred years at still higher rates is almost incredible: 340 times at 6 percent, 870 times at 7 percent, and—just to underline the spectacular effect of high compound rates—nearly 14,000 times at 10 percent in a century. If the rate of growth of industrial output is some 2 to 4 percent higher than population growth, the rise in per capita output over a century would be much higher than might be suggested by the rather modest difference in the rates of growth.

II. THE PATTERN OF INDUSTRIAL GROWTH

In recent years a number of countries have initiated programmes and plans of economic development in which special attention is paid to industrial growth. For them, decisions concerning the patterns of industrial development have assumed great practical importance. In view of the wide difference in the endowment of natural resources in various countries, a study of the development of specific industries in the industrial countries is not likely to furnish a useful guide to determining investment priorities in the pre-industrial countries at the present time. But a study of the historic evolution of the over-all sectoral pattern—the relationship between producer goods and the consumer goods—in the major industrial countries may be more relevant. Consumer goods,

---

[3] A similar conclusion for the growth of total per capita output for the last 120 years in the United States was advanced by Raymond Goldsmith. See United States Congress, Joint Economic Committee, *Employment, Growth, and Price Levels, Hearings* (86th Congress, 1st Session), Part II (Washington, April 7–10, 1959), pp. 230 ff.

as defined here, include all those finished goods and also semi-finished goods (e.g. yarn) which, although often used in industry, are largely bought by the public in a finished form—primarily for consumption in the home. Producer goods include raw materials, semi-manufactured articles and capital goods which are used by manufacturers.[4]

It is indeed striking that in all the major industrial countries for which data are shown in Table 3 there was a continuous decline over time in the share of consumer goods in total industrial output. At the beginning of industrialization in these countries, consumer goods accounted for two-thirds or more of total industrial output, and producer goods for the remainder. In the course of industrial development, however, the relative position of these two sectors was almost completely reversed—the share of consumer goods falling to around one-third of total industrial output and that of producer goods rising correspondingly. The rate of growth of the producer goods sector was thus throughout this period higher than that of the consumer goods sector.

In the early phase of industrialization—stretching from a few decades to half a century in the United Kingdom, France, Germany, the United States, Italy, Japan,[5] and the U.S.S.R.—the producer goods sector grew one and a half to more than two times as fast as the consumer goods sector (see Table 4). Once industrialization had reached a fairly high level and the proportion of consumer goods in total industrial output had fallen to around one-third, the differences in the rates of growth of both these sectors narrowed down significantly, with the producer goods sector expanding only a little faster than the consumer goods sector. This general pattern of industrial growth—producer goods expanding nearly twice as fast as consumer goods in the early phase of industrialization and the gap between the rates of growth for the two sectors narrowing down later on—appears to have been a characteristic feature of economic development in all the major industrial countries.[6] Among these

[4] The definition, and part of the data used in this section, are from Dr. W. Hoffmann's two studies, *British Industry, 1700–1950* (Oxford, 1955), and *Stadien und Typen der Industrialisierung* (Jena, 1931). The latter book has recently been published, in a somewhat revised and expanded version, in English translation under the title, *The Growth of Industrial Economies* (Manchester, 1958). The consumer and producer goods industries are defined to include four broad groups of industries under each—the consumer goods sector includes food, drink and tobacco, clothing (including footwear), leather goods and furniture (excluding other wood-working industries); the producer goods sector includes ferrous and non-ferrous metals, machinery, vehicle building and chemicals. These groups account for "two-thirds of the net output of all industry." For details, see *The Growth of Industrial Economies*, pp. 8–17.

[5] Owing to statistical limitations, the data for Japan are not shown in Table 4; but the developments there were essentially similar to those elsewhere. See W. W. Lockwood, "The Scale of Economic Growth in Japan, 1868–1938," in Simon Kuznets, W. E. Moore, and J. J. Spengler, editors, *Economic Growth: Brazil, India, Japan* (Durham, 1955), pp. 153–154.

[6] This pattern of growth, however, is not restricted to the major industrial countries only. As Hoffmann has shown by an analysis of changes in industrial structure over time, it applies to small industrial countries also. He has defined three basic stages in industrial growth in accordance with the changes in the ratio of the volume of consumer goods output to that of producer goods output; in the first stage, the ratio is $5(\pm 1):1$, in the second $2.5(\pm 1):1$ and in the third it is $1(\pm 0.5):1$. The fourth stage has a still lower ratio. See Hoffmann, *The Growth of Industrial Economies*, op. cit., pp. 2–3, also Chapter IV.

TABLE 3. DECLINE IN THE SHARE OF CONSUMER GOODS IN INDUSTRIAL OUTPUT
IN SELECTED COUNTRIES

Country	Year and Share in Percentages				
Great Britain	$\frac{1871}{52}$	$\frac{1901}{41}$	$\frac{1924}{40}$	–	$\frac{1946}{31}$
France	$\frac{1861-65}{65}$	$\frac{1896}{44}$	$\frac{1921}{35}$	–	$\frac{1952}{34}$
Germany	–	$\frac{1895}{45}$	$\frac{1925}{37}$	$\frac{1936}{25}$	$\frac{1951}{23}$
United States	$\frac{1880}{44}$	$\frac{1900}{34}$	$\frac{1927}{32}$	–	$\frac{1947}{30}$
Belgium	$\frac{1846}{80}$	$\frac{1896}{49}$	$\frac{1926}{37}$	$\frac{1936-38}{36}$	–
Switzerland	$\frac{1882}{62}$	$\frac{1895}{45}$	$\frac{1923}{38}$	–	$\frac{1945}{34}$
Italy	–	$\frac{1896}{72}$	$\frac{1913}{53}$	$\frac{1938}{37}$	–
Japan	–	–	$\frac{1925}{59}$	–	$\frac{1950}{40}$
U.S.S.R.	–	$\frac{1913}{67}$	$\frac{1928}{61}$	$\frac{1940}{39}$	$\frac{1955}{29}$

SOURCES: Data for Great Britain, France, Germany, the United States, Belgium, Switzerland and Japan from W. Hoffmann, *The Growth of Industrial Economies*, Statistical Appendix; for Italy, from A. Gerschenkron, "Rate of Industrial Growth in Italy, 1881–1913," in *Journal of Economic History*, XV, No. 4 (December, 1955), 365; data for Japan (1950) from United Nations, *Supplement to the Monthly Bulletin of Statistics* (1954) and for France (1952) from OEEC, *Statistical Bulletin, Definitions and Methods: Indices of Industrial Production* (Paris, 1957); and for the U.Ş.S.R. from *Narodnoye Khozyaistvo* (Moscow, 1956), p. 52.

NOTE: Owing to the limitations of statistical comparability, the figures are to be treated as crude indicators only. The data are based on "net value added" in manufacturing industries (excluding mining and building) for all countries except the U.S.S.R. where they refer to the gross value of output and include mining. For definitions, see the opening paragraph of this section and the footnote to it.

countries, there were very real differences in their natural resources endowment, in the accumulation of technical skills, in the period when they began industrialization, in the speed of their growth, in their attitude and actual experience regarding international trade and capital movements, in the proportion of capital goods output devoted to exports, in the fiscal and other forms of economic policies pursued, and in how industrial growth was promoted—through private enterprise (and therefore without a strict pre-determination of sectoral priorities) or through state encouragement and central planning. Despite these differences there was nevertheless a striking uniformity in the evolution of the sectoral pattern of their industrial growth.

In a broad historical sense, there is nothing surprising in such a development. It is only a common sense proposition that since output of producers goods is the least developed segment in the early phase of industrialization, it should

TABLE 4. RATES OF GROWTH OF CONSUMER AND PRODUCER GOODS AND THEIR RATIO IN SELECTED COUNTRIES

Country and Period	Total Industrial Output (a)	Consumer Goods Output (b)	Producer Goods Output (c)	Ratio of Producer Goods Output to Consumer Goods Output Col. $\frac{c}{b}$
	Percent per year			
Great Britain				
1812 to 1851	3.4	3.1	4.0	1.3
1851 to 1881	2.7	2.0	3.8	1.9
1881 to 1907	1.8	1.5	2.0	1.3
1907 to 1935	1.0	0.8	1.2	1.5
France				
1861–65 to 1896	2.4	1.2	3.3	2.7
1896 to 1921	0.5	–	1.1	–
Germany				
1860 to 1880	2.9	1.8	3.9	2.2
1880 to 1900	5.0	3.7	5.4	1.5
1900 to 1913	3.4	2.5	3.7	1.5
United States				
1880 to 1900	4.5	3.2	5.1	1.6
1900 to 1927	4.2	3.9	5.5	1.4
Italy				
1896 to 1913	5.4	3.5	8.7	2.5
U.S.S.R.				
1928 to 1940	17.0	12.0	21.2	1.8
1940 to 1955	8.1	6.1	9.1	1.5
1958 to 1965 (Plan)	8.8	7.3	9.3	1.3

SOURCES AND METHODS: W. Hoffmann, *British Industry, 1700–1950* (Oxford, 1955); Rolf Wagenführ, *Die Industriewirtschaft* (Berlin, 1932); for Italy and the U.S.S.R., the same as in Table 3; also N. S. Khrushchev's *Report to the XXI Congress of CPSU* (Moscow, 1957). The rates of growth for France and the United States derived by applying the proportions for each of the sectors given in the Statistical Appendix to Hoffmann's study, *The Growth of Industrial Economies*, to the movement of the index of manufacturing production for the periods concerned.

NOTE: See Note to Table 3.

expand much faster than the consumer goods sector. Moreover, the share of investment (and hence producer goods) in national output and expenditure usually rises in the process of economic growth and calls for a more rapid expansion of the supplies of producer goods than of consumer goods. This process is generally reinforced by an increasing substitution of imported producer goods by domestic output.[7] The relatively faster expansion of producer goods

[7] For elucidation of a similar conclusion reached by a discussion of export prospects, see Surendra J. Patel, "Export Prospects and Economic Growth: India," in the *Economic Journal*, LXIX, No. 275 (September, 1959), 490 ff.

often continues even at a later stage of economic growth when the share of investment in national expenditure becomes more or less stable largely due to a rise in the actual machinery and equipment content per unit of fixed asset formation and in the share of producer goods in exports.[8] Many economic historians have regarded such a development as an essential feature of industrial growth,[9] although other economists, perhaps owing to their limited acquaintance with long-term experience and their preoccupation with contemporary concerns, have been less than clear on this point.

III. CHANGING SHARES IN THE WORLD'S INDUSTRIAL OUTPUT

Differences in the rates of growth of industrial output, described above, have led to important changes in the relative position of various countries and areas in total world industrial output. An analysis of these changes is of great interest in elucidating the conditions under which the gap between the most advanced industrial nations and the late-comers was closed. Its relevance to the contemporary problem of closing the gap between rich industrial countries and poor pre-industrial areas needs no emphasis.

Great Britain was the seed-bed for the early phase of the industrial revolution. Although it had only about 2 percent of the world's population, more than one-half of the world's industrial output was concentrated in these islands throughout the first half of the nineteenth century. In a world in which the growth of output in relation to population was almost stagnant, Great Britain attained a decisive superiority by realizing rates of growth of 2 to 3 percent per year. Although these rates appear very modest in comparison with those current in many parts of the world in the last few decades, they were a powerful engine of massive expansion—particularly when cumulated over a long period—in a more or less stagnant world. The benefits they yielded in the nineteenth century to Great Britain in terms of wealth and power are now a matter of common knowledge. This was the period of which it is rightly said that England was the workshop of the world.

The growth of industrial output in other countries in Europe and in the United States at rates twice as high as in Great Britain had started making inroads into British industrial supremacy during the second half of the nineteenth century. To the contemporary Europeans, the economic race between Great Britain and Germany was not just a subject of idle curiosity; it was intimately bound up with the realities of power and influence over the rest of mankind. While this contest constituted a center of attention for the historians of the late nineteenth century, the rapid emergence of the United States as a

---

[8] This may also be explained to some extent by the fact that a part of the final output of the metal, vehicle and chemical industries is destined for consumers.

[9] See W. Hoffmann, *British Industry, 1700–1950, op. cit.*, p. 73; and *idem, The Growth of Industrial Economies, op. cit.*, p. 2. Also see A. Gerschenkron, "Rate of Industrial Growth in Italy, 1881–1931," in the *Journal of Economic History*, XV, No. 4 (December, 1955), 365.

world industrial power was of far greater significance.[10] Already by the close of the nineteenth century the United States had surpassed Great Britain in total volume of industrial output (see Table 5), which by the end of the century was one and a half times higher than in Great Britain, and total German output was not far behind the British. Since the First World War the United States has remained in the center of the industrial world, accounting for nearly 40 percent of its output.[11] Less than half a century was needed to accomplish this change.

TABLE 5. RELATIVE POSITION OF SELECTED COUNTRIES IN WORLD INDUSTRIES OUTPUT, PERCENTAGE SHARE IN WORLD INDUSTRIES OUTPUT

| | Private Enterprise Economies | | | | | | | Centrally Planned Economies | | | |
Period	Total	U.S.	United Kingdom	Germany^a	Total Western Europe	Japan	Others	Total	U.S.S.R.	Eastern Europe	China
1870	97	23	32	13	62	–	12	3	–	–	–
1896–1900	96	30	20	17	53	–	13	4	–	–	–
1913	95	36	14	16	44	1	14	5	–	–	–
1926–1929	95	42	9	12	35	2	16	5	(2)	–	–
1953	77	41	6	6	25	2	9	23	14	(7)	(2)
1958	69	31	5	7	25	3	10	31	18	–	–

SOURCES: Same as Table 1. Data for 1870 to 1926–1929 from League of Nations, *Industrialization and Foreign Trade* (Geneva, 1945), p. 13, and for 1953, as indicated in the general note to Table 1; those for 1958 derived by deflating the relative weights by the movement of the index of industrial output; the weight assigned in the League of Nations' study to the industrial output in the U.S.S.R. in 1926–29 adjusted to agree with the movement of the index for the U.S.S.R. in Table 1.

NOTE: The relative shares of countries are based on very crude data and any inter-country comparisons should be limited to broad order of magnitude rather than precise statistical measurement.

^a All of Germany up to 1926–29 and only western Germany thereafter.

During the first half of the twentieth century, other countries—Italy, Japan and the U.S.S.R.—began industrializing. Their pace of growth was still higher, but their share in world output in the initial period was so low that until the middle of this century their growth had little effect on the relative positions of other countries. This, however, was no longer the case by the end of the fifties. By then, the division of the world into two zones or regions was a fairly settled affair: the private enterprise economies, which basically maintained—although with considerable modifications in recent years—private ownership of means of production and depended on private enterprise for economic growth; the other, the centrally planned economies, where the resourcefulness and the financial ability of the individual daring entrepreneur of the Schumpeterian

[10] To the historians who study the present economic competition between the United States and the U.S.S.R., it may be suggested that the economic developments in contemporary China may not have an altogether dissimilar significance for the twenty-first century.

[11] Whatever the shift in the relative position of Great Britain and the United States, the total industrial output in these two English-speaking countries has continued to account for one-half or more of the world's industrial output throughout the nineteenth century and the first half of the twentieth century. Economics—the whole body of theoretical premises, the neat schemes of internal balances and disturbing elements, the bundle of logical deductions and policy conclusions—is in no small measure associated with this; for economics is for the most part a product of the English-speaking countries with occasional contributions from the outside.

type was replaced by the leadership of the state in planning and promoting industrial growth. The precise measurement of the rates of growth which the latter group has attained remains a subject of considerable controversy among western scholars, but there is general agreement that these rates have been high —they are usually placed in the range of 8 to 10 percent per year,[12] or more than twice as high as in the United States and nearly four times the rate common in the older industrial countries.

The relative position of the two groupings shown in Table 5 is very approximate, in fact only illustrative, and no attempt should be made to read into it any statistical precision. For the purpose of a broad survey of this type, it is not very important whether a few percentage points are added to or subtracted from either region. What is of decisive importance is the present relationship between their respective rates of growth. Given this relationship and given its continuation over the next decade or two, little arithmetical skill is needed to indicate that the industrial output of the centrally planned economies could approximate that of the rest of the world 15 to 25 years hence. Whether the level of industrial output in the centrally planned economies in recent years is taken as one-half, one-third or one-fourth (and these relative positions have been suggested by various scholars) of that in the private enterprise economies makes a difference of only a decade to the period—15 years or 25 years—in which the industrial output in both groupings could become approximately equal.

Whether the present differential in the rates of growth in these two areas will continue or will narrow is not the main concern of this paper. The important point is this: once the continuation of the differential in the rates is assumed, the closing of the gap in a relatively short period is an arithmetically inevitable consequence. It would merely be a repetition of what Great Britain attained in the first half and United States and Germany in the second half of the nineteenth century. In all these countries the underlying conditions were also the same, that is, the rate of growth of the newcomer was twice (or more) as high as that of the old-timer; and the period needed for closing the gap was less than half a century—the lifetime of a man in his twenties.

One further observation of some relevance may be made in this connection. Although a number of countries have become industrially strong over the last century, over 90 percent of the world's industrial output has continued to be concentrated in areas (including eastern Europe and the U.S.S.R.) inhabited by peoples of European origin—peoples now accounting for rather less than

[12] For details regarding rates of growth in the Soviet Union, see Donald R. Hodgman, *Soviet Industrial Production, 1928–51* (Cambridge, Mass., 1954), pp. 89, 134; Naum Jasny, *The Soviet Economy During the Plan Era* (Stanford, 1951), p. 23; Colin Clark, *The Conditions of Economic Progress*, second edition (London, 1951), p. 186, and F. Seton, "The Tempo of Soviet Industrial Expansion" in *Bulletin of the Oxford University Institute of Statistics* (February, 1958), 18. The rates of growth of industrial output in the U.S.S.R., estimated by western scholars for the period 1928 to 1940, are lower than official estimates, although the difference between these has continued to narrow with the passage of time. The annual rate of growth was 11 percent according to Jasny and Clark, 13 percent according to Hodgman and about 13 to 14 percent according to Seton; the official estimate was 16 to 17 percent.

one-third of the population of the world. There have been varying degrees of industrialization in other countries (Japan, India, and China) but the share of these countries in world output was very small until recent years. An unfortunate consequence of observing such a concentration was the cultivation of a belief in some quarters that industrial growth was somehow an exclusively European plant which might be grown with great care in a few and specially selected gardens in the rest of the world but could hardly be expected to become a matter of mass cultivation.

It is true that all new technical developments require attaining adequate training and in many instances adaptation of habits of thought and behavior.[13] But in a wide historical perspective, industrial growth, or more precisely the application of machinery to productive use, would seem to be no more the exclusive hall-mark of a particular geographic (and hence ethnic) region than were all the past landmarks in mankind's long development—early use of fire and later the taming of it, domestication of animals, agriculture and irrigation, smelting of ores and use of metals, invention of scripts, paper and the art of printing, ship's sternpost rudder and marine-compass, gunpowder, Indian numerals and the methods of calculation, and many others. Many areas of the world would recognize in such a list their own contribution—which was carried forward, enriched and brought to fruition in some other parts at another time. The experience of industrial growth in Japan, and in more recent years in India and China, should indicate that the idea of industrialization as an exclusive possession of the peoples of European origin is based on an arrogant ignorance of history rather than on facts. . . .

[13] A. Gerschenkron has drawn pointed attention to this. See his paper, "Economic Backwardness in Historical Perspective," in Bert F. Hoselitz, editor, *The Progress of Underdeveloped Areas* (Chicago, 1952), p. 23.

The Occupational Structure of the Labour Force: Patterns and Trends in Selected Countries

ABDELMEGID M. FARRAG

INTRODUCTION

In the course of development certain changes in the structure of the labour force by industry and occupation are usually entailed. In a developing country, past changes in this respect may provide some indication of the likely changes which are desirable, or are likely to take place, for the fulfilment or during the

Reprinted from *Population Studies*, 18 (July, 1964), pp. 17–34, by permission of the author and the publisher.

process of development. Short-term policies may be guided by past short-term trends, but for perspective planning and long-term policy making it is essential to foresee the emerging patterns over long periods of time and to base the forecasts on a long-term analysis of past trends.

Since historical data are hard to obtain over sufficiently long periods of time for many developing countries, it is possible that the analysis of similar data for countries which are at an advanced stage of economic growth may provide some useful indications of the likely future trends in the less advanced countries.[1] But one of the main difficulties here lies in the fact that for many of the advanced countries early data are not strictly comparable to more recent ones. This is particularly true of data on the occupational structure of the labour force. One of the main reasons for this incomparability is that the classification of the 'occupied population' or the 'labour force' by occupation, is a comparatively recent undertaking, and that earlier statistical surveys provided us with no more than a classification of the labour force by industry or by branch of economic activity.[2]

An attempt is made in this article to bring together somewhat scattered and fragmentary information on the occupational structure of the labour force for a limited number of countries where early data exist. The attempt is then extended, to try and match these early data with more recent data for the same countries with a view to constructing a more homogeneous time series over longer periods for each of these countries. The data are then presented in a form which approaches as closely as possible the nine major groups of the 'International Standard Classification of Occupations' (I.S.C.O.).[3]

The difficulties encountered in this attempt are discussed in the following section.* The analysis in the later sections, which are based on these constructed series, naturally suffers from certain limitations which are mainly due to these difficulties and to the type of adjustments which were made.

The object of the article is to fill some of the gaps in our knowledge of the long-term changes in the occupational structure of the labour force in the course of development. In the assessment of future manpower requirements for the economy the need for such data, together with other data on concomitant changes in production, investment, income, wages and various other indicators

[1] It is important to note, however, that even at earlier dates the advanced countries will probably have been much more advanced than most developing countries are at present. Besides, the process of development of the latter may also prove to be dissimilar, in nature and in speed, from that of the former. Historical trends in the advanced countries can, therefore, only serve as broad indicators of the likely and/or desirable future changes in the occupational structure of the labour force as the process of development gets under way in the developing countries of to-day.

[2] In a classification by industry the employed person is assigned to a branch of economic activity which is determined by the principal product produced or handled, or services rendered by the production unit to which he belongs. In a classification by occupation, on the other hand, the determining criterion is the nature of the work actually performed by the individual employed person or the types of functions attaching to his job.

[3] See *International Standard Classification of Occupations*, International Labour Office, Geneva, 1958.

* [The material referred to is not included—Editor.]

of general trends in the economy as a whole, could not be over-emphasized. The implications of such an assessment on educational and training policies, or on 'investment in man' in general, is more than obvious. . . .

ANALYSIS OF HISTORICAL TRENDS BY MAJOR OCCUPATIONAL GROUPS

One of the objects of analysing occupational trends is to see their implications on policies of training and formal education. Unfortunately, the relationship between any occupational classification and formal educational requirements is not easy to determine in precise terms. For some occupations the educational requirements are never static. They vary from one country to another and for the same country from time to time. At an advanced stage of development a primary school teacher, for example, may be required to have completed a university education or its equivalent. But at a less advanced stage a country may not require such teachers to have an education of such high level. 'In many underdeveloped countries the majority of elementary school teachers may have no more than a primary school education. . . . The requirements for managers, technicians and foremen likewise are difficult to define in educational terms. Indeed, . . . the educational level of persons in a wide variety of high-level occupations depends in part on the available supplies of educated manpower. In a relatively advanced country employers can, and do, insist on higher standards of formal education than in less developed countries.'[4]

In view of these divergencies in conditions and of differences in the production-mix of both goods and services in different countries, it is only logical to assume that different countries will place different emphasis on different occupations at different periods of time. The educational requirements for at least some of these occupations may also be different in different countries depending on their development objectives. Certain occupations could probably be made available to the labour market in a relatively short period of time. Other occupations or talents, on the other hand, take longer to develop, and require much earlier foresight of their future desirable magnitude. Priorities have to be assigned to the wide range of occupations which have to be developed. Each country has to develop its own criterion to determine what occupations are more 'critical,' or 'strategic' to its own development programmes.

In this article no attempt is made to formulate a definition of strategic manpower. Any definition of this sort is bound to be arbitrary unless it is related to a real situation of a given country at a given time. Nevertheless, for the analytical phase of this article, and since we do not propose to examine the whole range of occupations in the same degree of detail, it would be useful to determine the occupational groups to be examined against a background of a certain terminology, although this terminology may seem arbitrary.

---

[4] F. Harbison and C. Myers, *Education, Manpower and Economic Growth—Strategies of Human Resource Development*, 1964, pp. 191–192.

As suggested earlier, it is conceivable that some occupations may require longer periods of time to develop than others. These occupations will presumably require more education, and a minimum level of secondary education is usually attached to them. Occupations with such minimum educational characteristics may encompass most of such occupational groups of the I.S.C.O. as:

1. Professional Technical and Related Workers.
2. Administrative, Executive and Managerial Workers.
3. Clerical Workers.
4. Sales Workers.

An examination of the various components of these major occupational groups will show that only few do not require the secondary education specified above as a minimum.

In the following section we shall remark on the trends which have been observed in the four countries under consideration during the periods indicated for the four occupational categories mentioned above. In a subsequent section these categories are considered as a whole in order to compare trends in the whole body of white-collar as compared with blue-colour occupations. Finally, changes in sex differentials are examined and certain observations are made on this topic.* The occupational ratios presented in the various tables of this article are calculated on the basis of the numerical totals given in Table 1.

TABLE 1. TRENDS IN THE SITE OF THE LABOUR FORCE IN SELECTED COUNTRIES.* (IN THOUSANDS)

Year	Australia	Canada	England and Wales	U.S.A.[a]
1841	.	.	5,744	.
51	.	.	8,118	.
61	.	.	9,213	.
71	684	.	10,281	12,506
81	906	.	11,188	17,392
91	1,343	.	12,752	22,736
1901	1,595	1,782	14,328	{ 29,073 / 29,030
11	1,925	2,725	16,287	37,291
21	2,279	3,158	16,246	42,206
31	2,692[b]	3,922	18,421	48,686
41	.	4,186	.	51,741
51	3,141[b]	5,149	19,482	58,999
61	...	6,305	...	64,537

Explanation of signs used in this and all the following tables:

. = figure not available, or could not be obtained, or period not applicable.

... = figure not yet available.

A line (———) placed between two figures in a column indicates a new source and/or that a new series of comparable figures starts.

* = excluding those who did not report their occupations.

[a] = data relating to years immediately preceding the years indicated.

[b] = figures are for 1933 and 1947 respectively.

* [The material referred to is not included—Editor.]

Throughout the following sections it has to be remembered that the discussion is based on major occupational groups and that these are clusters of minor groups of occupations which in turn are made up of individual or unit occupations. In view of this fact, observed trends for any of the major occupational groups may be composed of similar or dissimilar trends for each of these components at the minor and/or unit level.[5]

(i) Professional Workers[6]

Trends in the relative importance of this group in the total labour force for the countries under consideration, are outlined in Table 2 below. It can be seen that with only a few exceptions, the ratio of professional workers in the total labour force has been rising consistently over the periods indicated, especially in England and Wales and the United States. It is interesting to note that, although these two countries had exactly the same proportions of their labour force classified as professionals around 1870, the United States has established a substantial lead over the years. It may also be observed that while a rising trend is common to all the four countries, that of the United States appears to be sharpest.

At the turn of the century the ratio of the professional group to the total labour force seems to have ranged between 4–5 per cent in three of these countries and about 7 per cent in Australia. Fifty years later the ratio was

TABLE 2. Professional Workers as a Percentage of Total Labour Force (Trends in Selected Countries)

Year	Australia	Canada	England and Wales	U.S.A.[a]
1841	.	.	2.8	.
51	.	.	3.0	.
61	.	.	3.1	.
71	.	.	3.3	3.3
81	.	.	3.7	3.8
91	.	.	4.0	4.9
1901	6.9	4.6	4.2	$\begin{cases} 5.4 \\ \overline{4.3} \end{cases}$
11	7.3	3.7	4.4	4.7
21	8.5	5.5	4.1	5.4
31	8.4[b]	6.1	4.3	6.8
41	.	6.7	.	7.5
51	7.3[b]	7.5	6.3	8.6
61	...	10.0	...	11.4

For explanations of signs see under Table 1 above.
[a] Data relating to years immediately preceding the years indicated.
[b] Data for 1933 and 1947 respectively.

[5] See footnote 9.
[6] According to the I.S.C.O. definition (p. 27), this group would include a variety of professions ranging from scientists, engineers, teachers, physicians, accountants, etc., to jurists, clergy, authors, actors, musicians, librarians, nurses, midwives, etc.

between 6 per cent for England and Wales and almost 9 per cent for the United States. In 1960 this ratio had already reached 11 per cent in the United States, and is expected to exceed 13 per cent in 1970 and 14 per cent by 1975.[7,8]

No useful purpose would be served by drawing a general observation on the rising trends of the proportions of this major group in the total labour force of different countries. Although it may be assumed that in the course of development there is a tendency for an increased utilization of scientists, engineers and technicians not only in research activities but also in industry, government and educational institutions, it would be mistaken to assume that all professional groups show similar tendencies. Indeed, even if a component group shows an increase over time in numerical terms, its proportion of the total major group will not increase unless the rate of growth of the former is higher than that of the latter.[9]

(II) MANAGERIAL WORKERS[10]

Trends in the relative importance of the managerial group as a percentage of the total labour force for the four countries under consideration which are given in Table 3 below should be approached with caution. This is mainly due to many areas of uncertainty as to possible changes and variations in the classification systems of occupations between countries and between different years for the same country. It is not clear, for example, in the original sources, whether working proprietors in wholesale and retail trade are included in, or excluded from, this group. Data for working proprietors by divisions of economic

[7] See *Manpower Report of the President* and *A Report on Manpower Requirements, Resources, Utilization and Training*, by the United States Department of Labor, transmitted to the Congress, March 1963, p. 100.

[8] Estimates based on data published in 'The active population of the U.S.S.R.', *International Labour Review*, 84, 3, September 1961, pp. 198–203, suggest that the ratio of professional workers has risen from 6.5 per cent in 1939 to 10.5 per cent in 1959. As for India, it is estimated that the ratio will rise from 1.9 per cent in 1961 to 4 per cent in 1976 (see V. R. K. Tilak, "The future manpower situation in India, 1961–76," *International Labour Review*, 87, 5, May 1963, Table IX, p. 444).

[9] U.S. data, for example, show that between 1950 and 1960 the total of the professional group has increased by 47 per cent, but its components have shown varying degrees of increase or decline. The increase in the number of electrical and electronic technicians, for example, was eightfold; for mathematicians it was sevenfold; for aeronautical engineers threefold, while the number of industrial engineers has more than doubled. On the other hand, the number of photographers has declined by 2 percent; of mining engineers by about 15 percent and of athletes by 64 percent. An increase in the absolute number of nurses by 45.5 per cent (from 400,000 to almost 600,000) left their percentage in the total professional group practically unchanged. The increase in the number of elementary school teachers from some 700,000 in 1950 to over 1 million in 1960 (an increase of 49 percent as compared to 47 percent increase in the total professional group), implied only a minor increase in their proportion of the total group (from 13.7 percent in 1950 to 13.9 percent in 1960). At the same time, the relative importance of the secondary school teachers within this major group declined from 7.5 percent over the period, despite the increase in their numbers.

[10] Workers in this group, as defined in the I.S.C.O. (p. 55), would include, basically, government, administrative and executive officials and directors, managers and working proprietors in all the different divisions of economic activity, except working proprietors in wholesale and retail trade.

TABLE 3. MANAGERIAL WORKERS AS A PERCENTAGE OF TOTAL
LABOUR FORCE. (TRENDS IN SELECTED COUNTRIES)

Year	Australia	Canada	England and Wales	U.S.A.[a]
1841	.	.	0.6	.
51	.	.	0.8	.
61	.	.	1.0	.
71	.	.	1.0	4.6
81	.	.	1.1	4.6
91	.	.	1.1	5.9
1901	0.5	4.3	1.4	{6.2 / 5.8
11	0.7	4.7	1.8	6.6
21	0.8	7.3	3.2	6.6
31	1.2[b]	5.6	2.1	7.4
41	.	5.4	.	7.3
51	4.3[b]	7.6	2.3	8.7
61	...	8.6	...	8.5

For explanations of signs see under Table 1 above.
[a] Data relating to years immediately preceding the years indicated.
[b] Data for 1933 and 1947 respectively.

activity are hardly available. Besides, for earlier years, some of the above figures refer, in published sources, to public administrators, a connotation which does not include, in principle, directors and managers of private business.

However, if the figures given in the table above are taken at their face value, bearing in mind that they may need adjustment, mainly to exclude working proprietors in commerce who should be re-allocated (according to the I.S.C.O. practices) to the sales workers group it may be observed that at the turn of the century the share of this managerial group in the total labour force ranged between 0.5 per cent in Australia and about 6 per cent in the United States. Around 1950 it had risen to a range of a little over 2 per cent in England and Wales and almost 9 per cent in the United States. Since it was not easy to probe into the classificatory difficulties over time and between countries, it is not safe to assume that the observed growth of this group's share in the total labour force is always real. For instance, the change in the relative importance of this group in Australia from 0.5 per cent in 1901 to 4.3 per cent in 1947 means more than an eightfold increase in less than 50 years. None of the other three countries has shown any comparable increases during the same period. It may be of interest to note that while the managerial group has increased from 7.3 per cent of the United States total labour force in 1940 to 8.5 per cent in 1960, it has declined in the U.S.S.R. from 1.7 per cent in 1939 to 1.4 per cent in 1959.[11] For India it is estimated that this group accounted for only 1 per cent of the total labour force in 1961 but is expected rise to 2.4 per cent by 1976.[12]

[11] "The active population of the U.S.S.R.," *op. cit.*
[12] V. R. K. Tilak, *loc. cit.*

The rising trend in the ratio of the managerial group may be conceived of partly as a function of the growth of large-scale organization of commerce. In early years large-scale establishments in commerce were less frequent than in more recent years. Besides, the number of managers and other salaried officials in private industry also tends to increase. The managerial functions to be performed in a continually developing society are bound to grow gradually and to assume broader dimensions, both inside and outside the government machinery. Development of the critical faculties of management receives increasing attention as the growth of the economy gets under way. Management or executive development programmes are found in many large companies, especially in advanced countries. With the development of the scientific approach to the study of management new concepts emerge. The recent distinction between various levels of management would suggest that the inventory of managers may include in more recent years persons who, in earlier years, used to be excluded. The extent to which these and other factors may affect the comparability of the data contained in Table 3 above for each of the countries under consideration is, however, difficult to ascertain.

(III) CLERICAL WORKERS

Data pertaining to this group for three of the countries under consideration are given in Table 4 below. It suggests that there has been a consistent rise from one census year to another in the proportion of clerical workers in the total labour force of these countries. At the beginning of the present century this category accounted for no more than 4 per cent of the total labour force, whereas fifty-odd years later the corresponding percentages have nearly trebled in Canada, and in England and Wales, and have shown a fourfold increase in the United States. In the latter country this figure has risen further in the subsequent decade so that in 1960 clerical workers made up 15 per cent of the labour force. In the

TABLE 4. CLERICAL WORKERS AS A PERCENTAGE OF
THE TOTAL LABOUR FORCE. (TRENDS IN SELECTED
COUNTRIES)*

Year	Canada	England and Wales	U.S.A.[a]
1891	.	3.3	.
1901	3.2	4.1	3.0
11	3.8	4.9	5.3
21	6.9	6.1	8.0
31	6.7	7.0	8.9
41	7.3	.	9.6
51	10.9	10.9	12.3
61	13.2	...	14.9

For explanations of signs see under Table 1 above.
* Data are not available separately for this category for Australia.
[a] Data relating to years immediately preceding the years indicated.

U.S.S.R., on the other hand, this group has declined from 6.2 per cent in 1939 to 5.5 per cent in 1959. In the United States also the projection of future trends foreshadows a slackening in the rate or growth of clerical workers with possibly an eventual stabilization of their share in the total labour force. It is anticipated, for example, that the ratio will creep up to only 15.9 per cent in 1970 and to 16.2 per cent in 1975.[13]

Apart from the fact that both ratios of the managerial and clerical workers have declined in the U.S.S.R. between 1939 and 1959, there is not enough evidence, at least on the basis of data contained in this article, to show a close relationship between these two groups. It is also interesting to note that, contrary to popular belief, the automation of many clerical functions in the United States during 1950–1960 did not affect the continuous rise in the demand for certain types of clerical workers. This is explained partly as due 'to the substantial expansion of industries which employ large numbers of clerical personnel, such as finance and insurance, and state and local governments.'[14]

(iv) Sales Workers[15]

The relative size of this group for three of the countries under consideration in their respective total labour force, over time, is shown in Table 5 below. It may be seen that, with the probable exception of England and Wales, the size of this group in the total labour force has been generally rising. There may be

TABLE 5. Sales Workers as a Percentage of the Total Labour Force. (Trends in Selected Countries)*

Year	Canada	England and Wales	U.S.A.[a]
1891	.	7.6[b]	.
1901	3.1	5.4[b]	4.5
11	4.7	4.6[b]	4.7
21	5.7	9.6	4.9
31	6.1	11.2	6.3
41	5.9	.	6.7
51	6.8	10.2	7.0
61	6.5	...	7.4

For explanations of signs see under Table 1 above.

* Data are not available separately for this category for Australia.

[a] Data relating to years immediately preceding the years indicated.

[b] In the original source, the corresponding absolute figures appear under 'general and undefined workers and dealers.'

---

[13] *Manpower Report of the President, op. cit.,* p. 100.

[14] *Ibid.,* p. 28.

[15] This major group includes working proprietors in wholesale and retail trade, auctioneers, salesmen of insurance, real estate, securities and services, commercial travellers and manufacturers' agents, shop assistants and related workers.

a certain element of overlap between this group and that of clerical workers. In some cases only combined figures for both groups are available. It is also probable, as has already been discussed, that the 'sales workers' are underestimated, at least for earlier years. If adjusted to include working proprietors the figures will increase. Taking the figures as they appear in Table 5, however, it is seen that this group represented between 3–5 per cent of the total labour force around 1900, whereas around 1950 the range was between 7 and 10 per cent. The increments from one census year to another do not, however, follow a definite pattern.

(v) WHITE-COLLAR AND BLUE-COLLAR WORKERS

For the sake of convenience and in view of the fact that for some of the occupational groups discussed above it was not always possible to obtain separate figures, the four occupational groups considered above will be treated here as a single group comprising the 'white-collar' occupations.[16] 'Blue-collar occupations,' on the other hand, are defined here to comprise three of the remaining five I.S.C.O. occupational groups, thus including miners, quarrymen and related workers; workers in transportation and communication; and craftsmen, production-process workers and labourers (except farm) not elsewhere classified.

Trends in the proportions of these two broad categories in the total labour force are obviously not complementary according to the definitions adopted here. A rising trend in the proportion of white collar workers need not be compensated by a declining trend in the proportion of blue-collar workers in the total labour force. Therefore, the analysis of occupational patterns of the total labour force in these two broad categories only will be incomplete, and consideration of the other two occupational groups, farmers and service workers, is therefore essential in such an analysis since neither of them falls neatly into either the white-collar or the blue-collar group.

Table 6 below gives a consolidated picture of trends in the occupational patterns of these countries for the years indicated. In the accompanying diagram, trends in the white-collar occupations are depicted.

It can be seen from the data given in Table 6 and from the accompanying diagram (Fig. 1) that the ratio of white-collar occupations in the total labour force has been growing consistently for each of the countries under consideration. The ratio has actually doubled during the first half of this century, except in Australia. Around 1950 it was ranging between 30 per cent for England and Wales and 37 per cent for the United States. In the latter country it is estimated

---

[16] Although the term 'white-collar workers' is frequently used in social analysis, full agreement as to its scope is lacking. If this concept is approached from the point of view of occupation, much controversy centres on the question of inclusion or exclusion of most groups of sales workers and certain types of supervisory personnel in industry such as foremen, etc. In the *Manpower Report of the President*, in the United States, the 'white-collar' occupations covered the four occupational groups covered by this term in this article. In any case there is little doubt that these groups account for the preponderant share of 'white-collar workers,' however they may be defined in most contexts.

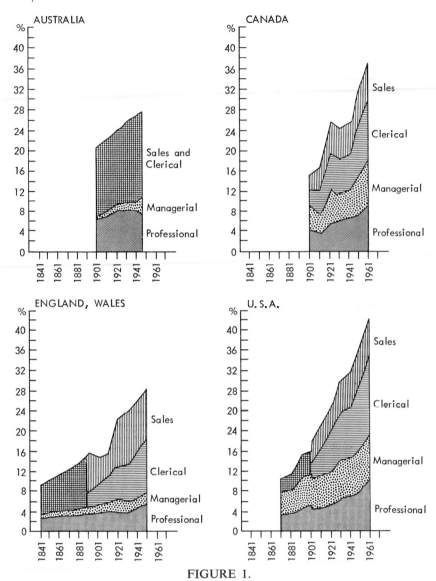

FIGURE 1.

that the ratio of white-collar workers in the American labour force will rise from 42 per cent in 1960 to a little over 46 per cent by 1970.[17] For India it is estimated that the group of white collar occupations will constitute a little over 14 per cent of the labour force by 1971 as against 10 per cent in 1961.[18] By the time this ratio rises to absorb almost half of the American labour force (48 per cent) by 1975, the corresponding ratio for India would just hit the 16 per cent mark.

[17] *Manpower Report of the President, op. cit.*, p. 100.
[18] V. R. K. Tilak, *loc. cit.*

TABLE 6.　Trends in Occupational Patterns for Selected Countries. (Percentages of Total Labour Force)

Country and Year of Reference	White-collar Workers	Blue-collar Workers	Farmers	Service Workers	Total
Australia					
1871	25.8[a]	30.3[b]	43.9[c]	[d]	100
81	27.1[a]	34.3[b]	38.6[c]	[d]	100
91	18.7	38.2[b]	31.3[c]	11.8	100
1901	20.7	41.6	25.5	12.2	100
11	22.5	42.4	24.8	10.3	100
21	23.9	43.7	23.1	9.3	100
33	26.3	42.7	22.0	9.0	100
47	28.0	48.3	17.1	6.6	100
Canada					
1901	15.2	33.8	42.8	8.2	100
11	16.9	38.3	37.1	7.7	100
21	25.4	32.8	34.7	7.1	100
31	24.5	35.3	31.1	9.1	100
41	25.3	35.2	29.0	10.5	100
51	32.8	39.4	19.1	8.7	100
61	38.3	37.0	12.1	12.6	100
England and Wales					
1841	9.2	47.7	23.0	20.1	100
51	10.2	52.7	22.1	15.0	100
61	11.3	53.5	19.0	16.2	100
71	12.7	54.7	15.0	17.6	100
81	14.1	55.9	12.4	17.6	100
91	16.0	59.6	10.2	14.2[e]	100
1901	15.1	63.7	8.5	12.7[e]	100
11	15.7	64.6	8.1	11.6[e]	100
21	23.0	56.1	7.9	13.0	100
31	24.6	55.2	6.5	13.7	100
41	.	.	.	.	.
51	29.7	54.4	5.5	10.4	100
United States					
1870	10.4	26.6	47.1	7.8	100[f]
80	11.4	30.5	43.7	6.2	100[f]
90	15.1	32.4	36.8	6.4	100[f]
1900	{ 16.2 / 17.6	{ 35.3 / 35.8	{ 35.0 / 37.6	{ 5.0 / 9.0	100[f] / 100
10	21.3	38.2	30.9	9.6	100
20	24.9	40.2	27.0	7.9	100
30	29.4	39.6	21.2	9.8	100
40	31.1	39.8	17.4	11.7	100
50	36.6	41.1	11.8	10.5	100
60	42.2	39.7	6.3	11.8	100

For explanation of signs see under Table 1 above.

[a] Includes 'services' which could not be separated.

[b] It is not clear in the original source whether miners, quarrymen and related workers are included in this group.

[c] Estimated as residual.

[d] Included in the group of white-collar workers.

[e] Original source indicates that these figures are not comparable.

[f] Components do not add up to 100, the difference represents persons who are not classified by occupations.

Table 6 also suggests that the ratio of blue-collar occupations as defined in this article tended to rise during the periods studied. Its rise, however, has not been as steady or as consistent as in the case of white-collar occupations. It is, in fact, shown that it has declined steadily since 1921 in England and Wales. Besides, in the United States, after an initial rise between 1900 and 1920, the ratio has remained almost stationary. On the whole, however, the examination of absolute figures suggests that while both groups were expanding, the rate of growth of white-collar occupations far exceeded that of blue-collar occupations. In other words, increases in the numbers and proportions in the total labour force of blue-collar workers may have been more modest than those of white-collar workers, but such increases were by no means negligible. At the turn of the century, for example, blue-collar workers may have constituted more than a third of the labour force in Canada and the United States as compared with almost two-thirds of the labour force of England and Wales. Around 1950 the corresponding shares had moved closer to 40 per cent in Canda and the United States.

It must be remembered in this connection that in contrast to the white-collar group of occupations, changes in the absolute and relative magnitude of blue-collar occupations are not only affected by science and research development, the size of businesses, the process of automation or the like, but are also a function of the availability and discovery of natural resources as in the case of workers in mines and quarries, for example.

Table 6 also suggests that in all the countries shown, the proportion of farmers in the total labour force has fallen substantially. Data on service workers, on the other hand, do not suggest any definite trend. Fluctuations in individual countries are for the most part irregular and can hardly be explained by simple or single factors.

'It is well-known that the countries with high proportions of the labour force in agriculture are low-income countries, and vice versa. In these countries the non-agricultural labour force nearly always finds employment to a greater extent in services than in industry, reflecting the lack of industrial development; but in countries in which industry is highly developed, too, there are often even more jobs in services. This is the case, for example, in Australia, Canada, Japan and the United States, but not in Germany (Federal Republic), Great Britain, Italy, Sweden or Switzerland.'[19]

This geographical observation could also be applied to time analysis, of the corresponding data in Table 6 above. In the course of their development, these countries have experienced higher incomes in recent years. This phenomenon could easily be associated with lower proportions of farmers in the total labour force.[20]

---

[19] *Employment Objectives and Policies*, Report I, Preparatory Technical Conference on Employment, 1963, International Labour Organization, Geneva, 1963, p. 15.

[20] On the basis of data for 29 countries, the author has found a significant correlation coefficient of -0.7 between income per head and the ratio of farmers in the total labour force.

Data on the proportions of service workers, shown to be oscillating in Table 6 above, are not easy to interpret in the context of the present article. According to the above quotation such oscillation is only natural, since the relative importance of service workers in the total labour force changes regardless of the level of industrial development. The increase in job availabilities in industry, however, stimulates greater increases in the total and relative size of this group in the total labour force.

I. SUMMARY OBSERVATIONS

A consistently rising trend in the share of the labour force has been detected for all white-collar occupations, namely the professional, the managerial, the clerical and, to a lesser extent, the sales workers groups. In contrast, the share of the occupational category embracing farmers, fisherman, etc., has shown a persistent downward trend. On the other hand, no definite trend could be detected for the remaining major groups of occupations. This emergent pattern is further confirmed in some recent studies on the subject, at any rate, in the industrialized countries.

Sources of Information

1. *Censuses of the Commonwealth of Australia*, 1921 (Vol. II) and 1947.
2. *Censuses of England and Wales* (Occupation Tables), 1921 and 1951.
3. Dominion Bureau of Statistics, Ottawa: *Censuses of Canada*, 1951, Vol. X, and 1961, Series 3.1, Bulletin 3.1–3, 26.2.1963.
4. P. H. Douglas, C. N. Hitchcock and W. E. Atkins: *The Worker in Modern Economic Society*, Chicago, 1923.
5. A. M. Edwards: *Comparative Occupation Statistics for the United States* 1870 *to* 1940, a report published in the 1940 Population Census of the United States as a separate volume.
6. International Labour Office: "The active population of the U.S.S.R." *International Labour Review*, 84, 3, Geneva, September 1961.
7. D. G. Jones: "Some notes on the census of occupations for England and Wales," *Journal of the Royal Statistical Society*, 78, London, 1915.
8. E. C. Snow: "The limits of industrial development (II), Influence of growth of population on the development of industry,' *Journal of the Royal Statistical Society*, **98**, London, 1935.
9. "The distribution of labour between industries," *Review of Economic Progress*, **2**, 5 (May 1950), and 7 (July 1950), a monthly publication issued by the Queensland Bureau of Industry, Brisbane, Australia.
10. United Nations: *Demographic Yearbook*, 1956.
11. U.S. Bureau of the Census: *Historical Statistics of the United States. Colonial Times to* 1957 Washington, D.C., 1960.
12. U.S. Bureau of the Census: *U.S. Census of Population*, 1960. *Detailed Characteristics, United States Summary*, Final Report PC(1)–1D, U.S. Government Printing Office, Washington, D.C., 1963.
13. United States: *Manpower Report of the President and A Report on Manpower Requirements, Resources, Utilization, and Training*, by the United States Department of Labor, transmitted to the Congress, March 1963.

Trends in Amount of Time Worked

HAROLD L. WILENSKY

... Here, as in all talk of the changing human condition, much depends on the places and times to be compared and the quality of the data. The data are weak, but certain tendencies appear likely.

1. *In the perspective of several centuries, time at work increased before it decreased.* The secular decline in hours and days of work is greatly exaggerated by the usual comparison of gross daily or weekly averages with those of the "take off" period of rapid economic growth in England, France, and America —a time of horrendous working schedules and conditions. Estimates of *annual* hours and days of work for populations of *earlier* times yield less confidence in great progress and surely suggest the absence of a unilinear downward trend in the past several centuries.

Among the citizens of antiquity, as well as among primitive agriculturalists, the number of days of leisure often approached half of every year. The transformation of tabooed or unlucky days into holy days, and the latter into holidays —what an early student of the matter calls "man's ineradicable tendency to convert his fast days into feast days"[1]—occurred long before the middle ages. "In the old Roman calendar, out of 355 days, nearly one-third (109) were marked as ... unlawful for judicial and political business."[2] In the last two centuries of the republic, festival days were stretched to accommodate more spectacles and public games. The Roman passion for holidays reached its climax in the middle of the fourth century when days off numbered 175. If we assume a 12-hour day, which is probably on the high side, total working time would be only about 2,160 hours a year. Whatever the work schedules of slaves and women, leisure for the ruling classes, for administrative and professional men, was never again so abundant. Hours of work for comparable populations in subsequent centuries seem to have increased sharply. Fourastié estimates that French "intellectual" workers in courts, ministries, and administrative agencies worked about 2,500 hours per year in 1800, 3,000 to 3,500 in 1950.[3] In short, historical

Reprinted from *Social Problems*, **9** (Summer, 1961), pp. 32–56, by permission of the author and the publisher, The Society for the Study of Social Problems.

[1] H. Webster, *Rest Days, A Study in Early Law and Morality*, New York: The Macmillan Company, 1916, p. 100. A recent expression is the Supreme Court's defense of blue laws as protection of secular rest.

[2] *Ibid.*, p. 304.

[3] J. Fourastié, *The Causes of Wealth*, translated and edited by T. Caplow, Glencoe, Illinois: The Free Press, 1960, pp. 171–173. A ten-month year in the upper civil service in Britain was usual in 1800 and prevailed until World War II. Since then, weekly hours increased from 38½ (6 days) to 42½ (5 days) and annual leave was cut back to a maximum of six weeks. That makes about 1,955 hours per year—close to the situation of antiquity but much more leisured than the American counterpart.

materials suggest a considerable loss of leisure for higher strata through the ages, although lower white-collar men (e.g., office messengers, clerks, notaries) have gained since 1800.

What about farmers and urban workers? The problem of estimation for both is the rhythm of the seasons and the day. Estimates for traditional European agriculture put annual hours at 3,500–4,000 throughout the early period; this did not change until the 20th century.[4] For urban areas, while daily schedules of 12–16 hours are reported as early as the 13th century (after the emergence of flourishing commercial cities in the West), the number of days off and the record of one- or two-hour lunch periods and ½-hour breaks suggests that annual hours were little more than they are for a fully employed worker today.

According to a basic sourcebook on work rules in 13th-century France, night work, Sunday work and work after Saturday vespers (4 to 5 P.M.) were forbidden in most trades, although some privileged artisans were exceptions to these rules.[5] In many trades (e.g., tapestry-makers in Beauvais) the 12-hour day included a ½-hour rest in the morning and an hour at lunch.[6] Craftsmen such as wire-drawers in Paris received 30-day vacations in addition to the normal 141 days off; they worked only about 194 days a year—a 16-hour day in "summer" (six months), an eight-hour day in "winter" (six months).[7] The total: 2,328 annual hours.

From the late middle ages to 1800, the drift in manual occupations was unmistakably toward longer hours. Dolléans and Dehove report workdays in the city crafts of 14 to 18 hours.[8] And the number of days off declined from the 15th century on.[9] By 1750, day laborers were working perhaps 3,770 hours.[10] By 1850 the average workweek in French cities was about 70 hours,[11] and some estimates put it higher.[12] The record of daily and weekly hours for England is similar—e.g., a climb from a 12-hour day with a two-hour rest in 1700 to a 14–18-hour day in 1800,[13] when the stage was set for humanitarian protest against the costs of industrialism.

---

[4] Fourastié, *op. cit.*, p. 164.

[5] *Le livre des métiers d'Etienne Boileau*, XIIIe Siecle, in the collection Les métiers et corporations de la ville de Paris, Paris: Imprimerie nationale, 1879, pp. 1–285 *passim*.

[6] Émile Levasseur, *Histoire des classes ouvrières et de l'industrie en France avant 1789*, Paris: Arthur Rousseau, 1901, second edition, Vol. I, pp. 320–322, 328–329, 690.

[7] Alfred Franklin, *La vie privée d'autrefois*, Paris: E. Plon, Nourrit et Cie, 1889, Vol. 5, pp. 125–216, 138.

[8] Edouard Dolléans and Gérard Dehove, *Histoire du travail en France*, Vol. I, Paris: Domat-Montchrestien, 1953, pp. 97–98.

[9] Levasseur, *op. cit.*, Vol. II, pp. 237, 385–388.

[10] Fourastié, *op. cit.*, p. 38.

[11] *Ibid.*, p. 91.

[12] For the 1840's, Woytinsky estimates an 80-hour week for unspecified populations of "Continental Europe," Wladimir S. and E. S. Woytinsky, *World Population and Production*, Twentieth Century Fund, 1953, p. 366; and a 78-hour week for U.S.A. and France, W. S. Woytinsky, "Hours of Labor," *Encyclopaedia of the Social Sciences*, Vol. VII, New York: Macmillan Co., 1935, p. 479.

[13] *Loc. cit.*

The burden of labor in our century, of course, has lessened,[14] today annual hours are down in the range 1,900–2,500—a return to the work schedules of medieval guildsmen.

2. *Recent increases in leisure have been unequally distributed by industry and occupational category.* Most of the real gain in leisure in the U.S. has come to private nonagricultural industries—especially since 1850—and most markedly in manufacturing and mining, and to agriculture in the last 50 years, especially since 1940. Professionals, executives, officials and other civil servants, and the self-employed have benefited little, and in some occupations have lost out. In such industries as all-year hotels, buslines and local railways, and telegraphic communications, the workweek did not drop below 44 hours until the 1950's.[15]

This disproportionate leisure gain in manufacturing and mining, and recently agriculture, is given emphasis by statistics on seasonal and part-year occupations. Table 1 shows that about one in five of those who worked in 1957 worked primarily at part-time jobs; one in ten, at full-time jobs, but 26 weeks or less; one in six, 26–50 weeks.

The part-timers and intermittent workers are heavily concentrated among women, non-whites, young workers, old workers, and rural workers. And the concentration by occupation is striking: a full year's work is typical of white-collar people—salesmen, clerks, proprietors, managers, officials, and professionals (excepting female teachers). But in 1949 only about half the laborers (farm and nonfarm) and female operatives worked the full year; only three in five of the private household workers and male operatives had a full year.[16]

This picture must be modified slightly by the longer voluntary vacation of upper strata. Table 4 shows that men who work very long hours tend to take long vacations.* This is especially clear among professional groups (short-hours

---

[14] C. D. Long gives the most reliable estimate for the average labor force member. In each of the four countries offering usable data, the "standard" workweek (not adjusted for layoffs, strikes, sickness, turnover, etc.), weighted by the number of persons in the major industry categories (including agriculture, domestic service, and government), declined as follows:

Country	Dates	Decrease per decade in weekly hours of work
U.S.A.	1890–1950	4.2
Great Britain	1911–1951	3.3
Canada	1921–1941	3.5
Germany	1895–1950	3.2

The Labour Force under Changing Income and Employment, Princeton University Press, 1958, pp. 140, 270–274.

[15] U.S. Department of Commerce, *Statistical Abstract of the United States 1960*, pp. 224–226. Industry variations in rates of technological progress is a major factor. Recently brewing, baking, printing, and the ladies garment industry, all undergoing rapid technological change, have moved to standard workweeks shorter than 40. S. Brandwein, "Recent Accomplishments," in *The Shorter Work Week*, Washington, D.C.: Public Affairs Press, 1957, pp. 65–75.

[16] Bogue, *op. cit.*, pp. 515–516.

* [The material referred to is not included—Editor.]

TABLE 1. ONLY ABOUT HALF OF THE LABOR FORCE WORKS YEAR-ROUND FULL-TIME*

Type of Worker	Percent of Persons Who Worked in 1957
Full-Time Workers (35 hours or more per week)	81.0
Year-round full-time workers—worked primarily at full-time jobs for 50 or more weeks during the year	55.1
Part-year full-time workers—worked primarily at full-time jobs for less than 50 weeks but more than 26 weeks	15.5
Intermittent workers—worked primarily at full-time jobs, but for 26 weeks or less	10.4
Part-Time Workers (less than 35 hours per week)	19.0
Year-round part-time workers	6.4
Part-year part-time workers	12.6

* D. J. Bogue's summary of U.S. Bureau of the Census' Annual survey of work experience. *The Population of the United States*. Glencoe, Illinois: The Free Press, 1959, p. 453.

short-vacation engineers vs. long-hours long-vacation lawyers and professors) and older white-collar workers.[17] But the main outlines nonetheless stand up. For instance, if a year-round full-time professional takes a four-week vacation and works about 2,400 hours per year (50 hours a week for 48 weeks) for only 40 years, his worklife total (96,000 hours) will still exceed that of the year-round full-time blue-collar worker who takes a two-week vacation, and works about 2,000 hours (40 a week for 50 weeks) for 47 years (94,000 hours). Since the blue-collar man seldom works year-round full-time, lifetime leisure seems heavily weighted toward the lower strata. Low-status jobs held by a majority of the labor force have shown the fastest drop in the workweek; they also provide more weeks off per year.

3. *Despite an increasing age of entry into the labor force and a decreasing age of exit, men today work more years over the life cycle than they did in 1900.* The fraction of the total life span worked, however, has changed little—because of increased longevity. Again there are crucial differences among occupational strata and groups. Tables of working life show that in 1900 the average labor force member who was 20 years old could expect to live another 42 years, of which only three would be retirement years. In 1950 his life expectancy was 49 years, of which nearly six would be spent in retirement. Length of working life has gone up about 15 per cent, length of retirement has doubled.[18]

---

[17] For the larger study a factor analysis of the combined samples was done to clean up 34 measures of control variables such as "opportunity to stylize leisure" and "preoccupational leisure training." Length of vacation loads .42 on a high SES factor defined by high family income, occupation, and education.

[18] Based on Stuart Garfinkle, "Changes in Working Life of Men, 1900–2000," *Monthly Labor Review*, 78 (March, 1955), Table 1, p. 299.

But look at the variations by occupational category in Table 2.

TABLE 2. ON AVERAGE HIGHER STRATA WORK FEWER YEARS THAN LOWER STRATA*

Major Occupational Category	Mean Number of Years in Working Force	Average Age of Entry	Average Retirement Age
Professional, technical and kindred workers	40 years	Late	Early
Managers, officials and proprietors, except farm	41	Late	Early
Craftsmen, foreman and kindred workers	44	Late	Average
Operatives and kindred workers	45	Early	Early
Sales workers	47	Early	Average
Clerical and kindred workers	47	Early	Average
Farmers and farm managers	48	Late	Late
Laborers, except farm and mine	51	Early	Late
Farm laborers and foremen	52	Early	Late
Service workers	52	Early	Late

* SOURCE: A. J. Jaffe and R. O. Carleton, *Occupational Mobility in the United States*, 1930–1960. New York: Columbia King's Crown Press, 1954, pp. 49-50. "Mean number of years" summarizes occupational differences in rates of new entries and retirements as of 1950; it is a synthetic figure, since few men spend their entire worklives in the same census category. The results are similar for 1940 and 1930. The actual distribution of employed older workers in 1959 as reported by M. S. Gordon shows a similar picture, but suggests later retirement for managers, proprietors, and officials. "Work and Patterns of Retirement" in R. W. Kleemeier, editor, *Aging and Leisure*, New York: Oxford University Press, 1961, pp. 19–20.

There is a correlation of $-.82$ between the quality of occupations (indicated by earnings and education) and the mean length of working life.[19] Clearly, men in better jobs spend less of their lives working. Variations on the main theme: extremely arduous or hazardous jobs (e.g., mining) bring very early retirement or death, while many professionals never stop working—they fade away, like old soldiers, pencils in hand. For reasons of both motive and opportunity (including job-linked health factors) the truck driver or the man on the assembly line, if he lives on, will sever his work ties earlier and more completely than the professor or physician.[20]

4. *While the labour force participation rate for women increases with economic growth, the trend by occupation is away from long-hours jobs*, such as domestic service and farm labor, into shorter-hour jobs, such as sales and clerical.[21] Whether this means more "leisure" for women is another matter; typically, work is added to traditional housewifery, and female *work*life expectancy is

[19] Jaffe and Carleton, *op. cit.*, p. 50. In keeping with a market definition of work, we make the wry assumption that the training period is "leisure."
[20] H. L. Wilensky, "Life Cycle, Work Situation, and Participation in Formal Associations," Chapter 8 of R. W. Kleemeier, editor, *Aging and Leisure*, New York: Oxford University Press, 1961, pp. 227 ff.
[21] C. Long, *op. cit.*, p. 275.

going up at a faster rate than life expectancy or nonworking years [22]—with a dubious net result, as we shall see below.*

In sum: If we begin either with antiquity or Europe before the Reformation, average hours of work per year, if not per week, moved upward into the 19th century. The 20th century decline in work has been grossly exaggerated by selective comparison with the shocking schedules of early English textile mills—an episode which dominates historical discussion of the evils of industrialism.

Moreover, the daily or weekly averages obscure important inequalities in the distribution of leisure. With economic growth the upper strata have probably lost leisure. Professionals, executives, officials, and proprietors have long workweeks, year-round employment. Their longer vacations and shorter worklives (delayed entry and often earlier retirement) do not offset this edge in working hours. Although lifetime leisure decreases with increased status, the picture is one of bunched, predictable leisure for elites whose worklives are shorter; and intermittent, unpredictable, unstable leisure for the masses, whose worklives are longer....

[22] Bogue, *op. cit.*, p. 463.
* [The material referred to is not included—Editor].

Work Satisfaction in Modern Society

ROBERT BLAUNER

... Before considering occupational differences and the factors that account for them, I shall briefly consider evidence on the general extent of job satisfaction by looking at the results of six representative sample studies. In Table 1 the figure in the extreme right-hand column indicates the percentage of workers who gave the dissatisfied response to such a question as "Taking into consideration all the things about your job (work), how satisfied or dissatisfied are you with it?"[1]

In the 1946 issue of the *Personnel and Guidance Journal*, Robert Hoppock began summarizing the results of all published studies of job satisfaction, most of which were non-representative samples of individual companies or occupations. When, by 1958, 406 percentages of the proportion of persons dissatisfied with their jobs in these several hundred studies had been averaged out, they yielded a median percentage of 13 per cent dissatisfied.[2] This figure is quite

Reprinted by permission of John Wiley and Sons, Inc. From *Labor and Trade Unionism* by Seymour Martin Lipset and Walter Galenson (eds.). Copyright © 1960 by John Wiley and Sons, Inc.

[1] This is the question used in the Morse and Weiss study.
[2] H. Alan Robinson, "Job Satisfaction Researches of 1958," *Personnel and Guidance Journal*, 37 (1959), p. 670.

TABLE 1. Proportion of Dissatisfied Workers in Major Job Satisfaction Studies

Researchers	Scope of Sample	Composition of Study	Date	Per cent Dissatified
Morse and Weiss*	Random national	401 employed men	1955	20
Centers†	Representative national	811 men	1949	17
Palmer‡	Norristown, Pa.	517 labor force members	1957	10
Shister and Reynolds §	New England city	800 manual workers	1949	12
				21**
Hoppock ‖	New Hope, Pa.	309 labor force members	1935	15
Kornhauser¶	Detroit area	324 employed persons	1952	11

* Nancy C. Morse and Robert S. Weiss, "The Function and Meaning of Work and the Job," *American Sociological Review*, 20 (1955), pp. 191–198.

† Richard Centers, *The Psychology of Social Classes* (Princeton: Princeton University Press, 1949), p. 172.

‡ Gladys L. Palmer, "Attitudes toward Work in an Industrial Community," *American Journal of Sociology*, 63 (1957), pp. 17–26.

§ Joseph Shister and L. G. Reynolds, *Job Horizons: A Study of Job Satisfaction and Labor Mobility* (New York: Harper, 1949), p. 33.

‖ Robert Hoppock, *Job Satisfaction* (New York: Harper, 1935), p. 246.

¶ Arthur Kornhauser, *Detroit as the People See It* (Detroit: Wayne University Press, 1952), p. 54.

** Two separate samples.

similar to the summary percentages of dissatisfaction resulting from more representative labor force samples.

Thus the most recent American research on satisfaction attitudes seems to support the generalization that: "Even under the existing conditions, which are far from satisfactory, most workers like their jobs. Every survey of workers' attitudes which has been carried out, no matter in what industry, indicates that this is so."[3]

But a caveat should be inserted at this point. Many of these studies, which seek to determine the proportion of workers who are satisfied or dissatisfied with their jobs, fail to specify sufficiently an inherently vague concept and ignore the cultural pressures on workers to exaggerate the degree of actual satisfaction. Despite this, the evidence shows that in the numerous samples of the labor force which have been interviewed, more than 80 per cent indicate general job satisfaction.[4] Even though the methodological limitations make it hard to

[3] J. C. Brown, *The Social Psychology of Industry* (Baltimore: English Pelican Edition, 1954), pp. 190–191. He proceeds to give supporting evidence from British studies.

[4] Of course, as the industrial psychologist Arthur Kornhauser has written, "Simple summary conclusions of this kind are dangerously inadequate. Feelings of satisfaction or dissatisfaction are complicated and varied. Working people may be satisfied with many of the conditions of their employment and still be markedly dissatisfied about other features of the job or of their working lives. The number considered dissatisfied will depend in large measure upon the arbitrary method of defining what the term dissatisfaction refers to in the given case." "Psychological Studies of Employee Attitudes," in S. D. Hoslett, ed., *Human Factors in Management* (Parkville, Mo.: Park College Press, 1946), p. 304. In this extensive critique of the methodology of job satisfaction research, Kornhauser also points out that respondents may not want or even be able to answer such questions honestly. There is a certain naivete in expecting frank and simple answers to job satisfaction questions in a society where one's work is so important a part of one's self that to demean one's job is to question one's own competence.

accept the findings of any one of these studies by itself, it is much harder to reject the weight of their cumulative evidence.

Although it is difficult, therefore, not to accept the proposition that at least the majority (and possibly a very large majority) of American workers are moderately satisfied in their work, such a finding is neither particularly surprising nor sociologically interesting. Under "normal" conditions there is a natural tendency for people to identify with, or at least to be somewhat positively oriented toward, those social arrangements in which they are implicated. Attitude surveys show that the majority of employees like their company, that the majority of members are satisfied with their unions, and undoubtedly research would show a preponderance of positive over negative attitudes toward one's own marriage, family, religion, and nation-state. It is the presence of marked occupational *differences* in work attitudes to which I turn in the next section that is of more theoretical interest.

OCCUPATIONAL DIFFERENCES IN WORK SATISFACTION

Work satisfaction varies greatly by occupation. Highest percentages of satisfied workers are usually found among professionals and businessmen. In a given plant, the proportion satisfied is higher among clerical workers than among factory workers, just as in general labor force samples it is higher among middle-class than among manual working class occupations. Within the manual working class, job satisfaction is highest among skilled workers, lowest among unskilled laborers and workers on assembly lines.

When a scale of relative job satisfaction is formed, based on general occupational categories, the resulting rank order is almost identical with the most commonly used occupational status classification—the Edwards scale of the Bureau of the Census. For example, the mean indexes of satisfaction in Table 2 resulted from a survey of all New Hope, Pa., jobholders in 1935.

TABLE 2

Occupational Group	*Mean Index*[5]	*Number in Sample*
Professional and managerial	560	23
Semiprofessional, business, and supervisory	548	32
Skilled manual and white collar	510	84
Semiskilled manual workers	483	74
Unskilled manual workers	401	55

[5] In this index, the figure 100 would indicate extreme dissatisfaction, 400 indifference, and 700 extreme satisfaction. Hoppock, *op. cit.*, p. 255. A rather similar rank order was found by Donald Super. In his study, the percentages of satisfied workers were 85.6 for professionals, 74.2 for managerial, 41.9 for commercial (lowest white collar), 55.9 for skilled manual and 47.6 for semiskilled. However, Super's study has serious weaknesses: the sample was not chosen randomly but taken from members of hobby groups, and it overrepresented workers with high education and in high status occupations. D. Super, "Occupational Level and Job Satisfaction," *Journal of Applied Psychology*, 23 (1939), pp. 547–564.

A similar rank order resulted in a national survey when the proportions of workers in each occupational group who would continue the same kind of work in the event they inherited enough money to live comfortably were computed[6] (Table 3).

TABLE 3

Occupational Group	Per cent Who Would Continue Same Kind of Work	Number in Sample
Professionals	68	28
Sales	59	22
Managers	55	22
Skilled manual	40	86
Service	33	18
Semiskilled operatives	32	80
Unskilled	16	27

The generally higher level of job satisfaction of white-collar over blue-collar workers is confirmed by a study of twelve different factories in 1934, in which the scores of clerical workers on job satisfaction were considerably higher than those of factory workers;[7] by the Centers national sample, which found that only 14 per cent of workers in middle-class occupations were dissatisfied with their jobs, compared to 21 per cent of those in working class occupations;[8] and by a 1947 *Fortune* poll, which revealed that the proportion of employees who said their jobs were interesting was 92 per cent among professionals and executives, 72 per cent among salaried employees and 54 per cent among factory workers.[9] However, a study of the Detroit area population found that only among such upper white-collar employees as secretaries, draftsmen, and bookkeepers was the incidence of job satisfaction greater than among manual workers; such lower white-collar employees as clerks, typists, and retail salespeople were somewhat less satisfied than blue-collar workers.[10]

Further evidence of the relation of job satisfaction to occupational status is provided by studies of retirement plans. Although there are a number of factors which affect the retirement decision, it is plausible to argue that the more satisfying a job is to the worker, the more likely will he choose not to retire.

[6] Morse and Weiss, *op. cit.*, p. 197.

[7] R. S. Uhrbock, "Attitudes of 4430 Employees," *Journal of Social Psychology*," 5 (1934), pp. 365–377, cited in Hoppock, *op. cit.*, p. 141.

[8] Centers, *op. cit.*, p. 134.

[9] Alexander R. Heron, *Why Men Work* (Stanford: Stanford University Press, 1948), pp. 71–72. A 1948 *Fortune* poll which asked the same question to *youth* between the ages of 18 to 25 found that the proportion of those who found their work interesting or enjoyable "all the time" was 85 percent for professionals and executives, 64 percent for white-collar workers, 59 percent for non-factory manual labor and 41 percent for factory labor. Cited in Lawrence G. Thomas, *The Occupational Structure and Education* (Englewood Cliff, N.J.: Prentice-Hall, 1956), p. 201, whose summary of studies on the extent of, and occupational differences in, job satisfaction is one of the best in the literature.

[10] Kornhauser, *Detroit* . . . , p. 55.

In a study of work and retirement in six occupations it was found that the proportion of men who wanted to continue working or had actually continued working after age sixty-five was more than 67 per cent for physicians, 65 per cent for department store salesmen, 49 per cent for skilled printers, 42 per cent for coal miners, and 32 per cent for unskilled and semiskilled steelworkers.[11]

As has been shown in the preceding section of this paper, the majority of workers in all occupations respond positively when asked whether or not they are satisfied with their jobs. But that does not mean they would not prefer other kinds of work. The average worker in a lower-status occupation says that he would choose another line of work if he had the chance to start his working life anew. This question then, is perhaps a more sensitive indicator of latent dissatisfactions and frustrations; the occupational differences it points to, though forming the same pattern as the other, are considerably greater. For example, when a survey of 13,000 Maryland youths was made during the depression it was found that 91 per cent of professional-technical workers preferred their own occupation to any other, compared to 45 per cent of managerial personnel and farm owners, 41 per cent of skilled manual workers, 37 per cent of domestic workers, 36 per cent of office and sales personnel, 14 per cent of unskilled, and 11 per cent of semiskilled manual workers.[12]

TABLE 4. PROPORTION IN VARIOUS OCCUPATIONS WHO WOULD CHOOSE SAME KIND OF WORK IF BEGINNING CAREER AGAIN

Professional Occupations %		Working Class Occupations§ %	
Mathematicians*	91	Skilled printers	52
Physicists*	89	Paper workers	52
Biologists*	89	Skilled automobile workers	41
Chemists*	86	Skilled steelworkers	41
Lawyers†	83	Textile workers	31
Journalists‡	82	Unskilled steelworkers	21
		Unskilled automobile workers	16

SOURCES: * "The Scientists: A Group Portrait," *Fortune*, October 1948, pp. 106–112.

† "The U.S. Bar," *Fortune*, May 1939, p. 176.

‡ Leo Rosten, *The Washington Correspondents* (New York: Harcourt, Brace and Company, 1938), p. 347.

§ These are unpublished data which have been computed from the IBM cards of a survey of 3,000 factory workers in 16 industries, conducted by Elmo Roper for *Fortune* magazine in 1947. A secondary analysis of this survey is being carried out by the Fund for the Republic's Trade Union Project. The general findings of the original study appeared in "The Fortune Survey," *Fortune*, May 1947, pp. 5–12, and June 1947, pp. 5–10.

[11] E. A. Friedmann and R. J. Havighurst, *The Meaning of Work and Retirement* (Chicago: University of Chicago Press, 1954), p. 183.

[12] Howard M. Bell, *Youth Tell Their Story* (Washington: American Council on Education, 1938), p. 134.

More detailed data for a number of professional and manual working class occupations strongly confirms these general findings. Note how for six different professions, the proportion of satisfied persons ranges from 82 per cent to 91 per cent, whereas for seven manual occupations it varies from 16 per cent for unskilled automobile workers to 52 per cent for skilled printers. (See Table 4.) . . .

Additional Readings

CLARK KERR and ABRAHAM SIEGEL, "The Interindustry Propensity to Strike—An International Comparison," in ARTHUR KORNHAUSER, ROBERT DUBIN, and ARTHUR M. ROSS (eds.), *Industrial Conflict* (New York: McGraw-Hill Book Company, Inc., 1954), pp. 189–212 (esp. 189–191).

WILLIAM SPINRAD, "Correlates of Trade Union Participation: A Summary of the Literature," *American Sociological Review*, 25 (April, 1960), pp. 237–244.

LEO TROY, "Trade Union Membership, 1897–1962," *The Review of Economics and Statistics*, 67 (February, 1965), pp. 93–113.

U.S. Department of Labor, *Manpower Report of the President* (Washington, D.C.: U.S. Government Printing Office, 1963).

IRVING BERNSTEIN, "The Growth of American Unions," *American Economic Review*, 44 (June, 1954), pp. 301–318.

IRVING BERNSTEIN, "The Growth of American Unions, 1945–1960," *Labor History*, 2 (Spring, 1961), pp. 131–157.

POLITY

Introduction

Political sociologists and political scientists distinguish three different types of *polity*: dictatorship, oligarchy, and democracy. A classic problem in these fields of study is the specification of the determinants of the different types of polity. The following three selections present factual information relevant to the determinants of democracy.

The first selection by Lipset, "The Distribution of Democracy," reports information about two areas, the European and English-speaking nations and the Latin American nations. The main criteria used to define European democracies are the uninterrupted continuation of political democracy since World War I and the absence over the past twenty-five years of a major political movement opposed to democracy. Application of these criteria reveals thirteen stable democracies and fifteen unstable democracies and dictatorships among European and English-speaking nations. The criterion used to define Latin American democracies is whether a country has had a history of more or less free elections for most of the post-World War I period. Application of this criterion reveals seven democracies and unstable dictatorships and thirteen stable dictatorships among Latin American nations.

The second selection by Lipset, "Economic Development and Democracy," contains a proposition and four factual generalizations. The proposition indicates a positive relationship between the level of economic development and the existence of democracy: the higher the level of economic development, the greater the likelihood of democracy. The factual generalizations indicate a positive relationship between wealth, industrialization, urbanization, and education—different measures of economic development—and the existence of democracy. The previous selection by Patel, "Rates of Industrial Growth in the Last Century, 1860–1958," measured industrialization by the growth of industrial output, that is, production in factories. Lipset, however, uses two different measures of industrialization: the percentage of males in agriculture and the amount of per capita energy consumed.[1]

A commonly suggested determinant of democracy is political participation: the greater the political participation, the greater the likelihood of democracy. The selection by Milbraith, "Political Participation as a Function of Social Position," summarizes factual information about the social characteristics of the individuals who participate in the political process. Milbraith distinguishes three types of political participation.[2] First, there are "spectator activities" which consist of exposing oneself to political stimuli, voting, initiating a political discussion, attempting to talk another into voting a certain way, and wearing a button or putting a sticker on the car. Second, there are "transitional activities" which consist of contacting a public official or a political leader, making a monetary contribution to a party or a candidate, and attending a political meeting or rally. Third, there are "gladiatorial activities" which consist of contributing time in a political campaign, becoming an active member in a political party, attending a caucus or a strategy meeting, soliciting political funds, being a candidate for office, and holding public and party office. Spectator activities are the least active form of political participation, whereas gladiatorial activities are the most active. Milbraith's main findings are that individuals who are located near the center of society, who are high class, have high income, more education, a high-prestige occupation, reside in an urban community, participate in general group activity, have high community integration, are between forty and sixty, male, white, and Jewish have a greater degree of political participation than individuals who are located near the periphery of society, who are low class, have low income, less education, a low-prestige occupation, reside in a rural community, do not participate in general group activity, have low community integration, are under forty and over sixty, female, Negro and non-Jewish.

[1] Lipset's material is also relevant to discussions of "industrialization," "urbanization," and "education."

[2] Lester W. Milbraith, *Political Participation* (Chicago: Rand McNally and Company, 1965), pp. 5–38.

The Distribution of Democracy

SEYMOUR MARTIN LIPSET

. . . Clearly in order to discuss democracy, or any other phenomenon, it is first necessary to define it. For the purposes of this paper, democracy (in a complex society) is defined as a political system which supplies regular constitutional opportunities for changing the governing officials. It is a social mechanism for the resolution of the problem of societal decision-making among conflicting interest groups which permits the largest possible part of the population to influence these decisions through their ability to choose among alternative contenders for political office. In large measure abstracted from the work of Joseph Schumpeter and Max Weber,[1] this definition implies a number of specific conditions: (a) a "political formula," a system of beliefs, legitimizing the democratic system and specifying the institutions—parties, a free press, and so forth—which are legitimized, i.e., accepted as proper by all; (b) one set of political leaders in office; and (c) one or more sets of leaders, out of office, who act as a legitimate opposition attempting to gain office.

The need for these conditions is clear. *First*, if a political system is not characterized by a value system allowing the peaceful "play" of power—the adherence by the "outs" to decisions made by "ins" and the recognition by "ins" of the rights of the "outs"—there can be no stable democracy. This has been the problem faced by many Latin American states. *Second*, if the outcome of the political game is not the periodic awarding of effective authority to one group, a party or stable coalition, then unstable and irresponsible government rather than democracy will result. This state of affairs existed in pre-Fascist Italy, and for much, though not all of the history of the Third and Fourth French Republics, which were characterized by weak coalition governments, often formed among parties which had major interest and value conflicts with each other. *Third*, if the conditions facilitating the perpetuation of an effective opposition do not exist, then the authority of officials will be maximized, and popular influence on policy will be at a minimum. This is the situation in all one-party states; and by general agreement, at least in the West, these are dictatorships. . . .

Comparative generalizations dealing with complex social systems must necessarily deal rather summarily with particular historical features of any one society within the scope of the investigation. In order to test these generalizations bearing on the differences between countries which rank high or low in possession of the attributes associated with democracy, it is necessary to establish some

Reprinted from *American Political Science Review*, 53 (March, 1959), pp. 71–74, by permission of the author and the publisher.

[1] Joseph Schumpeter, *Capitalism, Socialism and Democracy* (New York: Harper and Bros., 1947), pp. 232–302, esp. 269; Max Weber, *Essays in Sociology* (New York: Oxford University Press, 1946), p. 226.

empirical measures of the type of political system. Individual deviations from a particular aspect of democracy are not too important, as long as the definitions unambiguously cover the great majority of nations which are located as democratic or undemocratic. The precise dividing line between "more democratic" and "less democratic" is also not a basic problem, since presumably democracy is *not* a quality of a social system which either does or does not exist, but is rather a complex of characteristics which may be ranked in many different ways. For this reason it was decided to divide the countries under consideration into two groups, rather than to attempt to rank them from highest to lowest. Ranking *individual* countries from the most to the least democratic is much more difficult than splitting the countries into two classes, "more" or "less" democratic, although even here borderline cases such as Mexico pose problems.

Efforts to classify all countries raise a number of problems. Most countries which lack an enduring tradition of political democracy lie in the traditionally underdeveloped sections of the world. It is possible that Max Weber was right when he suggested that modern democracy in its clearest forms can only occur under the unique conditions of capitalist industrialization.[2] Some of the complications introduced by the sharp variations in political practices in different parts of the earth can be reduced by dealing with differences among countries within political culture areas. The two best areas for such internal comparison are Latin America as one, and Europe and the English-speaking countries as the other. More limited comparisons may be made among the Asian states, and among the Arab countries.

TABLE 1. CLASSIFICATION OF EUROPEAN, ENGLISH-SPEAKING AND LATIN AMERICAN NATIONS BY DEGREE OF STABLE DEMOCRACY

European and English-speaking Nations		Latin American Nations	
Stable Democracies	Unstable Democracies and Dictatorships	Democracies and Unstable Dictatorships	Stable Dictatorships
Australia	Austria	Argentina	Bolivia
Belgium	Bulgaria	Brazil	Cuba
Canada	Czechoslovakia	Chile	Dominican Republic
Denmark	Finland	Colombia	Ecuador
Ireland	France	Costa Rica	El Salvador
Luxemburg	Germany (West)	Mexico	Guatemala
Netherlands	Greece	Uruguay	Haiti
New Zealand	Hungary		Honduras
Norway	Iceland		Nicaragua
Sweden	Italy		Panama
Switzerland	Poland		Paraguay
United Kingdom	Portugal		Peru
United States	Rumania		Venezuela
	Spain		
	Yugoslavia		

[2] See Max Weber, "Zur Lage der bürgerlichen Demokratie in Russian," *Archiv für Sozialwissenschaft und Sozialpolitik*, Vol. 22 (1906), pp. 346 ff.

The main criteria used in this paper to locate European democracies are the uninterrupted continuation of political democracy since World War I, *and* the absence over the past 25 years of a major political movement opposed to the democratic "rules of the game."[3] The somewhat less stringent criterion employed for Latin America is whether a given country has had a history of more or less free elections for most of the post-World War I period. Where in Europe we look for stable democracies, in South America we look for countries which have not had fairly constant dictatorial rule (see Table I). No detailed analysis of the political history of either Europe or Latin America has been made with an eye toward more specific criteria of differentiation; at this point in the examination of the requisites of democracy, election results are sufficient to locate the European countries, and the judgements of experts and impressionistic assessments based on fairly well-known facts of political history will suffice for Latin America. . . .[4]

[3] The latter requirement means that no totalitarian movement, either Fascist or Communist, received 20 percent of the vote during this time. Actually all the European nations falling on the democratic side of the continuum had totalitarian movements which secured less than seven per cent of the vote.

[4] The historian Arthur P. Whitaker, for example, has summarized the judgments of experts on Latin America to be that "the countries which have approximated most closely to the democratic ideal have been . . . Argentina, Brazil, Chile, Colombia, Costa Rica, and Uruguay." See "The Pathology of Democracy in Latin America: A Historian's Point of View," this REVIEW, Vol. 44 (1950), pp. 101–118. To this group I have added Mexico. Mexico has allowed freedom of the press, of assembly and of organization, to opposition parties, although there is good evidence that it does not allow them the opportunity to win elections, since ballots are counted by the incumbents. The existence of opposition groups, contested elections, and adjustments among the various factions of the governing *Partido Revolucionario Institucional* does introduce a considerable element of popular influence in the system.

The interesting effort of Russell Fitzgibbon to secure a "statistical evaluation of Latin American democracy" based on the opinion of various experts is not useful for the purposes of this paper. The judges were asked not only to rank countries as democratic on the basis of purely political criteria, but also to consider the "standard of living" and "educational level." These latter factors may be conditions for democracy, but they are not an aspect of democracy as such. See Russell H. Fitzgibbon, "A Statistical Evaluation of Latin American Democracy," *Western Political Quarterly*, Vol. 9 (1956), pp. 607–619.

Economic Development and Democracy

SEYMOUR M. LIPSET

. . . Perhaps the most widespread generalization linking political systems to other aspects of society has been that democracy is related to the state of economic development. Concretely, this means that the more well-to-do a nation, the

Reprinted from *American Political Science Review*, 53 (March, 1959), pp. 75–80; by permission of the author and the publisher.

greater the chances that it will sustain democracy. From Aristotle down to the present, men have argued that only in a wealthy society in which relatively few citizens lived in real poverty could a situation exist in which the mass of the population could intelligently participate in politics and could develop the self-restraint necessary to avoid succumbing to the appeals of irresponsible demagogues. A society divided between a large impoverished mass and a small favored elite would result either in oligarchy (dictatorial rule of the small upper stratum) or in tyranny (popularly based dictatorship). And these two political forms can be given modern labels: tyranny's modern face is Communism or Peronism; oligarchy appears today in the form of traditionalist dictatorships such as we find in parts of Latin America, Thailand, Spain or Portugal.

As a means of concretely testing this hypothesis, various indices of economic development—wealth, industrialization, urbanization and education—have been defined, and averages (means) have been computed for the countries which have been classified as more or less democratic in the Anglo-Saxon world and Europe and Latin America.

In each case, the average wealth, degree of industrialization and urbanization, and level of education is much higher for the more democratic countries, as the data presented in Table I indicate. If we had combined Latin America and Europe in one table, the differences would have been greater.[1]

The main indices of *wealth* used here are per capita income, number of persons per motor vehicle and per physician, and the number of radios, telephones, and newspapers per thousand persons. The differences are striking on every score, as Table I indicates in detail. In the more democratic European countries, there are 17 persons per motor vehicle compared to 143 for the less democratic countries. In the less dictatorial Latin American countries there are 99 persons per motor vehicle, as against 274 for the more dictatorial ones.[2] Income differences for the groups are also sharp, dropping from an

[1] Lyle W. Shannon has correlated indices of economic development with whether a country is self-governing or not, and his conclusions are substantially the same. Since Shannon does not give details on the countries categorized as self-governing and non-self-governing, there is no direct measure of the relation between "democratic" and "self-governing" countries. All the countries examined in this paper, however, were chosen on the assumption that a characterization as "democratic" is meaningless for a non-self-governing country, and therefore, presumably, all of them, whether democratic or dictatorial, would fall within Shannon's "self-governing" category. Shannon shows that under-development is related to lack of self-government; my data indicate that once self-government is attained, development is still related to the character of the political system. See Shannon (ed.), *Underdeveloped Areas* (New York: Harper, 1957), and also his article, "Is Level of Government Related to Capacity for Self-Government?" *American Journal of Economics and Sociology*, Vol. 17 (1958) pp. 367–382. In the latter paper, Shannon constructs a composite index of development, using some of the same indices, such as inhabitants per physician, and derived from the same United Nations sources, as appear in the tables to follow. Shannon's work did not come to my attention until after this paper was prepared, so that the two papers can be considered as separate tests of comparable hypotheses.

[2] It must be remembered that these figures are means, compiled from census figures for the various countries. The data vary widely in accuracy, and there is no way of measuring the validity of compound calculated figures such as those presented here. The consistent direction of all these differences, and their large magnitude, is the main indication of validity.

average per capita income of $695 for the more democratic countries of Europe to $308 for the less democratic ones; the corresponding difference for Latin

TABLE I. A COMPARISON OF EUROPEAN, ENGLISH-SPEAKING AND LATIN AMERICAN COUNTRIES, DIVIDED INTO TWO GROUPS, "MORE DEMOCRATIC" AND "LESS DEMOCRATIC," BY INDICES OF WEALTH, INDUSTRIALIZATION, EDUCATION, AND URBANIZATION[1]

A. Indices of Wealth

Means	Per Capita Income[2] in $	Thousands of Persons Per Doctor[3]	Persons Per Motor Vehicle[4]	Telephones Per 1,000 Persons[5]	Radios Per 1,000 Persons[6]	Newspaper Copies Per 1,000 Persons[7]
European and English-speaking stable democracies	695	.86	17	205	350	341
European and English-speaking unstable democracies and dictatorships	308	1.4	143	58	160	167
Latin American democracies and unstable dictatorships	171	2.1	99	25	85	102
Latin American stable dictatorships	119	4.4	274	10	43	43
Ranges						
European stable democracies	420–1,453	.7–1.2	3–62	43–400	160–995	242–570
European dictatorships	128–482	.6–4	10–538	7–196	42–307	46–390
Latin American democracies	112–346	.8–3.3	31–174	12–58	38–148	51–233
Latin American stable dictatorships	40–331	1.0–10.8	38–428	1–24	4–154	4–111

B. Indices of Industrialization

Means	Percentage of Males in Agriculture[8]	Per Capita Energy Consumed[9]
European stable democracies	21	3.6
European dictatorships	41	1.4
Latin American democracies	52	.6
Latin American stable dictatorships	67	.25
Ranges		
European stable democracies	6–46	1.4 –7.8
European dictatorships	16–60	.27–3.2
Latin American democracies	30–63	.30–0.9
Latin American stable dictatorships	46–87	.02–1.27

C. Indices of Education

Means	Percentage Literate[10]	Primary Education Enrollment Per 1,000 Persons[11]	Post-Primary Enrollment Per 1,000 Persons[12]	Higher Education Enrollment Per 1,000 Persons[13]
European stable democracies	96	134	44	4.2
European dictatorships	85	121	22	3.5
Latin American democracies	74	101	13	2.0
Latin American dictatorships	46	72	8	1.3
Ranges				
European stable democracies	95–100	96–179	19–83	1.7–17.83
European dictatorships	55– 98	61–165	8–37	1.6– 6.1
Latin American democracies	48– 87	75–137	7–27	.7– 4.6
Latin American dictatorships	11– 76	11–149	3–24	.2– 3.1

TABLE I (continued)

D. *Indices of Urbanization*

Means	Per Cent in Cities over 20,000[14]	Per Cent in Cities over 100,000[15]	Per Cent in Metropolitan Areas[16]
European stable democracies	43	28	38
European dictatorships	24	16	23
Latin American democracies	28	22	26
Latin American stable dictatorships	17	12	15
Ranges			
European stable democracies	28–54	17–51	22–56
European dictatorships	12–44	6–33	7–49
Latin American democracies	11–48	13–37	17–44
Latin American stable dictatorships	5–36	4–22	7–26

[1] A large part of this table has been compiled from data furnished by International Urban Research, University of California, Berkeley, California.
[2] United Nations, Statistical Office, *National and Per Capita Income in Seventy Countries* 1949, Statistical Papers, Series E, No. 1, New York, 1950, pp. 14–16.
[3] United Nations, *A Preliminary Report on the World Social Situation, 1952*, Table 11, pp. 46–8.
[4] United Nations, *Statistical Yearbook, 1956*, Table 139, pp. 333–338.
[5] *Ibid.*, Table 149, p. 387.
[6] *Ibid.*, Table 189, p. 641. The population bases for these figures are for different years than those used in reporting the numbers of telephones and radios, but for purposes of group comparisons, the differences are not important.
[7] United Nations, *A Preliminary Report . . .*, *op. cit.*, Appendix B, pp. 86–89.
[8] United Nations, *Demographic Yearbook, 1956*, Table 12, pp. 350–370.
[9] United Nations, *Statistical Yearbook, 1956*, *op. cit.*, Table 127, pp. 308–310. Figures refer to commercially produced energy, in equivalent numbers of metric tons of coal.
[10] United Nations, *A Preliminary Report . . .*, *op. cit.*, Appendix A, pp. 79–86. A number of countries are listed as more than 95 per cent literate.
[11] *Ibid.*, pp. 86–100. Figures refer to persons enrolled at the earlier year of the primary range, per 1,000 total population, for years ranging from 1946 to 1950. The first primary year varies from five to eight in various countries. The less developed countries have more persons in that age range per 1,000 population than the more developed countries, but this biases the figures presented in the direction of increasing the percentage of the total population in school for the less developed countries, although fewer of the children in that age group attend school. The bias from this source thus reinforces the positive relationship between education and democracy.
[12] *Ibid.*, pp. 86–100.
[13] UNESCO, *World Survey of Education*, Paris, 1955. Figures are the enrollment in higher education per 1,000 population. The years to which the figures apply vary between 1949 and 1952, and the definition of higher education varies for different countries.
[14] Obtained from International Urban Research, University of California, Berkeley, California.
[15] *Ibid.*
[16] *Ibid.*

America is from $171 to $119. The ranges are equally consistent, with the lowest per capita income in each group falling in the "less democratic" category, and the highest in the "more democratic" one.

Industrialization—indices of wealth are clearly related to this, of course—is measured by the percentage of employed males in agriculture, and the per capita commercially produced "energy" being used in the country, measured in terms of tons of coal per person per year. Both of these indices show equally consistent results. The average percentage of employed males working in agriculture and related occupations was 21 in the "more democratic" European countries, and 41 in the "less democratic," 52 in the "less dictatorial" Latin American countries, and 67 in the "more dictatorial." The differences in per capita energy employed in the country are equally large.

The degree of *urbanization* is also related to the existence of democracy.[3] Three different indices of urbanization are available from data compiled by International Urban Research (Berkeley, California), the percentage of the population in places of 20,000 and over, the percentage in communities of 100,000 and over, and also the percentage residing in standard metropolitan areas. On all three of these indices of urbanization, the more democratic countries score higher than the less democratic, for both of the political culture areas under investigation.

Many have suggested that the better educated the population of a country, the better the chances for democracy, and the comparative data available support this proposition. The "more democratic" countries of Europe are almost entirely literate: the lowest has a rate of 96 per cent, while the "less democratic" nations have an average literacy rate of 85 per cent. In Latin America, the difference is between an average rate of 74 per cent for the "less dictatorial" countries and 46 per cent for the "more dictatorial."[4] The educational enrollment per thousand total population at three different levels, primary, post-primary, and higher educational, is equally consistently related to degree of democracy. The tremendous disparity is shown by the extreme cases of Haiti and the United States. Haiti has fewer children (11 per thousand) attending school in the primary grades than the United States has attending colleges (almost 18 per thousand).

The relationship between education and democracy is worth more extensive treatment since an entire philosophy of democratic government has seen in increased education the spread of the basic requirement of democracy.[5] As Bryce wrote with special reference to Latin America, "education, if it does

---

[3] Urbanization has often been linked to democracy by political theorists. Harold J. Laski asserted that "organized democracy is the product of urban life," and that it was natural therefore that it should have "made its first effective appearance" in the Greek city states, limited as was their definition of "citizen." See his article "Democracy" in the *Encyclopedia of the Social Sciences* (New York: Macmillan, 1937), Vol. V, pp. 76–85. Max Weber held that the city, as a certain type of political community, is a peculiarly Western phenomenon, and traced the emergence of the notion of "citizenship" from social developments closely related to urbanization. For a partial statement of his point of view, see the chapter on "Citizenship," in *General Economic History* (Glencoe: The Free Press, 1950), pp. 315–338. It is significant to note that before 1933 the Nazi electoral strength was greatest in small communities and rural areas. Berlin, the only German city of over two million, never gave the Nazis over 25 per cent of the vote in a free election. The modal Nazi, like the modal French Poujadist or Italian neo-Fascist today, was a self-employed resident of a small town or rural district. Though the communists, as a workers' party, are strongest in the working-class neighborhoods of large cities within countries, they have great electoral strength only in the less urbanized European nations, e.g., Greece, Finland, France, Italy.

[4] The pattern indicated by a comparison of the averages for each group of countries is sustained by the ranges (the high and low extremes) for each index. Most of the ranges overlap, that is, some countries which are in the low category with regard to politics are higher on any given index than some which are high on the scale of democracy. It is noteworthy that in both Europe and Latin America, the nations which are lowest on any of the indices presented in the table are also in the "less democratic" category. Conversely, almost all countries which rank at the top of any of the indices are in the "more democratic" class.

[5] See John Dewey, *Democracy and Education* (New York, 1916).

not make men good citizens, makes it at least easier for them to become so."[6] Education presumably broadens men's outlooks, enables them to understand the need for norms of tolerance, restrains them from adhering to extremist and monistic doctrines, and increases their capacity to make rational electoral choices.

The evidence bearing on the contribution of education to democracy is even more direct and strong in connection with individual behaviour *within* countries, than it is in cross-national correlations. Data gathered by public opinion research agencies which have questioned people in different countries with regard to their belief in various democratic norms of tolerance for opposition, to their attitudes toward ethnic or racial minorities, and with regard to their belief in multi-party as against one-party systems have found that *the most important single factor differentiating those giving democratic responses from others has been education.* The higher one's education, the more likely one is to believe in democratic values and support democratic practices.[7] All the relevant studies indicate that education is far more significant than income or occupation.

These findings should lead us to anticipate a far higher correlation between national levels of education and political practice than in fact we do find. Germany and France have been among the best educated nations of Europe, but this by itself clearly did not stabilize their democracies. It may be, however, that education has served to inhibit other anti-democratic forces. Post-Nazi data from Germany indicate clearly that higher education is linked to rejection of strong-man and one-party government.[8]

If we cannot say that a "high" level of education is a sufficient condition for democracy, the available evidence does suggest that it comes close to being a necessary condition in the modern world. Thus if we turn to Latin America, where widespread illiteracy still exists in many countries, we find that of all the nations in which more than half the population is illiterate, only one, Brazil, can be included in the "more democratic" group.

There is some evidence from other economically impoverished culture areas that literacy is related to democracy, The one member of the Arab League

---

[6] Quoted in Arthur P. Whitaker, *op. cit.*, p. 112; see also Karl Mannheim, *Freedom, Power and Democratic Planning* (New York, 1950).

[7] See C. H. Smith, "Liberalism and Level of Information," *Journal of Educational Psychology*, Vol. 39 (1948), pp. 65–82; Martin A. Trow, *Right Wing Radicalism and Political Intolerance*, Ph.D. dissertation, Columbia University, 1957, p. 17; Samuel Stouffer, *Communism, Conformity and Civil Liberties* (New York, 1955), pp. 138–9; K. Kido and M. Suyi, "Report on Social Stratification and Mobility in Tokyo, . . . Mobility in Tokyo, III: The Structure of Social Consciousness," *Japanese Sociological Review* (January 1954), pp. 74–100.

[8] Dewey has suggested that the character of the educational system will influence its effect on democracy, and this may shed some light on the sources of instability in Germany. The purpose of German education, according to Dewey, writing in 1916, was "disciplinary training rather than . . . personal development." The main aim was to produce "absorption of the aims and meaning of existing institutions," and "thoroughgoing subordination" to them. This point raises issues which cannot be entered into here, but indicates the complex character of the relationship between democracy and closely related factors, such as education. See Dewey, *Democracy and Education, op. cit.*, pp. 108–110. It suggests caution, too, in drawing optimistic inferences about the prospects of democratic developments in Russia, based on the great expansion of education now taking place there.

which has maintained democratic institutions since World War II, Lebanon, is by far the best educated (over 80 per cent literacy) of the Arab countries. In the rest of Asia east of the Arab world, only two states, the Phillipines and Japan, have maintained democratic regimes without the presence of large anti-democratic parties since 1945. And these two countries, although lower than any European state in per capita income, are among the world's leaders in educational attainment. The Phillipines actually ranks second to the United States in its proportion of people attending high school and university, while Japan has a higher level of educational attainment than any European state.[9]

Although the various indices have been presented separately, it seems clear that the factors of industrialization, urbanization, wealth, and education, are so closely interrelated as to form one common factor.[10] And the factors subsumed under economic development carry with it the political correlate of democracy.[11]. . .

[9] Ceylon, which shares with the Philippines and Japan the distinction of being the only democratic countries in South and Far Asia in which the Communists are unimportant electorally, also shares with them the distinction of being the only countries in this area in which a *majority* of the population is literate. It should be noted, however, that Ceylon does have a fairly large Trotskyist party, now the official opposition; and while its educational level is high for Asia, it is much lower than either Japan or the Philippines.

[10] A factor analysis carried out by Leo Schnore, based on data from 75 countries, demonstrates this. (To be published.)

[11] This statement is a "statistical" statement, which necessarily means that there will be many exceptions to the correlation. Thus we know that poorer people are more likely to vote for the Democratic or Labor parties in the U.S. and England. The fact that a large minority of the lower strata vote for the more conservative party in these countries does not challenge the proposition that stratification position is the main determinant of party choice, given the multivariate causal process involved in the behavior of people or nations. Clearly social science will never be able to account for (predict) all behavior.

Political Participation as a Function of Social Position

LESTER W. MILBRAITH

The greatest quantity of research on political participation has related that behavior to social-position variables. In part, this is because social-position and other demographic variables are so visible and so readily measured. They are included in nearly every study as a matter of custom and convenience. A related reason is that social-position variables "stand for" many of the attitudinal and personality variables . . ., which are so difficult to measure. Social-position variables, such as class or place of residence, do not "cause" any specific behavior in the sense that they are requisites for, or the immediate antecedents of, given acts. Social conditions, however, do form personalities, beliefs, and attitudes which, in turn, do "cause" (are requisite to) specific acts such as participation in politics.

It is a simple matter, then, to find correlational relationships between social-position variables and political participation, but the reader should keep in mind that the effects of social-position variables must be mediated through personality, beliefs, and opinions. Social environment also can affect the behavior through the stimuli which it presents to behaving organisms . . . . The reader should keep both channels of influence in mind throughout the following discussion.

SOCIAL POSITION TOWARD THE CENTER OR PERIPHERY OF SOCIETY

A general way to discuss the relationship of social position to political participation is to plot social position along a central-peripheral dimension. This is superior for heuristic purposes to the more commonly used social class or socio-economic status. For one thing, the center-periphery concept incorporates other variables in addition to SES, such as length of time at a given residence, amount of group activity, urban-rural residence, and integration into the community. Another reason is that position on the center-periphery dimension is more than an objective fact, it is also a psychological feeling of being close to the center of things or of being out on the periphery. This feeling of closeness to or distance from the center is an important correlate of political participation. Feeling or perception is closely entwined with reality here; the person whose life circumstances have placed him close to the center (as determined by an impartial observer) is quite likely to *feel* closer to the center than is a person whose life circumstances have placed him on the periphery (as determined by an impartial observer).

There is no objective center which every observer would immediately recognize as such, and this means it is necessary to try to define the concept. Defining it one way might show a stronger relationship to political participation than defining it another. We shall look at several definitions advanced by scholars which differ in specifics but which have many similarities. The precise nature of the concept may still be a bit vague at the conclusion of that examination, but the broad outlines of the dimension will be visible, and that will be adequate for our purposes.

Lane has defined centrality largely in terms of communication (1959, p. 196). Centrally located persons are more accessible, more likely to be informed, partake in more discussions, belong to more organizations, are more likely to be opinion leaders.[1] A study of decision-making in a housing project showed that apartment dwellers located at a crosspath or at the bottom of the stairs were more likely to become involved in a controversy over self-government

[1] This is similar to Berelson, et al. (1954).

for the project (Festinger, et al., 1950). Another aspect of Lane's definition of centrality is that the centrally located person is liked by many others, especially other "central" persons. As a consequence, he is involved in many more interactions and receives many more communications.

Rokkan and Valen (1962) have defined communes in Norway, instead of people, as central or peripheral. Peripheral communes have many persons engaged in primary occupations such as fishing and agriculture, whereas central communes have more secondary (manufacturing) and especially more tertiary (service) occupations. Peripheral communes lost, and central communes gained population. Per capita income is lower in peripheral communes than in central communes. Peripheral communes have more small farms and less favorable tax rates because of many subsistence incomes. Peripheral communes are relatively isolated from existing transport networks. This is a reasonably good operational definition of centrality-peripherality in Norway, but one would expect other factors, as well, to be relevant in other societies.

Sociologists sometimes speak of the "underdog" in society (Knupfer, 1947); this is the socially and economically underprivileged. The operational definition of the underdog is essentially socioeconomic status: underdogs have low income, little education, low prestige, and feel that they have little power. . . . The underdog might be thought of as on the periphery of society, while the top dog is at the center.

Agger and Ostrom isolated a community role they termed "active advisor" (Agger, 1956; Agger & Ostrom, 1956). Such persons are in close contact with the "top leadership" in the community. The characteristics of these active advisors are very similar to those generally defined here as persons near the center of society: they have higher educational attainment, membership in more groups, greater length of residence in the community, plan to continue to live in the community, read more out-of-town newspapers, associate more with school or governmental officials, are more likely to have held public office, are more likely to be men than women, and are not likely to be young persons.

Lazarsfeld and Katz developed the concept of "opinion leader" (Berelson, et al., 1954; Katz, 1957–1958; Katz & Lazarsfeld, 1955; Lazarsfeld, et al., 1944). Opinion leaders are important communication links in the message flows of a society. They attend more to the mass media and communicate more with leaders; in turn, when requested, they pass this information on to others who are not so closely tied in to the communications system. They have many of the characteristics of persons near the center: higher SES, strategic social location (to receive and send messages), high integration into social grouping, high competence (highly correlated with education), high gregariousness, more activity in groups, greater interest in a subject (public affairs), greater exposure to media, and they personify certain values (are admired). The intimate relationship between position factors and personality factors is illustrated by this listing of characteristics of opinion leaders.

The general central-peripheral dimension should now be visible to the reader. Persons close to the center occupy an environmental position which naturally links them into the communications network involved in policy decisions for the society. They become identified with the body politic. They receive from and send more communications to other persons near the center. They have a higher rate of social interaction, and they are active in more groups than persons on the periphery. This central position increases the likelihood that they will develop personality traits, beliefs, and attitudes which facilitate participation in politics. There are many more political stimuli in their environment, and this increases the number of opportunities for them to participate. . . .

One of the most thoroughly substantiated propositions in all of social science is that persons near the center of society are more likely to participate in politics than persons near the periphery (Agger, 1956; Agger & Goldrich, 1958; Agger & Ostrom, 1956; Berelson, et al., 1954; Buchanan, 1956; Campbell, et al., 1954; Campbell, et al., 1960; Campbell & Kahn, 1952; Dogan, 1961; Glaser, 1959; Gronseth, 1955; Guttsman, 1951; Karlsson, 1958; Katz & Lazarsfeld, 1955; Kitt & Gleicher, 1950; Kornhauser, et al., 1956; Lane, 1959; Lazarsfeld, et al., 1944; Lipset, 1950; Lipset, 1960; Lipset, et al., 1954; Marvick & Nixon, 1961; Masumi, 1961; M. Miller, 1952; Pesonen, 1960; Pesonen, 1961; Riesman & Glazer, 1950; Rokkan & Valen, 1962). . . .

SOCIOECONOMIC STATUS (SES) OR CLASS

It will not be necessary, for our purposes, to distinguish status and class; they will be treated as roughly the same concept. Status or class differences imply not only that some persons have more of the goods of life than others, but also that some persons are looked up to more than others. Status differences are found in every society, even though the components of status and the ways of measuring it differ from society to society. What is valued and looked up to in one society may not be valued in another.

Yet, no matter what things are valued in status and no matter how status is measured, it seems clear that persons of high status are close to the center of society and persons of low status usually are on the periphery. Center-periphery, as defined above, is a broader concept than status, so the two are not identical, but the correlation between them is very high.

In Western industrialized societies in the mid-twentieth century, SES is generally conceived of as having three components: education, income, and occupation. These three components are themselves highly intercorrelated, but they are sufficiently different to warrant measuring them separately and including all three in a combined "objective" index of class or status. In a typical index of this type (different scholars use somewhat different weightings), persons who scored high on all three factors would be placed in the upper SES. Those who scored high on two factors but medium or low on one factor would be in the next rank. Those who scored high on only one factor would be in the next rank, and so forth. The index is called "objective" because the researcher places the respondent in a particular status after he has gathered the relevant data on the person.

In contrast, a "subjective" measure of class allows the respondent to select the class that he thinks he falls into. One of the first questions of this type might have read something like this: "Do you usually think of yourself as being part of the upper class, the upper-middle class, the lower-middle class, or the lower class?" Researchers soon discovered several difficulties with this type of question: (1) some people never thought about class; (2) few people had the pride to place themselves in the upper class; (3) almost no one had the lack of pride to call himself lower class. Modern survey researchers now use a series of questions reading something like this: "There is a lot of discussion about class these days. Do you ever think of yourself as belonging to a class?" "If you had to pick a class for yourself, would you say you are middle class or working class?" "Do you think you are in the upper part of the ——— class or just average ——— class?" A small percentage of respondents in the United States refuse to pick any class, sometimes insisting there are no classes in a democracy. Most respondents, however, give answers that are readily codable into one of the four categories produced by the questions: upper middle, lower middle, upper working, and lower working.[2]

Naturally, some respondents "misperceive" their class when their judgment is compared to the scholar's "objective" measurement, but most correlations between the two types of measures are rather high. Most people do accurately perceive their class status. More importantly, subjective perception of class may be as significant, or more significant, an indication of behavioral predisposition than the person's "objective" status. People tend to take on the norms and behavior patterns of the class they aspire to join. As one might imagine, many people aspire upward and take on middle-class values; almost no one aspires downward. No matter how class is measured, studies consistently show that higher-class persons are more likely to participate in politics than lower-class persons (Agger, et al., 1964; Allardt & Pesonen, 1960; Campbell, et al., 1954; Campbell, et al., 1960; Connelly & Field, 1944; Dahl, 1961; Erbe, 1964; Eulau, 1962; Foskett, 1955; McPhee & Glaser, 1962; Tingsten, 1937; Woodward & Roper, 1950). . . .

INCOME

Similar to the finding for SES, studies in many Western countries show that income is positively correlated with political participation (Agger & Ostrom, 1956; Campbell, et al., 1954; Campbell, et al., 1960; Campbell & Kahn, 1952; Connelly & Field, 1944; Dahl, 1961; Gronseth, 1955; Korchin, 1946; Lane, 1959; Lipset, 1960; M. Miller, 1952; Riesman & Glazer, 1950; Tingsten, 1937; Valen, 1961). The tau beta correlation between income and the Campaign Activity Index* on the 1956 election data is .22.† The Evanston survey showed

---

[2] For an interesting political analysis working with these categories, see Eulau (1962).

* [The material referred to is not included—Editor.]

† [A tau beta correlation of 1.00 in this case would indicate a perfect positive relationship between income and the Campaign Activity Index, whereas a correlation of −1.00 would indicate a perfect negative relationship—Editor.]

that middle-income persons are significantly more likely to be active in politics than low-income persons, but that high-income persons are not significantly more likely to be active than middle-income persons (Jenson, 1960).[3] Lane, in studying some turnout figures by income levels, suggested "a kind of declining marginal productivity of income on voting" (1959, p. 326). For each thousand-dollar increment in income, the absolute increase and the rate of increase in turnout declined. It is partly because of this factor that income correlates somewhat less highly with political participation than some other indices of SES. . . .

EDUCATION

A trend for those with higher education to be more likely to participate in politics has also been found in many Western countries (Agger & Goldrich, 1958; Agger & Ostrom, 1956; Agger, et al., 1964; Allardt & Pesonen, 1960; Almond & Verba, 1963; Benny, et al., 1956; Berelson, et al., 1954; Buchanan, 1956; Campbell, 1962; Campbell, et al., 1954; Converse & Dupeux, 1961; Dahl, 1961; Gronseth, 1955; Jensen, 1960; Key, 1961; Kornhauser, et al., 1956; Kuroda, 1964; Lane, 1959; Lipset, 1960; McPhee & Glaser, 1962; M. Miller, 1952; Sussman, 1959; Woodward & Roper, 1950). The Survey Research Center's 1956 election data and the Evanston survey both show a tau beta correlation of .25 between education and an index of participation. The five-nation study shows that educational differences were more important in accounting for differences in participation in Italy, Germany, and Mexico than in the United Kingdom and the United States (Almond & Verba, 1963, p. 121). The investigators concluded from patterns found in all five nations that education has a greater impact on political behavior than the other components of socioeconomic status (income and occupation) (p. 400).[4] . . .

OCCUPATION

Occupation is a somewhat more tricky variable to interpret than education or income. What kinds of occupational distinctions are meaningful, and how can one compute quantitative differences in occupation (as one can for income and education)? A traditional distinction, which is rather broad and vague, is between white-collar and blue-collar occupations, but the color of his collar is not a sure guide to the most relevant characteristics of a person's occupation. This distinction produces inconclusive results when it is related to political participation. Some studies (Allardt & Bruun, 1956) show white-collar persons to be more likely to participate than blue-collar, while other studies (Jensen, 1960) show no relationship.

Another way of handling occupation is to rank the statuses of the various occupations. Occupations closer to the center usually are perceived as having higher status than those on the periphery. One way to create a status ranking is to have

---

[3] Kuroda (1964) found in a Japanese community that income did not relate significantly to participation.

[4] Agger & Ostrom (1956) also reported education to be more significant than income.

a random sample of citizens rate the prestige of various occupations. Such ratings have quite high inter-rater reliability, suggesting that there are widely shared beliefs about the prestige of occupations. A categorization based on such ratings was used to make an occupation status index for respondents in the 1956 election study. This index showed a clear tendency for higher-status persons to be more likely to be active in politics; the tau beta correlation with the CAI was .20. Several other studies report that persons of higher occupational status are more likely to participate in politics (Agger & Ostrom, 1956; Berelson, et al., 1954; Bonham, 1952; Buck, 1963; Campbell & Kahn, 1952; Connelly & Field, 1944; Dahl, 1961; Gronseth, 1955; Korchin, 1946; Lane, 1959; McPhee & Glaser, 1962). The exception for Norway, discussed under education, also applies here. The status-polarized party system there requires recruiting for political workers within occupations at all statuses; therefore, the over-all relationship between occupation status and participation is not very pronounced in Norway (Rokkan & Campbell, 1960). . . .

Turning now to somewhat more specific occupations, several studies show that professional persons are the most likely to get involved in politics (Anderson, 1935; Buck, 1963; Guttsman, 1951; Jensen, 1960; M. Miller, 1952; Schlesinger, 1957). This generalization seems especially true of political office-holding, being very evident for higher offices. It very probably would not hold for a setting where political activity, or the kind of office held, is not well respected. The Evanston survey showed professionals most likely to be active in politics, followed by businessmen, clerical, skilled, and unskilled workers in that order (Jensen, 1960). In Anglo-Saxon countries and in France, lawyers are especially likely to seek office and be active in other ways in politics; this pattern is not so prevalent in other countries, however. Almost half of the state governors in the United States from 1870 to 1950 (456 of 995) were practising lawyers (Schlesinger, 1957). Occupations of members of the British Parliament have followed a trend away from landowning and toward professional occupations (Buck, 1963; Guttsman, 1951). There is a pattern in some countries for government employees to be very active politically (Lipset, 1960b; Tingsten, 1937). Whether or not this occurs may depend on possible legal prohibitions against political activity by public employees. The Hatch Act (1940) controls the political activities of employees of the federal government in the United States. Certainly, the public nature of their job means that government job-holders have an important stake in political outcomes.

Businessmen, compared to the rest of the population, tend to be quite active in politics, although there is variation from business to business and perhaps also from community to community. A study of the political activity of Philadelphia businessmen reported these findings: A high propotion vote and contribute money, as a matter of course (40 per cent contributed money as compared to 10 per cent for a national sample) (Janosik, 1962). The percentage of businessmen who worked in a campaign (8 per cent) was just a little higher than the national average (3 or 4 per cent) and is a normal percentage for upper-middle SES persons. There were no public office-holders among these businessmen.

They tended to have a positive attitude toward politics and politicians, tended to be optimistic about politics, and tended slightly to inhibit political discussion for fear of offending associates. Top business executives were more likely to be active in politics than middle- and lower-level executives. Another study of the effects of political training classes, designed to involve businessmen in politics, reported modest to poor results for the training (Hacker & Aberbach, 1962). The positive attractions to politics often did not compensate for the costs of political action (especially diversion of time and energy).

Most studies show laboring persons disinclined, on the whole, to become involved actively in politics. There are exceptions to this generalization in countries with strong working-class movements and parties. . . . In the United States, labor unions have some success in mobilizing their members for political action, but the result is not very impressive; this effort will be discussed later under group memberships. Certain aspects of a laboring man's job make it difficult for him to become active in politics, especially to undertake gladiatorial activity.* He has a fixed work schedule, making it difficult to be free for meetings. His job usually does not emphasize or teach verbal skills that can be transferred to political action. The relevance of political outcomes for his income and job satisfaction is often not very clear. Farmers tend to have the lowest levels of political participation of all occupational groupings (Campbell, et al., 1960). The major reason for this is grounded in the relative isolation of rural life.

URBAN-RURAL

In the definitional terms of center-periphery discussed at the beginning of this chapter, it is clear that the urban dweller is generally closer to the center of most societies than is the rural dweller. This is largely due to the enhanced opportunity for interaction and communication that the urban dweller has when compared to rural people. Campbell was quoted on urban opportunities for communication in Chapter II† (p. 42); a few additional remarks are germane:

We . . . find very low levels of political interest and involvement among farmers in the United States. Despite the widespread ownership of automobiles and television sets by rural people, farm life in America is not only physically but socially remote. The typical farmer not only lives apart from his neighbors but has relatively little formal association with them. Most American farmers belong to no farm organizations and few of those who do express any great interest in them (Campbell, 1962, pp. 13–14).

It has been found in many studies that farmers are less likely to become active in politics than city dwellers (Berelson, et al., 1954; Campbell, 1962; Campbell, et al., 1960; McPhee & Glaser, 1962; Pesonen, 1960; Rokkan & Campbell, 1960; Rokkan & Valen, 1962; Tingsten, 1937, in all four Scandinavian countries). In addition to the communication disadvantages of the rural setting, another reason for the urban-rural difference is the striking difference in political activity levels of rural and urban women (Rokkan & Campbell, 1960). Women

---

* [See the Introduction to this section for a discussion of gladiatorial activities—Editor.]
† [The material referred to is not included—Editor.]

from families engaged in primary economic activity (agriculture, forestry, fishing) are much less likely to participate in politics. Women in a primary economy stay close to home and often are involved in production. This not only leaves little time for politics, but also limits social interaction to family members (once again, social interaction seems to be a central variable). An additional factor is that primary economies tend to be more tradition-oriented, and it is a strong tradition to think of politics as "man's work." As a greater proportion of the economic activity in a locality becomes secondary and tertiary, the differences in participation between men and women are reduced. Women in urban areas in Norway are just as likely to vote as men, they are just as likely as men to take part in party affairs, and they are more likely to become candidates for office than rural women, even though urban men are still more likely to become candidates than urban women (Rokkan & Campbell, 1960; Rokkan & Valen, 1962).

Some research evidence questions the generalization that rural people are less likely to be active in politics than urban people. A community study in Oregon found no urban-rural differences in general community participation (their index included nonpolitical activities) (Agger & Ostrom, 1956). In Sweden, farmers were more active in voting than persons employed in many other industries, but they were not as active as employers (Karlsson, 1958a). Slightly higher voting turnout rates were found for rural Indiana counties than for urban counties (Robinson & Standing, 1960). Rural voting is also high in France and Italy.

In Japan, the general urban-rural differences described above do not hold. Several studies in Japan since World War II show political participation, especially voting turnout, to be higher in the rural areas than in urban areas (Kyogoku & Ike, 1959; Masumi, 1961). Most of the reasons given for this finding suggest that urban persons are no closer to the center of Japanese society than rural persons. If anything, the tendency is in the other direction. Most urban areas, especially Tokyo, have grown very fast in recent years, and a large proportion of city dwellers are poorly integrated into their community. Rural areas show higher community integration; the houses are close together (not isolated, as farm-houses are in the United States); exposure to the mass media is generally higher in rural areas; and rural communities compete with one another in seeing who can produce the greater turnout.

A very important factor is the social structure of rural Japan, which is still semi-feudal in basic respects. Old and large landowning families are closely knit by kinship and friendship ties. There is an authoritarian tradition for the people to follow the political lead of the head of the clan; voting is taken as a sign of loyalty. These rural political machines are stronger than urban machines and are the basic strength of the conservative party in Japan. Rural people place more emphasis on the reputation and personality of candidates, whereas city dwellers must rely more on party labels as a guide to voting.

City areas in Japan have experienced a much higher percentage of candidates offering themselves for public office. Many of these candidates have little reputation and status and meager city background. This seriously increases the information demands and costs for city voters. As the evolution toward urbanization proceeds, and as more adequate means are found to integrate the masses into urban life, one would expect the center of Japanese life to shift to the cities and the participation rates of urban and rural dwellers to follow more closely the pattern found in Western countries. . . .

MEMBERSHIP AND ACTIVITY IN GROUPS

The point [has been] made . . . and supported by many studies, that general group activity is highly related to participation in politics. This close relationship occurs not only because many of the same personal and social characteristics lead to both political and nonpolitical participation, but also because groups are important mobilizers of political action by their members. Organizations facilitate turnout, recruit candidates, and boost party membership (Hartenstein & Liepelt, 1962; Lane, 1959; Lipset, 1960; McClosky & Dahlgren, 1959; Rokkan, 1962a). This holds, of course, only for organizations that desire to mobilize their membership politically; some organizations may have a norm favoring political apathy (Rosenberg, 1954–1955). . . .

COMMUNITY IDENTIFICATION

It was mentioned several times above that persons who are well integrated into their community tend to feel close to the center of community decisions and are more likely to participate in politics. One evidence of this is that the longer a person resides in a given community, the greater the likelihood of his participation in politics (Agger, et al., 1964; Allardt & Bruun, 1956; Birch & Campbell, 1950; Buchanan, 1956; Kitt & Gleicher, 1950; Lane, 1959; Lipset, 1960; Tingsten, 1937). Although length of residence correlates with voting turnout, it seems especially relevant to gladiatorial activities. A newcomer to town very likely begins to vote after a year or so, but it usually takes some additional time before he is drawn into party work. Only after a few years of testing will community residents be inclined to entrust party office to a newcomer or encourage his candidacy for public office.

Another bit of evidence is that *homeowners are more likely to vote than renters* (M. Miller, 1952). A study of a Mississippi community found that persons who identified strongly with it were more likely to feel that their vote had political impact, and they were less likely to perceive their community as run by a small elite not subject to popular guidance (Buchanan, 1956). It is curious, yet understandable, that persons most estranged from politics and their community are most likely to perceive their community as run by a small clique of autocratic rulers. Additional evidence relative to community integration comes from data relating age to participation: *young people are not likely to become enmeshed in politics until they have become established in a job, a home, and start to raise a family*—but that is the topic of the next section.

LIFE CYCLE AND AGE

The point just made helps to explain the typical curve found when age is related to political participation. Participation rises gradually with age, reaches its peak and levels off in the forties and fifties, and gradually declines above sixty (Allardt & Bruun, 1956; Benny, et al., 1956; Campbell, et al., 1960; Campbell & Kahn, 1952; Jensen, 1960; Kuroda, 1964; Lipset, 1960; Tingsten, 1937, reported supporting data from five countries). Other studies do not describe the curve but simply report that older persons are more likely to vote than younger (Berelson, et al., 1954; Birch & Campbell, 1950; Buchanan, 1956; Connelly & Field, 1944; Glaser, 1959; Korchin, 1946; Lazarsfeld, et al., 1944; McPhee & Glaser, 1962; M. Miller, 1952). A community study in Oregon found no relationship between age and turnout (Agger & Ostrom, 1956). In a recent study of four communities (two of which are in the South), it was found that young Negroes (under thirty-five) in the South were more active than older Negroes. Some of the active young Negroes were newcomers to their community, too, in contrast to the general finding for the four communities that newcomers are less likely to be active in politics (Agger, et al., 1964). Clearly, a dynamic emotional issue (civil rights) is at work here, creating an aberration on the normal pattern. . . .

VARIATIONS BY SEX

The traditional division of labor which assigns the political role to men rather than women has not vanished. The finding that men are more likely to participate in politics than women is one of the most thoroughly substantiated in social science (Agger, et al., 1964; Allardt, 1956; Allardt & Pesonen, 1960; Almond & Verba, 1963; Benny, et al., 1956; Berelson, et al., 1954; Birch, 1950; Buchanan, 1956; Campbell & Cooper, 1956; Connelly & Field, 1944; Dogan & Narbonne, 1955; Gronseth, 1955; Grundy, 1950; Korchin, 1946; Kuroda, 1964; Lane, 1959; Lazarsfeld, et al., 1944; McPhee & Glaser, 1962; Pesonen, 1960; Pesonen 1961; Rokkan, 1962b; Tingsten, 1937, data from five countries). Data supporting this proposition come from at least nine countries. The survey interviewer seeking respondents for a political study discovers after only a few house calls that there are significant remnants of the tradition in modern society. A favorite excuse for not wishing to be interviewed is to claim that the husband takes care of the family politics. The *Chicago Sun Times* on September 2, 1963, quoted a state representative from Arkansas about women meddling in politics: "We don't have that trouble up in Perry County. When our women get too nosey about something that doesn't concern them, we get another cow to milk or get them a little more garden to tend." Only a few years ago in Switzerland, a proposition to give women the right to vote failed of passage.

Economic and social modernization is slowly eroding this sex difference, however. The five-nation study found the differences in participation between the sexes least in the United States, followed by the United Kingdom, Germany,

Mexico, and Italy; the difference was especially great in Italy (Almond & Verba, 1963, Ch. 13). Two community studies in the United States found no differences in participation by sex (Agger & Ostrom, 1956; M. Miller, 1952). Researchers in Finland found that when they controlled for marital status and age, the difference by sex disappeared (Allardt & Bruun, 1956). A comparative study between Norway and the United States found for both countries that the sex difference in participation was quite pronounced in lower SES areas, especially areas of primary economy, but that the sex difference almost disappeared in urban, upper-middle SES, well-educated strata. At the upper levels of politics (running for and holding party and public office) in both countries, men and more likely to participate than women, even if both sexes are high SES (Rokkan & Campbell, 1960). The Evanston survey found women significantly less likely than men to be party actives (Jensen, 1960). The Survey Research Center 1956 election data show men more likely than women to wear a button or to proselyte but not significantly more likely to give money, attend meetings, do campaign work, or join a political club.

The erosion of the sex difference in participation does not necessarily mean that women are becoming independent of men in choosing whom they will support; it means only that politics is less and less considered strictly a man's role. A good deal of solid evidence still suggests that wives follow their husband's lead in politics (sometimes vice versa), or at least that husband and wife tend to support the same parties and candidates (Campbell, et al., 1960; Glaser, 1959; Gronseth, 1955; Tingsten, 1937).

RELIGION

It is difficult to know if religion per se influences political behavior, because religious groupings tend to coincide with SES, ethnic, and racial groupings. It is virtually impossible to separate out religion from these other factors. In any case, religious differences in participation are slight. The general pattern found in the United States is that Jews are slightly more active in politics than Catholics who, in turn, are slightly more active than Protestants (Campbell & Kahn, 1952; Connelly & Field, 1944; Korchin, 1946). The Survey Research Center 1956 election data show Catholics more likely than Protestants to vote but not more likely to engage in gladiatorial activities; Jews were more likely to engage in both spectator* and gladiatorial activities. . . .

Studies relating political participation to specific Protestant denominations show a slight trend for Episcopalians and Presbyterians to be more active than the average Protestant; Baptists seemed to be a bit less active than the average (Jensen, 1960; Milbraith, 1956a). However, since the first two groupings have above-average SES and the last has below-average SES, the denominational difference may merely reflect an SES difference. A study in Waukegan, Illinois, found persons affiliated with a church more likely to vote than nonaffiliates

---

* [See the Introduction to this section for a discussion of spectator activities—Editor.]

(M. Miller, 1952). The Survey Research Center 1956 election data show regular attenders at church more likely than average to vote but not more likely to engage in gladiatorial activities . . .; nonattenders and nonaffiliates were less likely to participate in both spectator and gladiator activities. The reader is reminded of the relevance of this to the relationship between group participation and political participation previously discussed.

RACIAL AND ETHNIC MINORITIES

Physiological racial characteristics do not account for participation differences between races; rather, it is the relative social position of racial groupings that create these differences. It seems clear that in the United States, Negro and other racial minorities are located toward the periphery rather than toward the center of society. Generally, they have less education, fewer job opportunities, lower incomes, and fewer opportunities to interact with prominent people. It has repeatedly been found in nationwide studies in the United States that Negroes participate in politics at a much lower rate than whites (Campbell, et al., 1954; Campbell, et al., 1960; Woodward & Roper, 1950). In the Survey Research Center 1956 election data, this difference held not only for the Campaign Activity Index but also for all the specific acts included in the index. Whites were especially more likely to contribute money than Negroes (the racial difference is also an income difference) but were only slightly more likely to proselyte, attent meetings, and join political clubs.

The survey in Evanston (a relatively wealthy northern suburb of Chicago) found no significant difference in political participation between whites and Negroes (Jensen, 1960). The Evanston situation may be similar to that found in a study of New Haven, Connecticut, where Negroes were more likely than whites to participate in local politics. In New Haven, channels of political influence and advancement are open equally to Negroes and whites. Private channels of influence (e.g., connections and advancement in private business), however, are relatively much less accessible to Negroes. Politics, then, probably seems more enticing to the ambitious Negro than to the ambitious white (Dahl, 1961). Lane (1959) has suggested that ethnic minorities are more likely to participate in local politics than nonethnics.[5] The recent study of four communities found higher participation rates for Negroes than for whites in one of the southern communities (Agger, et al., 1964, p. 269). These scattered findings suggest that racial and ethnic minorities are not always on the periphery; in certain communities they may be at the center or have very good access to it. One must be cautious in generalizing about behavior from a mere racial or ethnic category. . . .

---

[5] See Lane (1959, Ch. 17) for a full exposition.

Bibliography

AGGER, ROBERT E.
1956 "Power Attributions in the Local Community," *Social Forces*, XXXIV (May), 322–331.

AGGER, ROBERT E., and DANIEL GOLDRICH
1958 "Community Power Structures and Partisanship," *American Sociological Review*, XXIII (August), 383–392.

AGGER, ROBERT E., DANIEL GOLDRICH, and BERT E. SWANSON
1964 *The Rulers and the Ruled: Political Power and Impotence in American Communities*, New York: Wiley.

AGGER, ROBERT E., and VINCENT OSTROM
1956 "Political Participation in a Small Community," in Heinz Eulau, Samuel J. Eldersveld, and Morris Janowitz, eds., *Political Behavior*. Glencoe, Ill.: The Free Press. Pp. 138–148.

ALLARDT, ERIK
1956 *Social Struktur oc Politisk Activitet*. Helsinki: Soderstroms.

ALLARDT, ERIK, and KETTIL BRUUN
1956 "Characteristics of the Finnish Non-voter," *Transactions of the Westermarck Society*, III, 55–76.

ALLARDT, ERIK, and PERTTI PESONEN
1960 "Citizen Participation in Political Life in Finland," *International Social Science Journal*, XII, No. 1, 27–39.

ALMOND, GABRIEL, and SIDNEY VERBA
1963 *The Civic Culture*. Princeton: Princeton University Press.

ANDERSON, H. DEWEY
1935 "The Educational and Occupational Attainment of Our National Rulers," *Scientific Monthly*, XL (June), 511–518.

BENNY, MARK, A. P. GRAY, and R. H. PEAR
1956 *How People Vote: A Study of Electoral Behavior in Greenwich*. London: Routledge and Kegan Paul.

BERELSON, BERNARD R., PAUL F. LAZARSFELD, and WILLIAM N. McPHEE
1954 *Voting*. Chicago: University of Chicago Press.

BIRCH, A. H.
1950 "The Habit of Voting," *Journal of the Manchester School of Economic and Social Studies*, XVIII (January), 75–82.

BIRCH, A. H., and PETER CAMPBELL
1950 "Voting Behavior in a Lancashire Constituency," *British Journal of Sociology*, I (September), 197–208.

BONHAM, JOHN
1952 "The Middle Class Elector," *British Journal of Sociology*, III (September), 222–230.

BUCHANAN, WILLIAM
1956 "An Inquiry into Purposive Voting," *The Journal of Politics*, XVIII (May), 281–296. Also in Bobbs-Merrill Reprint Series, No. PS-34.

BUCK, PHILIP W.
1963 *Amateurs and Professionals in British Politics*. Chicago: University of Chicago Press.

CAMPBELL, ANGUS
1962 "The Passive Citizen," *Acta Sociologica*, VI (fasc. 1–2), 9–21.

CAMPBELL, ANGUS, PHILLIP CONVERSE, WARREN MILLER, and DONALD STOKES
1960 *The American Voter*. New York: Wiley.

CAMPBELL, ANGUS, and HOMER C. COOPER
1956   *Group Differences in Attitudes and Votes*. Ann Arbor: University of Michigan, Institute for Social Research, Survey Research Center.

CAMPBELL, ANGUS, GERALD GURIN, and WARREN MILLER.
1954   *The Voter Decides*. Evanston, Ill.: Row, Peterson.

CAMPBELL, ANGUS, and ROBERT L. KAHN
1952   *The People Elect a President*. Ann Arbor: University of Michigan, Institute for Social Research, Survey Research Center.

CONNELLY, GORDON M., and HARRY H. FIELD
1944   "The Non-Voter: Who He Is, What He Thinks," *Public Opinion Quarterly*, VIII (Summer), 175–187.

CONVERSE, PHILLIP and GEORGES DUPEUX
1961   "Some Comparative Notes on French and American Political Behavior." UNESCO Seminar, Bergen, Norway, June. (Mimeographed.)

DAHL, ROBERT A.
1961   *Who Governs? Democracy and Power in an American City*. New Haven: Yale University Press.

DOGAN, MATTEI
1961   "Political Ascent in a Class Society: French Deputies 1870–1958," in Dwaine Marvick, ed., *Political Decision-Makers*. Glencoe, Ill.: The Free Press. Pp. 57–90.

DOGAN, MATTEI, and J. NARBONNE
1955   *Les Francaises Face à la Politique*. Paris: Armand Colin.

ERBE, WILLIAM
1964   "Social Involvement and Political Activity," *American Sociological Review*, XXIX (April), 198–215.

EULAU, HEINZ
1962   *Class and Party in the Eisenhower Years*. New York: The Free Press of Glencoe.

FESTINGER, LEON, STANLEY SCHACHTER, and KURT BACK
1950   *Social Pressures in Informal Groups*, New York: Harper.

FOSKETT, J. M.
1955   "Social Structure and Social Participation," *American Sociological Review*, XX (August), 431–438.

GLASER, WILLIAM A.
1959   "The Family and Voting Turnout," *Public Opinion Quarterly*, XXIII (Winter, 563–570.

GRONSETH, ERIK
1955   *The Political Role of Women in Norway*. Oslo: Institute for Social Research. (Mimeographed.) Excerpts from a contribution to the Norwegian report to the UNESCO study of the political role of women. Oslo: Oslo University, Institute of Sociology, 1953. First published in Maurice Duverger, *The Political Role of Women*. Paris: UNESCO. Pp. 194–221.

GRUNDY, J.
1950   "Non-Voting in an Urban District," *Journal of the Manchester School of Economic and Social Studies*, XVIII (January), 83–99.

GUTTSMAN, W. L.
1951   "The Changing Social Structure of the British Political Elite, 1886–1935," *British Journal of Sociology*, II (June), 122–134.

HACKER, ANDREW, and JOEL D. ABERBACH
1962   "Businessmen in Politics," in *Symposium on the Electoral Process: Part I*, published as Spring, 1962, issue of *Law and Contemporary Problems*. Durham, N. C.: Duke University School of Law. Pp. 260–279.

HARTENSTEIN, WOLFGANG, and KLAUS LIEPELT
1962   "Party Members and Party Voters in West Germany," *Acta Sociologica*, VI (fasc. 1–2), 43–52.

JANOSIK, EDWARD G.
1962   *Report on Political Activity of Philadelphia Businessmen.* Philadelphia: University of Pennsylvania, Wharton School of Finance and Commerce.

JENSEN, JACK
1960   Political Participation: A Survey in Evanston, Illinois. Unpublished master's thesis, Northwestern University.

KARLSSON, GEORG
1958   "Voting Participation among Male Swedish Youth," *Acta Sociologica,* III (fasc. 2–3), 98–111.

KATZ, Elihu
1957   "The Two-Step Flow of Communication: An Up-to-Date Report on an Hypothesis," *Public Opinion Quarterly,* XXI (Spring), 61–78.

KATZ, ELIHU, and PAUL LAZARSFELD
1955   *Personal Influence.* Glencoe, Ill.: The Free Press.

KEY, V. O., Jr.
1961   *Public Opinion and American Democracy.* New York: Alfred A. Knopf.

KITT, ALICE S., and DAVID B. GLEICHER
1950   "Determinants of Voting Behavior," *Public Opinion Quarterly,* XIV (Fall), 393–412.

KNUPFER, GENEVIEVE
1947   "Portrait of the Underdog," *Public Opinion Quarterly,* XI (Spring), 103–114.

KORCHIN, SHELDON J.
1946   Psychological Variables in the Behavior of Voters. Unpublished doctoral dissertation, Harvard University.

KORNHAUSER, ARTHUR, ALBERT J. MAYER, and HAROLD SHEPPARD
1956   *When Labor Votes.* New York: University Books.

KURODA, YASUMASA
1964   *Measurement, Correlates, and Significance of Political Participation at the Community Level.* (Mimeographed.)

KYOGOKU, JUN-ICHI, and NOBUTAKA IKE
1959   *Urban-Rural Differences in Voting Behavior in Postwar Japan.* Reprinted as No. 66 of the Stanford University Political Science Series for the Proceedings of the Department of Social Sciences, University of Tokyo.

LANE, ROBERT E.
1959   *Political Life: Why People Get Involved in Politics.* Glencoe, Ill.: The Free Press.

LAZARSFELD, PAUL F., BERNARD BERELSON, and HAZEL GAUDET
1944   *The People's Choice.* New York: Duell, Sloan, and Pearce.

LIPSET, SEYMOUR MARTIN
1950   *Agrarian Socialism.* Berkeley: University of California Press.
1960   *Political Man.* Garden City, N. Y.: Doubleday.

LIPSET, SEYMOUR MARTIN, PAUL LAZARSFELD, ALLEN BARTON, and JUAN LINZ
1954   "The Psychology of Voting: An Analysis of Political Behavior," in Gardner Lindzey, ed., *Handbook of Social Psychology,* II, Cambridge, Mass.: Addison-Wesley, 1124–1175.

MCCLOSKY, HERBERT, and HAROLD E. DAHLGREN
1959   "Primary Group Influence on Party Loyalty," *American Political Science Review,* LIII (September), 757–776. Reprinted in S. Sidney Ulmer, *Introductory Readings in Political Behavior.* Chicago: Rand McNally, 1961. Pp. 221–237.

MCPHEE, WILLIAM N., and WILLIAM A. Glaser, eds.
1962   *Public Opinion and Congressional Elections.* New York: The Free Press of Glencoe.

MARVICK, DWAINE, and CHARLES NIXON
1961   "Recruitment Contrasts in Rival Campaign Groups," in Dwaine Marvick, ed., *Political Decision-Makers.* Glencoe, Ill.: The Free Press. Pp. 193–217.

MASUMI, JUNNOSUKE
1961 "Japanese Voting Behavior: A Changing Nation and the Vote," paper prepared for the Fifth World Congress of the International Political Science Association, Paris, September.
MILBRAITH, LESTER W.
1956 The Motivations and Characteristics of Political Contributors: North Carolina General Election, 1952. Unpublished doctoral dissertation, University of North Carolina.
MILLER, MUNGO
1952 "The Waukegan Study of Voter Turnout Prediction," Public Opinion Quarterly, XVI (Fall), 381–398.
PERSONEN, PERTTI
1960 "The Voting Behavior of Finnish Students," in Democracy in Finland. Helsinki: Finnish Political Science Association. Pp. 93–104.
1961 "Citizen Participation in Finnish Politics," paper prepared for the Fifth World Congress of the International Political Science Association, Paris, September.
RIESMAN, DAVID, and NATHAN GLAZER
1950 "Criteria for Political Apathy," in Alvin Gouldner, ed., Studies in Leadership. New York: Harper. Pp. 540–547. Also in Bobbs-Merrill Reprint Series No. S-236.
ROBINSON, JAMES A., and WILLIAM H. STANDING
1960 "Some Correlates of Voter Participation: The Case of Indiana," The Journal of Politics, XXII (February), 96–111.
ROKKAN, STEIN
1962a "Approaches to the Study of Political Participation," Introduction to special issue, edited by Rokkan, of Acta Sociologica, VI (fasc. 1–2), 1–8.
1962b "The Comparative Study of Political Participation: Notes toward a Perspective on Current Research," in Austin Raney, ed., Essays on the Behavioral Study of Politics. Urbana: University of Illinois Press. Pp. 47–90.
ROKKAN, STEIN, and ANGUS CAMPBELL
1960 "Norway and the United States of America," in Citizen Participation in Political Life, issue of International Social Science Journal, XII, No. 1, 69–99.
ROKKAN, STEIN, and HENRY VALEN
1962 "The Mobilization of the Periphery: Data on Turnout, Party Membership and Candidate Recruitment in Norway," Acta Sociologica, VI (fasc. 1–2), 111–158.
ROSENBERG, MORRIS
1954– "Some Determinants of Political Apathy," Public Opinion Quarterly, XVIII
1955 (Winter), 349–366.
SCHLESINGER, JOSEPH A.
1957 "Lawyers and American Politics: A Clarified View," Midwest Journal of Political Science, I (May), 26–39.
SUSSMAN, LEILA
1959 "Mass Political Letter Writing in America: The Growth of an Institution," Public Opinion Quarterly, XIII (Summer), 203–212.
TINGSTEN, HERBERT
1937 Political Behavior: Studies in Election Statistics. London: P. S. King.
VALEN, HENRY
1961 "The Motivation and Recruitment of Political Personnel," paper prepared for UNESCO Seminar, Bergen, Norway, June. (Mimeographed.)
WOODWARD, JULIAN L., and ELMO ROPER
1950 "Political Activity of American Citizens," American Political Science Review, XLIV (December), 872–885.

Additional Readings

ROBERT R. ALFORD, "The Role of Social Class in American Voting Behavior," *The Western Political Quarterly*, 16 (March, 1963), pp. 180–194.

HEINZ EULAU, "Perceptions of Class and Party in Voting Behavior, 1952," *The American Political Science Review*, 49 (June, 1955), pp. 364–384.

LEWIS A. FROMAN, Jr., *People and Politics* (Englewood Cliffs, N.J.: Prentice-Hall, Inc., 1962), pp. 80–102.

SEYMOUR MARTIN LIPSET, *Political Man* (Garden City, N.Y.: Doubleday and Company, Inc., 1959), pp. 45–60, 97–126, 179–216, 285–290, 310–343.

SIDNEY VERBA, "Political Participation and Strategies of Influence: A Comparative Study," *Acta Sociologica*, 6 (1962), pp. 22–42.

JULIAN L. WOODWARD and ELMO ROPER, "Political Activity of American Citizens," *The American Political Science Review*, 44 (December, 1950), pp. 872–885.

Introduction

The nature, types, and determinants of *social control* constitute important problems for sociological research. Four mechanisms of social control are frequently identified in this research: *kinship, religion,* education, and *stratification.*[1] The next four sections report factual information about these four mechanisms.

The *family* is the group most commonly used to illustrate the kinship system. The five selections used in this section report factual information about the family.

A classic problem in the study of the family is the determination of its extensiveness. Murdock, for example, has argued that a *nuclear family* which performs the four following functions is universal in all societies: socialization, economic cooperation, reproduction, and sexual relations.[2] The selection by Reiss, "The Universality of the Family," disagrees with Murdock's argument, and suggests instead that what is universal in all societies is some type of kinship group, not just the nuclear family, which performs the dominant share of nurturant socialization. Nurturant socialization, as defined by Reiss, refers to giving positive emotional responses to infants and small children. Murdock's definition of socialization is a more general term than Reiss' definition of nurturant socialization.

Specification of the determinants of group *stability* has long been a problem investigated by sociologists. When this problem is investigated in relation to families, divorce is a commonly used measure of stability. The selections by Plateris, "The National Divorce Trend," and Murdock, "Family Stability in

[1] "Education" is not italicized, because it is not a basic concept in sociology. Socialization is the basic concept which includes education.

[2] George P. Murdock, *Social Structure* (New York: The Macmillan Company, 1949), pp. 1–22.

Non-European Cultures," summarize factual information about divorce. Three main conclusions can be drawn from Plateris' information. First, there has been a long-term increase in the divorce rate in the United States. In 1920, the rate per 1,000 total population was 1.6; by 1963 this rate had increased to 2.3. A more refined measure of the divorce rate is the rate per 1,000 married females over 15 years of age. This more refined measure indicates divorce rates of 8.0 and 9.6, respectively, for 1920 and 1963. Second, there has been a decrease in the divorce rate since the end of World War II in the United States. In 1946, the rate per 1,000 total population was 4.3; by 1963 this rate had decreased to 2.3. The rates per 1,000 married females over 15 years of age—the more refined measure of divorce—were 17.9 and 9.6, respectively, for 1946 and 1963. Third, the comparative divorce rate of the United States is relatively high. In 1963, for example, the divorce rate per 1,000 population in the United States was 2.3; the country whose divorce rate came the closest to this figure was the United Arab Republic (Egypt) with 2.1.[3]

Most of the comparative information in Plateris' selection is about European societies; however, the comparative information in Murdock's selection is entirely about non-European societies. The main conclusion that emerges from Murdock's selection is that the family in the United States is relatively stable compared to the family in non-European countries. Murdock's information suggests that family stability in non-European societies is not as high as is often believed. Unfortunately, Murdock, because of the limitations of the information he is sampling, cannot present the type of detailed statistical information about divorce which Plateris presents.

The impact of industrialization and urbanization on the family is an important problem in the study of the family. Two basic propositions exist in this area: the greater the increase of industrialization and urbanization in a society, the greater the likelihood that the family will be an isolated nuclear family rather than an *extended family*. The next two selections by Sussman-Burchinal and Furstenberg, in addition to stating the two propositions, report factual information relevant to this problem. Sussman and Burchinal, in "Kin Family Network: Unheralded Structure in Current Conceptualizations of Family Functioning," present information about the type of family in one highly industrialized and urbanized society, the contemporary United States. Furstenberg, in "Industrialization and the American Family: A Look Backward," presents information about the type of family in the United States before the society was highly industrialized and urbanized. The main conclusion that emerges from the studies that Sussman and Burchinal summarize is that the family system in the contemporary United States, rather than being either the isolated nuclear family or the classical extended family, is an intermediate variety, the "modified extended family." The family system that Furstenberg describes in the United States between 1800 and 1850—before the society was highly industrialized and urbanized—strongly resembles the contemporary family in the United States.[4] The selections by Sussman-Burchinal and Furstenberg do not support the suggested relationship between industrialization and urbanization, on the one hand, and the existence of an isolated nuclear family, on the other hand.

[3] There is no comparative information about the divorce rates per 1,000 married females over 15 years of age.

[4] The selections by Sussman-Burchinal and Furstenberg present information which is often discussed in connection with "industrialization" and "urbanization."

The Universality of the Family

IRA L. REISS

During the last few decades, a revived interest in the question of the universality of the family has occurred. One key reason for this was the 1949 publication of George Peter Murdock's book *Social Structure*.[1] In that book, Murdock postulated that the nuclear family was universal and that it had four essential functions which it always and everywhere fulfilled. These four functions were: (1) socialization, (2) economic cooperation, (3) reproduction, and (4) sexual relations. Even in polygamous and extended family systems, the nuclear families within these larger family types were viewed as separate entities which each performed these four functions.

The simplicity and specificity of Murdock's position makes it an excellent starting point for an investigation of the universal functions of the human family. Since Murdock's position has gained support in many quarters, it should be examined carefully.[2] Brief comments on Murdock's position appear in the literature, and some authors, such as Levy and Fallers, have elaborated their opposition.[3] The present paper attempts to go somewhat further, not only in testing Murdock's notion but in proposing and giving evidence for a substitute position. However, it should be clear that Murdock's position is being used merely as an illustration; our main concern is with delineating what, if anything, is universal about the human family.

The four functions of the nuclear family are "functional prerequisites" of human society, to use David Aberle's term from his classic article on the topic.[4] This means that these functions must somehow occur for human society to exist. If the nuclear family everywhere fulfills these functions, it follows that this family should be a "structural prerequisite" of human society, i.e., a universally necessary part of society.[5] The basic question being investigated is

Reprinted from the *Journal of Marriage and the Family*, 27 (November, 1965), pp. 443–453, by permission of the author and the publisher.

[1] George P. Murdock, *Social Structure*, New York: Macmillan, 1949.

[2] Many of the textbooks in the family field fail to really cope with this issue and either ignore the question or accept a position arbitrarily. The Census definition also ignores this issue: "A group of two persons or more related by blood, marriage, or adoption and residing together." The recently published *Dictionary of the Social Sciences*, ed. by Julius Gould and William Kolb, Glencoe, Ill.: Free Press, 1964, defines the nuclear family as universal. See pp. 257–259. Parsons, Bales, Bell and Vogel are among those who also seem to accept Murdock's position. See: Talcott Parsons and Robert F. Bales, *Family, Socialization and Interaction Process*, Glencoe, Ill.: Free Press, 1955; Talcott Parsons, "The Incest Taboo in Relation to Social Structure and the Socialization of the Child," *British Journal of Sociology*, 5 (January 1954), pp. 101–117; *A Modern Introduction to the Family*, ed. by Norman Bell and Ezra Vogel, Glencoe, Ill.: Free Press, 1960.

[3] Marion J. Levy, Jr. and L. A. Fallers, "The Family: Some Comparative Considerations," *American Anthropologists*, 61 (August 1959), pp. 647–651.

[4] David F. Aberle *et al.*, "The Functional Prerequisites of a Society," *Ethics*, 60 (January 1950), pp. 100–111.

[5] *Ibid.*

not whether these four functions are functional prerequisites of human society—almost all social scientists would accept this—but whether these four functions are necessarily carried out by the nuclear family. If these functions are not everywhere carried out by the nuclear family, then are there any functional prerequisites of society which the nuclear family or any family form does fulfill? Is the family a universal institution in the sense that it always fulfills some functional prerequisite of society? Also, what, if any, are the universal structural features of the family? These are the ultimate questions of importance that this examination of Murdock's position is moving toward.

Murdock's contention that the nuclear family is a structural prerequisite of human society since it fulfills four functional prerequisites of human society is relatively easy to test. If a structure is essential, then finding one society where the structure does not exist or where one or more of the four functions are not fulfilled by this structure is sufficient to refute the theory. Thus, a crucial test could best be made by focusing on societies with rather atypical family systems to see whether the nuclear family was present and was fulfilling these four functions. The more typical family systems will also be discussed. A proper test can be made by using only groups which are societies. This limitation is necessary so as not to test Murdock unfairly with such subsocietal groups as celibate priests. For purposes of this paper, the author accepts that definition of society developed by Aberle and his associates:

A society is a group of human beings sharing a self-sufficient system of action which is capable of existing longer than the life-span of an individual, the group being recruited at least in part by the sexual reproduction of the members.[6]

A TEST OF MURDOCK'S THESIS

One of the cultures chosen for the test of Murdock's thesis is from his own original sample of 250 cultures—the Nayar of the Malabar Coast of India. In his book, Murdock rejected Ralph Linton's view that the Nayar lacked the nuclear family.[7] Since that time, the work of Kathleen Gough has supported Linton's position, and Murdock has accordingly changed his own position.[8] In letters to the author dated April 3, 1963 and January 20, 1964, Murdock took the position that the Nayar are merely the old Warrior Caste of the Kerala Society and thus not a total society and are more comparable to a celibate

6 *Ibid.*, p. 101.

7 Murdock, *op. cit.*, p. 3.

8 For a brief account of the Nayar, see: E. Kathleen Gough, "Is the Family Universal: The Nayar Case," pp. 76–92 in *A Modern Introduction to the Family, op. cit.* It is interesting to note that Bell and Vogel, in their preface to Gough's article on the Nayar, contend that she supports Murdock's position on the universality of the nuclear family. In point of fact, Gough on page 84 rejects Murdock and actually deals primarily with the marital and not the family institution. See also: *Matrilineal Kinship*, ed. by David M. Schneider and Kathleen Gough, Berkeley: U. of California Press, 1961, Chaps. 6 and 7. A. R. Radcliffe-Brown was one of the first to note that the Nayar lacked the nuclear family. See his: *African Systems of Kinship and Marriage*, New York: Oxford U. Press, 1959, p. 73.

group of priests. No such doubt about the societal status of the Nayar can be found in his book. Murdock rejects the Nayar only after he is forced to admit that they lack the nuclear family. In terms of the definition of society adopted above, the Nayar seem to be a society even if they, like many other societies, do have close connections with other groups.

The matrilineage is particularly strong among the Nayar, and a mother with the help of her matrilineage brings up her children. Her husband and "lovers" do not assist her in the raising of her children. Her brother typically assists her when male assistance is needed. Assistance from the linked lineages where most of her lovers come from also substitutes for the weak husband role. Since many Nayar women change lovers rather frequently, there may not even be any very stable male-female relation present. The male is frequently away fighting. The male makes it physiologically possible for the female to have offspring, but he is not an essential part of the family unit that will raise his biological children. In this sense, sex and reproduction are somewhat external to the family unit among the Nayar. Very little in the way of economic cooperation between husband and wife occurs. Thus, virtually all of Murdock's functions are outside of the nuclear family. However, it should be noted that the socialization of offspring function is present in the maternal extended family system. Here, then, is a society that seems to lack the nuclear family and, of necessity, therefore, the four functions of this unit. Even if we accept Gough's view that the "lovers" are husbands and that there really is a form of group marriage, it is still apparent that the separate husband-wife-child units formed by such a group marriage do not here comprise separately functioning nuclear families.

One does not have to rely on just the Nayar as a test of Murdock. Harold E. Driver, in his study of North American Indians, concludes that in matrilocal extended family systems with matrilineal descent, the husband role and the nuclear family are often insignificant.[9] It therefore seems that the relative absence of the nuclear family in the Nayar is approached particularly in other similar matrilineal societies. Thus, the Nayar do not seem to be so unique. They apparently demonstrate a type of family system that is common in lesser degree.

A somewhat similar situation seems to occur in many parts of the Caribbean. Judith Blake described a matrifocal family structure in which the husband and father role are quite often absent or seriously modified.[10] Sexual relations are often performed with transitory males who have little relation to the raising of the resultant offspring. Thus, in Jamaica one can also question whether the nuclear family exists and performs the four functions Murdock ascribed to it. Socialization of offspring is often performed by the mother's family without any husband, common law or legal, being present. Naturally, if the husband is absent, the economic cooperation between husband and wife cannot occur.

[9] Harold H. Driver, *Indians of North America*, Chicago: U. of Chicago Press, 1961, pp. 291–292.

[10] Judith Blake, *Family Structure in Jamaica*, Glencoe, Ill.: Free Press, 1961. Whether Jamaicans actually prefer to marry and have a more typical family system is a controversial point.

Also, if the male involved is not the husband but a short-term partner, sex and reproduction are also occurring outside the nuclear family.

The above societies are all "mother-centered" systems. A family system which is not mother-centered is the Israeli Kibbutz family system as described by Melford Spiro.[11] Here the husband and wife live together in a communal agricultural society. The children are raised communally and do not live with their parents. Although the Kibbutzim are only a small part of the total Israeli culture, they have a distinct culture and can be considered a separate society by the Aberle definition cited above. They have been in existence since 1909 and thus have shown that they can survive for several generations and that they have a self-sufficient system of action. The function which is most clearly missing in the Kibbutz family is that of economic cooperation between husband and wife. In this communal society, almost all work is done for the total Kibbutz, and the rewards are relatively equally distributed regardless of whether one is married or not. There is practically no division of labor between husbands and wives as such. Meals are eaten communally, and residence in one room which requires little in the way of housekeeping.

Here, too, Murdock denies that this is a real exception and, in the letters to the author referred to above, contends that the Kibbutzim could not be considered a society. Murdock's objection notwithstanding, a group which has existed for over half a century and has developed a self-sufficient system of action covering all major aspects of existence indeed seems to be a society by almost all definitions. There is nothing in the experience of the Kibbutzim that makes it difficult to conceive of such groups existing in many regions of the world or, for that matter, existing by themselves in a world devoid of other people. They are analogous to some of the Indian groups living in American society in the sense that they have a coherent way of life that differs considerably from the dominant culture. Thus, they are not the same as an average community which is merely a part of the dominant culture.

Melford Spiro concludes that Murdock's nuclear family is not present in the Kibbutz he and his wife studied. He suggests several alterations in Murdock's definition which would be required to make it better fit the Kibbutz. The alterations are rather drastic and would still not fit the Nayar and other cultures discussed above.[12]

There are other societies that are less extreme but which still create some difficulty with Murdock's definition of the nuclear family. Malinowski, in his

---

[11] Melford E. Spiro, *Kibbutz: Venture in Utopia*, Cambridge, Mass.: Harvard U. Press, 1956; and Melford E. Spiro, *Children of the Kibbutz*, Cambridge, Mass.: Harvard U. Press, 1958.

[12] Spiro suggests that "reference residence" be used in place of actual common residence. The Kibbutz children do speak of their parents' room as "home." He suggests further that responsibility for education and economic cooperation be substituted for the actual doing of these functions by the parents. The parents could be viewed as responsible for the education of their children, but since nothing changes in economic terms when one marries, it is difficult to understand just what Spiro means by responsibility for economic cooperation being part of the family. Spiro also would alter Murdock's definition of marriage so as to make emotional intimacy the key element.

study of the Trobriand Islanders, reports that except for perhaps nurturant socialization, the mother's brother rather than the father is the male who teaches the offspring much of the necessary way of life of the group.[13] Such a situation is certainly common in a matrilineal society, and it does place limits on the socialization function of the nuclear family *per se*. Further, one must at least qualify the economic function in the Trobriand case. The mother's brother here takes a large share of the economic burden and supplies his sister's family with half the food they require. The rigidity of Murdock's definition in light of such instances is apparent. These examples also make it reasonable that other societies may well exist which carry a little further such modifications of the nuclear family. For example, we find such more extreme societies when we look at the Nayar and the Kibbutz.

Some writers, like Nicholas Timasheff, have argued that the Russian experience with the family evidences the universality of the nuclear family.[14] While it is true that the Communists in Russia failed to abolish as much of the old family system as they wanted to, it does not follow that this demonstrates the impossibility of abolishing the family.[15] In point of fact, the family system of the Israeli Kibbutz is virtually identical with the system the Russian Communists desired, and thus we must admit that it is possible for at least some groups to achieve such a system. Also, the Communists did not want to do away with the family *in toto*. Rather, they wanted to do away with the patriarchal aspects of the family, to have marriage based on love, easy divorce, and communal upbringing of children. They ceased in much of this effort during the 1930's when a falling birth rate, rising delinquency and divorce rates, and the depression caused them to question the wisdom of their endeavors. However, it has never been demonstrated that these symptoms were consequences of the efforts to change the family. They may well have simply been results of a rapidly changing social order that would have occurred regardless of the family program. Therefore, the Russian experience is really not evidence pro or con Murdock's position.

The Chinese society deserves some brief mention here. Marion Levy contends that this is an exception to Murdock's thesis because in the extended Chinese family, the nuclear family was a rather unimportant unit, and it was the patrilineal extended family which performed the key functions of which Murdock

[13] Bronislaw Malinowski, *The Sexual Life of Savages in North-Western Melanesia*, New York: Harvest Books, 1929.

[14] Nicholas S. Timasheff, "The Attempt to Abolish the Family in Russia," pp. 55–63 in Bell and Vogel, *op. cit.*

[15] Timasheff refers to the family as "that pillar of society." But nothing in the way of convincing evidence is presented to support this view. The argument is largely that since disorganization followed the attempt to do away with the family, it was a result of that attempt. This may well be an example of a *post hoc ergo propter hoc* fallacy. Also, it should be noted that the love-based union of parents that the early communists wanted might well be called a family, and thus that the very title of Timasheff's article implies a rather narrow image of the family. For a recent account of the Soviet family see: David and Vera Mace, *The Soviet Family*, New York: Doubleday, 1963; and Ray Bauer *et. al.*, *How the Soviet System Works*, Cambridge, Mass.: Harvard U. Press, 1959.

speaks.[16] Regarding present day Communist China, it should be noted that the popular reports to the effect that the Chinese Communes either aimed at or actually did do away with the nuclear family are not supported by evidence. The best information indicates that the Chinese Communists never intended to do away with the nuclear family as such; rather, what they wanted was the typical communist family system which the Israeli Kibbutzim possess.[17] The Communists in China did not intend to do away with the identification of a child with a particular set of parents or vice-versa. If the Israeli Kibbutz is any indication, it would seem that a communal upbringing system goes quite well with a strong emphasis on affectionate ties between parent and child.[18] However, it is well to note that the type of communal family system toward which the Chinese are striving and have to some extent already achieved, clashes with Murdock's conception of the nuclear family and its functions in just the same way as the Kibbutz family does.

Overall, it appears that a reasonable man looking at the evidence presented above would conclude that Murdock's position is seriously in doubt. As Levy and Fallers have said, Murdock's approach is too simplistic in viewing a particular structure such as the nuclear family as always, in all cultural contexts, having the same four functions.[19] Robert Merton has said that such a view of a very specific structure as indispensable involves the erroneous "postulate of indispensability."[20] Certainly it seems rather rash to say that one very specific social structure such as the nuclear family will always have the same consequences regardless of the context in which it is placed. Surely this is not true of specific structures in other institutions such as the political, religious, or economic. The consequences of a particular social structure vary with the socio-cultural context of that structure. Accordingly, a democratic bicameral legislative structure in a new African nation will function differently than in America; the Reform Jewish Denomination has different consequences in Israel than in America; government control of the economy functions differently in England than in Russia.

The remarkable thing about the family institution is that in so many diverse contexts, one can find such similar structures and functions. To this extent, Murdock has made his point and has demonstrated that the nuclear family with these four functions is a surprisingly common social fact. But this is quite different from demonstrating that this is always the case or necessarily the case. It should be perfectly clear that the author feels Murdock's work has contributed greatly to the advancement of our knowledge of the family. Murdock is used

[16] Levy and Fallers, *op. cit.*, pp. 649–650.

[17] Felix Greene, *Awakened China*, New York: Doubleday, 1961, esp. pp. 142–144. Philip Jones and Thomas Poleman, "Communes and the Agricultural Crises in Communist China," *Food Research Institute Studies*, 3 (February 1962), pp. 1–22. Maurice Freedman, "The Family in China, Past and Present," *Pacific Affairs*, 34 (Winter 1961–2), pp. 323–336.

[18] Spiro, *op. cit.*

[19] Levy and Fallers, *op. cit.*

[20] Robert K. Merton, *Social Theory and Social Structure*, Glencoe, Ill.: Free Press, 1957, p. 32.

here because he is the best known proponent of the view being examined, not because he should be particularly criticized.

A safer approach to take toward the family is to look for functional pre-requisites of society which the family fulfills and search for the full range of structures which may fulfill these functional prerequisites. At this stage of our knowledge, it seems more valuable to talk of the whole range of family structures and to seek for a common function that is performed and that may be essential to human society. What we need now is a broad, basic, parsimonious definition that would have utility in both single and cross-cultural comparisons.[21] We have a good deal of empirical data on family systems and a variety of definitions —it is time we strove for a universal definition that would clarify the essential features of this institution and help us locate the family in any cultural setting.

Looking over the four functions that Murdock associates with the nuclear family, one sees that three of them can be found to be absent in some cultures. The Nayar perhaps best illustrate the possibility of placing sex and reproduction outside the nuclear family. Also, it certainly seems within the realm of possibility that a "Brave New World" type of society could operate by scientifically mating sperm and egg and presenting married couples with state-produced offspring of certain types when they desired children.[22] Furthermore, the raising of children by other than their biological parents is widespread in many societies where adoption and rearing by friends and relatives is common.[23] Thus, it seems that sex and reproduction may not be inexorably tied to the nuclear family.[24]

The third function of Murdock's which seems possible to take out of the nuclear family is that of economic cooperation. The Kibbutz is the prime example of this. Furthermore, it seems that many other communal-type societies approximate the situation in the Kibbutz.

The fourth function is that of socialization. Many aspects of this function have been taken away from the family in various societies. For example, the Kibbutz parents, according to Spiro, are not so heavily involved in the inculcation

---

[21] Zelditch attempted to see if the husband-wife roles would be differentiated in the same way in all cultures, with males being instrumental and females expressive. He found general support, but some exceptions were noted, particularly in societies wherein the nuclear family was embedded in a larger kinship system. Morris Zelditch, Jr., "Role Differentiation in the Nuclear Family: A Comparative Study," in Parsons and Bales, *op. cit.* The Kibbutz would represent another exception since both mother and father play expressive roles in relation to their offspring.

[22] Aldous Huxley, *Brave New World*, New York: Harper & Bros., 1950.

[23] See: *Six Cultures: Studies in Child Rearing*, ed. by Beatrice B. Whiting, New York: John Wiley, 1963. Margaret Mead reports exchange of children in *Coming of Age in Samoa*, New York: Mentor Books, 1949. Similar customs in Puerto Rico are reported in David Landy, *Tropical Childhood*, Chapel Hill: U. of North Carolina Press, 1959.

[24] Robert Winch, in his recent textbook, defines the family as a nuclear family with the basic function of "the replacement of dying members." In line with the present author's arguments, it seems that the actual biological production of infants can be removed from the family. In fact, Winch agrees that the Nayar lack the family as he defined it because they lack a permanent father role in the nuclear family. See: *The Modern Family*, New York: Holt, 1963, pp. 16, 31, and 750.

of values or the disciplinary and caretaking aspects of socialization. Nevertheless, the Kibbutz parents are heavily involved in nurturant socialization, i.e., the giving of positive emotional response to infants and young children. A recent book by Stephens also reports a seemingly universal presence of nurturance of infants.[25] It should be emphasized that this paper uses "nurturance" to mean not the physical, but the emotional care of the infant. Clearly, the two are not fully separable. This use of the term nurturant is similar to what is meant by "expressive" role.[26] Interestingly enough, in the Kibbutz both the mother and father are equally involved in giving their children nurturant socialization. All of the societies referred to above have a family institution with the function of nurturant socialization of children. This was true even for the extreme case of the Nayar.

The conception of the family institution being developed here has in common with some other family definitions an emphasis on socialization of offspring. The difference is that all other functions have been ruled out as unessential and that only the nurturant type of socialization is the universal function of the family institution. This paper presents empirical evidence to support its contention. It is important to be more specific than were Levy and Fallers regarding the type of socialization the family achieves since all societies have socialization occurring outside the family as well as within. It should be noted that this author, unlike Murdock, is talking of *any* form of family institution and not just the nuclear family.

As far as a universal structure of the family to fulfill the function of nurturant socialization is concerned, it seems possible to set only very broad limits, and even these involve some speculation. First, it may be said that the structure of the family will always be that of a primary group. Basically, this position rests on the assumption that nurturant socialization is a process which cannot be adequately carried out in an impersonal setting and which thus requires a primary type of relation.[27] The author would not specify the biological mother as the socializer or even a female, or even more than one person or the age of the person. If one is trying to state what the family must be like in a minimal sense in any society—what its universally required structure and function is— one cannot be too specific. However, we can go one step farther in specifying the structure of the family group we are defining. The family is here viewed as an institution, as an integrated set of norms and relationships which are socially defined and internalized by the members of a society. In every society in the world, the institutional structure which contains the roles related to the nurturant function is a small kinship structured group.[28] Thus, we can say that the primary group which fulfills the nurturant function is a kinship

[25] William N. Stephens, *The Family in Cross Cultural Perspective*, New York: Holt, Rinehart & Winston, 1963, p. 357. Stephens discusses the universality of the family in this book but does not take a definite position on the issue. See Chapter 1.

[26] Zelditch, *op. cit.*, pp. 307–353.

[27] The key importance of primary groups was long ago pointed out by Charles Horton Cooley, *Social Organization*, New York: Scribner's, 1929.

[28] The structural definition is similar to Levy and Fallers, *op. cit.*

structure. Kinship refers to descent—it involves rights of possession among those who are kin. It is a geneological reckoning, and people with real or fictive biological connections are kin.[29]

This specification of structure helps to distinguish from the family institution those nonkin primary groups that may in a few instances perform nurturant functions. For example, a nurse-child relation or a governess-child relation could, if carried far enough, involve the bulk of nurturant socialization for that child. But such a relationship would be a quasi-family at best, for it clearly is not part of the kinship structure. There are no rights of "possession" given to the nurse or the child in such cases, and there is no socially accepted, institutionalized, system of child-rearing involving nurses and children. In addition, such supervisory help usually assumes more of a caretaking and disciplinary aspect, with the parents themselves still maintaining the nurturant relation.

Talcott Parsons has argued, in agreement with the author's position, that on a societal level, only kinship groups can perform the socialization function.[30] He believes that socialization in a kin group predisposes the child to assume marital and parental roles himself when he matures and affords a needed stable setting for socialization. Clearly other groups may at times perform part of the nurturant function. No institution in human society has an exclusive franchise on its characteristic function. However, no society exists in which any group other than a kinship group performs the dominant share of the nurturant function. Even in the Israeli Kibbutz with communal upbringing, it is the parents who dominate in this area.

Should a society develop wherein nonkin primary groups became the predominant means of raising children, the author would argue that these nonkin groups would tend to evolve in the direction of becoming kin groups. The primary quality of the adult-child relation would encourage the notion of descent and possession. Kin groups would evolve as roles and statuses in the nonkin system became defined in terms of accepted male-female and adult-child relationships and thereby became institutionalized. Once these nonkin groups had institutionalized their sex roles and adult-child (descent) roles, we would in effect have a kinship-type system, for kinship results from the recognition of a social relationship between "parents" and children. It seems that there would be much pressure toward institutionalization of roles in any primary group child-rearing system, if for no other reason than clarity and efficiency. The failure of any one generation to supply adequate role models and adequate nurturance means that the next generation will not know these skills, and persistence of such a society is questionable. The importance of this task makes institutionalization quite likely and kinship groups quite essential. To avoid kinship groups, it seems that children would have to be nurtured in a formal secondary group setting. The author will present evidence below for his belief that the raising of children in a secondary group setting is unworkable.

[29] Radcliffe-Brown, *op. cit.*
[30] Parsons, *op. cit.*

In summation then, following is the universal definition of the family institution: *The family institution is a small kinship structured group with the key function of nurturant socialization of the newborn.* How many years such nurturant socialization must last is hard to specify. There are numerous societies in which children six or seven years old are given a good deal of responsibility in terms of care of other children and other tasks. It seems that childhood in the West has been greatly extended to older ages in recent centuries.[31] The proposed definition focuses on what are assumed to be the structural and functional prerequisites of society which the family institution fulfills. The precise structure of the kinship group can vary quite radically among societies, and even within one society it may well be that more than one small kinship group will be involved in nurturant socialization. The definition seeks to avoid the "error" of posting the indispensability of any *particular* family form by this approach. Rather, it says that any type of kinship group can achieve this function and that the limitation is merely that it be a kinship group. This degree of specification helps one delimit and identify the institution which one is describing. Some writers have spelled out more specifically the key structural forms in this area.[32] Adams has posited two key dyads: the maternal dyad and the conjugal dyad. When these two join, a nuclear family is formed, but these dyads are, Adams believes, more fundamental than the nuclear family.

There are always other functions besides nurturant socialization performed by the kinship group. Murdock's four functions are certainly quite frequently performed by some type of family group, although often not by the nuclear family. In addition, there are some linkages between the family kinship group and a larger kinship system. But this is not the place to pursue these interconnections. Instead, an examination follows of evidence relevant to this proposed universal definition of the family institution.

EVIDENCE ON REVISED CONCEPTION

The evidence to be examined here relates to the question of whether the definition proposed actually fits all human family institutions. Three types of evidence are relevant to test the universality of the proposed definition of the family. The first source of evidence comes from a cross-cultural examination such as that of this article. All of the cultures that were discussed were fulfilling the proposed functional prerequisite of nurturant socialization, and they all had some sort of small kinship group structure to accomplish nurturant socialization. The author also examined numerous reports on other cultures and found no exception to the proposed definition. Of course, other functions of these family groups were present in all instances, but no other specific universally present functions appeared. However, the author hesitates to say that these

[31] Phillippe Aries, *Centuries of Childhood*, New York: Alfred A. Knopf, 1962.
[32] Richard N. Adams, "An Inquiry into the Nature of the Family," pp. 30–49 in *Essays in the Science of Culture in Honor of Leslie A. White*, ed. by Gertrude E. Dole and Robert L. Carneiro, New York: Thomas Y. Crowell, 1960.

data confirm his position because it is quite possible that such a cross-cultural examination will reveal some function or structure to be universally *present* but still not universally *required*. Rather, it could merely be universally present by chance or because it is difficult but not impossible to do away with. As an example of this, one may cite the incest taboo. The evidence recently presented by Russell Middleton on incest among commoners in Ptolemaic Egypt throws doubt on the thesis that incest taboos are functional prerequisites of human society.[33] We need some concept of functional "importance," for surely the incest taboo has great functional importance even if it is not a prerequisite of society. The same may be true of the functional importance of Murdock's view of the nuclear family.

If being universally present is but a necessary and not a sufficient condition for a functional prerequisite of society, then it is important to present other evidence. One source of such evidence lies in the studies of rhesus monkeys done by Harry Harlow.[34] Harlow separated monkeys from their natural mothers and raised them with surrogate "cloth" and "wire" mother dolls. In some trials, the wire mother surrogate was equipped with milk while the cloth mother was not. Even so, the monkeys preferred the cloth mother to the wire mother in several ways. The monkeys showed their preference by running more to the cloth mother when threatened and by exerting themselves more to press a lever to see her. Thus, it seemed that the monkeys "loved" the cloth mother more than the wire mother. This was supposedly due to the softer contact and comfort afforded by the cloth mother. One might speculatively argue that the contact desire of the monkeys is indicative of at least a passive, rudimentary nurturance need. Yerkes has also reported similar "needs" in his study of chimpanzees.[35]

Further investigation of these monkeys revealed some important findings. The monkeys raised by the surrogate mothers became emotionally disturbed and were unable to relate to other monkeys or to have sexual relations. This result was produced irreversibly in about six months. One could interpret this to mean that the surrogate mothers, both cloth and wire, were inadequate in that they gave no emotional response to the infant monkeys. Although contact with the cloth mother seemed important, response seemingly was even more important. Those laboratory-raised females who did become pregnant became very ineffective mothers and were lacking in ability to give nurturance.

Harlow found that when monkeys were raised without mothers but with siblings present, the results were quite different. To date, these monkeys have

[33] Russell Middleton, "Brother-Sister and Father-Daughter Marriage in Ancient Egypt," *American Sociological Review*, 27 (October 1962), pp. 603–611.

[34] See the following articles, all by Harry F. Harlow: "The Nature of Love," *American Psychologist*, 13 (December 1958), pp. 673–685; "The Heterosexual Affection System in Monkeys," *American Psychologist*, 17 (January 1962), pp. 1–9; (with Margaret K. Harlow), "Social Deprivation in Monkeys," *Scientific American*, 206 (November 1962), pp. 1–10.

[35] Robert M. Yerkes, *Chimpanzees*, New Haven: Yale U. Press, 1943, esp. pp. 43, 68, 257–258; and Robert M. Yerkes and Ada W. Yerkes, *The Great Apes*, New Haven: Yale U. Press, 1929, passim.

shown emotional stability and sexual competence. In growing up, they clung to each other just as the other monkeys had clung to the cloth mother, but in addition they were able to obtain the type of emotional response or nurturance from each other which they needed.

Harlow's evidence on monkeys is surely not conclusive evidence for the thesis that nurturant socialization is a fundamental prerequisite of human society. There is need for much more precise testing and evidence on both human and nonhuman groups. Despite the fact that human beings and monkeys are both primates, there is quite a bit of difference in human and monkey infants. For one thing, the human infant is far more helpless and far less aware of its environment during the first few months of its life. Thus, it is doubtful if placing a group of helpless, relatively unaware human infants together would produce the same results as occurred when monkeys were raised with siblings. The human infant requires someone older and more aware of the environment to be present. In a very real sense, it seems that the existence of human society is testimony to the concern of humans for each other. Unless older humans care for the newborn, the society will cease to exist. Every adult member of society is alive only because some other member of society took the time and effort to raise him. One may argue that this care need be only minimal and of a physical nature, e.g., food, clothing, and shelter. The author believes that such minimal care is insufficient for societal survival and will try to present additional evidence here to bear this out.

One type of evidence that is relevant concerns the effect of maternal separation or institutional upbringing on human infants. To afford a precise test, we should look for a situation in which nurturant socialization was quite low or absent. Although the Kibbutzim have institutional upbringing, the Kibbutz parents and children are very much emotionally attached to each other. In fact, both the mother and father have expressive roles in the Kibbutz family, and there is a strong emphasis on parent-child relations of a nurturant sort in the few hours a day the family is together.

A better place to look would be at studies of children who were raised in formal institutions or who were in other ways separated from their mothers. Leon J. Yarrow has recently published an excellent summary of over one hundred such studies.[36] For over 50 years now, there have been reports supporting the view that maternal separation has deleterious effects on the child. The first such reports came from pediatricians pointing out physical and psychological deterioration in hospitalized infants. In 1951, Bowlby reviewed the literature in this area for the World Health Organization and arrived at similar conclusions.[37] More recent and careful studies have made us aware of the importance of distinguishing the effects of maternal separation from the effects of

---

[36] Leon J. Yarrow, "Separation from Parents During Early Childhood," pp. 89–136 in *Review of Child Development*, ed. by Martin L. Hoffman and Lois W. Hoffman, New York: Russell Sage Foundation, 1964, Vol. 1.

[37] John Bowlby, *Maternal Care and Mental Health*, Geneva: World Health Organization, 1951.

institutionalization. Certainly the type of institutional care afforded the child is quite important. Further, the previous relation of the child with the mother before institutionalization and the age of the child are important variables. In addition, one must look at the length of time separation endured and whether there were reunions with the mother at a later date. Yarrow's view is that while there is this tendency toward disturbance in mother separation, the occurrence can best be understood when we learn more about the precise conditions under which it occurs and cease to think of it as inevitable under any conditions. In this regard, recent evidence shows that children separated from mothers with whom they had poor relationships displayed less disturbance than other children. Further, infants who were provided with adequate mother-substitutes of a personal sort showed much less severe reactions. In line with the findings on the Kibbutz, children who were in an all-day nursery gave no evidence of serious disturbance.

Many studies in the area of institutionalization show the importance of the structural characteristics of the institutional environment. When care is impersonal and inadequate, there is evidence of language retardation, impairment of motor functions, and limited emotional responses toward other people and objects.[38] Interestingly, the same types of characteristics are found among children living in deprived family environments.[39] One of the key factors in avoiding such negative results is the presence of a stable mother-figure in the institution for the child. Individualized care and attention seem to be capable of reversing or preventing the impairments mentioned. Without such care, there is evidence that ability to form close interpersonal relations later in life is greatly weakened.[40] As Yarrow concludes in his review of this area:

> It is clear from the studies on institutionalization that permanent intellectual and personality damage may be avoided if following separation there is a substitute mother-figure who develops a personalized relationship with the child and who responds sensitively to his individualized needs.[41]

The evidence in this area indicates that some sort of emotionally nurturant relationship between the child in the first few years of life and some other individual is rather vital in the child's development. Disease and death rates have been reported to rise sharply in children deprived of nurturance. The author is not rash enough to take this evidence as conclusive support for his contention that nurturant socialization is a functional prerequisite of human society which the family performs. Nevertheless, he does believe this evidence lends some support to this thesis and thows doubt on the survival of a society that rears its children without nurturance. In addition, it seems to support the position that some sort of kin-type group relationship is the structural prerequisite of the nurturant function. Indeed, it seemed that the closer the institution approximated a stable, personal kinship type of relationship of the child and a nurse, the more

[38] Yarrow, *op. cit.*, p. 100.
[39] *Ibid.*, p. 101–102.
[40] *Ibid.*, p. 106.
[41] *Ibid.*, pp. 124–125.

successful it was in achieving emotional nurturance and avoiding impairments of functions.

SUMMARY

A check of several cultures revealed that the four nuclear family functions that Murdock states are universally present were often missing. The nuclear family itself seems either absent or unimportant in some cultures. An alternate definition of the family in terms of one functional prerequisite of human society and in terms of a broad structural prerequisite was put forth. The family was defined as a small kinship structured group with the key function of nurturant socialization of the newborn. The nurturant function directly supports the personality system and enables the individual to become a contributing member of society. Thus, by making adult role performance possible, nurturant socialization becomes a functional prerequisite of society.

Three sources of evidence were examined: (1) cross-cultural data, (2) studies of other primates, and (3) studies of effects on children of maternal separation. Although the evidence did tend to fit with and support the universality of the new definition, it must be noted that much more support is needed before any firm conclusion can be reached. . . .

The National Divorce Trend

ALEXANDER A. PLATERIS

. . . The national divorce total of 428,000 for 1963 was the highest annual number ever observed, except for the years 1945–47 when the post-World War II divorce peak occurred. The 1963 total represents an increase of 3.6 percent over the figure for 1962 and an increase of 8.9 percent over that for 1960. The 1963 divorce rate of 2.3 per 1,000 population was much lower than that for the early postwar years, when the maximum rate of 4.3 was observed in 1946. The 1963 rate is close to the levels observed since 1955.

The trend of the divorce rate since 1867, the first year for which this rate was computed, showed a long-term increase that lasted 80 years, reaching a record peak in 1946. During this period, the rate increased from 0.3 to 4.3 per 1,000 total population. The trend was accelerated by wars and reversed by economic depressions. During the 44 years shown in Table 1 and Figure 1, the rate first declined from the slight post-World War I peak, then resumed its upward trend (which was interrupted by the great depression), and almost doubled during the war and early postwar years—from 2.2 in 1941 to 4.3 in 1946. It declined rapidly afterwards, going back to 2.2 in 1957; since then it has remained approximately

Reprinted from *Divorce Statistics Analysis, United States—1963* by Alexander Plateris. Published October, 1967, by National Center for Health Statistics.

TABLE 1. Estimated Number of Divorces and Annulments and Rates, with Percent Changes from Preceding Year: United States, 1920–63*

Year	Number	Percent Change in Number	Rate per 1,000 Total Population[1]	Percent Change in Rate	Rate per 1,000 Married Female Population 15+ Years[2]	Percent Change in Rate
1963	428,000	+3.6	2.3	+4.5	9.6	+2.1
1962	413,000	−0.2	2.2	−4.3	9.4	−2.1
1961	414,000	+5.3	2.3	+4.5	9.6	+4.3
1960	393,000	−0.5	2.2	−	9.2	−1.1
1959	395,000	+7.3	2.2	+4.8	9.3	+4.5
1958	368,000	−3.4	2.1	−4.5	8.9	−3.3
1957	381,000	−0.3	2.2	−4.3	9.2	−2.1
1956	382,000	+1.3	2.3	−	9.4	+1.1
1955	377,000	−0.5	2.3	−4.2	9.3	−2.1
1954	379,000	−2.8	2.4	−4.0	9.5	−4.0
1953	390,000	−0.5	2.5	−	9.9	−2.0
1952	392,000	+2.9	2.5	−	10.1	+2.0
1951	381,000	−1.1	2.5	−3.8	9.9	−3.9
1950	385,144	−3.0	2.6	−3.7	10.3	−2.8
1949	397,000	−2.7	2.7	−3.6	10.6	−5.4
1948	408,000	−15.5	2.8	−17.6	11.2	−17.6
1947	483,000	−20.8	3.4	−20.9	13.6	−24.0
1946	610,000	+25.8	4.3	+22.9	17.9	+24.3
1945	485,000	+21.3	3.5	+20.7	14.4	+20.0
1944	400,000	+11.4	2.9	+11.5	12.0	+9.1
1943	359,000	+11.8	2.6	+8.3	11.0	+8.9
1942	321,000	+9.6	2.4	+9.1	10.1	+7.4
1941	293,000	+11.0	2.2	+10.0	9.4	+6.8
1940	264,000	+5.2	2.0	+5.3	8.8	+3.5
1939	251,000	+2.9	1.9	−	8.5	+1.2
1938	244,000	−2.0	1.9	−	8.4	−3.4
1937	249,000	+5.5	1.9	+5.6	8.7	+4.8
1936	236,000	+8.3	1.8	+5.9	8.3	+6.4
1935	218,000	+6.9	1.7	+6.3	7.8	+4.0
1934	204,000	+23.6	1.6	+23.1	7.5	+23.0
1933	165,000	+0.6	1.3	−	6.1	−
1932	164,241	−12.6	1.3	−13.3	6.1	−14.1
1931	188,003	−4.1	1.5	−6.2	7.1	−5.3
1930	195,961	−4.8	1.6	−5.9	7.5	−6.2
1929	205,876	+2.8	1.7	−	8.0	+2.6
1928	200,176	+2.0	1.7	+6.3	7.8	−
1927	196,292	+6.3	1.6	−	7.8	+4.0
1926	184,678	+5.3	1.6	+6.7	7.5	+4.2
1925	175,449	+2.6	1.5	−	7.2	−
1924	170,952	+3.5	1.5	−	7.2	+1.4
1923	165,096	+10.9	1.5	+7.1	7.1	+7.6
1922	148,815	−6.7	1.4	−6.7	6.6	−8.3
1921	159,580	−6.4	1.5	−6.2	7.2	−10.0
1920	170,505	+20.5	1.6	+23.1	8.0	−

* [Data refer only to events occurring within the United States. Includes Alaska beginning 1959, and Hawaii, 1960.]

[1] Population enumerated as of April 1 for 1940, 1950, and 1960, and estimated as of July 1 for all other years; includes Armed Forces abroad for 1941–46.

[2] Population enumerated as of January 1 for 1920 and as of April 1 for 1930, 1940, 1950, and 1960 and estimated as of July 1 for all other years.

at the same level. At the present moment it is too early to say whether the slight increases of the rate in 1961 and 1963 indicate the beginning of a new period of growth, but the provisional estimates of the national divorce totals for 1964 and 1965 (445,000 and 481,000, respectively, or 2.3 and 2.5 per 1,000 population) suggest that the upward trend may have resumed.

The crude divorce rate, computed for the total population, depends in part on the proportion of married persons in the population, as married persons only are subject to the risk of divorce. Therefore the divorce rate per 1,000 married women is a more refined measure of the incidence of divorce (Table 3). The divorce rate per 1,000 married women was 9.6 in 1963—slightly higher than the 1962 rate of 9.4, equal to the 1961 rate, and higher than the rates for all years from 1954 to 1960. These differences indicate that the increase in the number of divorces was partially due to reasons other than the growth of the married population. This statement can also be illustrated by ratios of the population to divorce: in 1963 a divorce was granted to 1 of every 104 married women, in 1962 to 1 of every 106, and in 1960 to 1 of every 109.

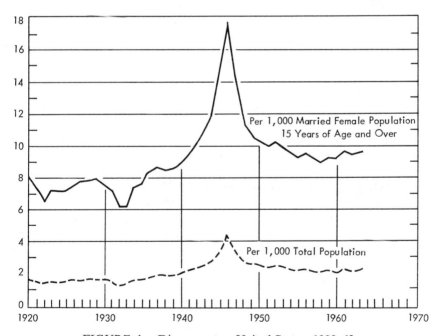

FIGURE 1. Divorce rates: United States, 1920–63.

Inasmuch as the number of persons divorced is twice the number of divorces granted, 856,000 persons were divorced in 1963. In addition, 583,000 children of divorced couples were involved in divorce cases. This brings the total number of persons involved in divorce to 1,439,000. The involvement rate was 7.6 per 1,000 population. Analogous figures for other years are shown in Table 2.

TABLE 2. NUMBER OF HUSBANDS, WIVES, AND CHILDREN INVOLVED IN DIVORCE AND RATES PER 1,000 TOTAL POPULATION, WITH PERCENT CHANGE FROM PRECEDING YEAR: UNITED STATES, 1953-63

Year	Total Involved	Percent Change	Rate
1963	1,439,000	+5.6	7.6
1962	1,363,000	+2.6	7.3
1961	1,329,000	+6.4	7.3
1960	1,249,000	−0.7	7.0
1959	1,258,000	+10.9	7.1
1958	1,134,000	−0.6	6.5
1957	1,141,000	+1.4	6.7
1956	1,125,000	+2.2	6.7
1955	1,101,000	+0.2	6.7
1954	1,099,000	−1.0	6.8
1953	1,110,000	−	7.0

INTERNATIONAL COMPARISONS

Almost all countries report their annual divorce totals and rates to the Statistical Office of the United Nations, and these data are published annually in the *Demographic Yearbook*. Twelve countries and dependencies whose laws do not provide legal means for the dissolution of legitimate marriages are Argentina, Brazil, Chile, Columbia, Ireland, Italy, Malta, Paraguay, Peru, the Phillippines, Santa Lucia, and Spain. Some annulments may have been granted in these countries, but they were not reported.

Table 3 shows the official divorce rates for other selected countries. These were listed according to the level of their latest divorce rate. In 1963 the United States had the highest crude rate among the reporting sovereign countries, but in 1960 and earlier years the rate for the United Arab Republic (Egypt) was highest. Three minor political areas not listed in the table reported higher rates than did the United States. One of them is the Virgin Islands, with a rate of 4.3. The remaining two areas were East Berlin, with a rate of 3.0, and Zanzibar and Pemba, with its latest reported rate of 4.4 for 1957.

All countries except Egypt and Japan, the only countries with a non-Western cultural background, experienced a considerable increase in the divorce rate during the 34-year period 1930–63. Although rates for the United States were highest for all years shown in Table 3 (except for some rates for Egypt), the relative increase was smaller than that for most other countries. The ratio between the divorce rate for 1963 and that for 1930 may be used to measure this increase. This ratio was 1.4 for the United States. Smaller ratios were found only for France, Switzerland, West Germany, and the Netherlands, where they were 1.3 or 1.4, and for Japan (0.9) and Egypt (0.8). In the remaining countries, the increase was larger than that for the United States—the largest ratios were 25.0 for Venezuela, 11.4 for Austria, 7.4 for England and Wales, 5.1 in both Canada and Romania, and 5.0 for Mexico. From the available data, it is

TABLE 3. Divorce Rates per 1,000 Population: United States and Selected Foreign Countries, 1930–63*

Country	1963	1960	1955	1950	1945	1940	1935	1930
United States	2.27	2.18	2.29	2.55	3.66	2.00	1.71	1.59
United Arab Republic (Egypt)[1]	2.11	2.50	2.39	2.95	3.45	2.44	2.80	–
Romania	1.92	2.01	1.80	1.47	0.89	0.59	0.50	0.38
Hungary	1.82	1.66	1.43	1.21	0.22	0.50	0.63	0.64
Denmark	1.38	1.46	1.53	1.61	1.45	0.91	0.81	0.65
East Germany[3]	1.33	1.34	1.35	2.47	–	0.75	0.75	0.63
U.S.S.R.	1.3	1.3	–	–	–	–	–	–
Czechoslovakia	1.22	1.12	1.05	1.06	0.71	0.61	0.50	0.40
Austria	1.14	1.13	1.29	1.52	0.67	0.93	0.11	0.10
Sweden	1.12	1.20	1.21	1.14	0.97	0.55	0.44	0.36
West Germany[3]	0.84	0.83	0.85	1.57	–	0.75	0.75	0.63
Switzerland	0.82	0.87	0.89	0.90	0.84	0.73	0.73	0.67
Japan	0.73	0.74	0.85	1.01	–	0.67	0.70	0.79
Australia	0.68	0.65	0.73	0.90	0.97	0.46	0.36	0.28
England and Wales	0.67	0.51	0.59	0.69	0.36	0.18	0.10	0.09
France	0.63	0.66	0.67	0.85	0.62	0.28	0.51	0.49
Belgium	0.56	0.50	0.50	0.59	0.38	0.22	0.31	0.31
Mexico	0.50	0.43	0.41	0.31	0.43	0.22	0.24	0.10
Netherlands	0.49	0.49	0.51	0.64	0.50	0.33	0.35	0.36
Scotland	0.42	0.35	0.40	0.42	0.43	0.15	0.10	0.10
Canada[4]	0.41	0.39	0.38	0.39	0.42	0.21	0.13	0.08
Venezuela	0.25	0.25	0.18	0.14	0.15	0.09	0.04	0.01

* [Based on the Demographic Yearbook of the United Nations, 1958, 1961, 1964, and 1965.]

[1] Beginning with 1955, data include revocable divorces among the Moslem population, which approximate legal separations.

[2] Provisional.

[3] Rates for 1930, 1935, and 1940 refer to Germany as a whole.

[4] Prior to 1950 excludes Newfoundland.

impossible to estimate how much of the change is due to a higher incidence of divorces and how much to improved registration practices in some of the reporting countries. Changes in crude rates may also reflect differences in age structure and marital status of the population.

Most of the reporting countries experienced a sharp increase of the divorce rate during or immediately after World War II. Afterwards, the rate declined in the United States and several other countries but continued to grow in others. This postwar growth was particularly pronounced in Hungary and Romania.

It is difficult to find an explanation for the differences in the divorce rates among various countries, except that most Communist countries have comparatively high rates. The usual explanations, such as differences in religion or in urbanization, do not seem to apply. It is particularly interesting to compare the United States and Canada, because Canada has always had one of the lowest rates listed in the *Demographic Yearbook* despite geographic proximity and cultural similarity. On the other hand, the Canadian rate grew much more rapidly than the American rate. In 1930 the ratio between the two rates was 19.9, but by 1963 it had declined to 5.5. . . .

Family Stability in Non-European Cultures

GEORGE PETER MURDOCK

This paper presents the conclusions of a special study of the stability of marriage in forty selected non-European societies undertaken in an attempt to place the family situation in the contemporary United States in cross-cultural perspective. Eight societies were chosen from each of the world's major ethnographic regions —Asia, Africa, Oceania, and native North and South America. Within each region the samples were carefully selected from widely scattered geographical locations, from different culture areas, and from levels of civilization ranging from the simplest to the most complex. The data were obtained from the collections in the Human Relations Area Files, formerly the Cross-Cultural Survey. The selection was made in as random a manner as possible except that it was confined to cultures for which the descriptive literature is full and reliable. Once chosen, a particular society was rejected and another substituted only in a few instances where the sources failed to provide (1) information on the relative rights of the two sexes in divorce, or (2) evidence permitting a solid judgment as to the degree of family stability relative to that in our own society.

SOCIETIES IN SAMPLE

The method, it is believed, comes as close to that of purely random sampling as is feasible today in comparative social science. The results, it must be admitted, contain a number of surprises—even to the writer, who has been steeped for years in the literature of world ethnography. The forty selected societies are listed and located below.

Asia: the Chukchi of northeastern Siberia, the Japanese, the Kazak of Turkestan, the Kurd of Iraq, the Lakher of Assam, the Mongols of Outer Mongolia, the Semang Negritos of Malaya, and the Toda of southern India.

Africa: the Dahomeans of coastal West Africa, the Ganda of Uganda, the Hottentot of South-West Africa, the Jukun of Northern Nigeria, the Lamba of Northern Rhodesia, the Lango of Kenya, the Siwans of the oasis of Siwa in Egypt, and the Wolof of Senegal.

Oceania: the Atayal aborigines of interior Formosa, the Balinese of Indonesia, the Kalinga of the northern Philippines, the Kurtatchi of the Solomon Islands in Melanesia, the Kwoma of New Guinea, the Murngin of northern Australia, the Samoans of Polynesia, and the Trukese of Micronesia.

North America: the Aztecs of ancient Mexico, the Creek of Alabama, the Crow of the high plains in Montana, the Haida of northern British Columbia and southern Alaska, the Hopi pueblo-dwellers of Arizona, the Iroquios of northern New York, the Klamath of interior Oregon, and the Yurok of coastal California.

Reprinted from the *Annals of the American Academy of Political and Social Sciences*; 272 (November, 1950), pp. 195–201, by permission of the author and the publisher.

South America: the Cuna of southern Panama, the Guaycuru or Mbaya of the Gran Chaco, the Incas of ancient Peru, the Kaingang of southern Brazil, the Macusi of Guiana, the Ona of Tierra del Fuego, the Siriono of lowland Bolivia, and the Witoto of the northwest Amazonian jungle.

From these cases it emerges, as a first conclusion, that practically all societies make some cultural provision for the termination of marriage through divorce. The Incas stand isolated as the solitary exception; among them a marriage, once contracted in the presence of a high official representing the emperor, could not subsequently be dissolved for any reason. None of the other thirty-nine societies in our sample compels a couple to maintain their matrimonial relationship where there are reasons for separation that would impress most contemporary Americans as genuinely cogent.

DIVORCE RIGHTS—BY SEX

Perhaps the most striking conclusion from the study is the extraordinary extent to which human societies accord both sexes an approximately equal right to initiate divorce. In thirty of the forty cultures surveyed it was impossible to detect any substantial difference in the rights of men and women to terminate an unsatisfactory alliance. The stereotype of the oppressed aboriginal woman proved to be a complete myth.

The author expected, in line with general thought on the subject, that males would be found to enjoy superior, though perhaps not exclusive, rights in a substantial minority of the cultures surveyed, if not in a majority. They were discovered to possess such prerogatives, however, in only six societies—a bare 15 per cent of the total. In two of the Moslem societies, the Kurd and the Siwans, a husband can dismiss his wife with the greatest of ease, even for a momentary whim. He needs only to pick up three stones and drop them, uttering to his spouse a routine formula of divorce. She has no comparable right; she can only run away and hope that her male relatives will support her. Among the Japanese, divorce is very easy for the husband or by mutual consent, but can be obtained by a woman against the will of her spouse only for serious cause and with considerable legal difficulty. A Ganda man, too, is free to dismiss his wife for any cause, whereas she has no right to initiate a permanent separation. If severely mistreated she can only run away to her male relatives, to whom the husband must justify himself and make amends in order to get her back. For the Siriono it is reported that only men, never women, initiate divorce. A Guaycuru man who wants to terminate his marriage for any reason merely removes for a few days to another hut in the same village, until his wife takes the hint and returns to her family. Women rarely seek a divorce directly, but not infrequently they deliberately act in such a manner as to provoke their husbands into leaving them.

In four societies, or 10 per cent of the total sample, women actually possess superior privileges as regards divorce. Among the Kwoma a wife is relatively free to abandon her husband, but he has no right to dismiss her. His only recourse is to make life so miserable for her that she will leave of her own accord. In the stable form of Dahomean marriage, i.e., that characterized by patrilocal residence and the payment of a bride price, a woman can readily desert her husband for cause, but he cannot initiate divorce proceedings directly; he can only neglect his wife, insult her relatives, and subject her to petty annoyances until she takes matters into her own hands and departs. A Yurok marriage can be terminated at the initiative of either partner, but it involves the return of a substantial bride price. A wife is in a much better position to persuade her male relatives of the justice of her cause than is her husband. His claims are scrutinized with great skepticism, and are often rejected. While in theory he could still agree to an uncompensated separation, no male in his right mind in this highly pecuniary culture would think of incurring voluntarily such a financial loss. A Witoto woman can secure a divorce by merely running away. In such a case the husband is always blamed, because people assume that no woman would leave her male protector unless cruelly mistreated. A man can dismiss his wife for cause, but this makes him a target of damaging ridicule and gossip, and unless he is able to justify his action to the complete satisfaction of the local council of adult men, he becomes a virtual social outcast.

FREQUENCY OF DIVORCE—BY SOCIETY

Analysis of the relative frequency of divorce reveals that, in addition to the Incas, the stability of marital unions is noticeably greater than in our society among Atayal, Aztecs, Creek, Dahomeans, Ganda, Hopi, Hottentot, Jukun, Kazak, Lakher, Lango, Murngin, Ona, Siriono, and Witoto. In the remaining twenty-four societies, constituting 60 per cent of the total, the divorce rate manifestly exceeds that among ourselves. Despite the widespread alarm about increasing "family disorganization" in our own society, the comparative evidence makes it clear that we still remain well within the limits which human experience has shown that societies can tolerate with safety.

In most of the societies with relatively infrequent divorce, the stability is achieved through the mores and the pressure of public opinion rather than through legal enactments and judicial obstacles. The Atayal, Aztecs, and Hottentot constitute partial exceptions. In the first of these tribes divorce is freely allowed for childlessness, but petitions on any other grounds must receive a hearing before the chief. He may refuse or grant the divorce, but in the latter case he usually sentences the guilty party to punishment and may even forbid him or her to remarry. Any other separation is likely to precipitate a feud between the families of the estranged spouses. Among the Aztecs, divorce cases were heard before a special court, and the party adjudged guilty forfeited half of his property to the other. Among the Hottentot, adequate grounds for a divorce have to be proved to the satisfaction of a council consisting of all the adult men of the clan, which may order a runaway wife to return to her husband, or award the property of a deserting husband to his wife.

In only two of the societies with frequent divorce is separation effected by the action of constituted authorities—by village officials among the Balinese and by the courts in an action brought by a Japanese woman. Except in these five societies and the Incas, divorce is everywhere exclusively a private matter, and such restraints as are exercised are imposed by informal social pressures rather than by legal restrictions.

STABILIZING DEVICES

The cases reveal clearly some of the devices whereby different peoples have attempted to make marital unions more stable. One of the most common is the payment of a bride price, which comparative studies have shown to be customary among approximately half of the societies of the earth. Contrary to the popular impression, the bride price is almost never conceived as a payment for a purchased chattel. Its primary function nearly everywhere is that of providing an additional economic incentive to reinforce the stability of marriage. In our sample, the sources on Dahomeans, Klamath, Lango, Mongols, Wolof, and Yurok reveal particularly clear evidence of the stabilizing effect of the bride price.

An even more frequent device is to take the choice of a marital partner largely out of the hands of young men and women and vest it in their parents. Most cultures reflect a marked distrust of sexual attraction as a primary motive in marriage, as it is likely to be in the minds of young people, and it seems to be widely recognized that parents, with their greater worldly experience, are more likely to arrange matches on the basis of factors better calculated to produce a durable union. Having been responsible for a marriage, parents tend to feel humiliated when it shows signs of breaking up, and are likely to exert themselves to restore harmony and settle differences. This is attested very specifically for the Haida and the Iroquois, and the evidence shows that the influence of relatives is also a prominent stabilizing factor among Creek, Hopi, Jukun, Kalinga, Murngin, and Ona.

The lengths to which this precaution can be carried in cases of infidelity is well illustrated by the Jukun. A wife first attempts to persuade her husband to give up an adulterous relationship about which she has learned, whereas the husband in a similar situation merely requests a relative or friend to remonstrate with his wife. If the relationship still continues, the innocent spouse reports the matter to the father, uncle, or elder brother of the other, who exerts all the pressure in his power to bring the delinquency to an end. Only after these steps prove fruitless, and the infidelity continues, is a separation effected.

Occasionally, of course, relatives break up a union that is satisfactory to both the parties primarily concerned. Among the Chukchi, for example, the parents of the groom can send the bride home if they become dissatisfied with her at any time within a year or eighteen months after the wedding, and a woman's relatives attempt to break up her marriage if they become estranged from her husband's family at any time, even going to the extreme of carrying off the unwilling wife by force.

In one of the societies of the sample, the Crow Indians—public opinion, instead of exerting its usual stabilizing influence, actually tends to undermine the marital relationship. Divorce is exceedingly frequent, and a man subjects himself to ridicule if he lives too long with one woman. Rivalrous military societies make a sport of stealing wives from one another, and any husband feels ashamed to take back a wife thus abducted from him, however much against her will and his own.

INCIDENCE OF DIVORCE

The sources rarely give precise statistics on the incidence of divorce in societies where it occurs most frequently. All we have is fragmentary statements, for instance, that one-third of all adult Chukchi women have been divorced, or that the ethnographer encountered Cuna of both sexes who had lived through from seven to nine successive marriages, or that it is not uncommon to meet a Siwan woman of forty who has been married and divorced more than ten times.

It is nevertheless possible to segregate one group of societies in which the excessive frequency of divorce is confined to recently contracted marriages and dwindles to a rarity after a union has endured for a year or more, especially after children have been born. This is attested, for example, among the Japanese, the Kaingang, the Kalinga, and the Macusi. Among the Trukese, marriages are very brittle and shifting with people in their twenties, but by the end of this early period of trial and error the majority have found spouses with whom they are content to live in reasonable harmony for the rest of their lives.

In other societies, like the Semang, while the rate of divorce subsides markedly after the birth of children, it still remains high as compared with our own. All in all, the sample reveals nineteen societies, or nearly half of the total, in which permanent separations appear substantially to exceed the present rate in the United States throughout the lifetime of the individual. Among them, either spouse can terminate the union with little difficulty and for slight or even trivial reasons among Balinese, Chukchi, Crow, Cuna, Haida, Iroquois, Klamath, Kurtatchi, Lamba, Mongols, Samoans, Semang, Toda, and Wolof. In matrilocal communities like the Cuna or the Iroquois, the husband simply walks out, or the wife unceremoniously dumps his effects outside her door. It is more surprising to encounter an equal facility in divorce among patrilocal and even patriarchal peoples like the Mongols, who see no reason for moral censure in divorce and say in perfectly matter-of-fact manner that two individuals who cannot get along harmoniously together had better live apart.

GROUNDS FOR DIVORCE

The societies which condone separation for a mere whim are few. The great majority recognize only certain grounds as adequate. The Lamba, for whom the information is particularly full, consider a man justified in seeking a divorce if he has been continually harassed by his parents-in-law, if his wife commits adultery or theft, if she has contracted a loathsome disease, if she is quarrelsome or disrespectful, or if she refuses to remain at his home after he has taken a second wife. For a woman the recognized grounds are impotence or loathsome disease in her spouse, his failure to prepare a garden or provide her with adequate clothing, persistent wife-beating, or mere cessation of her affection for him. If the marriage produces no issue, husband and wife argue as to who is responsible, and usually agree to separate. If the woman then bears a child to her new husband whereas the man fails to produce offspring by his next wife, the former husband is so overcome with shame that he usually either commits suicide or leaves the community.

Particular societies recognize interesting special grounds as adequate. Thus the Aztecs, who strongly disapproved of divorce and required proof of substantial cause before a special court, readily granted separation to a woman if she showed that her husband had done less than his share in attending to the education of their children. In general, however, a few basic reasons recur repeatedly as those considered justifiable in a wide range of societies. These are incompatibility, adultery, barrenness or sterility, impotence or frigidity, economic incapacity or nonsupport, cruelty, and quarrelsomeness or nagging. Desertion rarely appears, because it is, of course, not usually a reason for divorce, but the actual means by which a permanent separation is effected. The degree to which the more widespread grounds are recognized as valid in the forty sample societies is shown in Table 1. In order to provide comparability, an entry is made under each heading for every society. Judgments that are merely inferred as probable from the general context, however, are distinguished from evidence specifically reported or unmistakably implied in the sources.

The data in Table 1 reinforce the earlier comment concerning the extraordinary equality of the sexes in rights of divorce revealed by the present study. Where the table shows notable differences, these have relatively obvious explanations. That cruelty is recognized as an adequate ground for women far more often that for men merely reflects their comparative physical strength. The

TABLE 1.   REASONS FOR DIVORCE (FORTY SAMPLE SOCIETIES)

| | Permitted | | | | Forbidden | | | |
| | Definitely | | Inferentially | | Definitely | | Inferentially | |
Reasons	*To Man*	*To Wife*	*To Man*	*To Wife*	*To Man*	*To Wife*	*To Man*	*To Wife*
Any grounds, even trivial	9	6	5	6	14	13	12	15
Incompatibility, without more specific grounds	17	17	10	10	6	7	7	6
Common adultery or infidelity	19	11	8	12	8	10	5	7
Repeated or exaggerated infidelity	27	23	8	10	5	5	0	2
Childlessness or sterility	12	4	15	18	7	7	6	11
Sexual impotence or unwillingness	9	12	24	21	3	4	4	3
Laziness, non-support, economic incapacity	23	22	11	9	4	5	2	4
Quarrelsomeness or nagging	20	7	7	12	6	11	7	10
Mistreatment or cruelty	7	25	19	9	3	4	11	2

aggression of women toward their spouses is thus perforce directed more often into verbal channels, with the result that quarrelsomeness and nagging become an adequate justification for divorce much more commonly for the male sex.

CONCERN OVER DIVORCE PROBLEM

The demonstration that divorce tends to be easier and more prevalent in other societies than in our own does not warrant the conclusion that most peoples are indifferent to the stability of the marriage relationship and the family institution. In our sample, such a charge might be leveled with some justification at the Crow, the Kaingang, and the Toda, but for the most of the rest the data explicitly reveal a genuine concern with the problem. The devices of the bride price and the arrangement of marriages by parents, already alluded to, represent only two of the most common attempts to reach a satisfactory cultural solution. Others, demonstrated by the author in a previous study (*Social Structure*, 1949), may be briefly summarized here.

One such device is the taboo on primary incest, which is absolutely universal.* There is not a single society known to history or ethnography which does not prohibit and penalize, among the general run of its members, both sexual intercourse and marriage between father and daughter, mother and son, and brother and sister. These universal prohibitions are understandable only as an adaptive provision, arrived at everywhere by a process of mass trial and error, by which sexual rivalry is inhibited within the nuclear family so that the unity and integrity of this basic institution are preserved for the performance of its crucial societal services—economic co-operation, sexual reproduction, and the rearing and education of children.

Nearly as universal are prohibitions of adultery. A very large majority of all known societies permit relatively free sexual experimentation before marriage in their youth of both sexes, but this license is withdrawn when they enter into matrimony. In a world-wide sample of 250 societies, only five—a mere 2 per cent of the total—were found to condone adulterous extramarital liaisons. In many of the remaining 98 per cent, to be sure, the ideal of marital fidelity is more honored in the breach than in the observance. Its very existence, nevertheless, can only reflect a genuine and widespread concern with the stability of marriage and the family, which are inevitably threatened by the jealousy and discord generated by infidelity.

It is clear that approximately as many peoples disapprove in theory of divorce as of adultery. They have learned through experience, however, that the reasons are commonly much more urgent for the former than for the latter, and they consequently allow it wider latitude. The vital functions of the family are not likely to be well performed where husband and wife have become genuinely incompatible. Children raised by stepparents, grandparents, or adoptive parents may frequently find their new social environment more conducive to

* [The reader is referred to Reiss' comments about the universality of the incest taboo in "The Universality of the Family"—Editor.]

healthy personality development than a home torn by bitter internal conflict. Even though less desirable than an ideal parental home, since this is unattainable divorce may represent for them, as for their parents, the lesser of two evils.

No society in our sample, with the possible exception of the Crow, places any positive value on divorce. The general attitude is clearly that it is regrettable, but often necessary. It represents merely a practical concession to the frailty of mankind, caught in a web of social relationships and cultural expectations that often impose intolerable pressure on the individual personality. That most social systems work as well as they do, despite concessions to the individual that appear excessive to us, is a tribute to human ingenuity and resiliency.

AMERICAN FAMILY COMPARATIVELY STABLE

The cross-cultural evidence makes it abundantly clear that the modern American family is unstable in only a relative and not an absolute sense. From an absolute, that is, comparative, point of view, our family institution still leans quite definitely toward the stable end of the ethnographic spectrum. Current trends could continue without reversal for a considerable period before the fear of social disorganization would acquire genuine justification. Long before such a point is reached, however, automatic correctives, some of them already apparent, will have wrought their effect, and a state of relative equilibrium will be attained that will represent a satisfactory social adjustment under the changed conditions of the times.

Kin Family Network: Unheralded Structure in Current Conceptualizations of Family Functioning

MARVIN B. SUSSMAN AND LEE BURCHINAL

The major purpose of this paper is to reduce the lag between family theory and research in so far as it concerns the functioning of the American kin family network and its matrix of help and service among kin members . . . .

One assumption of the isolated nuclear family conceptualization is that the small nuclear family came into existence in Western Europe and the United States as a consequence of the urban-industrial revolution. Furthermore its small size is ideally suited for meeting requirements of an industrial society for a mobile workforce. The effect of the urban-industrial revolution is to produce a small sized family unit to replace the large rural one. This assumption can be challenged. A study of different societies reveals that industrialization and urbanization can occur with or without the small nuclear family.[1]

Reprinted from *Marriage and Family Living*, 24 (August, 1962), pp. 231–240, by permission of the author and the publisher.

[1] Sidney M. Greenfield, "Industrialization and the Family in Sociological Theory," *American Journal of Sociology*, 67 (November, 1961), pp. 312–22.

If household size reflects in any way the structure and characteristics of the joint extended family in India, then little changes have occurred in this system during the period of industrialization in India from 1911 to 1951.[2]

The uprooting of the rural family, the weakening of family ties, and the reshaping of the rural family form into a nuclear type as a consequence of the industrial revolution are disclaimed for one Swiss town in a recent investigation. On the contrary many fringe rural families were stabilized and further strengthened in their kin ties from earning supplementary income in nearby factories. Able-bodied members obtained work nearby and no longer had to leave the family unit in search of work. Families which moved closer to their place of employment were accommodated in row houses; these units facilitated the living together of large family groups.[3] These findings question the impact of industrialization upon the structure and functioning of the pre-industrial family.

It is difficult to determine if the conditions of living during the transition from a rural to an industrial society ended the dominance of the classical extended family and replaced it with a modified kin form, or if it was replaced by the nuclear one. The question is whether the modified extended family has existed since industrialization occurred; is it a recent phenomenon or an emergent urban familism, a departure from the traditional nuclear form; or is it non-existent? The evidence to support either of these positions is inconclusive. It remains however that the family network described variously as "an emergent urban familism" or "modified extended family" exists and functions in the modern community.

The family network and its functions of mutual aid has implications for the functioning of other social systems. With the growth of large metropolitan areas and concomitant occupational specialization, there is less need for the individual to leave the village, town, city or suburb of the urban complex in order to find work according to his training. Large urban areas supply all kinds of specialized educational and occupational training. The individual can remain in the midst of his kin group, work at his speciality and be the recipient of the advantages or disadvantages preferred by the kin family network. If individuals are intricately involved within a kin family network, will they be influenced by kin leaders and be less amenable to influence by outsiders; will they seek basic gratifications in kin relationships in lieu of the work place or the neighborhood; will they modify drastically current patterns of spending leisure time thus affecting current leisure forms and social systems?[4]

Empirical evidence from studies by investigations in a variety of disciplines substantiate the notion that the extended kin family carries on multitudinous activities that have implications for the functioning of other social systems of the society. The major activities linking the network are mutual aid and social

---

[2] Henry Orenstein, "The Recent History of the Extended Family in India," *Social Problems*, 8 (Spring, 1961), pp. 341–50.

[3] Rudolph Braun, *Industrialisierung Volksleben*, (Erbenback-Zierrich: Reutsch, 1960).

[4] A. O. Haller raises interesting questions on the significance of an emerging urban familism. See "The Urban Family," *American Journal of Sociology*, 66 (May, 1961), pp. 621–22.

activities among kin related families. Significant data have been accumulated on the "mutual aid network" between parents and their married child's family in a number of separate and independent investigations.[5,6,7] The conclusions are:

1. Help patterns take many forms, including the exchange of services, gifts, advice and financial assistance. Financial aid patterns may be direct as in the case of the young married couples Burchinal interviewed; or indirect and subtle, such as the wide range of help patterns observed by Sussman, Sharp and Axelrod.

TABLE 1. DIRECTION OF SERVICE NETWORK OF RESPONDENT'S FAMILY AND RELATED KIN BY MAJOR FORMS OF HELP

	Direction of Service Network				
Major Forms of Help and Service	Between Respondents' Family and Related Kin Per Cent*	From Respondents to Parents Per Cent*	From Respondents to Siblings Per Cent*	From Parents to Respondents Per Cent*	From Siblings to Respondents Per Cent*
Any form of help	93.3	56.3	47.6	79.6	44.8
Help during illness	76.0	47.0	42.0	46.4	39.0
Financial aid	53.0	14.6	10.3	46.8	6.4
Care of children	46.8	4.0	29.5	20.5	10.8
Advice (personal and business)	31.0	2.0	3.0	26.5	4.5
Valuable gifts	22.0	3.4	2.3	17.6	3.4

* Totals do not add up to 100 per cent because many families received more than one form of help or service.
Marvin B. Sussman, "The Isolated Nuclear Family: Fact or Fiction," *Social Problems*, 6 (Spring, 1959), p. 338.

2. Such help patterns are probably more widespread in the middle and working class families and are more integral a feature of family relationships than has been appreciated by students of family behavior. Very few families included in available studies reported neither giving nor receiving aid from relatives. However, these relationships until recently have not been the subject of extensive research.

3. The exchange of aid among families flows in several directions, from parents to children and vice versa, among siblings, and less frequently, from more distant relatives. However, financial assistance generally appears to flow from parents to children.

[5] Marvin B. Sussman, "The Help Pattern in the Middle Class Family," *American Sociological Review*, 18 (February, 1953), pp. 22–28. For related analyses by the same author see, "Parental Participation in Mate Selection and Its Effect Upon Family Continuity," *Social Forces*, 32 (October, 1953), p. 76–81; "Family Continuity: Selective Factors Which Affect Relationships Between Families at Generational Levels," *Marriage and Family Living*, 16 (May, 1954), pp. 112–20; "Activity Patterns of Post Parental Couples and Their Relationship to Family Continuity," *Marriage and Family Living*, 27 (November, 1955), pp. 338–41; "The Isolated Nuclear Family: Fact or Fiction," *Social Problems*, 6 (Spring, 1959), pp. 333–40; "Intergenerational Family Relationships and Social Role Changes in Middle Age," *Journal of Gerontology*, 15 (January, 1960), pp. 71–75.

[6] Harry Sharp and Morris Axelrod, "Mutual Aid Among Relatives in an Urban Population," in Ronald Freedman and associates, eds., *Principals of Sociology*, (New York: Holt, 1956), pp. 433–39.

[7] Lee G. Burchinal, "Comparisons of Factors Related to Adjustment in Pregnancy-Provoked and Non-Pregnancy-Provoked Youthful Marriages," *Midwest Sociologist*, 21 (July, 1959), pp. 92–96; also by the same author, "How Successful Are School-Age Marriages?" *Iowa Farm Science*, 13 (March, 1959), pp. 7–10.

4. While there may be a difference in the absolute amount of financial aid received by families of middle and working class status, there are insignificant differences in the proportion of families in these two strata who report receiving giving or exchanging economic assistance in some form.

5. Financial aid is received most commonly during the early years of married life. Parents are probably more likely to support financially "approved" than "disapproved" ones, such as elopements, interfaith and interracial marriages. Support can be disguised in the form of substantial sums of money or valuable gifts given at the time of marriage, at the time of the birth of children, and continuing gifts at Christmas, anniversaries or birthdays. High rates of parental support are probably associated with marriages of children while they are still in a dependency status; those among high school or college students are examples.

6. Research data are inadequate for assessing the effects of parental aid on family continuity and the marital relations of the couple receiving aid. Few studies report associations between the form and amount of aid given with the parent's motivations for providing aid. Additional studies on these points are necessary before the implications of aid to married children can be better known.[8]

Social activities are principal functions of the kin family network. The major forms are inter-family visitation, participation together in recreational activities, and ceremonial behavior significant to family unity. Major research findings are:

1. Disintegration of the extended family in urban areas because of lack of contact is unsupported and often the contrary situation is found. The difficulty in developing satisfactory primary relationships outside of the family in urban areas makes the extended family *more important* to the individual.[9]

2. Extended family get-togethers and joint recreational activities with kin dominate the leisure time pursuits of urban working class members.[10]

3. Kinship visiting is a primary activity of urban dwelling and outranks visitation patterns found for friends, neighbors, or co-workers.[11,12,13,14,15]

4. Among urban middle classes there is an almost universal desire to have

---

[8] Further analyses on the implications of parental aid to married children are found in a paper, "Parental Aid to Married Children: Implications for Family Functioning," forthcoming in *Marriage and Family Living*, November, 1962.

[9] William H. Key, "Rural-Urban Differences and the Family," *Sociological Quarterly*, 2 (January, 1961), pp. 49–56.

[10] F. Dotson, "Patterns of Voluntary Association Among Urban Working Class Families," *American Sociological Review*, 16 (October, 1951), pp. 689–93.

[11] Morris Axelrod, "Urban Structure and Social Participation," *American Sociological Review*, 21 (February, 1956), pp. 13–18.

[12] Scott Green "Urbanism Reconsidered," *American Sociological Review*, 21 (February, 1965), pp, 22–25.

[13] Wendell Bell and M. D. Boat, "Urban Neighborhoods and Informal Social Relations," *American Journal of Sociology*, 43 (January, 1957), pp. 381–98.

[14] Marvin B. Sussman and R. Clyde White, *Hough: A Study of Social Life and Change* (Cleveland: Western Reserve University Press, 1959).

[15] Paul J. Reiss, "The Extended Kinship System of the Urban Middle Class" (Unpublished Ph.D. Dissertation, Harvard University, 1959).

interaction with extended kin, but distance among independent nuclear related units is a limiting factor.[16]

5. The family network extends between generational ties of conjugal units. Some structures are identified as sibling bonds,[17] "occasional kin groups"[18] family circles and cousin clubs.[19] These structures perform important recreational, ceremonial, mutual aid, and often economic functions.

Services performed regularly throughout the year or on occasions are additional functions of the family network. The findings from empirical studies are:

1. Shopping, escorting, care of children, advice giving and counselling, cooperating with social agencies on counselling and welfare problems of family members, are types of day-to-day activities performed by members of the kin network.[20,21]

2. Services to old persons such as physical care, providing shelter, escorting, shopping, performing household tasks, sharing of leisure time, etc. are expected and practiced roles of children and other kin members. These acts of filial and kin responsibility are performed voluntarily without law or compulsion.[22,23, 24,25,26,27,28,29]

[16] E. Franklin Frazier, "The Impact of Urban Civilization Upon Negro Family Life," in P. K. Hatt and A. S. Reiss, Jr., editors. *Cities and Society*, (Glencoe: Illinois, Free Press, 1957, rev. ed.), pp. 495–96.

[17] Elaine Cumming and David M. Schneider, "Sibling Solidarity: A Property of American Kinship," *American Anthropologist*, 63 (June, 1961), pp. 498–507.

[18] Millicent Ayoub, "American Child and His Relatives: Kindred in Southwest Ohio," project supported by the Public Health Service, 1961. Dr. Ayoub is continuing her studies under the subtitle, "The Nature of Sibling Bond." She examines the solidarity or lack of it between siblings in four focal subsystems and at different stages of the life cycle.

[19] William E. Mitchell, "Descent Groups Among New York City Jews," *The Jewish Journal of Sociology*, 3 (1961), pp. 121–28; "Lineality and Laterability in Urban Jewish Ambi-lineages," read at the 60th Annual Meeting of the American Anthropological Association in Philadelphia, Pa., November 16, 1961; and William E. Mitchell and Hope J. Leichter, "Urban Ambilineages and Social Mobility," unpublished paper based on research from the project, "Studies in Family Interaction" sponsored jointly by the Jewish Family Service of New York City and the Russell Sage Foundation.

[20] Sussman, *op. cit.*, "The Help Pattern in the Middle Class Family."

[21] Hope J. Leichter, "Kinship and Casework," paper read at the meetings of the Groves Conference, Chapel Hill, North Carolina, 1959; "Life Cycle Changes and Temporal Sequence in a Bilateral Kinship System," read at the annual meetings of the American Anthropological Association, 1958, Washington, D.C.; "Normative Intervention in an Urban Bilateral Kinship System," paper read at the meetings of the American Anthropological Association, 1959.

[22] John Kosa, Leo D. Rachiele and Cyril O. Schommer, S. J., "Sharing the Home with Relatives," *Marriage and Family Living*, 22 (May, 1960), pp. 129–31.

[23] Alvin L. Schorr, *Filial Responsibility in a Modern American Family*, Washington, D.C.; Social Security Administration, U.S. Department of Health, Education and Welfare, 1960, pp. 11–18.

[24] Peter Townsend, *The Family Life of Older People: An Inquiry in East London* (London: Routledge and Kegan Paul, 1957).

[25] Michael Young and Peter Willmott, *Kinship and Family in East London* (Glencoe, Illinois: Free Press, 1957).

[26] Elizabeth Bott, *Family and Social Network* (London: Tavistock Publications, Ltd., 1957).

[27] See *Adjustment in Retirement*, by Gordon F. Streib and Wayne E. Thompson, *Journal of Social Issues*, 14 (1958). Streib and Thompson have done the most creative thinking and analysis of data on these points. Streib's paper "Family Patterns in Retirement," pp. 46–60 in this issue is most pertinent.

3. Families or individual members on the move are serviced by units of the family network. Services range from supplying motel-type accommodations for vacationing kin passing through town, to scouting for homes and jobs for kin, and in providing supportive functions during the period of in-migration and transition from rural to the urban pattern of living.[30,31,32,33,34]

4. Services on occasions would include those performed at weddings or during periods of crisis, death, accident, disaster, and personal trouble of family members. A sense of moral obligation to give service or acknowledgement of one's kin appropriate to the occasion is found among kin members. The turning to kin when in trouble before using other agencies established for such purposes is the mode rather than the exception.[35,36,37,38]

5. General supportive behavior from members of the kin family network facilitate achievement and maintenance of family and community status.[39] Supportive behavior of kin appears to be instrumental in affecting fertility rates among component family members.[40]

---

[28] Ethel Shanas, "Older People and Their Families," paper given at the meetings of the American Sociological Association, September, 1961. A more complete report is in *Family Relationships of Older People*, Health Information Foundation, 1961.

[29] The best treatment of uses of leisure during the later years of life is found in Robert W. Kleemeier, ed., *Aging and Leisure* (New York: Oxford University Press, 1961). See particularly the chapters by Wilensky, Streib and Thompson.

[30] M. B. Sussman and R. C. White, *op. cit., Hough: A Study of Social Life and Change.*

[31] C. Wright Mills, Clarence Senior and Rose K. Goldsen, *Puerto Rican Journey* (New York: Harper Bros., 1950), pp. 51–55.

[32] James S. Brown, Harry K. Schwarzweller, and Joseph J. Mangalam, "Kentucky Mountain Migration and the Stem Family: An American Variation on a Theme by LePlay," paper given at the meetings of the American Sociological Association, September 1, 1961.

[33] Peter H. Rossi, *Why Families Move* (Glencoe, Illinois: Free Press, 1955), pp. 37–38.

[34] Earl L. Koos, *Families in Trouble* (New York: Columbia University Press, 1946).

[35] Sussman, *op. cit.*, "Family Continuity: Selective Factors Which Affect Relationships Between Families at Generational Levels."

[36] Seymour S. Bellin, *Family and Kinship in Later Years*, N.Y. State Dept. of Mental Hygiene, Mental Health Research Unit Publication, 1960.

[37] Sharp and Axelrod, *op. cit., Mutual Aid Among Relatives.*

[38] Enrico L. Wuarantelli, "A Note on the Protective Function of the Family in Disasters," *Marriage and Family Living*, 22 (August, 1960), pp. 263–64.

[39] Bernard Barber, "Family Status, Local-Community Status, and Social Stratification: Three Types of Social Ranking," *Pacific Sociological Review*, Vol. 4, #1 (Spring, 1961), pp. 3–10. In this paper Barber challenges the current conceptualization of social class for designating an individual's position, and power within a community. He differentiates social class position, family status and local-community statuses into three types of social ranking. Each one has its own structure and functions; each allocates position, power and prestige; and each has its own range of variation. The family kin network and support received from it determines family status. President Kennedy's family and its extended family relations illustrates the point of this thesis.

[40] David Goldberg, "Some Recent Developments in Fertility Research," Reprint No. 7, *Demographic and Economic Change in Developed Countries*, Princeton University Press, 1960. Recent fertility research has focused upon the relationship of family organization to differential fertility since variations in family planning and family size cannot be explained by differences in socio-economic status. One variable of family organization is the family kin network. Goldberg observes, "—and incidentally one which may ultimately prove fruitful in cross-cultural studies, is a consideration of the relative benevolence of the environment in defraying the economic and social costs of having children. Here it is hypothesized that the greater the amount of help available from one's community or kinship system the weaker the desire to prevent or postpone pregnancy." *Ibid.*, p. 9.

A convergence of many of these findings occurs in the work of Eugene Litwak. In an extensive study of a middle class population Litwak tests several hypotheses on the functional properties of the isolated nuclear family for an industrial society: (a) occupational mobility is antithetical to extended family relations; (b) extended family relations are impossible because of geographical mobility. His findings summarized briefly are: (1) The extended kin family as a structure exists in modern urban society at least among middle class families; (2) Extended family relations are possible in urban industrial society; (3) Geographical propinquity is an unnecessary condition for these relationships; (4) Occupational mobility is unhindered by the activities of the extended family, such activities as advice, financial assistance, temporary housing, and the like provide aid during such movement; and (5) The classical extended family of rural society or its ethnic counterpart are unsuited for modern society, the isolated nuclear family is not the most functional type, the most functional being a modified extended kin family.[41]

CONCLUSIONS

There exists an American kin family system with complicated matrices of aid and service activities which link together the component units into a functioning network. The network identified by Litwak as extended family relations is composed of nuclear units related by blood and affinal ties. Relations extend along generational lines and bilaterally where structures take the form of sibling bonds and ambilineages, i.e., the family circle or cousin club.

As a consequence of limited historical work and particularistic developments in theory and research in sociology there is uncertainty concerning the impact of industrialization upon the structure and function of the pre-industrial family. Was the extended classical type found in rural society replaced by a nuclear one, or did it evolve into the modified kin form described in this paper? It is suggested that the notion of the isolated nuclear family stems from theories and research on immigrant groups coming into the city to work during the period of urbanization in Western society.[42] Anomie in family behavior resulted from individual and institutional failure to make appropriate adjustments required by this migration. The coldness and indifference of the workplace and the city as a steel and concrete bastion contributed to a feeling of aloneness and isolation. The basic concern of the in-migrant was survival in an unknown man-made jungle. Survival was related to dependence upon small family units. These could make quicker and more complete adjustment to the new ways of urban life. The ethos of a competitive and expanding industrial society supported the flexibility of movement now possible by an atomistic unit. Every man is

---

[41] Eugene Litwak, "The Use of Extended Family Groups in the Achievement of Social Goals: Some Policy Implications," *Social Problems*, 7 (Winter, 1959–60), pp. 177–87; Eugene Litwak, "Occupational Mobility and Extended Family Cohesion," *American Sociological Review*, 25 (February, 1960), pp. 9–21); Eugene Litwak, "Geographical Mobility and Extended Family Cohesion," *American Sociological Review*, 25 (June, 1960), pp. 385–394.

[42] Key, *op. cit.*, "Rural-Urban Differences and the Family," p. 56; Sussman, *op. cit.*, "The Isolated Nuclear Family: Fact or Fiction," p. 340.

for himself, every man should be unencumbered by ties that will hinder his economic or social progress, and every man should seize opportunities to better himself. One assumption of this position is that early urban man had little time for concern or activity with kinsmen. A more logical assumption is that isolation, a depressive workplace, and uncertainty produced greater reliance upon kin. Once new immigrants became established in the city they served as informants, innkeepers, and providers for later kin arrivals.[43] Once these followers arrived the kin family network then functioned most effectively to protect and acculturate their members into urban ways.

Major activities of this network are that members give to each other financial aid and good of value, and a wide range of services at specific times and under certain conditions. The aid and service provided within the network supplement rather than displace the basic activities of nuclear family units. Kinship behavior assists more than negates the achievement of status and occupational advance of component families and their members.

The main flow of financial aid is along generational lines, from parents to young married children and from middle-aged parents to aged parents. Such aid is not restricted to emergencies, but may be given at various occasions such as support for education, to start a family, at time of marriage, to begin a career, and the like.

The network is used among middle class families as a principal source of aid and service when member families or individuals are in personal difficulty, in times of disaster and crisis, and on ceremonial occasions. There are some indications that established working class families are following the same pattern. Some situations cannot be handled by the nuclear unit alone, e.g., destruction of the family home by a tornado; while other situations involve more than one nuclear family or individual member, e.g., the death of an aging parent. In such situations these are mutual expectations of going to the aid of kin. Aid is sought from the most immediate kin chiefly along sibling or generational lines. Then it is followed by help from more distant kin.

In many instances everyday or weekly activities link together the members of the kin family network. Joint participation in leisure time activities are possible because of reduction of the work week. Visiting among kin is facilitated by high speed highways and other conveyances of a modern transportation system. Constant communication among kin members is possible by the widespread adoption on all class levels of the telephone as a household necessity.[44,45]

The feasibility of the kin network in modern society is due to the existence

43 Key discusses this point in his paper "Rural-Urban Differences and the Family," *op. cit.* From studies on immigration to the United States and geographical movement of families within the country one concludes that family members perform invasion of scout roles and then attract other kin into their communities and neighborhoods.

44 Several empirical studies are currently in progress on the extensity of kin family network functions in metropolitan areas. Robert W. Habenstein and Alan D. Coult are conducting one in Kansas City on "The Functions of Extended Kinship in an Urban Milieu." "The purpose of this research is to discover, describe, and analyse the social correlates and functions of extended kinship in representative samples of blue collar and white collar socio-economic classes in Kansas City." p. 1, Research Proposal, July 1, 1961.

of modern communication and transportation systems which facilitate interaction among members; a bureaucratic industrial structure suited to modern society which removes the responsibility for job placement from the network will still permit the network to concentrate on activities intended to aid the social and economic achievement of network members;[46,47] and expansion of metropolitan areas in which individuals can obtain educational, occupational and status objectives without leaving their kin area. Kin members can live some distance from each other within the metropolitan area and still have relationships within the network. Nuclear units function autonomously. Decisions on what and when to act are responsibilities of the nuclear family. Influence may be exerted by the kin group upon the nuclear units so that the latter may make the "right" decision. However the kin group seldom directs the decision or action of the nuclear family in a given situation. Immunity from such control is guaranteed by legal and cultural norms which reaffirm the right and accountability of the nuclear family in such situations. The role of the family kin network is supportive rather than coercive in its relationship with the nuclear family. . . .

[45] A second study is being undertaken by Marvin B. Sussman and Sherwood B. Slater in Cleveland, Ohio. "The objectives of the Cleveland Study are to investigate the working and middle-class families; to compare the kinship networks of 'illness' and 'non-illness' families; to estimate the normative form of kinship networks for social class and family life cycle stages to variations in normative patterns," p. 1, Research Plan, September 27, 1961.

[46] One investigation being conducted by John Bennett is concerned with the variations in business operations due to kinship behavior. Business organization practice according to current theory operates with bureaucratic, universalistic, and impartial norms. Bennett is investigating the compatibility and conflict between these bureaucratic norms and those which characterize the kinship network, particularistic behavior for idiosyncratic situations, "Kinship in American Business Organization," meetings of the Central States Anthropological Society, May, 1961.

[47] William Mitchell, "Lineality and Laterality in Urban Jewish Ambilineages," *op. cit.*, finds some integration of kinship and business activity. There is a tendency to "Throw business to kin members."

Industrialization and the American Family: A Look Backward

FRANK F. FURSTENBERG, JR.

The proposition that industrialization destroys traditional family structures has long been accepted by sociologists and laymen alike. In industrial societies a new kind of family, the "isolated nuclear family," has been recognized; in societies presently industrializing, the older family systems are thought to be under great strain.[1] Analysts of the American family have both assumed and

Reprinted from the *American Sociological Review*, 31 (June, 1966), pp. 326–337, by permission of the author and the publisher.

[1] Talcott Parsons discusses how the family and the economy affect each other in *Family, Socialization and Interaction Process*, Glencoe, Ill.: The Free Press, 1955, especially Chapter 1. The most forceful expression of this view was made by William F. Ogburn in his *Technology and the Changing Family*, New York: Houghton Mifflin, 1955. This view is also expressed in George C. Homans, *The Human Group*, New York: Harcourt, Brace and Company, 1950, pp. 276–280. See also David and Vera Mace, *Marriage East and West*, Garden City, N.Y.: Dolphin Books, 1959, Chapter 1.

asserted that the transition from an agricultural to an industrial economy is accompanied by the weakening of a family system characterized by such traits as low social and geographical mobility, high parental authority over children, marital harmony and stability, dominance of husband over wife, and close ties within the extended family. It is similarly assumed that the modern family possesses few of the characteristics of the pre-industrial family. Just as the older family pattern served the needs of a farming economy, it is frequently said that the modern family serves the needs of an industrial economy.[2]

Widespread acceptance of an ideal image of the pre-industrial family has limited empirical investigation of family change. Waller wrote some years ago: "According to the Victorian ideology, all husbands and wives lived together in perfect amity; all children loved the parents to whom they were indebted for the gift of life; and if these things were not true, they should be, and even if one knew that these things were not true he ought not mention it."[3] Few sociologists today would want to conceal unflattering truths about the family of three or four generations ago. However, certain widely shared beliefs about the family of today have helped to preserve what Goode has labeled "the classical family of Western nostalgia."[4]

Goode's recent analysis of change in some of the world's major family systems suggests some general propositions that cast doubt on the traditional view of the relationship between industrialization and the family. Goode concludes: (1) there are indigenous sources of change in family systems, before industrialization takes place; (2) the relations between industrialization and family patterns are complex and still not sufficiently understood; (3) the family system itself may be an independent source of change facilitating the transition to industrialization; and (4) some apparently recent characteristics of the family may actually be very old social patterns.[5]

Each of these general propositions may be partially tested by using historical data from the United States. While this paper will touch on all four, it will concentrate on data pertaining to the fourth proposition—that certain "recent" family patterns are in fact evident in the family of a century ago. This is a particularly important theoretical point, for relatively stable family patterns would weaken the hypothesis that industrialization necessarily undermines the traditional family form. Further, it would force us to examine more carefully just which elements in the family are most responsive to changes in the economic system. A refutation of the assumption that trends in family change are well known may stimulate historians and historical sociologists to develop more

[2] Two excellent books on the social consequences of industrialization summarize the supposed changes in the family produced by industrialization: Harold L. Wilensky and Charles N. Lebeaux, *Industrial Society and Social Welfare*, New York: Russell Sage Foundation, 1958, pp. 67–83; and Eugene V. Schneider, *Industrial Society*, New York: McGraw-Hill Book Company, Inc., 1957, Chapter 18.

[3] *The Family: A Dynamic Interpretation*, New York: Cordon Company, 1938, p. 13.

[4] William J. Goode, *World Revolution and Family Patterns*, New York: The Free Press of Glencoe, 1963, p. 6.

[5] *Ibid.*, Chapter 1.

precise descriptions of family systems at different periods in the past and of the family's relations with other social institutions during these periods.

It is important to recognize that the sharp contrast between the pre-industrial family and the modern family has already been diminished to some extent. Recent research has brought into question the validity of the conception of the "isolated nuclear family." [6] Increasing evidence suggests that we must modify our picture of the modern family. It seems not to be nearly so isolated and nuclear as it has been portrayed by some sociologists.[7]

Thus, we may attack from two ends the view that considerable family change has occurred in the past century. On the near end, we are beginning to get a more balanced picture of what the family of today looks like. On the far end, we have less information. This paper attempts to assemble some limited but highly useful information on the family of a hundred or more years ago. This information may be used to explore certain theoretical issues concerning family change. Although industrialization may have placed added strains on the family, the extent to which the industrial system affected the family has been greatly exaggerated. Further, I contend that not only did strains exist prior to industrialization, but some of these very tensions in the family may have facilitated the process of industrialization. The long-recognized effect of the economy on the family has too often obscured the converse—that the family may have important consequences for the economic system. To understand the complicated relationship between the economy and the family, we cannot simply view the family as the dependent variable in the relationship.

METHOD

The data supporting these views are drawn from the accounts of foreign travelers visiting this country during the period 1800–1850.[8] Although prior to and during this period, American technical achievements were many—a canal system, the cotton gin, the steamship, a spreading rail network, etc.—the nation was almost entirely agricultural until the decade before the Civil War.

[6] See Marvin B. Sussman's "The Isolated Nuclear Family: Fact or Fiction" in his book of readings *Sourcebook in Marriage and the Family*, Boston: Houghton Mifflin Company, 1963, pp. 48–53.

[7] Marvin Sussman has done several studies on the relationship between middle-class couples and their families. See especially "The Help Pattern in the Middle-Class Family," in Sussman, *Sourcebook in Marriage and the Family*, ibid., pp. 380–385. Note the article by Gordon F. Streib in the same reader entitled "Family Patterns in Retirement." Also see Eugene Litwak, "Occupational Mobility and Extended Family Cohesion," Bobbs-Merrill Reprint Series in the Social Sciences, Sociology-177.

[8] Accounts of foreign travelers have been used in a few studies of the family. Arthur W. Calhoun made extensive use of such accounts in his three-volume study of the American family, *A Social History of the American Family*, 3 volumes, New York: Barnes & Noble, Inc., 1960 (first published 1917–1919). See also Willystine Goodsell, *A History of Marriage and the Family*, New York: The Macmillan Company, 1939, Chapter 11. More recently, Lipset has used foreign travelers' accounts in making some observations about the early American family (Seymour Martin Lipset, *The First New Nation: The United States in Historical and Comparative Perspective*, New York: Basic Books Inc., 1963, especially Chapter 3.)

In 1850 only 16 per cent of the labor force was engaged in manufacturing and construction industries, and this percentage had not greatly changed since 1820.[9] Although the country was beginning to industrialize and urbanize, over four-fifths of the population still resided in rural areas.[10] About two out of every three workers were farmers. This ratio had decreased only slightly over the previous four decades.[11] Thus, it seems safe to assert that the impact of industrialization on the American family cannot have been great prior to 1850.[12]

Travelers' accounts are a rich source of data on the American family in the first half of the nineteenth century.[13] Many of these accounts have both literary and historical merit, and some of the writings have become famous because of their perceptive observations on American society. While the writings of Alexis de Tocqueville, Harriet Martineau, and Frances Trollope are well known, thousands of little-known accounts were written during this period.[14] Europeans, anxious to observe what was still referred to as "the New World" became the precursors of the more systematic participant observers of today.

To what extent can we place confidence in these travelers' accounts? Do they accurately portray American society as it actually was in the nineteenth century? Naturally the same cautions apply in using this source of historical data as apply to any other source of data. There are several methodological qualifications about the use of travelers' accounts that should be made. While these travelers may be viewed in certain respects as sociological observers of the nineteenth century, it must be remembered that they did not possess the basic qualifications of trained sociological observers. Many of the accounts of American society lack a neutral and value-free perspective. The biases of the observers are especially evident in the area of the family. For many travelers, the family was the source of great moral concern.

Without dismissing the possibility of distortion, such moral sentiments may to a degree enhance the value of these accounts as sociological data when we can ascertain and control for such biases. Generally, liberal and conservative Europeans evaluated the American family differently, reflecting their own biases. Liberals, as one might expect, viewed the American family in a more favorable

[9] U.S. Bureau of the Census, *Historical Statistics of the United States: Colonial Times to 1957*, Washington, D.C.: U.S. Government Printing Office, 1960, Series D, 57–71. It should be noted that more change appeared in the decade between 1840–1850 than in previous decades.

[10] *Ibid.*, Series A, 34–50.

[11] *Ibid.*, Series D, 36–45.

[12] A limited amount of industrialization could be found in the Northeastern states prior to 1850. However, Wilensky and Lebeaux, and Schneider report that industrialization was quite confined until after the Civil War. Wilensky and Lebeaux, *op. cit.*, p. 49; Schneider, *op. cit.*, chapter 4. The beginnings of an industrial economy, however, were apparent in such places as Lowell, Massachusetts. A number of travelers visited Lowell during this period and commented with great interest on the Lowell factories.

[13] There are many bibliographies of accounts of foreign travelers written during this period. Two extensive bibliographies are: Max Berger, *The British Traveler in America*, New York: Columbia University Press, 1943, and Frank Monaghan, *French Travelers in the United States 1765–1932*, New York: The New York Public Library, 1953.

[14] Berger and Monaghan each list many thousands of accounts and they are only partial listings for two countries.

light; conservatives, in an unflattering glare.[15] The possibility of bias from political persuasion is not great, however, because most of the observations reported in this paper are common to observers of all political points of view. That travelers of very different prejudices made *similar* observations enhances the reliability and validity of these observations. Where, on the other hand, the observer's bias may have affected the accuracy of his accounts, I shall try to note such bias. When they do occur, these biases are more likely to be the result of the traveler's sexual status than his political status.[16]

The accounts used here do not represent a systematically selected sample of European travelers during the period. There are literally thousands of published and unpublished accounts, and a good sample of the observations of European travelers would be difficult to obtain. The sample used here is composed of forty-two accounts and selections from accounts, most of them containing extensive commentary on the family. To arrive at this sample, I examined over one hundred accounts, the majority of which made either no reference, or only an oblique reference, to family life in America.[17]

One final caution: most of the travelers base their comments on a view of the middle-class American family.[18] These travelers usually observed the family during their stay in residential hotels or during brief visits to American homes in rural areas of the country. More likely than not, these homes were middle-class. Since most of the comments and generalizations about the modern family of today also apply largely to the middle class, this limitation in the data will probably not affect the comparison adversely.

FAMILY OBSERVATIONS

COURTSHIP AND MATE SELECTION

To begin this discussion with the first stage in the life cycle of the family, we shall discuss some of the foreign travelers' observations on the courtship

[15] Portions of the travelers' accounts used in this study were rated by the author and an associate and placed into three categories: positive, neutral, or negative. It was found that accounts could be reliably coded. There was complete agreement in 78 per cent of the cases. Where disagreement occurred, it never involved cases where one person coded a positive evaluation and the other a negative evaluation. The traveler's general evaluation was related to his political ideology. Although this information could be obtained for only about half of the sample, it showed a distinct relationship to evaluation. All three travelers who were conservatives had a negative view of America, while only one of twelve liberals had an overall negative impression of the country.

[16] The females in the sample were inclined to view the position of married American women less favorably. They were more skeptical about the desirability of the position of women in the United States.

[17] The sample of accounts examined does not represent a systematic selection of travelers' accounts. A large proportion of the sample was located from the bibliography of Oscar Handlin, *et al.* (eds.), *Harvard Guide to American History*, Cambridge, Mass.: The Belknap Press, 1954, pp. 151–159, which includes a diverse selection of accounts. Handlin also edited a book of selections from travelers' accounts. This book contains some writings not listed in the *Harvard Guide*. See *This Was America*, New York: Harper & Row, 1949.

[18] Middle-class, in this context, refers to persons engaged in small business, professionals, and prosperous landowners. Travelers in the sample were more likely to comment on the habits and customs of the farmer than the farmhand.

patterns of American youth. The American system of courtship and mate selection is sometimes said to be one of the consequences of the urbanized and industrialized economy in the United States.[19] Free mate selection and the "romantic-love complex" are often linked to the demands of the economic system or to the weakened control by family elders in an industrialized society.[20] In fact, however, the same system of mate selection and emphasis on romantic love appear to have existed here prior to industrialization.

Although few of the travelers described the actual process of courtship in America, it is evident from their accounts that free choice of mates was the prevailing pattern as well as the social norm. Foreign visitors expressed diverse opinions on the desirability of this norm, but there was complete agreement that such a norm existed. Chevalier wrote in the 1830's that the dowry system, common in France, was almost nonexistent in the United States. He observed that American parents played only a nominal role in selecting the person their child married.[21] Parental consent was formally required, but this requirement was seldom taken very seriously. In 1842, Lowenstern wrote:

A very remarkable custom in the United States gives girls the freedom to choose a husband according to their fancy; practice does not permit either the mother or the father to interfere in this important matter.[22]

The general expectation in America was that the choice of a mate should be based on love. Some travelers were skeptical about whether love actually dictated the marriage selection. Buckingham writes, "Love, among the American people, appears to be regarded rather as an affair of the judgment, than of the heart; its expression seems to spring from a sense of duty, rather than from a sentiment of feeling."[23] A few travelers already noted that, in spite of the previously mentioned tendency of young people to spurn financial considerations in choosing a mate, there were matches that seemed to be based on material considerations. This touch of cynicism, however, occurs in only a minority of the travelers' writings. Most of the observers praised the American marriage system because it permitted young people to select mates whom they loved and with whom they could enjoy a happy marriage. Some persons, however, noted that free mate selection resulted in certain family strains. Lowenstern states that marriage between people of different social classes, a pattern sometimes asserted to be

[19] This is suggested in Harry Johnson's chapter on the family in *Sociology: A Systematic Introduction*, New York: Harcourt, Brace and Company, 1960, Chapter 6. Parsons advocates this view in his article "Age and Sex in the Social Structure" in his *Essays in Sociological Theory*, Glencoe, Ill.: The Free Press, 1954.

[20] David and Vera Mace, *op. cit.*, chapter 5; also Robert F. Winch, *The Modern Family*, rev. ed., New York: Holt, Rinehart and Winston, 1963, pp. 318–320.

[21] Michael Chevalier, *Society, Manners, and Politics in the United States*, New York: Doubleday Anchor Books, 1961, p. 294. Six other travelers substantiate Chevalier's observations on the freedom of mate selection.

[22] Isidore Lowenstern, "Les Etats-Unis et La Havane: souvenirs d'un Voyage, 1842," in Handlin, *This Was America, op. cit.*, p. 183.

[23] James Silk Buckingham, *The Eastern and Western States of America*, 2 vols., London: Fisher, Son & Co., 1867, p. 479.

typical of an industrial society, was not uncommon.[24] Several other travelers support this view. By no means were all the comments on interclass marriages favorable. Women, it was sometimes noted with bitterness, not infrequently married beneath themselves.[25]

Another source of strain in the marriage system in the view of some travelers, was the American habit of marrying at an extremely early age. Many observers noted that there seemed to be a great pressure for young people to marry. "In view of the unlimited freedom of the unmarried woman," Moreau writes, "it is astonishing to discover the eagerness of all to be married, for marriage brings about an absolute change in the life of the girl."[26] The tendency for an early marriage and the feelings of pressure to marry may be related to the "unlimited freedom" of which Moreau speaks.

Almost half of the travelers in the sample comment on freedom given to youth before marriage. Particularly striking to the travelers was the amount of freedom given to young women. But this freedom was tempered by considerable self-restraint. Adolescents were permitted to be alone together, but they were expected to behave according to strict moral standards. In the view of at least one observer, apparently this restraint led to a pronounced lack of responsiveness. Moreau stated that a young couple could be left alone in the house together without any fear of improper behavior. In fact, ". . . sometimes on returning, the servants find them fallen asleep and the candle gone out—so cold is love in this country!"[27]

While these extraordinary feats of self-restraint may be reminiscent of the privileges of courtly love, lauded by poets but not reported by objective observers,[28] there is general consensus among the travelers that the behavior of American women, particularly of young women, was exemplary. More often, young women in America came under criticism for being cold. No doubt, the combination of the freedom granted and the strong sanctions against misbehaving have something to do with the common observation that American women lacked warmth and spontaneity. On this matter, though, there is a dissenting view. Abdy commented: "Many women, who seem cold as flint in general, give out fire enough when they find a 'blade' that suits them."[29]

The pressure to marry at an early age may have been generated by strains on the young woman. She was permitted to travel alone, to socialize with the

---

[24] Lowenstern, *op. cit.* James Fenimore Cooper, the American novelist, in a book on his observations of American life, notes the same pattern of interclass marriage. See his *Notions of the Americans*, vol. I, London: Henry Colburn, 1828.

[25] Among others, Sir Charles Lyell made this observation in his *A Second Visit to the United States of North America*, New York: Harper & Brothers, 1849.

[26] Mederic Louis Elie Moreau de Saint-Mery, "Voyage aux Stat-Unis de L'Amerique, 1793–1798," in Handlin, *This Was America, op. cit.*, p. 100. Similar observations on the early marriage age were made by nine other travelers.

[27] *Ibid.*, p. 99.

[28] Sidney Painter in his book, *French Chivalry*, Ithaca, N.Y.: Great Seal Books, 1957, presents a superb account of courtly love in mediaeval France. See especially Chapter 4.

[29] E. S. Abdy, *Journal of a Residence and Tour in the United States of North America*, vol. I, London: John Murray, 1935, p. 74.

opposite sex, and even to leave home alone for extended periods; but with this freedom went an enormous responsibility. She was expected to remain chaste, to conform to strict standards of propriety, and to respect the privileges of her freedom. The strain created by such a combination of freedom and moral restraint could well explain the tendency toward early marriage.[30]

Several observers note the problems that arise from early marriage. In her characteristically incisive way, Frances Trollope commented:

They marry very young; in fact, in no rank of life do you meet with young women in that delightful period of existence between childhood and marriage, wherein, if only tolerably well spent, so much useful information is gained, and the character takes a sufficient degree of firmness to support with dignity the more important parts of wife and mother.[31]

The Pulszkys concurred with Trollope that American girls got too little opportunity to see life before they settled down to marriage.[32] It was also suggested that the rapid push toward marriage led young people to marry without knowing each other sufficiently; courtships were considered excessively casual. As one observer wrote, "Meet your girl in the morning, marry in the afternoon, and by six in the evening you are settled in your home, man and wife."[33]

To sum up, travelers perceived several strains in the American system of courtship and mate selection. Freedom of choice did not always lead to the selection of a mate on the basis of love; and it sometimes resulted in crossing of class lines and unwise marriages. The pressures toward early marriage seemed to result in inadequate preparation for marriage. These strains were observed by both critics and supporter of America alike. Their frequency and consistency suggest that they were very real problems. It is perhaps obvious to point out similarities in the criticisms of American marriages that were observed in the nineteenth century and the criticisms of American marriages today. At the time these criticisms were made, they were not thought to be related to incipient industrialization. The problems in the courtship process were regarded as the consequence of other political and economic factors, such as American ideological commitment to democracy, the opportunity for achievement in the society, and the emphasis on equality and individualism.[34]

---

[30] It is possible to develop a fourfold table based on the two variables of amount of moral restraint (permissiveness toward sexual expression before marriage) and degree of freedom permitted young people to associate together. I predict that marriage age will be early when freedom to associate is high and moral restraint is also high. Where freedom to associate is high and moral restraint is low, marriage age will be somewhat later. It may be even later when freedom to associate is low and moral restraint is high. It is difficult to predict how the fourth case would turn out. A study on this problem is being undertaken.

[31] Frances Trollope, *Domestic Manners of the Americans*, New York: Alfred A. Knopf, 1949, p. 118.

[32] Theresa and Kossuth Pulszky, "White Red Black," in Handlin, *This Was America, op. cit.*

[33] Karl T. Freisinger, "Lebende Bilder Aus America," Handlin, *This Was America, op. cit.*, p. 254.

[34] This view is advocated by Tocqueville throughout his writings on the American family. Alexis de Tocqueville, *Democracy in America*, 2 vols., New York: Vintage Books, 1954. See especially vol. 2, Chapter 8.

THE CONJUGAL RELATION

The aspect of married life which drew the most attention was the great loss of freedom the woman suffered when she married. As already noted, single girls were granted considerable freedom before marriage. Almost a fourth of all the travelers commented on the loss of this freedom for the woman in married life. On this situation, there are no views to the contrary. Although Tocqueville[35] and Murat[36] see the loss of this freedom as voluntary on the part of the female, other observers view it as imposed upon her. A number of writers state their belief that the American wife is neglected in favor of the single woman. She is, as one traveler put it, "laid on the shelf."[37]

Why this was so, few travelers ventured to speculate. Several travelers imply that the retirement of married women from social life gives them greater moral protection.[38] Most of the writers feel that married women suffer unnecessary discrimination. Some of our contemporary sociological notions might suggest that the women, after consenting to marry, had little left to bargain with.[39] Furthermore, there were really no alternatives open to the women which would permit them to get out of the home more often and at the same time fulfill their domestic obligations. It is also possible that the intense pressures for early marriage prohibited married women from competing with single girls for men's attentions.

The primary cause for the withdrawal of married women from social life seems to have been their demanding domestic obligations. It is commonly assumed that women were more satisfied in their domestic role a century ago, before industrialization tempted them into the job market.[40] Yet the frequent complaint that married women were "laid on the shelf" belies this picture of domestic felicity. Lacking the alternative of employment, women did not face the possibility of role conflict that the modern woman may encounter. Yet boredom and dissatisfaction with this domestic withdrawal may have encouraged women into the labor market when the possibility arose some decades later.

There was general consensus that American women made dutiful and affectionate wives. Lieber wrote:

[35] *Ibid.*, Chapter 10.

[36] Achille Murat, *The United States of America*, London: Effingham Wilson, 1833.

[37] Alex Macay uses this expression in *The Western World*, vol. I, London: Richard Bentley, 1850.

[38] Grattan suggests that married women are particularly visible and thus, to a great extent, safeguarded from moral dangers. He also notes that American women do not stop flirting after they are married. Thomas Colley Grattan, *Civilized America*, 2 vols., second edition, London: Bradbury and Evans, 1859.

[39] This notion of a role bargain is implicit in Willar Waller's article "The Rating and Dating Complex," *American Sociological Review*, 2 (October, 1937), pp. 727–734 and in his book on the family, *op. cit.*, pp. 239–254. Goode uses the conception of a "role bargain" in "A Theory of Role Strain," *American Sociological Review*, 25 (August, 1960), pp. 483–496.

[40] Ralph Linton, in an otherwise quite illuminating discussion of the dilemma of the modern woman, states, "Even fifty years ago the comfortably married woman looked with smug pity on the poor working girl in her drab, mannish clothes." "Women in the Family" in Marvin B. Sussman, *op. cit.*, p. 170.

I must mention the fact, that American women make most exemplary wives and mothers, and strange, be a girl ever so coquettish—yea, even a positive flirt, who, in Europe would unavoidably make her future husband unhappy as soon as she were married, here she becomes the domestic and retired wife.[41]

The coldness that was attributed to single girls was not mentioned in the descriptions of married women. Even the most critical observers acknowledged the braveness and devotion that pioneer wives demonstrated in following their husbands into the Western wilderness.

There were a few travelers who dissented from the prevailing view that American women made good wives and mothers. A single traveler, Israel Benjamin, wrote, "The women have a characteristic, innate, and ineradicable aversion to any work and to household affairs."[42] This opinion, however, is so disparate from the vast majority of observers that it may indicate nothing more than Benjamin's generally negative attitude toward family life in America.

Although observers seemed to agree that the young women gave up an advantageous position when they married, several travelers noted that women wielded considerable power inside the home. Along with Tocqueville, these observers felt that the division of labor between husband and wife permitted the wife to have a great deal of authority over household matters.[43] One observer commented bitterly: "The reign of the women is here complete."[44] But generally, observers remarked that women deferred to their husbands' decisions in cases of disagreement. Clearly, the picture of the patriarchal household is only partially accurate. The authority of the husband was uncontested, but it seemed to be a limited authority which did not interfere with the woman's domestic power.[45] Bremer sums up the situation: "Of the American home I have seen and heard enough for me to say that women have, in general, all the rule there they wish to have. Woman is the centre and lawgiver in the home of the New World, and the American man loves that it should be so."[46]

There is a lack of consensus among the travelers on the closeness of the American family. Some observers commented that family members are united. Tocqueville interprets the close ties between husband and wife, father and sons, and between siblings as resulting from the greater equality of family members and the absence of arbitrary authority.[47]

Although Tocqueville's theory of family relations is probably sound, there was considerable opinion that family ties were not as close as in Europe. Here,

---

[41] Francis Lieber, *The Stranger in America*, London: Richard Bentley, 1835, p. 132.

[42] Israel Joseph Benjamin, "Drei Jahre in Amerika 1859–1862," in Handlin, *This Was America, op. cit.*, p. 274.

[43] Tocqueville, *op. cit.*

[44] Benjamin, *op. cit.*, p. 273.

[45] Rose Coser identifies the same pattern in the Eastern European Jewish family in her article "Authority and Structural Ambivalence in the Middle-Class Family" in the book of readings she edited, *The Family: Its Structure and Functions*, New York: St. Martin's Press, 1964, pp. 370–383.

[46] Fredrika Bremer, *The Homes of the New World*, 2 vols., New York: Harper & Brothers, 1853, p. 190.

[47] Tocqueville, *op. cit.*

the particular experiences of travelers to the United States may have created certain observational biases which cannot easily be checked. Specifically, many travelers did not observe families in their homes, but saw them in hotels and boarding houses. Families that lived in such residences were frequently engaged in business and represented the urban middle class. The observations of the urban middle class family tend to increase the appearance of similarity between the nineteenth century family and the family of today.

Most of the travelers who commented on family life in boarding houses were appalled at what they saw. Young married couples neither desired nor got privacy.[48] Young women were denied the opportunity to develop domestic skills which they would need when they moved into their own homes. Above all, boarding house life for women was exceedingly dull. Men went off to work leaving women with nothing to do. Trollope remarked that she saw the most elaborate embroidered apparel there because women had little else with which to occupy their time.[49] Several descriptions of life in the boarding house paint a dismal picture of women's pathetic attempts to occupy themselves until their husbands came home from work. A few travelers also felt the inactivity and lack of privacy endangered the wife's morals.

The claim that husbands neglected their wives for business was not restricted to accounts of boarding house life. It was one of the most frequent criticisms of American marriages. Vivid detail is supplied to give testimony to this situation. The husband left for his business early in the morning, perhaps came home for lunch, but usually did not return until late at night. This situation was frequently used to explain the dull marriages and the lack of intimacy between family members. Bishop gives a curious picture of the husband's role in the family:

The short period which they can spend in the bosom of their families must be an enjoyment and relaxation to them; therefore, in the absence of any statements to the contrary, it is but right to suppose that they are affectionate husbands and fathers.[50]

Marryat, among others, felt that the family was disintegrating in America though he was not specific about why this was so.

Beyond the period of infancy there is no endearment between the parents and children; none of that sweet spirit of affection between brother and sisters; none of those links which unite one family; of that mutual confidence; that rejoicing in each other's success; that refuge, when they are depressed or afflicted, in the bosoms of those who love us.[51]

[48] Boarding house life is discussed by W. E. Baxter in *America and the Americans*, London: Geo. Routledge & Co., 1855. Auguste Carlier associated the spread of boarding houses with the decline of domestic life in America. See his *Marriage in the United States*, Boston: De Bries, Ibarra & Co., 1867.

[49] Trollope, *op. cit.*

[50] Anne Bishop, *The Englishwomen in America*, London: John Murray, 1856, p. 365.

[51] Frederick Marryat in Sydney Jackman (ed.), *A Diary in America*, New York: Alfred A. Knopf, 1962, p. 355.

Thus we find there is some disagreement about the closeness of the family in America at this time, despite the widespread assumption in our generation that family life then was cohesive and intimate. Perhaps the most interesting insight on this problem is offered by Chevalier, who wrote:

It may be objected that in the United States family sentiment is much weaker than it is in Europe. But we must not confound what is merely accidental and temporary with the permanent acquisitions of civilization. The temporary weakness of family sentiment was one of the necessary results of the general dispersion of individuals by which the colonization of America has been accomplished . . . As soon as they have their growth, the Yankees whose spirit now predominates in the Union quit their parents, never to return, as naturally and with as little emotion as young birds desert forever their native nests as soon as they are fledged.[52]

This statement suggests a reformulation of the common latter-day hypothesis that industrialization and urbanization weaken family cohesion. There are a number of general centrifugal forces which may weaken the family. These forces are not always accompanied by industrialization and urbanization. When, for example, the family cannot offer opportunities locally to its younger men and women that are equal to those opportunities elsewhere, we would expect that family ties will be weakened.

American morality drew praise from many of the European visitors. The American woman's self-imposed restraint was often attributed to the childhood freedom granted to her. Though a few of the travelers scoffed at the reputed moral purity of American women, the great majority of travelers who commented on morality found American women to be almost beyond reproach. Tocqueville[53] and Wyse[54] even indicate that there is less of a double standard for men than in Europe; moral restraints are binding on the males as well as the female. But Marryat counters, "To suppose there is no conjugal infidelity in the United States is to suppose that human nature is not the same everywhere."[55] Several travelers heard stories of infidelity but few actual encounters are reported. Martineau claims that disgrace is less permanent in the United States.[56]

DIVORCE

Although divorce is touched upon in the travelers' accounts, it obviously is not a matter of intense concern for most of the observers.[57] Grattan[58] and Griesinger[59] point out that a divorce is more difficult to obtain in America than

---

[52] Chevalier, *op. cit.*, p. 398.

[53] Tocqueville, *op. cit.*

[54] Francis Wyse, *America, Its Realities and Resources*, vol. I, London: T. C. Newby, 1846.

[55] Marryat, *op. cit.*, p. 431.

[56] Harriet Martineau in Seymour M. Lipset (ed.), *Society in America*, New York: Anchor Books, 1962.

[57] The intense concern with divorce does not begin until the rise of industrialization in the post-Civil War period. Then the divorce rate slowly rises, and public discussion of divorce rapidly increases. The Census did not begin to report divorce rates until after the Civil War.

[58] Grattan, *op. cit.*

[59] Griesinger, *op. cit.*

in Europe. Marryat[60] and Marjoribanks[61] report just the opposite. Several observers found that divorce was increasing in this country. Wyse notes that the problem had grown to the point where divorces were said to exceed two thousand a year.[62] The fact that all the mention of divorce occurs in accounts written after 1845 suggests an increasing concern in the latter part of the century. Still, this subject was relatively neglected, and did not take on great significance until after the Civil War.

AGING

One family problem is conspicuous by its absence. This is the problem of aging. Not a single account discusses the place of old people in the society or even the position of the grandparent in the family. Indeed, the subject of the extended family is rarely, if ever, discussed. There are several possible explanations for this absence. The proportion of older persons in the population was quite small: less than 4 per cent of the population was over 60 years old.[63] Not only were there proportionally fewer old people, but they were less likely to be living in urban areas where they might be viewed as a problem to the family. In rural areas, the older person might easily live with his children. The accounts make no mention of parents living with their grown children. However, it is likely that foreign travelers, accustomed to seeing the same pattern in their own country, did not think it was worthy of notice. A careful historical study of how old people were cared for in this country would be most interesting.

PARENT-CHILD RELATIONS

Many travelers point out the loving care that was given to children in America. Because of early marriages and the domestic emphasis placed on the married woman's role, large families were common.[64] There was almost complete agreement that children were well taken care of in America.

The most significant observation about American children was the permissive child-rearing patterns that apparently were widespread at this time. A fifth of the sample stated that youth in America were indulged and undisciplined. Marryat put it bluntly, "Now, anyone who has been in the United States must have perceived that there is little or no parental control." [65] Many of the Europeans were shocked by the power children had over their parents, their defiance of their parents' authority, and the way the children were spoiled and pampered.

The lack of restraints on children was justified by some travelers who felt this rejection of authority was a necessary preparation for a democratic citizen. Martineau argues:

---

[60] Marryat, *op. cit.*

[61] Alexander Marjoribanks, *Travels in South and North America*, New York: Simpkin, Marshall, and Company, 1853.

[62] Wyse, *op. cit.*

[63] *Historical Statistics, op. cit.*, Series A 71–85.

[64] Calhoun reports the frequency of large families in his study of the American family, *op. cit.*, vol. II, Chapter 1.

[65] Marryat, *op. cit.*, p. 351.

Freedom of manners in children of which so much complaint has been made by observers . . . is a necessary fact. Till the United States ceases to be republican—the children there will continue as free and easy and as important as they are.[66]

Some observers even took delight in the spontaneity and independence shown by American children.

The above suggests that the controversy between permissive and authoritarian child-rearing has not been confined to the twentieth century.[67] Also the great respect and reverence for parental authority that is generally assumed to have existed at this time is not as pervasive as the defenders of the traditional nineteenth-century family would suggest. Furthermore, the picture of the close Victorian family is not entirely supported by these accounts. Some travelers observed disharmony as well as harmony in the family, though not enough observers commented on this subject to make any conclusive statements.

Grattan, among others, comments on the enormous push for children to grow up and become independent of their families.[68] This may be part of the "business" stereotype that is present in some of these writings, but the move toward early maturity is consistent with the prevalence of early marriages. Girls over the age of 21 were considered by some as old maids, and boys, according to Marryat,[69] left home in their middle teens. This picture may be somewhat exaggerated. Yet the impression is that children were not inclined to stay in the bosom of the family for any longer than they had to. Children are frequently characterized as self-confident, independent, poised, and mature.

This contention is supported by description of the American adolescent. Freedom is the most frequent word used to describe adolescent behavior in America. However, as already noted, the freedom which existed between the sexes was tempered by considerable restraint.

There is surprisingly little criticism of the behavior of adolescents. It is said by a few observers that there was much frivolous dancing and partying. Adolescents were not given nearly as much attention in these accounts as would be devoted to the subject today. The stress on growing up and assuming adult responsibilities seems to take precedence over what is today called "youth culture."[70]

From the little information that is reported, there appeared to be less discontintinuity between the role of an adolescent and the role of an adult. This is one point where the industrialized society may have placed added strains on the family. At least there is some reason to believe that adolescence as a period of great stress had not yet been generally identified in America.

[66] Martineau, *op. cit.*, p. 28. Four other travelers concur with Martineau.

[67] Miller and Swanson make a similar observation in their review of childrearing practices. Daniel R. Miller and Guy E. Swanson, *The Changing American Parent*, New York: John Wiley & Sons, Inc., 1958, pp. 8–9.

[68] Grattan, *op. cit.*

[69] Marryat, *op. cit.*

[70] Parsons, "Age and Sex in the Social Structure," *op. cit.*

THE POSITION OF WOMEN IN SOCIETY

The final topic that emerges from the travelers' accounts is the position of women in American society. This subject has been touched upon throughout the paper. There are, however, some additional observations to be reported. Over a fourth of the travelers comment favorably on female beauty in America. Cobden describes the ladies as "petite but elegant."[71] At the same time, he notes that Boston ladies were "still deficient in preface and postscript." [72] Several writers consider the women unhealthy in appearance. It is quite interesting that so many observers find that American looks fade at an early age. Moreau expresses a common view when he writes about American women: "... they are charming, adorable at fifteen, dried-up at twenty-three, old at thirty-five, decrepit at forty or fifty." [73] This observation is consistent with the comments discussed earlier about the withdrawal of the older women from social life. There was probably little motivation or need for the women to keep up their appearance. In view of the strong emphasis on morality, the attractive older woman may have been viewed with a certain suspicion.

Almost all of the sample remarked that American women were treated with extraordinary deference and respect. As a matter of course, men were expected to give women any seat they desired in a public place even though someone might be sitting there and other seats be available. One traveler commented that he saw a man grab a chicken wing off another man's plate to give to a woman who had asked for it.[74] Some Europeans found this almost compulsive chivalry quite proper. To them it indicated the high esteem in which the female was held in America. Thornton wrote, "Attention and deference to women, if carried to a faulty extreme, is an error on the right side; but I deem it rather praiseworthy than faulty ..." [75] Tocqueville suggested that the respect for women was a sign of a growing equality between the sexes.[76]

Many observers do not agree with these views. They saw the respect as superficial and deceptive. The Pulszkys had an extremely sophisticated analysis of this cult of politeness:

It appears as if the gentlemen would atone for their all-absorbing passion for business by the privilege they give to the ladies of idling time away ... And as business is a passion with the Americans, not the means, but the very life of existence, they are most anxious to keep this department exclusively to themselves; and, well aware that there is no more infallible way to secure noninterference, than by giving the general impression that they never act for themselves, *the lady's rule* has become a current phrase, but by no means a fact in the United States.[77]

[71] Richard Cobden in Elizabeth Hoon Cawley (ed.), *The American Diaries of Richard Cobden*, Princeton: Princeton University Press, 1952, p. 89.

[72] *Ibid.*, p. 14.

[73] Moreau, *op. cit.*, p. 98. Eight other travelers make the same observation.

[74] Marryat, *op. cit.*

[75] Major John Thornton, *Diary of a Tour Through the Northern States of the Union and Canada*, London: F. Barker ... and Co., 1850, p. 110.

[76] Tocqueville, *op. cit.*

[77] Pulszky and Pulszky, *op. cit.*, p. 239.

Though others do not see the degree of rationalization in the cult of politeness, there is support for the Pulszkys' view. Hall[78] and Martineau[79] state that women occupy an inferior position in American society. The elaborate courtesy and deference are only substitutes for real respect.

Although several of the observers see the American woman as satisfied with her place in society and two visitors see her fulfilling a valuable function of maintaining morality in the society, others feel strongly that the woman occupies an ambiguous position. Her lower status in the society is at odds with the democratic ideology. She cannot be considered an equal to men as long as she is confined completely to the home. The single woman must give up a good deal of her freedom when she marries. This loss of freedom is not fully compensated for by the respect she gains by mothering her husband's children and supervising his household. The discontinuity in the role of a woman is, in certain respects, similar to the conflict between career and family that exists today. It would be valuable to look at the diaries and letters of women from this period to see whether there is any indication of such a strain.

The great deference paid to women may have compensated them, in part, for this loss of standing. But many of the observers seemed to feel that the reward was not adequate compensation. It should be said, however, that some of the observers were crusaders for women's rights in Europe, and their dissatisfaction with the cult of politeness is to be expected.

Finally, it should be noted that this kind of strain, like many of the other strains in the family which we have pointed out, did not directly derive from emerging industrialization. No doubt, post-Civil War industrialization aggravated the ambiguous position of women in American society, but women by this time may have been ripe for emancipation from the home. Thus, we might find a convergence of social patterns rather than the often-assumed cause-and-effect relationship between industrialization and the emancipation of women.

CONCLUSION

The accounts of foreign travelers visiting the United States in the first half of the nineteenth century contain valuable observations on the American family. These observations suggest the following conclusions:

1. Changes in the American family since the period of industrialization have been exaggerated by some writers. The system of mate selection, the marital relationship, and parent-child relations in the pre-industrial family all show striking similarities to those in the family of today. Family strains commonly attributed to industrialization are evident to observers of the family prior to industrialization.

2. Although the American family is for the most part viewed favorably by the foreign travelers, it is in no way viewed as a tension-free, harmonious

[78] Captain Basil Hall, *Travels in North America in the Years 1827 and 1828*, Edinburgh: Robert Cadell, 1830.

[79] Martineau, *op. cit.*

institution. Strains resulting from the voluntary choice of mates, the abrupt loss of freedom for women at marriage, women's discontent arising from total domesticity, lack of discipline of American children, the inferior position of women in American society—these were some of the common points of stress in the American family at that time.

3. It is not unlikely that some of these tensions may have eased the adaptation to an industrial society. The lack of parental restrictions on American children and the desire for women to improve their position in society and escape the demands of domestic duties may have facilitated the growth of the industrial system.

4. It should also be pointed out that certain strains in the American family which are sources of widespread concern today were not noted by foreign travelers. Few comments were directed at adolescence, old age, or divorce, perhaps indicating that at that time these areas were not sources of strain.

Additional Readings

WILLIAM D. ALTUS, "Birth Order and Its Sequelae," *Science*, 151 (January 7, 1966), pp. 44–49.

LARRY D. BARNETT, "Research in Interreligious Dating and Marriage," *Journal of Marriage and Family Living*, 24 (May, 1962), pp. 191–194.

THOMAS K. BURCH, "The Size and Structure of Families: A Comparative Analysis of Census Data," *American Sociological Review*, 32 (June, 1967), pp. 347–363.

PAUL C. GLICK, DAVID M. HEER, and JOHN C. BERESFORD, "Family Formation and Family Composition: Trends and Prospects," in Marvin B. Sussman (ed.), *Sourcebook in Marriage and the Family* (Boston: Houghton Mifflin Company, 1955), pp. 30–40.

PETER JACOBSOHN and ADAM P. MATHENY, JR., "Mate Selection in Open Marriage Systems," *International Journal of Comparative Sociology*, 3 (September, 1962), pp. 98–123 (esp. 105–106).

PAUL H. JACOBSON, *American Marriage and Divorce* (New York: Holt, Rinehart & Winston, Inc., 1959), pp. 20–36 and 88–96.

JOEL J. MOSS, "Teen-age Marriage: Cross-National Trends and Sociological Factors in the Decision of When to Marry," *Journal of Marriage and the Family*, 27 (May, 1965), pp. 230–242.

GEORGE P. MURDOCK, *Social Structure* (New York: The Macmillan Company, 1949), pp. 284–289.

IRA L. REISS, "The Sexual Renaissance: A Summary and Analysis," *The Journal of Social Issues*, 22 (April, 1966), pp. 123–137.

MARVIN B. SUSSMAN and LEE G. BURCHINAL, "Parental Aid to Married Children: Implications for Family Functioning," in Bernard Farber (ed.), *Kinship and Family Organization* (New York: John Wiley and Sons, Inc., 1966), pp. 240–254.

MARVIN B. SUSSMAN, "Relationships of Adult Children with Their Parents in the United States," in Ethel Shanas and Gordon F. Streib (eds.), *Social Structure and the Family: Generational Relations* (Englewood Cliffs, N.J.: Prentice-Hall, Inc., 1965), pp. 62–93.

CHARLES F. WESTOFF, ROBERT G. POTTER, JR., PHILIP C. SAGI, and ELLIOT G. MISHLER, *Family Growth in Metropolitan America* (Princeton, N.J.: Princeton University Press, 1961), pp. 178–193.

RELIGION

Introduction

The selection by Bogue, "Religious Affiliation," summarizes factual information about religious preference. Some of Bogue's information will not be surprising. Most individuals, for example, will not be surprised to learn that religious preference is distributed in the following manner among the three major religious groups in the United States: Protestants, 66.2 per cent; Roman Catholics, 25.7 per cent; and Jews, 3.2 per cent. However, there are some surprises in Bogue's data; five are noteworthy. First, the Baptists are the most fertile religious group. Many individuals would have probably thought the Roman Catholics more fertile. Second, three religious groups stand out as having exceptionally high concentrations of their membership in metropolitan areas:[1] Jewish, Episcopal, and Roman Catholic. Many individuals would probably not have included the Episcopal group with the Jews and Roman Catholics. Third, Episcopalians have the highest average level of educational attainment. Many individuals would have probably nominated the Jews as the most educated religious group. (The Jews are second, however.) Fourth, Roman Catholic and Protestants tend to have similar occupational compositions. Many individuals who are aware of the heavy immigration of unskilled Roman Catholics at the turn of the century think of the Roman Catholics as primarily blue-collar workers and the Protestants as primarily white-collar workers. Fifth, when comparisons are made for all categories in the occupational scale, household heads whose religious preference is Roman Catholic tend to receive higher incomes than those who are Protestant. Similarly, Roman Catholic household heads tend to have higher incomes, for a given amount of schooling completed, than Protestant

[1] Metropolitan areas are generally counties which include a city of 50,000 or more inhabitants.

household heads. Many individuals, because of the immigration mentioned earlier, view the Roman Catholics as having lower incomes than the Protestants.

Ever since Weber suggested that ascetic Protestantism constituted one element in the growth of capitalism,[2] scholars have investigated this problem. The next two selections are within the Weberian tradition. The first selection, Glenn and Hyland's "Religious Preference and Worldly Success: Some Evidence From National Surveys," reports factual information about the relationship between religion and success. In the mid-1940's, Protestants ranked well above Roman Catholics in income, occupation, and education; however, by the mid-1960's Roman Catholics ranked above Protestants in most measures of income, occupation, and education. The most important remaining Protestant advantage was that a larger percentage of Protestants had at least some college training.[3] These findings signify that Roman Catholics as a group have experienced more net upward *mobility* during the post-World War II period than Protestants. Glenn and Hyland's findings confirm some of the surprises in Bogue's data, and are at variance with predictions based on Weber's study of ascetic Protestantism and capitalism.[4]

The second selection which is relevant to the Weberian tradition, Hadden's "Theological Belief and Political Ideology Among Protestant Clergy," reports factual information about the relationship between religion and politics. In a series of widely cited papers, Johnson—whose three case studies Hadden is checking with a national sample—advances two main points. First, conservative theological views are related to preference for the Republican party, and similarly, liberal theological views are related to preference for the Democratic party.[5] Second, theologically liberal ministers have a liberalizing influence on the political behavior of their laity who by class should tend toward conservative political behavior, whereas theologically conservative ministers have a moderating influence on laity who by class should tend toward liberal political behavior. Hadden's data directly and inferentially support, respectively, Johnson's first and second points. The studies by Johnson and Hadden are in accordance with predictions based on Weber's study of ascetic Protestantism and capitalism.[6]

The selection by Lazarwitz, "Some Factors Associated with Variations in Church Attendance," contains factual information about a topic that none of the other selections consider, church attendance. Analysis of the Christian group reveals five patterns: first, women, both in and out of the labor force, attend church more frequently than men; second, Negroes attend church somewhat more often than whites; third, the higher the education and occupation levels, the greater the rate of church attendance; fourth, no associations exist between frequency of church attendance and age, number of children, or family income; and fifth, there is an increased regularity of church attendance by Protestants with children five years old and over. In the Jewish group, men attend synagogue more frequently than women, and the older group more frequently than the younger group. There are no significant associations between church attendance and education, occupation, or income within the Jewish group. A distinction between "belief" and "practice"

[2] Max Weber, *The Protestant Ethic and the Spirit of Capitalism*, trans. Talcott Parsons (New York: Charles Scribner's Sons, 1930).

[3] Glenn and Hyland suggest that even this difference seems to have disappeared among the youngest adults.

[4] The information summarized by Glenn and Hyland is also relevant to the discussion of "mobility" in the section on "Stratification."

[5] Johnson also argues that theological views and party affiliation are manifestations of ascetic Protestant values.

[6] Hadden's selection presents information which is relevant to the section on "Culture" in Part I, "The Individual and the Group" and the section on "Polity" in Part II, "The Social Structure of the Group."

is customarily made in sociology of religion.[7] Church attendance, as described by Lazarwitz, would be an example of a religious practice. Lazarwitz's findings, therefore, must not be generalized to include religious belief. Church attendance, it should also be noted, does not have the same meaning as "church membership," another topic which is frequently studied in sociology of religion. An individual may attend church without being a member; similarly, church members do not always attend church activities. Lazarwitz's findings also must not be confused with information relating to church membership.

Many individuals believe that religious beliefs and practices in the United States have become stronger since the early nineteenth century. The selection by Lipset, "All-Pervasiveness, a Consistent Characteristic of American Religion," argues that religious beliefs and practices have always been strong in the United States. There has, in short, been no recent "religious revival" in the United States. Although he primarily presents information about the United States, Lipset also suggests that from the early nineteenth century until the present, the United States has been among the most religious countries in the Christian world.

---

[7] This distinction corresponds to the distinction between "prejudice" and "discrimination" discussed in connection with the selections by Stember, "Attitudes Toward Jews," and Sheatsley, "White Attitudes Towards the Negro." "Belief" and "prejudice" are examples of "internal orientations," whereas "practice" and "discrimination" are examples of "behavior."

Religious Affiliation

DONALD J. BOGUE

Most sociologists consider religious affiliation a factor of paramount importance in explaining many aspects of human behavior. Like the factors of educational attainment, occupation, and income, it is an axis around which much of a person's life is oriented. Even for the purposes of formal demography, a knowledge of the religious affiliations of the population is important, since it helps to explain the level and trend of fertility, the willingness of some persons to migrate to particular localities, etc. Many nations of the world collect statistics concerning religious affiliation, and report them in full detail as a part of the regular official census.[1] The United States, unfortunately, is not one of those nations.[2]

In March of 1957, the U.S. Bureau of the Census included the question, "What is your religion?" on its monthly Current Population Survey. The Census wanted to determine the attitude of the public toward answering such a question, and also to experiment with the wording in case the question should become an item on the 1960 census. Only a negligible number refused to answer, and much valuable information was obtained concerning the general religious affiliation of the population. Sample surveys made by private research organizations routinely ask questions concerning religion; their experience has been that it

Reprinted with permission of The Macmillan Company from *The Population of the United States* by Donald J. Bogue. © The Free Press, a Corporation 1959.

[1] "Among the countries with 500,000 or more inhabitants for which censuses have been published in recent years . . . about half have included at least one question on religion. By continental divisions, these totaled seven in North America, three in South America, twelve in Europe (including all the German governments as one), sixteen in Africa, and two in Oceania." Dorothy Good, "Questions on Religion in the United States Census," *Population Index*, January, 1959.

[2] Despite strong appeals from a wide array of analysts and administrators (including leaders of religious groups), a question on religious affiliation has never been included in the regular decennial census enumerations. For example, the American Sociological Society, the Census Users Advisory Committee (representing more than 75 professional organizations), and the Population Association of America supported the asking of a question on religious affiliation in the 1960 census. The Bureau of the Census has received strong representation directly and indirectly, through purse-string-holding congressmen, not to include questions on religion in its enumerations. It has been held by some that to ask a census question on religious affiliation would violate those constitutional rights of the citizen which assure freedom of religious belief. A small minority has feared that, at some future date, census records showing religious affiliation could be used as a weapon against persons belonging to particular religious groups. This is a fallacious argument. The religious affiliation of almost every citizen, or of his family, is already recorded or indicated in a number of different places. The titles of the ministers, priests, and rabbis who perform wedding ceremonies, the names of cemeteries and funeral directors on death certificates, the membership registers of churches, census records showing the birthplace of parents, the records of grammar schools, high schools, and colleges— even military and veterans' records—contain information that could be used to determine religious affiliation. Finally, if a dictator were abroad in the land, he probably would not rely on out-of-date census records, but would call for a new and compulsory registration involving severe penalties for noncompliance or falsification. This is what happened in Germany before World War II.

is one of the easiest question to enumerate, and causes no more anxiety or resentment than questions on such matters as age or marital status. A question on religious affiliation will not appear in the 1960 census, but its absence is due to policy considerations, not technical problems.

This brief chapter is an attempt to document the proposition that much scientific knowledge would be gained by including a question on religious affiliation once each year in the sample surveys, and also in the decennial census.[3] This chapter is based on the fraction of the results of the Census survey of March, 1957 that was released, and on a tabulation of the data concerning religious affiliation that were collected by the National Opinion Research Center of the University of Chicago in two of its recent nationwide surveys.[4]

CENSUS MATERIALS ON RELIGION: NUMBER AND DISTRIBUTION

Table 1 and Figure 1 show the religious composition of the population.

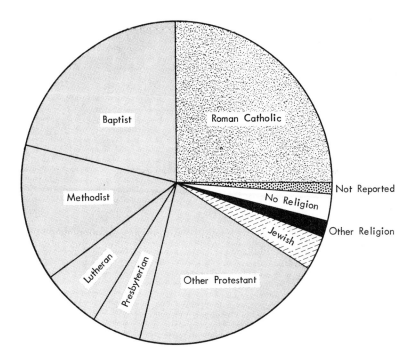

FIGURE 1. Religion reported by persons 14 years old and over: civilian population, March 1957. (*Source: Current Population Reports, Series P-20, No. 79, Table 1, Feb. 1958.*)

---

[3] This could be done at no additional cost, by substituting the question on religious affiliation for the question on veterans' status, which yielded such unreliable information at the 1950 census that detailed tabulations were not published.

Summarized in its broadest terms, the religious affiliation of persons 14 years old and over is as follows:

Religion	Total	White	Nonwhite
Total	100.0	100.0	100.0
Protestant	66.2	63.9	87.5
Roman Catholic	25.7	27.9	6.5
Jewish	3.2	3.6	–
Other religion	1.3	1.2	1.5
No religion	2.7	2.5	3.5
No information	0.9	0.9	1.0

Thus, two of every three persons 14 years of age or older identifies himself with one of the Protestant denominations, while about one in four reports himself as a Roman Catholic. The Jewish group is much smaller; only about one person in 31 in the population is Jewish. Almost all of the population (96.4 percent) claimed some religious affiliation; only 2.7 percent reported themselves as having no religion.

Within the Protestant class, the Bureau of the Census identified four major denominations:

	Percent of Population 14 and Over		
	Total	White	Nonwhite
Baptist	19.7	15.2	60.7
Lutheran	7.1	7.8	0.2
Methodist	14.0	13.7	17.3
Presbyterian	5.6	6.2	0.9
Other Protestant	19.8	21.1	8.5

This shows that about one-third of the population (and one-half of all Protestants) is either Methodist or Baptist, one-eighth is either Lutheran or Presbyterian, while about one-fifth belongs to the many dozens of smaller denominations or hundreds of sects. . . .

Distribution of Religious Groups. The religious composition of the population of the four census regions is reported in Table 2; the composition by urban and rural areas is shown in Table 3. From the information in these tables, it may be concluded that:

---

4 In February, 1958, the Bureau of the Census published a report, "Religion Reported by the Civilian Population of the United States: March, 1957," *Current Population Reports*, Series P-20, No. 79. These data furnish much of the material for this chapter. The release stated: "This is the first report containing nationwide statistics on religion of the population, based on data collected from individuals by the Bureau of the Census. . . . Other Reports presenting results of this survey are being prepared." When the supplementary reports of the Census Bureau are released, they will replace the NORC tabulations presented in this chapter, which were assembled only because the additional reports mentioned in the first census report had not yet been made available.

TABLE 1. RELIGION REPORTED FOR PERSONS 14 YEARS OLD AND OVER, BY COLOR AND SEX, FOR THE UNITED STATES: CIVILIAN POPULATION, MARCH 1957

Religion	Total (000)	White (000)		Nonwhite (000)		Percent distribution					
		Male	Female	Male	Female	Total	White		Nonwhite		Percent Nonwhite
							Male	Female	Male	Female	
Total, 14 years and over	119,333	51,791	55,570	5,679	6,293	100.0	100.0	100.0	100.0	100.0	100.0
Protestant	78,952	32,320	36,155	4,851	5,626	66.2	62.4	65.1	85.4	89.4	13.3
Baptist	23,525	7,822	8,450	3,354	3,899	19.7	15.1	15.2	59.1	62.0	30.8
Lutheran	8,417	4,084	4,301	17	15	7.1	7.9	7.7	0.3	0.2	0.4
Methodist	16,676	6,788	7,821	968	1,099	14.0	13.1	14.1	17.0	17.5	12.4
Presbyterian	6,656	3,000	3,549	57	50	5.6	5.8	6.4	1.0	0.8	1.6
Other Protestant	23,678	10,626	12,034	455	563	19.8	20.5	21.7	8.0	8.9	4.3
Roman Catholic	30,669	14,396	15,499	361	413	25.7	27.8	27.9	6.4	6.6	2.5
Jewish	3,868	1,860	1,999	1	8	3.2	3.6	3.6	...	0.1	0.2
Other religion	1,545	688	676	88	93	1.3	1.3	1.2	1.5	1.5	11.7
No religion	3,195	2,051	730	306	108	2.7	4.0	1.3	5.4	1.7	13.0
Religion not rept.	1,104	476	511	72	45	0.9	0.9	0.9	1.3	0.7	11.5

In this report, the "civilian population" includes about 809,000 members of the Armed Forces living off post or with their families on post, but excludes all other members of the Armed Forces. Four largest Protestant groups shown separately. Percent not shown where less than 0.1.

TABLE 2. REGION OF RESIDENCE OF PERSONS 14 YEARS OLD AND OVER, BY RELIGION REPORTED, CIVILIAN POPULATION, MARCH 1957

Religion	United States (000)	Northeast (000)	North Central (000)	South (000)	West (000)
Total, 14 years old and over	119,333	31,264	34,825	36,551	16,693
Protestant	78,952	13,225	24,025	30,249	11,453
White	68,475	11,675	21,978	24,037	10,785
Nonwhite	10,477	1,550	2,047	6,212	668
Roman Catholic	30,669	14,106	8,587	4,254	3,722
Jewish	3,868	2,671	460	299	438
Other Religion	1,545	647	410	269	219
No Religion	3,195	358	1,024	1,108	705
Religion not reported	1,104	257	319	372	156
Percent by Religion					
Total, 14 years old and over	100.0	100.0	100.0	100.0	100.0
Protestant	66.2	42.3	69.0	82.8	68.6
White	57.4	37.3	63.1	65.8	64.6
Nonwhite	8.8	5.0	5.9	17.0	4.0
Roman Catholic	25.7	45.1	24.7	11.6	22.3
Jewish	3.2	8.5	1.3	0.8	2.6
Other religion	1.3	2.1	1.2	0.7	1.3
No religion	2.7	1.1	2.9	3.0	4.2
Religion not reported	0.9	0.8	0.9	1.0	0.9
Percent by Residence					
Total, 14 years old and over	100.0	26.2	29.2	30.6	14.0
Protestant	100.0	16.8	30.4	38.3	14.5
White	100.0	17.1	32.1	35.1	15.8
Nonwhite	100.0	14.8	19.5	59.3	6.4
Roman Catholic	100.0	46.0	28.0	13.9	12.1
Jewish	100.0	69.1	11.9	7.7	11.3
Other religion	100.0	41.9	26.5	17.4	14.2
No religion	100.0	11.2	32.1	34.7	22.1
Religion not reported	100.0	23.3	28.9	33.7	14.1

(a) The South is strongly Protestant in its religious affiliation. Only 12 percent of the South's population is Roman Catholic, and less than 1 percent is Jewish.

(b) Roman Catholics are heavily concentrated in the Northeastern states. In the population of the North Central states and the West, they constitute just about the same proportion as they do of the nation's total population. Roman Catholics are predominantly urban; they are concentrated in and about large cities, and are comparatively scarce in rural areas.

(c) Persons of Jewish religion are highly concentrated in Northeastern states and in large cities. There are almost no Jewish farmers, and very few Jewish residents of rural-nonfarm areas.

(d) The "Other Religion" category has a distribution pattern roughly similar to that of the Roman Catholics. Persons whose religious belief is other than Protestant, Catholic, or Jewish are somewhat concentrated in the Northeast and in large urban centers. Because of its large Oriental population, the West also has a slight concentration of persons in the "Other Religion" category.

TABLE 3. URBAN-RURAL RESIDENCE OF PERSONS 14 YEARS OLD AND OVER, BY RELIGION REPORTED, FOR THE UNITED STATES: CIVILIAN POPULATION, MARCH 1957

Religion	United States	Urban Total	Urbanized Areas of 25,000 or More	Other Urban	Rural Nonfarm	Rural Farm
Percent by Residence Total, 14 years old and over	100.0	63.9	36.6	27.3	24.4	11.7
Protestant	100.0	56.6	27.2	29.5	28.7	14.7
White	100.0	55.2	24.5	30.7	30.1	14.7
Nonwhite	100.0	66.1	44.6	21.6	19.3	14.5
Roman Catholic	100.0	78.8	53.9	24.9	15.8	5.4
Jewish	100.0	96.1	87.4	8.7	3.6	0.2
Other religion	100.0	77.4	52.9	24.5	14.9	7.7
No religion	100.0	54.2	29.5	24.7	31.3	14.5
Religion not reported	100.0	68.2	49.5	18.7	23.4	8.4

POPULATION CHARACTERISTICS OF RELIGIOUS GROUPS: CENSUS MATERIALS

Sex Composition (Table 1). A slightly higher percentage of men than of women claim no religion. Among men and women who do identify themselves with a religious group, there is almost no difference between the sexes with respect to religious affiliation, although a slightly higher percentage of women than of men are members of Protestant denominations. This sex imbalance is greatest in the Methodist and the "Other Protestant" churches.

Color Composition (Table 1). The nonwhite population is almost exclusively Protestant (87.5 percent). Only about one nonwhite person in 16 is a Roman Catholic. More than 60 percent of the nonwhite population belongs to one denomination, the Baptist, and an additional 17 percent belongs to the Methodist denomination. (Approximately 31 per cent of all Baptists are nonwhite.) Hence, more than 3/4 of all nonwhites belong to these two denominations. A very small percentage of the membership of the Lutheran, Presbyterian, Roman Catholic, and Jewish groups is nonwhite. The remaining nonwhite population tends to belong to one of the many minor sects or small denominations. Nonwhite males and females both are more inclined than is the white population to report that they have no religion.

Age Composition. Inasmuch as almost all of the population reported one religion or another, any differences between religious groups with respect to age composition must be due entirely to the operation of basic demographic processes—fertility, mortality, immigration—within the groups. (As noted below, there is comparatively little evidence that persons change their religious affiliation after they reach maturity.) Assuming that mortality has only a minor

TABLE 4.   AGE OF PERSONS 14 YEARS OLD AND OVER, BY RELIGION REPORTED FOR THE
UNITED STATES: CIVILIAN POPULATION, MARCH 1957

Religion	Total 14 Years and Over (000)	14 to 19 Years (000)	20 to 24 Years (000)	25 to 34 Years (000)	35 to 44 Years (000)	45 to 64 Years (000)	65 Years and Over (000)	Median Age (Years)
Total	119,333	13,960	9,743	23,437	23,113	34,399	14,681	40.4
Protestant	78,952	9,334	6,332	15,188	14,919	22,907	10,272	40.8
White	68,475	7,850	5,288	12,916	12,899	20,181	9,341	41.3
Nonwhite	10,477	1,484	1,044	2,272	2,020	2,726	931	37.2
Roman Catholic	30,669	3,707	2,675	6,555	6,407	8,266	3,059	38.7
Jewish	3,868	350	233	660	729	1,393	503	44.5
Other religion and not reported	2,649	280	209	424	482	847	407	43.5
No religion	3,195	289	294	610	576	986	440	42.0
Percent by age								
Total	100.0	11.7	8.2	19.6	19.4	28.8	12.3	–
Protestant	100.0	11.8	8.0	19.2	18.9	29.0	13.0	–
White	100.0	11.5	7.7	18.9	18.8	29.5	13.6	–
Nonwhite	100.0	14.2	10.0	21.7	19.3	26.0	8.9	–
Roman Catholic	100.0	12.1	8.7	21.4	20.9	27.0	10.0	–
Jewish	100.0	9.0	6.0	17.1	18.8	36.0	13.0	–
Other religion and not reported	100.0	10.6	7.9	16.0	18.2	32.0	15.4	–
No religion	100.0	9.0	9.2	19.1	18.0	30.9	13.8	–

differentiating effect, being roughly the same in all groups (with the possible exception of nonwhite Protestants), fertility and immigration seem the logical factors by means of which to explain age differences. An examination of Table 4 shows that the Roman Catholic and the nonwhite Protestant groups contain disproportionately large numbers of persons aged 14 to 34, in comparison with the general population. This situation is due to the higher fertility of these groups. In the case of Roman Catholics, it may also be due partially to immigration, for there has been a large immigration of Puerto Rican and Mexican families to the United States in recent years. (On the other hand, the presence in the population of many elderly Italian and Polish immigrants who arrived in the United States shortly after the turn of the century helps to account for the fact that there is a larger percentage of Catholics than of nonwhite Protestants in the age group 65 and over.)

Religion of Married Partners.   Husbands and wives tend to belong to the same religious groups. Considering only three major religious divisions, the Protestant, the Roman Catholic, and the Jewish, the census survey showed the following percentages:

Religion	Percentage of Married Couples
Husband and wife in the same major religious group	93.6
Husband and wife in different major religious groups	6.4

Protestant Intermarriage. Where at least one spouse is Protestant, the census reports the following distribution for the religion of the other spouse:

	Percent
Total	100.0
Protestant (both spouses Protestant)	91.4
Roman Catholic	8.4
Jewish	0.2

Thus approximately 1 married Protestant in 12 currently has a religion different from that of his spouse.

Catholic Intermarriage. In families where one spouse is Roman Catholic, the religion of the other spouse is as follows:

	Percent
Total	100.0
Roman Catholic (both spouses Catholic)	78.5
Protestant	21.2
Jewish	0.4

Thus, a higher percentage of Catholics than of Protestants have married across religious lines.

Jewish Intermarriage. In families where one spouse is Jewish, the religion of the other spouse is as follows:

	Percent
Total	100.0
Jewish (both spouses Jewish)	92.8
Protestant	4.2
Roman Catholic	3.0

The Jewish group seems to be more endogamous than either of the other two groups. Thus, on an absolute basis, Roman Catholics are considerably more exogamous than Protestant or Jewish persons. This characteristic seems to be due largely to the fact that a majority of their potential mates are non-Catholic. On a relative basis, taking into account the difference in the number of potential mates of their own religions, and of religious affiliations, Catholics and Protestants tend to marry outside their group to about the same general extent, while out-marriage is much less frequent among Jewish persons.

FERTILITY OF RELIGIOUS GROUPS: CENSUS MATERIALS

Demographers have long been interested in the differences between religious groups with respect to fertility, because of the different attitudes toward family

TABLE 5. NUMBER OF CHILDREN EVER BORN PER 1,000 WOMEN, MARRIED AND HUSBAND PRESENT, BY RELIGION: 1957

Religion	Women 15 to 44 Years Old		Women 45 Years Old and Over	Ratio to Nation	
	Per 1,000 Women	Per 1,000 Women, standardized for Age[a]	Per 1,000 Women	Standardized, Women 15–44	Women 45 Years Old and Over
Total	2,218	2,188	2,798	1.00	1.00
Protestant	2,220	2,206	2,753	1.01	.98
Baptist	2,359	2,381	3,275	1.09	1.11
Lutheran	2,013	1,967	2,382	.90	.85
Methodist	2,155	2,115	2,638	.97	.94
Presbyterian	2,001	1,922	2,188	.88	.78
Other Protestant	2,237	2,234	2,702	1.02	.97
Roman Catholic	2,282	2,210	3,056	1.01	1.09
Jewish	1,749	(b)	2,218	.79	.79
Other, none, and not reported	2,069	2,075	2,674	.95	.96

a Standard is the distribution by age of all women of corresponding marital status in the United States in 1950.

b Standardized rate not computed where there are fewer than 150,000 women in several component 5-year age groups.

SOURCE: Department of Commerce, Bureau of the Census; *Current Population Reports*, Series P-20.

size and family planning that are expressed or implied by the ideologies of the various groups. Table 5 reports measures of the fertility of each of the leading religious groups, in terms of the number of children ever born per 1,000 women of each group who are married and living with the husbands. Data are reported separately for women still in the childbearing ages (15 to 44), standardized for age, and for women past the ages of fertility (45 years old and over).

Comparison of these measures with the corresponding measures for earlier periods of American history, and with those of other nations that have high fertility . . . makes it very obvious that no one of the religious groups is subject to uncontrolled fertility. The practices of family planning and family limitation have evidently become widely diffused throughout the population. Although the fertility of every religious group is above the replacement level, no group is characterized by rates of children ever born that imply an average of 5 or 6 children per married woman, an average which is typical of high fertility groups. Thus, fertility control is a widely-accomplished fact throughout all major American religious groups.

Baptists are the most fertile group; their standardized measures of fertility are 9 to 11 percent above the national average. A part of this differential is due to the fact that about one-third of the Baptists are Negroes; the fertility of Negroes is 40 percent higher than that of whites, so it boosts the average. In addition, a large share of the white Baptists either now live in rural areas of the South, or were born and reared in those areas, where fertility rates for the white population are above the national average.

Among older women, Roman Catholics are more fertile than any other religious group except Baptists, although this differential is much smaller (only 9 percent) than many people have believed. Moreover, younger Catholic women appear to have adopted the family-planning practices of the general population to such an extent that their age-standardized fertility measure in 1957 was only 1 percent above that of the nation. This is due in part, but not entirely, to the fact that the national level of fertility has climbed somewhat and is thus closer to the moderately higher Roman Catholic level.

The lowest rates of fertility shown are for Jewish and Presbyterian women. These groups are 20 to 25 percent below the general population in fertility, and are scarcely reproducing themselves. Lutherans also have moderately low rates of fertility—about 10 percent below the national average. Methodists have average fertility.

A substantial share of the differences in fertility among the religious groups is due to differences in urban-rural residence. For example, the fact that Lutherans tend to be more urban than Methodists in distribution may account for most, if not all, of the differences between them. The differential between Roman Catholics and Protestants probably would be larger if these two groups were compared separately by urban and rural residence, because a much higher percentage of Protestants than of Catholics live in rural areas and are farmers. Also, compositional factors as well as distributional factors may underlie some of the fertility differences between religious groups. Intergroup differences with respect to age at marriage, occupation, and education must be controlled simultaneously in a fertility analysis before it can be claimed that such an analysis has measured the independent effect of religious affiliation upon fertility. For example, the very low fertility level of Jewish and Presbyterian women may be due to a combination of other factors associated with low fertility —their residence in large metropolises, and the fact that their husbands are well-educated, hold white-collar jobs, and have high incomes (see section following).

In reviewing the census materials on fertility recently, Paul C. Glick, Census expert on family and fertility statistics, concluded, ". . . the differences between the major religious groups with respect to fertility patterns reflect differences in the age, color, geographic, and socio-economic distributions of these groups— perhaps as much as, or more than, they reflect differences in religious doctrines with regard to family behavior. . . . Differences between rates for those under and over childbearing age suggest a trend toward convergence of the fertility levels among women in the major religious groups."[5] There is also unmistakable evidence that differences in religious doctrines *do* stimulate fertility differences,

---

[5] "Intermarriage and Fertility Patterns among Persons in the Major Religious Groups," unpublished paper presented at the annual meeting of the American Sociological Society held in Seattle, Washington, August, 1958.

independently of these other traits. One of the unfinished and important tasks of demography is to measure and analyze the independent effect of religious affiliation upon fertility. It is to be hoped that the necessary data will be made available soon—if not by the Bureau of the Census, then by private research organizations.

NORC MATERIALS ON RELIGION: NUMBER AND DISTRIBUTION

The special tabulation of materials from the National Opinion Research Center used the results of two nationwide sample surveys—study 335, conducted in the summer of 1953, and study 367, conducted in the summer of 1955. Jacob J. Feldman, Senior Study Director, was the principal designer, the supervisor of coding, and the analyst for both these surveys. In each case there was a sample of approximately 2,500 households. In both surveys a question was asked concerning the religious preference of the respondent (and, presumably, of the entire household), who was also questioned as to the standard population characteristics of the household head.[6] Hence, by retabulating the data from these surveys it was possible to obtain information concerning the spatial distribution and the population characteristics of household heads, according to their religious preference.[7]

The NORC statistics given for Protestants and Roman Catholics, as total groups, have only small sampling variances. However, the statistics for individual Protestant denominations are subject to a larger sampling error. And the data for the three small groups—"Jewish," "No Religion," and "Other Religion"— are subject to very large sampling errors, since the data for each of these groups are based on less than 75 households in each survey. However, as modern sampling theory asserts, and as has been demonstrated empirically hundreds of times, probability samples of this size are capable of yielding much valuable information about particular homogeneous groups, so the results concerning these three smallest groups should not be disregarded entirely.

[6] These questions were answered in a straightforward and matter-of-fact way in each survey. It is the experience of NORC that such questions are among the easier items on its interviews attempt to obtain information.

[7] These tabulations were made separately for each survey, and the desired analytical tables were prepared independently from each survey's results. These duplicate tables were then compared, item by item. In most cases the twin tables were simply averaged to obtain the most accurate possible unbiased estimate; for a few cells in most of the tables, however, the results of one survey were arbitrarily accepted in preference to those of the other survey—if one survey had a substantial number of cases with which to make the particular calculation and the other survey, as a result of sampling fluctuations, had almost none. Although this procedure yields results that are internally consistent in almost every way, and which agree remarkably well with the much larger sample taken by the Bureau of the Census in its March, 1957 survey, it must be kept in mind that the possibility of large sampling errors exists, especially for some of the more detailed cross-tabulations. These NORC data are submitted as tentative evidence, until statistics based upon larger samples of the population are available.

The close correspondence between the results of the NORC surveys and the Census Bureau's survey of March, 1957, may be observed from the following comparison of religious composition as reported by each survey:

Religion	NORC Surveys	Census Bureau Survey	Difference (NORC minus Census)
Total	100.0	100.0	–
Protestant	71.5	66.2	5.3
Baptist	22.0	19.7	2.3
Methodist	17.4	14.0	3.4
Presbyterian	6.7	5.6	1.1
Lutheran	7.6	7.1	1.1
Episcopal	2.8	(n.a.)	−2.1
Other Protestant	14.9	19.8	
Roman Catholic	21.1	25.7	−4.6
Jewish	3.0	3.2	−0.2
Other	1.4	1.3	0.1
No religion	2.8	2.7	0.1
Religion not reported	–	0.9	−0.9

Considering that the NORC data refer to *household heads* (most of whom are male, and heavily concentrated at ages above 35 years), whereas the Census data refer to all *persons* aged 14 and over, much of the overcount of Protestants and undercount of Catholics in the NORC sample, in comparison with the Census data, may be attributed to differences in the age composition of the two samples. Also, the training of NORC interviewers, who are taught to probe until their questions are answered fully, may have meant that a considerable number of persons who belong to small offshoots of the Baptist and Methodist denominations were correctly allocated to those denominations rather than grouped with "Other Protestant." Also, minor differences in coding instructions could create small differences in the final distribution.

Region of Residence of Household Heads (Table 6).   A comparison of Table 6 (NORC) and Table 2 (Census), with respect to regional distribution of household heads by religious affiliation, shows very similar proportions for the major religious groups in the two surveys. However, Table 6 provides additional valuable information by showing the regional distribution of the individual Protestant denominations. Nearly two-thirds of all *Baptists* are concentrated in the South, and one-half of those living outside the South are found in the North Central states (to which southerners have been migrating). Baptists are a minority religious group outside these two regions, but within these two regions they are quite numerous. *Methodists* and *Presbyterians* tend to be more widely distributed among all regions; however, a slightly above-average share of Methodists live in the South, and the Presbyterians have a similar concentration in the

TABLE 6.   REGION OF RESIDENCE OF HOUSEHOLD HEADS, BY RELIGIOUS AFFILIATION

		Region			
Religion	All	North-east	North-central	South	West
Total	100.0	25.4	28.8	31.2	14.6
Protestant total	100.0	17.6	29.2	40.0	13.2
Baptist	100.0	8.3	15.6	69.4	6.7
Methodist	100.0	20.1	32.6	35.2	12.2
Presbyterian	100.0	30.1	32.0	21.6	16.4
Episcopal	100.0	37.2	15.6	26.4	21.0
Lutheran	100.0	24.0	54.4	6.6	15.0
Other Protestant	100.0	15.0	33.5	29.6	21.8
Roman Catholic	100.0	46.0	29.8	7.7	16.6
Jewish	100.0	61.2	11.4	9.4	18.0
Other	100.0	34.2	34.4	6.0	25.4
No religion	100.0	20.8	30.6	22.6	26.0

SOURCE: Special tabulations of survey data from National Opinion Research Center, Jacob J. Feldman, Senior Study Director.

Northeast and North Central regions. The membership of the *Episcopal* religion is quite concentrated in the Northeast and the West, although there is a substantial share in every region. *Lutherans*, by contrast, are almost nonexistent in the South; they are heavily concentrated in the North Central states, which have large populations of German descent.

To summarize: All religious groups for which data are available, except three, tend to be rather widely distributed among the regions, and to show only a moderate degree of concentration. Four generalizations that may be made concerning the distribution of religious groups are:

Baptists are concentrated in the South, and are very scarce in the Northeast and the West.
Lutherans are concentrated in the Midwest, and are very scarce in the South.
Jews are concentrated in the Northeast, and are very scarce in the South.
Roman Catholics are concentrated in the Northeast, and are very scarce in the South.

Religious Affiliation and Metropolitan and Nonmetropolitan Residence.   In Table 7 the household heads of each religious affiliation are classified according to residence inside or outside a standard metropolitan area (S.M.A.). Those living inside standard metropolitan areas are further dichotomized, according to whether the S.M.A. in which they live had more or less than 1 million inhabitants at the 1950 census. Nonmetropolitan areas are also dichotomized, according to whether the largest city in the county contained more or fewer than 10,000 inhabitants in 1950. Approximately one-fourth of the NORC sample of households falls into each of these four categories. Three religious groups stand out as having exceptionally high concentrations of their membership in metropolitan areas: Jewish, Episcopal, and Roman Catholic. Whereas roughly one-half of

TABLE 7. Type of County of Residence of Household Head, by Religious Affiliation

		Metropolitan Areas		Nonmetropolitan Areas	
Religion	*Total*	*Large— 1 Million or more Inhabitants*	*Small— less than 1 Million Inhabitants*	*Largest Town in County 10,000 or More*	*Largest Town in County Less than 10,000*
Total	100.0	30.4	28.2	19.2	22.2
Protestant total	100.0	22.8	28.8	21.6	26.8
Baptist	100.0	15.6	31.7	22.8	30.0
Methodist	100.0	21.6	29.0	19.0	30.4
Presbyterian	100.0	29.9	32.8	16.0	21.2
Episcopal	100.0	52.7	25.0	8.8	13.6
Lutheran	100.0	30.1	21.8	29.6	18.5
Other Protestant	100.0	22.4	26.0	22.4	29.0
Roman Catholic	100.0	45.3	28.4	14.7	11.6
Jewish	100.0	84.0	14.8	1.2	–
Other	100.0	55.8	28.1	8.4	7.7
No religion	100.0	38.2	26.4	19.4	16.0

Source: Special tabulations from National Opinion Research Center, Jacob J. Feldman, Senior Study Director.

the total sample of households falls in the S.M.A.'s, 98 percent of Jewish, 78 percent of Episcopal, and 74 percent of Roman Catholic household heads lived in an S.M.A. Moreover, all three of these groups were much more heavily concentrated in the very largest S.M.A.'s than they were in the smaller ones; 23 percent of the household heads in the total sample lived in S.M.A.'s having a population of one million or more, but 84 percent of Jewish, 53 percent of Episcopal, and 45 percent of Roman Catholic household heads live in these largest places. Also, persons reporting "other religion" and "no religion" are highly concentrated in places with one million or more inhabitants.

Baptists as one would suspect from their regional distribution, have a substantial concentration in the nonmetropolitan areas and the small S.M.A.'s. Methodists have a similar tendency to be concentrated in these areas. Presbyterians tend to be slightly metropolitanized, but a substantial share of their membership also lives in nonmetropolitan areas.

Religious Affiliation and Degree of Industrialization of Community of Residence. Table 8 classifies household heads by religion, and also according to the degree of industrialization of the county in which they reside. (Industrialization is measured in terms of the percentage of employed persons who were working in mining or manufacturing industries at the time of the 1950 census.)

TABLE 8. Degree of Industrialization of County of Residence, by Religious Affiliation

| | Percentage of Employed Labour Force in County of Residence Who Are Employed in Mining or Manufacturing Industries | | | | | | | |
Religion	All County Residence	44.3 Percent or More	37.2 to 42.8 Percent	31.9 to 37.1 Percent	27.3 to 31.9 Percent	23.5 to 27.0 Percent	18.0 to 23.3 Percent	11.1 to 17.8 Percent	Less than 11.1 Percent
Total	100.0	13.0	12.4	12.5	11.7	12.3	12.8	11.7	13.7
Protestant	100.0	12.2	11.9	10.8	12.0	11.0	14.0	12.4	15.5
Baptist	100.0	6.8	11.7	15.4	12.1	10.4	17.7	14.4	11.5
Methodist	100.0	12.0	10.2	10.4	16.8	8.7	11.5	10.2	20.2
Presbyterian	100.0	13.3	14.5	6.6	8.4	12.7	17.5	15.1	12.0
Episcopal	100.0	12.2	12.2	12.2	9.5	20.3	14.9	12.2	6.8
Lutheran	100.0	18.8	11.6	8.3	13.5	11.6	3.9	14.0	18.4
Other Protestant	100.0	15.3	13.1	8.7	8.7	11.6	15.2	11.0	16.5
Roman Catholic	100.0	15.9	14.9	15.5	10.0	14.9	8.3	11.4	9.2
Jewish	100.0	10.1	6.1	31.3	20.2	22.2	8.1	–	2.0
Other	100.0	20.8	14.6	4.2	6.2	14.6	22.9	8.3	8.3
No religion	100.0	8.8	11.2	12.5	7.5	13.8	15.0	11.2	20.0

Source: Special tabulations of survey materials from National Opinion Research Center, Jacob J. Feldman, Senior Study Director.

The outstanding fact brought out by this table is that Roman Catholics comprise a disproportionately large share of the population in the most heavily industrialized areas, whereas the other highly urbanized and metropolized populations— the Jewish and the Episcopal—tend to be distributed in the counties that are moderately, but not extremely, industrialized. Methodists and Presbyterians tend to be concentrated toward each of the two extremes; disproportionately large shares of these groups are found both in the more-industrialized and in the less-industrialized counties.

RELIGIOUS PREFERENCE AND EDUCATIONAL ATTAINMENT (NORC MATERIALS)

Two religious groups stand out above all others as well-educated: those with Jewish and those with Episcopal religious preference. A third group, the Presbyterian, had attained an educational level considerably above the average. More than one-fifth of the members of each of these groups were college graduates (Table 9), and only a comparatively small percent had less than 8 years of schooling. More than 60 percent of the household heads in each of these groups were high school graduates, whereas among the general population only 40 percent had this much schooling.

Among the white population, Protestant household heads showed a slightly higher level of education than Roman Catholic: Proportionately fewer Protestants had less than a grammar school education, and proportionately more Protestants had a college education, than was the case among Catholics (Table 9).

TABLE 9.   EDUCATIONAL COMPOSITION OF HOUSEHOLD HEADS, BY RELIGIOUS AFFILIATION
1955 TO 1956

| | | Education: Highest Grade of School Completed | | | | | | |
| | | Elementary School | | | High School | | College | |
Religious Preference	Total	0–4 Years	5–6 Years	7–8 Years	1–3 Years	4 Years	1–3 Years	4 or More
Total	100.0	8.9	7.8	24.0	20.2	21.1	9.6	8.4
Protestant total	100.0	8.8	7.8	24.2	20.6	20.8	9.8	8.2
Baptist	100.0	16.9	11.6	26.0	20.4	14.8	6.1	4.2
Methodist	100.0	5.3	6.2	20.9	21.5	26.0	11.6	8.6
Presbyterian	100.0	3.2	3.2	17.6	23.6	24.6	14.9	13.0
Episcopal	100.0	2.0	4.2	16.4	10.3	23.2	21.2	22.6
Lutheran	100.0	5.4	5.2	29.3	22.4	22.4	8.5	7.0
Other Protestant	100.0	6.7	8.7	27.0	18.5	20.5	9.2	9.4
Roman Catholic	100.0	8.0	7.4	25.8	20.6	22.4	8.9	6.8
Jewish	100.0	8.3	4.2	13.4	13.2	27.8	10.9	22.3
Other	100.0	23.4	13.6	11.0	11.0	22.4	5.7	12.8
No religion	100.0	10.7	8.7	23.4	20.4	16.9	8.8	11.0

SOURCE: Special tabulations of survey materials from National Opinion Research Center, Jacob J. Feldman, Senior Study Director.

This difference may be due in part to the fact that among the Roman Catholics there were many elderly and less-educated immigrants.

Baptists reported a much lower level of educational attainment than any other denomination or religious group. Almost one-fifth of the white Baptists had less than 7 years of schooling, whereas only about one-eighth of the Protestant population as a whole had this small an amount of education. Although 42 percent of Protestants had graduated from high school or attended college, only 31 percent of Baptists had attained this level.

Lutherans and Presbyterians were noteworthy for having a great concentration of their household heads near the average level of education; this group contained comparatively few very poorly-educated persons, as well as a somewhat below-average percentage of college-trained persons.

The various religious groups could be ranked as follows with respect to their average level of educational attainment:

Episcopal
Jewish
Presbyterian
Methodist
Other Protestant
Lutheran
No Religion
Roman Catholic
Baptist

Undoubtedly, the "Other Protestant" category hides some denominations which, if tabulated separately, using samples large enough to be reliable, would rank near the top with the Episcopal and Jewish groups. Unitarians, for example, might well out-rank both. Such groups as Christian Scientist and Congregationalist might rank near, or even above, the Presbyterian and Methodist groups.

Table 10, which shows separately the educational attainment of white and

TABLE 10. EDUCATIONAL ATTAINMENT OF HOUSEHOLD HEAD, BY COLOR AND RELIGIOUS AFFILIATION

| | | Education: Highest Grade of School Completed | | | | | | |
| | | Elementary School | | | High School | | College | |
Religious Preference	Total	0–4 Years	5–6 Years	7–8 Years	1–3 Years	4 Years	1–3 Years	4 or More Years
White, Total	100.0	6.8	6.6	24.2	20.5	22.4	10.3	9.1
Protestant total	100.0	6.0	6.1	24.6	21.0	22.4	10.8	9.1
Baptist	100.0	10.4	8.4	28.3	22.1	17.7	7.6	5.4
Methodist	100.0	4.3	5.2	21.0	21.8	26.5	12.2	9.0
Presbyterian	100.0	3.2	3.2	17.4	23.6	24.7	15.1	12.8
Episcopal	100.0	2.1	2.9	17.1	8.8	22.5	23.1	23.5
Lutheran	100.0	5.4	5.1	29.2	21.8	22.5	8.5	7.5
Other Protestant	100.0	6.1	7.1	26.9	19.0	21.4	9.8	9.8
Roman Catholic	100.0	7.5	7.6	25.8	20.8	22.5	9.0	6.8
Jewish	100.0	8.3	4.2	13.4	13.2	28.2	10.8	21.8
Other	100.0	25.2	13.4	12.4	9.8	21.2	3.7	14.2
No religion	100.0	11.0	9.5	23.6	19.1	16.3	9.5	11.0
Nonwhite	100.0	27.1	18.0	21.4	17.5	10.7	3.4	2.1
Baptist	100.0	32.0	18.4	21.6	16.4	7.8	2.8	1.2
Other	100.0	18.6	17.6	20.6	18.9	16.4	4.3	3.6

SOURCE: Special tabulations of survey data from National Opinion Research Center, Jacob J. Feldman, Senior Study Director.

nonwhite persons in each religious group, shows that the average level of educational attainment is much lower among nonwhite household heads where the head is a Baptist than where he is a member of some other denomination. This suggests that as Negroes obtain more education and move out of the rural South, they or their children tend to change their religious preference.

RELIGIOUS PREFERENCE AND OCCUPATIONAL COMPOSITION (NORC MATERIALS)

Quite a large amount of diversity exists among the various religious groups with respect to occupational composition of household heads (see Table 11). Three religions standout distinctively as having large percentages of their groups in "white-collar" employment: the Episcopal, the Jewish, and the Presbyterian.

TABLE 11. OCCUPATIONAL COMPOSITION OF HOUSEHOLD HEADS, BY RELIGIOUS AFFILIATION

Religious Affiliation	Total	Occupation—Percent Distribution									
		Prop. Prof. Tech.	Farm Oper. or Mgrs.	Mgrs. Off. Prop.	Clerical Workers	Sales Workers	Crafts-men	Opera-tives	Service Workers	Farm Laborers	Laborers, Non-Farm
Total	100.0	10.0	10.8	12.6	6.4	4.8	19.4	20.3	7.6	2.0	6.1
Protestant total	100.0	9.5	12.9	11.8	6.3	4.5	19.2	19.7	7.4	1.6	7.0
Baptist	100.0	6.0	13.3	7.6	4.1	3.0	18.2	25.3	10.0	2.4	10.0
Methodist	100.0	10.2	15.7	13.2	7.5	4.8	19.2	16.6	5.6	1.4	5.5
Presbyterian	100.0	15.3	8.0	16.1	8.2	10.6	16.7	15.8	4.8	1.2	3.6
Episcopal	100.0	19.6	1.5	20.4	11.0	5.4	16.7	9.6	10.7	–	5.3
Lutheran	100.0	8.0	15.6	15.4	5.4	4.4	24.0	15.1	6.2	0.6	5.2
Other Protestant	100.0	10.4	11.6	10.2	7.0	3.4	19.9	21.6	6.8	2.4	6.8
Roman Catholic	100.0	9.6	5.4	11.4	7.6	4.6	21.6	23.8	8.6	3.0	4.6
Jewish	100.0	17.6	1.3	36.0	9.6	15.0	7.2	12.0	–	–	1.3
Other	100.0	17.7	4.6	15.2	2.2	3.0	18.0	16.9	14.4	1.2	6.8
No religion	100.0	11.7	13.0	13.0	0.8	4.2	20.2	19.6	10.8	3.7	3.0

SOURCE: Special tabulations of survey data from National Opinion Research Center, Jacob J. Feldman, Senior Study Director.

Of these three, the Episcopal group contains the largest percentage of professional and technical persons, while the Jewish group has substantial proportions in managerial and proprietary jobs. At the other extreme are three religions with above-average proportions of "blue-collar" workers: Baptists, Methodists, and Lutherans. All three of these last-named groups contain substantial numbers of farmers, craftsmen, operatives, and unskilled workers.

Except for a comparative scarcity of farmers, and a compensating small excess of factory workers and service workers, Roman Catholics and Protestants tend to have quite similar occupational compositions. In the past, there has been a tendency to think of Catholics as being considerably lower in socio-economic status than Protestants. A close examination of Table 11 will show that in the Catholic group the proportion of household heads who are professional, proprietary, and clerical workers is about as large as it is among Protestants. The major difference is that such Protestant religions as Baptist, Methodist, and Lutheran contain a large proportion of farmers; Catholics have an excess of urban working-class persons, which compensates for the scarcity of Catholic farmers.

To what extent are the occupational differences noted above due to religious affiliation, and to what extent are they due simply to the fact, noted in the preceding section, that some religious groups have had more education than others? For example, are Baptist household heads concentrated in the blue-collar occupational group because they are Baptists, or because a preference for the Baptist religion is more common among socio-economic groups whose members have not had an opportunity to complete as many years of schooling as the rest of the population? A completely valid answer to this question would require much more detailed data than are available at the present time; it would require a simultaneous cross-tabulation of religious affiliation by single years of schooling, by occupation (using a fairly detailed breakdown), by color, by sex, and by age. The sample of data available at the present time is much too small to permit a full control even of education as a general factor in explaining the broad occupational groups.[8] Table 12 shows the median years of schooling completed by the members of each religious group who are in each of the broad occupational categories. These data permit only a few tentative statements. It seems that *educational attainment is a much more powerful factor in determining occupation than is religious preference.* Support for this conclusion is provided in Table 11, which shows that household heads employed in a particular occupation have generally reached the same educational level, irrespective of their religious preference. Some variations, however, are too large to be explained on the basis of sampling error, and are not easily accounted for except by attributing them to variations within the occupational groups. These variations probably arise from the fact that the Census fails to count postgraduate college training separately. For example, a person with an

---

[8] This is especially true for the Jewish, the "Other Religion" and the "No Religion" groups, where the number of cases in the sample is extremely small.

TABLE 12. MEDIAN YEARS OF SCHOOL COMPLETED BY HOUSEHOLD HEADS, BY OCCUPATION AND RELIGIOUS AFFILIATION: 1955

Religious Affiliation	Total	Prop. Prof. Tech.	Farm Oper. or Mgrs.	Mgrs. Off. Prop.	Clerical Workers	Sales Workers	Crafts-men	Opera-tives	Service Workers	Farm Laborers	Laborers, Non-Farm
				Median Years of School Completed by Occupation							
Total	9.5	16+	7.4	11.2	11.5	11.4	9.0	7.9	7.4	6.2	6.7
Protestant total	9.5	16+	7.6	11.2	11.5	11.6	9.0	8.0	7.3	6.9	6.7
Baptist	7.8	15.0	6.4	10.5	11.0	11.0	8.2	7.2	7.0	5.1	6.0
Methodist	10.7	16+	8.1	11.4	11.7	11.6	9.6	9.4	7.8	8.0	7.0
Presbyterian	11.0	16+	9.5	11.4	11.9	12.0	9.8	8.8	7.5	7.5	8.2
Episcopal	11.8	16+	13.5	12.5	12.2	13.5	11.6	8.8	9.5	–	7.2
Lutheran	9.6	16+	7.4	10.8	10.6	11.4	8.7	9.2	7.0	7.0	7.5
Other Protestant	9.3	16+	8.2	10.0	11.8	11.6	9.0	7.6	7.1	6.6	7.0
Roman Catholic	9.4	14.6	7.0	10.7	11.3	11.0	9.2	8.0	8.2	5.4	6.5
Jewish	11.4	16+	–	11.4	11.6	9.2	8.2	8.6	–	–	9.2
Other	8.8	12.8	5.0	8.5	–	–	7.2	5.5	2.0	5.0	–
No religion	9.2	16+	7.2	11.0	12.0	12.5	8.8	8.0	7.4	6.7	5.3

NOTE: Each median is based upon comparatively few cases. The over-all pattern of differences between entire rows or entire columns may be considered as general evidence. Individual cells should not be accepted as precise estimates.
SOURCE: Special tabulations of survey data from National Opinion Research Center, Jacob J. Feldman, Senior Study Director.

A.B. degree and a person with an M.D. or Ph.D. degree are both simply classed as having had "4 years or more of college." The fact that professional persons, except Baptists and Roman Catholics, have an average educational attainment of four years of college does not necessarily mean that these two religious groups have a "special pipeline" that allows their members to reach the nations' upper socio-economic levels without bothering to complete the amount of schooling that is generally considered a prerequisite. Instead, it probably means that a high proportion of Jewish, Episcopal, and Presbyterian professionals are physicians, college professors, or lawyers, while an unusually high percentage of Baptist and Catholic professionals may be artists, entertainers, photographers, or employed in other occupations which are classified by the Census as "professional" but which require much less schooling. Similarly, household heads who are Roman Catholic, Baptist, or Lutheran appear to have reached a status enabling them to be classified as proprietors, managers, or officials with the aid of less formal education than was obtained by the members of other religious groups who are classified as proprietors, managers or officials. It is quite possible that Episcopal, Jewish, and Presbyterian household heads, again because of higher educational achievement, hold very responsible positions in banks, manufacturing concerns, or as self-employed proprietors in wholesale and retail establishments, and that a higher proportion of Baptist, Catholic, and Lutheran workers with less education may be employed as railroad conductors, postmasters, or managers, or may be owners of small neighborhood grocery stores, restaurants, or filling stations—jobs which the Census also classifies as managerial or proprietary.[9]

From the materials in Table 12, one might expect to obtain the answer to a different kind of question: "Are the members of any religious group discriminated against, in their efforts to find employment, simply because of their particular religious preference?" One might conclude that they are if, in any religious group, the household heads have jobs that are low in the socio-economic scale and levels of educational attainment that are extraordinarily high. An examination of Table 12 shows that three groups seem to fit this pattern. the Presbyterian, the Methodist, and the Episcopal.[10] If the data are accepted as valid, one would be forced to conclude that the Episcopal group is more severely discriminated against than any other. Common-sense reflection suggests that such is not the case; if there is discrimination of the type defined above, it should show up among the Baptists, a group having a very large Negro population. Probably nothing more is involved than the fact that Episcopalians, Presbyterians, and Methodists place a stronger emphasis on educational achievement than many other religious groups do, and, hence, that their members tend to attain above-average educational levels irrespective of the occupational levels at which they may eventually work.

[9] Also, the use of median education, which does not show the full education distribution for each combination of occupation and religion, is a very crude approach to this problem, but is made necessary by lack of a larger sample.

[10] However, it will be shown in the next section that there are proportionately few Episcopalians and Presbyterians with low socio-economic status.

To summarize: the meager data available gives little evidence either that any religious group is extraordinarily favored, or that there is severe discrimination (independent of any other factors) against any religious group because of its beliefs—with respect to broad categories of occupational attainment. Although the religious groups differ substantially with respect to occupational composition, in general the members of each religion seem to be located just about as high on the occupational ladder as the level of their educational attainment would lead one to expect.

RELIGIOUS PREFERENCE AND INCOME (NORC MATERIALS)

There is a high concentration of poverty among the Baptist population, while being in the upper income brackets is closely related to a preference for the Episcopal or Jewish religion (see Table 13). Methodists, Presbyterians, and

TABLE 13. INCOME DISTRIBUTION OF HOUSEHOLD HEADS BY RELIGIOUS AFFILIATION

		Income							
Religious Affiliation	Total	Less than $1,000	$1,000 to $1,999	$2,000 to $2,999	$3,000 to $3,999	$4,000 to $4,999	$5,000 to $7,499	$7,500 to $9,999	$10,000 and Over
Total	100.0	7.3	10.0	13.8	17.4	17.7	21.3	7.0	5.6
Protestant total	100.0	8.2	11.0	14.6	17.6	17.4	19.8	6.4	5.2
Baptist	100.0	12.6	15.2	19.0	17.8	15.2	13.8	4.0	2.1
Methodist	100.0	7.0	9.6	11.3	18.2	16.6	24.0	7.5	5.9
Presbyterian	100.0	2.4	8.5	9.2	18.0	20.8	23.5	9.0	8.7
Episcopal	100.0	6.4	8.4	10.9	11.2	15.8	23.6	9.7	14.1
Lutheran	100.0	3.6	8.1	13.2	19.4	19.2	23.0	8.2	5.2
Other Protestant	100.0	8.4	9.6	15.7	16.2	20.2	18.6	6.2	5.2
Roman Catholic	100.0	5.0	7.2	11.7	18.4	19.6	25.0	8.4	4.6
Jewish	100.0	1.3	7.3	6.2	11.6	11.8	31.5	11.4	18.9
Other	100.0	2.2	16.4	17.4	16.2	15.1	22.1	7.2	3.4
No religion	100.0	10.2	7.2	13.0	12.2	19.7	18.4	7.6	11.6

SOURCE: Special tabulations from National Opinion Research Center, Jacob J. Feldman, Senior Study Director.

Roman Catholics tend to be concentrated in the upper middle income brackets, while Lutherans and other Protestants seem to be in the lower-middle grades. Persons who claim no religion tend to be distributed more or less evenly throughout all income levels. This means that, in comparison with the general population, disproportionately large numbers of people who have no religious preference are located at the extremely high and the extremely low income levels. If one were to rank and classify the leading religions according to "high income," "median income," and "low income" these groups would be listed as follows:

Religion
High income
Jewish
Episcopal
Presbyterian
Median income
Catholic
Lutheran
No religion
Methodist
Low income
Baptist
Small Protestant sects

How much of this income difference between religious groups is due to the differences in occupational composition that are described above? Here again, an answer to this question requires a multiple-variable cross-tabulation, which the sample of NORC data was too small to support. Since the measure of income employed here is family income, such items as the number of earners in the family, the occupational and educational level of the secondary earners, etc., could also affect the comparisons. Even such aspects of family structure and composition as age of head and family reaction to poverty (some groups support elderly low-income parents in their own households, while other groups may allow them to live apart) may affect these data to a marked degree. As a very rough substitute for completely adequate evidence, Table 14 reports the median family income for each occupational group, subdivided according to religious preference. Except in the case of the Baptists, most of the income differentials between religions, mentioned above, tend to disappear and become simply income differentials between occupations.

When comparisons are made for all categories in the occupational scale, household heads whose religious preference is Roman Catholic tend to receive higher incomes than those who are Protestant. For example, the family incomes of Catholic craft workers tend to be higher than the family incomes of Protestant craft workers, and so on for most occupational groups. Since Catholics have a lower educational level than Protestants, one might expect that some factor specifically associated with religion as such would explain this situation. However, the facts that most farmers have small cash incomes, and that most farmers are Protestants, probably constitute one of the major reasons for this differential. Also, because they have more children, there may be more earners in Catholic families (working children as well as working mothers) than in Protestant families.

Jewish and Episcopal household heads who are employed as professional, proprietary, or managerial workers tend to have higher median incomes than the members of other religious groups employed in these same broad occupational categories. This is probably due to the kind of internal variation between

TABLE 14. MEDIAN INCOMES OF HEADS OF HOUSEHOLDS BY OCCUPATION AND RELIGIOUS AFFILIATION

Religious Affiliation	Total	Median Income by Occupation									
		Prof. and Tech.	Farm Oper. or Mgrs.	Mgrs. Off. Prop.	Clerical Wkrs.	Sales Wkrs.	Craftsmen	Operatives	Service Wkrs.	Farm Laborers	Laborers, Nonfarm
Total	4,094	5,876	2,838	5,936	4,032	4,882	4,462	3,762	2,610	1,779	2,852
Protestant total	3,933	5,457	2,703	5,570	3,960	4,893	4,418	3,656	2,399	1,726	2,659
Baptist	3,174	4,529	1,639	4,116	4,111	4,250	4,056	3,310	1,868	1,798	2,311
Methodist	4,235	5,586	3,134	5,992	3,901	4,929	4,756	4,018	2,155	2,000	3,326
Presbyterian	4,586	5,794	4,479	6,405	4,958	5,178	3,916	4,106	3,750	2,000	2,666
Episcopal	5,000	6,156	–	7,208	5,500	4,750	5,250	3,146	3,375	–	2,000
Lutheran	4,278	5,858	2,854	5,802	4,333	6,372	4,662	3,800	2,375	–	2,834
Other Protestant	4,008	5,458	2,708	5,188	3,778	3,916	4,574	3,613	2,842	2,250	2,598
Roman Catholic	4,340	6,334	4,250	6,281	4,118	5,688	4,636	3,964	3,562	1,792	3,450
Jewish	5,954	7,333	–	6,924	4,775	4,300	5,000	3,792	–	–	–
Other	3,875	–	4,000	5,334	–	–	4,000	3,625	2,542	–	–
No religion	4,320	10,000+	3,250	6,010	–	4,125	4,250	3,854	2,125	2,000	–

NOTE: Each median is based upon comparatively few cases. The over-all pattern of differences between entire rows or entire columns may be considered as general evidence. Individual cells should not be accepted as precise estimates.

SOURCE: Special tabulations of survey data from National Opinion Research Center, Jacob J. Feldman, Senior Study Director.

occupations within each of the broad occupational categories that was described and illustrated in connection with educational attainment. Thus, occupation is a much more potent factor than religious preference in determining the income level of household heads.

How completely do inter-faith differences with respect to educational attainment explain the differences in income between religious groups? Table 15,

TABLE 15. MEDIAN INCOME OF HEADS OF HOUSEHOLDS, BY EDUCATIONAL ATTAINMENT AND RELIGIOUS AFFILIATION

		Elementary School			High School		College	
Religious Affiliation	Total	0–4 Years	5–6 Years	7–8 Years	1–3 Years	4 Years	1–3 Years	4 or More Years
Total	4,012	1,932	2,560	3,320	4,050	4,644	5,134	6,500
Protestant total	3,850	1,710	2,360	3,096	3,946	4,588	4,935	5,900
Baptist	3,032	1,629	2,312	2,839	3,670	4,034	4,128	4,614
Methodist	4,077	2,688	2,208	3,088	4,019	4,670	5,260	6,245
Presbyterian	4,494	2,250	3,125	3,500	4,282	4,682	5,625	6,000
Episcopal	4,750	–	–	3,250	3,375	5,475	4,584	7,062
Lutheran	4,230	1,688	3,300	3,526	4,103	4,759	5,458	6,584
Other Protestant	3,916	1,734	2,274	3,242	4,036	4,628	4,538	5,416
Roman Catholic	4,354	2,710	3,219	3,992	4,368	4,612	5,644	6,789
Jewish	5,956	2,916	–	4,334	5,500	5,472	6,050	8,500
Other	3,822	2,292	2,500	3,500	4,875	3,875	4,000	6,667
No religion	4,184	2,666	2,125	3,300	3,708	6,000	4,875	8,638

NOTE: Each median is based upon comparatively few cases. The over-all pattern of differences between entire rows or entire colums may be considered as general evidence. Individual cells should not be accepted as precise estimates.

SOURCE: Special tabulations of survey data from National Opinion Research Center, Jacob J. Feldman, Senior Study Director.

which reports the median income of each educational group, for each religion, provides very rough data with which to examine this question. This table shows that the differences in income between religious groups are greatly reduced when the factor of education is introduced. A general, over-all difference does seem to remain, however. Roman Catholic household heads tend to have higher incomes, for a given amount of schooling completed, than Protestant household heads. Similarly, Jewish household heads tend to receive larger incomes than Catholic household heads for a given amount of schooling completed. The difference between the Roman Catholic and the Protestant groups are of about the same magnitude as those between the Catholic and the Jewish. Within the protestant group, the Episcopalians, Presbyterians, and Methodists who had had college educations received higher incomes than the Baptists. All of these differences may be due to differences in age of head, number and type of secondary earners, family structure, and occupation—as well as to cultural factors associated with religious affiliation. Clarification of this point must await the availability of data.

It should not be concluded hastily that any of the socio-economic differences shown here are due directly to religious membership as such. The kind of occupational use to which a given amount of educational attainment is put has a great deal to do with the amount of income received. People with college degrees who choose law, medicine, or business administration as a career (as a high proportion of Jewish and Episcopal members do), and who have spent 5 to 8 years in college, will almost certainly receive much larger incomes than other college graduates who have spent 4 years in college and have chosen to teach elementary school or to hold other kinds of low-paying jobs as professionals or officials. Moreover, persons who live in large metropolitan areas (as a high proportion of Jews and Episcopalians do) receive higher incomes for a given occupation than workers living in other places. To summarize: *education is a much more potent factor than religious preference in determining the income level of households*, and even observed differences between religious groups, when amount of education is controlled, may be due to "intervening variables" other than religious affiliation.

SUMMARY AND CONCLUSION

The various religious groups differ greatly from each other in their distribution among regions, metropolitan and nonmetropolitan areas, and with respect to the size of places in which they live. They also differ as to age of the family head, ethnic composition, propensity to intermarry, and educational, occupational, and income levels. However, these differences are not due solely to religious affiliation as such. For example, it has been demonstrated in this chapter that occupational differences and educational differences each "explain" a large part of the income difference between religious groups. (Data were not available with which to measure how much of the total income differences between religious groups would be explained by both occupation and education considered simultaneously, but these factors probably would explain by far the larger part of these differences, if detailed occupation and education categories were used in the analysis.) There is comparatively little evidence that any particular group is receiving favored social or economic treatment simply on the basis of its religious affiliation. Neither is there much evidence to support a conclusion that any major religious group is being persecuted or disadvantaged in an economic sense solely because of its beliefs. Nevertheless, there is evidence that some economic and other differences between religious groups would still be found to persist, independent of other variables.

It would be very wrong to assert that because religious affiliation does not always have a strong effect, independent of all other variables, it is not an important variable for demographic and sociological analysis. This chapter has made it abundantly clear that unique "clusters of traits" are associated with each of the various religious groups. The hypothesis that these clusters are part of a tradition or culture which is transmitted from one generation to another is plausible, and is worthy of test and study. For example, in order to explain the results of this chapter it is almost mandatory to develop the hypothesis that members of the Episcopal, Jewish, and Presbyterian religions place a very high value on obtaining as much education as possible, that they strive to gain employment in the professional, managerial, or proprietary occupations, and that they attempt to save from current income so they can invest and increase their future income. This complex of traits or ambitions may lead to later marriage, fewer children, metropolitan residence, greater willingness to migrate, the accumulation of above-average amounts of wealth, and many other demographic and social phenomena reflecting values that our society deems praiseworthy. On the other hand, if we are familiar with the population composition of particular denominations, it helps us to understand the position these groups take with respect to particular social and economic issues. For this reason, and because religion *sometimes* is an important explanatory factor even when it is considered independently of other variables (as in the case of fertility analysis), much scientific and public good could be accomplished if religion were added as an item on the decennial census.

The analysis presented in this chapter concerning the interrelationships between religious affiliation and other population variables has had to be based on incomplete and inadequate data. These materials have enabled the analysis to demonstrate only that some highly meaningful relationships exist; as data with which to measure the magnitude of these relationships, however, they have permitted only approximate conclusions. There was not enough data to permit exploration of the reasons behind the existence of these relationships, and how they varied with changes in other circumstances. Further research must await more adequate information. It is to be hoped that the Bureau of the Census will give a high priority to this item in 1970, as penance for the policy forced on it in 1960.

Religious Preference and Worldly Success: Some Evidence from National Surveys

NORVAL D. GLENN AND RUTH HYLAND

The relationship of religion to economic and occupational success is the most viable topic of debate in the sociology of religion in the United States.[1] The issues raised by Weber in his famous essay on the Protestant Ethic continue to evoke vociferous exchanges. During recent years the controversy has become centered

Reprinted from the *American Sociological Review*, 32 (February, 1967), pp. 73–85, by permission of the authors and the publisher.

[1] Much of the debate deals not directly with economic and occupational success but with achievement motivation, deferred gratification, and similar variables that are assumed to underlie success.

on the influence of religion in contemporary American society.[2] Some scholars who accept Weber's basic thesis object to its application, in modified form, to contemporary societies.

The focus of the present controversy is on the relative rates of upward mobility of Protestants and Catholics, since there is clearcut evidence that Jews, for reasons that may or may not be essentially religious, experienced more rapid upward movement for several decades than either Protestants or Catholics.[3] Although there are some "hard data" that throw light on the relative advancement of Protestants and Catholics, these data are somewhat contradictory, or at least are subject to contradictory interpretations. One national study found no difference between the upward mobility of Protestant and of Catholic men;[4] this finding has been interpreted to mean both that religious differences do not lead to differences in mobility and that the Protestants equalled the Catholics in spite of palpable handicaps.[5] A study in the Detroit metropolitan area found greater upward mobility of Protestants than of Catholics;[6] this finding has been interpreted both as an indication of the importance of the religious factor and as a mere reflection of sampling variability or differences in ethnic background.[7] One author, in reporting selectively the findings of a national survey, noted that an equal percentage of Protestant and Catholic men under age 40 in metropolitan areas had incomes of $8,000 or more; he used these data to support a claim that Catholicism is not detrimental to worldly success.[8] However, he could have selected data from the same survey to support the opposite conclusion.[9]

[2] For instance, see Raymond W. Mack, Raymond J. Murphy, and Seymour Yellin, "The Protestant Ethic, Level of Aspiration, and Social Mobility: An Empirical Test," *American Sociological Review*, 21 (June, 1956), pp. 295–300; Bernard C. Rosen, "Race, Ethnicity, and the Achievement Syndrome," *American Sociological Review*, 26 (February, 1959), pp. 47–60; Gerhard Lenski, *The Religious Factor*, rev. ed., Garden City, New York: Doubleday, 1963; Joseph Veroff, Sheila Feld, and Gerald Gurin, "Achievement Motivation and Religious Background," *American Sociological Review*, 27 (April, 1962), pp. 205–217; Albert J. Mayer and Harry Sharp, "Religious Preference and Worldly Success," *American Sociological Review*, 27 (April, 1962), pp. 218–227; Andrew M. Greeley, "Influence of the 'Religious Factor' on the Career Plans and Occupational Values of College Students," *American Journal of Sociology*, 68 (May, 1963), pp. 658–671; Marvin Bressler and Charles F. Westoff, "Catholic Education, Economic Values, and Achievement," *American Journal of Sociology*, 69 (November, 1963); pp. 225–233; Andrew M. Greeley, "The Protestant Ethic: Time for a Moratorium," *Sociological Analysis*, 25 (Spring, 1964), pp. 20–33; Ralph Lane, Jr., "Research on Catholics as a Status Group," *Sociological Analysis*, 26 (Summer, 1965); and Seymour Warkov and Andrew M. Greeley, "Parochial School Origins and Educational Achievement," *American Sociological Review*, 31 (June, 1966), pp. 406–414.

[3] See Nathan Glazer, "The American Jew and the Attainment of Middle-Class Rank: Some Trends and Explanations," in Marshall Sklare, ed., *The Jews*, New York: The Free Press of Glencoe, 1958, pp. 138–146.

[4] Seymour Martin Lipset and Reinhard Bendix, *Social Mobility in Industrial Society*, Berkeley and Los Angeles: University of California Press, 1959, pp. 48–56.

[5] Lenski, *op. cit.*, p. 84.   [6] *Ibid.*

[7] Greeley, "The Protestant Ethic . . . ," *op. cit.*   [8] *Ibid.*

[9] Our similar national data show important differences in the distributions of Protestants and Catholics above this level (see Table 9).* Also, one could point out that Protestants equalled Catholics in spite of the heavy concentration of the former in the South and in the smaller metropolitan areas, where incomes in general were relatively low.

* [The material referred to is not included—Editor.]

It is not our ambition to end the controversy once and for all in this article; a secondary analysis of national survey data not gathered for the purpose of assessing mobility cannot provide conclusive evidence. However, we are convinced that the potential of such an analysis to help resolve the controversy has not been realized. All too frequently partisans in the debate have judiciously selected national survey data to support preconceived conclusions. Never, to our knowledge, has anyone done a comprehensive, thorough and objective analysis of the relevant national data.[10] Although the analysis reported here is not completely comprehensive, we strive for an objective treatment of the most relevant information.

Using data from 18 national surveys conducted from 1943 to 1965, we . . . assess trends in the relative economic, occupational, and educational status of Protestants and Catholics. . . . We also include data for Jews and, on occasion, for those with no religious preference, but the sample sizes usually allow reasonably confident conclusions only for Protestants and Catholics. In order to control influences related to race, we analyze data only for white respondents.

Seventeen of the surveys were conducted by the Gallup Organization (also known as the American Institute of Public Opinion) and one was conducted by the National Opinion Research Center. The two earliest polls (1943 and 1945) used quota samples; all of the others used some kind of probability sample.[11] Four of the surveys were selected expressly for this study; they were the four most recent Gallup polls using national probability samples which were available from the Roper Public Opinion Research Center when we started our research. The data from the other surveys were on hand for other purposes. In no case did we have any knowledge of the relevant frequency distributions before we selected a survey, and in no case did we exclude a survey after we examined the data.

POSTWAR TRENDS

Since the mid-1940's, the relative standings of white Protestants and Catholics in the country as a whole have changed dramatically (see Tables 1, 2,

[10] The best treatments of national data on status differences by religious preference are primarily descriptive rather than attempts to assess the relative impact of Protestantism and Catholicism on worldly success. See Hadley Cantril, "Education and Economic Composition of Religious Groups: An Analysis of Poll Data," *American Journal of Sociology*, 47 (March, 1943), pp. 574–579; Donald J. Bogue, "Religious Affiliation," *The Population of the United States*, New York: The Free Press of Glencoe, 1959, pp. 688–709; and Bernard Lazerwitz, "A Comparison of Major United States Religious Groups," *Journal of the American Statistical Association*, 56 (September, 1961), pp. 568–579. Lazerwitz's data are the most recent and come from two 1957 samples and one 1958 sample.

[11] None of the samples are simple random samples, however; they are therefore not amenable to analysis with the usual textbook statistical formulae. The standard errors for the more recent Gallup polls are estimated to be usually about 1.4 to 1.6 times the standard errors for simple random samples. In addition, the recent Gallup samples are inflated about 100 per cent by a weighting procedure used instead of callbacks; therefore the N's reported for the combined 1963, 1964, and 1965 data in the tables of this article are usually about twice the number of respondents represented. For statistical procedures for analysis of these samples, see Leslie Kish, *Survey Sampling*, New York: John Wiley and Co., 1965. We are indebted to Mr. Andrew Kohut of the Gallup Organization for additional guidance in analyzing the Gallup data.

TABLE 1. Distribution (%) by Economic Level of White Respondents to a 1943 NORC Survey and to Four Recent Gallup Polls, by Religious Preference*

Economic Level	1943 NORC Survey			
	Protestants	Catholics	Jews	Total
Upper	26.3	21.6	50.0	25.9
Middle	51.4	48.1	41.2	50.2
Lower	22.3	30.2	8.8	23.9
	100.0	100.0	100.0	100.0
N	1,638	485	67	2,190

Four Recent Gallup Polls (December, 1963 to March, 1965)

Economic Level	Protestants	Catholic	Jews	Total
Upper	35.9	41.0	58.0	37.8
Middle	41.5	43.3	26.7	41.5
Lower	22.7	15.6	15.3	20.7
	100.0	100.0	100.0	100.0
N	8,660	2,884	435	12,209

* The respondents to the 1943 NORC survey were divided into four economic levels largely on the basis of rent or, if they were home owners, estimated rental value of home. Here the two upper levels are combined into one. The Gallup respondents were divided into economic levels on the basis of the income data in Table 6.* The upper level starts at $7,000 and the lower level is below $3,000.

The original 1943 NORC data give religious identification for church members only. The nonmembers had lower average status than the members; they were allocated between the Protestants and Catholics on the basis of information on church membership from a 1945 Gallup poll. Jewish members and nonmembers do not differ appreciably in economic status; therefore the 1943 Jewish data presented here are for members only.

* [The material referred to is not included—Editor.]

and 3). For instance, in 1943 Protestants were well above Catholics in economic status, whereas by 1964 Catholics were clearly above Protestants (Table 1). The differences between the proportions of Protestants and Catholics at both the highest and lowest economic levels around 1964 are statistically significant. Since the 1943 data come from a quota sample, they do not meet the strict requirements for tests of significance, but the difference in the proportions of Protestants and Catholics at the lowest level is so large that we are rather confident that it did not result solely from sampling error.

The change in relative economic status may not have been quite as great as these data suggest. We delineated the 1964 levels on the basis of the income

TABLE 2. RATIO OF ACTUAL TO EXPECTED PROPORTION OF WHITE PROTESTANT, CATHOLIC, AND JEWISH HEADS OF HOUSEHOLDS AT BROAD URBAN OCCUPATIONAL LEVELS, 1945, 1953, AND 1964*

	Protestants			*Catholics*			*Jews*		
	1945	1953	1964	1945	1953	1964	1945	1953	1964
Upper nonmanual[a]	.99	.99	.94	.81	.82	.98	1.86	2.11	2.11
Lower nonmanual[b]	.95	.92	.92	1.06	1.08	1.17	1.60	1.64	1.60
Upper manual[c]	.89	.99	1.03	1.37	1.10	1.04	.86	.56	.22
Lower manual[d]	.95	.95	.97	1.23	1.03	1.14	.57	.51	.49
N	1,748	4,178	7,150	587	1,616	2,462	121	286	341

* The 1945 data are from one Gallup poll, the "1953" data are from five Gallup polls ranging in date from October, 1953 to March, 1954, and the "1964" data are from four Gallup polls ranging in date from December, 1963, to March, 1965.

The "expected" proportion at each occupational level is the proportion of white heads of households of all religious preferences at that level.

[a] Professional and semi-professional workers, businessmen, and executives.

[b] Clerical and sales workers.

[c] Skilled workers.

[d] Service workers, operatives, and laborers.

TABLE 3. RATIO OF ACTUAL TO EXPECTED PROPORTION OF WHITE PROTESTANTS, CATHOLICS, AND JEWS AT EACH BROAD EDUCATIONAL LEVEL, AGES 30 AND OVER, 1945 AND 1964*

	Protestants		*Catholics*		*Jews*	
Educational Level	1945	1964	1945	1964	1945	1964
No more than 8 years of school	.96	1.04	1.09	.95	.70	.55
At least some high school but no college	1.00	.97	1.08	1.11	1.11	.94
At least some college	1.05	.98	.75	.82	1.26	2.09
N	1,473	7,294	426	2,274	93	376

* The 1945 data are from one Gallup poll and the "1964" data are from four Gallup polls ranging in date from December, 1963, to March, 1965.

The "expected" proportion at each educational level is the proportion of white respondents of all religious preferences at that level.

data in Table 6,* whereas the levels for the 1943 respondents were determined at least partly on the basis of the interviewers' impressions of the life styles of the respondents and their families. Consequently the standards of placement of the 1943 respondents may have varied somewhat by community and region according to the average level of affluence. If so, the effect undoubtedly was to raise the Protestants relative to the Catholics, because Protestants were (and

* [The material referred to is not included—Editor.]

TABLE 4.   DISTRIBUTION (%) BY SIZE OF COMMUNITY OF RESIDENCE OF WHITE RESPONDENTS
TO FOUR RECENT GALLUP POLLS, BY RELIGIOUS PREFERENCE*

Community Size	Protestants	Catholics	Jews	No Religion	Total
Rural	39.5	15.1	2.9	18.8	32.1
2,500–9,999	9.4	5.8	–	9.0	8.3
10,000–49,000	9.3	7.6	1.4	12.6	8.7
50,000–249,999	15.0	19.8	11.9	16.3	16.1
250,000–999,999	16.2	22.1	15.6	15.8	17.6
1,000,000 and over	10.5	29.5	68.1	27.4	17.2
Total	100.0	100.0	100.0	100.0	100.0
N	9,097	2,940	436	277	12,750

* Dates of the polls range from December, 1963, to March, 1965. Therefore, the data are essentially for 1964.

TABLE 5.   DISTRIBUTION (%) BY REGION OF RESIDENCE OF WHITE RESPONDENTS TO FOUR
RECENT GALLUP POLLS, BY RELIGIOUS PREFERENCE*

Region	Protestants	Catholics	Jews	No Religion	Total
New England	2.5	12.3	7.8	5.8	5.0
Middle Atlantic	16.7	39.0	70.1	11.9	23.6
East Central	18.4	18.6	5.7	18.4	18.0
West Central	12.7	8.4	1.1	8.3	11.2
South	34.4	7.8	7.1	14.8	26.9
Rocky Mountain	4.3	3.2	0.9	12.3	4.1
Pacific	10.9	10.6	7.1	28.5	11.1
Total	100.0	100.0	100.0	100.0	100.0
N	9,099	2,940	435	277	12,751

* Dates of the polls range from December, 1963, to March, 1965. Therefore, the data are essentially for 1964.

still are) disproportionately in the South and in small communities, where average incomes are relatively low.[12]

Nevertheless a marked change in relative economic status undoubtedly resulted from the pronounced changes in relative occupational and educational standings. The occupational changes are shown in Table 2. The "expected" proportion of each religious category at each occupational level is simply the proportion of respondents of all religions at that level; accordingly ratios below and above unity indicate disproportionately low and high representation. Whereas Protestant representation decreased at both levels of nonmanual occupations

[12] See Tables 4 and 5. One should not place much confidence in the apparent increase, in Table 1, in the proportion of Jewish families at the lowest economic level. The Jewish samples for both dates are small and subject to considerable sampling variability, and the occupational and educational data in Tables 2 and 3 show an increase in the relative standing of Jews.

and increased at both manual levels, Catholic representation increased sharply in nonmanual occupations and declined in manual work.[13] In 1945 and in 1954 Protestants were more highly represented than Catholics at the upper nonmanual level, but in 1964 representation of Catholics at this level slightly exceeded that of Protestants. Although the small N's do not allow us to place much confidence in the Jewish data, it appears that Jews gained on Christians during the two decades. According to the data, Jewish representation increased at the highest level, remained the same at the lower nonmanual level, and declined at both manual levels.[14]

The changes in representation at three broad educational levels were similar to the occupational changes (Table 3). Protestant representation increased at the lowest level and declined at the two higher levels, while Catholic representation declined at the lowest level and increased at the high school and college levels. Protestants ranked clearly ahead of Catholics in educational status in 1945, but by 1964 the relative standings of the two religious categories had become ambiguous. Catholics had moved ahead in median years of school completed . . . but were still underrepresented at the college level. During the 20-year period Jewish representation apparently increased at the college level and declined at all lower levels.

It is clear that Catholics as a whole have experienced more net upward mobility during the postwar period than Protestants. In part, this is simply a matter of Catholics overcoming an initial disadvantage growing out of their more recent immigration. The Catholic immigrants, as all others, usually became employed at first at the lower occupational levels, and as long as they were incompletely acculturated in nonreligious American culture, many of their cultural characteristics may have impeded their upward movement. Culture not detrimental to worldly success in the home country became detrimental in the context of American culture; probably some of the culture of the Southern and Eastern Europeans in its original context was adverse to economic advancement. Consequently the acculturation of European immigrant groups during the past few decades has, in the absence of many new immigrants, tended in itself to close the socio-economic gap between Protestants and Catholics.

However, Catholics are now pulling ahead of Protestants; their greater advancement is therefore more than just a catching-up process. If, as is widely believed, the values, beliefs and practices of Protestantism are more conducive to worldly success than those of Catholicism, then clearly the Catholics have some advantage that more than offsets their religiously-based disadvantage.

Catholics in the United States do have one obvious and important advantage. They are highly concentrated in the larger metropolitan areas in the non-Southern regions (Tables 4 and 5)—precisely the communities with the highest average

[13] The underrepresentation of Protestants in 1945 and 1954 at all levels in Table 2 results from their overrepresentation in the farm category, which is not shown in the table.

[14] The fact that Jewish representation declined from 1954 to 1964 in three of the urban levels and stayed the same in the other reflects decreased total representation of Jews in urban occupations as Christians became more urbanized.

incomes, most favorable occupational distributions, and highest average educational attainments.[15] Thus, if Catholics in each community only equal or approach their Protestant neighbors in these status variables, Catholics in the country as a whole will exceed Protestants by a fairly wide margin. Furthermore, the probability of upward mobility of sons of manual workers apparently varies directly with size of community of orientation.[16] Consequently, with other relevant factors held constant, one would expect upward mobility to be substantially greater for Catholics than for Protestants. If this were not the case, then indeed it would seem that religiously-related values, ethnicity, high fertility, or some other factor or factors were holding Catholics back. However, Catholics apparently *are* advancing more rapidly than Protestants, and one cannot tell from the greater Catholic mobility alone whether or not it is occurring *in spite of* religiously-based handicaps. . . .

SUMMARY AND CONCLUSIONS

At the end of World War II, Protestants in the United States ranked well above Catholics in income, occupation and education; since then Catholics have gained dramatically and have surpassed Protestants in most aspects of status. A lingering crucial difference is in the percentages who have been to college. However, this may be only a residue of lower parental status, and even this difference seems to have disappeared among the youngest adults.

An important reason for the more rapid advancement of Catholics is their heavy concentration in the larger non-Southern metropolitan areas, where earnings, occupational distributions, educational opportunities, and rates of upward mobility are more favorable than in the typical home communities of

[15] For 1960 census data showing variation in income, occupation, and education by community size, see Leo F. Schnore, "Some Correlates of Urban Size: A Replication," *American Journal of Sociology*, 69 (September, 1963), pp. 185–193. The relationship between community size and median family income was monotonic, the median varying from $5,222 in urban places with 2,500 to 10,000 residents to $6,863 in urbanized areas with 3,000,000 or more residents. The relationship between community size and percentage of workers in nonmanual occupations was not as simple, but the percentages were generally higher in the larger classes of communities. Percentage of high school graduates did not vary consistently with community size, but the smallest percentage was in the communities with only 2,500 to 10,000 residents.

The median income of white persons with income in 1959 was $3,332 in the Northeast, $3,099 in the North Central Region, $3,322 in the West, but only $2,529 in the South. The percentage of employed white males in nonmanual occupations in 1960 was 39.4 in the Northeast, 33.7 in the North Central Region, 39.4 in the West, and 36.9 in the South. Median years of school completed by white persons 25 years old and older in 1960 were 10.8 in the Northeast and North Central Regions, 12.1 in the West, and 10.4 in the South. The more pronounced disadvantage of Southerners in income than in occupation and education reflects lower earnings within occupations in the South.

Bogue presents data from a 1955 NORC survey showing lower incomes for Protestants than for Catholics within broad occupational categories and educational levels (*op. cit.*, pp. 705–707). The variation in income within occupations by community size and region can account for this difference; therefore it is not, as Greeley argues ("The Protestant Ethic . . . , *op. cit.*, p. 32), evidence against an adverse economic effect of Catholicism.

[16] Lipset and Bendix, *op. cit.*, chapter 8.

Protestants. Protestants still rank above Catholics in the large non-Southern metropolitan areas, but among young adults the gap in most aspects of status is not great. If the recent trend continues Catholics in the nation as a whole will surge well ahead of Protestants in all major status variables in the next few years. However, Catholics may continue to lag slightly behind Protestants in their home communities.

Our primary concern here is with a Protestant-Catholic comparison, and therefore we refer only incidentally to the Jewish data. It is important to note, however, that Jews are maintaining a wide lead over other religious categories and apparently have improved their relative standing since World War II. . . .

Theological Belief and Political Ideology

Among Protestant Clergy

JEFFREY K. HADDEN

INTRODUCTION

Three developments during the 1960's have served to heighten interest in the relationship between religion and political behavior. The first was the election of a Catholic to the presidency in 1960. The second development has been the alliance between radical right political groups and a number of religious figures. The third development has been the unprecedented involvement of clergy in a variety of expressions of protest for social justice.

Social scientists in America have been slow to explore the relationships between religious and political beliefs. While Lazarsfeld and his colleagues reported in studies conducted as early as 1940 that religious identification is significantly associated with party choice, other social scientists have remained skeptical of these findings.[1] Others have argued that the observed relationships could be accounted for by social class differences and ethnic-minority statuses.[2] As late as 1959 one of the leading pollsters in this nation sought to dispel the "myth of the Catholic vote."[3]

Numerous studies and polls have demonstrated a strong tendency for Protestants to identify with and vote for Republican candidates, while Jews are

Original paper, adapted from a paper read at the Annual Meetings of The Society for the Scientific Study of Religion, Chicago, October, 1966. Copyright, Jeffrey K. Hadden, 1968.

[1] Paul Lazarsfeld, Bernard Berelson, and Hazel Gaudet, *The People's Choice* (New York: Columbia University Press, 1948).

[2] For example, see Wesley and Beverly Allensmith, "Religious Affiliation and Politico-Economic Attitude," *Public Opinion Quarterly*, Vol. 12 (Fall, 1948), pp. 377–389.

[3] Elmo Roper, "The Myth of the Catholic Vote," *Saturday Review*, October 31, 1959.

more frequently aligned with the Democratic party.[4] However, there have been few attempts to explore variance in voting or other forms of political behavior *within* any of the major religious faiths. If theological belief is related to political ideology, then studies which distinguish only between broad religious categories (i.e., Protestant, Catholic, and Jew) may be of limited value, particularly in light of recent studies which have demonstrated that religious belief varies significantly both within and between Protestant denominations.[5]

In a sense, examining the relationship between political preference or voting behavior and broad religious categories may be analogous to asking the question, "Do you believe in God?" While such studies may give us some *very general* clues as to the relationship between religion and political ideology, they may not begin to explore the complexity of subtlety of relationships between these two belief systems.

Thus far, Benton Johnson is the only scholar who has attempted to move beyond the broad categories of religious identification, and his work is particularly important in clarifying the relationship between religion and political preference.[6] Focusing within Protestantism, Johnson has argued that individuals who adhere strongly to the theological tradition which Weber described as "ascetic" Protestantism will be inclined to support political traditions which emphasize free enterprise, limited government, and individualism.[7] Operationalized, this means that persons who adhere to a Fundamentalist or Conservative theology (also referred to as orthodoxy or Biblical literalism) are more likely to identify with the conservative political tradition of the Republican party than those who hold more liberal theological views.

In two parallel studies of church laity in Oregon and Florida, and a study of clergy in two denominations in Oregon, Johnson found considerable support for this thesis. While the replication of his findings in three settings is suggestive of an empirical relationship in the general population, the limited samples in Johnson's studies necessitates cautious interpretation.

The purpose of this paper is to replicate and extend the Johnson findings with data from a national sample of Protestant clergymen in six major denominations. The findings reported here are based on more than seven thousand cases

[4] Gerhard Lenski, *The Religious Factor* (Garden City, New York: Doubleday, 1961); Bernard Berelson, *et al.*, *Voting: A Study of Opinion Formation in a Presidential Campaign* (Chicago: University of Chicago Press, 1954); Oscar Gantz, "Protestant and Catholic Voting Behavior in a Metropolitan Area," *Public Opinion Quarterly*, Vol. 23 (Spring, 1959); Scott Greer, "Catholic Voters and the Democratic Party," *Public Opinion Quarterly*, Vol. 25 (Winter, 1961); Angus Campbell, *et al.*, *The American Voter*, (New York: Wiley, 1960); Philip Converse, "Religion and Politics: The 1960 Election," University of Michigan, unpublished paper.

[5] Jeffrey K. Hadden, "A Protestant Paradox—Divided They Merge," *Trans-Action*, July/August, 1967, pp. 63–69; Charles Y. Glock and Rodney Stark, *Religion and Society in Tension* (Chicago: Rand McNally and Company, 1965), Chapter 5, "The New Denominationalism."

[6] Benton Johnson, "Ascetic Protestantism and Political Preference," *Public Opinion Quarterly*, Vol. 26 (Spring, 1962); "Ascetic Protestantism and Political Preference in the Deep South," *American Journal of Sociology*, Vol. 69 (January, 1964); "Theology and Party Preference Among Protestant Clergymen," *American Sociological Review*, Vol. 31 (April, 1966).

[7] Max Weber, *The Protestant Ethic and the Spirit of Capitalism* (New York: Charles Scribner's Sons, 1930).

of white parish clergy and represent a 62 percent response rate from the sample which was conducted in early 1965.[8] Theological position is measured by the clergy's self-designation within traditional theological categories.[9]

THE RELIGIOUS AND SOCIAL BELIEFS OF CLERGY

Our analysis begins by examining the relationship between the minister's theological position and his preference for political party. Table 1 confirms the findings of Johnson in the smaller regional sample. Fundamentalists and Conservatives are much more likely to identify with the Republican party than are Neo-orthodox or Liberals. Sixty-eight and 62 percent, respectively, indicated that the Republican party was their usual party preference compared with 39 and 36 percent of those calling themselves Neo-orthodox and Liberal. Similarly, persons identifying themselves as Liberals and Neo-orthodox were more likely to claim usual preference for the Democratic party. Thirty-six and 35 percent, respectively, of the latter two groups indicated a Democratic preference. Only 13 and 15 percent of the Fundamentalists and Conservatives indicated a Democratic party preference and this is partially accounted for by persons in the sample from the South. However, Neo-orthodox ministers choose the Republican party with a slightly greater frequency than they select the Democratic party. Approximately one-fifth in all theological groups indicate that they are political independents, but the proportion is slightly higher for the Liberals. The most dramatic differences are clearly between the Fundamentalist–Conservative groups on the one hand and the Neo-orthodox–Liberal groups on the other.

TABLE 1. PARTY PREFERENCE × THEOLOGICAL POSITION

	(N)	Republican	Independent	Democrat
Fundamentalist	(342)	68%	18%	13%
Conservative	(3,182)	62%	22%	15%
Neo-orthodox	(2,032)	39%	26%	35%
Liberal	(1,560)	36%	28%	36%

[8] For a more detailed description of the study and a statement of objectives, see: Jeffrey K. Hadden, "A Study of the Protestant Ministry of America," *Journal for the Scientific Study of Religion*, Vol. V., No. 1, 1965, pp. 10–23.

[9] The question asked was: "Admittedly, there are difficulties associated with describing oneself in terms of broad theological positions. However, within the following categories, which of the following best describes your own theological position at each point in your career?" Theological position was ascertained for four points in time: "On entering college," "On entering seminary," "On leaving seminary," and "Now." The data reported here are for the current position. The theological categories offered were as follows: "Fundamentalist," "Conservative," "Neo-orthodox," "Liberal," "Universalist-Unitarian," and "Other." The categories of "Universalist-Unitarian" and "Other" were selected by only a small proportion of the clergy and therefore are not reported in this analysis. Only among Episcopalians did more than one or two percent select the last two categories. Seventeen percent of the Episcopalians identified themselves as other and the large majority of this group wrote in that they were "Anglican" or "Anglican Catholic." As a group, they tend to score between the Conservatives and the Neo-orthodox on responses to social issues, though they tend to be more closely aligned with Neo-orthodox clergy than Conservatives.

Table 2 shows the relationship between theological position and party preference for each denomination. While there is noticeable denominational variance, the pattern remains essentially the same for all groups. In every denomination, the Fundamentalists and Conservatives identify with the Republican party to a much greater extent than do the Neo-orthodox and Liberal groups. This difference is least in the Methodist and Episcopalian denominations which, again, can be partially accounted for by the fact that these two groups have large representations in the South, while the other denominations do not.

With the exception of the Baptists, Fundamentalists are more likely to select the Republican party than the Conservatives. Neo-orthodox and Liberals are more likely to identify with the Democratic party, with Liberals tending to select the Democratic party with a somewhat greater frequency than those calling

TABLE 2. PARTY PREFERENCE × THEOLOGICAL POSITION AND DENOMINATION

	(N)	Republican	Independent	Democrat
American Baptist				
Fundamentalist	(49)	62%	20%	18%
Conservative	(369)	70%	20%	10%
Neo-orthodox	(101)	40%	31%	30%
Liberal	(117)	38%	29%	33%
American Lutheran				
Fundamentalist	(59)	80%	12%	9%
Conservative	(593)	69%	22%	9%
Neo-orthodox	(213)	49%	28%	23%
Liberal	(117)	31%	34%	34%
Episcopalian				
Fundamentalist	(3)	*	*	*
Conservative	(340)	50%	22%	27%
Neo-orthodox	(382)	35%	26%	39%
Liberal	(326)	31%	31%	38%
Methodist				
Fundamentalist	(84)	44%	27%	29%
Conservative	(734)	43%	28%	29%
Neo-orthodox	(799)	31%	28%	41%
Liberal	(850)	34%	29%	37%
Missouri Synod Lutheran				
Fundamentalist	(130)	79%	17%	4%
Conservative	(697)	69%	23%	9%
Neo-orthodox	(44)	43%	36%	20%
Liberal	(12)	*	*	*
Presbyterian				
Fundamentalist	(17)	82%	6%	12%
Conservative	(449)	75%	15%	10%
Neo-orthodox	(493)	49%	21%	29%
Liberal	(221)	49%	22%	30%

* N too small to compute percentages.

themselves Neo-orthodox. While there tends to be a linear order from Fundamentalist to Liberal, the sharpest break is clearly between the Conservatives and
Neo-orthodox. Conservatives respond more like Fundamentalists and Neo-
orthodox respond more like Liberals.

The proportion identifying with the Democratic party does not approach
50 percent for any group. However, the more theologically liberal are more
likely to consider themselves independent. These observations suggest the possible influence of their middle class congregations who are probably predominantly Republican. We will return to this question later.

In summary, the findings from the national survey strongly corroborate the
regional conclusions of Johnson. Fundamentalist and Conservative clergyman
are much more likely to identify with the Republican party, while Neo-orthodox
and Liberals are more likely to claim loyalty to the Democratic party.

It is important to emphasize that the hypothesized relationship between conservative theology, and preference for the Republican party is derived from the
historic value orientations of "ascetic" Protestantism which proclaimed the
virtuousness of free enterprise and individualism. In other words, the logic of
the hypothesis is that preference for the Republican party is only an *indicator*
of an underlying political ideology. If this is correct, we would expect conservative theology to be even more strongly aligned with value statements which represent this ideology.

Table 3 shows the responses of clergy by theological position and denomination to three value statements concerning free enterprise, government, and
individual accountability for his own welfare. The belief statements were again

TABLE 3. POLITICAL IDEOLOGY × THEOLOGICAL POSITION AND DENOMINATION

	American Baptist	American Lutheran	Episcop-alian	Methodist	Missouri Synod Lutheran	Presby-terian
"The free enterprise system is the single economic system compatible with the requirements of personal freedom and constitutional government." (% agreeing)						
Fundamentalist	82%	76%	*	71%	76%	88%
Conservative	65%	51%	45%	61%	56%	52%
Neo-orthodox	31%	28%	29%	38%	20%	24%
Liberal	18%	29%	28%	33%	*	26%
"The government is providing too many services that should be left to private enterprise." (% agreeing)						
Fundamentalist	70%	75%	*	68%	88%	76%
Conservative	62%	62%	47%	55%	63%	56%
Neo-orthodox	33%	40%	34%	32%	25%	24%
Liberal	14%	26%	26%	27%	*	22%
"Most people who live in poverty could do something about their situation if they really wanted to." (% agreeing)						
Fundamentalist	52%	51%	*	61%	60%	53%
Conservative	39%	37%	54%	40%	36%	26%
Neo-orthodox	17%	19%	16%	22%	14%	12%
Liberal	14%	23%	16%	19%	*	11%

* N too small to compute percentages.

responded to on a six point continuum and the percentages shown are the combined responses of "agree" and "definitely agree." The ranking of "probably agree" is not included.

It is clear from an inspection of Table 3 that there is a strong relationship between belief in free enterprise and conservative theology. The first statement, "The free enterprise system is the single economic system compatible with the requirements of personal freedom and constitutional government," is the key item. For every denomination there is a sharp break in the proportion who agree with the statement as theological position shifts. The proportion of Fundamentalists who agree with this statement ranges from 71 percent in the Methodist church to 88 percent among Presbyterians. When these responses are compared with party affiliation in Table 2, it is seen that the proportion of Fundamentalists and Conservatives who agree with the free enterprise statement is *greater* than the proportion indicating preference for the Republican party. Also, the proportion of Neo-orthodox and Liberals who agree with the statement is *less* than the proportion in these groups who identify with the Republican party.

While the figures are not shown here, it should be mentioned that if the "probably agree" response is added to the "agree" response on this item, the proportion of Fundamentalists agreeing and tending to agree ranges from 88 percent to 100 per cent across the denominations. Furthermore, the proportion who "probably agree" with the statement is greater for the two conservative groups than for the two more liberal groups, thus increasing even further the distance between conservatives and liberals. These findings are clearly consistent with the hypothesized relationship between theological orientation and political ideology.

The second item in Table 3 states that "The government is providing too many services that should be left to private enterprise." Again the proportion agreeing with the statement varies dramatically with theological position. Approximately three-fourths of the Fundamentalists agree as compared with only about one-fourth of the Liberals. Though slightly less dramatic than the response to the first statement, the pattern of response is identical.

The third item in Table 3 states that "Most people who live in poverty could do something about their situation if they really wanted to." The distribution of responses to this item is much less dramatic, but the pattern is the same. The more conservative a minister's theology, the more likely he is to agree with the statement. There are a number of explanations which may account for the failure of this item to elicit as wide a range of responses as the other two items. Probably most important is the fact that the mass media have made Americans increasingly aware of the plight of the poor, not only in this nation, but throughout the world. What this item suggests, thus, is that sensitivity to the dilemma of poverty is significantly influenced by a person's ideology.

The 1964 presidential election was unique inasmuch as the Republican candidate, Senator Barry Goldwater, unambiguously articulated the ideology which Weber described as "ascetic Protestantism." Goldwater's campaign attempted to appeal to an ideology as much, if not more, than to a party. Thus, support for Goldwater can be viewed as another way of measuring the relationship between theological outlook and political ideology. We would expect support for Goldwater to be stronger among Fundamentalists and Conservatives than Neo-orthodox and Liberals independent of party preference. Table 4 shows the proportion who favored Goldwater for president controlled by theological position for each denomination. Support for Goldwater is strongest among the Fundamentalists and is roughly proportional to their preference for the Republican party. Conservatives favored Goldwater to a lesser degree than they identified with the Republican party. The proportion of theological Conservatives favoring Goldwater, however, is greater than the proportion of the general population of the nation who voted for the Republican candidate. The proportion favoring Goldwater among Neo-orthodox and Liberals drops off very dramatically. Among Presbyterians, for example, only 11 percent of the Neo-orthodox and 10 percent of the Liberals indicated that Goldwater was their choice for president. Only six percent of the Liberal Baptists stated a preference for Goldwater. In short, those who consider themselves theologically liberal (Neo-orthodox or Liberal) eschewed the ideology which Goldwater represented. This is true even among theological liberals who normally consider themselves Republican.

TABLE 4. CANDIDATE PREFERENCE × THEOLOGICAL POSITION AND DENOMINATION

	American Baptist	American Lutheran	Episco-palian	Methodist	Missouri Synod Lutheran	Presby-terian
% Favoring Goldwater in 1964 Presidential Election						
Fundamentalist	68%	64%	*	61%	78%	76%
Conservative	53%	52%	39%	39%	66%	42%
Neo-orthodox	13%	23%	20%	15%	27%	11%
Liberal	6%	17%	13%	10%	*	10%

* N too small to percentage.

Table 5 shows the proportion favoring Goldwater controlling for theological position and party preference. Eighty-two percent who are Fundamentalist and Republican favored Goldwater. Among those who are Fundamentalist and politically independent, 56 percent favored Goldwater. Defections from the Republican ranks are enormous among those who are Neo-orthodox and Liberal. Only 30 and 22 percent of Neo-orthodox and Liberals respectively who were Republicans favored the Republican candidate. Among Democrats, 29 percent who consider themselves Fundamentalist favored Goldwater compared with only three percent and two percent who are theologically Neo-orthodox and Liberal.

In summary, the data support the thesis that both theological position and party affiliation are manifestions of a more basic ideology or world view which

TABLE 5. Percent Favoring Goldwater for President ×
Theological Position and Party Preference

	% Favoring Goldwater		
	Republican	*Independent*	*Democrat*
Fundamentalist	82%	56%	29%
Conservative	62%	39%	14%
Neo-orthodox	30%	12%	3%
Liberal	22%	7%	2%

Weber described as "ascetic" Protestantism. While both theological position and party preference are significant indicators of this ideology, theology is a better predictor. This is especially obvious in Table 5 where theological position is a much stronger predictor of endorsement of Goldwater among Republicans.

RECIPROCAL INFLUENCES OF CLERGY AND LAITY

Johnson's studies have also been provocative in suggesting that clergy have an influence on the political views of their congregations. Specifically, he finds that theologically liberal ministers have a liberalizing influence on the political behavior of their laity who by social status should tend toward conservative political behavior, while theologically conservative ministers have a moderating influence on laity who by social status should tend toward liberal political behavior. While Republicanism was directly related to higher social class among a sample of laity, frequent church attendance tended to reduce the class based political differences in the direction of the minister's views. In congregations where the minister was theologically liberal, persons who attended church frequently were *less* likely to be Republican than those who attended seldom. On the other hand, in congregations where the minister was theologically conservative, persons who attended church frequently were *more* likely to be Republican than those who seldom attended church. In other words, where active church laity are caught in a cross pressure between class based political tendencies and the theological position of their ministers, there is a tendency for the minister to affect their political outlook. The result, thus, is a "muting effect" with theologically liberal ministers tending to influence middle class congregations away from the Republican party and theologically conservative ministers drawing working class congregations toward the Republican party.

The data from this study lend inferential support to the Johnson thesis. While Republicanism is *positively* related to social status in the general population, Table 6 shows that among clergy, Republican party preference in *inversely* related to the social class of their parish.[10] Forty-two percent of the clergy serving congregations that are predominately professional and managerial indicated a preference for the Republican party compared with 53 percent of those serving blue collar congregations. Preference for the Democratic party, on the other hand, is positively aligned with social status. Thirty-five percent serving professional and managerial congregations compared with only 23 percent serving blue collar congregations stated a preference for the Democratic party.

TABLE 6. PARTY PREFERENCE OF CLERGY × SOCIAL STATUS OF THEIR CONGREGATIONS

Congregation's Social Status	(N)	Party Preference		
		Republican	Independent	Democrat
Predominately professional and managerial	(787)	42%	23%	35%
Majority salaried white collar with considerable professional and managerial	(1,608)	48%	25%	27%
Majority salaried white collar with considerable blue collar	(1,130)	51%	25%	24%
Draws membership about equally from all occupational groups	(1,177)	50%	26%	24%
Majority blue collar with some white collar	(1,893)	53%	24%	23%
Predominately blue collar	(846)	53%	25%	23%

The relationship between the social status of ministers' congregations and the choice of presidential candidates is presented in Table 7. As in the relationship between social status and party affiliation, social status is inversely related to preference for the Republican candidate. Only 21 percent of the clergy serving professional and managerial congregations favored Goldwater compared with 39 percent who serve blue collar congregations.

This consistent inverse relationship between the political views of clergy and the laity they serve presents a perplexing dilemma. How does it happen that organizations manage so persistently to hire professional leadership who differ dramatically from their own views regarding matters so basic as political ideology? The dilemma, in large part, grows out of the nature of the market place of available clergy. Higher status churches desire to recruit ministers who have acquired maximum quality education from high status institutions. Many of

---

[10] Social class is based on the minister's ranking of the occupational background of the members of his church. The options on the questionnaire were as follows: (1) professional and managerial; (2) majority salaried white collar workers, but also a considerable number of professional and managerial people; (3) majority salaried white collar workers, but there are also a considerable number of blue collar workers; (4) majority blue collar workers, but there are some white collar, professional, and managerial people; (5) membership predominately blue collar; and (6) membership about equally drawn from all occupational groups. The analyses presented here collapse categories 2 and 3 as white collar and categories 4 and 5 as blue collar. Personal interviews with 85 clergy, using the same categories, indicated that their perceptions of the social class of their congregations correlated very highly with independent criteria.

TABLE 7. POLITICAL CANDIDATE FAVORED BY CLERGY × SOCIAL STATUS OF THEIR CONGREGATIONS

	Candidate Favored		
Congregation's Social Status	*Gold-water*	*John-son*	*Neither*
Predominately professional and managerial	21%	77%	2%
Majority salaried white collar with considerable professional and managerial	28%	68%	4%
Majority salaried white collar with considerable blue collar	31%	66%	4%
Draws membership about equally from all occupational groups	33%	63%	4%
Majority blue collar with some white collar	38%	57%	5%
Predominately blue collar	39%	57%	4%

the high status and high quality seminaries in America have long traditions as centers of liberal theology and progressive political thought. Thus, higher status churches in seeking out clergy who have the credentials of the higher status educational institutions are systematically hiring men who are politically more liberal than the constituency of the congregation. This is one of the important built-in structural sources of conflict between clergy and laity in Protestantism, particularly in the free church tradition, where the processes of selecting ministers tend to maximize rather than reduce the possibility for conflict.

That Liberal ministers should have at least a modest liberalizing influence on their congregations, as reported by Johnson, seems altogether plausible. By the same token, one would expect congregations to have a moderating influence on their ministers. This is not, however, suggested by the data in Tables 6 and 7 which show the relationship between congregational social status and the political views of ministers. Table 8 shows the relationship between congregational social status and clergymen's party preference and presidential candidate choice controlling for theological position. Again there is no strong evidence to suggest that higher status congregations influence their ministers' political views. Thirty-four percent of the liberal ministers serving middle class congregations compared with 42 percent who serve professional and managerial congregations indicate a preference for the Democratic party. Liberal ministers in the two higher status groups overwhelmingly pick Johnson as their presidential candidate. Of the liberal ministers in professional and managerial and middle class congregations, 88 percent and 84 percent respectively favor Johnson. This is a stronger endorsement of Johnson than among liberal ministers in congregations of mixed and working class status.

An examination of the relationship between ministers' political views and congregational social status among theologically conservative ministers also fails to suggest any noticeable influence of the congregation on the ministers' views. The smallest proportion of theologically conservative ministers who indicate that they are Republican is found in the group serving professional and managerial congregations. In that group the proportion who identify with

TABLE 8. PARTY PREFERENCE AND CANDIDATE FAVORED BY CLERGY × THEIR THEOLOGICAL
POSITION AND THEIR CONGREGATION'S SOCIAL STATUS

	Neo-orthodox and Liberal				Fundamentalist and Conservative			
	Managerial and Professional	Middle Class	Mixed Class	Working Class	Managerial and Professional	Middle Class	Mixed Class	Working Class
Party Preference								
Republican	34%	38%	37%	39%	60%	63%	63%	63%
Independent	24%	28%	30%	26%	19%	21%	22%	23%
Democrat	42%	34%	33%	35%	21%	16%	15%	14%
Candidate Favored								
Goldwater	10%	13%	14%	16%	43%	49%	51%	54%
Johnson	88%	84%	82%	81%	53%	46%	45%	40%
Neither	1%	3%	4%	3%	4%	5%	4%	5%

the Republican party is 60 percent. The proportion reporting that they are Republican is 63 percent for all three other social status groups. Similarly, preference for Goldwater is inversely related to the social status of the minister's congregation. That is, the higher the social status of the congregation the less likely the clergyman will favor Goldwater.

In brief these data fail to confirm the proposition that congregations affect the political *beliefs* of their clergy. Clergy appear to remain fiercely independent in their political beliefs in the presence of laity who hold contrary views. While clergy may hold political views that are incongruent with their congregations, this does not mean that congregations do not affect their *behavior*.

We asked clergy whether they had endorsed one of the candidates for president during the 1964 campaign, either from the pulpit or in some other religious gathering. Only 14 percent said that they did. This small percentage who endorsed a political candidate takes on significance when we consider the fact that 60 percent of the ministers in the study believe that ministers should have a right to publicly indicate their views on political issues. Responses to two additional statements further illumine the constraining influence of laity on their public behavior. Sixty-seven percent of the clergy agreed with the statement "The John Birch Society and other extremist groups constitute a grave threat to our society." Furthermore 51 percent reject the statement that "The identification of Goldwater with extremist groups during the recent election was nothing more than a great political smear by his opposition."[11] In other words, a large proportion of the clergy view extremist groups as a serious threat to our society, and furthermore refuse to disidentify Goldwater from these extremists elements. Nevertheless, they did not speak out on the election, in spite of the fact that they felt that the issue was of grave importance and that they should have the right to do so. Thus, the data strongly suggest that clergy maintain a private

11 The percentages reported in these two paragraphs are for the "agree" and "disagree" responses on a six point scale. If the "probably agree" or "probably disagree" responses are added to the responses reported, all three figures will increase approximately 15 percent.

posture which is dissonant from their public behavior. Their public behavior would seem to be significantly affected by what they perceive to be the expectations of their laity.

SUMMARY

The results of this investigation clearly confirm the findings of Johnson that conservative religious views are associated with preference for the Republican party, and similarly, that liberal theological views are associated with preference for the Democratic party. The data from this study further support the proposition that theological views and party preference are both reflections of an underlying ideology or world view.

The consistency of the findings across six denominations which represent a wide range of theological views leaves us with little reason to doubt that the findings would be replicated in clergy samples from other denominations. A possible exception might occur among a few small sectarian fundamentalist groups. Elinson, for example, recently analyzed the content of the writing of A. A. Allen, a Pentecostal evangelist, and found that his teachings encourage withdrawal from political activities rather than espousal of right wing political views.[12] Other sectarian groups, however, have been in the public light as strong supporters of radical right wing political views.

The data presented in this study provide only an inferential basis for assessing the influence of clergy's views on their laity. We found that ministers who are theologically and politically liberal disproportionately serve higher status churches, while conservative ministers are disproportionately serving lower status churches. Thus, if clergy do influence their congregation's views, it would tend to be in the direction suggested by Johnson. However, other interpretations of these findings seem plausible and cannot be easily dismissed. For example, it may be that laity who find themselves in sharp disagreement with the political and social ideologies expressed by their minister become less involved in church activities. In other words, a minister draws the greatest support in terms of church attendance from those who agree with his social pronouncements. The available data are insufficient to resolve this dilemma of interpretation, but if this latter interpretation should be correct, the long range inplications are extremely important. If younger clergy continue to become more liberal in their social ideologies, we can anticipate increasing alienation and decline in support from higher status congregations.

While congregations seem to have little influence on a minister's political *beliefs*, the evidence is substantial that they affect his *behavior*. In spite of the fact that a large proportion of ministers feel that they should have the right to speak out on significant political issues, only a very small proportion actually do so. This discrepancy between belief and action apparently results from their desire to avoid head-on conflict with their congregations. A minister is entitled to believe as he likes so long as he doesn't try to proselytize his own views.

[12] Howard Elinson, "The Implications of Pentecostal Religion for Intellectualism, Politics, and Race Relations," *The American Journal of Sociology*, Vol. 70 (January, 1965).

Some Factors Associated with Variations
in Church Attendance

BERNARD LAZERWITZ

The development of the sociology of religion has been handicapped by a lack of data on large populations. While many fine studies have been made of the religious behavior of restricted populations and some on communities as large as Indianapolis or Detroit, reliable data for regions or the entire nation have not been available.[1]

To help extend the empirical basis for treatment of religious behavior, this article presents data on the association of several demographic and social factors with variations in church attendance. The data should enable the establishment of national averages against which studies of more restricted populations can be contrasted.

SOURCE OF INFORMATION

This article gives information gathered on three national surveys conducted by the Survey Research Center of The University of Michigan. Of these three surveys, two were conducted in the spring of 1957, and each adult respondent[2]

Reprinted from *Social Forces*, 39 (May, 1961), pp. 301–309, by permission of the author and the publisher.

[1] Some of the studies that have investigated the associations between church attendance or interest and various other characteristics are: (a) Gerhard Lenski, "Social Correlates of Religious Interest," *American Sociological Review*, 18 (October 1953), pp. 533–544. This article deals with Indianapolis. (b) Harry Sharp and Albert Mayer, *Religious Characteristics in the Detroit Metropolitan Area* (Ann Arbor, Michigan: The Detroit Area Study, 1960, mimeographed). (c) Joseph H. Fichter, *Social Relations in the Urban Parish* (Chicago: University of Chicago Press, 1954). (d) Basil Zimmer and Amos Hawley, "Suburbanization and Church Participation," *Social Forces*, 37 (May 1959), pp. 348–354. This article deals with Flint, Michigan. (e) Harold L. Orbach, "Aging and Religion: Church Attendance in the Detroit Metropolitan Area," *Geriatrics* (in press, 1961). (f) Joseph B. Schuyler, *Northern Parish* (Chicago: Loyola University Press, 1960). (g) Anonymous, "How Important Religion Is to Americans," *Catholic Digest*, 17 (February 1953), pp. 6–12. While this article presents some national data, it does not seem to be based on a probability sample. (h) Wesley Allinsmith and Beverly Allinsmith, "Religious Affiliation and Politico-Economic Attitude," *Public Opinion Quarterly*, 12 (Fall 1948), pp. 377–389. Their data are not based on a probability sample but do pertain to the entire population of the United States. (i) Michael Argyle, *Religious Behavior* (London: Routledge and Kegan Paul, 1958, and recently published by the Free Press). This book presents the results of various community studies done in the United States and Great Britain. (j) Louis Bultena, "Church Membership and Church Attendance in Madison, Wisconsin," *American Sociological Review*, 14 (June 1949), pp. 384–389. (k) Benson Y. Landis, "A Guide to the Literature on Statistics of Religious Affiliation with References to Related Social Studies," *Journal of the American Statistical Association*, 54 (June 1959), pp. 335–357. This last article presents an extremely fine discussion on the available types of religious statistics and an excellent bibliography.

[2] The three surveys accepted interviews with respondents under 21 years of age in certain cases. However, the tables apply only to respondents 21 years of age or older. (Very few respondents were under 21 years of age.)

was asked his religious preference and his denominational preference if the respondent was Protestant. The third survey was conducted in November 1958, and asked only for religious preference.[3]

It is important to insure that the inclusion of a third survey, conducted 18 months after the first two surveys, does not disturb our ability to view the data as representing a cross section in time. This possibility has been explored by running percentages for the 1957 surveys and then for all three surveys combined. Comparisons of these two sets of percentages indicating the passage of 18 months produced only random changes.[4] With these three surveys combined into one, the data may be thought of as referring to a point in time midway between the Spring of 1957 and November 1958, namely, December 1957.[5]

The probability that the dependent variable employed in this study, namely church attendance, is subject to upward bias has been pointed out by Argyle and Bultena.[6] Whatever bias exists in the church attendance data presented here is equally present in its relationships with other study variables. Consequently, the various differences in associations between church attendance and these other variables should not be appreciably distorted by possible overestimations of church attendance.

The associations between church attendance and other study variables are presented for all Protestants, Roman Catholics, Jews, Baptists, and Methodists. Because a sufficiently large number of interviews was obtained with Baptists and Methodists, it has been possible to include members of these denominations in the detailed analysis. Although the number of interviews with Jews is relatively small (188), they have been included in order to provide some contrast to the data on the Christian religious groups.[7]

---

[3] The three surveys are described in: (a) Gerald Gurin, Joseph Veroff, and Sheila Feld, *Americans View Their Mental Health* (New York: Basic Books, 1960). (b) Robert Davis, *The Public Impact of Science in the Mass Media* (Ann Arbor, Michigan: Institute for Social Research, 1958, mimeographed). (c) Warren C. Miller, *The Party and the Representative Process: A Progress Report on Research* (Ann Arbor, Michigan: Institute for Social Research, 1959, mimeographed). The lack of a question on Protestant denominational preference on the November, 1958, survey confines denominational data to the first two studies. The reader should bear this in mind when contrasting the number of interviews reported for all Protestants with that reported for Baptists and Methodists.

[4] For a comparison of these surveys with the one on religion conducted by the United States Bureau of the Census, see Bernard Lazerwitz, *A Comparison of Major United States Religious Groups* (Ann Arbor, Michigan: Institute for Social Research, 1960, dittoed), Table 3.

[5] Sampling error tables, prepared for individual percentages and for the difference between any two percentages, are available upon request. For a discussion of the function of such tables and illustrations of their use see the appendix to Gurin, Veroff, and Feld, *Americans View Their Mental Health*.

[6] Argyle, *op. cit.*, pp. 5–7; Bultena, *op. cit.*, pp. 387–388.

[7] The results of the investigation into the association between church attendance and the other study variables for the smaller Protestant denominations (Lutherans, Presbyterians, Episcopalians, other Fundamentalists, other non-Fundamentalists, and Protestants without a denominational preference) are available upon request. The number of such interviews is customarily too small to give reliable results. On the whole, the trends which can be observed in the data for these groups follow those of the Protestant group.

FINDINGS

SEX

Table 1 presents the relationship between sex and church attendance classified into regular attendance (once a week or more), often (once, twice, or three times a month), seldom (a few times a year or less), and never attending. Clearly, women attend church more frequently than men. This sex differential has been repeatedly reported by other investigations and has been frequently commented upon in the popular literature.[8]

TABLE 1. FREQUENCY OF CHURCH ATTENDANCE BY SEX (IN PERCENTAGES)

		Frequency of Church Attendance				
Religious Groups	*N*	*Regularly*	*Often*	*Seldom*	*Never*	*Total*
Protestants						
M	1,883	30	23	37	10	100
F	2,302	46	23	25	6	100
Roman Catholics						
M	584	67	14	14	5	100
F	686	75	13	9	3	100
Jews						
M	79	19	20	43	18	100
F	109	8	22	57	13	100
Baptists						
M	394	35	29	28	8	100
F	545	47	30	18	5	100
Methodists						
M	324	25	29	36	10	100
F	406	43	27	22	8	100

The sex differential is greater for all Protestants, Baptists, and Methodists than for Catholics but, surprisingly, reverses among Jews. Jewish men attend synagogue more frequently than Jewish women.

Undoubtedly, this reversal is the product of the Orthodox Jewish norm that men, not women, are supposed to attend religious services. While many Jews are no longer Orthodox, it is probable that this norm still operates among non-Orthodox Jews most of whom are children or grandchildren of Orthodox forebearers.

Why do Christian women attend church more frequently than men? Either norms in the Christian groups encourage such a sex differentiation, or there is something in the socialization and social roles of the sexes that results in Christian women wanting to go to church more frequently than their men. Argyle emphasizes a socialization explanation.[9] Lenski hypothesizes that the

[8] Similar sex differentials are reported by: Lenski, *op. cit.*; Sharp and Mayer, *op. cit.*; Orbach, *op. cit.*; *Catholic Digest, op. cit.*; Argyle, *op. cit.*; and Bultena, *op. cit.*
[9] Argyle, *op. cit.*, chap. 7, pp. 71–79.

TABLE 2. Frequency of Church Attendance by Sex and Labour Force Membership (in Percentages)

Religious and Labour Force Groups	N	Regularly	Often	Seldom	Never	Total
			Frequency of Church Attendance			
Protestants						
Men in Labor Force	1,512	30	24	37	9	100
Men Not in Labor Force	279	25	20	40	15	100
Women in Labor Force	832	46	25	24	5	100
Women Not in Labor Force	1,562	46	23	25	6	100
Catholics						
Men in Labor Force	502	68	14	14	4	100
Men Not in Labor Force	62	66	11	12	11	100
Women in Labor Force	243	77	14	9	0	100
Women Not in Labor Force	463	74	12	9	5	100
Jews						
Men in Labor Force[a]	72	19	19	43	19	100
Women in Labor Force	36	12	8	67	13	100
Women Not in Labor Force	73	6	29	52	13	100

[a] The category Jewish Men Not in Labor Force contains only seven cases.

sex difference may result from the greater male participation in the labor force.[10]

Table 2 refutes Lenski's hypothesis by presenting separate church attendance percentages with controls for religious preference, sex, and labor force participation. There is little, if any, change in the differences between the sexes even when women in the labor force are compared with men in the labor force. Notice how much alike the church attendance percentages are for women in the three religious groups who are in or out of the labor force and again, for men who are in and out of the labor force.

RACE

Of the Negro Baptists 84 percent attend church regularly or often in contrast to 69 percent of the white Baptists. United States Negroes are heavily Baptist; Baptists attend church most frequently of all major Protestant denominations.[11] This serves to underscore the strong Negro religious attachments commented upon by students of race relations.

AGE

It has long been thought that adults become more religious as they age. Orbach has recently completed a thorough study of the association between age and church attendance in Detroit. He found no meaningful change in

[10] Lenski, *op. cit.*, pp. 535–536.

[11] For data on these points see: (a) Lazerwitz, *op. cit.* (b) Donald J. Bogue, "Religious Affiliation," *The Population of the United States* (Glencoe, Illinois: Free Press, 1959), pp. 688–709. (c) United States Bureau of the Census, "Religion Reported by the Civilian Population of the United States: March 1957," *Current Population Reports*, Series P-20, No. 79.

TABLE 3. FREQUENCY OF CHURCH ATTENDANCE BY AGE (IN PERCENTAGES)

Religious Groups	N	*Frequency of Church Attendance*				
		Regularly	*Often*	*Seldom*	*Never*	*Total*
Protestants						
21–24 yrs.	251	27	25	39	9	100
25–29 yrs.	502	37	26	31	6	100
30–34 yrs.	498	41	26	26	7	100
35–39 yrs.	460	41	25	29	5	100
40–44 yrs.	494	37	23	32	8	100
45–49 yrs.	452	39	22	30	9	100
50–54 yrs.	419	42	25	28	5	100
55–59 yrs.	335	40	22	31	7	100
60–64 yrs.	259	40	24	28	8	100
65 and over	515	40	24	28	8	100
Roman Catholics						
21–24 yrs.	81	70	11	17	2	100
25–29 yrs.	158	69	16	13	2	100
30–34 yrs.	168	72	12	11	5	100
35–39 yrs.	157	72	17	9	2	100
40–44 yrs.	184	77	12	8	3	100
45–49 yrs.	117	72	13	13	2	100
50–54 yrs.	110	66	15	15	4	100
55–59 yrs.	80	78	9	5	8	100
60–64 yrs.	68	74	12	13	1	100
65 and over	147	66	14	12	8	100
Jews						
21–34 yrs.	48	6	17	56	21	100
35–49 yrs.	73	8	23	54	15	100
50–65 and over	67	25	22	43	10	100
Baptists						
21–24 yrs.	79	27	30	35	8	100
25–29 yrs.	107	41	38	19	2	100
30–34 yrs.	124	43	32	18	7	100
35–39 yrs.	110	45	29	22	4	100
40–44 yrs.	108	40	32	24	4	100
45–49 yrs.	105	42	27	23	8	100
50–54 yrs.	82	49	28	18	5	100
55–59 yrs.	60	40	33	24	3	100
60–64 yrs.	53	32	42	17	9	100
65 and over	111	47	22	20	11	100
Methodists						
21–24 yrs.	41	24	37	32	7	100
25–29 yrs.	72	26	36	31	7	100
30–34 yrs.	90	38	28	27	7	100
35–39 yrs.	81	41	32	22	5	100
40–44 yrs.	82	36	27	29	8	100
45–49 yrs.	72	34	19	40	7	100
50–54 yrs.	71	41	27	27	5	100
55–59 yrs.	59	29	27	34	10	100
60–64 yrs.	41	47	32	13	8	100
65 and over	121	33	16	35	16	100

church attendance for different age groups among Protestant and Catholics and an increase for Jews.[12]

His findings are confirmed for the United States, as a whole, by the percentages of Table 3. Here, too, there is no meaningful change in church attendance for different age groups among both Protestants and Catholics (with the exception of the Protestant 21–24 year old group). The change within the Jewish group is probably a product of the greater orthodoxy of older Jews.

Two other points should be commented upon. First of all, the Catholic young people's group (21–24 years old) does not show a drop in attendance as does the equivalent Protestant age group. This is another illustration of the success of the very strong Catholic emphasis upon church attendance. Secondly, Argyle supports his proposition of increasing religious activity with age by several measures—attitudes toward religion, certainty of an after-life, reading the Bible, daily prayer, and attending church.[13] Among these measures the least activity and variation appear in church attendance. Two pieces of negative evidence against one particular measure of religious activity does not invalidate the idea of changes in religious activity throughout adulthood. It may be that church attendance, itself, is based upon patterns established fairly early in life and subject to little (if any) change throughout adulthood. A more thorough investigation by age cohorts of church attendance and other forms of religious activity would go a long way toward resolving these questions.

NUMBER OF CHILDREN

The presence of varying numbers of children in the home does not appear to be associated with meaningful variations in church attendance. Protestants with no children in the home do exhibit slightly less regularity in church attendance than do Protestants with children. However, the small percentage differences between these groups are, at best, barely at the five percent level of significance. The other religious groups show no meaningful differentiation.

FAMILY LIFE CYCLE

Table 4 shows Protestants exhibiting changes in church attendance at different stages of the family life cycle. Young, single Protestants attend church the least. After marriage, regularity of church attendance rises, and it peaks for those families having children five years old and over. Apparently, when children are old enough to be sent to Sunday School, their parents stay for the religious services which are conducted at the same time. With children no longer in the home, regularity of attendance drops. Both the Baptists and Methodists display similar patterns.

It should be pointed out that Protestants with children five years old and over seem to shift from often to regular attendance. This category's seldom and never percentages differ only slightly from equivalent percentages for the

12 Orbach, *op. cit.*
13 Argyle , *op. cit.*, pp. 67–69.

TABLE 4. Frequency of Church Attendances by Family Life Cycle (in Percentages)

Religious Groups	N	Frequency of Church Attendance				
		Regularly	Often	Seldom	Never	Total
Protestants						
R. single and under 35 yrs.	96	31	26	31	12	100
Married, R. under 35 yrs., no children	154	38	32	24	6	100
Married, youngest child under 5 yrs.	1008	36	25	32	7	100
Married, youngest child 5 yrs. and over	1016	44	22	28	6	100
No children in home, R. 35 yrs. and over	1632	38	22	32	8	100
Catholics						
R. single and under 35 yrs.	45	77	5	15	3	100
Married, R. under 35 yrs., no children	59	71	9	17	3	100
Married, youngest child under 5 yrs.	350	72	14	11	3	100
Married, youngest child 5 yrs. and over	340	72	16	9	3	100
No children in home, R. 35 yrs. and over	404	71	12	11	6	100
Jews						
No children in home, R., under 35 yrs.	16	1	19	53	27	100
Married, youngest child under 5 yrs.	47	11	24	45	20	100
Married, youngest child 5 yrs. and over	60	9	19	56	16	100
No children in home, R. 35 yrs. and over	59	20	23	40	8	100
Baptists						
No children in home, R. under 35 yrs.	67	36	30	23	11	100
Married, youngest child under 5 yrs.	229	38	36	22	4	100
Married, youngest child 5 yrs. and over	235	47	28	20	5	100
No children in home, R. 35 yrs. and over	321	42	27	24	7	100
Methodists						
No children in home, R. under 35 yrs.	47	22	42	29	7	100
Married, youngest child under 5 yrs.	180	33	30	29	8	100
Married, youngest child 5 yrs. and over	164	41	25	29	5	100
No children in home, R. 35 yrs. and over	285	36	24	29	11	100

other life cycle categories. Protestants who are poor church attenders seem to display little change in their church-going habits with changes in family life.

When sample sizes are considered, one must conclude that the Catholic data do not indicate changes in church attendance with changes in family life cycle. Again, small sample sizes restrict conclusions about the Jewish group. Here, Jews with no children appear to be poor synagogue attenders; those with children show an increase in synagogue attendance. Those homes with older respondents display the higher synagogue attendance rates characteristic of older Jews.

EDUCATION

Table 5 indicates that church attendance increases with increasing number of years of schooling for all Protestants and Catholics, Baptists, and Methodists. The percentage increases are fairly sizable as one moves up the educational scale. A fairly good breaking point appears to occur at the 4 years of high school level. Christian adults with less than a high school education clearly attend church considerably less than those adults who do have a high school education

TABLE 5. Frequency of Church Attendance by Years of School Completed (in Percentages)

		Frequency of Church Attendance				
Religious Groups	*N*	*Regularly*	*Often*	*Seldom*	*Never*	*Total*
Protestants						
0–8 Grades	1381	33	26	31	10	100
Some High School	880	35	23	34	8	100
4 Yrs. High School	1128	42	21	31	6	100
1–3 Yrs. College	422	47	23	24	6	100
4 Yrs. or More of College	374	52	20	24	4	100
Roman Catholics						
0–8 Grades	436	63	17	13	7	100
Some High School	256	67	14	15	4	100
4 Yrs. High School	397	80	10	8	2	100
1–2 Yrs. College	117	79	10	9	2	100
4 Yrs. or More of College	64	89	9	1	1	100
Jews						
0–8 Grades and Some High School	66	21	27	44	10	100
4 Yrs. High School	58	6	14	62	18	100
1–4 Yrs. or More College	64	10	22	50	18	100
Baptists						
0–8 Grades	422	35	37	21	7	100
Some High School	225	44	26	23	7	100
4 Yrs. High School	193	46	23	28	3	100
1–3 Yrs. College	63	56	25	11	8	100
4 Yrs. or More of College	36	71	14	11	4	100
Methodists						
0–8 Grades	229	26	30	32	12	100
Some High School	143	26	29	33	12	100
4 Yrs. High School	200	37	30	26	7	100
1–3 Yrs. College	76	51	20	26	3	100
4 Yrs. or More of College	82	60	25	12	3	100

or better. The hypothesis that church attendance should decrease with increasing education or that college-educated adults attend church less frequently than adults without a college degree is not supported by the data.

The differences within the Jewish group are not significant. Assuming the percentages really differ in the manner shown by the table, one could attribute the variations to the smaller amount of education obtained by Orthodox Jews who are more heavily concentrated in the older, foreign-born, low income, and less desirable occupation categories than are non-Orthodox Jews. Since contemporary non-Orthodox Jews are frequently the children and grandchildren of Orthodox Jews, the percentages, again, tend to picture generational differences within the Jewish community.

OCCUPATION

The association between occupation of the family head and church attendance is introduced in Table 6. Among Christians, adults whose family heads have white-collar occupations show more regularity of church attendance than adults whose family heads have nonfarm, blue collar occupations. Protestant

TABLE 6. FREQUENCY OF CHURCH ATTENDANCE BY OCCUPATION OF FAMILY HEAD (IN PERCENTAGES)

Religious Groups	N	Frequency of Church Attendance				
		Regularly	Often	Seldom	Never	Total
Protestants						
Professions	372	47	23	23	7	100
Owners, Managers, and Officials	502	41	22	30	7	100
Clerical and Sales	419	43	23	29	5	100
Skilled	711	35	21	36	8	100
Semi-Skilled	628	34	23	36	7	100
Unskilled	411	35	27	31	7	100
Farmers	410	44	30	20	6	100
Roman Catholics						
Professions	106	81	11	7	1	100
Owners, Managers, and Officials	139	83	8	5	4	100
Clerical and Sales	132	81	11	5	3	100
Skilled	279	68	15	13	4	100
Semi-Skilled	254	66	16	13	5	100
Unskilled	131	62	21	11	6	100
Farmers	51	67	9	20	4	100
Jews						
Professions, Owners, Managers and Officials	93		85[a]		15	100
All other occupations	65		81[a]		19	100
Baptists						
Professions	47	66	13	18	3	100
Owners, Managers, and Officials	77	45	27	21	7	100
Clerical and Sales	67	51	30	16	3	100
Skilled	154	33	29	30	8	100
Semi-Skilled	181	38	31	24	7	100
Unskilled	140	42	36	17	5	100
Farmers	105	43	40	15	2	100
Methodists						
Professions	75	47	23	23	7	100
Owners, Managers, and Officials	82	45	28	22	5	100
Clerical and Sales	78	40	28	28	4	100
Skilled	118	30	25	37	8	100
Semi-Skilled	100	26	23	44	7	100
Unskilled	58	30	33	29	8	100
Farmers	66	40	36	21	3	100

[a] Represents combined percentages for regularly, often, and seldom.

adults whose family heads are farmers attend church as frequently as the white collar categories. This does not hold for the small group of Catholic farmers. Among all Protestants, Baptists, and Methodists the greatest regularity of attendance is found in the professional category. No significant differences are found within the Jewish group.

INCOME

Apart from a slight reduction in church regularity for the very bottom income categories, no pattern of association is found between income and church attendance within any of the religious groups. This lack of association is surprising in view of the associations previously observed between education, occupation, and church attendance. Additional research with added controls for education, occupation, and urbanization is needed to help identify the factors that prevent the development of a relationship between income and church attendance.

CONCLUSIONS

Clearly, Christian women go to church more than Christian men. The different labor force participation rates for men and women do not account for the differences in their church attendance rates. On the other hand, Jewish men have a greater percentage attending synagogue regularly than do Jewish women. Here the difference is accounted for by the Orthodox Jewish norm emphasizing male religious attendance which probably influences attendance patterns in the two newer Jewish denominations.

Could, then, the Christian differences be accounted for by a similar norm urging women to attend church more than men? Or, is one to hypothesize that women, as a result of differential social-psychological experiences between the sexes, always will attend church more than men in the absence of norms that discourage this behavior? The data raise these questions. Future research will have to answer them.

The lack of association between the age groups and church attendance points to the need for several measures to tap properly religious activity and interest. Studies of age cohorts and of changes in their religious activity through time would be extremely valuable. The life cycle approach indicates a probable shift to greater regularity of church attendance on the part of Protestants when their children are attending Sunday School. However, no association occurs between number of children in a family and church attendance.

The rather sizable associations between church attendance, years of schooling, and occupation of family head lend added support to previous research indicating that participation in voluntary organizations varies directly with status.[14] Church attendance is, at least in part, a manifestation of the greater rate of participation in voluntary organizations (in this case the church) of better educated, higher occupational status adults.[15]

Such a conclusion is neither supported nor refuted by the lack of association between income and church attendance.

Occasionally, it has been asserted that middle-class people exhibit greater frequency of church attendance than upper-class people. The opposite assertion is supported by the percentages presented in this article. Whatever association

[14] For data showing the association between measures of social status and number of organizational memberships and for a discussion of research in this area, see Charles R. Wright and Herbert H. Hyman, "Voluntary Association Memberships," *American Sociological Review*, 23 (June 1958), pp. 284–294.

[15] This conclusion is suggested by Lenski, Bultena, Cantril, and Reissman and supported by data presented by Cantril and Reissman. See Lenski, *op. cit.* pp. 539–540; Bultena, *op. cit.*, pp. 385–388; Hadley Cantril, "Educational and Economic Composition of Religious Groups: An Analysis of Poll Data," *American Journal of Sociology*, 48 (March 1943), pp. 574–579 (especially p. 579); and Leonard Reissman, "Class, Leisure, and Social Participation," *American Sociological Review*, 19 (February 1954), pp. 76–84 (especially Table 1).

is found between church attendance and status indicates that the highest status groups, adults possessing college degrees and adults whose family heads are professionals, have the greatest regularity of church attendance within the Protestant, Catholic, Baptist, and Methodist groups.

The different patterns found within the Jewish group appear to be a reflection of the differences between older, foreign-born, more heavily Orthodox Jews with lower educational and occupational status and their children and grand-children who possess considerably more education and have better occupational status. However, it would be an oversimplification to assume that the Jewish group will completely reproduce the Protestant patterns as it becomes more composed of third generation Americans. Both the Jewish religious tradition and its minority status should help maintain different Jewish associations between church attendance and demographic, social, and economic factors.

The associational patterns of the entire Protestant group can be expected to apply to other Protestant denominations as it does to Baptists and Methodists. The extent of this application and the amounts of variation among the Protestant denominations is another question for future research.

All-Pervasiveness, a Consistent Characteristic

of American Religion

SEYMOUR M. LIPSET

Widespread interest in religion is not a new aspect of American society. For almost a century, prominent European visitors who wrote on American life have been unanimous in remarking on the exceptional religiosity of the society. After his visit to America in 1830, Tocqueville commented: ". . . there is no country in the world where the Christian religion retains a greater influence over the souls of men than in America."[1] Martineau in 1834, Trollope in 1860, Bryce in 1883, and Weber in 1904, all arrived at similar conclusions.[2] Their accounts agree substantially with that of a historian's summary of the impressions of pre-Civil War English travelers who

pointed to the fact that America, though still largely a primitive country, had as many churches as the British Isles, that religious assemblages were being held at once place

From *The First New Nation*, © 1963 by Seymour Martin Lipset, Basic Books, Inc., Publishers, New York.

[1] Alexis de Tocqueville, *Democracy in America* (New York: Vintage Books, 1954), Vol. I, p. 314.

[2] Harriet Martineau, *Society in America* (New York: Saunders and Otlay, 1837), II, p. 317; Anthony Trollope, *North America* (New York: Alfred A. Knopf, 1951), p. 277; James Bryce, *The American Commonwealth* (New York: Macmillan, 1912), Vol. II, pp. 770, 778; H. H. Gerth and C. Wright Mills, ed., *From Max Weber: Essays in Sociology* (New York: Oxford University Press, 1946), pp. 302–303.

or another practically all the time; that large donations were constantly being made for religious purposes, America, they concluded, was basically a very religious country. . . . Church services were always crowded on Sundays. . . . Church-going, reported Maxwell, was all the rage in New York. . . . the high percentage of males in the audience was in sharp contrast to their paucity at English services.[3]

Religious practitioners reached similar conclusions. Thus Robert Baird, an American Presbyterian minister who spent eight years in Europe between 1835 and 1843, wrote on his return home:

In no other part of the world, perhaps, do the inhabitants attend church in a larger proportion than in the United States; certainly no part of the Continent of Europe can compare with them in that respect. The contrast between the two must strike anyone who, after having travelled much in the one, comes to see any of the cities of the other.[4]

Philip Schaff, a Swiss theologian who eventually emigrated to America, reported in similar terms to German Lutheran bodies. He witnessed much greater church attendance in New York and Brooklyn than in Berlin. He stated unequivocally: "There are in America probably more awakened souls, and more individual effort and self-sacrifice for religious purposes, proportionately, than in any other country, Scotland alone perhaps excepted."[5]

And a German liberal foe of religion, who found the prevalence of religious practice in America distasteful to his agnostic sentiments, testified to the same set of facts which he, like others, linked in a very materialistic fashion to the effects of the separation of church and state:

Clergymen in America must . . . defend themselves to the last, like other businessmen; they must meet competition and build up a trade, and it's their own fault if their income is not large enough. Now is it clear why heaven and hell are moved to drive the people to the churches, and why attendance is more common here than anywhere else in the world?[6]

The statistical data which bear on the question also suggest that the increase in church affiliation in recent times is not as significant as has been claimed. The earliest quantitative estimates of religious adherence in America that I have been able to locate are those reported in *The American Almanac and Repository of Useful Knowledge* which was published regularly for some years beginning about 1830. These volumes reported detailed statistcs for members *and adherents* of the various denominations. The membership data were taken from statements by the different church groups while the estimates of the number

---

[3] Max Berger, *The British Traveller in America, 1836–1860* (New York: Columbia University Press, 1943), pp. 133–134.

[4] Robert Baird, *Religion in America* (New York: Harper & Bros., 1844), p. 188.

[5] Philip Schaff, *America: A Sketch of the Political, Social, and Religious Character of the United States of North America* (New York: C. Scribner, 1855), pp. 94, 118.

[6] Karl T. Griesinger, "Lebende Bilder aus Amerika" (1858), a section of which is translated in Oscar Handlin, ed., *This Was America* (Cambridge, Mass.: Harvard University Press, 1949), p. 261.

of adherents were derived from various unmentioned publications. In 1831 the total number of adherents listed was 12,136,953, in 1832 the total was 12,496,953, and in 1837 it had risen to 14,585,000. Since in 1831 the total national population was 13,321,000 and in 1837 it was 15,843,000,[7] these data testify to an almost universal religious adherence by Americans in the 1830's, comparable to the results obtained by public opinion surveys in the past few decades which report that almost every American identifies with a given denomination.

In 1856 Robert Baird published statistical data which also differentiated between members and "those under the influence of the evangelical denominations." The total identified with these groups was 17,763,000. (The total population of the country at the time was 26,500,000.) These figures do not include Catholics, Unitarians, Universalists, Mormons, Jews, and various other small, non-evangelical groups. Without describing how he obtained his estimate of over 17 million supporters of the evangelical groups, Baird states: "Accuracy in such a calculation is hardly to be expected, but I have taken the best data I could find, and doubt not that the estimate I have made is not much wide of the truth. Including all the evangelical 'Friends,' this estimate would fall but little short of eighteen million." [8]

While the obvious problems of reliability and validity involved in the use of American church membership statistics make it difficult to reach any conclusions, the available evidence does suggest that, from some time early in American history down to the present, the United States has experienced a continuous "boom" in religious adherence and belief.

These data and observations pose the problem of how to reconcile the estimates concerning the general commitment to religion in the first half of the nineteenth century with the various estimates reported in the *Year Book of American Churches* which indicates a steep rise in membership in religious groups, particularly in the twentieth century.[9] There are many methodological problems concerning the reliability of any historical estimates of church membership, since all of them are presumably based on voluntary replies of church officers to questionnaires, and it is difficult to find out how the reports for much of the nineteenth century were compiled.[10] To some considerable degree,

[7] For estimates of religious adherence see William G. Ouseley, *Remarks on the Statistics and Political Institutions of the United States* (Philadelphia: Carey and Lea, 1832), p. 207; *The American Almanac and Repository of Useful Knowledge for the Year 1833* (Boston: Gray and Bowen, 1832), p. 156; *The American Almanac and Repository of Useful Knowledge for the Year 1838* (Boston: Charles Bowen, 1837), p. 172. For population statistics see U.S. Bureau of the Census, *Historical Statistics of the United States, Colonial Times to 1957* (Washington: U.S. Government Printing Office, 1960), p. 7.

[8] Baird, *Religion in America* (1856 edition), pp. 530–532.

[9] Benson Y. Landis, ed., *Year Book of American Churches* (New York: National Council of the Churches of Christ in the U.S.A., 1961), p. 247.

[10] The lack of reliability of church membership data, even in recent times, has been pointed out in a critique of the statistics assembled by the *Year Book of American Churches*, which indicates considerable growth in church membership since 1940. Winthrop Hudson concludes that the supposed boom is "largely an illusion." Among the many problems with the statistics is the fact that increases often reflect reports from denominations which had never reported before, as well as peculiar and suspicious increases, the validity of which are never questioned.

however, the rapid growth in reported membership after 1890 is a result of the considerable increase in the non-Protestant denominations, whose concept of a church member differed greatly from those of the Protestants. These groups, largely Catholic and Orthodox, reported as a member every person born in the faith, regardless of age or religious status, while most Protestant denominations all through the nineteenth century only considered as members those who had joined the church as adults, often after fulfilling a rigorous set of requirements.

The discrepancy between the travelers' reports that most Americans attended church regularly and the relatively small proportion of the population who actually belonged to a church may be accounted for by the fact that *during this period most of those who attended churches did not belong to a given denomination.* Baird, for example, described the situation as of the 1840's in the following terms:

Not only do persons who have not yet become members, by formal admission as such, attend our churches; they form a very large part of our congregations. In many cases they constitute two thirds, three fourths, or even more; this depending much on the length of the period during which the congregation has been organized, and hardly ever less than a half, even in the most highly-favoured churches. Nor do they attend only; they are cheerful supporters of the public worship, and are often found as liberal

---

For example "when thè Christ Unity Church was listed for the first time in the 1952 *Year Book* with 682,172 members, it alone accounted for more than one-third of the 1,842,515 gain reported that year. The following year, the American Carpatho-Russian Orthodox Greek Catholic Church and the Ukrainian Orthodox Church, each with 75,000 members, were listed for the first time. The year after that, five bodies listed for the first time contributed 195,804 to the total increase in church membership." Winthrop S. Hudson, "Are Churches Really Booming?" *The Christian Century*, 72 (1955), p. 1494. A critique of the reliability of data indicating Catholic growth may be found in B. G. Mulvaney, "Catholic Population Revealed in Catholic Baptisms," *American Ecclesiastical Review*, 133 (1955), pp. 183–193. A number of large denominations simply report their membership in round figures, such as one million for the Greek Orthodox. Others have reported amazing differences from year to year such as "the Romanian Orthodox Church, which reported an increase in the 1952 *Year Book* from 390 to 50,000. What these figures mean can best be seen in terms of a single year's report. The greatest gain in church membership that has been reported was in 1952—3,604,124. For this year, nine bodies with a total membership of 335,528 were listed for the first time. The Russian Orthodox Church reported an increase of membership from 400,000 to 750,000; the Churches of Christ, an increase from 209,615 to 1,500,000; Christ Unity Science Church, from 682,172 to 1,112,123. (The following year the Christ Unity Science Church reported a further 469,163 increase, making a total gain of 1,581,286 for the three year period.) These items alone account for 2,405,864 of the 3,604,124 gain in church membership for the year. If one subtracts the reported gain in Roman Catholic membership [which is also very dubious], all other religious bodies are left with no increase in membership, to say nothing of keeping up with the increase in population." A further difficulty rests in the extensive geographical mobility in the United States which "may have resulted in . . . duplications of church membership, with many people joining a new church without removing their names from the roll of the old church. Some spot checks of membership have tended to confirm this conjecture." Hudson, *op. cit.*, p. 1495.

A detailed look at the data provided by the twelve largest affiliates of the National Council of Churches, who together account for 30 million of the 35 million affiliated to the Council, indicates that their membership, relative to total population, actually "declined" between 1940 and 1954, the period dealt with by Hudson. He concludes that far "from offering 'proof' of a boom in church membership, the statistics . . . show that the boom is largely a fiction." *Ibid.*, p. 1496.

in contributing of their substance for the promotion of good objects, as the members of the church themselves, with whom they are intimately connected by the ordinary business of life, and by family ties. . . . The non-professing hearers of the Word, then, are to be considered as simply what we call them, members of the congregation, not of the church. . . .[11]

The reasons why men might attend church and support a given denomination without becoming a member are not difficult to understand, given the conditions for membership which existed for most of the nineteenth century:

Certainly by modern standards, church membership was a strenuous affair. All evangelical sects required of communicants a personal experience of conversion and a consistent life. Two worship services and Sunday School on the Sabbath were customary. The Methodists invariably kept new converts on "probation" for many months. Wesley's followers also attended a weekly class meeting. . . . Laymen of most denominations were responsible for a large amount of missionary and benevolent work. . . .[12]

Perhaps the most comprehensive attempt to specify the number of "adherents" as distinct from "communicants" of the different Protestant denominations is the study by H. K. Carroll, who was in charge of the Division of Churches for the 1890 U.S. Census.[13] His efforts led him to conclude that in 1890 with a population of 62,622,250, only 5 million people were *not* communicants or adherents. In percentage terms, he estimated that 92 per cent of the population in 1890 and 91 per cent in 1910 were linked to a denomination. These estimates are comparable to those suggested by Ouseley for the 1830's and by Baird for the 1840's and 1850's, and are similar to the results of public opinion surveys since the mid-1930's and to the 1957 U.S. Census Sample Survey of Religious Affiliation. And these statistical conclusions, of course,

[11] Baird, *Religion in America*, p. 188.

[12] Timothy L. Smith, *Revivalism and Social Reform in Mid-Nineteenth Century America* (New York: Abingdon Press, 1957), p. 18; Baird, *Religion in America*, pp. 185–187.

[13] He secured an estimate of the ratio of communicants to adherents by "a comparison between the census returns of the religious populations of various communions in Canada [where the Census asks each person his religious affiliation] with those which the denominations give themselves of communicants." H. K. Carroll, *The Religious Forces in the United States* (New York: The Christian Literature Co., 1893), p. xxxv. The average of Canadian Protestant adherents to communicants was 3.2. To be on the safe side, Carroll suggested, however, that this ratio was probably higher than in the United States since there were many smaller and obscure denominations here, and he concluded that he would be safe in assuming "that there are at least 2.5 adherents in the United States to each Protestant communicant." Relating reports on Protestant membership to this estimate, he derived a total estimate of 49,630,000 for the aggregate of Protestant communicants and adherents. He also determined the adherents and communicants for Catholic, Jewish, and other religious groups. Some similar procedures were employed by Dr. Carroll two decades later using 1910 materials. Carroll, *op. cit.* (1912 edition), pp. lxxi–lxxii. The ratio of communicants to adherents, however, had to be reduced from 2.5 to 2 in view of the large gain in actual church membership reported. In seeking to interpret the great gain in church memberships in the 1910 report, we must note that little, if any resulted from any significant growth in Protestant religious enthusiasm. Rather, as Dr. Carroll pointed out, the churches had changed their definition of a member. "All Churches receive children into that relation much earlier in life than formerly and there are other factors tending to reduce the ratio of adherents to communicants, particularly the relaxation of discipline. . . ." *Ibid.*, p. lxxii.

reiterate the almost unanimous comments made for close to a century and a half by various foreign travelers, who have never ceased to indicate their amazement at the rarity of atheists or anti-religious people in America.[14]

More precise historical data which belie the claim of drastic changes in religious practice are provided by the Census reports for the second half of the nineteenth century, which present the number of seats available in all American churches. These data indicate an increase in the ratio of church seats to population of from 62 to 69 per cent,[15] although the *Year Book of American Churches*, the most frequently quoted source on church affiliation in the United States, estimates a growth in membership between 1850 and 1900 of from 15 to 36 per cent of the total population. Since the 1850 population included two million slaves (almost one-seventh of the population), a group which on the whole lacked substantial church accommodations, it seems probable that the relatively small increase in available church facilities was added by the Negroes. All during the second half of the nineteenth century, the churches kept up with the tremendous population expansion in providing accommodations for almost the entire adult population.

Figures on number of clergymen in America from 1850 to 1950 also reveal a striking constancy. In each census year there has been approximately one clergyman for every 1,000 persons. In 1850 there were 1.16 clergymen per 1,000 population; by 1960, the figure had changed to 1.13. Actually, there has been *no effective change* in the ratio of clergy to total population during the past century, although the proportions of others in professional occupations increased sharply, a difference which is shown in Table 1.

This lack of an increase in the proportion of ministers adds further support to the idea that there has been little change in the strength of institutionalized religion, although in itself it is not conclusive evidence. Certainly the ratio of parishioners to clergy may have changed, so that modern clergymen may serve more members than those of the past. However, arguing against this possibility is the fact that the proportion of ministers has failed to rise with the long-term increasing wealth of the American people. That a congregation's ability to pay

[14] It is undoubtedly significant that the major change in the requirements for church membership among the traditionally evangelical denominations occurred within two or three years after the 1906 Census of Religion. This Census (gathered like previous ones through reports by church bodies of their membership) followed two decades of massive, largely non-Protestant, immigration. The difference between the Protestant and the Catholic-Greek Orthodox-Jewish concept of member resulted in a gross underestimate of the actual numerical strength of the Protestant groups. While the reasons advanced for the changes made by the various denominations in their membership standards did not allude to such competitive considerations, there can be little doubt that these played a role. The decision to admit children to membership simply added numbers. Other modifications in the requirements, however, made it much easier for adults to join, as may be seen in the example of the Methodists. The 1908 Conference of the Methodist Episcopal Church dropped the requirement that a new member must have "met for at least six months in class," and the further condition that he be "on trial" for six months "under the care of the leaders" for the simple obligation that he be "properly recommended." Franklin Hamlin Littell, *From State Church to Pluralism* (Garden City, N.Y.: Doubleday Anchor, 1962), p. 81.

[15] Unfortunately, the Census stopped reporting this datum so that we have no comparable figures for this century.

TABLE 1. NUMBER OF CLERGYMEN AND
PROFESSIONALS PER 1,000 POPULATION FOR
CENSUS YEARS 1900–1960

	Clergymen	Professionals
1900	1.22	14.2
1910	1.28	18.6
1920	1.20	20.6
1930	1.21	26.5
1940	1.09	26.2
1950	1.12	32.8
1960	1.13	40.3

SOURCES: *Data for Clergy in G. Stigler*,
Trends in Employment in the Service Industries (*Princeton, N.J.: Princeton University
Press, 1956*), *p. 108; data for professionals
calculated from Alba M. Edwards*, Comparative Occupational Statistics for the United
States, 1870 to 1940, *Bureau of the Census,
1943, and* Statistical Abstracts, 1952.

for religion would be a factor is suggested by the sharp drop in the depression decade revealed in the above table.

Some of those who contend that religious adherence in American society has reached an all time high in recent times point to evidence, derived from public opinion surveys and the 1957 U.S. Sample Survey of Religious Affiliation conducted by the Census Bureau, which indicate that over 95 per cent of the population state a belief in God and declare an identification with some specific religious group. There are, of course, no comparable interview data for the nineteenth century except for the nearly unanimous reports by foreign travelers that almost everyone they spoke to expressed religious beliefs and commitments. It is possible, however, to contrast the answers given by undergraduates in American colleges before World War I and in 1952 to questionnaires concerning their religious beliefs.

In a study made in 1913, 927 students in nine colleges of "high rank" replied to questions concerning their belief in God. Eighty-seven per cent of the men and 93 per cent of the women reported belief.[16] The same author received replies from 90 per cent of the students in "one college of high rank," of whom 70 per cent believed in immortality and after-life.[17] Four decades later, in 1952, a group of Cornell sociologists administered questionnaires to 4,585 students selected through statistical sampling procedures to be representative of *male* undergraduates at eleven colleges and universities. Twenty-four per cent of the men were atheists or agnostics.[18] Comparing the findings of these

[16] James H. Leuba, *The Belief in God and Immortality* (Chicago: Open Court Publishing Co., 1921), pp. 184–202.

[17] *Ibid.*, pp. 213–216.

[18] Philip E. Jacob, *Changing Values in College* (New York: Harper & Bros., 1957), p. 108. Universities differed: Almost one-third (32 per cent) of the Harvard College students do not believe in God as compared with 13 per cent of those at the University of Texas.

two studies suggests that at least for college students the supposed religious "revival" of the 1950's still has considerable distance to go before belief reaches a point comparable to that of 1913.[19]

Such statistical data as we have examined all argue against the thesis that religious practice in America in the mid-twentieth century is at its high point. Rather, one concludes from these data that, although there have been ebbs and flows in enthusiasm, basic long-term changes in formal religious affiliation and practice have not occurred, and the current high level of religious belief and observance existed in the past as well. As the foreign travelers noted in their books, Americans have been and continue to be a highly religious people. In fact, the one empirical generalization which does seem justified about American religion is that from the early nineteenth century down to the present, the United States has been among the most religious countries in the Christian world. Considerably lower proportions of religious responses (belief in God) are reported by pollsters for European countries than for the United States.[20] With respect to attendance, it is misleading to compare national rates because of the varying proportions of Catholics and Protestants (who manifest divergent church-going patterns) within populations. But American Protestants attend church more frequently than Protestants in Sweden, Denmark, Czechoslovakia (before the Communist coup), and Great Britain.[21] . . .

Additional Readings

LARRY D. BARNETT, "Religious Differentials in Fertility Planning and Fertility in the United States," *Family Life Coordinator*, 14 (October, 1965), pp. 161–169.

MICHAEL P. FOGARTY, *Christian Democracy in Western Europe 1820–1953* (Notre Dame, Ind.: University of Notre Dame Press, 1957), pp. 345–357.

NATHAN GLAZER, "The American Jew and the Attainment of Middle-Class Rank: Some Trends and Explanations," in Marshall Sklare (ed.), *The Jews* (New York: The Free Press, 1958), pp. 138–146.

WILL HERBERG, *Protestant-Catholic-Jew* (Garden City, N.Y.: Anchor Books, 1960), pp. 211–230.

BERNARD LAZERWITZ, "A Comparison of Major United States Religious Groups," *American Statistical Association Journal*, 56 (September, 1961), pp. 568–579.

[19] Actually, such a conclusion—that there is less belief today than four decades ago—would not be warranted since the sampling methods and questions asked differed greatly.

[20] Leo Rosten, *A Guide to the Religions of America* (New York: Simon & Schuster, 1955), p. 247.

[21] Hadley Cantril, *Public Opinion 1935–1946* (Princeton, N.J.: Princeton University Press, 1951), p. 699.

EDUCATION

Introduction

Education and occupation are widely used variables in sociological analysis, because they are related to so many other variables. The first three selections contain factual information about the relationships between education, occupation, income, and prejudice. The fourth selection summarizes factual information about academic performance.[1]

The first selection, by Folger and Nam, "Trends in Education in Relation to the Occupational Structure," suggests that, for men at prime working ages between 1940 and 1960, the relationship between education and occupation is moderate but declining. The relationship in 1940 was $+.52$; by 1960 this relationship had declined to $+.39$.[2] (If education and occupation were perfectly related in a positive manner, the score would have been $+1.00$.)

Miller, in "Annual Income in Relation to Education: 1939–1959," makes two main points. First, in every year for which data are presented, the completion of an additional level of schooling is related to higher average incomes for men. Contrary to the beliefs of some individuals, the economic advantages accruing from the completion of additional years of schooling have not diminished in recent years. Second, there is some evidence that elementary school graduates have had smaller relative income gains than high school graduates. In contrast, the income differential between high school and college graduates has remained fairly constant over time, and there is even some evidence that it has increased in favor of college graduates during the past few years. Therefore, the relative advantages of high

---

[1] Despite some references to education as a "determinant"—especially in the material about education and prejudice—and to the "determinants" of academic performance, the information in the four selections is basically factual.

[2] Folger and Nam also present information about occupational trends between 1900 and 1960; this information is relevant to the occupational material presented in connection with the "Economy."

school graduates compared to elementary school graduates, and college graduates compared to high school graduates, have not declined, despite the large increase in the numbers of high school and college graduates.

Previous research has generally indicated that education is negatively related to prejudice: the more the education, the less the prejudice. The selection by Stember, "Education and Attitude Change," basically suggests that the relationship between education and prejudice is more complicated than previous research has indicated. It is true that the educated are "less likely" to hold traditional stereotypes, to favor discriminatory policies, and to reject casual contacts with minority-group members. However, the educated are "more likely" to hold certain highly charged and derogatory stereotypes, to favor informal discrimination in some areas of behavior, and to reject intimate contacts with minority-group members.[3]

The selection by Lavin, "Demographic and Ecological Determinants of Academic Performance," indicates that individuals with higher socioeconomic status, who are females, Jews, who reside in the North, and who live in urban areas have higher academic performance than individuals with lower socioeconomic status, who are males, non-Jews, who reside in the South, and who live in rural areas. Although academic performance is usually related positively to socioeconomic status (the higher the socioeconomic status, the higher the academic performance), the relationship on the college level is negative when the range of socioeconomic status runs from the upper class to the middle class.[4]

[3] This selection is also pertinent to the previous selections by Stember, "Attitudes Toward Jews," and Sheatsley, "White Attitudes Toward the Negro."

[4] Lavin's selection is relevant to the previous selections by Cohen, "The Middle-Class Norms," and Miller-Riessman, "The Working-Class Norms" in Part I, "The Individual and the Group."

Trends in Education in Relation to the Occupational Structure

JOHN K. FOLGER AND CHARLES B. NAM

The role of education in shaping and modifying the social structure is a topic of considerable interest to educational sociologists and students of social stratification.[1] Of particular concern has been the economic benefits deriving from various levels of education attained,[2] and the association of different educational attainments with life styles and social mobility.[3]

The present article examines one specific aspect of the relationship, that between formal education and occupation. . . . The analysis is restricted to men because the relationships are different for the sexes and, as a means of limiting discussion, we have concentrated on those more likely to be family heads and breadwinners. . . .

EDUCATIONAL AND OCCUPATIONAL TRENDS

The long-term rise in educational attainment, deriving from continued expansion of the school systems and the extension of schooling to all groups and areas of the country, is well documented and needs only brief mention. Looking at data for men 25 to 64 years old, who closely approximate the males of labor force age, we find that, in 1910, 25 per cent of these men had less than five years of schooling; by 1960, about 7 per cent of their counterparts had that little schooling. In 1910, 13 per cent of the men were high school graduates and less than 4 per cent were college graduates; by 1960, the corresponding percentages were 44 and 11 per cent.[4]

This "educational revolution" had its strongest surge during the World War II and postwar periods, although improvements in educational attainment

Reprinted from *Sociology of Education*, 38 (Fall, 1964), pp. 19–33, by permission of the authors and the publisher.

[1] Jean Floud and A. H. Halsey, "The Sociology of Education; a Trend Report and Bibliography," *Current Sociology*, 8 (3), 1958, pp. 174–179; and Leonard Reissman, *Class in American Society*, Glencoe, Illinois: The Free Press, 1959.

[2] Paul C. Glick, "Educational Attainment and Occupational Advancement," Transactions of the Second World Congress of the International Sociological Association held at Liege, Belgium, 1953 (published in London, 1954); and Herman P. Miller, "Annual and Lifetime Income in Relation to Education, 1939–59," *American Economic Review*, 50 (1960), pp. 962–986.

[3] Bernard Barber, "Social-Class Differences in Educational Life Chances," *Teachers College Record*, 63 (November 1961), pp. 102–113; C. Arnold Anderson, "A Skeptical Note on the Relation of Vertical Mobility to Education," *The American Journal of Sociology*, 66 (May 1961), pp. 560–570; and Otis Dudley Duncan and Robert W. Hodge, "Education and Occupational Mobility; a Regression Analysis," *The American Journal of Sociology*, 68 (May 1963), pp. 629–644.

[4] The estimates for 1910 were prepared in connection with the authors' forthcoming census monograph on *Education of the American Population*.

TABLE 1. Educational Attainment of the Male Population 25 to 64 Years old: 1910 to 1980

	Estimated		Reported		Projected	
Years of School Completed	*1910*	*1920*	*1940*	*1960*	*1970*	*1980*
Number (in millions)						
Total	21.2	25.1	33.1	40.6	44.2	52.3
No school years completed	1.8	1.7	1.1	0.6	0.4	0.4
Elementary:						
1 to 4 years	3.6	3.9	3.4	2.2	1.7	1.5
5 to 7 years	4.7	5.4	6.1	5.3	4.0	3.2
8 years	7.0	8.1	9.4	6.6	5.1	4.0
High School:						
1 to 3 years	1.4	2.2	5.2	8.2	9.5	11.6
4 years	1.3	1.9	4.3	9.6	13.4	17.8
College:						
1 to 3 years	0.6	0.9	1.7	3.8	4.6	6.1
4 or more years	0.7	1.0	1.9	4.3	5.5	7.8
Per Cent Distributions						
Total	100.0	100.0	100.0	100.0	100.0	100.0
No school years completed	8.2	6.8	3.4	1.5	0.9	0.8
Elementary:						
1 to 4 years	17.0	15.5	10.2	5.4	3.9	2.8
5 to 7 years	22.3	21.6	18.5	13.1	9.0	6.1
8 years	32.8	32.3	28.3	16.3	11.6	7.7
High school:						
1 to 3 years	6.8	8.7	15.6	20.2	21.4	22.1
4 years	6.3	7.5	13.1	23.6	30.2	34.0
College:						
1 to 3 years	3.0	3.5	5.2	9.3	10.4	11.7
4 or more years	3.5	4.0	5.8	10.6	12.5	14.9

SOURCE: Data for 1910 and 1920 are estimates based on retrojection of 1940 age cohorts by education. Data for 1940 are from 1950 Census of Population, Volume I, U.S. Summary. Data for 1960 are from 1960 Census of Population, Volume I, Part 1, U.S. Summary. Projections for 1970 and 1980 are from U.S. Bureau of the Census, *Current Population Reports*, Series P-20, No. 91, and are based on Series B assumption at younger ages.

have been noted each decade at least back to 1910 (the earliest date for which estimates are available). Projections to 1980, according to Census Bureau reports, indicate that we can still expect substantial increases in the educational level of the population. The proportion of "functional illiterates" among men 25 to 64 years old may well be cut in half by that date, the percentage who are high school graduates is projected to be 61 per cent of the group at that time, and the proportion who are college graduates may reach 15 per cent.[5]

The trend in the occupational composition of the male population since the turn of the century has been one of numerical increases among white-collar occupations and among skilled, semi-skilled, and service workers. There was

[5] U.S. Bureau of the Census, *Current Population Reports*, Series P-20, No. 91, "Projections of Educational Attainment in the United States, 1960 to 1980."

some increase early in the century and decrease in later decades in the number of nonfarm laborers, and a general decline in the number of persons in farm occupations. The relative occupational composition has also changed significantly. White-collar workers constituted $17\frac{1}{2}$ per cent of the male work force in 1900 and double that percentage in 1960, with the professional and technical fields expanding most rapidly during the last couple of decades. The proportions in craft, operative, and service jobs rose gradually over the decades, although they leveled off some during the last decade or so. The percentages in nonfarm laboring occupations, which were steady during the early decades of the century, dropped rapidly in later decades, while percentages in farm occupations continued the sharp drop in recent years that had already been observed at the turn of the century.[6]

Projections to 1975, based on Labor Department records, indicate a general continuation of the occupational trends noted in the past. Most rapid increases can be expected in the professional and managerial fields. The proportion of white-collar jobs among men will be approaching half of the male labor force. Skilled and semi-skilled manual jobs, while increasing in number, will be a decreasing percentage of all occupations. Nonfarm labor may possibly increase slightly whereas the farm segment of the male labor force can be expected to continue to decline, both relatively and absolutely.[7]

ASSOCIATION OF EDUCATION AND OCCUPATION

Since most persons who enter the labor force are prepared to occupy only jobs that are suitable for the amount of education they have received, and since higher levels of education are usually required for entry into higher status jobs, it is not surprising that there is a direct association between level of education and occupation. The 1960 Census shows, as did the 1940 and 1950 Censuses, that the average level of educational attainment is highest for professional and technical occupations, not quite so high for other white-collar jobs, less for skilled and semiskilled jobs than for white-collar jobs, and lowest for farm occupations and unskilled nonfarm laborers.[8]

Granted that there is an association between education and occupation, however, how strong is it and is the relationship getting stronger or weaker? Because of data limitations, we have analyzed the relationship for white males 35 to 54 years old in nonfarm occupations in 1940, 1950, and 1960. (The data for 1940, in fact, are limited to native persons in the group and this probably has some effect on the results.) Using gamma as a measure of association, we

---

[6] David L. Kaplan and M. Claire Casey, Bureau of the Census Working Paper No. 5, *Occupational Trends in the United States, 1900 to 1950* (Washington: U.S. Department of Commerce, 1958); and *1960 Census of Population*, Volume I, Part 1, U.S. Summary (Washington: Government Printing Office, 1964), p. 216.

[7] Projections for 1975 are based on unpublished data provided by the U.S. Bureau of Labor Statistics.

[8] For analysis of the 1940 and 1950 relationships, see Glick, *op. cit.;* and Edmund deS. Brunner and Sloan Wayland, "Occupation, Labor Force Status, and Education," *Journal of Educational Sociology* (September 1958), pp. 3–15.

TABLE 2.   EMPLOYMENT OF MEN BY MAJOR OCCUPATION GROUP: 1900 TO 1975*

Major Occupation Group	Estimated			Reported	Projected
	1900	1920	1940	1960	1975
Numbers (in millions)					
Total	23.7	33.6	39.2	43.5	56.5
Professional, technical, and kindred workers	0.8	1.3	2.3	4.7	7.9
Mgrs., officials, and propr., exc. farm	1.6	2.6	3.4	4.9	7.9
Clerical and kindred workers	0.7	1.8	2.3	3.2	4.6
Sales workers	1.1	1.5	2.5	3.1	3.6
Craftsmen, foremen, and kindred workers	3.0	5.4	6.1	8.9	10.9
Operatives and kindred workers	2.5	4.8	7.1	9.1	10.3
Service workers	0.7	1.2	2.4	2.8	4.5
Laborers, exc. farm and mine	3.5	4.7	4.7	3.1	3.6
Farmers and farm managers	5.5	6.2	5.2	2.5	1.8
Farm laborers and foremen	4.4	4.1	3.3	1.3	1.3
Per Cent Distribution					
Total	100.0	100.0	100.0	100.0	100.0
Professional, technical, and kindred workers	3.4	3.8	5.8	10.8	14.0
Mgrs., officials, and propr., exc. farm	6.8	7.8	8.6	11.3	14.0
Clerical and kindred workers	2.8	5.3	5.8	7.4	8.1
Sales workers	4.6	4.5	6.4	7.1	6.4
Craftsmen, foremen and kindred workers	12.6	16.0	15.5	20.5	19.3
Operatives and kindred workers	10.4	14.4	18.0	20.9	18.2
Service workers	3.1	3.7	6.1	6.4	8.0
Laborers, exc. farm and mine	14.7	14.0	12.1	7.1	6.4
Farmers and farm managers	23.0	18.4	13.3	5.7	3.2
Farm laborers and foremen	18.7	12.1	8.4	3.0	2.3

SOURCE: Data for 1900, 1920, and 1940 are from David L. Kaplan and M. Claire Casey, *Occupational Trends in the United States, 1900 to 1950*, Bureau of the Census Working Paper No. 5, Washington, D.C., 1958. Data for 1960 are from 1960 Census of Population, Volume I, Part 1, U.S. Summary. Projections for 1975 are based on unpublished data provided by the U.S. Bureau of Labor Statistics, and are consistent with projections of occupations for both sexes published in the March 1963 issue of the *Monthly Labor Review*.

* Data for 1900 and 1920 refer to civilian gainful workers 10 years old and over; data for 1940 refer to persons 14 years old and over in the experienced civilian labor force; data for 1960 and projections to 1975 refer to employed persons 14 years old and over.

arrived at indexes of +.52 in 1940, +.50 in 1950, and +.39 in 1960.[9] The index for 1940 probably would have been higher if we had been able to include foreign-born persons.[10] At any rate, the results clearly show in summary fashion that

[9] Gamma can take values from +1.00 to −1.00. It is necessary that the variables used have ordered distributions. For a discussion of gamma as a measure of association, see Leo A. Goodman and William H. Kruskal, "Measures of Association for Cross Classifications," *Journal of the American Statistical Association*, 49:268 (December 1954), pp. 747–754. Procedures for computing gamma are shown in Morris Zelditch, *Basic Course in Sociological Statistics* (New York: Holt and Co., 1959).

[10] Likewise, different index values probably would be obtained if we included farm occupations, nonwhites, and persons in other age groups. It is doubtful, however, that the degree of association would change a great deal or that the downward trend of the index values would vary significantly.

TABLE 3. PER CENT WHO HAVE COMPLETED SPECIFIED LEVELS OF SCHOOLING BY MAJOR OCCUPATION GROUP: EMPLOYED NATIVE WHITE MALES 35 TO 54 YEARS OLD IN 1940, AND ALL WHITE MALES 35 TO 54 YEARS OLD IN THE EXPERIENCED CIVILIAN LABOR FORCE IN 1960

Major Occupation Group	Per Cent With Less Than 5 Years of School		Per Cent Who Are High School Graduates		Per Cent Who Completed 1 or More Years of College	
	1940	1960	1940	1960	1940	1960
Professional, technical and kindred workers	0.4	0.2	84.7	91.3	72.7	74.5
Farmers and farm managers	13.4	6.1	9.5	32.5	4.1	7.5
Mgrs., officials, and proprietors, exc. farm	2.2	1.0	46.7	68.0	23.5	35.4
Clerical, sales, and kindred workers	1.2	0.8	47.1	65.6	20.4	28.0
Craftsmen, foremen, and kindred workers	4.9	3.0	15.8	36.4	4.4	8.0
Operatives and kindred workers	8.1	5.7	10.9	24.9	2.9	4.0
Service workers	5.4	5.2	15.2	34.0	4.4	8.1
Farm laborers and foremen	21.2	29.2	6.3	12.1	1.9	2.7
Laborers, exc. farm and mine	13.5	12.3	7.3	17.2	2.0	2.8

SOURCE: Data for 1940 are from the 1940 Census of Population, Special Report on *Educational Attainment by Economic Characteristics and Marital Status*. Data for 1960 are from 1960 Census of Population, report PC(2)–5B, *Educational Attainment*.

the association of education and occupation has been moderate but is declining.[11]. . .

[11] For somewhat conflicting findings, however, see Duncan and Hodge, *op. cit.*, who conclude from regression analysis of more detailed data from a labor mobility survey that "education was no less important as a determinant of occupational status in 1950 than in 1940." Our data indicate, however, that the sharpest decline was between 1950 and 1960.

Annual Income in Relation to Education: 1939–1959

HERMAN P. MILLER

Nearly one-quarter of a century has elapsed since Harold F. Clark and his colleagues produced their pioneer study on life earnings in selected occupations [1]. Clark expressed the hope that his rough procedures would be improved upon with time and that the figures would be recalculated at least annually. Aside from a relatively few attempts, however, the challenge has not been taken up by contemporary economists or statisticians despite an increased need for such information. In part, this neglect must be attributed to a lack of data. Although a vast amount of data can be found on hourly, daily, or weekly wages for many skilled trades, information on annual earnings, which are used as a

Reprinted from the *American Economic Review*, 50 (December, 1960), pp. 962–986, by permission of the author and the publisher.

basis for computing lifetime earnings, is still quite scarce. The picture has changed somewhat as a result of the past two decennial censuses and the annual income surveys conducted by the Bureau of the Census since 1945. It is the purpose of this study to examine the relationship between income and education as revealed in these data. . . .

ANNUAL INCOME IN RELATION TO EDUCATION: 1939–1958

. . . Some of the basic statistics pertaining to the relationship between annual income and educational attainment are presented in Table 1, which shows the variations in average (mean) annual income over the past generation for men with different amounts of schooling.[1] The data are presented separately for each age group, as well as for all men 25 years old and over, in order to permit an examination of the figures without having to take account of changes in the age distribution of the population. Women have been excluded from the analyses; since a large proportion of them do not enter the labor market and many of those who do are employed on a part-time basis only, the relationship between their income and education may be distorted. In contrast, practically all adult men are full-time workers and it can therefore be assumed that any advantages which may accrue from more schooling are reflected in their incomes.

Table 1 shows that in every year for which data are presented the completion of an additional level of schooling was associated with higher average incomes for men. This finding parallels that obtained in numerous other studies of the relationship between education and income dating back to the early part of this century [3, p. 115]. Although the income levels have changed considerably during the past 20 years, the basic relationship between the extent of schooling and income appears to have remained much the same. Contrary to the expectations of some analysts, the economic advantages accruing from the completion of additional years of schooling have not diminished in recent years.

Although income generally tends to increase with education, Table 1 shows that a year spent in completing a given level of schooling (e.g., the fourth year in high school) yields a greater return than any of the years leading up to graduation. This difference may reflect a selection in terms of ability between those who do and those who do not complete their schooling. Thus in 1958, men who started high school but did not graduate, received on the average an annual income of about $400 more per year of schooling than men who

[1] For each year, the mean income was obtained as a summation of the product of the average income and the proportion of persons for each income level. For income levels below $10,000 in 1949, 1956, and 1958, below $6,000 for 1946, and below $5,000 for 1939, the midpoint of each class interval was assumed to be the average. For 1949, 1956, and 1958, $20,000 was used for the "$10,000 and over" interval; for 1946, $12,000 was used for the "$6,000 and over" interval; and for 1939, $9,000 was used for the "$5,000 and over" interval. Medians corresponding to the means shown in Table 1 May be obtained from the author. Tax return data for recent years suggest a drop in the average for the open-end interval. An alternative calculation made for 1958, using a mean of $17,000 for the "tail," revealed no substantial changes in the relationships.

TABLE 1. MEAN INCOME (OR EARNINGS) FOR MALES 25 YEARS OF AGE AND OVER, BY YEARS OF SCHOOL COMPLETED AND AGE: 1939, 1946, 1949, 1956, AND 1958

Years of School Completed and Age	*1939*[a]	*1946*[b]	*1949*[c]	*1956*[c]	*1958*[c]
Total: 25 Years Old and Over:					
Elementary: Total	$1,036	$2,041	$2,394	$3,107	$3,096
Less than 8 years[d]	(e)	1,738	2,062	2,613	2,551
8 years	(e)	2,327	2,829	3,732	3,769
High School: 1 to 3 years	1,379	2,449	3,226	4,480	4,618
4 years	1,661	2,939	3,784	5,439	5,567
College: 1 to 3 years	1,931	3,654	4,423	6,363	6,966
4 years or more	2,607	4,527	6,179	8,490	9,206
25 to 34 Years:					
Elementary: Total	837	1,729	2,185	3,061	3,143
Less than 8 years[d]	(e)	1,394	1,880	2,662	2,670
8 years	(e)	2,011	2,540	3,685	3,663
High School: 1 to 3 years	1,150	2,062	2,837	4,407	4,341
4 years	1,335	2,335	3,246	4,813	4,909
College: 1 to 3 years	1,566	2,875	3,444	5,437	5,774
4 years or more	1,956	3,237	4,122	6,307	7,152
35 to 44 Years:					
Elementary: Total	1,110	2,095	2,610	3,694	3,686
Less than 8 years[d]	(e)	1,730	2,244	3,169	3,023
8 years	(e)	2,425	3,029	4,256	4,403
High School: 1 to 3 years	1,574	2,607	3,449	4,799	5,035
4 years	1,979	3,463	4,055	5,992	6,007
College: 1 to 3 years	2,270	4,069	5,014	7,131	8,015
4 years or more	3,141	5,054	7,085	9,790	10,106
45 to 54 Years:					
Elementary: Total	1,199	2,349	2,797	3,672	3,660
Less than 8 years[d]	(e)	2,027	2,418	3,078	3,008
8 years	(e)	2,629	3,247	4,289	4,337
High School: 1 to 3 years	1,732	2,959	3,725	4,876	4,864
4 years	2,256	3,744	4,689	6,104	6,295
College: 1 to 3 years	2,428	4,671	5,639	7,426	8,682
4 years or more	3,575	5,242	8,116	11,702	12,269
55 to 64 Years:					
Elementary: Total	1,057	2,082	2,577	3,462	3,436
Less than 8 years[d]	(e)	1,814	2,278	2,922	2,956
8 years	(e)	2,365	3,010	3,932	3,960
High School: 1 to 3 years	1,551	2,648	3,496	4,398	5,034
4 years	2,104	3,179	4,548	5,920	6,510
College: 1 to 3 years	2,065	3,888	5,162	6,677	6,992
4 years or more	3,247	5,461	7,655	9,595	10,966
65 Years Old and Over:					
Elementary: Total	(e)	1,541	1,560	1,875	1,903
Less than 8 years[d]	(e)	1,434	1,366	1,686	1,672
8 years	(e)	1,670	1,898	2,247	2,337
High School: 1 to 3 years	(e)	1,894	2,379	2,560	2,661
4 years	(e)	2,601	3,115	3,314	3,036
College: 1 to 3 years	(e)	2,720	3,435	4,269[f]	4,180
4 years or more	(e)	3,902	5,421	5,835	6,091

completed their schooling with graduation from elementary school. High school graduates, however, received about $500 more of annual income per year of schooling than men who started high school but never graduated. Similarly, men who attended college but did not graduate had, on the average, about $700 more per year of schooling than high school graduates. The comparable differential for college graduates was about $900 per year of schooling.[2]

The educational attainment of the population has grown considerably during the past generation. The proportion of college graduates has nearly doubled during the period and the proportion of high school graduates has also risen dramatically (Table 2). How has this change in the relative supply of more highly educated workers affected income differentials? Have the incomes of college graduates, relative to other groups in the population, been pushed down because of the relative increase in their numbers or has the demand for their services increased sufficiently to offset any tendency for their incomes to be lowered?

Although these questions cannot be answered categorically, there is some evidence that elementary school graduates have had smaller relative income gains then high school graduates, despite the reduction in their relative numbers.

---

[a] Restricted to persons reporting $1 or more of wage or salary income and less than $50 of other income for native white and Negro males 25 to 64 years old only.

[b] Total money earnings.

[c] Total money income.

[d] Includes persons reporting no years of school completed, not shown separately.

[e] Not available.

[f] Base is less than 100 sample cases.

SOURCE: Data for 1939 derived from *1940 Census of Population, Education: Educational Attainment by Economic Characteristics and Marital Status*, Tables 29 and 31. Data for 1949 derived from *1950 Census of Population*, Ser. P-E, No. 5B, *Education*, Tables 12 and 13. Data for 1946, 1956, and 1958 derived from the consumer income supplements to the April 1947, March 1957, and March 1959 *Current Population Survey*.

Note regarding comparability of the figures: Neither the income concept nor the universe covered is directly comparable for all the years shown. Most of the differences, however, are relatively small and are not believed to seriously distort the relationships. Thus, for example, the figures for 1956 and 1958 are entirely comparable since they are based on the Current Population Survey and represent the total money income of the civilian noninstitutional male population 25 years old and over. The 1949 figures are based on the 1950 Census and also represent the total money income of all males 25 years old and over, including a relatively small number of institutional inmates. The 1946 figures are based on the Current Population Survey and represent the total money earnings (not total income) of the civilian noninstitutional male population 25 years old and over. Although the conceptual differences between income and earnings are substantial, the actual differences in the averages are quite small, primarily because the amount of nonearned income is small relative to the total and this type of income tends to be seriously underreported in household surveys of income. The figures for 1939 are based on the 1940 Census and are restricted to males 25–64 years of age with $1 or more of wage or salary income and less than $50 of nonwage income. For this group, of course, the averages represent total money income; however, the universe has been restricted, because of the way in which the data were collected, to those persons who received only wage or salary income. Only about three-fifths of all men 25–64 years old in 1940 were in this category. The effects of this restriction cannot be measured, but it is undoubtedly more important than restrictions cited for other years. It is also possible that this restriction affects college graduates more than persons with less schooling and for them tends to create an adverse selection since college graduates are more likely to have income other than earnings.

[2] For similar findings based on earlier data see [2].

TABLE 2. Per Cent Distribution by Years of School Completed for Males 25 Years Old and Over, for the United States: 1940, 1947, 1950, 1957, and 1959

Years of School Completed		1940	1947	1950	1957	1959
Total		100	100	100	100	100
Elementary School:	Total	62	51	49	42	39
	Less than 8 years[a]	34	(b)	28	23	22
	8 years	28	(b)	21	18	17
High School:	1 to 3 years	14	16	16	17	18
	4 years	12	18	18	22	23
College:	1 to 3 years	5	7	7	7	8
	4 years or more	5	6	7	9	10
Not reported		2	2	3	2	2

[a] Includes persons reporting no years of school completed, not shown separately.
[b] Not available.
Source: Data for 1940 derived from *1940 Census of Population*: Pt. 1, Vol. IV, *Characteristics by Age*, Table 18. Data for 1950 derived from *1950 Census of Population*, Ser. P-E, No. 5B, *Education*, Table 12. Data for 1947, 1957, and 1959 derived from the educational attainment supplements to the April 1947, March 1957, and March 1959 *Current Population Survey*, P-20, No. 15, Table 1; P-20, No. 77, Table 1; and P-20, No. 99, Table 1.

In contrast, the income differential between high school and college graduates has remained fairly constant over time and there is even some evidence that it has increased in favor of college graduates during the past few years (Table 3).

In the absence of 1939 income data for elementary school graduates, comparisons between the incomes of elementary and high school graduates must be restricted to the period since 1946. If attention is focused on these years, it is evident that the incomes of high school graduates have risen considerably more, in percentage terms, than those of elementary school graduates. In 1946, the differential between these two groups was only $600 or about 26 per cent. By 1958, the differential rose to about $1,800 or 48 per cent. This change is in part related to the fact that a large proportion of the elementary school graduates are employed in occupations such as farmers, farm laborers, and nonfarm laborers which tended to have lower relative income gains in recent years than most other occupations.[3] It is also possible, of course, that even for occupations such as operatives and craftsmen, in which a relatively large number of elementary school graduates are employed, high school graduates received relatively greater increases than persons who never attended high school. There is also a possibility that the reduction in the relative number of elementary school graduates reflects a constant transfer of the "cream" of that group to the high school group, so that the average elementary school graduate in 1958 may have been a less "able" person than in 1946; but there is no objective evidence on this point.

In contrast to the changing relationship between the incomes of elementary school and high school graduates, there has been relatively little change in the

[3] [4, Table E] shows that median total money income of employed males increased between 1950 and 1958 by 3 per cent for farm laborers, 51 per cent for nonfarm laborers, and 27 per cent for farmers. In contrast the median income during this period increased by 57 per cent for professional workers, 54 per cent for managers and officials, and 55 per cent for craftsmen.

TABLE 3. MEAN INCOME (OR EARNINGS) BY LEVEL OF SCHOOL COMPLETED, FOR MALES 25 YEARS OLD AND OVER, FOR THE UNITED STATES: 1939, 1946, 1949, 1956, AND 1958

	Elementary–High School Differential			High School–College Differential		
	Average Income			Average Income		
Year	Elementary School Graduate	High School Graduate	Per Cent Difference	High School Graduate	College Graduate	Per Cent Difference
1939	(a)	$1,661	(a)	$1,661	$2,607	57
1946	$2,327	2,939	26	2,939	4,527	54
1949	2,829	3,784	34	3,784	6,179	63
1956	3,732	5,439	46	5,439	8,490	56
1958	3,769	5,567	48	5,567	9,206	65

a Not available.
SOURCE: Table 1.

income differential between high school and college graduates. In 1939, the average income of college graduates was about $900, or 57 per cent more than for high school graduates. In 1956, the absolute difference between the incomes of these two groups increased to $3,100, but the relative difference was unchanged. By 1958, the absolute difference rose to $3,600 and the relative difference also increased to 65 per cent. The data suggest that during the recession years 1949 and 1958 the incomes of college graduates were less affected than other groups, reflecting, perhaps, a greater tendency for persons with lesser schooling to be subject to unemployment. There is also some possibility that the income gains for college graduates partly reflect a rise in the proportion of men in this group with graduate school training. The influence of this factor is probably quite small, however, since there is no evidence of a sharp rise in the proportion of college men with graduate training. Moreover, the income differential between all college graduates and those with graduate training is quite small, amounting to only about $200 in 1958 [4, p. 38].

Why has the relative income differential between high school and college graduates been maintained, and indeed recently increased, despite the large relative increase in the size of the college-trained population? One important part of the explanation must be that the demand for college graduates has kept pace with the supply. Due to our changing technology, the demand for trained workers has accelerated since the end of the second world war, and industry has absorbed the increased flow of graduates from our universities. The nature of this change can be seen most clearly by the sharp rise in the proportion of the labor force engaged in professional and managerial work, the two occupations in which the great majority of college graduates are employed. Table 4 shows that since 1940 there has been a relative increase of about 50 per cent in the proportion of men employed in the two major occupation groups which serve as the major outlet for men with college training . . . .

TABLE 4. Number and Per Cent of Males Employed in Professional and Managerial Occupations, for the United States: 1940, 1950, 1957, and 1959
(Numbers in thousands)

Major Occupation Group	Number				Per Cent			
	1940	1950	1957	1959	1940	1950	1957	1959
Total employed males	33,750	40,519	43,273	42,842	100.0	100.0	100.0	100.0
Professional, technical and kindred workers	2,075	2,971	4,141	4,471	6.1	7.3	9.6	10.4
Managers, officials and proprietors, except farm	3,231	4,341	5,598	5,695	9.6	10.7	12.9	13.3

Source: Data for 1940 and 1950 from *U. S. Census of Population: 1950*, Vol. II, *Characteristics of the Population*, Pt. 1, Table 54. Data for 1957 and 1959 from Bureau of the Census, *Current Population Reports*, Ser. P-60, No. 27 and No. 33.

CONCLUSION

This study largely represents an attempt to ascertain if the marked increase in the number and proportion of high school and college graduates during the past generation has been associated with a reduction in income differentials for these groups. On theoretical grounds, such a reduction could be expected *in the long run*, assuming no changes in the demand for more highly educated workers. The period under consideration, however, is relatively short and is one in which there were changes in the demand for, as well as in the supply of, such workers. Therefore, no fundamental theoretical issues are involved in this paper. The problem is merely one of ascertaining what has taken place and why.

The figures show that despite large relative reductions in the supply of workers whose schooling did not extend beyond the eighth grade, this group had smaller relative income gains than high school graduates. On the other hand, the large relative increase in the supply of college-trained workers did not adversely affect their relative income position. On this basis it is concluded that the demand for more highly educated workers has kept pace with the increased supply of such workers and, as a result, their relative income position has not changed. The fact that the proportion of men employed in professional and managerial work—the two major outlets for college-trained men—increased by 50 per cent during the past generation suggests that industry has absorbed the increased flow of graduates from our universities. . . .

References

1. H. F. CLARK, *Life Earnings in Selected Occupations in the United States*. New York 1937.
2. P. C. GLICK AND H. P. MILLER, "Educational Level and Potential Income," *Amer. Soc. Rev.*, June 1956, 21, 307–12.

3. Educational Policies Commission, *Education and Economic Well-Being in American Democracy*. Nat. Education Assoc. and Am. Assoc. of School Admin., Washington, D.C., 1940.
4. U. S. Bureau of the Census, *Current Population Reports*, Ser. P-60, No. 33, Jan. 1960.

Education and Attitude Change

CHARLES H. STEMBER

In presenting some conclusions derived from our data, we shall try to answer questions raised in the introduction to this report.* . . .

. . . The bulk of the data examined in the past indicated an inverse relationship between education and prejudice. Except for Campbell's 1942 study, most research suggested that the educated were less prejudiced. The present study finds no such clear-cut relationship; on many issues, the educated show as much prejudice as the less educated, and on some issues they show more. They appear no more concerned than others with problems of discriminations and prejudice.

In brief, the educated are *less likely* to:

hold *traditional* stereotypes;
favor discriminatory *policies*;
reject *casual* contacts with minority-group members.

The educated are *more likely* to:

hold certain highly charged and derogatory stereotypes;
favor *informal* discrimination in some areas of behavior;
reject *intimate* contacts with minority-group members.

LIMITATIONS IN EXISTING RESEARCH

Our research shows that past findings are partly a function of (1) the particular type of prejudice measured; (2) the time at which measurement occurred; and (3) the phrasing of questions.

FINDINGS AFFECTED BY TYPES OF PREJUDICE STUDIED

Investigators could reach opposite conclusions simply because of wide differences in focus. Samelson's data on attitudes toward Negroes are based primarily on opinions about formal and legal segregation—issues on which the

    * [The material referred to is not included. This selection is the concluding chapter of a book—Editor.]

educated really appear to take a less prejudiced position; but when testing issues of other kinds, she found no relationship. Campbell classified his respondents largely according to anti-Jewish statements made in the course of a narrative interview. Sentiments generally more characteristic of educated persons figure prominently in his classification system.

Similarly, Allport cites evidence from a South African study which demonstrated a marked effect of education, but the conclusion is derived from questions which educated persons customarily answer in less prejudiced terms.

FINDINGS AFFECTED BY TIME OF STUDY

Even though we have made no systematic attempt to trace changes in attitudes over the years, it seems certain that the educated have been more prejudiced at certain times than at others, which may partly explain the seeming discrepancies between Campbell's findings and those of most other investigators.

Our study suggests rather strongly that the relation of education to prejudice has varied with the political and social climate. In this sense there is no fixed relation between the two variables apart from prevalent community norms. We find the educated considerably more labile than others, and more responsive to changing values and beliefs. Thus, when anti-Semitism in American society has risen or fallen, the changes have been sharpest among educated people, judging by the data at our disposal. Similarly, the Supreme Court's school desegregation decision of 1954 at first found its most enthusiastic support among educated groups; but as resistance in the South stiffened, many of the educated withdrew their backing and became the staunchest supporters of the emerging doctrine of gradualism.

In contrast, the less educated seem more bound by traditional images, established policies and fixed forms of behavior. They often show more prejudice than the educated, but are less easily swayed by changes in the climate of opinion.

FINDINGS AFFECTED BY PHRASING OF QUESTIONS

Our analysis points up the crucial importance of language in measuring prejudice. For it is evident that different wording of identical issues may elicit distinctly different patterns of response. The finding confirms a point made by others, especially Hyman and Sheatsley in their criticism of *The Authoritarian Personality*.[1] It seems that some questions as commonly worded in public-opinion studies succeed in isolating only one type of prejudiced person, and thus, however useful for measuring this type, may provide misleading evidence on attitudinal correlates.

Much prejudice research has succumbed to the temptation to word questions as they presumably are phrased in people's minds. This approach tends to bypass the educated, whose prejudices are expressed more subtly, and who probably

---

[1] H. H. Hyman and P. B. Sheatsley, "The Authoritarian Personality—A Methodological Critique," *Studies in the Scope and Method of "The Authoritarian Personality,"* ed. R. Christie and M. Jahoda (Glencoe, Illinois: The Free Press, 1954).

recognize and avoid the trap set by a crudely phrased question. While rejecting, as they often do, a stereotype phrased in obviously biased clichés, they may nevertheless agree with its substance. This may explain why results of questions expressing extreme positions—for example, the widely used scales developed by the Berkeley group—have so often indicated a negative relation between prejudice and education. When the same issues are posed in more neutral terminology, no such relationship is evidenced. This is apparent in the few instances where our material contained alternate formulations of a particular issue.

It has been commonly assumed that agreement with statements couched in openly bigoted language reflects strongly bigoted feelings. But this assumption is not warranted. Various subcultural segments of the population (and some types of individuals) have their own modes of speech, some characteristically vehement or uninhibited, others more restrained. The educated tend to shun the vocabulary of the blatant bigot. But one cannot assume that the tone of language necessarily reflects the content, strength or direction of the underlying sentiment.

NATURE OF PREJUDICE AMONG THE EDUCATED

In the present report we have divided the data into three categories: (1) beliefs and perceptions concerning minorities; (2) attitudes toward discrimination; and (3) acceptance of personal relationships with minority-group members. It was our hypothesis that these were separate dimensions of prejudice, which must be measured separately, and that the relation of education to prejudice might be positive in one dimension but negative in another.

The data have not borne out this hypothesis. There is no uniformity in the effects of education within any of these dimensions; both negative and positive effects occur in each. We therefore cannot conclude that prejudice among the educated is more likely to take one of these forms than another.

The better schooled seem less hospitable than others to primitive misconceptions—that members of a given minority are all alike, or that their blood is somehow different. The stereotypes of the educated show more sophistication, reflecting contemporary concerns such as communism, draft evasion or racketeering.

This tendency to see minorities as social deviants probably rests on some underlying beliefs about their "inherent traits." Since public-opinion studies have usually concentrated on the more widely held images, these underlying beliefs of the educated have not been identified. But whatever they may be, they are not the same as those typically harbored by persons of less schooling.

When questions are posed in policy terms, or when legal or formal discrimination is at issue, we usually find the educated less prejudiced than the uneducated. Legal measures against discrimination are most vigorously supported by educated groups.

But apparently the educated do not take equally strong positions against informal discrimination. Although the data here are sketchy, it would seem that in this area education alters expressed attitudes rather than actual behavior.

A similar, more definite picture emerges on issues of personal acceptance. The educated are more inclined toward casual relationships with minority-group members, but less willing to accept contacts that verge on the intimate.

Taken together, the data suggest that the educated and the uneducated have distinct forms of prejudice, but the distinction does not correspond to our categories. Instead, the forms that characterize different levels of education are found within each category.

There is little evidence that schooling consistently causes stereotypes to be rejected, or that the educated are less prejudiced or discrimination-minded in their personal lives. All that can be said is that they are more likely to reject certain kinds of stereotypes, to support non-discrimination as a policy, and to accept casual personal contact with minorities. To the degree that current problems of prejudice revolve around such issues, the influence of education is positive.

Yet, as we go up the educational ladder, old images of minorities are replaced by new ones, often no less harmful. Covert discrimination continues to be acceptable and, most important perhaps, the desire to keep minorities at some social distance remains.

It would thus appear that the impact of education is limited. Its chief effect is to reduce traditional provincialism—to counteract the notion that members of minorities are strange creatures with exotic ways, and to diminish fear of casual personal contact. But the limits of acceptance are sharply drawn; while legal equality is supported, full social participation is not.

INSTABILITY OF ATTITUDES AMONG THE EDUCATED

The goal of our educational system, as most frequently described, is to enable people to "think for themselves." We regard the educated person as possessing a distinct set of values, and we assume that education makes the individual less susceptible to outside influences.

The present study indicates that education may not always have this effect where minority groups are concerned; as previously noted, educated persons may be *less* likely than the uneducated to have stable attitudes in this area. The data can only reveal, not explain, this phenomenon. But several hypotheses may be advanced:

1. The educational philosophy of the open mind—"everyone has a right to an opinion," "every question has two sides"—may discourage formulation of a clear set of values and cause all questions to be viewed as open questions. Persons with this outlook are likely to be especially responsive to the arguments of the moment and the panaceas of movements hostile to minority groups. Thus the educational process, by scrupulously refraining from teaching specific doctrines, may in effect be creating a vacuum which the prevailing winds of prejudice might rush in to fill. Some data in our study, as in earlier ones, suggest that the better

educated may be more susceptible to certain kinds of propaganda, particularly when the capacity to make inferences is involved.[2]

2. Thanks largely to wider personal contacts and greater exposure to media of opinion, the better educated are the first to sense changes in the climate of opinion and quickly respond to new fashions in social thought. Opinions and theories about minority groups, originating among small, highly articulate segments of the educated stratum, circulate rapidly among the educated at large. Among the rest of the population, on the other hand, lack of schooling tends to cut the individual off from the principal channels by which ideas are communicated, and to that extent inhibits changes in norms. In some degree, the educated person's greater awareness of changes may also be a result of generally higher social status; the effects of education and status in this instance are mutually reinforcing.

3. The better educated may well adhere to certain patterns of behavior and opinion simply because they consider them social requirements. This point has been made by many critics of American society who see conformity as the distinguishing characteristic of our middle-class life. The tendency of the better educated to shift with the tide of opinion thus may reflect middle-class status, not schooling.

Other hypotheses may occur to the reader. But whatever the reasons, it is clear that the relation of education and prejudice has undergone various changes within the past twenty years. That alone may explain why different investigations have yielded different results. The changing relationship of the two variables severely limits the conclusions which may be drawn from any one study and underlines the desirability of using a variety of studies for any analysis.

EFFECTS OF EDUCATION ON PREDUDICES AGAINST DIFFERENT GROUPS

Our introduction suggested that earlier research treated the relation of education and prejudice in too general a fashion—that education might not have the same effect on attitudes toward different minority groups.

In the few instances in our study where identical questions concerning Negroes and Jews could be compared, similar results were obtained. While prejudice against Negroes is more prevalent, the influence of education takes the same direction, whichever the target group. But the specific levels of education at which changes occur are not the same. In the case of anti-Jewish prejudice, the positive effects of education, where present, usually are visible at each step of the school ladder. But reduction of prejudice against Negroes is principally a function of college training; earlier schooling generally produces little favorable change.

It would appear, then, that not all increments in education are equally significant. Only a high level of schooling seems to exert any appreciable impact on the more deeply rooted prejudices.

---

[2] C. I. Hovland, A. A. Lumsdaine and F. D. Sheffield, *Experiments on Mass Communication* (Princeton, New Jersey: Princeton University Press, 1949), p. 183; H. Stember, "Which Respondents are Reliable?" *International Journal of Opinion and Attitude Research*, V (1949), pp. 475–479.

In a sense, this finding bears out our earlier conclusion that the influence of education is more superficial than profound—reaching most strongly those aspects of prejudice which are least entrenched in the normative system.

THE INFLUENCE OF SOCIO-ECONOMIC STATUS

Thus far, we have considered only the correlation between education and prejudice. Now that we have some idea of the conditions under which these two factors are inversely linked, there still remains the question of causality. To what extent are the observed relationships attributable to the educational process itself, and to what extent are they produced by other factors characteristic of the educated?

It has been widely held that educated people show less prejudice simply because they usually come from the higher socio-economic strata, where prejudice is allegedly less prevalent. Our data, by and large, do not support this hypothesis. More often than not, effects of education persist when socio-economic factors are controlled.

There is no conclusive evidence that those in the higher socio-economic strata are, in fact, less prejudiced. High status seems to exert a systematic positive effect only on some of the cruder stereotypes; on many other issues, persons of lower socio-economic status actually show less prejudice. Even the degree of crudeness with which negative attitudes are expressed is a function of schooling, not social status; education, rather than class position, causes the higher status groups to reject statements couched in the language of the bigot.

Although the independent effect of education remains apparent when socio-economic status is controlled, the interaction of the two variables produces varying effects. First, the positive effects of education are strongest and most systematic among persons of lower status, rendering them considerably less prejudiced than even the educated of the upper status group. At higher status levels the effects of education diminish and occasionally disappear altogether.

Second, on some issues the effect of socio-economic status varies with the education of respondents. Among the least educated, those of high status show the lowest degree of prejudice. Among the most educated the reverse is true; those of low status show the least prejudice. This tendency is apparent principally in connection with discrimination against Negroes and personal relations with them.

The effects of education then, are circumscribed by subcultural factors. *Only where education differentiates the individual sharply from his previous subculture does it appreciably affect his attitudes toward minorities.* Thus, the educated from the lower class show attitudes markedly different from those of the uneducated in their class, probably because education has changed their life situation sharply. Among the upper class, on the other hand, the educated are not marked off in life-style or condition. A certain level of prejudice characterizes the upper class, and those who are part of that milieu incline toward this level, whatever their education.

Interestingly enough, the upper class apparently tends to establish not only a minimum but also a maximum acceptance limit—or so it would appear in view of the finding that the educated of high status do not go as far toward acceptance of minorities as the educated of lower status. The latter, unhampered by the norms of their socio-economic group, are apparently free to respond much more fully to the influence of education.

THE INFLUENCE OF OTHER VARIABLES

Whatever positive attitude changes occur with increased education are evidently induced by education itself. They cannot be attributed principally to other factors.

True, the *better informed* usually are less prejudiced; and where the educated normally tend to be more prejudiced than the uneducated, information sometimes mitigates the condition. But information alone is not the determining factor.

The *urbanized*, too, usually are less prejudiced. The influence of education is not present in all types of communities; in less urbanized places it occasionally disappears. But in most instances, education remains visibly effective when urbanization is controlled.

Insofar as it has been possible to isolate *ideological differences*, we have found only one instance where the effects of education remain visible among persons with a liberal viewpoint while disappearing among the less liberal; in all other cases they are discernible among both groups. Liberal ideology itself frequently reduces prejudice, though not uniformly at all stages of schooling. Among the least educated, general political attitudes are not necessarily reconciled with attitudes toward minorities; only at higher levels of education do the two seem consistently related.

As noted in the introductory chapter, the educated are more likely to have *contact with the minority-group members*; and our data indicate that personal acquaintance with Negroes of the respondent's own educational level reduces prejudice independently of education. Yet contact of this sort cannot entirely account for the lower prejudice of the educated; on the less controversial issues the effect of education remains discernible both among persons who have met Negro status equals and among those who have not. Still, in one instance, the effects of education disappear among persons without such contact; and several issues which are usually viewed with more prejudice by the educated provoke no such reaction among the educated who have met Negro equals.

We conclude that factors associated with education generally do not explain instances of lesser prejudice among the educated. *By and large, the favorable effects of education* per se *remain evident when other possible causes are controlled.*

CONDITIONS MINIMIZING THE FAVORABLE EFFECTS OF EDUCATION

It has been found throughout our study that on a considerable number of issues the educated are *more* prejudiced than others. They are inclined to entertain some adverse beliefs about minorities, adhere to certain patterns of discrimination, and reject intimate personal association. What factors underlie these attitudes?

Socio-Economic Status

It has been noted that certain characteristics associated with educational attainment—high information level, urban environment, liberalism and personal contact with status equals in the minority—consistently tend to reduce prejudice and reinforce any positive effects education may have. But high socio-economic status frequently has the opposite effect above the grammar-school level.

That the upper socio-economic groups generally tend toward greater prejudice against both Jews and Negroes is illustrated by a number of issues in each of our three dimensions. For example, the inclination of the better educated to regard the intelligence of Negroes as inferior is not really a function of education but of socio-economic status; at any given level of schooling, the upper class holds this belief more widely than the lower. The apparently greater prejudice of the educated on certain discrimination and social-distance issues is also frequently due to socio-economic status rather than education.

This conclusion applies particularly to personal acceptance of Negroes. In the data on that topic, a pattern is clearly evident. As we move up the educational ladder, the effects of socio-economic status shift; at the grammar-school level, high status frequently has positive effects, whereas at the college level it has pronounced negative ones.

Similarly, moving from casual contacts toward more intimate relations, or from legal toward social equality, the differential effects of status on educational groups become more distinct.

The same pattern is apparent where discrimination against Jews or personal relations with them are at issue; in several instances, low prejudice among the educated occurs despite, not because of, high socio-economic status.

Other Factors

Only twice do we observe a negative effect of education independently of socio-economic status. First, the educated of all status levels are more likely to report hearing criticism about Jews than those of less schooling. Second, the educated are more likely to withdraw their acceptance of school integration when the possibility of a Negro majority in the schools is posed. In two occupational groups of contrasting status, this pattern was found characteristic of the better educated.

In our opinion, neither of these issues is a pure measure of prejudice; both also reflect other factors. . . . Reports of hearing criticism of Jews are not known to be correlated in any way with belief in their truth. Rejection of a Negro majority in the schools may reflect concern about the effect of integration on academic standards as much as attitudes toward the minority group as such.

The implied willingness of the respondents to sacrifice the rights of minorities (as exemplified by true school integration) to a major personal concern (the quality of their children's education) probably reflects the relative importance which the educated attach to the two issues. The finding is of interest in this respect, but it is not a measure of prejudice in the ordinary sense.

CONDITIONS MAXIMIZING THE FAVORABLE EFFECTS OF EDUCATION

We next assess the effect of education in interaction with the other variables examined, so as to determine under what conditions education may be expected to reduce prejudice against minorities. Our concern here is not with the independent effect of those other factors. We will consider education most effective when the attitudes of persons at different educational levels are most clearly differentiated. That the effect is especially marked at the lowest socio-economic level has already been emphasized.

Education makes more difference in urban areas and in the South than elsewhere. Differences between the grammar-school and college groups are largest in these areas, particularly in attitudes toward Negroes.

Education usually exerts about the same influence on Republicans and Democrats. Among non-voters its effects are generally greater. The differential effect on liberals and non-liberals is not clear; it seems to vary with the measures applied. The same is true of information level: some measures indicate more effect, others less, among the well informed.

The effects of education are occasionally found to be stronger among Catholics than Protestants, but this seems to be true only of issues in which the Church has an interest, such as voting for minority candidates, or on which it has taken a position, such as school integration. By and large, education exerts the same impact on both religious groups. Its influence is generally greater among the non-religious.

The visible effects are consistently greater among persons with a foreign-born parent than among those of native parentage.

By and large, women seem more influenced by education than men, though not consistently in all issues. The differential appears principally on questions dealing with Negroes.

We have very few data on the effect of contact with status equals in the minority group. Among persons who have had contact with Negro equals, education produces markedly increased acceptance. The picture is less clear with respect to Jews.

One pattern consistently emerges: *Education is most effective where subcultural differences between the educated and uneducated are greatest.* Thus we find maximal effects among persons of low socio-economic status, in urban areas and in the South—environments where education would tend to set the individual apart from the community in a number of ways. In the upper class and in the small town, on the other hand, a more defined subculture may be presumed to exist, with transcendent group norms that would minimize the effect of education.

Although the subculture of the South is also well defined, differences between the educated and the uneducated probably are greater in this than in any other region of the country. College-trained Southerners resemble the college educated of other areas far more than the "poor-white" sharecroppers of their own.

They probably are less in harmony with their regional subculture than the educated elsewhere.

Parallel patterns emerge from some of our other findings. Where individuals are tied together by adherence to either of the major political parties, the effects of education seem minimized. Non-voters are a less homogeneous lot, ranging from the politically ignorant and apathetic to the sophisticated who reject both parties; in this broad range of individuals, education is much more potent than among persons with traditional party ties.

Likewise in the religious sphere, commitment to traditional religion permits education to exert only a limited influence; its effects are stronger among the non-religious.

The marked impact of schooling on the children of foreign-born parents illustrates the same point, suggesting that persons still somewhat removed from the institutional or cultural dictates of their American environment are freer to respond to life experiences—schooling being one of these.

In the case of immigrants' offspring, empathetic identification may also play a role; as former or potential victims of prejudice, the better educated of foreign parentage are likely to draw inferences from their own situation which apply to prejudice against others. The same might be true of Catholics in situations where they think of themselves as members of a minority.

The suggestion that women are more responsive to education than men, though not consistently validated by our data, would seem to agree with our thesis: To the extent that educated women still are deviants from the feminine world, schooling may have more influence on their attitudes toward minorities.

The finding that education has more impact among those who have had contact with Negroes of their own status needs no special elucidation. We should note, however, that in the absence of such contact, schooling has little effect—a fact which points up how severely its potential is limited where segregation, formal or informal, continues to exist.

EFFECTS OF COLLEGE EXPERIENCE

Although our data on the effects of college experience derive from a single study conducted more than ten years ago, certain inferences are warranted.

SOCIO-ECONOMIC FACTORS

College students from families in the lower occupational strata tend to be less prejudiced than those of higher status. Neither status group seems to change greatly during the college years—which supports the notion that early training may be a more important factor in prejudice than college experience.

However, certain so-called answers to minority problems seem to be endemic in the campus environment and apparently are adopted by students of the most varied backgrounds. There is some evidence that a common denominator of attitudes toward minorities—including prejudice as well as some forms of acceptance—is learned in college.

FRATERNITY MEMBERSHIP

The fraternity system apparently tends to select those who initially are more prejudiced, but the effect of college in reducing prejudice seems to be as great among members of Greek-letter societies as among others. Our data contain no evidence that fraternities or sororities produce attitudes appreciably different from those generally current on campus.

FIELDS OF STUDY

Freshmen who select different fields of college work do not differ markedly in their attitudes toward minorities. But there is some evidence that social-science students are most likely, and business students least likely, to shed some of their prejudices. Among all students, increased prejudices usually concern the more intimate situations and involve both Jews and Negroes. Decreased prejudices most frequently relate to less intimate issues and to Negroes rather than Jews. In assessing initial differences among students in various fields in combination with differential changes during the college years, we find that seniors in the physical and social sciences and the humanities share fairly similar attitudes, while business seniors are more prejudiced on each of eight issues measuring general acceptance of Jews and Negroes.

FINAL OBSERVATIONS

The data in this study have extended considerably our knowledge of the influence of education on prejudice. We can be fairly certain at this point that:

1. *The impact of education is not the simple one it was previously thought to be.* It varies in direction and strength with specific issues, with time periods and forms of measurement.

2. *The influence of education remains substantially the same regardless of the particular targets of prejudice.* Its effect on attitudes toward America's principal minority groups—Jews and Negroes—is more or less similar. Furthermore, both positive and negative effects are visible in all three dimensions: in beliefs and stereotypes, in attitudes toward discrimination and in personal acceptance of minority-group members.

3. *Education's potentialities are greatest when the less profound intergroup problems are at issue.* It is most successful in promoting democratic values where institutionalized policies, old clichés about minorities or casual transient relations with minority-group members are concerned. But when the issues are sensitive or controversial, the effect of education is either nil or inverse.

4. *Within these limits, the positive effects of education are real and not spurious.* None of the other variables examined accounts for the correlations observed. Where democratic values show gains with increased education, the cause lies in some aspect of education itself, not in the sociological characteristics

of the population from which the educated are drawn. The data strongly suggest that such gains derive from the tendency of education to create a distinct subcultural milieu, rather than from formal learning.

5. *The effects are usually strongest where education tends to set off a group more or less distinctly from its environment.* Conversely, where other subcultural or institutional forces are most potent, education has the least effect—a finding that may be important in gauging how a general increase in educational attainment would affect prejudice.

6. *Merely raising the educational level will not necessarily reduce prejudice against minorities.* Whether it will do so, and to what extent, depends on how sharply other cultural and institutional factors impinge on individuals. Any force for change is circumscribed by the influence of other factors at work in the situation. Thus, if some other central institution in our society—business, politics or religion, for example—were to become overwhelmingly powerful in the lives of Americans, its values presumably would modify the effects of increased education.

7. *Formal learning by itself is unlikely to change deep-rooted attitudes toward minorities.* Although this study reveals little about the impact of the actual educational process in beliefs about minorities, or attitudes and behavior toward them, the data suggest that the effects are minimal. This seems to be as true of college training as of education generally, although there is some opposing evidence, by no means conclusive, that the effects of college are partly a function of curriculum content and independent of group relations.

Our study has established that education produces certain effects; it has defined their limits and has suggested the conditions under which they are heightened or lessened. But no amount of correlational analysis can illuminate the dynamics of the process whereby prejudices are altered or redefined, or normative behavior is changed. Nor can such research reveal what crucial life experiences produce the attitudes toward minority groups characteristic of persons at different levels of education.

Other types of research are required to give depth to the picture. Intensive studies of contrasted subcultures are needed to determine the extent of subcultural influences on attitudes, and the ways in which they may limit individual change. Studies of individuals over extended periods of time should be made, in an effort to trace the pattern of their education and their attitudes toward minorities. Future research might also fruitfully repeat some of the questions asked twenty years ago to determine generational differences, if any, among persons at corresponding age levels.

Attitudes toward minority groups not covered in this report need to be examined. This applies especially to Puerto Ricans, who are becoming the prime targets of prejudice in the East, in order to establish base lines for future measurement of changes. Since the Puerto Rican "problem" is intertwined with issues of special concern to the educated (the school system) and to the middle class (the problem of violence), such an investigation is particularly needed. . . .

Demographic and Ecological Determinants of Academic Performance

DAVID E. LAVIN

SOCIOECONOMIC STATUS AS A DETERMINANT OF ACADEMIC PERFORMANCE

... Of all the ecological and demographic factors to be discussed, the major variable in terms of the sheer quantity of research is socioeconomic status (SES). Most of the studies to be reviewed measure SES by some objective technique rather than by subjective ratings. The objective techniques all involve the combining or weighting of scores on variables such as occupation, education, income, attendance at private or public school, area of residence, and the like so as to produce an index of the position of the student's family in the status hierarchy.

We wish first to consider how such a measure of SES can be predictive of school performance. The answer is that SES is a *derivative* or summarizing variable. Persons of different socioeconomic status face different kinds of life situations, and in adapting to them, they may develop different sets of values and life styles.[1] In short, SES symbolizes a variety of values, attitudes, and motivations related to academic performance. There are two major factors symbolized by SES: one is intelligence; the other is what may be referred to as the "achievement syndrome."

SES and Intelligence. One factor positively associated with SES is intelligence. This finding is well documented,[2] but it raises a question concerning the degree to which SES and intelligence are independently related to academic performance. One study found that when SES is controlled, the correlation between intelligence and grades is not lowered.[3] On the other hand, when intelligence was controlled, correlations between SES and grades were lowered

---

From *The Prediction of Academic Performance* by David E. Lavin, Copyright © 1965 by the Russell Sage Foundation. Reprinted by permission of the Russell Sage Foundation.

[1] Of course it is also possible that in many cases given types of value systems may predispose persons to gravitate into given kinds of life situations.

[2] Crowley, Francis J., "The Goals of Male High School Seniors," *Personnel and Guidance Journal*, vol. 37, 1959, pp. 488–492; Friedhoff, W. H., "Relationships Among Various Measures of Socio-economic Status, Social Class Identification, Intelligence, and School Achievement," *Dissertation Abstracts*, vol. 15, 1955, p. 2098; Knief, Lotus M., and James B. Stroud, "Intercorrelations Among Various Intelligence, Achievement, and Social Class Scores," *Journal of Educational Psychology*, vol. 50, 1959, pp. 117–120; Miner, John B., *Intelligence in the United States: A Survey with Conclusions for Manpower Utilization in Education and Employment*, Springer Publishing Co., New York, 1957; Mitchell, James V., Jr., "A Comparison of the Factorial Structure of Cognitive Functions for a High and Low Status Group," *Journal of Educational Psychology*, vol. 47, 1956, pp. 397–414; Noll, Victor H., "Relation of Scores on Davis-Eells Games to Socioeconomic Status, Intelligence Test Results, and School Achievement," *Educational and Psychological Measurement*, vol. 20, 1960, pp. 119–129; Pinneau, Samuel R., and Harold E. Jones, "Development of Mental Abilities," *Review of Educational Research*, vol. 28, 1958, pp. 392–400.

[3] Friedhoff, W. H., *op. cit.*

from a range of .37 to .47 to a range of .20 to .32.* In another study, a traditional intelligence test and a "culture free" test were used to predict achievement test scores.[4] When SES was controlled, none of the correlations between intelligence and the criterion decreased very much. When intelligence was controlled, the original correlations between SES and the criterion were reduced from about .30 to .20.

If, as we have said, SES is a summarizing variable, it is to be expected that when any of the variables it summarizes (such as IQ) are controlled, relationships between SES and performance should be decreased. Since the relationship of SES to achievement was not totally erased when IQ was controlled, SES appears to summarize more than intelligence. In other words, if students are equated for intelligence, variations in social class are still associated with variations in achievement. Therefore, SES must also summarize other variables.

SES and the Achievement Syndrome. Another variable associated with SES is achievement motivation—or more appropriately perhaps, an achievement syndrome. Rosen found that achievement motivation is directly related to SES.[5] Students who exhibit high levels of motivation tend to come from higher status levels. Both achievement motivation and SES were directly related to the grades of high school students. However, when motivation was controlled, the relation between SES and grades was almost erased. This illustrates what was stated before; namely, that SES summarizes other variables.

Another aspect of the achievement syndrome is what may be called achievement values. They include, among others, these beliefs: (1) that it is possible to manipulate the environment; (2) that there is value in delaying immediate pleasure for the sake of long run gratifications; and (3) that there is value in shedding affective ties to the family of orientation if these will interfere with mobility.[6] Students who adhere to these values tend to exhibit higher levels of career aspiration.

Evidence indicates that this set of beliefs is related to SES and is also associated with educational aspiration.[7] As with achievement motivation, when achievement values are controlled, the relation between SES and educational aspiration disappears. Strodtbeck found that achievement values were related to over- and underachievement, and that they were independent of achievement motivation.[8] His findings suggest, therefore, that the use of achievement values and achievement motivation together may increase the efficiency of predicting academic performance. Schneider and Lysgaard showed that belief in the value

---

* [If SES and grades were perfectly related in a positive manner, the correlation would be 1.00—Editor.]

[4] Knief, Lotus M., and James B. Stroud, *op. cit.*

[5] Rosen, Bernard C., "The Achievement Syndrome: A Psychocultural Dimension of Social Stratification," *American Sociological Review*, vol. 21, 1956, pp. 203–211.

[6] *Ibid.*

[7] *Ibid.*

[8] Strodtbeck, Fred L., "Family Interaction, Values and Achievement," in McClelland, David C., and associates, *Talent and Society*, D. Van Nostrand Co., Inc., Princeton, N.J., 1958, pp. 135–194.

of delayed gratification varies directly with SES.[9] Brim and Forer also demonstrated that the belief in the value of planning for the future is directly associated with SES.[10] Other studies find a direct association between SES and level of educational and occupational aspiration.[11] With the exception of the work by Rosen and by Strodtbeck, these investigations are not concerned with the prediction of academic performance. However, the achievement syndrome seems to be directly relevant to this question.

Research Findings. Of the research reviewed here, 13 studies report that SES is directly related to academic performance.[12] That is, the higher one's social status, the higher his level of performance. This relationship holds for all educational levels.

Of special interest are six studies whose findings contrast with these results.[13] They find that SES is inversely related to performance.

[9] Schneider, Louis, and Sverre Lysgaard, "The Deferred Gratification Pattern: A Preliminary Study," *American Sociological Review*, vol. 18, 1953, pp. 142–149.

[10] Brim, Orville G., Jr., and Raymond Forer, "A Note on the Relation of Values and Social Structure to Life Planning," *Sociometry*, vol. 19, 1956, pp. 54–60.

[11] Crowley, Francis J., *op. cit.*, Hyman, Herbert H., "The Value Systems of Different Classes: A Social Psychological Contribution to the Analysis of Stratification," in Bendix, Reinhard, and Seymour M. Lipset, editors, *Class, Status and Power: A Reader in Social Stratification*, The Free Press, Glencoe, Ill., 1953, pp. 426–442; Sewell, William, Archie O. Haller, and Murray A. Straus, "Social Status and Educational and Occupational Aspiration," *American Sociological Review*, vol. 22, 1957, pp. 67–73; Wilson, Alan B., "Residential Segregation of Social Classes and Aspirations of High School Boys," *American Sociological Review*, vol. 24, 1959, pp. 836–845.

[12] Bresee, Clyde W., "Affective Factors Associated with Academic Underachievement in High-School Students," *Dissertation Abstracts*, vol. 17, 1957, pp. 90–91; Coster, John K., "Some Characteristics of High School Pupils from Three Income Groups," *Journal of Educational Psychology*, vol. 50, 1959, pp. 55–62; Friedhoff, W. H., *op. cit.*; Gerritz, Harold G. J., "The Relationship of Certain Personal and Socio-economic Data to the Success of Resident Freshmen Enrolled in the College of Science, Literature and the Arts at the University of Minnesota," *Dissertation Abstracts*, vol. 16, 1956, p. 2366; Gibboney, Richard A., "Socio-economic Status and Achievement in Social Studies," *Elementary School Journal*, vol. 59, 1959, pp. 340–346; Knief, Lotus M., and James B. Stroud, *op. cit.*; McKnight, A. James, "The Relation of Certain Home Factors to College Achievement," *Dissertation Abstracts*, vol. 19, 1958, pp. 870–871; McQuary, John P., "Some Relationships Between Non-Intellectual Characteristics and Academic Achievement," *Journal of Educational Psychology*, vol. 44, 1953, pp. 215–228; Mueller, Kate H., and John H. Mueller, "Class Structure and Academic and Social Success," *Educational and Psychological Measurement*, vol. 13, 1953, pp. 486–496; Noll, Victor H., *op. cit.*; Ratchick, Irving, "Achievement and Capacity: A Comparative Study of Pupils with Low Achievement and High Intelligence Quotients with Pupils of High Achievement and High Intelligence Quotients in a Selected New York City High School," *Dissertation Abstracts*, vol. 13, 1953, pp. 1049–1050; Rosen, Bernard C., *op. cit.*; Travers, Robert M. W., "Significant Research on the Prediction of Academic Success," in Donahue, W. T., C. H. Coombs, and R. M. W. Travers, editors, *The Measurement of Student Adjustment and Achievement*, University of Michigan Press, Ann Arbor, 1949.

[13] Boyce, E. M., "A Comparative Study of Overachieving and Underachieving College Students on Factors Other Than Scholastic Aptitude," *Dissertation Abstracts*, vol. 16, 1956, pp. 2088–2089; Davis, Junius A., "Differential College Achievement of Public vs. Private School Graduates," *Journal of Counseling Psychology*, vol. 3, 1956, pp. 72–73; Davis, Junius A., and Norman Frederiksen, "Public and Private School Graduates in College," *Journal of Teacher Education*, vol. 6, 1955, pp. 18–22; McArthur, Charles C., "Personalities of Public and Private School Boys," *Harvard Educational Review*, vol. 24, 1954, pp. 256–262; McArthur, Charles C., "Subculture and Personality During the College Years," *Journal of Educational*

The apparent contradiction in these studies needs to be resolved. It is important to note at the outset that the samples used in the studies that find SES to be directly related to performance are different in certain respects from the samples used in those that observe an inverse relationship. Of the latter, five of the six studies show inverse relationships when the college performance of public school graduates is compared with that of private school graduates. Furthermore, in four of these investigations, the subjects were males who attended some of the very top eastern Ivy League colleges,[14] where the preparatory school graduates (largely from the most prestigious eastern preparatory schools) were likely to come mainly from upper-class backgrounds, while the public school graduates were likely to be largely of middle- and upper-middle-class origins.

Since most of the research on SES and academic performance does not sample the upper-class segment of the SES range, we suggest that the inconsistency between the results of the various studies referred to at the outset can be accounted for by differences in the SES range sampled. The situation is probably as follows: The relationship between SES and academic performance is positive through most of the SES range, but at the upper SES levels, it is inverse. When the SES sample does not include this upper segment, positive relations will be found. When the sample does include the upper range and does not go below the middle class, inverse relations will be found.

The preceding explanation is, of course, a statistical one. There remains the question of the meaning of the discrepancy on a theoretical level. We turn now to this question.

Two studies of the performance of Princeton students found that public school graduates are superior academically to private school graduates during the freshman year and that this superiority is maintained during the sophomore year, even though the two groups do not differ with regard to ability.[15] It seems reasonable to assume, as have the authors in this research, that private school students tend to be of higher SES than public school students. Another writer, in discussing findings of this sort, also suggests that private school graduates represent mainly the upper classes. [16] In the Princeton studies the authors present a possible explanation for the findings. First, since the public school graduates are from somewhat lower SES, college is an important means of enhancing status; private school graduates, on the other hand, need only to maintain their status level. For the latter group, therefore, simply graduating from college may be more important than the academic record they establish. Thus, differential motivation may be operative.

Sociology, vol. 33, 1960, pp. 260–268; Shuey, Audrey M., "Academic Success of Public and Private School Students in Randolph Macon Women's College: I. The Freshman Year," *Journal of Educational Research*, vol. 49, 1956, pp. 481–492.

[14] Davis, Junius A., *op. cit.*; Davis, Junius A., and Norman Frederiksen, *op. cit.*; McArthur, Charles C., "Personalities of Public and Private School Boys . . . ," *op. cit.*; McArthur, Charles C., "Subculture and Personality . . . , *op. cit.*

[15] Davis, Junius A., *op. cit.*; Davis, Junius A., and Norman Frederiksen, *op. cit.*

[16] McArthur, Charles C., "Personalities of Public and Private School Boys . . . ," *op. cit.*

A second interpretation would be that because private schools have a more directed regimen, their graduates encounter difficulty in adapting to the less structured college environment. If true, differences in college performance would be due to structural differences between private schools and public schools. At the present time, this remains an open question awaiting the results of additional research.

The first interpretation has received attention from McArthur,[17] who asserts that the eastern upper classes hold values that are not consistent with the American success orientation. Whereas this orientation stresses the future as the important time, the individual as the important person, and doing (achieving) as the important aspect of the person, among the upper-class group the important time is the past, the important persons are lineal ancestors, and "being" (a gentleman) is the most important aspect of the person. The latter is a portrayal of an aristocratic ideal in which behavior is oriented toward propriety in contrast to achievement. Presumably, the upper and middle classes differ in terms of these values.

These status groups also differ in terms of methods of child training. The parents of the middle-class public school group gear early training toward achievement and mobility; the parents of the upper-class private school group orient early training toward proper, gentlemanly behavior. These training and value differences may be reflected in the school achievement of the children. This probably constitutes the underlying theoretical meaning expressed in the earlier statistical explanation. In short, the inconsistency in the two sets of studies relating socioeconomic status to academic performance is more apparent than real. It can be resolved on both a statistical and a theoretical level.

Summary and Evaluation. The research shows that socioeconomic status is usually positively related to academic performance, but that on the college level the relationship is inverse when the range of SES runs from the upper to the middle class. The apparent inconsistency is interpretable in terms of personality and value differences between social status categories.

SES is a significant variable in the study of performance because it summarizes systematic variations in attitudes, motivations, and value systems that are related to such performance. While two underlying factors have been pointed out (intelligence and the achievement syndrome), this is probably not an exhaustive list. What is needed is a thorough review of the differences in personality, value systems, and behavior that are related to SES. Such class-related variables can then be applied to the study of achievement in school.

Another neglected area of research concerns the question of sex differences in the relation of SES to academic performance. It might be that SES is directly related to performance for males, but not for females. In addition, the class-related personality characteristics that are predictive of academic performance might be qualitatively different for males and females. These possibilities have not yet been researched.

---

[17] *Ibid.*; McArthur, Charles C., "Subculture and Personality . . . ," *op. cit.*

Social class differences may also partly determine the quality of student-teacher interaction. For example, one might ask how the interaction of middle-class teachers with lower-class students affects characteristics of the student-teacher relationship. Davidson and Lang found that children's perceptions of their teacher's favorability or unfavorability toward them were directly related to social class.[18] This suggests that SES-related behavioral characteristics may affect the treatment students receive from teachers.

In short, SES may summarize a number of other factors in addition to the ones noted earlier. Further research is needed.

SEX DIFFERENCES IN ACADEMIC PERFORMANCE

Throughout this review, sex has been used as one major point of reference for describing the research findings. However, most studies are not concerned with the study of sex differences. We now examine those studies that are concerned with this question.

The Findings.   The studies that assess the relation between sex and academic performance show that females have higher academic performance than males.[19] The evidence in Chapter 4* also clearly suggests that the correlation between intelligence and performance is higher for females than for males; that is, the performance of females more nearly in accord with their measured ability than is the case for males.

In addition, a few more specialized findings are of interest. In a longitudinal study on the elementary school level, Hughes found that when ability was controlled, the reading achievement of girls was superior to boys through the fourth grade; however, beyond this grade the sex differences were not significant and did not consistently favor the girls.[20]

In a most interesting study, Shaw and McCuen attempted to determine whether there is any specific academic level at which underachievement begins.[21] They used students in the top 25 per cent of the school population with regard to ability and classified them as achievers or underachievers on the basis of their cumulative grade-point averages in grades 9, 10, and 11. A student whose IQ

---

[18] Davidson, Helen H., and Gerhard Lang, "Children's Perceptions of Their Teachers' Feelings Toward Them Related to Self-Perception, School Achievement and Behavior," *Journal of Experimental Education*, vol. 29, 1960, pp. 107–118.

[19] Gerritz, Harold G. J., *op. cit.*; Hoyt, Donald P., "Size of High School and College Grades," *Personnel and Guidance Journal*, vol. 37, 1959, pp. 569–573; Hughes, Mildred C., "Sex Differences in Reading Achievement in the Elementary Grades," *Supplementary Educational Monographs*, no. 77, 1953, pp. 102–106; Jackson, Robert A., "Prediction of the Academic Success of College Freshmen," *Journal of Educational Psychology*, vol. 46, 1955, pp. 296–301; Northby, Arwood S., "Sex Differences in High-School Scholarship," *School and Society*, vol. 86, 1958, pp. 63–64; Shaw, Merville C., and John T. McCuen, "The Onset of Academic Underachievement in Bright Children," *Journal of Educational Psychology*, vol. 51, 1960, pp. 103–108.

* [The material referred to is not included—Editor.]

[20] Hughes, Mildred C., *op. cit.*

[21] Shaw, Merville C., and John T. McCuen, *op. cit.*

was higher than 110 and whose grade-point average was below the mean for his class was classified as an underachiever;[22] one whose grade-point average was above his class mean and whose IQ was above 110 was classified as an achiever. By eliminating some students, the authors ensured that the comparison groups had equal means and variances in their intelligence scores. They also controlled for sex. After the groups were selected, the academic record of each student for grades 1 through 11 was obtained and the performance of each group at each level was computed. When the higher- and lower-achieving males were compared, the data showed a significant difference between the two groups beginning at the third grade and increasing at each grade level up to grade 10, where it began to decrease, though it remained statistically significant.

Comparison of higher- and lower-achieving females presents quite a different picture. Through grade 5 those females who are later to become low achievers tend to exceed the higher achievers in grade-point average. At grade 6 the higher achievers attain a higher grade-point average for the first time, and this difference increases every year until grade 10. It is interesting to note that the start of the drop for the lower-achieving group roughly coincides with the onset of puberty. In contrast, the low-achieving males show a predisposition toward lower performance very early in their elementary school careers.

Summary and Evaluation. The findings on sex differences indicate that the level of academic performance of females is higher than that of males. Second, they suggest that the development of underachievement may follow a different pattern for females than for males. In all likelihood the significance of these findings can be understood in terms of a variety of differences in attitudes and behavior which result from the fact that males and females are socialized differently. Each sex must learn to play a different role, and the attitudes and values associated with sex-role learning may help to explain sex differences in academic performance.

In the first place, academic success probably has different significance for males than for females. Within the context of the cultural definition of the male role, academic success is an instrumental goal having important implications for later career success. For females the instrumental aspect of academic performance may not be as important, since integration with the occupational system is less crucial for the female role. Because academic success for males is considered more significant in terms of later occupational success, family pressures on them to do well in school are probably stronger than they are for females. If academic success is more directly involved with the male's affective ties to his family, the school might be more likely to become an arena in which either compulsive conformity to, or rebelliousness from, parental expectations may occur. Compulsive conformity would lead to overachievement, and rebelliousness to underachievement.

---

[22] This method of defining underachievement does not meet the criteria discussed in Chapter 2. [The material referred to is not included—Editor.] It would be more accurate simply to state that within a sample of students comparable as to ability, there are significant differences in level of academic performance.

Another consideration is that female teachers far outnumber male teachers, especially in the elementary and high schools. This being the case, we might speculate that teacher definitions of the student role include more characteristics of the female sex role. That is, the model of a good student is a female model. If this is true, then for the male, deviation from the student role actually constitutes a confirmation of his masculinity. This point has been made by Parsons in an attempt to account for certain patterns of aggressive behavior.[23]

If these interpretations have any validity, they may help to explain why the phenomena of over- and underachievement are more often observed for males than for females.[24] While it is interesting to speculate about these sex differences, more research is required both to document this evidence further and to specify the sources of the differences. Particularly interesting are the questions raised by the longitudinal studies—such as why the development of underachievement for girls follows a different pattern than that for boys.

MISCELLANEOUS ECOLOGICAL AND DEMOGRAPHIC CHARACTERISTICS

The scattering of research on the relationship between academic performance and other ecological and demographic factors includes studies on religion, school size, age, geographic region, and academic load.

Religious Background. Some evidence suggests that with regard to religion, Jewish students outperform non-Jewish students. Strodtbeck found this to be true when he compared Jewish high school students with their Italian Catholic counterparts.[25] However, many of the differences between these two groups seemed attributable to the effects of socioeconomic status rather than religion. That is, while Jews were more likely to have characteristics related to high academic achievement, when SES was controlled, the effects of religion disappeared. One other study found that Jews were more likely to be high achievers than students of other religions.[26]

Because some evidence suggests the presence of differences in the value systems of different religious groups further study is warranted. The work to date indicates, for example, that relative to the Italian Catholic value system, the Jewish culture places greater emphasis on the value of education and confers more prestige upon the scholar. Presumably this emphasis upon scholarship fits into a value system which places great importance upon rationality, future time orientation, and the like. Whether such achievement-related values are unique to particular religious groups or are associated more generally with

---

[23] Parsons, Talcott, "Certain Primary Sources and Patterns of Aggression in the Social Structure of the Western World," in Patrick Mullahy, editor, *A Study of Interpersonal Relations,* Hermitage House, New York, 1949, pp. 284–287.

[24] If, as we have stated earlier, the academic performance of females is more predictable than that of males when intellective factors are used as the predictors, then it follows that over- and underachievement should be more frequent for the males.

[25] Strodtbeck, Fred L., *op. cit.*

[26] Gerritz, Harold G. J., *op. cit.*

differences in socioeconomic status should be ascertained through further investigation.

Regional and Rural-Urban Variation. A few studies have looked at the effects of regional and community differences upon academic performance. In a summary of some of these findings, Rossi states that students in the South score lower on achievement tests than do students in the North.[27] He points out, however, that these studies do not hold intelligence constant. Therefore, the poorer achievement of southern students could be due to lower ability, to inferior schools, or perhaps to both.

Studies of rural-urban background find that students from urban areas have higher levels of academic performance than students from less populated areas.[28] However, the study by Washburne finds that the relation of urbanism to academic performance does not hold for the students who come from major metropolitan areas (500,000 or more), perhaps because of the greater heterogeneity of students from such areas. Another study found that while urban students were higher on aptitude than rural students, they were no different in academic performance.[29] However, the rural students tended to be registered in schools of agriculture, and urban students in business or arts and sciences colleges; consequently, it is difficult to interpret the results of these studies because the grades are not comparable.

While these findings indicate that northern students outperform southern students and that urban students outperform their rural counterparts, the meaning of such findings is ambiguous. A number of factors, either singly or in combination, could account for these results. Thus, urban students may obtain higher scores on intelligence tests. Moreover, they may come from higher SES levels and the urban schools may be educationally superior to rural schools. At present, the research findings do not allow us to assess these possibilities.

Age. Three studies of the effects of age on academic performance in the elementary school reach contradictory conclusions. One of these finds that under-age children have lower school achievement than children of normal age for the grade and equivalent ability.[30] Another finds that under-age children are somewhat superior in achievement,[31] and a third shows little effect of age.[32]

[27] Rossi, Peter H., "Social Factors in Academic Achievement: A Brief Review," in Halsey, A. H., Jean Floud, and C. A. Anderson, editors, *Education, Economy, and Society,* The Free Press, New York, 1961, pp. 269–272.

[28] Shaw, Merville C., and Donald J. Brown, "Scholastic Underachievement of Bright College Students," *Personnel and Guidance Journal,* vol. 36, 1957, pp. 195–199; Washburne, Norman F., "Socioeconomic Status, Urbanism and Academic Performance in College," *Journal of Educational Research,* vol. 53, 1959, pp. 130–137.

[29] Sanders, William B., R. Travis Osborne, and Joel E. Greene, "Intelligence and Academic Performance of College Students of Urban, Rural, and Mixed Backgrounds," *Journal of Educational Research,* vol. 49, 1955, pp. 185–193.

[30] Carter, Lowell, "The Effect of Early School Entrance on the Scholastic Achievement of Elementary School Children in the Austin Public Schools," *Journal of Educational Research,* vol. 50, 1956, pp. 91–103.

[31] Stephany, Edward Oscar, "Academic Achievement in Grades Five Through Nine," *Dissertation Abstracts,* vol. 16, 1956, p. 1846.

[32] Miller, Vera V., "Academic Achievement and Social Adjustment of Children Young for Their Grade Placement," *Elementary School Journal,* vol. 57, 1957, pp. 257–263.

While no generalization can be made on the basis of these studies, on other educational levels—for example, on the high school level—one might expect that students who are older than the average would exhibit lower levels of academic performance, since academic difficulty may have slowed their progress. This could be the case even if ability were controlled.

High School Size. Two studies examine the relationship between size of high school and academic performance in college. One of these finds that graduates of smaller high schools tend to receive lower grades, even though they are not lower on intelligence.[33] The other study finds size to be unrelated to college performance.[34]

While these studies permit no generalization, it is suggested that if school size were found to have a consistent relation with college performance, this would probably be a result of differences in facilities, teacher salaries, and the like. Should this factor be systematically assessed, we would expect a curvilinear relationship between size and performance. Small high schools are probably found more frequently in rural areas, and their facilities and teacher salaries are likely to be inferior. At the other extreme, very large high schools are most likely to be found in congested urban areas where the schools suffer from overcrowding, inadequate facilities, and the presence of large proportions of economically and socially underprivileged youth. Medium-sized schools would be representative of communities able to provide facilities at a pace more or less in keeping with population increases.

Academic Load. Five studies find that academic load (number of courses carried) has little or no effect upon school performance.[35] For low-ability students, however, academic load is inversely related to grades. Because there is so little variability in load at any educational level, this probably cannot be considered to be an important factor.

Additional Readings

FABIO L. CAVAZZA, "The European School System: Problems and Trends," *Daedalus*, 93 (Winter, 1964), pp. 394–415.

JAMES A. DAVIS, "Higher Education: Selection and Opportunity," *The School Review*, 71 (Autumn, 1963), pp. 249–265.

[33] Hoyt, Donald P., *op. cit.*

[34] Altman, Esther R., "The Effect of Rank in Class and Size of High School on the Academic Achievement of Central Michigan College Seniors, Class of 1957," *Journal of Educational Research*, vol. 52, 1959, pp. 307–309.

[35] Andrew, Dean C., "Relationship Between Academic Load and Scholastic Success of Deficient Students," *Personnel and Guidance Journal*, vol. 34, 1956, pp. 268–270; Hountras, Peter Timothy, "The Relationship Between Student Load and Achievement," *Journal of Educational Research*, vol. 51, 1958, pp. 355–360; Merrill, Reed M., and Hal W. Osborn, "Academic Overload and Scholastic Success," *Personnel and Guidance Journal*, vol. 37, 1959, pp. 509–510; Schwilk, Gene L., "Academic Achievement of Freshmen High School Students in Relationship to Class Load and Scholastic Aptitude," *Personnel and Guidance Journal*, vol. 37, 1959, pp. 455–456; Shaw, Merville C., and Donald J. Brown, *op. cit.*

PAUL HEIST, "The Entering College Student—Background and Characteristics," *Review of Educational Research*, 30 (October, 1960), pp. 285–297.

A. J. JAFFE and WALTER ADAMS, "College Education for U.S. Youth: The Attitudes of Parents and Children," *American Journal of Economics and Sociology*, 23 (July, 1964), pp. 269–283.

MARTIN TROW, "The Democratization of Higher Education in America," *European Journal of Sociology*, 3 (1962), pp. 231–262.

MARTIN TROW, "The Second Transformation of American Secondary Education," *The International Journal of Comparative Sociology*, 2 (September, 1961), pp. 144–166.

STRATIFICATION

Introduction

The selections in this section include information about four of the major topics commonly investigated in research about stratification: income, prestige, the correlates of *class*, and *vertical mobility*. The first two selections present information about income stratification.

The first selection by Miller, "The Distribution of Income," contains information relevant to contemporary discussions of the extent of poverty in the United States. Four facts are relevant. First, if an income of $4,000 is used as the line between poverty and nonpoverty, then 25 million families and individuals were below this line in 1959.[1] Second, half of the young and old "unrelated individuals" received less than $1,000 in 1959.[2] Third, one half of the working-age unrelated individuals had incomes under $2,500. Fourth, 14 million families had incomes under $4,000 in 1959. Miller also presents comparative information about income distribution. The major conclusion of the comparative information is that there is no evidence that incomes are more widely distributed in any country than they are in the United States. Thus, although there is a "sizable" amount of poverty in the United States, the rich apparently do not get a larger share of income in the United States than they do in other countries.

It is commonly believed that incomes are gradually becoming more evenly distributed in the United States. The second selection by Miller, "Trends in the Distribution of Income," presents information relative to this belief. Miller's main point is that the share of income received by the lower income groups has not changed in twenty years. This conclusion is based on an examination of income differentials between whites and nonwhites and between the different types of

[1] This type of division probably overstates the extent of poverty, because there are large variations in the income requirements of individuals who earn less than $4,000 a year.

[2] There were 13 million unrelated individuals in 1959, two fifths of whom were young and old.

occupations.[3] It should be noted that the two selections by Miller describe the distribution of *income*; the distribution of *wealth* is a different topic about which no conclusions should be drawn on the basis of Miller's information.

The next two selections present information about prestige stratification. The selection by Hodge, Siegel, and Rossi, "Occupational Prestige in the United States, 1925–63," indicates that no appreciable changes in the prestige structure of occupations have occurred in the United States between 1925 and 1963. The lowest product-moment correlation observed is .934.[4] (If there had been no change in occupational prestige between 1925 and 1963, the product-moment correlation would have been 1.00.) The stability of occupational prestige is remarkable in view of the many changes that have occurred in the United States during the past four decades.

The selection by Inkeles and Rossi, "National Comparisons of Occupational Prestige," presents information about the prestige of comparable occupations in six countries: United States, Great Britain, New Zealand, Japan, the Union of Soviet Socialist Republics, and Germany. High correlations are found with respect to occupational prestige in the six countries. Twelve of the fifteen product-moment correlations are above .9 and one is below .8. These high correlations indicate that the occupations are ranked in a relatively standard hierarchy, despite the cultural differences among the six nations. The material relating to the "structuralist" and "culturalist" positions, which is propositional rather than factual, is included, because it is so intertwined with the factual information that it could not easily be deleted. Hodge, Treiman, and Rossi have a later, more comprehensive, and much more complicated treatment of national comparisons of occupational prestige.[5]

The selection by Bronfenbrenner, "Socialization and Social Class Through Time and Space," is the first of three selections presenting information about the "correlates of class." Bronfenbrenner summarizes information about trends in infant care and child training between 1930 and 1955. With respect to infant care, his main point is that from about 1930 till the end of World War II, working-class mothers were uniformly more permissive than middle-class mothers; however, since World War II it is the middle-class mother who is the more permissive. With respect to child training, he makes four main points: first, middle-class mothers are more permissive toward the child's expressed needs and wishes than working-class mothers; second, middle-class parents have higher expectations for the child than working-class parents; third, working-class parents are more likely to employ physical punishment as discipline and middle-class parents to rely more on "love-oriented" techniques; and fourth, parent-child relationships in the middle class tend to be more acceptant and equalitarian, while they tend to be more oriented toward maintaining order and obedience in the lower class.[6]

The selection by Alford, "Class Voting in Anglo-American Countries," indicates that between 1952 and 1962 class voting is consistently higher in Australia and Great Britain than in Canada and the United States. The countries are ranked in the following order: Great Britain, Australia, the United States, and Canada. Class

[3] The nonwhites and the members of unskilled occupations are the low income groups examined.

[4] The product-moment correlations are in Table 2. The product-moment correlation is a statistic designed to measure the relationship between two variables which, in this instance, are occupational prestige rankings at two points in time.

[5] Robert W. Hodge, Donald J. Treiman, and Peter H. Rossi, "A Comparative Study of Occupational Prestige," in Reinhard Bendix and Seymour M. Lipset (eds.), *Class, Status, and Power* (New York: The Free Press, 1966), pp. 309–334.

[6] The selection by Bronfenbrenner could have been discussed in connection with a section on "Socialization" in Part I, "The Individual and the Group" or with the section on "Kinship" in Part II, "The Social Structure of the Group."

voting, as defined by Alford, refers to the extent to which manual and nonmanual occupational strata divide in their support for political parties. If all the manual workers in the United States, for example, voted for the Democrats, and if all the nonmanual workers voted for the Republicans, then class voting in the United States would be maximal.[7]

The main finding in the selection by Goode, "A Cross-Cultural Analysis of Class Differentials in Divorce Rates," is that there is a negative relationship between class and divorce rates (the higher the class, the lower the divorce rate) in highly industrialized Western nations. This finding is contrary to the popular belief that, at least in the United States, class and divorce rates are positively related.[8]

Rates of vertical mobility are frequently used to distinguish *open* and *closed* systems of stratification: the higher the rate of vertical mobility, the more open the system of stratification. The selection by Jackson and Crockett, "Occupation Mobility in the United States: A Point Estimate and Trend Comparison," is the first of two selections that present information about vertical mobility. Two major conclusions emerge from Jackson and Crockett's information. First, the rate of occupational mobility in the United States in 1957 was closer to that of a system of maximum mobility the "full-equality model," than to a system of minimum mobility, the "maximum inheritance model." (A system of maximum mobility exists when the occupation of the father has no effect on the occupation of the son; a system of minimum mobility exists when the occupation of the father completely determines the occupation of the son.) Second, the rate of occupational mobility has increased somewhat since the end of World War II. In other words, the United States has moved even closer to a system of maximum mobility between the end of World War II and 1957. Jackson and Crockett's information disagrees with a widely held belief that rates of vertical mobility are declining in the United States (or that "the United States is becoming a more closed type of society"). Jackson and Crockett follow the common practice of using the amount of "occupational" vertical mobility to measure the amount of vertical mobility.

The common belief has been that the rate of vertical mobility is much higher in the United States than in the modern industrial countries of Europe. The selection by Barber, "A Comparison of the Amount of Social Mobility in the United States and Europe," indicates that there is no good evidence to support this belief. Like the selection by Jackson and Crockett, the information which Barber summarizes uses occupational vertical mobility to measure the amount of vertical mobility. Barber's information is qualified by the recent work of S. M. Miller.[9]

[7] Robert R. Alford, *Party and Society* (Chicago: Rand McNally and Company, 1963), pp. 79–86. Alford's selection is also relevant to the discussion of the "Polity."

[8] Goode's information is also relevant to the section on "Kinship."

[9] Seymour M. Miller, "Comparative Social Mobility," *Current Sociology*, 9 (1960), No. 1.

The Distribution of Income

HERMAN P. MILLER

To start with, you must take my word for it that figures on income distribution are reasonably accurate. . . .

The American people received one-third of a trillion dollars in cash income in 1959. That is a lot of money: too much for anyone to imagine comfortably. But this vast sum had to be shared by fifty-eight million families and individuals. If each one got an equal share, it would only be $5,700. There is a number with some meaning! And to many it will seem surprisingly low.

There are many reasons why the average is low. For one thing, it assumes that each family gets exactly the same amount of money. That doesn't make much sense. Some families are larger than others; they "need" more. Some

FIGURE 1. Families and individuals by income levels: 1959. (*U.S. Bureau of the Census*, How Our Income Is Divided, *Graphic Pamphlet No. 2, 1963.*)

people work harder than others; they "deserve" more. Some people take bigger risks than others; they gain (or lose) accordingly. But there are also other reasons for the low average.

Above are figures showing the spread of income in the United States. They come from the last census. You may be interested in finding out where you fit in the income picture. Since only six different income groups are shown, these figures give an unrealistic view of the actual spread of incomes. It is really much greater than most people imagine. The noted economist Paul Samuelson has described income distribution in the following terms: "If we made an income pyramid out of a child's blocks, with each layer portraying $1,000 of income, the peak would be far higher than the Eiffel Tower, but almost all of us would be within a yard of the ground." This gives you some idea of the diversity that is compressed within these six income groupings.

The average factory worker earns about $100 a week, or more than $5000 a year. In addition, many families have more than one worker. How then can there be 25 million families and individuals—nearly one-half of the total—with incomes under $4,000? There must be a joker somewhere.

Notice that unrelated individuals (a technical term for "one-person" families who live alone or as boarders in other people's homes) have been lumped with family groups consisting of two or more persons. That makes a big difference. One person living alone has only his own income and only himself to support. Where there are two or more people in a home, more than one can work—but there are also more mouths to feed.

It is obvious that before any more can be said about income, the unrelated individuals must first be separated from the families.

UNRELATED INDIVIDUALS BY INCOME LEVELS

At the time of the last census, there were 13 million unrelated individuals in the United States. They are often overlooked in the figures because their number is so small relative to the 165 million people who live in families. But they are a special group and they deserve special attention.

9% are under 25
34% are over 65 } Young and old
57% are 25–64　　Working age

Together, the young and the old constitute more than two-fifths of all unrelated individuals. Many in the group called unrelated individuals are widows and widowers who spent most of their lives as family members. When their mates died, they kept their own homes and did not move in with children or enter old-age homes. Their incomes are low by all standards—half received less than $1,000 in the prosperous year of 1959. It was received largely as pensions and public assistance—although many of these people work.

Younger persons are also important in the unrelated individual population; they account for about one-tenth of the total. The average income of the youngsters was also low ($1,500), largely because their lack of skill and experience prevented them from commanding high wages.

Unrelated individuals in the most productive age brackets (twenty-five to sixty-four years) make up about three-fifths of the total. Their incomes are considerably higher than those cited for the younger and older persons; but they are nevertheless quite low by most standards. One-half had incomes under $2,500. The relatively low incomes of this group can be blamed on their inability to work, failure to find work, or their concentration in low-paying jobs when they are employed.

FAMILIES BY INCOME LEVELS

The distribution of families by income levels is considerably different from that shown for unrelated individuals. At the time of the last census there were forty-five million families in the United states and they received nearly $300 billion. If this total had been equally divided, each would have received $6,600. In 1959, about six families out of every ten received less than that amount.

Millions of families in the United States still try to get by on less than $40 a week. There were six million such families, to be exact, in 1959. They represented 13 percent of all families but they received only 2 percent of the income. Many of them lived on farms where their cash incomes were supplemented by food and lodging that did not have to be purchased. Yet, even if this income were added to the total, it would not change the results very much.

At the golden apex of the income pyramid there were about one-half million families with incomes over $25,000. They represented 1 percent of the total but they received 8 percent of the income.

Another way to view these figures is to examine the share of income received by each fifth of the families ranked from lowest to highest by income. In Table 2 you will see that in 1959 the poorest fifth of the families had incomes under $2,800; they received 5 percent of the total. In that same year, the highest fifth of the families had incomes over $9,000; they received 43 percent of the total.

Who sits at the top of the heap? The figures show that until you get to the very top the incomes are not so high. The top 5 percent of the families had incomes over $14,800. They received 18 percent of all the income. Families with

TABLE 1. FAMILIES BY INCOME LEVELS IN 1959

Income Level	Number of Families	Percent	
		Families	Income
All families	45 million	100%	100%
Under $2,000	6 million	13	2
Between $2,000 and $4,000	8 million	18	8
Between $4,000 and $6,000	11 million	23	18
Between $6,000 and $8,000	9 million	19	20
Between $8,000 and $10,000	5 million	12	15
Between $10,000 and $15,000	5 million	11	19
Between $15,000 and $25,000	1½ million	3	10
$25,000 and over	½ million	1	8
Median income		$5,660	

U.S. Bureau of the Census, *How Our Income Is Divided*, Graphic Pamphlet No. 2, 1963.

TABLE 2. SHARE OF INCOME RECEIVED IN 1959 BY EACH FIFTH OF U.S.
FAMILIES AND BY TOP 1% AND 5%

Families Ranked from Lowest to Highest	Income Range	Percent of Income Received
Lowest fifth	Less than $2,800	5%
Second fifth	Between $2,800 and $4,800	12
Middle fifth	Between $4,800 and $6,500	17
Fourth fifth	Between $6,500 and $9,000	23
Highest fifth	$9,000 and over	44
Top 5%	$14,800 and over	18
Top 1%	$25,000 and over	8

U.S. Bureau of the Census, *How Our Income Is Divided*, Graphic
Pamphlet No. 2, 1963.

incomes over $25,000 were in the top 1 percent and they received 8 percent of
the total. Is $15,000 or $25,000 a year a very high income? To those near the
base of the pyramid, it might be; but to a skilled worker with a working wife,
an annual income of $15,000 may not seem like an unattainable goal. Economist
Henry Wallich remarks that in America "the $25,000 family enjoys a variety of
extras, but its basic form of living is not very obviously distinguishable from
that of the $6,000 family."

If $25,000 a year is not a very high income, what is? Sociologist C. Wright
Mills, in his book *The Power Elite*, defines the corporate rich as those with
incomes of $100,000 a year or more. Relatively few American families have
incomes this high. In 1959, there were only 28,000 individual income tax returns
filed with adjusted gross incomes over $100,000. These returns accounted
for about $5 billion or slightly more than 1 percent of the total distributed to the
entire economy. These people certainly got more than their share; but the figures
hardly support the view that the lower-income groups would be much better
off if these very high incomes were confiscated and spread around more evenly.
The fact of the matter is that they might be worse off if the golden goal of an
income this high were removed.

The top income receivers are highly concentrated in the large metropolitan
areas. The hundred largest urban centers contain about one-half of the population but about four-fifths of those who pay taxes on incomes over $100,000.
In 1959, the New York metropolitan area provided 6,700 tax returns reporting
incomes over $100,000. Chicago and Los Angeles followed New York with
about 1,800 high-income returns each.

ARE U.S. INCOMES TOO UNEQUALLY DISTRIBUTED?

These is no objective answer to this question. It all depends on how unequally
you think incomes should be distributed.

Around the turn of the century, the French poet and philosopher Charles Péguy wrote: "When all men are provided with the necessities, the real necessities, with bread and books, what do we care about the distribution of luxury?" This point of view went out of style with spats and high-button shoes. There is an intense interest in the distribution of luxury in the modern world.

Since we all cannot have as many material things as we should like, many people are of the opinion that those who are more productive should get more both as a reward for past performance and as an incentive to greater output in the future. This seems like a reasonable view, consistent with the realities of the world. Lincoln said: "That some should be rich shows that others may become rich and hence is just encouragement to industry and enterprise." The fact is that all modern industrial societies, whatever their political or social philosophies, have had to resort to some forms of incentives to get the most work out of their people.

Despite its reasonableness, this view has its critics. Some have argued that a man endowed with a good mind, drive, imagination, and creativity, and blessed with a wholesome environment in which these attributes could be nurtured, has already been amply rewarded. To give him material advantages over his less fortunate fellows would only aggravate the situation. The British historian R. H. Tawney wrote in his book *Equality:* ". . . some men are inferior to others in respect to their intellectual endowments. . . . It does not, however, follow from this fact that such individuals or classes should receive less consideration than others or should be treated as inferior in respect to such matters as legal status or health, or economic arrangements, which are within the control of the community."

Since there is no objective answer to the question as it has been formulated, it may be fruitful to set it aside and turn to the comparison of income in the United States and other major countries for which such data are available.

Anyone who doubts that real incomes—purchasing power—are higher in the United States than in all other major countries just hasn't been around. But, how much higher? That is hard to say. How do you compare dollars, pounds, rubles, and francs? Official exchange rates are often very poor guides. Differences in prices, quality of goods, and living standards add to the complexity. In view of these problems, international comparisons are often made in terms of the purchasing power of wages. But even this measure has serious limitations. What constitutes a representative market basket in different countries, and how does one compare the market basket in one country with another? For example, Italians may like fish, which is relatively cheap, whereas Americans may prefer beef, which is quite expensive. How then would one compare the cost of a "typical" meal for families in the two countries? Because of this kind of problem, and many others, international comparisons of levels of living must be made with great caution. One study that casts some light on the subject was published in 1959 by the National Industrial Conference Board. It shows the amount of work it would take to buy the following meal for a family of four in several different countries. The items were selected from an annual survey of retail prices conducted by the International Labor Office:

Beef, sirloin	150 grams
Potatoes	150 grams
Cabbage	200 grams
Bread, white	50 grams
Butter	10 grams
Milk	.25 liter
Apples	150 grams

The results are shown in the pictograph (Fig. 2). The industrial worker in the United States had to work one hour to buy the meal above. The Canadian worker, whose level of living is not far behind that of his American cousin, had to work nine minutes more to buy the same meal. In Europe, the Danes came closest to the American standard, but even in Denmark the average worker had to toil one-half hour longer to feed his family. In West Germany and Great Britain it took more than two hours of work to buy the same meal and in Italy it took five hours. These and many other figures of a similar nature show that American workers are paid more in real terms than the workers of any other major country.

If international comparisons of levels of income are difficult, comparisons of the distribution of income are virtually impossible. There are many opinions on the subject, but few of them are solidly based. Aldous Huxley, for example, believes that incomes are more unequally distributed in England than in France

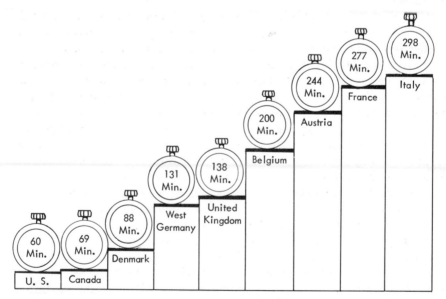

FIGURE 2. Work time to buy a meal in 1958. (*Zoe Campbell, "Food Costs in Work Time Here and Abroad,"* Conference Board Business Record, December, 1959.)

because "the highest government servants in England are paid forty or fifty times as much as the lowest." Following a similar line of reasoning, Max Eastman finds inequality greater in Russia than in the U.S. because the managing director of an American mining firm receives about forty times as much as one of his miners whereas a man in the same position in Russia may earn up to eighty times as much as a miner. This type of evidence might satisfy a literary man. The statistician is harder to please.

The United Nations, which has done some work in this field, cautions that "despite the intense interest in international comparisons of the degree of inequality in the distribution of income . . . surprisingly little incontrovertible evidence has been amassed. The margins of error of the available statistics . . . combined with differences in the underlying definitions . . . make it extremely hazardous to draw conclusions involving any but possibly a very few countries." No reputable scholar would deny the wisdom of these remarks. Yet judgments must be made and some figures, if they are carefully considered and properly qualified, are better than none. Even the world's leading authority on income distribution, Professor Simon Kuznets of Harvard University, agrees that international comparisons of income distribution, despite their serious limitations, have value because they are based on "a variety of data . . . rather than irresponsible notions stemming from preconceived and unchecked views on the subject."

Do the rich get a larger share of income in the United States than they do in other countries? According to the available evidence this is not the case. The

TABLE 3. PERCENT OF INCOME RECEIVED BY TOP
5% OF FAMILIES IN SELECTED COUNTRIES

United States	(1950)	20%*
Sweden	(1948)	20
Denmark	(1952)	20
Great Britain	(1951–52)	21
Barbados	(1951–52)	22
Puerto Rico	(1953)	23
India	(1955–56)	24
West Germany	(1950)	24
Italy	(1948)	24
Netherlands	(1950)	25
Ceylon	(1952–53)	31
Guatemala	(1947–48)	35
El Salvador	(1946)	36
Mexico	(1957)	37
Colombia	(1953)	42
Northern Rhodesia	(1946)	45
Kenya	(1949)	51
Southern Rhodesia	(1946)	65

* The numbers represent total income before taxes received by families or spending units.
Simon Kuznets, "Quantitative Aspects of the Economic Growth of Nations," *Economic Development and Cultural Change*, Vol. XI, No. 2, January, 1963, Table 3.

United States has about the same income distribution as Denmark, Sweden, and Great Britain and a much more equal distribution than most of the other countries for which data are shown. There is no evidence that incomes are more widely distributed in any country than they are in the United States.

The figures in Table 3 classify the top 5 percent as "rich." This is a rather low point on the income scale. In the United States it would include all families receiving more than $15,000 a year. A more interesting comparison would be the share of income received by the top 1 percent ($25,000 or more per year) or perhaps even a higher income group. Such information, however, is not available for most other countries.

A comprehensive study of international comparisons of income was made in 1960 by Professor Irving Kravis of the University of Pennsylvania. He summarized the income distribution among the countries for which data are available in the following way:

More nearly equal distribution than the U.S.
  Denmark
  Netherlands
  Israel (Jewish population only)
About the same distribution as U.S.
  Great Britain
  Japan
  Canada
More unequal distribution than U.S.
  Italy
  Puerto Rico
  Ceylon
  El Salvador

Source Notes

(The numbers on the left refer to the pages on which the data and quotations appear.)

313 *The New York Times*, November 11, 1962.

314 Paul A. Samuelson, *Economics: An Introductory Analysis*, 5th ed. New York, McGraw-Hill Book Co., Inc., 1961, p. 113.

314 Facts cited for unrelated individuals are from U.S. Bureau of the Census, *How Our Income Is Divided*, Graphic Pamphlet No. 2, 1963.

315–16 Henry Wallich, *The of Cost Freedom*. New York, Harper & Row, Publishers, 1960, p. 114.

316 C. Wright Mills, *The Power Elite*. New York, Oxford University Press, 1956 (Galaxy Books, 1959, p. 149).

316 The 1959 tax figures for persons with incomes above $100,000 are from U.S. Bureau of the Census, *Statistical Abstract of the United States: 1962*, p. 392.

316 The 1959 figures for high incomes in New York, Chicago, and Los Angeles are from Internal Revenue Service, *Statistics of Income: Individual Income Tax Returns for 1959*, Table 19.

317 Charles Péguy, *Basic Verities*. New York, Pantheon Books, 1943, p. 61.

317 Lincoln's statement was a reply to the New York Workingmen's Democratic Republican Association, March 21, 1864. It is quoted in *The Collected Works of Abraham Lincoln*, Vol. 7, ed. by Roy P. Basler. New Brunswick, N.J., Rutgers University Press, 1953, p. 259.

317 R. H. Tawney, *Equality*. New York, G. P. Putnam's Sons (Capricorn Books), 1961, p. 40.

318 For additional comparisons between the United States and other countries, see Leonore Epstein, "Unmet Need in a Land of Abundance," *Social Security Bulletin*, May, 1963.

319 Aldous Huxley, *Ends and Means*. New York, Harper & Row, Publishers, 1937, p. 187.

319 For Max Eastman's ideas, see the above source.

319 United Nations, Economic and Social Council, *Statistics of Income Distribution*, E/CN.3/184, January, 1954, p. 6.

319 Simon Kuznets, "Quantitative Aspects of the Economic Growth of Nations," *Economic Development and Cultural Change*, Vol. XI, January, 1963, p. 12.

Trends in the Distribution of Income

HERMAN P. MILLER

A myth has been created in the United States that incomes are gradually becoming more evenly distributed. This view is held by prominent economists of both major political parties. It is also shared by the editors of the influential mass media.

Arthur F. Burns, chief economist for the Eisenhower Administration, stated in 1951 that "the transformation in the distribution of our national income ... may already be counted as one of the great social revolutions of history." Paul Samuelson, one of President Kennedy's leading economic advisers, stated in 1961 that "the American income pyramid is becoming less unequal." Several major stories on this subject have appeared in the *New York Times*, and the editors of *Fortune* magazine announced ten years ago: "Though not a head has been raised aloft on a pikestaff, nor a railway station seized, the U.S. has been for some time now in a revolution."

In the preceding chapter,* several basic facts were presented regarding trends in the inequality of income distribution in the United States. It was shown that there has been no appreciable change in income shares for nearly twenty years. This question will now be examined a little more intensively.

Despite the existence of much poverty in the United States, there is general agreement that real levels of living are much higher than they were only ten years ago and that the prospects for future increases are very good. Since conditions are improving you may wonder why it is important to consider the gap between the rich and the poor. Isn't it enough that the *amount* of income received by the poor has gone up substantially? Why be concerned about their share? Many who have thought about this problem seriously regard the *share* as the critical factor. When Karl Marx, for example, spoke about the inevitability of increasing misery among workers under capitalism he had a very special definition of misery in mind. Sumner Slichter, in summarizing the Marxian position on this point, states: "Marx held that wages depend upon the customary wants of the laboring class. Wages, so determined, might rise in the long run. Hence, Marx conceded that real wages *might* rise, but not the relative share of labor. Even if real wages rose, misery would grow, according to Marx, since workers would be worse off relative to capitalists."

Arnold Toynbee has approached the problem of income shares in still another way. He notes that minimum standards of living have been raised considerably and will continue to be raised in the future, but he observed that this rise has not stopped us from "demanding social justice; and the unequal distribution of the world's goods between a privileged minority and an underprivileged majority has been transformed from an unavoidable evil to an intolerable injustice."

In other words "needs" stem not so much from what we lack as from what our neighbors have. Veblen called this trait our "pecuniary standard of living" and modern economists refer to it as the "relative income hypothesis," but it all comes back to the same thing. Except for those rare souls who have hitched their wagons to thoughts rather than things, there is no end to "needs." So long as there are people who have more, others will "need" more. If this is indeed the basis for human behavior, then obviously the gap between the rich and the poor cannot be ignored, however high the *minimum* levels of living may be raised.

Although the figures show no appreciable change in income shares for nearly twenty years, the problem is complex and there is much that the statistics cannot show. It is conceivable, for example, that a proportional increase in everybody's real income means more to the poor than to the rich. The gap in "living levels" may have closed more than the gap in incomes. Even if exact comparisons are not possible, many believe that by satisfying the most urgent and basic needs of the poor, there has been some "leveling up" in the comforts of life.

Other examples of a similar nature can be cited. The extension of government services benefits low-income families more than those who have higher incomes —by providing better housing, more adequate medical care, and improved educational facilities. The increase in paid vacations has surely brought a more equal distribution of leisure time—a good that is almost as precious as money. Finally, improved working conditions—air conditioning, better light, mechanization of routine work—has undoubtedly reduced the painfulness of earning a living more for manual workers than for those who are in higher paid and more responsible positions.

When allowance is made for all of these factors, and for many others not mentioned, it may well be that some progress has been made during recent years in diminishing the inequality of levels of living. But it is hard to know how much allowance to make and our judgments could be wrong. Most opinions regarding changes in inequality, including those held by professional economists, are based on statistical measures of income rather than on philosophical concepts. With all their limitations, the income figures may well serve as a first approximation of changes in welfare. These figures show that the share of income received by the lower income groups has not changed for twenty years. Let us look at some other evidence that supports this view and then examine the implications of the findings.

WHITE-NONWHITE INCOME DIFFERENTIALS ARE NOT NARROWING

The narrowing of income differentials between whites and nonwhites (92 percent of whom are Negroes) is sometimes cited as evidence of a trend toward equilization. Several years ago, Professor Joseph Kahl of Washington University stated: "The poorest section of the country, the South, and the poorest group in all the country, the Negroes, made the greatest gains of all."

What are the facts? Surely one would expect a change here in view of the major relocation of the Negro population in recent years. Migration and technological change during the past twenty years have altered the role of the nonwhite from a southern farmhand or sharecropper to an industrial worker. In 1940, about three-fourths of all nonwhites lived in the South and were largely engaged in agriculture. By 1950, the proportion residing in the South had dropped to about two-thirds, and today it is down to a little more than half. Even in the South, nonwhites are now more concentrated in urban areas than ever before.

The change in the occupations of nonwhite males tells the story of their altered economic role even more dramatically. Twenty years ago, four out of every ten nonwhites who worked were laborers or sharecroppers on southern farms. At present, less than two out of every ten are employed in agriculture and about five out of ten work as unskilled or semiskilled workers at nonfarm jobs. The change in the occupational status of nonwhites has been accompanied by a marked rise in educational attainment, proportionately far greater than for whites. In 1940, young white males averaged four years more of schooling than nonwhites in the same age group. Today the gap has been narrowed to one and a half years.

The income gap between whites and nonwhites did narrow during World War II. During the last decade, however, it shows some evidence of having widened again (see Table 1 and Fig. 1). The census statistics demonstrate this dismaying fact.

In 1947, the median wage or salary income for nonwhite workers was 54 percent of that received by the whites. In 1962, the ratio was almost identical (55 percent). Prior to 1947 there was a substantial reduction in the earnings gap between whites and nonwhites. In view of the stability of the earnings gap

TABLE 1. THE INCOME GAP: WHITE VS. NONWHITE MALE WORKERS
AGED 14 AND OVER, IN 1939, AND 1947 TO 1962

Year	White	Nonwhite	Nonwhite as Percent of White
All persons with wage or salary income:			
1939	$1,112	$ 460	41%
1947	2,357	1,279	54
1948	2,711	1,615	60
1949	2,735	1,367	50
1950	2,982	1,828	61
1951	3,345	2,060	62
1952	3,507	2,038	58
1953	3,760	2,233	59
1954	3,754	2,131	57
1955	3,986	2,342	59
1956	4,260	2,396	56
1957	4,396	2,436	55
1958	4,596	2,652	58
1959	4,902	2,844	58
1960	5,137	3,075	60
1961	5,287	3,015	57
1962	5,462	3,023	55
Year-round full-time workers with wage or salary income:			
1939	$1,419	$ 639	45
1955	4,458	2,831	64
1956	4,710	2,912	62
1957	4,950	3,137	63
1958	5,186	3,368	65
1959	5,456	3,339	61
1960	5,662	3,789	67
1961	5,880	3,883	66
1962	6,025	3,799	63

during the postwar period, however, the reduction during the war years cannot be viewed as part of a continuing process, but rather as a phenomenon closely related to war-induced shortages of unskilled labor and government regulations such as those of the War Labor Board designed generally to raise the incomes of lower paid workers, and to an economy operating at full tilt.

This conclusion is reinforced by details of the 1960 census which show that in the twenty-six states (including the District of Columbia) which have 100,000 or more Negroes, the ratio of Negro to white income for males increased between 1949 and 1959 in two states (District of Columbia and Florida) and it was unchanged in two others (New Jersey and Oklahoma). In every other state there was a widening of the gap between the incomes of whites and Negroes and in some cases it was fairly substantial.

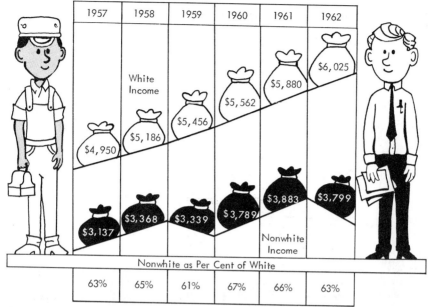

FIGURE 1. The income gap—white vs. nonwhite workers: 1957 to 1962. (*U.S. Bureau of the Census*, Current Population Reports—Consumer Income, *Series P-60, annual issues.*)

OCCUPATIONAL DIFFERENTIALS IN EARNINGS ARE NOT NARROWING

One of the most widely and strongly held misconceptions about income concerns the narrowing of the difference in earnings between skilled and unskilled workers. The prevailing view holds that the decrease in the earnings gap between the skilled and the unskilled in the United States is part of a historical process that has been going on since the the the turn of the century. The Department of Labor reports that in 1907 the median earnings of skilled workers in manufacturing industries was about twice that received by unskilled workers. By the end of World War I, it was only 75 percent greater, and by the end of World War II only 55 percent greater. Thus, during a forty-year period, this income gap was reduced by about 50 percent, an average of about 1 percent per year.

Recent trends in income differentials between skilled and unskilled workers are shown in Fig. 2 and Table 2. These figures represent the median wages and salaries received during the year in the major occupation groups for men. Women are excluded because their earnings are highly influenced by the fact that a large proportion of them work intermittently rather than full time.

There was not too much variation among occupation groups in the rate of income growth during the entire twenty-two year period. The average income for most of the occupations quadrupled. But an examination of the growth rates for two different periods, 1939–50, and 1950–61, reveals striking differences.

FIGURE 2.   Men's income by occupation in 1939, 1950, and 1961.

TABLE 2. MEN'S INCOME BY OCCUPATION: PERCENT CHANGE

Year	Professional and Managerial Workers	Craftsmen	Semiskilled Factory Workers	Service Workers and Nonfarm Laborers
1939–61	243%	322%	331%	314%
1939–50	96	160	172	180
1950–61	75	62	59	48

U.S. Bureau of the Census, *Current Population Reports—Consumer Income,* Series P-60, Nos. 9 and 39 (for Fig. 2 and Table 2).

During the decade that included World War II, the lower paid occupations made the greatest relative gains in average income. Thus, laborers and service workers (waiters, barbers, janitors, and the like), two of the lowest paid groups among nonfarm workers, had increases of about 180 percent. The gains for craftsmen, who are somewhat higher paid, was 160 percent; professional and managerial workers, the highest paid workers of all, had the lowest relative gains—96 percent.

During the past decade the picture has been reversed. Laborers and service workers made the smallest relative gains, 48 percent; craftsmen had increases of 62 percent, and the professional and managerial workers had the greatest gains of all, 75 percent. The narrowing of the income gap between the skilled and the unskilled, the high-paid and the low-paid workers, which was evident up to and including the war years, has stopped during the past decade and the trend seems to be moving in the opposite direction.

The above figures are national averages in which all industries and regions are combined. They are very useful for identifying major trends, but they can also be very misleading because they average together so many different things. It is important to examine the figures for a particular industry in a particular region to get a better understanding of the underlying trends. The primary and fabricated metals industries have been selected for this purpose. The same analysis was also made for about ten other major American industries and the results are generally the same as those presented below.

About 2,200,000 men were engaged in the production of metals or the fabrication of metal products in 1960. This employment was about equally divided between production and fabrication.

The production of primary metals consists of three major components: blast furnaces and steel mills with about 600,000 men; other primary iron and steel works (mostly foundries) with about 300,000 men; and primary nonferrous metal (mostly aluminium) plants, with about 300,000 men. The iron and steel industry is highly concentrated in the Northeast and North Central states and within these states it can be further pinpointed to the following areas: Pittsburgh-Youngstown, Cleveland-Detroit, and Chicago.

The fabrication industry has a similar geographic distribution. About one-third of the workers are employed in the Northeastern states and a somewhat larger proportion are in the North Central region. This industry is divided into several major components, two of which are dominant and account for about nine-tenths of the employment. The largest component manufactures structural metal products—a miscellany ranging from bridge sections to bins, metal doors, windows, etc. It employs 200,000 men. The second major category, called "miscellaneous fabricated metal products," makes everything from dog chains to missiles and employs 700,000 men.

An examination of employment in this industry shows that the total number of workers increased by 24 percent between 1950 and 1960. Professional, managerial, and other white-collar workers increased 62 percent; skilled and semiskilled production workers increased by about 20 percent, but unskilled laborers decreased 9 percent. Thus, despite the general rise in employment and output in this industry, there was a drop in the demand for unskilled labor.

FIGURE 3. Men employed in the metal industries: 1950 and 1960. (*U.S. Census of Population, 1960, Vol. II,* Occupation by Industry, *Table 2; and* U.S. Census of Population: *1950, Vol. II, Table 84.*)

In view of these changes in the demand for labor in this industry, what happened to earnings? The figures for the eight major metal-producing and fabricating states are shown in Table 3. The states are shown in order of the size of their employment in this industry. They accounted for nearly three-fourths of the entire employment in this industry in 1960. The actual dollar earnings for unskilled, semiskilled, and all other workers (largely craftsmen and white-collar

TABLE 3. REGIONAL DIFFERENCES IN INCOME OF MEN IN THE METAL INDUSTRIES IN
1939, 1949, AND 1959

| | Amount of Earnings | | | | | | | |
| | Laborers | | | Operatives | | | Other Workers | |
State	1939	1949	1959	1939	1949	1959	1949	1959
Pennsylvania	$ 947	$2,414	$3,939	$1,153	$2,767	$4,597	$3,220	$5,624
Ohio	1,006	2,403	4,077	1,091	2,841	4,885	3,367	5,920
California	1,056	2,411	4,136	1,231	2,814	5,002	3,639	6,866
Illinois	950	2,506	4,448	1,124	2,931	5,034	3,517	6,321
New York	918	2,503	3,940	1,060	2,703	4,458	3,318	5,796
Michigan	962	2,645	4,134	1,150	2,997	4,726	3,691	6,246
Indiana	1,074	2,526	4,054	1,286	2,918	4,897	3,454	5,792
Alabama	701	2,032	3,565	887	2,316	4,301	3,073	5,864

| | Percent Increase, 1939–49 | | Percent Increase, 1949–59 | | |
State	Laborers	Operatives	Laborers	Operatives	Other Workers
Pennsylvania	155%	140%	63%	66%	75%
Ohio	139	160	70	72	76
California	128	129	72	78	89
Illinois	164	161	77	72	80
New York	173	155	57	65	75
Michigan	175	161	56	58	69
Indiana	134	127	60	68	68
Alabama	190	161	75	86	91

U.S. Census of Population: 1960, Detailed Characteristics, Tables 124 and 130; *U.S. Census of Population: 1950*. Vol. II, Tables 78 and 86; and *U.S. Census of Population: 1940*, Vol. III, Table 16.

workers) for 1939, 1949, and 1959 are shown in the first part of the table; percentage changes are shown in the second part. It is the latter figures that are of greatest interest because they show which groups made the greatest relative gains. There are some differences in the definition of earnings for each of the years shown, but they are not believed to create serious distortions in the figures for these workers.

In all states except Ohio and California, unskilled workers in this industry made greater relative gains than the semiskilled between 1939–49. Similar figures are not available for the higher paid "other" workers for 1939. Thus there was a tendency toward a narrowing of earnings differentials in this industry between 1939–49. But, during the decade 1949–59, the reverse was true. In every state there was a widening of differentials, with the highest paid "other" workers making the greatest relative gains, followed by the semiskilled workers and then the unskilled. In Pennsylvania, for example, laborers had a 63 percent increase in earnings between 1949–59, semiskilled operatives had a 66 percent increase, and professional, managerial, and other white-collar workers had a 75 percent increase. The same general pattern of wage movement was found in each of the other states shown. . . .

Source Notes

(The numbers on the left refer to the pages on which the data and quotations appear.)
321 Editors of *Fortune, The Changing American Market*. New York, Garden City Books (Hanover House), 1955, p. 52.
322 Sumner H. Slichter, *Economic Growth in the United States*. Baton Rouge, La., Louisiana State University Press, 1961 (New York, The Crowell-Collier Publishing Co., Collier Books, 1963, pp. 29–30).
322 Arnold J. Toynbee, *Civilization on Trial*. New York, Oxford University Press, 1948, p. 25.
322 Thorstein Veblen, *The Theory of the Leisure Class*. New York, The Modern Library, 1934, pp. 102–114.
323 Joseph A. Kahl, *The American Class Structure*. New York, Holt, Rinehart and Winston, Inc., 1957, p. 99.
325-27 Department of Labor figures used to compare earnings of skilled and unskilled factory workers are from Harry Ober, "Occupational Wage Differentials, 1907–1947," *Monthly Labor Review*, August, 1948.

Occupational Prestige in the United States, 1925–63

ROBERT W. HODGE, PAUL M. SIEGEL, AND PETER H. ROSSI

The research reported in this paper represents an attempt to add historical depth to the study of the prestige of occupations in the United States. It reports mainly on a replication conducted in 1963 of the National Opinion Research Center's well-known 1947 study of the prestige positions accorded to ninety occupations by a national sample of the American adult population.[1] We also deal with several fragmentary earlier studies, which together with the two main NORC studies, provide a rough time series going back to 1925. Since the two NORC studies were not replications of the earlier ones, we shall dwell mainly on change and stability in the prestige of occupations during the period from 1947 to 1963. . . .

Reprinted from the *American Journal of Sociology*, 70 (November 1964), pp. 286–302, by permission of the authors and the University of Chicago Press.

[1] The replication was undertaken as the first stage of a larger project supported by a National Science Foundation grant (NSF G85, "Occupations and Social Stratification") aimed at providing definitive prestige scores for a more representative sample of occupations and at uncovering some of the characteristics of occupations which generate their prestige scores. The replication was undertaken as the first step in the research program to determine whether appreciable shifts occurred in prestige scores in the time period 1947–63 so that the effects of improvements in technical procedures could be sorted out from effects of historical changes in any comparisons which would be undertaken between the 1947 study and the more definitive researches presently under way.

METHODS AND PROCEDURES

A small-scale replication of the 1947 study was undertaken in the spring of 1963. In order properly to compare the replication with the original, it was necessary to replicate the study using procedures as nearly identical as possible with those of the earlier study. The same question was used to elicit ratings, and the ninety job titles were rated in the same orders (using rotated blocks) in the same way. Most of the items (with the exception of those that were historically obsolete) were repeated. Even the sample was selected according to the outmoded quota sampling methods employed in 1947. The few new items included in the restudy were placed in the questionnaire after the occupational ratings.

Because of the stability of prestige positions of occupations from subgroup to subgroup in the 1947 study, it was felt that a relatively small national sample would be sufficient for the replication. In all a total of 651 interviews was collected according to quota sampling methods from a national sample of adults and youths.[2]

As in the 1947 study, occupational ratings were elicited by asking respondents to judge an occupation as having *excellent, good, average, somewhat below average, or poor* standing (along with a "don't know" option) in response to the item: "For each job mentioned, please pick out the statement that best gives *your own personal opinion* of the *general standing* that such a job has."

One indicator of prestige position is the proportion of respondents (among those rating an occupation) giving either an "excellent" or a "good" response. Another measure which can be derived from a matrix of ratings by occupation requires weighting the various responses with arbitrary numerical values: We can assign an excellent rating a numerical value of 100, a good rating the value of 80, an average rating the value of 60, a somewhat below average rating the value of 40, and a poor rating the value of 20. Calculating the numerical average of these arbitrarily assigned values over all respondents rating the occupation yields the NORC prestige score. This latter measure has received rather widespread use despite arbitrariness in the numerical weights assigned to the five possible ratings.[3]

---

[2] Justification for our claim that 651 cases suffice to give a reliable intertemporal comparison can be derived from examination of sampling error estimates based on the assumption of a random sample. Such estimates indicate that confidence limits at the 0.90 level for $p = 0.50$ and $N = 651$ are 0.47 and 0.53. For $N = 60$ (smaller than any subgroup used in this paper) the corresponding error estimates are 0.39 and 0.61. Thus for even relatively small subgroups any dramatic changes are likely to be detected, although it must be clearly understood that error estimates for quota sampling are only approximated by assuming that formulas for random samples apply.

[3] The reader will observe that the correlation between the two ways of ordering occupations need not be unity. Of the two measures mentioned above, the proportion of excellent or good ratings enjoys some advantages over the NORC prestige scores. Its range and variance are somewhat larger than the NORC prestige scores, which tend to obscure differences between occupations in the middle of the prestige hierarchy. However, the two measures are, in fact, highly intercorrelated ($r = .98$) and the advantages of the proportion of excellent or good ratings over the NORC prestige scores are largely statistical in nature. Throughout this paper, the bulk of our analysis employs the NORC prestige scores—a decision based largely on the wide use and popularity of the prestige scores derived from the original 1947 study.

The ratings and derived scores for each of the ninety occupations obtained in 1947 and in 1963 are shown in Table 1. We present the findings in such detail because of their intrinsic interest. However, the bulk of the analysis contained in this paper is more concerned with characteristics of the distributions of these ratings than with the positions of particular occupations.

CONGRUITIES IN OCCUPATIONAL PRESTIGE: 1947–63

The major result of the 1963 restudy is dramatically summarized in the product-moment correlation coefficient of .99 between the scores in 1947 and the scores in 1963. . . .

. . . The results indicate a striking similarity between the structure of the 1947 and the 1963 NORC scores. While we shall subsequently document a number of systematic shifts in the prestige of specific occupational groups,* it is abundantly clear that these shifts are small and did not produce any substantial re-ordering of the relative prestige of the ninety occupations under consideration here.

There are several good reasons for this observed stability. First, relative differential educational requirements, monetary rewards, and even something as nebulous as the functional importance of occupations are not subject to rapid change in an industrial society.[4] Second, any dramatic shifts in the prestige structure of occupations would upset the dependency which is presumed to hold between the social evaluation of a job, its educational prerequisities, its rewards, and its importance to society. Finally, instabilities would further ambiguities or status inconsistencies if the prestige structure were subject to marked and rapid change. Indeed, the meaning of achievement, career, seniority, and occupational mobility would be fundamentally altered if occupational prestige were subject to large-scale changes. No small amount of intragenerational mobility between prestige classes would, for example, be induced solely by the changing structure of occupational prestige *even though individuals did not change their occupations over time.* . . .

OCCUPATIONAL PRESTIGE SINCE 1925

Since the appearance of George S. Count's pioneering 1925 study of occupational prestige, a number of readings have been taken on the distribution of occupational prestige. These studies have utilized a variety of different measurement techniques and different types of samples of raters, college students being quite popular. However, there is evidence that the over-all structure of prestige

---

* [The material referred to is not included—Editor.]

[4] For a discussion of this point see Otis Dudley Duncan, "Properties and Characteristics of the Socio-economic Index," in Reiss *et al., op. cit.,* pp. 152–53. A correlation of .94 was found between an aggregate measure of the income of an occupation in 1940 and a similar indicator in 1950; a correlation of .97 was found between the proportion of high-school graduates in an occupation in 1940 and the same measure in 1950.

TABLE 1. DISTRIBUTION OF PRESTIGE RATINGS, UNITED STATES, 1947 AND 1963

| | March, 1947 | | | | | | | | June, 1963 | | | | | | | |
| | Per Cent | | | | | | | | Per Cent | | | | | | | |
Occupation	Excellent*	Good	Average	Below Average	Poor	Don't Know†	NORC Score	Rank	Excellent‡	Good	Average	Below Average	Poor	Don't Know§	NORC Score	Rank
U.S. Supreme Court justice	83	15	2	=	=	3	96	1	77	18	4	1	1	1	94	1
Physician	67	30	3	=	=	1	93	2.5	71	25	4	=	=	1	93	2
Nuclear physicist	48	39	11	1	1	51	86	18	70	23	5	1	=	10	92	3.5
Scientist	53	38	8	1	=	7	89	8	68	27	5	=	1	2	92	3.5
Government scientist	51	41	7	1	=	6	88	10.5	64	30	5	=	1	2	91	5.5
State governor	71	25	4	=	=	1	93	2.5	64	30	5	=	=	1	91	5.5
Cabinet member in the federal government	66	28	5	1	=	6	92	4.5	61	32	6	1	1	2	90	8
College professor	53	40	7	=	=	1	89	8	59	35	5	=	=	1	90	8
U.S. representative in Congress	57	35	6	1	1	4	89	8	58	33	6	2	=	2	90	8
Chemist	42	48	9	1	=	7	86	18	54	38	8	=	=	3	89	11
Lawyer	44	45	9	1	1	1	86	18	53	38	8	1	1	=	89	11
Diplomat in U.S. foreign Service	70	24	4	1	=	9	92	4.5	57	34	7	=	=	3	89	11
Dentist	42	48	9	1	=	=6	86	18	47	45	6	=	=	=	88	14
Architect	42	48	9	1	=	6	86	18	47	47	6	=	=	2	88	14
County judge	47	43	9	1	=	1	87	13	50	40	8	1	=	1	88	14
Psychologist	38	49	12	1	=	15	85	22	49	41	8	1	=	6	87	17.5
Minister	52	35	11	1	1	1	87	13	53	33	13	1	1	1	87	17.5
Member of the board of directors of a large corporation	42	47	10	1	=	5	86	18	42	51	6	1	=	1	87	17.5
Mayor of a large city	57	36	6	1	=	1	90	6	46	44	9	1	=	=	87	17.5
Priest	51	34	11	2	2	6	86	18	52	33	12	2	1	6	86	21.5
Head of a department in a state government	47	44	8	=	1	3	87	13	44	48	6	1	=	1	86	21.5
Civil engineer	33	55	11	1	=	5	84	23	40	52	8	1	=	2	86	21.5
Airline pilot	35	48	15	1	1	3	83	24.5	41	48	11	1	=	1	86	21.5
Banker	49	43	8	1	1	1	88	10.5	39	51	10	1	=	=	85	24.5
Biologist	29	51	18	1	1	16	81	29	38	50	11	1	=	6	85	24.5
Sociologist	31	51	16	1	1	23	82	26.5	35	48	15	1	1	10	83	26
Instructor in public schools	28	45	24	2	1	1	79	34	30	53	16	1	=	=	82	27.5

TABLE 1—Continued

Occupation	March, 1947 — Per Cent Excellent*	Good	Average	Below Average	Poor	Don't Know†	NORC Score	Rank	June, 1963 — Per Cent Excellent‡	Good	Average	Below Average	Poor	Don't Know§	NORC Score	Rank
Captain in the regular army	28	49	19	2	2	2	80	31.5	28	55	16	2	=	1	82	27.5
Accountant for a large business	25	57	17	1	=	3	81	29	27	55	17	1	=	=	81	29.5
Public school teacher	26	45	24	3	2	=	78	36	31	46	22	1	=	=	81	29.5
Owner of a factory that employs about 100 people	30	51	17	1	1	2	82	26.5	28	49	19	2	1	1	80	31.5
Building contractor	21	55	23	1	=	1	79	34	22	56	20	1	1	=	80	31.5
Artist who paints pictures that are exhibited in galleries	40	40	15	3	2	6	83	24.5	28	45	20	5	2	4	78	34.5
Musician in a symphony orchestra	31	46	19	3	1	5	81	29	25	45	25	3	1	3	78	34.5
Author of novels	32	44	19	2	2	9	80	31.5	26	46	22	4	2	5	78	34.5
Economist	25	48	24	2	1	22	79	34	20	53	24	2	1	12	78	34.5
Official of an international labor union	26	42	20	5	7	11	75	40.5	21	53	18	5	3	5	77	37
Railroad engineer	22	45	30	3	1	=	77	37.5	19	47	30	3	1	=	76	39
Electrician	15	38	43	4	1	1	73	45	18	45	34	2	1	=	76	39
County agricultural agent	17	53	28	2	=	5	77	37.5	13	54	30	2	1	4	76	39
Owner-operator of a printing shop	13	48	36	3	=	2	74	42.5	13	51	34	2	=	2	75	41.5
Trained machinist	14	43	38	5	1	2	73	45	15	50	32	4	=	1	75	41.5
Farm owner and operator	19	46	31	3	1	1	76	39	16	45	33	5	1	=	74	44
Undertaker	14	43	36	5	2	2	72	47	16	46	33	3	2	3	74	44
Welfare worker for a city government	16	43	35	4	2	4	73	45	17	44	32	3	2	2	74	44
Newspaper columnist	13	51	32	3	1	5	74	42.5	10	49	38	3	1	1	73	46
Policeman	11	30	46	11	2	1	67	55	16	38	37	6	2	1	72	47
Reporter on a daily newspaper	9	43	43	4	1	2	71	48	7	45	44	3	1	1	71	48
Radio announcer	17	45	35	3	=	2	75	40.5	9	42	44	3	1	1	70	49.5
Bookkeeper	8	31	55	6	=	1	68	51.5	9	40	45	5	1	=	70	49.5
Tenant farmer—one who owns livestock and machinery and manages the farm	10	37	40	11	2	1	68	51.5	11	37	42	8	3	1	69	51.5
Insurance agent	7	34	53	4	2	2	68	51.5	6	40	47	5	3	1	69	51.5
Carpenter	5	28	56	10	1	=	65	58	7	36	49	8	2	=	68	53
Manager of a small store in a city	5	40	50	4	1	1	69	49	7	40	48	7	2	=	67	54.5
A local official of a labor union	7	29	41	14	9	11	62	57	8	36	42	9	5	4	67	54.5
Mail carrier	8	26	54	10	2	1	66	57	7	29	53	10	1	=	66	57
Railroad conductor	8	30	52	9	1	1	67	55	6	33	48	10	3	=	66	57
Traveling salesman for a wholesale concern	6	35	53	5	1	2	68	51.5	4	33	54	7	3	2	66	57

Occupation	March, 1947 — Per Cent Excellent*	Good	Average	Below Average	Poor	Don't Know†	NORC Score	Rank	June, 1963 — Per Cent Excellent‡	Good	Average	Below Average	Poor	Don't Know§	NORC Score	Rank
Plumber	5	24	55	14	2	1	63	59.5	6	29	54	9	2	‖	65	59
Automobile repairman	5	21	58	14	2	‖	63	59.5	5	25	56	12	2	‖	64	60
Playground director	7	33	48	10	2	‖	67	55	6	29	46	15	4	3	63	62.5
Barber	3	17	56	20	4	1	59	66	4	25	56	13	4	1	63	62.5
Machine operator in a factory	4	20	53	20	3	2	60	64.5	6	24	51	15	4	1	63	62.5
Owner-operator of a lunch stand	4	24	55	14	3	1	62	62	4	25	57	11	3	2	63	65.5
Corporal in the regular army	5	21	48	20	6	3	60	64.5	6	25	47	15	6	1	62	65.5
Garage mechanic	4	21	57	17	1	‖	62	62	4	22	56	15	3	‖	62	67
Truck driver	2	11	49	29	9	‖	54	71	3	18	54	19	5	2	59	68
Fisherman who owns his own boat	3	20	48	21	8	7	58	68	1	19	51	19	8	4	58	68
Clerk in a store	2	14	61	20	3	1	58	68	3	14	56	22	6	1	56	70
Milk route man	2	10	52	29	7	‖	54	71	3	12	55	23	8	‖	56	70
Streetcar motorman	3	16	55	21	7	2	58	68	2	16	46	27	7	2	56	70
Lumberjack	3	11	48	29	10	8	53	73	4	16	46	29	8	3	55	72.5
Restaurant cook	3	13	44	29	11	3	54	71	2	15	44	26	11	3	55	72.5
Singer in a nightclub	1	9	43	23	18	6	52	74.5	2	16	43	24	14	3	54	74
Filling station attendant	2	7	48	34	8	1	52	74.5	3	11	41	34	11	1	51	75
Dockworker	2	9	34	37	20	8	47	81.5	3	9	43	33	14	3	50	77.5
Railroad section hand	3	8	35	33	21	3	48	79.5	3	10	39	29	17	2	50	77.5
Night watchman	3	11	33	35	21	1	47	81.5	2	13	39	32	19	1	50	77.5
Coal miner	4	8	33	31	17	2	49	77.5	2	8	34	31	16	2	50	77.5
Restaurant waiter	2	8	37	36	17	1	48	79.5	3	8	42	32	18	1	49	80.5
Taxi driver	2	8	38	35	19	1	49	77.5	1	8	39	31	22	1	49	80.5
Farm hand	3	12	35	31	25	1	50	76	2	12	31	32	19	2	48	83
Janitor	1	7	30	37	25	4	44	85.5	1	9	35	35	21	1	48	83
Bartender	1	6	32	32	29	2	44	85.5	2	7	42	28	22	2	48	85
Clothes presser in a laundry	2	6	35	36	21	2	46	83	‖	7	31	38	21	1	45	85
Soda fountain clerk	1	5	34	40	20	2	45	84	‖	5	30	44	20	1	44	86
Sharecropper—one who owns no livestock or equipment and does not manage farm	1	6	24	28	41	3	40	87								
Garbage collector	1	4	16	26	53	2	35	88	1	8	26	28	37	2	42	87
Street sweeper	1	3	14	29	53	1	34	89	2	5	21	32	41	1	39	88
Shoe shiner	1	2	13	28	56	2	33	90	‖	3	17	30	46	2	34	89
Average	22	31	30	11	7	4	70	—	22	32	29	11	6	2	72	—

* Bases for the 1947 occupational ratings are 2,920 less "don't know" and not answered for each occupational title.

† Base is 2,920 in all cases.

‡ Bases for the 1963 occupational ratings are 651 less "don't know" and not answered for each occupational title.

§ Base is 651 in all cases.

‖ Less than 0.5 per cent.

Source of 1947 distributions: Albert J. Reiss, Jr., and others, *Occupations and Social Status* (New York: Free Press of Glencoe, 1963), Table ii-9.

is invariant under quite drastic changes in technique.[5] Furthermore, one of the major findings of the original 1947 NORC survey was that *all* segments of the population share essentially the same view of the prestige hierarchy and rate occupations in much the same way.[6] With these findings in mind, we may utilize selected prestige studies conducted since 1925 to ascertain whether any substantial changes in the prestige structure of occupations have occurred since that date.

A pre-World War II and post-Depression bench mark is provided by the investigations of Mapheus Smith, who provides the mean ratings of one hundred occupations as rated by college and high-school students in the academic years 1938–39, 1939–40, and 1940–41. The rating technique used by Smith differs considerably from that employed in the NORC study. Respondents were originally required to *rank* occupations according to how far an average incumbent would be seated from the guest of honor at a dinner honoring a celebrity and then to *rate* the occupations on a 100-point scale of prestige (according to the rater's personal estimation).[7]

A pre-Depression bench mark of occupational prestige is provided by Counts's study, which provides rankings of forty-five occupations according to their "social standing." The data were collected from high-school students, high-school teachers, and college students.[8] Unlike the NORC and Smith studies, rankings rather than ratings were obtained by Counts. Counts provides rankings for six groups of respondents, and a continuous type variable can be derived by taking the average rank of an occupation over the six groups, weighting for the number of respondents in each group.

These four studies, then, provide an opportunity to examine occupational prestige since 1925. A fairly large number of titles are shared in common between each pair of studies, so that the number of titles utilized in any given comparison is larger than the total number of titles that have been rated in many prestige studies.[9]

Product-moment correlations between the prestige ratings of occupations common to each pair of studies are presented in Table 2, together with the number of matching titles. It is evident from the data presented in Table 2 that *there have been no substantial changes in occupational prestige in the United States since 1925*. The lowest correlation observed is .934, and this occurs between

[5] One study, e.g., requested respondents to sort seventy of the occupations in the NORC list into groups of *similar* occupations. The respondent was then asked to order the groups of similar occupations he had formed into social levels. Nevertheless, a rank-order correlation of .97 was found between scores derived from this study and scores obtained from the 1947 NORC study (see John D. Campbell, "Subjective Aspects of Occupational Status" [unpublished Ph.D. thesis, Harvard University, 1952], chap. ii).

[6] Reiss *et al.*, *op. cit.*, pp. 189–90.

[7] Mapheus Smith, "An Empirical Scale of Prestige Status of Occupations," *American Sociological Review*, VIII (April, 1943), 185–92.

[8] George S. Counts, "The Social Status of Occupations: A Problem in Vocational Guidance," *School Review*, XXXIII (January, 1925), 16–27.

[9] See, e.g., the national studies cited by Alex Inkeles and Peter H. Rossi, "National Comparisons of Occupational Prestige," *American Journal of Sociology*, LXI (January, 1956), 329–39.

TABLE 2. Correlations Between Occupational Prestige Ratings at Selected Time Periods, 1925–63*

Study and Time Period	C	S	X	Y
C (Counts' mean ranks, 1925)	–	.968	.955	.934
S (Smith's mean ratings, *ca.* 1940)	23	–	.982	.971
X (NORC scores, 1947)	29	38	–	.990
Y (NORC scores, 1963)	29	38	90	–

* Correlations placed above diagonal; no. of matching titles placed below diagonal.
Sources: George S. Counts, "The Social Status of Occupations: A Problem in Vocational Guidance," *School Review*, XXXIII (January, 1925), 20–21, Table 1; Mapheus Smith, "An Empirical Scale of Prestige Status of Occupations," *American Sociological Review*, VIII (April, 1943), 187–88, Table I; National Opinion Research Center, "Jobs and Occupations: A Popular Evaluation," *Opinion News*, IX (September 1, 1947), 3–13. See text for details.

the 1963 NORC scores and the mean ranks derived from the 1925 study of Counts. In view of the high correlation between 1947 and 1963 NORC scores, it is not particularly surprising that high correlations are found between any pair of studies from adjacent points in time. That no substantial changes are observed over a span of approximately 40 years is a bit more surprising and is further evidence of constraints toward the stability of prestige hierachies. . . .

CONCLUSIONS

The theme of this paper has been accurately captured by an eminent pathologist who remarked of biochemical phenomena: "Universal instability of constituents seems to be compatible with a stability and even monotony of organized life."[10] Such is the picture one gleans of occupational structures from the present endeavor. Between 1947 and 1963 we are fully aware that many *individual* changes in occupation were under way as men advanced in their career lines, retired, or entered the labor force. Yet, despite the turnover of incumbents, occupational morphology, at least insofar as prestige is concerned, remained remarkably stable. To be sure, systematic patterns of change could be detected, but one would miss the import of this paper if one failed to recognize that these changes were minor relative to the over-all stability. The view developed here is that a stable system of occupational prestige provides a necessary foundation to which individuals may anchor their careers.

System maintenance is, however, only part of the story. Small, but nevertheless systematic, changes can be detected between 1947 and 1963. In some cases these changes appear to be attributable to increasing public knowledge of occupations, but it was suggested that any complete understanding of prestige shifts and their causes would require a time series pertaining to the standing of particular occupations. The present study is a step in that direction. Our purposes

[10] René Dubos, *The Dreams of Reason: Science and Utopias* (New York: Columbia University Press, 1961), p. 124.

will be adequately accomplished if others are stimulated to make periodic readings of, as it were, the occupational weather.

National Comparisons of Occupational Prestige

ALEX INKELES AND PETER H. ROSSI

During the latter part of the nineteenth and the first half of the twentieth centuries the factory system of production was introduced, at least on a small scale, to most areas of the world. The factory has generally been accompanied by a relatively standard set of occupations, including the factory manager (sometimes also owner) and his administrative and clerical staff, engineering and lesser technical personnel, foremen, skilled, semiskilled, and unskilled workers. In the factory, authority and responsibility are allocated largely according to the degree of technical or administrative competence required for the job. In addition, the allocation of material and social rewards, the latter generally in the form of deference, is closely adjusted to levels of competence and degrees of authority and responsibility. The pattern of differentiation of authority is undoubtedly functionally necessary to the productive activity of the factory, and it may be that the associated pattern of reward differentiation is also functionally necessary.

There is, however, no clear-cut imperative arising from the structure of the factory as such which dictates how the incumbents of its typical statuses should be *evaluated* by the population at large. One possibility is that in popular esteem the typical occupations will stand relative to one another in a rank order strictly comparable to their standing in the formal hierarchy of competence, authority, and reward in the factory. It is also possible, however, that the popular evaluation of these occupations will be quite different. Indeed, where the factory system has been introduced into societies like those of Spain or Japan, with well-established values based on tradition and expressive of the culture, one might expect significant differences between an occupation's standing in the formal hierarchy of the industrial system and its position in the popular ranking scheme.

Thus the interaction of the two systems—the standardized modern occupational system and the individual national value pattern for rating occupations—presents an interesting and important problem in comparative sociology.

We may posit two extreme positions in his interaction, while granting that it might be difficult to find live exponents of either. The extreme "structuralist" would presumably insist that the modern industrial occupational system is a highly coherent system, relatively impervious to influence by traditional culture patterns. Indeed, he might go so far as to insist that the traditional ranking system would in time have to be subsumed under, or integrated into, the industrial

Reprinted from the *American Journal of Sociology*, 61 (January, 1956), pp. 329–339, by permission of the authors and the University of Chicago Press.

system. Consequently, his argument would run, even such occupations as priest, judge, provincial governor, not part of the modern occupational system and often given unusual deference, would come in time to have roughly the same standing relative to one another and to other occupations, no matter what their national cultural setting.

By contrast, an extreme "culturalist" might insist that within each country or culture the distinctive local value system would result in substantial—and, indeed, sometimes extreme—differences in the evaluation of particular jobs in the standardized modern occupational system. For example, he might assume that in the United States the company director would be rated unusually high because of our awe of the independent businessman and large corporations or that in the Soviet Union the standing of industrial workers would be much higher relative to managerial personnel than in Germany, with its emphasis on sharply differentiated status hierarchies. Furthermore, he might argue that the more traditional occupational roles assigned special importance in particular cultures would continue to maintain their distinctive positions in the different national hierarchies. Indeed, he might hold that the characteristic roles of the modern industrial system would come to be subsumed within the traditional rating sytem, each factory occupation being equated with some traditional occupation and then assigned a comparable rank.

A systematic test of these contrasting positions is not beyond the capacity of contemporary social research. A standard list of occupations—say thirty or forty in number— might be presented for evaluation to comparable samples from countries presenting a range of culture types and degrees of industrialization. The list should contain both standard industrial occupations and the common, but differentially valued, traditional roles (e.g., priest, legislator, etc.).

Data are available which, though far from completely adequate, will carry us a long way beyond mere speculation on these matters. In the postwar years studies of occupational ratings have been conducted in and reported on five relatively industrialized countries: the United States, Great Britain, New Zealand, Japan, and Germany.[1] In addition, the authors have available previously unpublished data for a sixth country, the Soviet Union.

Since these six studies[2] were, on the whole, undertaken quite independently, our ideal research design is clearly far from being fulfilled. Nevertheless, the data do permit tentative and exploratory cross-national comparisons.

[1] Additional studies of occupational prestige are available for the United States and for Australia. The authors decided to restrict the United States data to the most comprehensive study available. The Australian case (Ronald Taft, "The Social Grading of Occupations in Australia," *British Journal of Sociology*, Vol. IV, No. 2 [June, 1953]) was not included in this report because it was felt that little was to be gained by the inclusion of another Anglo-Saxon country.

[2] (1) A. A. Congalton, "The Social Grading of Occupations in New Zealand," *British Journal of Sociology*, Vol. IV, No. 1 (March, 1953) (New Zealand data); (2) John Hall and D. Caradog Jones, "The Social Grading of Occupations," *British Journal of Sociology*, Vol. I, No. 1 (January, 1950) (Great Britain); (3) National Opinion Research Center, "Jobs and Occupations: A Popular Evaluation," in Reinhard Bendix and S. Martin Lipset, *Class, Status, and Power* (Glencoe, Ill.: Free Press, 1953) (United States data); (4) the Schleswig-Holstein

THE COMPARABILITY OF RESEARCH DESIGNS

The elements of similarity and difference in the six studies may be quickly assessed from the following summary of their essential features:

A. Population studied

United States: National sample of adults fourteen years and over; 2,920 respondents

Japan: Sample of males twenty to sixty-eight years of age in the six large cities of Japan; 899 respondents

Great Britain: Written questionnaires distributed through adult-education centers and other organizations; 1,056 returns (percentage returned unspecified)

U.S.S.R.: Sample of displaced persons, mostly in DP camps near Munich, Germany, and some former DP's now residing on eastern seaboard of U.S.; 2,100 written questionnaires

New Zealand: Sample collected mainly by interviews with inhabitants of town of 2,000, partly by mailed questionnaires (12 per cent returns) sent out to town of 4,000; 1,033 questionnaires and interviews used

Germany: 1,500 Schleswig-Holsteiners: vocational-school students, university students, and male adults (not otherwise specified); adult sample only used here

B. Overlap among occupations studied

Each study involved a different number of occupations, ranging from 88 in the case of the National Opinion Research Center American study to 13 in the Soviet research. Only the New Zealand and the British groups studied exactly the same occupations. Each of the remaining four studies used a different, but partially overlapping, set of occupations.

In order to make comparisons between pairs of countries, each occupation studied in each research was matched, when possible, with an occupation in the data gathered in the other country. In many cases it was necessary to disregard the information about an occupation in one of the paired countries because no comparable occupation was studied in the other. In other instances, in order to increase the number of occupations which could be compared for any given pair of countries, occupations were matched which were only very roughly comparable, e.g., Buddhist priest and minister, or collective farm chairman and farm owner and operator. In most cases, however, a direct correspondence characterizes the pairs of occupations which

data are taken from an article published in *Der Spiegel*, June 30, 1954, reporting a study by Professor Karl-Martin Bolte, of Christian-Albrecht University, in Kiel, Germany, to be published early in 1955; (5) Research Committee, Japan Sociological Society, "Report of a Sample Survey of Social Stratification and Mobility in the Six Large Cities of Japan" (mimeographed; December 1952) (the authors are grateful to Professor Kunio Odaka, of the University of Tokyo, for bringing this valuable study to their attention); and (6) the Soviet materials were collected by the Project on the Soviet Social System of the Russian Research Center at Harvard University. The authors plan to publish several articles dealing with the special features of the occupational ratings secured from former Soviet citizens.

are being equated. The reader is invited to turn to Table 3 (below), where the lists of occupations used from each of the researches are printed. The occupations listed on any row or line were matched. The number of pairs of similar or identical occupations for each cross-national comparison is shown in Table 1.

TABLE 1. Number of Identical or Similar Occupations Rated Between Six Countries

	U.S.	Great Britain	U.S.S.R.	Japan	New Zealand	Germany
United States	–	24	10	25	24	20
Great Britain	–	–	7	14	30	12
U.S.S.R.	–	–	–	7	7	8
Japan	–	–	–	–	14	19
New Zealand	–	–	–	–	–	12
Total occupations studied	88	30	13	30	30	38

C. Nature of rating task

United States: Respondents were asked: ". . . Please pick out the statement that best gives your own *personal opinion* of the *general standing* that such a job has. Excellent standing, good standing, average standing, somewhat below average, poor standing."

Japan: Respondents were given a set of thirty cards and asked: ". . . Think of the general reputations they have with people, and sort them into five or more groups, from those which people think highly of to those which are not thought so well of."

Great Britain: Respondents were told: "We should like to know in what order, *as to their social standing*, you would grade the occupations in the list given to you. [Rate them] . . . in terms of five main social classes . . . ABCDE."

U.S.S.R.: Respondents were asked: "Taking everything into consideration, how desirable was it to have the job of (_____) in the Soviet Union? Very desirable? Desirable? So-so? Undesirable? Very undesirable?"

New Zealand: Same as in Great Britain.

Germany: The source is unfortunately not very specific about the rating task assigned. The respondents were apparently asked to rank-order a list of 38 occupations presented as one slate.

D. Computing prestige position

With the exception of the German study, each research presents a "prestige score" for each of the occupations studied. These scores, computed variously, represent in each case the "average" rating given to each of the occupations by the entire sample of raters used. The German study presented only the rank-order positions of the occupations.

One is not sure whether differences between nations are generated by the differences in the questionnaires or the differences in the nations themselves.

However, similarities in the prestige hierarchies, particularly when they are striking, are somewhat strengthened by the same lack of comparability in research designs and in the occupations matched to one another. Similarities may be interpreted as showing the extent to which design and other differences are overcome by the comparability among the prestige hierarchies themselves.

COMPARABILITY OF OCCUPATIONAL PRESTIGE HIERARCHIES

Since each study included some occupations used in another study, it is possible to compare the prestige hierarchies of occupations in pairs of countries by computing correlation coefficients for the scores (or ranks) of occupations. The fifteen correlation coefficients which result are presented in Table 2.[3] It

TABLE 2*. CORRELATIONS BETWEEN PRESTIGE SCORES (OR RANKS) GIVEN TO COMPARABLE OCCUPATIONS IN SIX NATIONAL STUDIES

	U.S.S.R.	Japan	Great Britain	New Zealand	U.S.	Germany†
U.S.S.R.	–	.74	.83	.83	.90	.90
Japan	–	–	.92	.91	.93	.93
Great Britain	–	–	–	.97	.94	.97
New Zealand	–	–	–	–	.97	.96
United States	–	–	–	–	–	.96
Av. correlation	.84	.89	.93	.93	.94	.94

* See Table 1 for numbers of occupations involved in each comparison.

† All coefficients are product-moment correlations, with the exception of those involving Germany, which are rank-order coefficients.

will be seen immediately that the levels of correlation are considerably higher than the magnitude to be expected if there were only rough agreement on placement in the top and bottom halves of the prestige hierarchy. Indeed, twelve of the fifteen coefficients are above .9, and only one is below .8. The three coefficients below .9 all concern the Soviet ratings, which, it will be recalled, involve only a very small number of occupations, maximizing the chances for lower correlations arising from merely one or two "mismatches."

For most of the comparisons, furthermore, the findings go beyond establishing mere comparability of rank orders. With the exception of the correlations involving Germany, each coefficient represents the relationships between prestige *scores* given to the same occupations in two different nations. Hence there is a high relationship between the relative "distance" between occupations, as expressed in score differences, as well. In other words, if, of two occupations,

[3] Note that the correlation coefficients are all product-moment correlations, with the exception of the five coefficients involving the German study, which are rank-order correlations. With the exception noted, these coefficients represent the degree of similarity between the prestige *scores* given to the occupations.

one is given a much lower score than the other by the raters in one country, this difference in prestige scores and not merely crude rank order also obtains in another country.

It should also be noted that these high correlations were obtained by using samples of occupations which were not strictly identical from country to country, including such very crude comparisons already mentioned as that of collective farm chairman and farm owner and operator. One may anticipate that if the occupations studied were more uniform, the similarities of prestige hierarchies from country to country would be even higher.

In other words, *despite the heterogeneity in research design, there exists among the six nations a marked degree of agreement on the relative prestige of matched occupations.* To this extent, therefore, it appears that the "structuralist" expectation is more nearly met than is the expectation based on the culturalist position.

Each of the six nations differs in the extent to which its prestige hierarchy resembles those of other nations. The average of the correlations for each nation, contained in the bottom row of Table 2, expresses these differences among nations quantitatively. Thus we may see that the American and German occupational prestige hierarchies are most similar to those of other nations, while the Soviet and Japanese hierarchies are most dissimilar. When we consider that the Soviet Union and Japan are, of the six, the more recently industrialized cultures, we may see there some small degree of evidence for the culturalist position.

Furthermore, if we examine the correlations among the three nations which have the closest cultural ties and which share a common historical background and language—Great Britain, the United States, and New Zealand—we find these coefficients to be among the highest in Table 2. Again, the evidence to some extent supports the interpretation of a small "cultural" effect. However, the coefficients in question are not sufficiently distinguished in size from those involving Germany[4] and the three Anglo-Saxon nations to allow much weight to be given to the influence of the common Anglo-Saxon culture. In other words, whatever the national differences between the six, they do not greatly affect the general pattern of the prestige hierarchy. . . .

SUMMARY

To sum up, our examination of occupational ratings in six modern industrialized countries reveals an extremely high level of agreement, going far beyond chance expectancy, as to the relative prestige of a wide range of specific occupations, despite the variety of sociocultural settings in which they are found.

[4] Since the correlations involving Germany are rank-order correlations, it is difficult to make comparisons of such coefficients with others in Table 1. However, the relationship between rank-order correlations and product-moment correlations is rather high in the upper ranges, and it can be taken for granted that if prestige scores were available for the German ratings, the analysis shown in Table 2 would not be materially altered.

TABLE 3

United States	Score	Germany	Rank	Great Britain	Score	New Zealand	Score	Japan	Score	U.S.S.R.	Score
United States:		*Germany:*		*Great Britain:*		*New Zealand*		*Japan:*		*U.S.S.R.:*	
Physician	93	Doctor	2	Medical officer	1.3	Medical officer	1.4	Doctor	7.0	Doctor	75
State governor	93	Univ. professor	1					Prefectural gov.	3.8		
College professor	89							Univ. professor	4.6	Scientific worker	73
Scientist	89										
County judge	87							Local court judge	4.7		
Head of dept. in state government	87	High civil servant (Regierungsrat—höherer Beamter)	4	Civil servant	6.0	Civil servant	7.0	Section head of a government office	7.2		
Minister	87	Minister (Pfarrer)	6	Non-conformist minister	6.4	Non-conformist minister	5.9	Priest of a Buddhist temple	12.5		
Architect	86	(Elec. engineer)*	10					(Architect)	9.5		
Lawyer	86			Country solicitor	2.6	Country solicitor	3.8				
Member of board of directors of large corporation	86	Factory director (Fabrikdirektor)	5	Company director	1.6	Company director	3.6	Officer of large company	5.5	Factory manager	65
Civil engineer	84	Elec. engineer	10					(Architect)†	9.5	Engineer	73
Owner of a factory that employs about 100 people	82							Owner of a small or medium-sized factory	10.2		
Accountant for a large business	81			Chartered accountant	3.2	Chartered accountant	5.7	(Company office clerk)‡	16.1	Bookkeeper	62
Captain in regular army	80	Major (in armed forces)	8							Officer in the armed services	58
Building contractor	79			Jobbing master builder	11.4	Jobbing master builder	10.7				
Instructor in public schools (teacher)	78	Elem.-school teacher (Volksschullehrer)	11	Elem.-school teacher	10.8	Elem.-school teacher	10.3	Elem.-school teacher	11.7	Teacher	55
Farm owner and operator	76	Farmer (Bauer—mittelgrosser Betrieb)	13	Farmer	7.3	Farmer	8.1	Small independent farmer	16.4	Chairman of collective farm	38
Official of international labor union	75							Chairman of national labor federation	10.8		
Electrician	73										
Trained machinist	73	Skilled industrial worker (Industriefacharbeiter)	24	Fitter (elec.)	17.6	Fitter (elec.)	15.8				
Reporter on daily newspaper	71			News reporter	11.8	News reporter	13.8	Newspaper reporter	11.2		
Bookkeeper	68	Bank teller (bookkeeper in bank)	19	Routine clerk	16.1	Routine clerk	16.4	Company office clerk	16.1	(Bookkeeper)§	62

* Used here only for comparison with Japan. For comparison with other countries, see line beginning "United States civil engineer."
† Architect is the only occupation of a technical nature in Japan and was used here as a comparison only with the Soviet Union.
‡ Used here only for comparison with the Soviet Union. For comparison with other countries, see line beginning "United States bookkeeper."
§ Used here only for comparison with Japan. For comparison with other countries, see line beginning "United States accountant for a large business."

United States		Germany		Great Britain		New Zealand		Japan		U.S.S.R.	
Occupation	*Score*	*Occupation*	*Rank*	*Occupation*	*Score*	*Occupation*	*Score*	*Occupation*	*Score*	*Occupation*	*Score*
Insurance agent	68	Insurance agent	20	Insurance agent	14.6	Insurance agent	16.1	Insurance agent	20.2	Rank-and-file worker	48
Traveling salesman for wholesale concern	68			Commercial traveler	12.0	Commercial traveler	14.1				
Policeman	67	Postman	23	Policeman	16.1	Policeman	15.5	Policeman	16.4		
Mail carrier	66	Carpenter	18	Carpenter	18.6	Carpenter	17.0	Carpenter	20.2		
Carpenter	65	Non-commissioned officer	31								
Corporal in regular army	60										
Machine operator in factory	60	Machine operator (Maschinen-schlosser-Geselle)	26	(Composite of fitter, carpenter, bricklayer, tractor driver, coal hewer)‖	20.5	(Composite of fitter, carpenter, bricklayer, tractor driver, coal hewer)‖	20.9	Latheman	21.1		
Barber	59	Barber	16					Barber	20.5		
Clerk in a store	58	Store clerk (Verkäufer im Lebensmittel geschäft)	28	Shop assistant	20.2	Shop assistant	20.2	Department-store clerk	19.8		
Fisherman who owns own boat	58							Fisherman	22.0		
Streetcar motorman	58	Conductor	33					Bus driver	20.9		
Restaurant cook	54			Chef	13.8	Chef	21.8				
Truck driver	54			Carter	25.8	Carrier#	20.2				
Farm hand	50	Farm laborer (worker)	36	Agricultural laborer	25.5	Agricultural laborer	24.4			Rank-and-file collective farmer	18
Coal miner	49			Coal hewer	23.2	Coal hewer	24.7	Coal miner	23.7		
Restaurant waiter	48	Waiter (Kellner)	30	Dock laborer	27.0	Dock laborer	28.3				
Dock worker	47			Barman	26.4	Barman	28.3				
Bartender	44			Road sweeper	28.9	Road sweeper	28.9	Road worker	24.8		
Street sweeper	34	(Unskilled laborer)**	38								
Shoe shiner	33	Bricklayer	27	Bricklayer	20.2	Bricklayer	19.3	Shoe shiner	26.9		
		Clothing-store owner	12	Business manager	6.0	Business manager	5.3	Owner of a retail store	15.3		
		Tailor	14	Works manager	6.4	Works manager	7.9	Tailor	17.7		
		Street peddler	35	News agent and tobacconist	15.0	News agent and tobacconist	15.4	Street-stall keeper	24.9		
				Tractor driver	23.0	Tractor driver	22.8				
				Railway porter	25.3	Railway porter	25.3				

‖ Used here only for comparison with the Soviet Union. For comparison with other countries, see individual occupations as they appear later in the table.
As there was no comparable occupation in New Zealand, the occupation substituted was carrier.
** Used here only for comparison with Japan.

This strongly suggests that there is a relatively invariable hierarchy of prestige associated with the industrial system, even when it is placed in the context of larger social systems which are otherwise differentiated in important respects. . . .

Socialization and Social Class Through Time and Space

URIE BRONFENBRENNER

BACKGROUND AND RESOURCES

During the past dozen years, a class struggle has been taking place in American social psychology—a struggle, fortunately, not *between* but *about* social classes. In the best social revolutionary tradition the issue was joined with a manifesto challenging the assumed superiority of the upper and middle classes and extolling the neglected virtues of the working class. There followed a successful revolution with an overthrow of the established order in favor of the victorious proletariat, which then reigned supreme—at least for a time. These dramatic changes had, as always, their prophets and precursors, but they reached a climax in 1946 with the publication of Davis and Havighurst's influential paper on "Social Class and Color Differences in Child Rearing."[1] The paper cited impressive statistical evidence in support of the thesis that middle-class parents "place their children under a stricter regimen, with more frustration of their impulses than do lower-class parents." For the next eight years, the Davis–Havighurst conclusion was taken as the definitive statement of class differences in socialization. Then, in 1954, came the counterrevolution; Maccoby and Gibbs published the first report[2] of a study of child-rearing practices in the Boston area which, by and large, contradicted the Chicago findings: in general, middle-class parents were found to be "more permissive" than those in the lower class.

In response, one year later, Havighurst and Davis[3] presented a reanalysis of their data for a subsample more comparable in age to the subjects of the Boston study. On the basis of a careful comparison of the two sets of results, they concluded that "the disagreements between the findings of the two studies

From "Socialization and Social Class Through Time and Space" by Urie Bronfenbrenner from *Readings in Social Psychology*, Third Edition, edited by E. E. Maccoby, T. M. Newcomb, and E. L. Hartley. Copyright 1947, 1952, © 1958 by Holt, Rinehart and Winston, Inc. Reprinted by permission of Holt, Rinehart and Winston, Inc.

[1] A. Davis and R. J. Havighurst, "Social Class and Color Differences in Child Rearing," *Am. Sociol. Rev.*, 1948, XI, 698–710.

[2] E. E. Maccoby, P. K. Gibbs, and the staff of the Laboratory of Human Development at Harvard University, "Methods of Child Rearing in Two Social Classes," in W. E. Martin and C. B. Standler (eds.), *Readings in Child Development* (New York: Harcourt, Brace & Co., 1954).

[3] Havighurst and Davis, "A Comparison of the Chicago and Harvard Studies of Social Class Differences in Child Rearing," *Am. Sociol. Rev.* 1955, XX, 438–442.

are substantial and large" and speculated that these differences might be attributable either to genuine changes in child-rearing practices over time or to technical difficulties of sampling and item equivalence.

A somewhat different view, however, was taken by Sears, Maccoby, and Levin[4] in their final report of the Boston study. They argued that Davis and Havighurst's interpretation of the Chicago data as reflecting greater permissiveness for the working-class parent was unwarranted on two counts. First, they cited the somewhat contrasting results of still another research—that of Klatskin[5] in support of the view that class differences in feeding, weaning, scheduling, and toilet training "are not very stable or customary." Second, they contended that the Chicago findings of greater freedom of movement for the lower class child were more properly interpreted not as "permissiveness" but as "a reflection of rejection, a pushing of the child out of the way." Such considerations led the Boston investigators to conclude:

This re-examination of the Chicago findings suggests quite clearly the same conclusion that must be reached from Klatskins' study and from our own: the middle-class mothers were generally more permissive and less punitive toward their young children than were working-class mothers. Unfortunately, the opposite interpretation, as presented by Davis and Havighurst, has been widely accepted in education circles during the past decade. This notion of working-class permissiveness has been attractive for various reasons. It has provided an easy explanation of why working-class children have lower academic achievement motivation than do middle-class children—their mothers place less restrictive pressure on them. It has also provided a kind of compensatory comfort for those educators who have been working hard toward the goal of improving educational experiences for the noncollege-oriented part of the school population. In effect, one could say, lower-class children may lack the so highly desirable academic motivation, but the lack stems from a "good" reason—the children were permissively reared.[6]

It would appear that there are a number of unresolved issues between the protagonists of the principal points of view—issues both as to the facts and their interpretation. At such times it is not unusual for some third party to attempt a reappraisal of events in a broader historical perspective with the aid of documents and information previously not available. It is this which the present writer hopes to do. He is fortunate in having at his disposal materials not only from the past and present, but also seven manuscripts unpublished at the time of this writing, which report class differences in child-rearing practices at four different places and five points in time. To begin with, Bayley and Schaefer[7] have reanalyzed data from the Berkeley Growth Study to provide information on class differences in maternal-behavior ratings made from 1928 to 1932, when

---

[4] R. R. Sears, Maccoby, and H. Levin, *Patterns of Child Rearing* (Evanston, Ill.: Row, Peterson & Co., 1957).

[5] E. H. Klatskin, "Shifts in Child Care Practices in Three Social Classes under an Infant Care Program of Flexible Methodology," *Am. J. Orthopsychiat.*, 1952, XXII, 52–61.

[6] Sears, Maccoby, and Levin, *op. cit.*, pp. 446–447.

[7] N. Bayley and E. S. Schaefer, "Relationships between Socioeconomic Variables and the Behavior of Mothers toward Young Children," unpublished manuscript, 1957.

TABLE 1. DESCRIPTION OF SAMPLES

Sample	Principal Investigator Source	Date of Field Work	Age	No. of Cases			Description of Sample
				Total	Middle Class	Working Class	
National Cross Section,* I II III IV	Anderson	1932	0–1 1–5 6–12 1–12	494 2,420 865 3,285	217 1,131 391 1,522	277 1,289 474 1,763	National sample of white families "having child between 1 and 5 years of age" and "representing each major geographic area, each size of community and socioeconomic class in the United States." About equal number of males and females. SES (seven classes) based on Minnesota Scale for Occupational Classification.
Berkeley, Cal., I–II	Bayley and Schaefer	1928–32 1939–42	1–3 9–11	31 31	Information not available		Subjects of both sexes from Berkeley Growth Study, "primarily middle class but range from unskilled laborer, relief, and three-years education to professional, $10,000 income and doctoral degrees." SES measures include education, occupation (Taussig Scale), income, home and neighborhood rating, and composite scale.
Yellow Springs, Ohio	Baldwin	1940	3–12	124	Information not available		Families enrolled in Fels Research Institute Home Visiting Program. "Above average" in socioeconomic status but include "a number of uneducated parents and from the lower economic levels." No SES index computed but graphs show relationships by education and income. Middle-class sample "mainly" from mothers of nursery-school children; lower class from "areas of poor housing." All mothers native born.
Chicago, Ill., I*	Davis and Havighurst	1943	5 (approx.)	100	48	52	Two-level classification SES following Warner based on occupation, education, residential area, type of home, etc.
Chicago, Ill., II	Duvall	1943–44	5 (approx.)	433	230	203	Negro and white (Jewish and non-Jewish) mothers. Data collected at "regular meetings of mothers' groups." SES classification (four levels) following Warner.

Location	Author	Year	Age				Description
New Haven Conn., I*	Klatskin	1949–50	1 (approx.)	222	114	108	Mothers in Yale Rooming-in Project returning for evaluation of baby at one year of age. SES classification (three levels) by Hollingshead, following Warner.
Boston, Mass.*	Sears, et al.	1951–52	4–6	372	198	174	Kindergarten children in two suburbs. Parents American born, living together. Twins, adoptions, handicapped children, and other special cases eliminated. Two-level SES classification follows Warner.
New Haven, Conn., II	Strodtbeck	1951–53	14–17	48	24	24	Third-generation Jewish and Italian boys representing extremes of under- and over-achievement in school. Classified into three SES levels on basis of occupation.
Detroit, Mich., I*	Miller and Swanson	1953	12–14	112	59	53	Boys in grades 7–8 above borderline intelligence within one year of age for grade, all at least third-generation Americans, Christian, from unbroken, nonmobile families of Northwest European stock. SES (four levels) assigned on basis of education and occupation.
Detroit, Mich., II*	Miller and Swanson	1953	0–18	479	Information not available	Information not available	Random sample of white mothers with child under 19 and living with husband. Step-children and adoptions eliminated. SES (four levels) based primarily on U.S. census occupation categories.
Palo Alto, Cal.*	White	1953	2½–5½	74	36	38	Native-born mothers of only one child, the majority expecting another. Unbroken homes in suburban area SES (two levels) rated on Warner scale.
Urban Connecticut	McClelland et al.	1953–54	6–18	152	Information not available	Information not available	Parents between 30–60 having at least one child between six and eighteen and representing four religious groups. "Rough check on class status" obtained from educational level achieved by parent.
Upstate New York	Boek, et al.	1955–56	3–7 months	1,432	595	837	Representative sample of N.Y. state mothers of newborn children, exclusive of unmarried mothers. SES classification (five levels) as given on Warner scale.
Eugene, Oregon*	Littman, et al.	1955–56	0–14	206	86	120	Random sample of children from preschool classes and school rolls. Two SES levels assigned on same basis as in Boston study.
Washington, D.C.	Kohn and Clausen	1956–57	10–11	339	174	165	Representative samples of working- and middle-class mothers classified by Hollingshead's index of social position.

* Denotes studies used as principal bases for the analysis.

the children in the study were under three years old, and again from 1939 to 1942, when most of them were about ten years old. Information on maternal behavior in this same locale as of 1953 comes from a recent report by Martha Sturm White[8] of class differences in child-rearing practices for a sample of preschoolers in Palo Alto and environs. Miller and Swanson have made available relevant data from their two comprehensive studies of families in Detroit, one based on a stratified sample of families with children up to 19 years of age,[9] the other a specially selected sample of boys, ages 12 to 14 years.[10] Limited information on another sample of adolescent boys comes from Strodtbeck's investigation of "Family Interaction, Values, and Achievement."[11] Also, Littman, Moore, and Pierce-Jones[12] have recently completed a survey of child-rearing practices in Eugene, Oregon for a random sample of parents with children from two weeks to 14 years of age. Finally, Kohn[13] reports a comparison of child-training values among working and middle-class mothers in Washington, D.C.

In addition to these unpublished sources, the writer has made use of nine published researches.[14] In some instances—notably for the monumental and regrettably neglected Anderson report—data were reanalyzed and significance tests computed in order to permit closer comparison with the results of other investigations. A full list and summary description of all the studies utilized in the present review appear in Table 1. Starred items designate the researches which, because they contain reasonably comparable data, are used as the principal bases for analysis. . . .

SOCIAL CLASS DIFFERENCES IN INFANT CARE, 1930–1955

In interpreting reports of child-rearing practices it is essential to distinguish between the date at which the information was obtained and the actual period

[8] M. S. White, "Social Class, Child Rearing Practices, and Child Behavior," *Am. Sociol. Rev.* 1957, XXII, 704–712.

[9] D. R. Miller and G. E. Swanson, *The Changing American Parent* (New York: John Wiley & Sons, Inc., in press).

[10] Miller and Swanson, *Inner Conflict and Defense* (New York: Henry Holt & Co., Inc., to be published in 1959).

[11] F. L. Strodtbeck, "Family Interaction, Values, and Achievement," in A. L. Baldwin, Bronfenbrenner, D. C. McClelland, and F. L. Strodtbeck, *Talent and Society* (Princeton, N.J.: D. Van Nostrand Co., 1958).

[12] R. A. Littman, R. A. Moore, and J. Pierce-Jones, "Social Class Differences in Child Rearing: A Third Community for Comparison with Chicago and Newton, Massachusetts," *Am. Sociol. Rev.*, 1957, XXII, 694–704.

[13] M. L. Kohn, "Social Class and Parental Values," paper read at the Annual Meeting of the American Sociological Society, Washington, D.C., August, 27–29, 1957.

[14] H. E. Anderson (Chrmn.), *The Young Child in the Home*, report of the Committee on the Infant and Preschool Child, White House Conference on Child Health and Protection (New York: D. Appleton-Century, 1936); A. L. Baldwin, J. Kalhorn, and F. H. Breese, *Patterns of Parent Behavior*, Psychol. Monogr., 1945, LVIII, No. 3 (Whole No. 268); W. E. Boek, E. D. Lawson, A. Yankhauer, and M. B. Sussman, *Social Class, Maternal Health, and Child Care* (Albany: New York State Department of Health, 1957); Davis and Havighurst, *op. cit.*; E. M. Duvall, "Conceptions of Parenthood," *Am. J. Sociol.*, 1946–1947, LII, 190–192; Klatskin, *op. cit.*; E. E. Maccoby and P. K. Gibbs, *op. cit.*; D. C. McClelland, A. Rindlisbacher, and R. DeCharms, "Religious and Other Sources of Parental Attitudes toward Independence Training," in McClelland (ed.), *Studies in Motivation* (New York: Appleton-Century-Crofts, Inc., 1955); Sears, Maccoby, and Levin, *op. cit.*

to which the information refers. This caution is particularly relevant in dealing with descriptions of infant care for children who (as in the Eugene or Detroit studies) may be as old as 12, 14, or 18 at the time of the interview. In such instances it is possible only to guess at the probable time at which the practice occurred by making due allowances for the age of the child. The problem is further complicated by the fact that none of the studies reports SES differences by age. The best one can do, therefore, is to estimate the median age of the group and from this approximate the period at which the practice may have taken place. For example, the second Detroit sample, which ranged in age from birth to 18 years, would have a median age of about nine. Since the field work was done in 1953, we estimate the date of feeding and weaning practices as about 1944.[15] It should be recognized, however, that the practices reported range over a considerable period extending from as far back as 1935 to the time of the interview in 1953. Any marked variation in child-rearing practices over this period could produce an average figure which would in point of fact be atypical for the middle year 1944. We shall have occasion to point to the possible operation of this effect in some of the data to follow.

TABLE 2.   FREQUENCY OF BREAST FEEDING

1. *Sample*	2. *Approx.* *Date of* *Practice*	*No. of Cases Reporting*			*Percentage Breast Fed*			9. *Differ-* *ence**
		3. *Total* *Sample*	4. *Middle* *Class*	5. *Work-* *ing* *Class*	6. *Total* *Sample*	7. *Middle* *Class*	8. *Work-* *ing* *Class*	
National I	1930	1,856	842	1,014	80	78	82	−4†
National II	1932	445	201	244	40	29	49	−20†
Chicago I	1939	100	48	52	83	83	83	0
Detroit I	1941	112	59	53	62	54	70	−16
Detroit II	1944	200	70	130	Percentages not given			+
Eugene	1946–47	206	84	122	46	40	50	−10
Boston	1947–48	372	198	174	40	43	37	+6
New Haven I	1949–50	222	114	108	80	85	74	+11†
Palo Alto	1950	74	36	38	66	70	63	+7
Upstate New York	1955	1,432	594	838	24	27	21	+6†

* Minus sign denotes lower incidence for middle class than for working class.

† Denotes difference significant at 5-percent level of confidence or better.

If the dates of practices are estimated by the method outlined above, we find that the available data describe social-class differences in feeding, weaning, and toilet training for a period from about 1930 to 1955. The relevant information appears in Tables 2 and 4.

[15] It is true that because of the rising birth rate after World War II the sample probably included more younger than older children, but without knowledge of the actual distribution by age we have hesitated to make further speculative adjustments.

TABLE 3. Scheduled Versus Self-demand Feeding

		No. of Cases Reporting			Percentage Fed on Demand			
1.	2.	3.	4.	5.	6.	7.	8.	9.
	Approx.			Work-			Work-	
	Date of	Total	Middle	ing	Total	Middle	ing	Differ-
Sample	Practice	Sample	Class	Class	Sample	Class	Class	ence*
National I	1932	470	208	262	16	7	23	−16†
Chicago I	1939	100	48	52	25	4	44	−40†
Detroit I	1941	297	52	45	21	12	53	−41†
Detroit II	1944	205	73	132	55	51	58	−7
Boston	1947–48	372	198	174	Percentages not given			−
New Haven I	1949–50	191	117	74	65	71	54	+17
Palo Alto	1950	74	36	38	59	64	55	+9

* Minus sign denotes lower incidence of self-demand feeding in middle class.
† Denotes difference significant at 5-percent level of confidence or better.

TABLE 4. Duration of Breast Feeding (for Those Breast Fed)

		Number of Cases††			Median Duration in Months			
	Approx.			Work-			Work-	
	Date of	Total	Middle	ing	Total	Middle	ing	Differ-
Sample	Practice	Sample	Class	Class	Sample	Class	Class	ence**
National II*	1930	1,488	654	834	6.6	6.2	7.5	−1.3†
Chicago I	1939	83	40	43	3.5	3.4	3.5	−.1
Detroit I*	1941	69	32	37	3.3	2.8	5.3	−2.5
Eugene	1946–47	95	34	61	3.4	3.2	3.5	−.3
Boston	1947–48	149	85	64	2.3	2.4	2.1	+.3
New Haven I*	1949–50	177	97	80	3.6	4.3	3.0	+1.3
Upstate New York	1955	299	145	154	1.2	1.3	1.2	+.1

* Medians not given in original report but estimated from data cited.
† Denotes difference significant at 5-percent level of confidence or better.
** Minus sign denotes shorter duration for middle class than for working class.
†† Number of cases for Chicago, Eugene, Boston, and Upstate New York estimated from percentages cited.

It is reasonable to suppose that a mother's reports of whether or not she employed a particular practice would be somewhat more reliable than her estimate of when she began or discontinued that practice. This expectation is borne out by the larger number of statistically significant differences in tables presenting data on prevalence (Tables 2 and 3) rather than on the timing of a particular practice (Tables 4–6). On the plausible assumption that the former data are more reliable, we shall begin our discussion by considering the results on frequency of breast feeding and scheduled feeding, which appear in Tables 2 and 3.

General Trends. We may begin by looking at general trends over time irrespective of social-class level. These appear in column 6 of Tables 2 and 3. The data for breast feeding are highly irregular, but there is some suggestion of decrease in this practice over the years.[16] In contrast, self-demand feeding is becoming more common. In both instances the trend is more marked (column 8) in the middle class; in other words, it is they especially who are doing the changing. This fact is reflected even more sharply in column 9 which highlights a noteworthy shift. Here we see that in the earlier period—roughly before the end of World War II—both breast feeding and demand feeding were less common among the middle class than among the working class. In the later period, however, the direction is reversed; it is now the middle-class mother who more often gives her child the breast and feeds him on demand.

The data on duration of breast feeding (Table 4) and on the timing of weaning and bowel training (Tables 5 and 6) simply confirm, somewhat less reliably, all

TABLE 5.   AGE AT COMPLETION OF WEANING (EITHER BREAST OR BOTTLE)

		Number of Cases			Median Age in Months			
Sample	*Approx. Date of Practice*	*Total Sample*	*Middle Class*	*Working Class*	*Total Group*	*Middle Class*	*Working Class*	*Difference**
Chicago I	1940	100	48	52	11.3	10.3	12.3	−2.0†
Detroit I	1942	69	32	37	11.2	10.6	12.0	−1.4†
Detroit II	1945	190	62	128	—Under 12 months—			—
Eugene	1947–48	206	85	121	13.6	13.2	14.1	−.9
Boston	1948–49	372	198	174	12.3	12.0	12.6	−.6
New Haven I	1949–50	222	114	108	—Over 12 months—			—
Palo Alto	1951	68	32	36	13.1	14.4	12.6	+1.8

* Minus sign denotes earlier weaning for middle than for working class.
† Denotes difference significant at 5-percent level of confidence or better.

of the above trends. There is a general tendency in both social classes to wean the child earlier from the breast but, apparently, to allow him to suck from a bottle till a somewhat later age. Since no uniform reference points were used for securing information on toilet training in the several studies (i.e., some investigators report percentage training at six months, others at ten months, still others at 12 or 18 months), Table 6 shows only the direction of the difference between the two social classes. All these figures on timing point to the same generalization. In the earlier period, middle-class mothers were exerting more pressure; they weaned their children from the breast and bottle and carried out bowel and bladder training before their working-class counterparts. But in the

[16] As indicated below, we believe that these irregularities are largely attributable to the highly selective character of a number of the samples (notably, New Haven I and Palo Alto) and that the downward trend in frequency and duration of breast feeding is probably more reliable than is reflected in the data of Tables 2 and 4.

TABLE 6. Toilet Training

Sample	Approx. Date Practice Begun	Number of Cases		Direction of Relationship			
		Bowel Training	Bladder Training	Beginning Bowel Training	End Bowel Training	Beginning Bladder Training	End Bladder Training
National II	1931	2375	2375		−†		−*
National I	1932	494	494		−	−	
Chicago I	1940	100	220†	−†		−†**	+†
Detroit I	1942	110	102		−	+	−
Detroit II	1945	216	200	+†		−	
Eugene	1947–48	206	206	+	−	+	+
Boston	1948–49	372		−	+†		
New Haven I	1950–51	214		+†			
Palo Alto	1951	73		+†			

* Minus sign indicates that middle class began or completed training earlier than lower class.
† Denotes difference significant at 5-percent level of confidence or better.
** Based on data from 1946 report.

last ten years the trend has been reversed—it is now the middle-class mother who trains later.

These consistent trends take on richer significance in the light of Wolfenstein's impressive analysis [17] of the content of successive editions of the United States Children's Bureau bulletin on *Infant Care*. She describes the period 1929–38 (which corresponds to the earlier time span covered by our data) as characterized by:

. . . a pervasive emphasis on regularity, doing everything by the clock. Weaning and introduction of solid foods are to be accomplished with great firmness, never yielding for a moment to the baby's resistance. . . . Bowel training . . . must be carried out with great determination as early as possible. . . . The main danger which the baby presented at this time was that of dominating the parents. Successful child training meant winning out against the child in the struggle for domination.

In the succeeding period, however,

. . . all this was changed. The child became remarkably harmless . . . His main active aim was to explore his world . . . When not engaged in exploratory undertakings, the baby needs care and attention; and giving these when he demands them, far from making him a tyrant, will make him less demanding later on. At this time mildness is advocated in all areas: thumbsucking and masturbation are not to be interfered with; weaning and toilet training are to be accomplished later and more gently.[18]

The parallelism between preachment and practice is apparent also in the

[17] M. Wolfenstein, "Trends in Infant Care," *Am. J. Orthopsychiat.*, 1953, XXIII, 120–130. Similar conclusions were drawn in an earlier report by Stendler surveying 60 years of child-training practices as advocated in three popular women's magazines. *Cf.* C. B. Stendler, "Sixty Years of Child Training Practices," *J. Pediatrics*, 1950, XXXVI, 122–134.
[18] Wolfenstein, *op. cit.*, p. 121.

use of breast feeding. Up until 1945, "breast feeding was emphatically recommended," with "warning against early weaning." By 1951, "the long-term intransigence about breast feeding is relaxed." States the bulletin edition of that year: "Mothers who find bottle feeding easier should feel comfortable about doing it that way."

One more link in the chain of information completes the story. There is ample evidence that, both in the early and the later period, middle-class mothers were much more likely than working-class mothers to be exposed to current information on child care. Thus Anderson cites table after table showing that parents from higher SES levels read more books, pamphlets, and magazines, and listen to more radio talks on child care and related subjects. This in 1932. Similarly, in the last five years, White, in California, and Boek, in New York, report that middle-class mothers are much more likely than those in the working class to read Spock's best-seller, *Baby and Child Care*[19] and similar publications.

Our analysis suggests that mothers not only read these books but take them seriously, and that their treatment of the child is affected accordingly. Moreover, middle-class mothers not only read more but are also more responsive; they alter their behavior earlier and faster than their working-class counterparts.

In view of the remarkably close parallelism in changes over time revealed by Wolfenstein's analysis and our own, we should perhaps not overlook a more recent trend clearly indicated in Wolfenstein's report and vaguely discernible as well in the data we have assembled. Wolfenstein asserts that, since 1950, a conservative note has crept into the child-training literature; "there is an attempt to continue . . . mildness, but not without some conflicts and misgivings . . . May not continued gratification lead to addiction and increasingly intensified demands?"[20] In this connection it is perhaps no mere coincidence that the differences in the last column of Tables 2 to 4 show a slight drop after about 1950; the middle class is still more "relaxed" than the working class, but the differences are not so large as earlier. Once again, practice may be following preachment—now in the direction of introducing more limits and demands—still within a permissive framework. We shall return to a consideration of this possibility in our discussion of class differences in the training of children beyond two years of age.

Taken as a whole, the correspondence between Wolfenstein's data and our own suggests a general hypothesis extending beyond the confines of social class as such: *child-rearing practices are likely to change most quickly in those segments of society which have closest access and are most receptive to the agencies or agents of change (e.g., public media, clinics, physicians, and counselors)*. From this point of view, one additional trend suggested by the available data is worthy of note: rural families appear to "lag behind the times" somewhat in their practices of infant care. For example, in Anderson's beautifully detailed report, there is evidence that in 1932 farm families (Class IV in his sample) were still

[19] Benjamin Spock, *Baby and Child Care* (New York: Pocket Books, Inc., 1957).

[20] Wolfenstein, *op. cit.*, p. 121.

breast feeding their children more frequently but being less flexible in scheduling and toilet training than nonfarm families of roughly comparable socioeconomic status. Similarly, there are indications from Miller and Swanson's second Detroit study that, with SES held constant, mothers with parents of rural background adhere to more rigid techniques of socialization than their urban counterparts. Finally, the two samples in our data most likely to contain a relatively high proportion of rural families—Eugene, Oregon and Upstate New York—are also the ones which are slightly out of line in showing smaller differences in favor of middle-class permissiveness.

The above observations call attention to the fact that the major time trends discerned in our data, while impressive, are by no means uniform. There are several marked exceptions to the rule. True, some of these can be "explained" in terms of special features of the samples employed. A case in point is the New Haven study, which—in keeping with the rooming-in ideology and all that this implies—shows the highest frequency and duration of breast feeding for the postwar period, as well as the greatest prevalence of feeding on demand reported in all the surveys examined. Other discrepancies may be accounted for, at least in part, by variations in time span encompassed by the data (National 1930 *vs.* 1932), the demonstrated differential rate in breast feeding for first *vs.* later children (Palo Alto *vs.* National 1930 or Boston), ethnic differences (Boston *vs.* Chicago), contrasting ages of mothers in middle- *vs.* working-class samples (Chicago), etc. All of these explanations, however, are "after the fact" and must therefore be viewed with suspicion.

Summary. Despite our inability to account with any confidence for all departures from the general trend, we feel reasonably secure in our inferences about the nature of this trend. To recapitulate, over the last 25 years, even though breast feeding appears to have become less popular, American mothers—especially in the middle class—are becoming increasingly permissive in their feeding and toilet training practices during the first two years of the child's life. The question remains whether this tendency is equally apparent in the training of the child as he becomes older. We turn next to a consideration of this issue.

CLASS DIFFERENCES IN THE TRAINING OF CHILDREN BEYOND THE AGE OF TWO

Once we leave the stage of infancy, data from different studies of child training become even more difficult to compare. There are still greater variations in the questions asked from one research to the next, and results are reported in different types of units (e.g., relating scales with varying numbers of steps diversely defined). In some instances (as in the Chicago, Detroit II, and, apparently, Eugene surveys) the questions referred not to past or current practices but to the mother's judgment about what she would do at some later period when her child would be older. Also, when the samples include children of widely varying ages, it is often difficult to determine at what period the behavior described by the mother actually took place. Sometimes a particular age was specified in the interviewer's question and when this occurred, we have made use of that

TABLE 7. PERMISSIVENESS TOWARD IMPULSE EXPRESSION

Sample	Approx. Date of Practice	Number of Cases Reported	Direction of Trend for Middle Class			
			Oral Behavior	Toilet Accidents	Sex	Aggression
National I	1932	470			More infants allowed to play on bed unclothed.*	
Chicago	1943	100		Treated by ignoring,* reasoning or talking,* rather than slapping,* scolding, or showing disgust.*		More children allowed to "fight so long as they don't hurt each other badly.""*
Detroit II	1946	70–88	Less often disciplined for thumb sucking.		Less often disciplined for touching sex organs.	
New Haven	1949–50	216	Less often disapproved for thumb sucking, eating habits, mannerisms, etc.*			
Eugene	1950	206		Less often treated by spanking or scolding.	More permissive toward child's sexual behavior.*	Fewer children allowed "to fight so long as they don't hurt each other badly." More permissiveness toward general aggression.
Boston	1951–52	372	Less restriction on use of fingers for eating.*	Less severe toilet training.*	Higher sex permissiveness (general index).*	More permissive of aggression toward parents,* children† and siblings. Less punishment of aggression toward parents.*
Palo Alto	1953	73		Less severe toilet training.*		More permissive of aggression toward parents.* Less severe punishment of aggression toward parents.

* Indicates difference between classes significant at the 5-percent level or better.
† The difference between percentages is not significant but the difference between ratings is significant at the 5-percent level or better.

fact in estimating the approximate date of the practice. More often, however, such information was lacking. Accordingly, our time estimates must be regarded as subject to considerable error. Finally, even though we deal with substantially the same researches considered in the analyses of infant care, the total period concompassed by the data is appreciably shorter. This is so because the mothers are no longer being asked to recall how they handled their child in infancy; instead they are reporting behavior which is contemporary, or at least not far removed, from the time of the interview.

All of these considerations combine to restrict severely our ability to identify changes in practices over time. Accordingly, the absence of evidence for such changes in some of the data is perhaps more properly attributed to the limitations of our measures than to the actual course of events.

Permissiveness and Restriction on Freedom of Movement. The areas of impulse expression documented in Table 7 reflect a continuity in treatment from babyhood into early childhood. With only one minor, statistically insignificant exception, the results depict the middle-class parent as more permissive in all

TABLE 8. RESTRICTION ON FREEDOM OF MOVEMENT

Sample	Approx. Date of Practice	Number Cases Reported	Age	Item	Direction of Relationship*
National II	1932	2,289	1–5	Play restricted to home yard	—
				Play restricted to block	+
				Play restricted to neighborhood	+ †
				No restriction on place of play	+ †
National III	1932	669	6–12	Child goes to movie with parents	+
				Child goes to movie with other children	+
National IV	1932	2,414	1–12	Child goes to bed earlier	+
Chicago	1943	100	5	Age at which child is allowed to go to movie alone or with other children	+ †
				Age at which child is allowed to go downtown	− †
				Time at which children are expected in at night	+ †
New Haven I	1949–50	211	1	Definite bed time	− †
Boston	1951–52	372	5	Restriction on how far child may go from home	—
				Frequency of checking on child's whereabouts	− **
				Strictness about bed time	− †
				Amount of care taken by persons other than parents	− †
Detroit II	1953	136	0–18	Child supervised closely after 12 years of age	− †
Palo Alto	1953	74	2½–5½	Extent of keeping track of child	0

* Plus sign denotes greater restriction for middle class.

† Denotes difference significant at 5-percent level or better.

** The difference between percentages is not significant but the difference between mean ratings is significant at the 5-percent levels or better.

four spheres of activity: oral behavior, toilet accidents, sex, and aggression. There is no suggestion of a shift over the somewhat truncated time span. The now-familiar trend reappears, however, in the data on restriction of freedom of movement shown in Table 8.

In Table 8 we see a gradual shift over time with the middle class being more restrictive in the 1930's and early 1940's but becoming more permissive during the last decade.

Training for Independence and Achievement. Thus far, the trends that have appeared point predominantly in one direction—increasing leniency on the part of middle-class parents. At the same time, careful consideration of the nature of these data reveals that they are, in a sense, one-sided: they have been concerned almost entirely with the parent's response to the expressed needs and wishes of the child. What about the child's response to the needs and wishes of the parent, and the nature of these parental demands? The results presented in Table 9 are of especial interest since they shed light on all three aspects of the problem. What is more, they signal a dramatic departure from the hitherto unchallenged trend toward permissiveness.

Three types of questions have been asked with respect to independence training. The first is of the kind we have been dealing with thus far; for example, the Boston investigators inquired about the mother's reaction to the child's expression of dependence (hanging on to the mother's skirt, demanding attention, etc.). The results for this sort of query, shown in column 6 of Table 9, are consistent with previous findings for the postwar period; middle-class mothers are more tolerant of the child's expressed needs than are working-class mothers. The second type of question deals with the child's progress in taking care of himself and assuming responsibility (column 7). Here no clear trend is apparent, although there is some suggestion of greater solicitousness on the part of the middle-class mother. For example, in the 1932 material the middle-class child excelled in dressing and feeding himself only "partially," not "completely." In the 1935 Palo Alto study, the middle-class mother viewed her child as more dependent even though he was rated less so by the outside observer. It would appear that middle-class mothers may be on the alert for signs of dependency and anxious lest they push too fast.

Yet, as the data of column 8 clearly indicate, they push nevertheless. By and large, the middle-class mother expects more of her child than her working-class counterpart. All five of the statistically significant differences support this tendency and most of the remaining results point in the same direction. The conclusion is further underscored by the findings on class differences in parental aspirations for the child's academic progress, shown in column 9. The only exception to the highly reliable trend is in itself noteworthy. In the Boston study, more middle-class mothers expected their children to go to college, but they were less likely to say that it was important for their child to do well in school. Are these mothers merely giving what they consider to be the socially acceptable response, or do they really, as Sears and his colleagues suggest, have less cause for concern because their children are living up to expectations?

TABLE 9. TRAINING FOR INDEPENDENCE AND ACADEMIC ACHIEVEMENT

1. Sample	2. Approx. Date of Practice	3. Number of Cases Reported	4. Age	5. Item	Direction of Relationship			
					6. Parents' Response to Child's Dependency	7. Child's Behavior*	8. Parental Demands and Expectations	9. Academic Aspirations for Child*
National II	1932	2,380	1–5	Dress self not at all		+		
				Dress self partially		+		
				Dress self completely		−		
		2,391		Feed self not at all		−		
				Feed self partially		+ !		
				Feed self completely				
National III	1932	2,301	6–12	Children read to by parents				+
		865		Runs errands		0		
				Earns money		−		
				Receive outside lessons in music, art, etc.				
National IV	1932	2,695	1–12	Age child expected to dress self			0	
Chicago I	1943	100	5	Expected to help at home by age 5			+ †	+ †
				Expected to help with younger children			+ †	+ †
				Girls expected to begin to cook			+ +	
				Girls expected to help with dishes			+	
				Child expected to finish high school only				+ †
				Child expected to finish college				+ †
				Father teaches and reads to children				+ †

TABLE 9 (Continued)

Location	Year	N	Age	Variable		
Detroit II	1946	128	0–18	All right to leave three-year-old with sitter	0	
	1947	127		Expected to pick up own toys	+	
	1948	126		Expected to dress self by age 5	+	
	1948			Expected to put away clothes by age 5	+ †	
				Children requested to run errands at age 7	0	
				Agree child should be on his own as early as possible	+	
Urban						
Connecticut	1950	152	6–18	Age of expected mastery (Winterbottom scale)	+ †	
Eugene	1950	206	0–18	Household rules and chores expected of children	+	
Boston	1951–52	372	5	Parent permissive of child dependency	– †	
				Punishment, irritation for dependency	– †	
				Parents give child regular job around house	0	
				Importance of child's doing well at school		– †
				Expected to go to college		+ †
New Haven II 1951–53		48	14–17	Father subscribes to values of independence and mastery	+ †	
		1,151**	14–17	Expected to go to college		+ †
				Family checks over homework		+ †
Palo Alto	1953	74	2½–5½	M's report of child's dependency	–	
				Amount of attention child wants	+	
				Child objects to separation	–	
				Judge's rating of dependency	+	
Upstate New York	1955	1,433	0–1	Mother's educational aspirations for child		+ †

* Plus sign denotes greater independence or achievement required for middle-class child.
† Difference between classes significant at the 5-percent level or better.
** This is the entire high-school sample which Strodtbeck surveyed in order to select his experimental and control group.

The preceding question raises an even broader and more significant issue. Our data indicate that middle-class parents are becoming increasingly permissive in response to the child's expressed needs and desires. Yet, these same parents have not relaxed their high levels of expectations for ultimate performance. Do we have here a typical instance of Benedict's "discontinuity in cultural conditioning,"[21] with the child first being encouraged in one pattern of response and then expected to perform in a very different fashion? If so, there are days of disappointment ahead for middle-class fathers and mothers. Or, are there other elements in the parent-child relationship of the middle-class family which impel the child to effort despite, or, perhaps, even because of, his early experiences of relatively uninhibited gratification? The data on class differences in techniques of discipline shed some light on this question.

Techniques of Discipline. The most consistent finding documented in Table 10 is the more frequent use of physical punishment by working-class parents. The middle class, in contrast, resort to reasoning, isolation, and what Sears and his colleagues have referred to as "love-oriented" discipline techniques.[22] These are methods which rely for their effect on the child's fear of loss of love. Miller and Swanson referred to substantially the same class of phenomena by the term "psychological discipline," which for them covers such parental behaviors as appeals to guilt, expressions of disappointment, and the use of symbolic rather than direct rewards and punishments. Table 10 shows all available data on class differences in the use of corporal punishment, reasoning, isolation and "love-oriented" techniques. Also, in order to avoid the risks, however small, involved in wearing theoretical blinders, we have listed in the last column of the table all other significant class differences in techniques of discipline reported in the studies we have examined.

From one point of view, these results highlight once again the more lenient policies and practices of middle-class families. Such parents are, in the first place, more likely to overlook offenses, and when they do punish, they are less likely to ridicule or inflict physical pain. Instead, they reason with the youngster, isolate him, appeal to guilt, show disappointment—in short, convey in a variety of ways, one the one hand, the kind of behavior that is expected of the child; on the other, the realization that transgression means the interruption of a mutually valued relationship.

These consistent class differences take on added significance in the light of the finding, arrived at independently both by the Boston and Detroit investigators, that "love-oriented" or "psychological" techniques are more effective than other methods for bringing about desired behavior. Indeed, both groups of researchers concluded on the basis of their data that physical punishment for aggression tends to increase rather than decrease aggressive behavior. From the point of view of our interest, these findings mean that middle-class

[21] R. Benedict, "Continuities and Discontinuities in Cultural Conditioning," *Psychiat.*, 1938, I, 161–167.

[22] These investigators also classify "isolation" as a love-oriented technique, but since this specific method is reported on in several other studies as well, we have tabulated the results separately to facilitate comparison.

TABLE 10. TECHNIQUES OF DISCIPLINE

Sample	Approx. Date of Practice	Number of Cases Reporting	Age	Direction of Relationship*				Nature of Love-Oriented Technique	Other Significant Trends for Middle Class
				Physical Punishment	Reason-ing	Isola-tion	Love-Oriented Technique		
National II	1932	1,947	1–5	–†					
National III	1932	839	6–12						Infractions more often ignored† More children deprived of pleasure as punishment
National IV	1932	3,130	1–12		+†	+†			
Chicago I	1943	100	5	+		–	+†	Praise for good behavior.	Soiling child more often ignored,† rather than spanked† or shown disgust
Detroit I	1950	115	12–14	–†			+†	Mother expresses disappointment or appeals to guilt	
Detroit II	1950	222	0–19	–			+	Mother uses symbolic rather than direct rewards and punishments	
Eugene	1950	206	0–18	–	0	+†	0	No difference in overall use of praise or withdrawal of love	
Boston	1951–52	372	5	–†	+	+	0		Less use of ridicule,† deprivation of privileges** or praise for no trouble at the table†

* Plus sign indicates practice was more common in middle class than in working class.

† Denotes difference between classes significant at 5-percent level or better.

** The difference between percentages is not significant but the difference between mean ratings is significant at the 5-percent level or better.

parents, though in one sense more lenient in their discipline techniques, are using methods that are actually more compelling. Moreover, the compelling power of these practices, rather than being reduced, is probably enhanced by the more permissive treatment accorded to middle-class children in the early years of life. The successful use of withdrawal of love as a discipline technique implies the prior existence of a gratifying relationship; the more love present in the first instance, the greater the threat implied in its withdrawal.

In sum, to return to the issue posed in the preceding section, our analysis suggests that middle-class parents are in fact using techniques of discipline which are likely to be effective in evoking the behavior desired in the child. Whether the high levels of expectation held by such parents are actually achieved is another matter. At least, there would seem to be some measure of functional continuity in the way in which middle class parents currently treat their children from infancy through childhood.

Before we leave consideration of the data of Table 10, one additional feature of the results deserves comment. In the most recent study reported, the Boston research, there were three departures from the earlier general trend. First, no class difference was found in the over-all use of praise. Second, working-class parents actually exceeded those of the middle class in praising good behavior at the table. Third, in contrast to earlier findings, the working-class mother more frequently punished by withdrawing privileges. Although Sears *et al.* did not classify "withdrawal of privileges" as a love-oriented technique, the shift does represent a change in the direction of what was previously a method characteristic of the middle-class parent. Finally, there is no clear trend in the differential use of love-oriented techniques by the two social classes. If we view the Boston study as reflecting the most recent trends in methods of discipline, then either middle-class mothers are beginning to make less use of techniques they previously relied upon, or the working class is starting to adopt them. We are inclined toward the latter hypothesis in the belief that the working class, as a function of increasing income and education, is gradually reducing its "cultural lag." Evidence from subsequent studies, of course, would be necessary to confirm this speculative interpretation, since the results cited may merely be a function of features peculiar to the Boston study and not typical of the general trend.

Over-all Character of the Parent-child Relationship. The material considered so far has focused on specific practices employed by the parent. A number of researches document class differences as well in variables of a more molar sort—for example, the emotional quality of the parent-child relationship as a whole. These investigations have the additional advantage of reaching somewhat further back in time, but they also have their shortcomings. First of all, the results are not usually reported in the conventional form of percentages or means for specific social-class levels. In some studies the findings are given in terms of correlation coefficients. In others, social status can only be estimated from educational level. In others still, the data are presented in the form of graphs from which no significance tests can be computed. Partly to compensate for this lack of precision and comparability, partly to complete the picture

TABLE 11. OVERALL CHARACTER OF PARENT-CHILD RELATIONSHIP

Sample	Approx. Date of Practice	Number of Cases Reported	Age	Middle-Class Trend	Working-Class Trend
Berkeley I	1928–32	31	1–3	Grants autonomy Cooperative Equalitarian	Expresses affection Excessive contact Intrusive Irritable Punitive Ignores child
National I	1932	494	0–1		Baby picked up when cries†
National IV	1932	3,239	1–12	Higher percentage of children punished†	Nothing done to allay child's fears†
Yellow Springs, Ohio	1940	124	3–12	Acceptant-democratic	Indulgent Active-rejectant
Berkeley II	1939–42	31	9–11	Grants autonomy Cooperative Equalitarian Expresses affection	Excessive contact Intrusive Irritable Punitive Ignores child
Chicago I	1943	100	5		Father plays with child more†
Chicago II	1943–44	433	1–5	"Developmental" conception of "good mother" and "good child."†	"Traditional" conception of "good mother" and "good child."†
New Haven I	1949–50	219	1	More necessary discipline to prevent injury or danger.†	More prohibitive discipline beyond risk of danger or injury.
Boston	1951–52	372	5	Mother warmer toward child† Father warmer toward child* Father exercises more authority* Mother has higher esteem for father† Mother delighted about pregnancy† Both parents more often share authority*	Father demands instant obedience† Child ridiculed† Greater rejection of child† Emphasis on neatness, cleanliness, and order† Parents disagree more on child-rearing policy*
New Haven II	1951–53	48	14–17	Fathers have more power in family decisions† Parents agree in value orientations†	
Palo Alto	1953	73	2½–5½	Baby picked up when cries†	Mother carries through demands rather than dropping the subject†
Eugene	1955–56	206	0–18	Better relationship between father and child†	
Washington, D.C.	1956–57	400	10–11	Desirable qualities are happiness,* considerateness,* curiosity,* self-control*	Desirable qualities are neatness-cleanliness,* obedience*

* Trend significant at 5-percent level or better.
† The difference between percentages is not significant but the difference between mean ratings is significant at the 5-percent level or better.

of available data on class differences in child rearing, we cite in Table 11 not only the results from these additional studies of molar variables but also all other statistically significant findings from researches considered previously which might have bearing on the problem at hand. In this way, we hope as well to avoid the bias which occasionally arises from looking only at those variables in which one has a direct theoretical interest.

The data of Table 11 are noteworthy in a number of respects. First, we have clear confirmation that, over the entire 25-year period, middle-class parents have had a more acceptant, equalitarian relationship with their children. In many ways, the contrast is epitomized in Duvall's distinction between the "developmental" and "traditional" conceptions of mother and child. Duvall asked the mothers in her sample to list the "five things that a good mother does" and the "five things that a good child does." Middle-class mothers tended to emphasize such themes as "guiding and understanding," "relating herself lovingly to the child," and making sure that he "is happy and contented," "shares and cooperates with others," and "is eager to learn." In contrast, working-class mothers stressed the importance of keeping house and child "neat and clean," "training the child to regularity," and getting the child "to obey and respect adults."

What is more, this polarity in the value orientation of the two social classes appears to have endured. In data secured as recently as 1957, Kohn[23] reports that working-class mothers differ from those of the middle class in their choice of characteristics most desired in a child; the former emphasize "neatness, cleanliness, and obedience," while the latter stress "happiness, considerateness, and self-control."

Yet, once again, it would be a mistake to conclude that the middle-class parent is exerting less pressure on his children. As the data of Table 11 also show, a higher percentage of middle-class children are punished in some manner, and there is more "necessary" discipline to prevent injury or danger. In addition, though the middle-class father typically has a warmer relationship with the child, he is also likely to have more authority and status in family affairs.

Although shifts over time are difficult to appraise when the data are so variable in specific content, one trend is sufficiently salient to deserve comment. In the early Berkeley data the working-class parent is more expressive of affection than his middle-class counterpart. But in the follow-up study of the same children eight years later the trend is reversed. Perhaps the same mothers behave differently toward younger and older children. Still, the item "Baby picked up when cries" yields a significant difference in favor of the working-class mother in 1932 and a reliable shift in the opposite direction in 1953. *Sic transit gloria Watsoniensis!*

Especially with terms as heavily value laden as those which appear in Table 11, one must be concerned with the possibility that the data in the studies examined document primarily not actual behavior but the middle-class mother's superior knowledge of the socially acceptable response. Undoubtedly, this factor operates to inflate the reported relationships. But there are several reassuring

---

23 Kohn, *op. cit.*

considerations. First, although the items investigated vary widely in the intensity of their value connotations, all show substantially the same trends. Second, four of the studies reported in Table 11 (Berkeley I and II, Yellow Springs, and New Haven II) are based not on the mother's responses to an interview but on observation of actual interaction among family members. It seems highly unlikely, therefore, that the conclusions we have reached apply only to professed opinions and not to real behavior as well.

RETROSPECT AND PROSPECT

It is interesting to compare the results of our analysis with the traditional view of the differences between the middle- and lower-class styles of life, as documented in the classic descriptions of Warner,[24] Davis,[25] Dollard,[26] and the more recent accounts of Spinley,[27] Clausen,[28] and Miller and Swanson.[29] In all these sources the working class is typically characterized as impulsive and uninhibited, the middle class as more rational, controlled, and guided by a broader perspective in time. Thus Clausen writes:

The lower class pattern of life . . . puts a high premium on physical gratification, on free expression of aggression, on spending and sharing. Cleanliness, respect for property, sexual control, educational achievement—all are highly valued by middle class Americans—are of less importance to the lower class family or are phrased differently.[30]

To the extent that our data even approach this picture, it is for the period before World War II rather than for the present day. The modern middle class has, if anything, extended its time perspective so that the tasks of child training are now accomplished on a more leisurely schedule. As for the lower class the fit is far better for the actual behavior of parents rather than for the values they seek to instill in their children. As reflected in the data of Tables 10 and 11, the lower-class parent—though he demands compliance and control in his child— is himself more aggressive, expressive, and impulsive than his middle-class counterpart. Even so, the picture is a far cry from the traditional image of the casual and carefree lower class. Perhaps the classic portrait is yet to be seen along the skid rows and Tobacco Roads of the nation, but these do not lie along the well-trodden paths of the survey researcher. He is busy ringing doorbells, no less, in the main section of the lower-class district, where most of the

[24] W. L. Warner and P. S. Lunt, *The Social Life of a Modern Community* (New Haven: Yale University Press, 1942); Warner, Meeker, and Others, *op. cit.*

[25] A. Davis, B. Gardner, and M. R. Gardner, *Deep South* (Chicago: University of Chicago Press, 1941).

[26] J. Dollard, *Caste and Class in a Southern Town* (New Haven: Yale University Press, 1937).

[27] B. M. Spinley, *The Deprived and the Privileged: Personality Development in English Society* (London: Routledge & Kegan Paul, Ltd., 1953).

[28] J. A. Clausen, "Social and Psychological Factors in Narcotics Addiction," *Law and Contemporary Problems*, 1957, XXII, 34–51.

[29] Miller and Swanson, *The Changing American Parent, op. cit.*

[30] Clausen, *op. cit.*, p. 42.

husbands have steady jobs and, what is more important, the wife is willing to answer the door and the interviewer's questions. In this modern working-class world there may be greater freedom of emotional expression, but there is no laxity or vagueness with respect to goals of child training. Consistently over the past 25 years, the parent in this group has emphasized what are usually regarded as the traditional middle-class virtues of cleanliness, conformity, and control, and although his methods are not so effective as those of his middle-class neighbors, they are perhaps more desperate.

Perhaps this very desperation, enhanced by early exposure to impulse and aggression, leads working-class parents to pursue new goals with old techniques of discipline. While accepting middle-class levels of aspiration he has not yet internalized sufficiently the modes of response which make these standards readily achievable for himself or his children. He still has to learn to wait, to explain, and to give and withhold his affection as the reward and price of performance.

As of 1957, there are suggestions that the cultural gap may be narrowing. Spock has joined the Bible on the working-class shelf. If we wish to see the shape of the future, we can perhaps do no better than to look at the pages of the newly revised edition of this ubiquitous guidebook. Here is a typical example of the new look—a passage not found in the earlier version:

> If the parent can determine in which respects she may be too permissive and can firm up her discipline, she may, if she is on the right track, be delighted to find that her child becomes not only better behaved but much happier. Then she can really love him better, and he in turn responds to this.[31]

Apparently "love" and "limits" are both watchwords for the coming generation of parents. As Mrs. Johnson, down in the flats, puts away the hairbrush and decides to have a talk with her unruly youngster "like the book says," Mrs. Thomas, on the hill, is dutifully striving to overcome her guilt at the thought of giving John the punishment she now admits he deserves. If both ladies are successful, the social scientist may eventually have to look elsewhere in his search for ever larger F's and t's.

Such speculations carry us beyond the territory yet surveyed by the social scientist. Perhaps the most important implication for the future from our present analysis lies in the sphere of method rather than substance. Our attempt to compare the work of a score of investigators over a score of years will have been worth the labor if it but convinces future researchers of the wastefulness of such uncoordinated efforts. Our best hope for an understanding of the differences in child rearing in various segments of our society and the effects of these differences on personality formation lies in the development of a systematic long-range plan for gathering comparable data at regular intervals on large samples of families at different positions in the social structure. We now have survey organizations with the scientific competence and adequate technical facilities to perform the task. With such hopes in mind, the author

[31] Spock, *op. cit.*, p. 326.

looks ahead to the day when the present analysis becomes obsolete, in method as well as substance.

RECAPITULATION AND CODA

A comparative analysis of the results of studies of social-class differences in child rearing over a 25-year period points to the following conclusions.

A. TRENDS IN INFANT CARE

1. Over the past quarter of a century, American mothers at all social-class levels have become more flexible with respect to infant feeding and weaning. Although fewer infants may be breast fed, especially over long periods of time, mothers are increasingly more likely to feed their children on demand and to wean them later from the bottle.

2. Class differences in feeding, weaning, and toilet training show a clear and consistent trend. From about 1930 till the end of World War II, working-class mothers were uniformly more permissive than those of the middle class. They were more likely to breast feed, to follow a self-demand schedule, to wean the child later both from breast and bottle, and to begin and complete both bowel and bladder training at a later age. After World War II, however, there has been a definite reversal in direction; now it is the middle-class mother who is the more permissive in each of the above areas.

3. Shifts in the pattern of infant care—especially on the part of middle-class mothers—show a striking correspondence to the changes in practices advocated in successive editions of U.S. Children's Bureau bulletins and similar sources of expert opinion.

4. In addition to varying with social-class level, methods of infant care appear to differ as a function of cultural background, urban vs. rural upbringing, and exposure to particular ideologies of child rearing.

5. Taken together, the findings on changes in infant care lead to the generalization that socialization practices are most likely to be altered in those segments of society which have most ready access to the agencies or agents of change (e.g., books, pamphlets, physicians, and counselors).

B. TRENDS IN CHILD TRAINING

6. The data on the training of the young child show middle-class mothers, especially in the postwar period, to be consistently more permissive toward the child's expressed needs and wishes. The generalization applies in such diverse areas as oral behavior, toilet accidents, dependency, sex, aggressiveness, and freedom of movement outside the home.

7. Though more tolerant of expressed impulses and desires, the middle-class parent, throughout the period covered by this survey, has higher expectations for the child. The middle-class youngster is expected to learn to take care of himself earlier, to accept more responsibilities about the home, and—above all— to progress further in school.

8. In matters of discipline, working-class parents are consistently more likely to employ physical punishment, while middle-class families rely more on reasoning, isolation, appeals to guilt, and other methods involving the threat of loss of love. At least two independent lines of evidence suggest that the techniques preferred by middle-class parents are more likely to bring about the development of internalized values and controls. Moreover, the effectiveness of such methods, should, at least on theoretical grounds, be enhanced by the more acceptant atmosphere experienced by middle-class children in their early years.

9. Over the entire 25-year period studied, parent-child relationships in the middle class are consistently reported as more acceptant and equalitarian, while those in the working class are oriented toward maintaining order and obedience. Within this context, the middle class has shown a shift away from emotional control toward freer expression of affection and greater tolerance of the child's impulses and desires.

In the past few years, there have been indications that the gap between the social classes may be narrowing. Whatever trend the future holds in store, let us hope that the social scientist will no longer be content to look at them piecemeal but will utilize all the technical resources now at his command to obtain a systematic picture of the changes, through still more extended space and time, in the way in which humanity brings up its children.

Class Voting in the Anglo-American Countries

ROBERT R. ALFORD

A number of public opinion surveys taken between 1952 and 1962 indicate that class voting is consistently higher in Australia and Great Britain than in

TABLE 1. CLASS VOTING, 1952–1962

Country	Index of Class Voting*			Based on Number of Surveys
	Mean	Lowest	Highest	
Great Britain	40	35	44	8
Australia	33	27	37	10
United States	16	13	23	5
Canada	8	−1	17	10

* The index of class voting was computed by subtracting the percentage of non-manual workers voting for "Left" parties from the percentage of manual workers voting for "Left" parties. For Great Britain, the Labour party was used; for Australia, the Australian Labor party; for the United States, the Democratic party; for Canada, the CCF (or NDP) and Liberal parties. Where two parties were classified as "Left," their votes among each strata were combined. . . .

Canada and the United States. The countries may be ranked in the following order: Great Britain, Australia, the United States, and Canada. Table 1 and Fig. 1 summarize these results. . . .

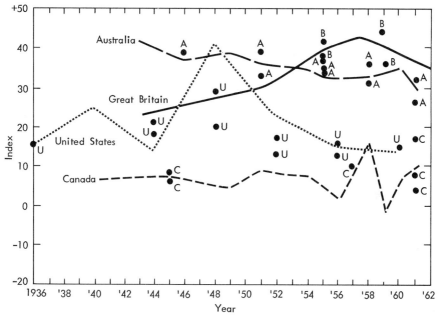

FIGURE 1.   Class voting in the Anglo-American countries, 1936–1962.

Class voting is almost always above zero; only one Canadian survey falls below that mark. Great Britain is consistently higher than Australia in the 1952–1962 period; it has a mean index of 40 and a range of 35 to 44. Australia is consistently higher than the United States and has a mean index of 33 and a range of 27 to 37. The United States is consistently higher than Canada, except for one 1958 Canadian survey, and has a mean index of 16 and a range of 13 to 23. Canada always has the lowest level of class voting, with the single exception mentioned.[1]

Particular shifts in each country and the contribution of each social stratum to class voting will be discussed in the chapters on each country, but it must be stressed that no particular figure has any great significance. It is probable, however, that the over-all patterns of differences from country to country override any possibilities of sampling error.

The "true" level of class voting may actually have shifted, as Fig. 1 indicates. Given the lack of tight integration of social groups, whether they be social classes or others, and the lack of close correspondence of class and party, a rather high level of shifting back and forth of the social bases of the parties is likely,

[1] Table 1 includes only the 1952–1962 period for summary purposes. Prior data are more unreliable for the various countries because of greater sampling variability and the unavailability of really comparable British data prior to 1955.

as different issues both class and non-class become salient, and as the parties jockey for support from various groups. But what is striking here is not the variation within the countries, but that, regardless of that variation, the differences in class voting between the countries are so sharp and consistent.

But before these results are accepted, we must consider the possibility that they are due to particular social groups within each country. It is possible, for example, that the solid Democratic loyalties in the South account for the lower level of class voting in the United States than in Australia. It is possible that the solid Liberal loyalties of Quebec (until 1958) account for the lower level of class voting in Canada than in the United States. It is possible that class voting is manifested in Great Britain and Australia mainly among older persons, in whom class loyalties are more deeply felt and depressions and oppression more bitterly remembered, on one side, or callously forgotten, on the other. If the differences between the four Anglo-American nations disappear when certain subgroups of the population are examined, then the difference between political systems is a statistical artifact produced by strong antipathies among certain segments of the population and equally strong ties overriding those of class among other segments.

As Table 2 shows, the differences in the level of class voting between the four Anglo-American countries do not disappear when class voting is examined

TABLE 2. Class Voting Within Selected Demographic Groups, Between 1952 and 1962

Mean Index of Class Voting

Country	Age-Group† 20–30	30–40	40–50	50–60	Religion Protestants	Catholics	Region‡ Highest	Lowest	Cities over 100,000
Great Britain	39	36	37	42	46	44	47	23	41
Australia	30	28	35	39	36	29	47	22	36
United States	13	13	22	13	21	16	31	4	20
Canada	5	9	13	9	10	2	26	−12	11

Sources: The surveys upon which the figures are based are:

Great Britain, CQ 82 (1955), CQ 1717 (1957), CQ 116–118 (1959), and CQ 275 (1962); *Australia,* Nos. 115 (1955), 135 (1958), 140 (1960), 149 (1961), and 154 (1961); *United States, Michigan* (1952); Nos. 573 (1956), 636K (1960), and 75 (1960); Canada, Nos. 238 (1954), 250 (1956), 266X (1958), 285 (1960), 286 (1961), and 292 (1961). Not all information was available on every survey. See Appendixes A and B for details on the surveys.*

* [The material referred to is not included. The meaning of these symbols is explained in Appendix A—Editor.]

† The age-groups for Michigan 1952 and the British surveys are not precisely as indicated above.

‡ For Michigan 1952, the regions are slightly different from those used in the other United States surveys, and the "urban" category is a combination of urban and suburban metropolitan areas. All figures are + except as indicated.

within different age groups, within two religious groups (Protestants and Catholics), within the regions highest and lowest in their level of class voting, and in large cities. By and large, the rank order of class voting is not affected. Within each age-group, among either Protestants or Catholics, Great Britain has the highest class voting of any of these countries; Australia is next followed by the United States and then Canada. It may be noted that the difference between Britain and Australia disappears when the regions highest and lowest in class voting are considered. (To some extent the figures are artifacts of extremely high or low component index figures, so that here, as before, no particular number has any great significance.)

Table 2 shows that regionalism and religion have marked effects upon class voting in each country—in that class voting is consistently higher among Protestants than among Catholics and that a considerable difference appears between the regions with the highest and the lowest average levels of class voting. . . .

The differences between the countries remain when class voting in cities of over 100,000 population is considered. Urbanization does not (or has not yet) reduce the international differences in class voting. (It may be noted here that two surveys of urban constituencies in New Zealand found a level of class voting very close to Great Britain's.)[2]

As a final check on the validity of the differences between these political systems in their level of class voting (and as a check on the adequacy of the manual–non-manual distinction as a measure of class), it is possible to define social class more narrowly in terms of two criteria of class position instead of one and to compute a more refined measure of class voting. It seems reasonable to predict that the validity of the principal finding of the differences in class voting will be reinforced if the rank order remains when social class is defined in terms of either education, income, subjective class identification, of trade-union membership in addition to occupation. Table 3 shows that the rank order of class voting in the four countries remains the same even when a more narrow (one should say more rigorous) definition of the social class position of the respondents is used. The level of class voting is indeed higher in each country when social classes are defined more narrowly than by manual and non-manual occupation, but the differences between the four countries remain the same.

Survey data from four Anglo-American countries have shown that clear and consistent differences between the countries exist, regardless of whether class voting is examined for the total electorate divided into manual and non-manual occupations, for the same division within various demographic groups,

[2] Class voting in one metropolitan area of New Zealand (Dunedin Central) was +40 in a 1961 election. The figure was computed from Austin Mitchell, "Dunedin Central," *Political Science* (New Zealand), XIV (March, 1962), 27–80. A detailed breakdown of occupations allowed a recombination into a manual–non-manual dichotomy. A 1958 survey of voting in a New Zealand urban constituency (Wellington Central) showed parallel results, although precise comparisons are not possible since the data were not given in sufficient detail. See Robert S. Milne, "Voting in Wellington Central, 1957," *Political Science* (New Zealand), X (September, 1958), 34–37.

TABLE 3.   CLASS VOTING DEFINED BY TWO CLASS CHARACTERISTICS, BETWEEN 1952 AND 1962

	Mean Class Index*			
Country	Education and Occupation	Income and Occupation	Subjective Social Class and Occupation	Trade-Union Membership and Occupation
Great Britain	57	52	53	51
Australia	43	46	47	46
United States	26	31	35	22
Canada	10	11	12	16

* Figures given are means computed from the same surveys listed under Table 2 where the question was asked. In Australia, education and class identification were asked only in No. 154 (1961). In Canada, class identification was asked only in No. 292 (1961). In the United States, class identification was asked only in Michigan (1952). Otherwise the figures are derived from at least two surveys in each country. All figures are +. The figures are based upon a definition of "working class" and "middle class" defined by two class characteristics, as follows:

Great Britain: Manual workers were included who either (1) left school before the age of fifteen, (2) were judged to be in one of the lower two positions on a four-point socio-economic status scale by interviewers, (3) identified themselves as "working-class" when asked: "What social class would you say you are in?" or (4) had a member of a trade union in their family. Non-manual persons were included who either (1) remained in school past age fifteen, (2) were judged to belong in one of the higher two positions on a socio-economic status scale by interviewers, (3) identified themselves as "lower-middle-class" or higher, or (4) did not have a trade-union member in the family.

Australia: Manual workers were included who either (1) had primary, secondary, some technical or commercial education, who finished technical or commercial school, or who had an intermediate certificate; (2) were judged to be in one of the lower two positions on a four-point socio-economic status scale by interviewers; (3) identified themselves as "working-class," or (4) had a trade-union member in the family. Non-manual persons were included who either (1) had some university training or a university degree, or either a leaving or a matriculation certificate, (2) were judged to belong in one of the upper two positions on a four-point socio-economic scale by interviewers, (3) identified themselves as "middle-class" or higher, or (4) did not have a trade-union member in the family.

United States: Criteria in the United States surveys varied considerably. For education, the division was between high school or less for manual workers, and some college or more for persons in non-manual occupations. The income criteria for the Gallup and Roper surveys were parallel to the British and Australian surveys, but for Michigan (1952), manual workers were included who earned less than $3,000 per year and non-manuals who earned more than $7,500.

Canada: The educational criteria were the same as in the United States; the others, the same as Britain and Australia.

or for a more rigorous definition of classes. Great Britain and Australia have higher levels of class voting than the United States and Canada. . . .

In none of these countries is the voting of one stratum for "its" party unanimous. Political consensus in these countries is shown by the constant shifting back and forth from Right to Left, but never does the vote by manual workers for the Right party, or non-manual workers for the Left party, drop below about 20 per cent. Never does the index of class voting rise above 60 percentage points (80 per cent of the manual workers voting Left, 20 per cent of the non-manual workers voting Left, for example) even when, as in Table 3, classes are defined more narrowly than by occupation only. This narrower definition leaves out so much of the potential electorate that it is meaningless as an over-all measure of class voting. The imperfect "status crystallization" of these four countries produces a high level of "cross-class" voting, no matter how class is defined. The fairly even impact of politically relevant events upon the classes is also shown clearly by the parallel moves to the Right or Left in most election periods. . . .

A Cross-Cultural Analysis of Class Differentials in Divorce Rates

WILLIAM J. GOODE

. . . Prior to the first world war, social analysts had guessed that the social relations of certain occupations created a greater proneness to divorce: the travelling salesman because he lived much of the time away from the social control of his neighbours; the bartender and entertainers because of the temptations to which their lives exposed them; the physician because of the emotional responses ('transference phenomenon' in the modern psychodynamic vocabulary) he aroused; and so on. Occupational data were indeed collected at that time although registration procedures were poor.[1] Most American textbooks that dealt with the topic in succeeding decades repeated these findings in one form or another. But through predictions could be made from a few specific occupations, (clergymen, physicians, teachers, dancers) our knowledge of most occupations permitted no prediction at all, and occupation was soon dropped from most records.

By contrast, it seems likely that class position, with its concomitant patterning of social relations and styles of life, might affect divorce rates in at least a rough fashion. Popular belief, and to some extent that of social scientists, supposed until recently that United States divorce rates were higher among the upper strata and lower among the lower strata, where desertion was and is a common occurrence. However, a summary of the available data extending over half a century, together with new calculations from national surveys and censuses, shows that in fact there was an inverse correlation between class position and divorce rates. These findings may be summarized briefly:

1. The findings do not negate the hypothesis that specific occupations in any class position may have high or low divorce rates. Thus clergymen and

Reprinted from the *International Social Science Journal*, 14 (1962), pp. 507–526, by permission of the author and the publisher.
[1] *Marriage and Divorce*, 1867–1906, Washington, Bureau of the Census, 1909. See my critique of these items in *After Divorce*, Glencoe, Ill., The Free Press, 1956, pp. 52 ff.

professors will have relatively low rates, while psychiatrists, surgeons, and perhaps general practitioners may have higher rates.

2. Negroes have a higher divorce rate than whites.
3. When occupation is used as an indicator of class, roughly following the Alba Edwards system used by the Census Bureau, the upper occupational groups have lower rates of divorce.
4. When income is used as an indicator, the upper income groups have lower rates of divorce.
5. When education is used as an indicator, the upper groups have lower rates of divorce.
6. However, the relationship between the education of non-whites and divorce rates is positive: the higher the education, the higher the proneness to divorce. . . .

CLASS DIFFERENTIALS IN OTHER SOCIETIES: PHASES OF DEVELOPMENT

The relationship between social structure and divorce seems general enough to apply to other societies. Let us explore the matter. Where there is a well-developed stratification system it would seem likely that the lower class does not count on the stability of the marriage, that the marriage itself costs less, less is invested in it than in the upper strata, the kin ties are less important and therefore the ambiguity created by divorce would not be taken so seriously as in the upper strata.

In the past, on the other hand, without any questions the divorce rate (as distinguished from the general rate of instability) was higher in the upper strata of the United States. In some states' jurisdictions, an act of the legislature was necessary to obtain a divorce and generally divorce was costly. Consequently at some unknown point in American history, the lower strata began to surpass the upper strata in the divorce rate, just as happened with respect to the Negro-White divorce differential. Thus a fuller exploration must at some point introduce the notion of phase in these considerations. In other words, the lower strata may generally have a higher rate of marital instability, but their divorce rate may not always be higher until some stage of development in the marriage and divorce system occurs.

This general theory of the relationship between the larger social structure and class divorce rates may correctly apply to the Western culture complex where Church dogma with respect to the family was translated into State laws in every nation, and where the administration of these restrictive laws was until recently in the hands of the *élite*. However, those laws have been altered greatly over the past half-century in most Western States. Moreover, if the theory is to be generalized, it must be modified to fit those cultures such as China, India, Japan and Arab Islam where marriage and divorce were not generally under the jurisdiction of State officials (except for extreme cases) and where marriage was not primarily a sacred affair (Japan, China).

Finally, the use of occupation as a class index, perhaps the best in view of the necessarily crude data available for cross-national comparisons, may at times introduce a new variable into the analysis, the peculiar style of life of certain occupations. For example, clergymen and teachers (in the West) will have low divorce rates but physicians and artists will have high ones—yet in most national tabulations of divorce these will all be classified together. In the West, farmers have lower divorce rates, but in Japan a special pattern of 'trial marriage' creates high divorce rates among agriculturalists—though many of these are never recorded.

If these necessary modifications are integrated, several inferences can be tested. (a) In the pre-industrial or early industrialization period of Western nations the upper classes will have higher divorce rates. Indeed, there may be almost no lower class divorces. (b) As a Western nation industrializes, its divorce procedures are gradually made available to all classes. Since family strain toward the lower strata is greater, the proportion of lower strata divorces will increase, and eventually there should be an inverse relation between class and divorce rate, as in the United States. (c) In China, India, Japan and Arab Islam, where the power to divorce remained in the hands of the groom's family, no such set of phases will occur. Indeed—though very likely precise data do not exist—I hypothesize that the relation between class and divorce rate moves in the opposite direction: that is though the lower strata will continue to furnish more than their 'share' of the divorces, the class differential will narrow somewhat as the upper strata begin to divorce more. (d) Finally (though here again the data will very likely never become available) since the dominant pattern of respectability was set by the urban *élite*, and the rural marriage and divorce patterns seem to have been looser, it is likely that in China, Japan, India and Arab Islam any modern changes would be toward a decline in the divorce rate agriculturalists.

Let us look at the data that bear on the first of these three hypotheses.

New Zealand. The ratio of divorced to married by income distribution shows clearly that toward the lower strata the divorce rate is higher.

RATIO OF PERCENTAGE OF DIVORCED TO PERCENTAGE OF MARRIED, WITHIN INCOME GROUPS

Income Group	Ratio*	Income Group	Ratio*
Under £100	1.78	£400–£449	.67
£100–£149	1.84	£450–£549	.58
£150–£199	1.86	£550–£649	.56
£200–£249	1.50	£650–£749	.48
£250–£299	1.10	£750 and over	.34
£300–£349	.96	Not specified	2.01
£350–£399	.87		

* Figures higher than 1.00 indicate that the income group concerned contributes more than its numerical 'share' to the total number of divorces.

SOURCE: A. J. Dixon, *Divorce in New Zealand*, Auckland, Auckland University College Bulletin No. 46, 1954, p. 42 (Sociology Series No. 1).

The same relationship shows by occupation; the ratio of comparative frequency of divorce to numbers in each of various occupational groups being:

PRONENESS TO DIVORCE BY OCCUPATION, NEW ZEALAND

Occupation	Ratio*	Occupation	Ratio*
Architect, dentist, lawyer, lecturer,		Mechanic	.96
doctor	.07	Railway employee	.80
Engineer	.72	Clerk	.55
Farmer	.17	Salesman	1.17
Manager (not company)	.32	Barman	4.73
Carpenter	.78	Labourer	2.30
Butcher	1.05		

* Figures higher than 1.00 indicate that the occupation concerned contributes more divorces than its numerically proportionate 'share' within all occupations.
SOURCE: *ibid.*

United States. Although an extensive summary of the relevant data is available for the United States,[2] it may be relevant to note that a more recent summary has corroborated these findings, and from one of these the following table has been taken.

RATIO OF DIVORCED TO 1,000 OF EVER-MARRIED MEN BY OCCUPATION OF CIVILIAN LABOUR FORCE, 14 YEARS AND OVER, 1950 UNITED STATES CENSUS

Occupations	Number Divorced per 1,000 Ever-Married Men
Professional technical and kindred workers	18.49
Managers, officials and proprietors (excluding farm)	16.59
Clerical and kindred workers	25.70
Craftsmen, foremen and kindred workers	24.15
Operatives and kindred workers	26.18
Farm labourers and foremen	40.76

SOURCE: Karen G. Hillman, *Marital Instability and Its Relation to Education, Income and Occupation: An Analysis Based on Census Data*, Evanston, Illinois, Northwestern University, 1961, p. 19, mimeographed.

Australia. In Australia, too, the relationship holds:

RATIO OF DIVORCED TO 1,000 MARRIED MALES BY OCCUPATIONAL CLASS, 1947 CENSUS OF AUSTRALIA*

Occupational Level	Number Divorced per 1,000 Married Males	Occupational Level	Number Divorced per 1,000 Married Males
Employer	9	Employee (on wage)	15
Self-employed	9	Helper (not on wage)	23

* Calculated from: *Census of the Commonwealth of Australia, 30 June 1947. Statistician's Report*, Canberra, 1952, p. 268.

2 *After Divorce, op. cit.*, pp. 52 ff. *et passim.*

Sweden. A similar ratio may be found in the 1950 Swedish census:

RATIO OF DIVORCED PER 1,000 MARRIED MEN, BY OCCUPATIONAL CATEGORY *

Category	Number Divorced per 1,000 Married Men	Category	Number Divorced per 1,000 Married Men
Employers	12	Wage-earners	28
Salaried employees	21		

* Calculated from: Personal correspondence, Central Bureau of Statistics, Sweden. Statistiska Centralbyran, Folkräkningen, Den 31 December 1950, V, VI, Totala Räkningen, Folkmängden Efter Yrke. Hushall. Utrikes Födda Och Utlänningar: Tab. 8., 'Förvärvsarbetande befolkning efter näringsgren (huvudoch undergrupper) och yrkesstallning i kombination med kön, alter och civilstand den 31 december 1950' (Economically active population by industry (divisions and major groups) and occupational status, and by sex, age and marital status), pp. 162–3 (Males only).

Belgium. In the following table calculated from the 1947 Belgian census, a similar relation appears, although here the differences are very small.

RATIO OF DIVORCED PER 1,000 MARRIED MEN, BY OCCUPATIONAL CATEGORY (EXCLUDING AGRICULTURE, FARMING AND FISHING) *

Category	Number Divorced per 1,000 Married Men	Category	Number Divorced per 1,000 Married Men
Employers	13	Skilled and unskilled workers	15
Salaried workers	14	Auxiliary personnel	31

* Calculated from: Institut national de Statistique, *Recensement Général de la Population, de l'Industrie et du Commerce au 31 Décembre 1941.* Vol. 8: *Répartition de la Population d'après l'Activité et la Profession.* Tableau 18—Répartition de la population active masculine de nationalité belge d'après l'État Civil, l'État Social et les Sections d'Activité, pp. 34–5.

France. The relationship also holds here.

RATIO OF DIVORCED PER 1,000 MARRIED MEN, BY OCCUPATIONAL CATEGORY *

Category	Number Divorced per 1,000 Married Men	Category	Number Divorced per 1,000 Married Men
Liberal professions and senior cadres	17	Skilled and unskilled workers	24
Intermediate cadres	20	Domestic servants	78
Salaried workers	21		

* Calculated from: *Résultats du sondage au 1/20ᵉ*, Institut National de la Statistique et des Études économiques, Presses Universitaires de France, 1960 (Recensement général de la Population de Mai 1954), p. 61, p. 62, p. 63.

England. A special study of the occupational structure of the divorcing and the 'continued married relations population' in England and Wales in 1951 reveals that the proportions of the divorcing population in the selected occupational categories were almost exactly those of the proportions in the continued married population. Thus the 'professional and managerial class' accounted for 13.5 per cent of the divorcing sample and 13.9 per cent of the continuing married.

Much more instructive, however, and strongly confirming our second hypothesis is the change in the distribution of the husband's occupation at divorce. Such a comparison is presented below, showing how the 'gentry, professional and managerial workers' dropped from 41.4 per cent of the total divorcing population, to 11.4 per cent between 1871 and 1951. During the same period, the proportion furnished by the manual workers increased from 16.8 to 58.5 per cent.

HUSBAND'S OCCUPATION AT DIVORCE, 1871 AND 1951, ENGLAND AND WALES*

Year	Gentry, Professional and Managerial Workers %	Farmers and Shop-keepers %	Black-coated Workers %	Manual %	Unknown Occupation %	Total of Occupations
1871	41.4	12.7	6.3	16.8	22.8	285
1951	11.4	6.7	7.6	58.5	15.8	1,813

* Calculated from: Griselda Rowntree and Norman H. Carrier, 'The Resort to Divorce in England and Wales, 1858–1957,' in: *Population Studies*, No. 11, March 1958, p. 222.

South Africa. Up to the time of writing, I have been unable to make a similar comparison for South Africa because the categories used for occupation and divorce do not correspond to one another in the sources available to me.[3]

Netherlands. The data from the Netherlands do not fit the hypothesis because of the extremely high divorce ratio among the free professions, which

RATIO OF DIVORCE PER 1,000 MARRIED MALE HEADS OF HOUSEHOLDS, NETHERLANDS 1955–57 (EXCLUDING AGRICULTURE)*

Categories	Number of Divorces per 1,000 Male Household Heads	Categories	Number of Divorces per 1,000 Male Household Heads
Heads of enterprises	18	Teaching	15
Free professions	50	Other bureaucrats	37
Civil Service and office employees	21	Manual workers	30

* Calculated from: Number of households taken as of 30 June 1956; divorces as of 1955–57.
SOURCE: *Echtscheidingen in Nederland*, 1900–57, Central Bureau Voor De Statistiek, Zeist, W. de Haan, 1958, Appendix II, Table D, p. 63.

[3] See the table on divorce and occupation in *Egskeiding in Suid-Afrika* by Hendrik Johannes Pick, Pretoria Ph.D., 1959, p. 262.

include both the established professions of medicine and law, and such occupations as musician, artist, writer, and so on. Teaching is separate and of course has a low ratio. Unfortunately, skilled workers seem to be classified with manual labourers. Thus, although the extreme categories in the Netherlands do fit our thesis, the 'free professions' do not fit.

Yugoslavia. Yugoslavia has recently begun to industrialize, and our hypothesis would suggest that the divorce ratio would be higher towards the upper strata. If education is used as an index, this appears to be so as of 1959.

RATIO OF DIVORCE TO 1,000 MARRIED MALES, BY EDUCATION

School Achievement of Husband	Number of Divorced per 1,000 Married	School Achievement of Husband	Number of Divorced per 1,000 Married
Without school	124	Secondary school (completed)	148
Primary school	124		
Secondary school (incomplete)	144	Faculty, high and higher school	144

SOURCE: *Statistical Yearbook of the Federal People's Republic of Yugoslavia*, Federal People's Republic of Yugoslavia Federal Statistical Institute, Belgrade, August 1961. Calculated from: Table 202–23—Contracted Marriages by School Qualifications of Bridegroom and Bride in 1959 (preliminary data), p. 83; Table 202–27—Divorces by School Qualifications of Husband and Wife in 1959 (preliminary data), p. 85.

However, the ratios by occupations are puzzling. Here the technical problem of the ratio itself is important: if the ratio used is actual divorces and marriages in one given year, the result may be an anomaly: e.g., a high divorce-marriage ratio among pensioners because they do experience some divorces, but very few marriages on account of their age. However, this result is a function of age level rather than of a high propensity to divorce.

In any event, with this warning, the following table presents data comparable in part to the previous tables.

RATIO OF DIVORCES TO MARRIAGES BY OCCUPATION OF HUSBAND *

Occupation of Husband	Number of Divorces per 1,000 Marriages	Occupation of Husband	Number of Divorces per 1,000 Marriages
Unskilled	144	Administrative and managing personnel	256
Workers in manufacturing industries, arts, crafts	140	Professional and technical occupations and artists	132

* Calculated from: *Statistical Yearbook of the Federal People's Republic of Yugoslavia*, Federal Statistical Institute, Belgrade, August 1961. Data calculated from: Table 202–21—Contracted Marriages by Occupation of Bridegroom and Bride in 1959 (preliminary data), p. 83; Table 202–28—Divorces by Occupation of Husband and Wife in 1959 (preliminary data), p. 85.

These figures are also somewhat different from those which Milič has calculated, apparently from the same sources.[4]

Egypt. Egyptian data on such a matter raises the problem, common to all countries in which divorce has been a limited concern of the State, of how adequate the coverage of divorces is, and whether the more literate or better educated couples who divorce are more likely to record their divorces. As can be seen in the succeeding table, the divorce/married ratio predicted holds good primarily for the distinction between employers on the one hand and all other occupations on the other.

RATIO OF DIVORCES TO MARRIAGES BY OCCUPATION OF HUSBAND (EXCLUDING AGRICULTURE FISHING AND HUNTING)*

Categories	Number of Divorces per 1,000 Marriages	Categories	Number of Divorces per 1,000 Marriages
Employers	9	Employees	11
On own account	18	Labourers and artisans	18
Directors and sub-directors	12	Unemployed	117

* Calculated from: *Population Census of Egypt*, 1947, General Tables, Ministry of Finance and Economy, Statistical and Census Department, Government Press, Cairo, 1954. Table XXIX (concluded)—Working Status for Persons engaged in Industries by Sex, Age Group and Civil Status (excluding children below 5 years). Table refers to males and excludes occupations in agriculture, fishing, and hunting, pp. 362–3.

However, one comparison of illiteracy and divorce shows no difference in the literacy of bridegrooms and divorced males in 1956 (47 and 45 per cent).[5]

Ratios calculated for those engaged in agriculture, fishing and hunting in Egypt follow the pattern presented above for occupations outside these categories.[6]

Jordan. Corresponding data do not exist for Jordan, but it is at least possible to calculate that in 1959 75 per cent of the males who married were literate, but only 59 per cent of those who divorced; and 25 per cent of the females who married were literate, but only 5 per cent of the divorcees.[7] Therefore we can conclude that the better educated divorced less than the less educated. This general conclusion also emerges from many non-quantitative analyses of divorce

4 Vojin Milič, 'Sklapanje I Razvod Braka Prema Zanimanju,' in: *Statisticka Revija* No. 7, March 1957, pp. 19–44, especially p. 38.
5 United Arab Republic (Egypt), Presidency of the Republic, Statistics and Census Department, *Vital Statistics, 1956*, Vol. II, Table XXIII, p. 340—Classification of Divorced Males by Locality according to Literacy for year 1956; Table VI, pp. 274–5—Classification of of Bridegrooms by Locality according to Literacy (and Marital Condition) for the year 1956. Perhaps the literate are more likely to record their divorces officially.
6 Population Census of Egypt, 1947, General Tables, op. cit., Table XXIX,—Working Status for Persons engaged in Industries by Sex, Age Group and Civil Status (excluding children under 5 years). This table refers to those engaged in agriculture, fishing and hunting only.
7 *Statistical Yearbook*. 1959. Hashemite Kingdom of Jordan, Jerusalem, pp. 45–50.

in Arabic Islam. Specifically, it is sometimes asserted that divorce and remarriage are the 'poor man's polygyny.'[8]

Finland. Allardt found that in 1947 the divorce rate per 100,000 of the main supporters of the family was higher toward the upper strata, which would fit our first hypothesis. Using these three classes, labouring, middle, and upper, he found rates of 527, 543, and 1,022.

However, most of the *élite* are to be found in Helsinki, where the divorce rates are higher than elsewhere in Finland and a comparison of the divorce applications in different classes in 1945–46 showed no statistically significant differences among them, i.e., in the more industrialized areas, the older class pattern had already changed. Allardt notes that the differences among the classes were greater at the beginning of the century but that there is now very little difference (second hypothesis).[9]

Hungary. As a newly industrializing nation, Hungary would be expected to have a somewhat lower divorce rate toward the lower strata. Our data suggest caution but do conform.

RATIO OF DIVORCES TO MARRIAGES, 1958

Occupation	Number of Divorces	Number of Marriages	Number of Divorces per 1,000
Agricultural workers	1,827	25,154	72
Manual workers	9,133	51,017	179
Intellectuals	3,481	15,156	223

SOURCE: *Statisztikai Evkonyv, 1958*, Kozponti Statisztikai Hivatal, Budapest, 1960. Table 20—Marriages by the Professional Status of Husband and Wife, p. 20; Table 26—Divorces by Professional Status of Husband and Wife, p. 22.

India. The Indian pattern is, of course, very well known though no quantitative data exist. Divorce has been impossible for Brahmans until very recently (1955). On the other hand, the lower castes and the outcasts, as well as tribal groups, have long permitted divorce. As a consequence there is no doubt that the general relationship presented earlier fits at least the observed differences among the strata—though in this instance it is perhaps not possible to make a strong case for differential strain.[10]

[8] Lester Mboria, *La Population de l'Égypte*, University of Paris Faculty of Law Thesis, Cairo, Procaccia, 1938, p. 68.

[9] Erik Allardt, *The Influence of Different Systems of Social Norms on Divorce Rates in Finland*, Columbia University, 1954, mimeographed. These data are taken from Allardt's *Miljöbetingade differenser i skilsmässofrekvensen i Finland 1891–1950*, Helsingfors, Finska Vetenskaps-Societeten, 1953.

[10] See *India: Sociological Background*, HRAF-44 Cornell 8, Vol. 1 (M. Opler, ed.) New Haven, Yale University Press, 1958, p. 25; P. V. Kane, *Hindu Custom and Modern Law*, Bombay, University of Bombay Press, 1950, p. 82; Mohindar Singh, *The Depressed Classes*, Bombay, Hind Kitebs, 1947, p. 168.

China. The case of China is similar to that of Japan. Though China has permitted divorce from at least the T'ang period, divorce has not been a respectable step in Chinese culture and thus would tend to be more common towards the lower strata. Indeed among the *élite*, other solutions were open to the dissatisfied husband.[11]

Japan. The divorce rate in Japan has been dropping over the past half century, though at the same time divorce has been much more completely recorded than formerly. Again, our hypothesis is confirmed. . . .

THE RATIO OF DIVORCE PER 1,000 MARRIED MALE WORKERS 15 YEARS AND OVER, JAPAN, JULY 1957*

Occupation	Number Divorced per 1,000 Male Workers
Technicians and engineers	7
Professors and teachers	3
Medical and public health technicians	5
Managers and officials	4
Clerical and related workers	8
Farmers, lumbermen, fishermen and related workers	10
Workers in mining and quarrying	18
Craftsmen, production process workers, and labourers not else where included	18
Domestic	238

* Calculated from: Japan, Bureau of Statistics, Office of the Prime Minister, *1955 Population Census of Japan*, Vol. II: *One Percent Sample Tabulation*, Part III, 'Occupation, July 1957,' Table 3—Occupation (Intermediate Group) of Employed Persons 15 Years Old and Over by Marital Status and Sex, for all Japan, all *Shi* and all *Gun*, pp. 136–7 (Males only).

[11] A good historical analysis of divorce in China is Wang Tse-Tsiu, *Le Divorce en Chine*, Paris, Lovitow, 1930.

Occupational Mobility in the United States: A Point Estimate and Trend Comparison

ELTON F. JACKSON AND HARRY J. CROCKETT, JR.

Vertical mobility has come to be recognized as a crucial attribute of systems of structured inequality. Stimulated and to some extent foreshadowed by Sorokin's classic *Social Mobility*,[1] studies of social origins and mobility are an outstanding example of cumulative research in modern sociology. Most of this research has concentrated either on the individual effects of mobility or on

Reprinted from the *American Sociological Review*, 29 (February, 1964), pp. 5–15 by permission of the authors and the publisher.
[1] Pitirim A. Sorokin, *Social Mobility*, New York: Harper, 1927.

comparing rates of mobility between societies or within the same society at different times.[2]

This paper reports research in the latter area, the study of mobility trends. We shall first present a reading as of 1957 on intergenerational occupational mobility in the United States and then compare the 1957 findings with several earlier national studies of mobility, paying particular attention to the hypothesis of growing rigidity in the system of occupational inheritance.

OCCUPATIONAL MOBILITY IN 1957

The data for our 1957 estimate of mobility come from a national sample survey conducted in the spring of that year by Gurin, Veroff and Feld at the University of Michigan Survey Research Center.[3] The area probability (cluster) sample consisted of American adults living in private households. We shall confine our analysis to the 1023 males in the sample for whom occupational data were available for themselves and their fathers.[4]

Occupational mobility is measured from responses to the following questions: "What kind of work do you do?" and "What kind of work did your father do for a living while you were growing up?" In order to match our occupational categories, for a trend comparison, with those used by Centers in 1945, we employed his criteria[5] to recode both fathers' and sons' occupations into a seven category scale: (1) Professional, (2) Business, (3) White Collar, (4) Skilled Manual, (5) Semi-Skilled, (6) Unskilled, and (7) Farmer.[6] For other comparisons

[2] For a recent survey and discussion of findings on rates, consequences and conditions of social mobility, see Seymour Martin Lipset and Reinhard Bendix, *Social Mobility in Industrial Society*, Berkeley: University of California Press, 1959.

[3] The major findings of this survey are reported in Gerald Gurin, Joseph Veroff and Sheila Feld, *Americans View Their Mental Health*, New York: Basic Books, 1960. The complete interview schedule is given in Appendix I and details of the sampling procedure in Appendix II.

[4] Fifty-four males had to be dropped for lack of such occupational data. The remaining 1,023 males include 885 employed full-time, 103 retired, 24 unemployed, and 11 employed part-time. Since our object was to estimate the mobility experience of all adult U.S. males, we did not restrict the analysis to full-time employees (except when necessary for comparative purposes). The white, full-time employed sample yields very similar findings, however.

[5] Centers' analysis of male mobility is presented in Richard Centers, "Occupational Mobility of Urban Occupational Strata," *American Sociological Review*, 13 (April, 1948), pp. 197–203. Somewhat more detailed statements of his occupational coding criteria can be found in his "Marital Selection and Occupational Strata," *American Journal of Sociology*, 54 (May, 1949), pp. 530–535, esp. fn. 6, and *The Psychology of Social Classes*, Princeton: Princeton University Press, 1949, pp. 48–50.

[6] The following occupational codes from the 1957 survey were included in the seven categories: (1) Professional: professional, technical and kindred workers, and officers in the Armed Forces; (2) Business: managers, proprietors and officials; (3) White Collar: minor technicians, clerical and kindred workers, and sales workers; (4) Skilled Manual: craftsmen, foremen and kindred workers, skilled and semi-skilled service workers, and government service workers; (5) Semi-Skilled: operatives and kindred workers, Armed Forces enlisted men, and unskilled service workers dealing primarily with people (barbers, beauticians, etc.); (6) Unskilled: unskilled nonfarm laborers and private household workers; and (7) Farmer: farm owners, managers, tenants, and laborers. The content of these categories follows Centers as closely as possible so as to permit an accurate comparison between the 1945 and 1957 data (Table 3).

TABLE 1. Occupation of Males, by Father's Occupation, 1957

Occupation of Respondent's Father	Occupation of Male Respondents (in percentages and mobility ratios)[a]							N(100.0%)[b]
	Professional	Business	White Collar	Skilled Manual	Semi-Skilled	Unskilled	Farmer	
Professional	40.4% (4.81)	19.1% (1.45)	12.8% (.91)	19.1% (.72)	2.1% (.12)	4.3% (.47)	2.1% (.18)	47
Business	18.3 (2.18)	25.8 (1.96)	22.5 (1.61)	15.0 (.57)	12.5 (.72)	1.7 (.18)	4.2 (.36)	120
White collar	20.3 (2.41)	17.4 (1.32)	24.6 (1.76)	20.3 (.77)	10.1 (.59)	5.8 (.64)	1.4 (.13)	69
Skilled manual	8.5 (1.02)	13.6 (1.03)	15.6 (1.11)	42.2 (1.59)	14.6 (.84)	4.5 (.50)	1.0 (.09)	199
Semi-skilled	2.3 (.28)	6.3 (.47)	17.2 (1.23)	28.9 (1.09)	32.8 (1.90)	10.2 (1.12)	2.3 (.20)	128
Unskilled	1.5 (.18)	6.1 (.46)	10.6 (.76)	36.4 (1.37)	27.3 (1.58)	15.2 (1.66)	3.0 (.26)	66
Farmer	2.5 (.30)	11.2 (.85)	8.4 (.60)	21.6 (.81)	16.5 (.95)	13.5 (1.48)	26.4 (2.29)	394
All respondents (N's)	86	135	143	271	177	93	118	1,023

Summary Mobility Measures: Per cent mobile:

Observed	70.0%
Structural movement	27.0
Circulation	43.0
Full-equality model	84.8
Cramér's V	.246

[a] Cell entries in parentheses are mobility ratios, defined as the ratio of the observed cell frequency to the cell frequency expected under conditions of full equality of opportunity.

[b] Some rows do not total to exactly 100.0% because of rounding.

these are collapsed into the familiar Non-Manual-Manual-Farm scale by combining categories 1, 2, and 3 and categories 4, 5, and 6.[7]

Table 1 presents occupational origins and destinations for the 1957 sample, using the seven-point occupational scale. These data show that in every origin category (except unskilled worker) the most common destination is the occupational category of the father—30 per cent of the men in the sample had, in this sense, "inherited" their fathers' occupational level. When movement does occur, it is usually to an adjacent or near-adjacent category. Sons of farmers who do not remain in farming tend to go into manual occupations. Although farmers' sons do not move into nonmanual jobs as often as sons of skilled manual workers, they are more likely than sons of semi-skilled and unskilled workers to go into business positions.

If we assume that our six urban occupational categories are ranked roughly in order of prestige, despite considerable intra-category variation, we can categorize urban movers as upwardly or downwardly mobile. Under this assumption, nearly a quarter of the men in the sample have moved up from an urban origin to a higher urban occupation and about a sixth have moved down.

Information beyond these simple descriptive statements may be garnered from Table 1 by comparing the observed data with two analytic models—one of maximum stability, the other of equal opportunity.

Comparison with a maximum stability model allows us to divide occupational circulation from structural movement.[8] We see in Table 1 that the number of sons in each urban occupational category is larger than the corresponding number for fathers, and that the reverse is true for the farmer category. This, of course, is partly due to the national expansion of urban occupations and contraction of rural occupations. Another source of the discrepancy is the differential fertility of fathers in various occupational groups, producing a surplus of sons in some categories and an insufficient number for full replacement in others. These differences between the fathers' and sons' marginal distributions reflect structural conditions which, in a sense, *force* occupational mobility.

Our figures indicate that if inheritance, or stability, had been at a maximum, all sons of urban fathers could have inherited their fathers' occupational level, about a quarter of the farmers' sons could have inherited, and the remaining farmers' sons would have been forced by lack of farm positions to go into the

[7] It would have been fruitful to assess mobility using a regression analysis based on Duncan's socio-economic index of occupations. Many of the interviews, however, did not provide sufficient detail for coding in the Duncan scheme, and, in any case, comparison with earlier studies required that we match their methods as closely as possible. For details of this index see Otis Dudley Duncan, "A Socioeconomic Index for All Occupations" and "Properties and Characteristics of the Socioeconomic Index," Chs. 6 and 7 in Albert J. Reiss, Jr., *et al.*, *Occupations and Social Status*, New York: Free Press, 1961, pp. 109–161. For an example of regression analysis of social mobility employing these scores, see Otis Dudley Duncan and Robert W. Hodge, "Education and Occupational Mobility: A Regression Analysis," *American Journal of Sociology*, 68 (May, 1963), pp. 629–644.

[8] A similar analysis, employing Swedish data, can be found in Gösta Carlsson, *Social Mobility and Class Structure*, Lund: Gleerup, 1958, pp. 103–104.

vacant urban occupations. In other words, under conditions of maximum inheritance or stability, 73 per cent of the sample would have inherited and 27 per cent (all farmers' sons) would necessarily have moved due to structural change.

The observed data, on the other hand, show much more movement than this necessary minimum generated by structural conditions. Even in urban occupations, where complete inheritance was possible, in no case did a majority of sons of a given origin inherit their fathers' occupational level. Comparison with the maximum stability model, then, indicates that of the 70 per cent who did in fact move, the movement of 27 per cent can be attributed to structural conditions; the remaining 43 per cent may be counted as circulators. "Circulation" represents mutual exchange among the occupational categories, for example, upward mobility balanced by downward, and (less frequently) movement from the farm balance by movement from urban to rural employment. The amount of circulation suggests how open the system would be in times of structural stability.

In our second comparison, we calculate how the mobility table would look if all sons had equal occupational opportunity. This full-equality model assumes that the occupation of the father has no effect on that of the son and therefore depicts, in a sense, a situation of maximum mobility. The expected figures are computed using the marginals in exactly the manner employed in a chi-square test. Since the full-equality model thus reflects the structural conditions expressed in the marginal distributions, deviations from the model cannot be simply attributed to structural conditions.

Several sorts of deviation from the full equality model will be of interest to us here. In parentheses below the percentages in Table 1 are shown ratios of the observed frequency in that cell to the frequency predicted by the full-equality model. These mobility ratios indicate whether each form of movement or inheritance occurs more often than expected (ratios greater than one) or less often than expected (ratios less than one).[9] The ratios show a pattern similar to that of the percentages—a tendency for sons disproportionately to enter their father's occupational category or one nearby. Inheritance beyond random expectation is especially marked for sons of professionals and farmers. Among sons of urban workers, deviations in the direction of upward mobility are larger and more common than those indicating disproportionate downward mobility. The model figures can also be summed to yield the expected proportion experiencing all types of movement. About 85 percent of the sample would have moved (i.e., would not have inherited) under conditions of full equality; this compares to an observed movement of 70 per cent of the men.

An overall comparison between the observed and the full-equality figures can be obtained by computing Cramér's V, a measure of association that is based on chi-square and thus reflects the divergence of the observed from the

---

[9] For a discussion of these ratios and an extended example of their use and interpretation, see Natalie Rogoff, *Recent Trends in Occupational Mobility*, Glencoe, Ill.: Free Press, 1953 esp. pp. 29–33.

model figures.[10] In other words, the value of V indicates the strength of the relation between fathers' and sons' occupations, reflecting all forms of contingency and not only direct occupational inheritance. The value of V, .246, is consistent with the above analysis, showing that movement in our sample departs only moderately from a system of full occupational equality.[11]

Gross Occupational Mobility. When we collapse the relatively fine occupational scale of Table 1 into a simple Nonmanual-Manual-Farm scale, the data show that almost one-third of the sons of nonmanual workers fall into the manual stratum and the same proportion of manual sons rise into nonmanual jobs; about two-thirds of the sons from both origins are stable (detailed figures are given in Table 4). Farmers are recruited almost entirely from the sons of farmers, but almost three-quarters of the sons of farmers move into urban occupations, over half into the manual stratum. Farmer's sons do not attain nonmanual positions quite as often as do sons of urban manual workers.

The gross mobility table, of course, counts part of the movement appearing in Table 1 as stability, and thus gives the impression of less mobility than Table 1. When the gross mobility figures are compared with the maximum stability model (Table 4), the percentage of mobility attributable to structural change is still 27 per cent, because the only structural movement is from farm to urban occupations and the farm category was not collapsed when the occupational scale was reduced to three categories. The percentage of men who can be regarded as circulators thus drops to about 21 per cent. In our second comparison, the full-equality model predicts movement of about two-thirds of the sample, compared to an observed figure of about 48 per cent. The value of Cramér's V for the gross table is .348, still a moderate relation between the occupations of father and son.

Occupational Mobility and Age. In Table 2 we present the gross occupational mobility of our sample within 10-year age groups (the small sample size prevented finer age or occupational breaks). Age should have two opposed effects in occupational mobility in modern urban industrialized societies. In the first place, as a man grows older he has more opportunity to gain education, accumulate capital and experience and in other ways improve his chances for attaining or maintaining a high occupational position. Also, young men who are training for high-status occupations often must delay their entry into the labor force until a later age than persons entering low-status positions. For these reasons, age should be *positively* correlated with upward mobility and with inheritance of high occupational status. This is a cyclic effect, recurring as each generation passes through the occupational structure. On the other hand, a long-term trend effect stems from expanding educational opportunities and an increasing number of high-status positions. Age here indicates the period during which

[10] For a description of this measure, see Hubert M. Blalock, Jr., *Social Statistics*, New York: McGraw-Hill, 1960, p. 230.

[11] Duncan and Hodge, *op. cit.*, pp. 634–635, obtained a similarly modest zero-order correlation between father's and sons' occupations, using 1950 data from Chicago (r = approx. .30). Of course, the values of the two coefficients are not directly comparable, since ours is a chi-square measure and theirs a product-moment correlation.

TABLE 2. Occupation of Males, by Father's Occupation and Age, 1957

	Respondent's Father Nonmanual Worker			
	Respondent's Occupation			
Respondent's Age in 1957	Nonmanual	Manual	Farm	N (100.0%)ᵃ
21–29	63.8%	36.2%	0.0%	47
30–39	72.7	25.0	2.3	44
40–49	73.8	26.2	0.0	65
50–59	67.6	24.3	8.1	37
60 and over	52.4	40.5	7.1	42

	Respondent's Father Manual Worker			
	Respondent's Occupation			
	Nonmanual	Manual	Farm	N (100.0%)ᵃ
21–29	33.3%	65.4%	1.3%	78
30–39	33.6	65.5	.9	110
40–49	29.9	68.8	1.3	77
50–59	27.0	68.3	4.8	63
60 and over	25.0	73.4	1.6	64

	Respondent's Father Farmer			
	Respondent's Occupation			
	Nonmanual	Manual	Farm	N (100.0%)ᵃ
21–29	17.1%	53.7%	29.3%	41
30–39	23.0	60.9	16.1	87
40–49	30.9	49.4	19.8	81
50–59	29.2	48.6	22.2	72
60 and over	12.5	46.4	41.1	112

ᵃ Some rows do not total to exactly 100.0% because of rounding. These N's total to only 1,020 because the ages of three respondents were not ascertained.

the man trained for and began his occupational career. Younger men entered the system at a later period and thereby received more advantages, thus producing a *negative* relation between age and upward mobility.

To separate these two effects, we need comparative data by age for different time periods.[12] Lacking such data, we present our age analysis in relatively simple

[12] For an attempt to separate these factors through an age-cohort analysis, see Gerhard E. Lenski, "Trends in Inter-Generational Occupational Mobility in the United States," *American Sociological Review*, 23 (October, 1958), pp. 514–523. Our age categories mask some of the effects of the economic depression which Lenski identified, since the 1903–1912 cohort is split and combined with adjacent five-year groups. When the same cohorts as used by Lenski are examined, sons of nonmanual workers in the depression cohort were less likely to remain nonmanual and more likely to move down to a manual job than in adjacent older or younger cohorts.

form, expecting the two opposing effects to produce a curvilinear relationship —men of middle age should enjoy some of the benefits and avoid most of the hardships of both effects, and thus should hold better occupational positions than younger or older men. The data in Table 2 do indeed show such a curvilinear relationship for sons of nonmanual workers and sons of farmers. Middle-aged sons of nonmanual workers are more likely than either older or younger sons to have remained in or returned to a nonmanual job, and less likely to have moved down to a manual job. Among sons of farmers, the middle-aged cohorts are the most likely to have attained nonmanual urban employment. Among the sons of manual workers, however, the relationship is roughly monotonic—the older a man, the more likely he is to have remained in the manual category, the less likely to have moved up to a nonmanual job. Apparently the educational and occupational trends discussed above affect sons of manual workers, but the career mobility cyclic effect is weaker than in other origin groups, perhaps because manual sons in the early years of their working careers are less likely to accumulate the financial or educational capital necessary for upward career mobility.

In summary, our 1957 estimate of mobility rates in the U.S. suggests that despite a clear tendency for sons to follow occupations within or near the occupational categories of their fathers, the influence of father's occupation on son's is only moderate. In other words, the behavior of the system of occupational transmission is closer to that of a full-equality model than to a model of maximum inheritance. We now turn to comparisons of our findings with those of earlier national studies of mobility.

TREND COMPARISONS OF OCCUPATIONAL MOBILITY

In 1955 Ely Chinoy[13] assessed the empirical and theoretical studies on mobility trends in the U.S. and concluded that they had failed to establish with any convincing degree of accuracy whether national mobility rates were rising, falling, or remaining stationary. Few empirical studies on the question have appeared in the ensuing years. Lenski, employing age cohort estimates,[14] concluded that upward mobility increased in the last half-century (largely for structural reasons), that downward mobility rose and then fell to the original rate, and that upward mobility opportunities for sons of farmers declined relative to those of urban sons. Perrucci's study of engineers[15] concluded that the structure of opportunities for this group became more rigid from 1911 to 1950, since the father's position increasingly influenced the (engineering) position of the son.

[13] Ely Chinoy, "Social Mobility Trends in the United States," *American Sociological Review*, 20 (April, 1955), pp. 180–186.

[14] Lenski, *op. cit.* This is the only previous attempt known to the authors to estimate mobility trends empirically using national sample data.

[15] Robert Perrucci, "The Significance of Intra-Occupational Mobility: Some Methodological and Theoretical Notes, Together with a Case Study of Engineers," *American Sociological Review*, 26 (December, 1961), pp. 875–883.

In this section we shall attempt to estimate mobility trends by comparing our 1957 findings to the three available national reports on U.S. occupational mobility: Centers' 1945 study,[16] the 1947 "Jobs and Occupations" survey of the National Opinion Research Center,[17] and the Survey Research Center's 1952 election study, as reported by Lenski.[18] Our comparisons do not span nearly as long a time period as some earlier studies; but they do make a start at the *direct* measurement of national mobility trends.

It is important to examine the comparability of these surveys, both with regard to the sampling procedure and to the questions on occupation. None of these studies was primarily directed toward the assessment of occupational mobility; hence, neither the sampling designs nor the questions on occupation are especially adapted to mobility research.

The 1952 and 1957 Survey Research Center studies use area cluster samples, which are usually closely representative of the national population of non-institutionalized adults.[19] The 1945 and 1947 studies, however, employ quota sampling procedures, which typically over-represent persons from higher social strata.[20] (Centers reports such a bias in a comparison of the occupational distribution of his sample with the 1940 U.S. Census distribution.[21]) We assume that the effect of this bias is not so great nor so focused as to distort any overall mobility trend.

The occupational questions in the three comparison studies were as follows:

1945:[22] "What do you do for a living?"
     "What was or is your father's occupation?"
1947:[23] "What kind of work do you do?"
     "What is (was) your father's main occupation?"
1952:[24] "What is your occupation? I mean, what kind of work do you do?"
     "What kind of work did your father do for a living while you were growing up?"

The minor variations in the questions concerning respondent's occupation do not seem likely to make for serious difficulties in comparing the four studies. Variations in questions regarding occupation of respondent's father seem more troublesome: the questions used in the 1952 and 1957 studies focus on father's

[16] Centers, "Occupational Mobility of Urban Occupational Strata," *op. cit.*

[17] National Opinion Research Center, "Jobs and Occupations," *Opinion News*, (September 1, 1947), pp. 3–13. The data used in the present paper are those derived from the NORC report by Natalie Rogoff and published in Lipset and Bendix, *op. cit.*, p. 21.

[18] Lenski, *op. cit.*

[19] For a detailed statement of the sampling design of the 1952 study, see Angus Campbell, Gerald Gurin, and Warren E. Miller, *The Voter Decides*, Evanston, Illinois: Row, Peterson, 1954.

[20] For a description of these samples, see: 1945 study—Centers, *The Psychology of Social Classes*, pp. 34–38; 1947 study—Reiss, *et al.*, *op. cit.*, p. 6.

[21] Centers, *The Psychology of Social Classes*, p. 38.

[22] *Ibid.*, pp. 232, 234.

[23] Reiss, *op. cit.*, pp. 259–260.

[24] Campbell, *et al.*, *op. cit.*, p. 226.

occupation while the respondent was "growing up," but the 1945 and 1947 questions do not specify the period for which father's occupation should be given. Respondents in these earlier studies might have tended to take advantage of the less restrictive question by reporting as father's occupation the most prestigeful job he ever held; this might produce lower rates of upward mobility and higher rates of downward mobility in the two earlier studies as compared with the 1952 and 1957 studies. The size of this bias, if any, unfortunately cannot be estimated.

1945–1957 Comparison. Centers' is the earliest national sample study on male occupational mobility of which we are aware. We compare his findings with ours separately from the other two studies since he uses a relatively fine occupational break and also because he presents no data on sons of farmers, as the other studies do. To make this comparison two sorts of alteration were necessary: (1) in order to match occupational categories, we merged Centers' two Business categories into one and his two Farmer categories into one, since our 1957 occupational data were not sufficiently precise to permit such fine distinctions; (2) we reduced our sample of adult males to whites, employed full- or part-time, whose fathers were not farmers, since Centers presented data for this group only. The comparison, then, is in terms of six occupational origins and seven destinations and applies only to white employed men of urban occupational origin.

The general pattern of occupational movement and stability is similar in the 1945 and 1957 samples. Inheritance or movement to an adjacent occupational group is the most common destination for sons of all origins in both studies. The summary mobility measures in Table 3, however, reveal several differences between the two samples.

First, somewhat more mobility was observed in the later sample: 67.7 per cent had moved from their father's occupation in 1957, compared to 61.5 per cent in 1945.[25] The bottom line of Table 3 indicates that more urban sons experienced upward mobility in 1957 than in 1945 (urban upward and downward mobility are defined as in the first section). When the observed mobility figures are compared to the model of maximum stability, the percentage who were "forced" to move by structural conditions is similar in the two samples; the difference between the two studies is essentially in the amount of circulation.

Mobility differences are also indicated by comparing the deviations of the two samples from their respective models of equal opportunity. Mobility ratios are presented in Table 3 for men from each origin and for the whole sample; these are the ratios of the observed numbers inheriting, moving up, or moving down to the numbers expected under a situation of full equality. For each occupational origin, the 1945 inheritance ratio is higher than that for 1957, indicating that the tendency to depart from full equality was greater in the earlier sample. The tendency toward upward mobility was uniformly higher in 1957.

[25] Unfortunately, this comparison and those to follow all involve quota samples; tests of statistical significance were not applied because the assumption of random sampling is not met.

TABLE 3. OCCUPATIONAL MOBILITY OF WHITE, EMPLOYED MALES OF URBAN ORIGIN, 1945 AND 1957 COMPARED

Summary Mobility Measures

	1945	1957
N	(637)	(538)
Per cent mobile:		
Observed	61.5%	67.7%
Structural movement	16.8	14.5
Circulation	44.7	53.2
Full-equality model	81.9	81.1
Cramér's V	.297	.233

	Inheritance		Upward Mobility		Downward Mobility	
	1945	1957	1945	1957	1945	1957
Mobility ratios by origin:						
Professional	3 54	3.41	–	–	.71	.62
Business	2.05	1.80	1.32	1.49	.63	.71
White collar	2.25	1.21	.91	1.39	.46	.72
Skilled manual	1.66	1.47	.76	.83	1.03	.82
Semi-skilled	2.26	2.07	.61	.72	1.36	1.48
Unskilled	4.85	1.79	.67	.93	–	–
Overall mobility:						
Ratios	2.13	1.71	.74	.90	.73	.74
Percentages[a]	38.5%	32.3%	29.7%	39.8%	27.0%	25.7%

[a] These percentages do not sum to 100% either for 1945 or 1957 because movement into farm occupations is not included in any column.

Lastly, the values of Cramér's V indicate that in the 1945 sample the son's occupation was more closely related to his father's than the 1957 sample.

Although these differences are not strikingly large, the figures consistently indicate, then, that white, employed, urban-born men in the 1957 sample experienced somewhat more mobility than did those in the 1945 sample. Our task is now to account for this result. Our analysis rules out structural change as an explanation. Unfortunately, we cannot definitely dismiss the possibility that the mobility "trend" is due at least partly to differences in the age distributions of the two samples. Centers' study was completed just before World War II ended. Therefore, despite a quota sample control for persons above and below 40 years of age, his interviewers were unable to sample the millions of men who were at that time serving in the Armed Forces. The proportion below age 30 in his sample is therefore smaller than in ours, and the proportion in the age 30–40 category larger.[26] Our data on age and mobility presented in the previous

[26] These remarks are based on an age distribution presented in Centers' The Psychology of Social Classes, p. 167. This distribution includes 825 of his 1,100 respondents. Since the degree of correspondence between this 825-person sample and the 637-person mobility sample is unknown, these figures cannot be used for an indirect age standardization of the two mobility samples, which might otherwise have indicated the extent to which age differences produced the mobility differences.

section indicate that if this complement of young men had been added to the 1945 sample, that sample would probably have shown more mobility, thus reducing the differences between the two compared studies.

A second interpretation, which could either supplement or replace the first is that the effect of military service on many men was to broaden their occupational aspirations and, in the form of post-war assistance in technical and academic training, provide for implementation of some of these aspirations. In many cases, too, by interrupting careers, military service might also have produced downward mobility. In other words, the war might have loosened the ties between fathers' occupation and sons' occupation for the cohort beginning their careers at that time. Therefore, even if the 1945 sample had included more young men, the 1957 sample might still have had a higher mobility rate, since it includes those veterans after the effects of military service have had time to emerge.

A third explanation is that the findings represent at least in part a long-term relaxation in the system of occupational transmission, due to such factors as increased educational opportunities and the decreasing importance of inherited financial capital in occupational success. The postwar comparisons, to which we now turn, tend to support this conclusion.

1947–1952–1957 Comparison. Our second comparison differs from the previous one in that all three samples consist of all adult U.S. males, including nonwhite and sons of farmers, thus yielding a more comprehensive picture of occupational mobility in the U.S. at three points in time. The nature of the reported data for the two earlier studies, however, restricts our occupational measurement to simple Nonmanual, Manual, and Farm categories. Centers' 1945 study is not included here because his sample included no nonwhites and because he did not report data for sons of farmers.

Table 4 indicates that the general pattern of occupational movement is similar for all three samples. The only consistent difference of any size is the rise from 1947 to 1957 in the percentage of farmers' sons going into manual occupations, and the corresponding fall in the percentage remaining on the farm. The mobility ratios for this row, however, show only a small variation over time, indicating that this trend is mainly attributable to structural shifts in the availability of farm and manual occupations.

As for the amount of mobility, Table 4 shows a slight increase in the percentage of movers in the samples from 1947 to 1957. When the observed figures are broken down into the movement due to structural conditions (from the maximum stability model) and the remaining circulation, we see that the percentage of structural movement increased between 1947 and 1952, producing a small drop in the movement attributable to circulation, despite the increased total amount of movement. Neither of these changes continued from 1952 to 1957. The context of this change, however, is such that it may be spurious. In all three samples, structural movement is entirely due to the excess of sons with farmer fathers over sons currently employed in farming, meaning that considerable numbers of farm sons could not inherit their fathers' occupation and

TABLE 4. OCCUPATIONAL MOBILITY OF MALES IN THREE NATIONAL SAMPLES

Occupation of Male Respondents
(in percentages and mobility ratios)[a]

Occupation of Respondent's Father	Nonmanual			Manual			Farm			N's (100.0%)[b]		
	1947	1952	1957	1947	1952	1957	1947	1952	1957	1947	1952	1957
Nonmanual	70.8% (1.74)	64.7% (1.90)	66.5% (1.87)	25.1% (.58)	34.0% (.67)	30.5% (.58)	4.1% (.26)	1.3% (.09)	3.0% (.26)	319	153	236
Manual	35.1 (.86)	31.1 (.91)	30.5 (.86)	60.9 (1.41)	67.1 (1.32)	67.7 (1.28)	4.0 (.25)	1.8 (.12)	1.8 (.15)	430	280	393
Farm	23.0 (.56)	22.0 (.64)	22.1 (.62)	39.1 (.90)	44.3 (.87)	51.5 (.97)	37.9 (2.37)	33.8 (2.23)	26.4 (2.29)	404	314	394
All respondents (N's)	470	255	364	499	379	541	184	113	118	1,153	747	1,023

Summary mobility measures:

	1947	1952	1957
Per cent mobile:			
Observed	44.4%	47.4%	48.5%
Structural movement	19.1	26.9	27.0
Circulation	25.3	20.5	21.5
Full-equality model	67.0	67.6	67.0
Cramér's V	.390	.372	.348

[a] Cell entries in parentheses are mobility ratios.
[b] Some rows do not total to exactly 100.0% due to rounding.

were "forced" to move to urban jobs. The true percentage of men with farmer fathers in the U.S. is probably decreasing consistently over time. [27] The percentage is indeed smaller in the 1957 sample than in the 1952 sample, but the percentage of men with farmer fathers in the 1947 sample is lower than in either of the two later studies. This suggests that the 1947 quota interviewers failed to contact a representative number of respondents with farm fathers. If the percentage of farmer fathers in the 1947 sample had been even one percentage point higher than in 1952, the structural movement percentage would have been practically constant for all three samples. We may plausibly infer, then, that the increase in structural mobility and the resultant decrease in circulation from 1947 to 1952 are probably due to undersampling of farmers' sons in the earlier study.

At any rate, the difference stems solely from the movement of farm sons. If the three samples are compared in terms of the mobility of urban workers' sons alone, no such trend is apparent. If anything, the amount of movement attributable to structural conditions decreased slightly, as our 1945–1957 comparison, confined to sons of urban workers, indicated.

The final comparison involves the deviations of each of the three samples from the distributions expected under a random, or full-equality model. The value of Cramér's V decreases somewhat over the period, suggesting a decrease in the degree to which the samples depart from the model. If the pattern of occupational transmission has changed at all in the U.S. in these years, it has moved toward a situation of full equality of opportunity.

SUMMARY AND CONCLUSIONS

The following conclusions are suggested by our data:

1. In 1957 differential replacement rates and changes in occupational structure had produced movement of about a quarter of U.S. men from farm origin into urban, especially manual, occupations. Considerable circulation, however, occurred beyond this minimal structural mobility: using a relatively fine measure of occupation, the amount of movement was much closer to that expected in a situation of full equality of opportunity than to the minimum imposed by the differences between fathers' and sons' occupational distributions. The relation between fathers' and sons' occupations was only moderate.

2. Comparisons with earlier national mobility studies yield an impression that no striking changes have occurred in mobility patterns and rates since World War II. The conservative interpretation might be that of essentially no change. What movement has occurred, however, is in the direction of increasing rates of movement and decreasing influence of father's occupation on that of his son.

The scope of these findings should be carefully qualified. They pertain only to intergenerational occupational mobility, they are based on total national

[27] Our age data and those of Lenski, *op. cit.*, support this assumption. In both samples the percentage of men who are sons of farmers falls consistently from the older to the younger age cohorts. Also, with one exception, each of the age cohorts in the 1957 sample had a smaller percentage of farmers' sons than did the same age cohort in the 1952 sample.

samples, and they cover only the years since World War II. Entirely different forms of change may have occurred in educational, financial, or other forms of mobility; the national data may mask important variations among communities, occupations, and other sub-groups; and mobility changes in earlier (or later) periods might be of quite a different order. The data suggest, however, that the rate of occupational mobility in the United States has increased somewhat since the end of World War II. At the least, we found scant evidence that the system of occupational inheritance is growing more rigid.

A Comparison of the Amount of Social Mobility in the Contemporary United States and Europe

BERNARD BARBER

. . . a cross-national comparison of occupational rating scores in several different modern industrialized societies—the United States, Great Britain, New Zealand, Japan, Germany, and Soviet Russia—shows fundamental similarities in these ratings in the different countries. The similar ratings are presumably the results of similarities and near-similarities both in their social structural arrangements and value systems. Since this is so, we might expect that these social structural and value similarities would produce further similarities in other aspects of the structure and processes of their stratification systems, and specifically in the processes and amounts of social mobility.

But popular images in this respect have been quite different. Both in the United States and in Europe. the common popular view—and indeed also the prevalent view among social scientists—has been that the amount of social mobility in the United States is much larger than in other modern industrialized societies. Both in the United States and in Europe, the view has gone almost unchallenged that the United States is the premier "land of opportunity," that it is a much more "open" society than any other. Perhaps this is so in fact. Perhaps this view will eventually be shown to be correct by satisfactory comparative national studies of social mobility. But recently Lipset and his colleagues have performed the useful service of pointing out that there is no good evidence to support the belief that America does have a much larger amount of social mobility than its modern industrial counterparts in Europe.[1]

From *Social Stratification* by Bernard Barber, © 1967 by Harcourt, Brace & World, Inc. and reprinted with their permission.

[1] Seymour Martin Lipset and Natalie Rogoff, "Class and Opportunity in Europe and the U.S.: Some Myths and What the Statistics Show," *Commentary*, Dec. 1954, 562–68. See also critical letters in *Commentary* by Lewis A. Coser, Jan. 1955, and Kurt B. Mayer, April 1955. See also the following unpublished documents by Lipset and H. L. Zetterberg: *Proposal for a Comparative Study of Social Mobility; A Theory of Social Mobility; Class and Mobility— Definitions and Measurements for a Comparative Survey;* and *Memorandum on the Relevance of Business Elite Studies for a Comparative Analysis of Class and Mobility*; all documents of the Bureau of Applied Social Research, Columbia U.

They have raised the question whether this belief may not be more the product of various American and European ideologies than of scientifically established fact. In the United States, for example, at least until recently, there seems to have been an ideological tendency to exaggerate the amount of social mobility occurring in this country, a tendency expressed partly in overstating the amount, and partly in giving full publicity to all the mobility that did in fact occur. That is, the predominant American ideology has consisted both in false and in highly selective perception. Moreover, since ideology often has a comparative reference, Americans have tended to minimize the amount of mobility in Europe, which was the natural standard of reference for a society that has a great many of its own historical and social roots there. In modern Europe, on the other hand, ideological distortion about the amount of mobility there in comparison with the United States has sprung from different social sources. In modern Europe, because of its historical roots in an aristocratic, caste type of society, there has been an ideological tendency to minimize the amount of social mobility and to exaggerate, in comparison, the amount occurring in the United States.

We may examine this question somewhat more objectively by looking at the data which Lipset and his colleagues have collected from studies of social mobility made on national samples of eight different American and European populations. These data have several important deficiencies; nevertheless they do shed some light on the matter in hand. Before examining these comparative data, then, let us identify some of their deficiencies.[2]

First of all, the eight different samples are not all properly comparable with one another. They use somewhat different occupational and class categories for classifying the fathers and sons for whom the mobility is being measured. Even the three American samples are not strictly comparable in this respect. Secondly, apart from non-comparability of categories, the evidence is often weak. In six of the eight studies, the mobility data were collected only quite incidentally to some other major purpose. For example, in at least one study, the reports by sons about their fathers' social class position are known to have been ideologically distorted by "working class" identifications. And, finally, after these two deficiencies have been recognized and the data are made as comparable as possible, the social categories in which fathers and sons can be classified are still so rough that they constitute adequate indicators of class position and of social mobility only in the sense that there is nothing much better available.

Lipset and Zetterberg have reclassified the data under the three categories, "nonmanual," "manual," and "farm." Movement from "farm" or "manual" into "nonmanual" is assumed to represent social mobility; but of course this can be assumed only quite tentatively. All the studies, as we shall see, show considerable movement from "farm" or "manual" into "nonmanual," and this is one kind of mobility that reflects important changes in the social structure

---

[2] Lipset and Zetterberg, *A Theory of Social Mobility*, Publication A-185 of the Bureau of Applied Social Research, Columbia U., 1955, have discussed these deficiencies themselves in some detail. See especially p. 22.

of modern industrialized societies. The proportion of "nonmanual" jobs has been steadily increasing. But whether movement into "nonmanual" positions represents social mobility in the sense of moving into a more highly evaluated social position is a matter which cannot be ascertained from the data as they

SOCIAL MOBILITY IN REPRESENTATIVE COUNTRIES*

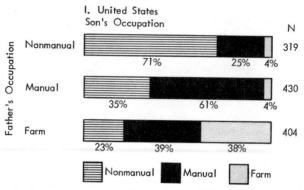

(SOURCE: Derived by Natalie Rogoff from data published in National Opinion Research Center, "Jobs and Occupations: A Popular Evaluation," *Publ. Opin. News*, 9 (1947), 3–13.)

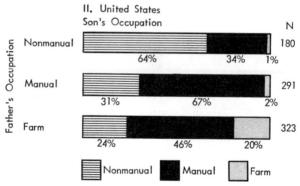

(SOURCE: Computed from data obtained by the Survey Research Center, U. of Michigan, in its study of the 1952 Presidential election.)

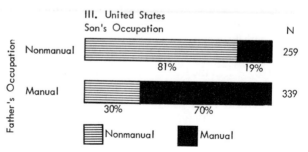

(SOURCE: Richard Centers, *The Psychology of Social Classes*, Princeton U. Press, 1949, p. 181.)

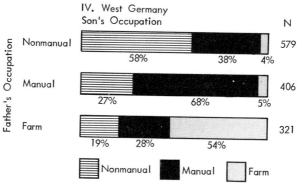

(SOURCE: Computed from data obtained by the Unesco Institute, Cologne, in its study of West German attitudes in 1953.)

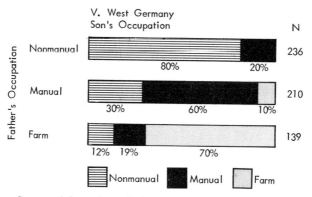

(SOURCE: Computed from data obtained by the *Institut fuer Demoskopie*, Allensbach, Germany, in one of its surveys of West German opinion.)

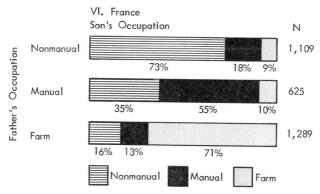

(SOURCE: M. Brésard, "Mobilité Social et Dimension de la Famille," *Population*, 5 (1950), 533–67. Also on France see Natalie Rogoff, "Social Stratification in France and in the United States," *Amer. J. Social.*, 58 (1953), 347–57.)

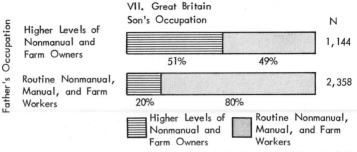

(Source: Adapted from David V. Glass, ed., *Social Mobility in Britain*, Routledge and Kegan Paul, London, 1954.)

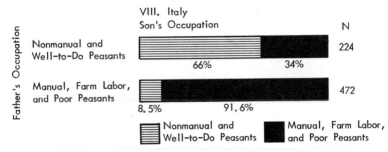

(Source: L. Livi, "Sur la Mesure de la Mobilité Sociale," *Population, 5* (1950), 65–76.)

(Source: Robert A. Feldmesser, "The Persistence of Status Advantages in Soviet Russia," *Amer. J. Sociol., 59* (1953), 19–27. Based on a study of a group of émigrés from Soviet Russia. Representativeness of sample is unknown.)

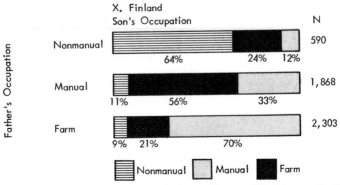

[Source: Tauno Hellevuo, "Poimintatutkimus, Säätykierrosta" ("A Sampling Study of Social Mobility"), *Suomalainera Suomi*, No. 1, 1952, 93–96.]

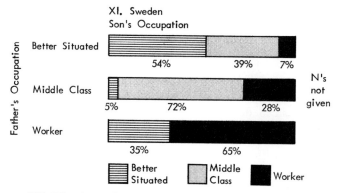

(SOURCE: Ellis Håstad, "*Gallup*" *Och Den Svenska Väljarkåren*, Hugo Gebers Förlag, Uppsala, 1950, p. 271.)

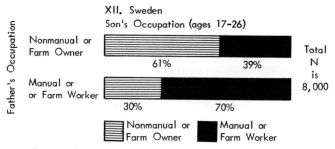

(SOURCE: Computed from materials in Ungdomsvårdskommitten, *Ungdomen möter sambället*, Statens Offentliga Utredningar, 41, Stockholm, 1951, pp. 32–34.)

* All twelve of these graphs are adapted from tables in Lipset and Zotterberg, *A Theory of Social Mobility*, Publication A-185 of the Bureau of Applied Social Research, Columbia University, 1955, p. 21, the original sources of which are indicated here by a note accompanying each graph. With the exception of those on Russian émigrés (Graph IX), all data are based on national samples of the respective countries. In all cases, the respondents are taken as sons.

have been collected. Some movement from "farm" or "manual" into "non-manual" consists only in a change of occupations at the same class level.

Despite all these weaknesses, the data on social mobility in eight different countries presented in the following twelve graphs provide more factual information on this subject than was previously available.

These, then, are the somewhat inadequate but still interesting data available on amounts of mobility in the United States and in several European countries at the present time. Lipset and Zetterberg put their conclusions about relative amounts of mobility in the United States and Europe in this way:

When examining results of these studies, especially the ones for the United States, France, and Germany (which are most comparable), there can be little doubt that the advanced European countries for which we have data have "high" rates of social mobility, if by a high rate we mean one which is similar to that in the United States. In each country, a large minority is able to rise above the occupational position of their fathers, while a smaller but still substantial minority falls in occupational status.

In all these modern industrialized, open-class societies, then, there is considerable social mobility.[3] But as the authors themselves go on to say, "Whether there are significant differences among these countries can only be decided after the completion of an integrated comparative research project, which employs the same methods of collecting, classifying, and processing the data. Thus far, no such study exists." Lipset and Zetterberg have cleared the ground for the necessary next steps in comparative research on the amounts of mobility that occur in different modern societies of the open-class industrial type. Probably it will not be long before such research is forthcoming.

Additional Readings

REINHARD BENDIX and FRANK W. HOWTON, "Social Mobility and the American Business Elite," *The British Journal of Sociology*, 8 (December, 1957), pp. 357–369.

REINHARD BENDIX and FRANK W. HOWTON, "Social Mobility and the American Business Elite," *The British Journal of Sociology*, 9 (March, 1958), pp. 1–14.

ROBERT C. DAVIS, "Poverty in the Affluent Society. A Review Article," *Sociological Quarterly*, 4 (Autumn, 1963), pp. 335–343.

OTIS D. DUNCAN, "The Trend of Occupational Mobility in the United States," *American Sociological Review*, 30 (August, 1965), pp. 491–498.

ARCHIBALD O. HALLER and DAVID M. LEWIS, "The Hypothesis of Intersocietal Similarity in Occupational Prestige Hierarchies," *American Journal of Sociology*, 72 (September, 1966), pp. 210–216.

ROBERT W. HODGE, DONALD J. TREIMAN, and PETER H. ROSSI, "A Comparative Study of Occupational Prestige," in Reinhard Bendix and Seymour Lipset (eds.), *Class, Status, and Power* (New York: The Free Press, 1966), pp. 309–321.

CHARLES KADUSHIN, "Social Class and the Experience of Ill Health," *Sociological Inquiry*, 34 (Winter, 1964), pp. 67–80.

GABRIEL KOLKO, *Wealth and Power in America* (New York: Frederick A. Praeger, 1962).

SEYMOUR MARTIN LIPSET and REINHARD BENDIX, *Social Mobility in Industrial Society* (Berkeley: University of California Press, 1959), pp. 11–75 and 114–143.

ALAN LITTLE and JOHN WESTERGAARD, "The Trend of Class Differentials in Educational Opportunity in England and Wales," *British Journal of Sociology*, 15 (December, 1964), pp. 301–316.

HAROLD LYDALL and JOHN B. LANSING, "A Comparison of the Distribution of Personal Income and Wealth in the United States and Great Britain," *American Economic Review*, 49 (March, 1959), pp. 43–67.

DWIGHT MACDONALD, "Our Invisible Poor," *The New Yorker*, 38 (January 19, 1963), pp. 82–132.

DENNIS H. WRONG, "Trends in Class Fertility in Western Nations," *The Canadian Journal of Economics and Political Science*, 24 (May, 1958), pp. 216–229.

---

[3] And, with regard to comparisons between the United States and Europe for periods in the recent past, Lipset and Zetterberg say, *A Theory of Social Mobility*, p. 24 and n. 32: "Furthermore, available historical material tends to indicate that much of Europe had occupational mobility rates from 1900 to 1940 which are similar to the present, and which did not lag behind the American one."

PART III

Types of Groups

Introduction

Part III, "Types of Groups," contains three sections: "Community," "Organization," and "Collective Behavior." As in Part I, a single Introduction will serve for
the three sections.

COMMUNITY. The first two selections present factual information about the
growth of *urban communities*. The selection by Hauser, "The Growth of Metropolitan Areas in the United States," emphasizes at least six points. First, the population
has become increasingly concentrated in metropolitan areas. (A metropolitan area
is generally a county which contains a city—termed the "central city"—with 50,000
or more inhabitants.) In 1900, about 32 per cent of the population lived in metropolitan areas; by 1960 the figure had increased to about 63 per cent. Second, the
population within metropolitan areas has become increasingly decentralized.
Between 1900 and 1950, the central cities within the metropolitan areas increased
their population by about 178 per cent; during the same period of time, the suburban areas ringing the central cities increased their population by about 208 per
cent. Third, lower income groups generally live in the center of the central city of
the metropolitan area, whereas higher income groups live toward the periphery.
Fourth, the longer an immigrant group has been in the metropolitan area, the
farther from the center of the city is their median location point and the more
dispersed is their residential pattern. Fifth, the longer an immigrant group has been
in the metropolitan area, the higher its class position tends to be.[1] Sixth, the most
recent newcomers to metropolitan areas are "in-migrants" from other parts of the
country rather than "immigrants." The largest group of in-migrants are Negroes.
In 1910, 27 per cent of the Negroes lived in urban places; by 1960 the figure had
increased to about 66 per cent.[2] (An urban place is basically a population center
having 2,500 or more inhabitants.)

[1] Hauser refers, not to "class," but to "economic status" and "social status."
[2] Hauser's information is also relevant to the material presented in Part IV, "Population
and Ecology."

Davis, in "The Urbanization of the World," makes three main points. First, the percentage of the world's population living in cities—Davis' definition of urbanization—has increased. In 1820, about 2 per cent of the world's population was living in cities of 20,000 or more; by 1950 the figure had increased to about 21 per cent. Second, the highest levels of urbanization are found in northwestern Europe and in those regions where northwest Europeans have settled and extended their industrial civilization. Oceania is the most urbanized of the world's major regions, because Australia and New Zealand are its principal components; Asia and Africa are the least urbanized of the world's major regions. Third, the difference between the industrial and preindustrial nations with respect to urbanization is beginning to diminish. The rate of urbanization in the older industrialized countries is slowing down, whereas the rate of urbanization in the preindustrial nations is increasing.

The selection by Spinrad, "Power in Local Communities," distinguishes two views regarding the distribution of *power* in local American communities. First there is the view which suggests a pyramidal, quasi-monolithic power structure dominated by a business elite. Spinrad associates the business dominant view with Delbert Miller. Second, there is the view which suggests a relatively pluralistic power structure. Spinrad associates the pluralistic view with Robert Dahl. After surveying the literature, Spinrad, like Dahl, suggests that most American communities reveal a relatively pluralistic power structure.[3]

ORGANIZATION. An important problem in the study of *organizations* has been the relative output of large and small organizations. One way to investigate this problem has been through the study of "concentration." The assumption is that concentration is positively related to size: the greater the amount of concentration, the greater the relative output of large organizations. Means, in "A Contemporary View of Industrial Concentration," distinguishes concentration in the economy from concentration in the manufacturing sector of the economy. With respect to concentration in the economy, Means believes that by 1929 the dominantly small-enterprise economy which existed in 1860 had been largely replaced by one in which the large corporation was the most characteristic feature. The degree of concentration in the economy is not significantly less in 1963 than it was in 1929. With respect to the manufacturing sector of the economy, Means believes that there has been an increase in concentration. In 1929, the 100 largest manufacturing corporations had legal control of approximately 40 per cent of the "total assets" of all manufacturing corporations and 44 per cent of their "net capital assets"; by 1962, the two percentages were, respectively, 49 and 58.[4]

Administrative employees are commonly distinguished from production employees. In a business firm, for example, the administrative employees are usually white-collar employees paid by salaries, whereas the production employees are usually blue-collar employees paid by wages. Administrative employees are often referred to as "bureaucrats" and the relative increase of this type of employee as "bureaucratization." The selection by Bendix, "The Growth of Bureaucracy," indicates that the ratio of administrative to production employees (the "A/P" in Table 1) has increased in the United States, France, Great Britain, Germany, and Sweden. For example, the ratio for the United States in 1899 was about 8; by

[3] Spinrad's information, if viewed as "power stratification," could have been included in the section on "Stratification" in Part II, "The Social Structure of the Group."

[4] "Total assets" include total current assets (such as inventories, accounts receivable, and government securities) and fixed assets (such as land, buildings and equipment after depreciation and depletion). Excluded from total assets are estimated holdings of securities of other corporations. "Net capital assets" include only the net property—the land, buildings, and equipment less depreciation and depletion. Net capital assets constitute the instruments of production.

1947 this figure had increased to about 22. Bendix's information is in agreement with the general belief that there is a trend toward greater bureaucratization in Western nations.

Ownership and control are commonly distinguished. Ownership refers to a legally defined *property* right, whereas control refers to the exercise of power. Historically, the individuals who owned a business corporation also controlled the activities of the corporation. The nineteenth-century capitalist in the United States, for example, both owned and controlled his business. Berle and Means argued, in their classic *The Modern Corporation and Private Property*, that by 1929 ownership and control were no longer exercised by the same individuals in large nonfinancial corporations. The individuals who controlled did not own and the individuals who owned did not control. The selection by Larner, "Ownership and Control in the 200 Largest Nonfinancial Corporations, 1929 and 1963," attempts to check the accuracy of the Berle and Means thesis for 1963. Larner's main point is that management control (as contrasted with various degrees of control by owners) has substantially increased among the 200 largest nonfinancial corporations since 1929. Forty-four per cent of the corporations in 1929 and 58 per cent of their assets were management-controlled; in 1963, 84.5 per cent of the corporations and 85 per cent of their assets were management-controlled. The separation of ownership and control which Berle and Means described in 1929 was even greater in 1963.

COLLECTIVE BEHAVIOR. *Social movements* are frequently studied in the field of *collective behavior*. The selection by Pinard, "Poverty and Political Movements," presents factual information about political social movements. Based primarily on data from four political social movements in Canada, France, and the United States, Pinard suggests that middle-income individuals, rather than low-income and high-income individuals, are the first joiners of new political social movements.[5] (In presenting his findings, Pinard uses the terms "hypothesis" and "proposition" to refer to what this anthology refers to as "factual statements.")

[5] Pinard's information is also relevant to the section on "Polity" in Part II, "The Social Structure of the Group."

COMMUNITY

The Growth of Metropolitan Areas in the United States

PHILIP M. HAUSER

I

Even more dramatic than the national resurgence in total population growth in the United States is the explosive increase in the urban and particularly in the metropolitan area population. Throughout the history of this nation, population has become increasingly concentrated in urban and metropolitan places.

When our first census was taken in 1790 there were only 24 urban places in this country—places having 2,500 or more persons. They contained only 5 per cent of the nation's population, some 200,000 out of almost 4 million. Only two of these places had more than 25,000 persons—New York and Philadelphia. By 1950, there were over 4700 such urban places, including almost two-thirds of the national population—nearly 100 million persons (Table 1). In 1960, about 122 million persons lived in urban places—some 68 per cent of the total population.

The tendency of the American population to become increasingly concentrated in large clumpings is even more manifest in the growth of metropolitan areas, the nucleus of which is the city of 50,000 or more.[1] In 1900, areas which would have qualified as Standard Metropolitan Areas in 1950 contained about a third of the total population, about 24 million persons (Table 2). Between 1900 and 1950, while the population of the country doubled, that outside the metropolitan areas increased by only 50 per cent; and that in metropolitan areas more than tripled. In consequence, by 1950 some 57 per cent of the population lived in 168 Standard Metropolitan Areas—about 85 million persons.[2] In 1960, about 63 per cent of the total population, about 112 million persons, resided in 211 "Standard Metropolitan Statistical Areas," the nomenclature adopted by the federal government in 1959. . . .[3]

From *Population Perspectives* by Philip M. Hauser. Copyright © 1960, by Rutgers University Press. Reprinted with permission of Rutgers University Press.
[1] The Standard Metropolitan Area was defined by the federal government in 1950, as, in general, one or more central cities of 50,000 or more inhabitants, the county in which the central city (or cities) were located, and such contiguous counties as by various social and economic criteria were oriented to the central city (or cities). For details of the definition see Bureau of the Census, *County and City Data Book, 1956* (Washington, D.C.: Government Printing Office, 1957).

[2] Donald J. Bogue, *Population Growth in Standard Metropolitan Areas, 1900–1950* (Housing and Home Finance Agency) (Washington, D.C.: Government Printing Office, 1953), p. 13; and United States Bureau of the Census, *Census of Population: 1950*, Vol. I, pp. 1–3 and 1–69.

[3] United States Department of Commerce, Bureau of the Census, *1960 Census of Population*, "Preliminary Reports," PC(P3)–4, pp. 2 and 19.

TABLE 1.   URBAN AND RURAL POPULATION FOR THE UNITED STATES, 1790 TO 1950, ESTIMATED FOR 1960 AND PROJECTED TO 1980.

	Population (*thousands*)			
Selected Dates	*Total*	*Urban*	*Rural*	*Per cent Urban*
1790	3,929	202	3,728	5.1
1800	5,308	322	4,986	6.1
1850	23,192	3,544	19,648	15.3
1900	75,995	30,160	45,835	39.7
1920	105,711	54,158	51,552	51.2
1950*				
Old def. urban	150,697	88,927	61,770	59.0
New def. urban	150,697	96,468	54,230	64.0
1960	180,000	122,000	58,000	68.0
1970	214,000	150,000	64,000	70.0
1980	260,000	190,000	70,000	73.0

* New definition, in general, includes places having 2,500 or more persons whether incorporated or unincorporated in contrast with old definition which included only incorporated places of this size.

SOURCE: Data for 1790 to 1940: Bureau of the Census, *Historical Statistics of the United States*, Government Printing Office, Washington, D.C., 1949, p. 25.

Data for 1950: Bureau of the Census, *Statistical Abstract of the United States, 1959*, Government Printing Office, Washington, D.C., 1959, p. 17. Data for 1960 to 1980: Percent urban drawn from estimates by Bogue and applied to total population projections of U.S. Bureau of the Census, assuming continuation of postwar birth rate (see Chapter 2) Donald J. Bogue, *The Population of the United States* (Glencoe, Illinois: Free Press, 1959), p. 784.

TABLE 2.   POPULATION OF METROPOLITAN AREAS OF THE UNITED STATES, 1900 TO 1960 AND PROJECTED TO 1980.

Date	*Number of SMA's*	*Population (millions)*	*Percent of U.S. Pop.*	*Percent in Ring*
	Estimates for Principal Standard Metropolitan Areas			
1900	52	24.1	31.9	38.1
1910	71	34.5	37.6	35.9
1920	94	46.1	43.7	34.7
1930	115	61.0	49.8	36.4
1940	125	67.1	51.1	38.2
1950	147	84.3	56.0	42.4
	Standard Metropolitan Areas			
1950	168	84.5	56.1	41.5
	Standard Metropolitan Statistical Areas			
1960	211	111.7	62.8	48.7
	Projections			
1970	–	139*	65*	54*
1980	–	174*	67*	58*

* See Note 4*.

SOURCES: U.S. Bureau of the Census and Donald J. Bogue, except as noted above—see Notes 2 and 3.

* [Another note is not included which is as follows: "Based on percentage by Ray P. Cuzzort, *op. cit.*" The Cuzzort refers to what is now Note 4—Editor.]

II

During the first half of the century, urban places absorbed about 79 per cent and metropolitan areas 73 per cent of the increase in the total population of the United States (Table 3). Under the impact of mobilization for war, urban areas absorbed 76 per cent and metropolitan areas over 80 per cent of the total

TABLE 3. Percent of Total U.S. Population Increase in Standard Metropolitan Areas by Central City and Ring 1900–1950.

			Percent of U.S. Increase			
Date	U.S. Increase	Standard Metropolitan Area	Central Cities	Rings	Urban	Rural
1950–60*	100.0	81	16	65	86†	14†
1940–50	100.0	80.6	31.6	49.0	76.2	23.8
1930–40	100.0	61.6	24.8	36.8	61.5	38.5
1920–30	100.0	80.9	46.4	34.5	86.7	13.3
1910–20	100.0	75.0	52.5	22.6	88.5	11.5
1900–10	100.0	61.6	43.7	17.9	74.1	25.9
1900–50	100.0	73.2	40.6	32.7	78.7	21.3

* From preliminary census release—see Note 3.
† Estimated from Table 1.
Source: See Note 2 except for 1950–60.

national population gain between 1940 and 1950. Between 1950 and 1960 both urban and metropolitan places absorbed over 80 per cent of the total population increase of the nation. Should the observed trends continue it is possible that by 1970 some 70 per cent of the population, or 150 million, and by 1980 some 73 per cent, or 190 million people, will be living in urban places (Table 1). By 1970 some 65 per cent of the population, or about 137 million persons, and by 1980 some 67 per cent, or over 174 million persons, may be resident in metropolitan areas[4] (Table 2).

III

Throughout the course of this century, while population was becoming increasingly metropolitanized, it was also becoming more decentralized within metropolitan areas (Fig. 1). Between 1900 and 1950, suburban populations grew at a rate about one and one third times that of the central city populations (Table 4). Between 1940 and 1950, the last decade of this period, suburban population growth was two and one half times that of central cities. Between 1950

[4] Projections of metropolitan area population based on percentages estimated by Cuzzort applied to census population projections (assuming continuation of postwar fertility). Percentages in Ray P. Cuzzort, "The Size and Distribution of Metropolitan Areas in 1975," in *Applications of Demography, The Population Situation in the U.S. in 1975*, ed. D. J. Bogue, pp. 62 ff.

TABLE 4. PERCENT POPULATION INCREASE IN STANDARD METROPOLITAN AREA BY CENTRAL CITIES AND RINGS, AND URBAN AND RURAL POPULATION FOR THE U.S. 1900 TO 1960

			Percent Increase			
Date	*U.S. Population*	*Standard Metropolitan Areas*	*Central Cities*	*Rings*	*Urban*	*Rural*
1950–60*	17.5	25.3	9.4	47.7	†	†
1940–50	14.5	21.8	13.9	34.7	19.5‡	7.9‡
1930–40	7.2	8.5	5.4	13.9	7.9	6.4
1920–30	16.1	27.1	23.8	33.2	27.3	4.4
1910–20	14.9	25.4	27.7	21.3	29.0	3.2
1900–10	21.0	32.0	36.6	24.3	39.3	9.0
1900–1950	98.3	177.8	159.2	208.1	295	125

* From preliminary census release—see Note 3.
† 1960 census data not yet available when table prepared.
‡ Old definition—see Table 1.
SOURCE: See Note 2 except for 1950–60.

and 1960, metropolitan areas manifested even greater rates of decentralization, with suburban populations growing about five times as fast as central cities—48 per cent as compared with 9 per cent.

Suburbia, then, has been absorbing increasingly larger proportions of total metropolitan growth. Between 1900 and 1950, suburbia accounted for 45 per cent of the total gain in metropolitan areas. During the last decade of this period, 1940 to 1950, the suburbs contributed 61 per cent of the total metropolitan growth, and during the fifties, about 80 per cent.

As the result of these growth differentials, the relative size of central city and suburb has, of course, been affected. In 1900, 38 per cent of the population of metropolitan areas was in suburbia (Table 2). By 1950, the proportion had risen to 42 per cent. In 1960, suburban population constituted 49 per cent of metropolitan area population. . . .

Although metropolitan United States as a whole is experiencing rapid growth, some areas are actually losing population, and the explosive growth is confined mainly to the suburbs. Of the 211 Standard Metropolitan Statistical Areas, 9 lost population between 1950 and 1960; and of 256 central cities in metropolitan areas, 73 lost population.[5]

Individual metropolitan areas, and especially the smaller ones, are subject to population losses by reason of the changing economy, relatively large industrial shifts, or the denudation of resources on which local industries may depend. Central cities, on the whole, and especially the older and larger ones, have reached a point of relative stability in size. Apart from annexations, they will

[5] See Note 3.*
* [The material referred to is not included—Editor.]

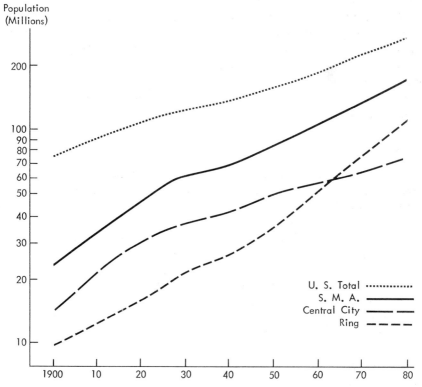

FIGURE 1. Growth of population of metropolitan areas by central city and ring compared with growth of United States, 1900–1980. *Note:* Drawn on logarithmic scale so that slope of line indicates rate of increase. (*Source: U.S. Bureau of the Census and projections. See text.*)

probably experience relatively small gains or losses from now on, depending largely on how changing land use patterns may increase or decrease population densities within their boundaries.

It should also be noted that the non-metropolitan population, and especially the rural-farm population, is not experiencing explosive growth. Over the first half of this century population in non-metropolitan areas increased by only 50 per cent while metropolitan populations more than tripled. Between 1950 and 1960, non-metropolitan population increased by only 7 per cent, as compared with a metropolitan increase of over 25 per cent.

Rural-farm population has actually decreased over the period in which it has been counted in this country—that is, since 1910. From a level of about 32 million it declined to about 30 million by 1930, despite great total population gains. During the depression thirties farm population rose again, but with improved economic conditions at the end of the decade farm out-migration increased, and by 1940 farm population had again declined to about its 1930 level. During World War II farm population decreased rapidly and although there was some increase with demobilization it had declined to about 25 million by 1950. In 1960, farm population numbered about 17 million. Should the trend continue farm population may have shrunk to about 12 million by 1980, despite explosive national growth.[6] The decline in rural-farm population reflects the increased mechanization and productivity of American agriculture. Acreage under cultivation throughout the period of decline of farm population has changed relatively little, whereas productivity per acre has, of course, continued to increase greatly.

IV

Basic changes in land use patterns and the structure of the metropolitan area have accompanied metropolitan area explosive population growth and decentralization. Further changes may be anticipated with the tremendous population expansion which is projected.

Present patterns of land use in our metropolitan districts reflect the origin and growth of the area's economic base and the process of peopling. Urban and metropolitan places had their origin at a point or points which encompassed their first economic functions. Such a point was frequently a break in means of transportation. In Chicago, for example, the major point of origin was the point of junction of the Chicago River and Lake Michigan. From this point the city developed and expanded. It grew to the South, to the North, and to the West, but, for obvious reasons, not so much to the East.

Residential land use patterns were a function of the geometry of urban growth and the play of market forces. Since the city necessarily grew away from its point of origin, the newer residential areas were always farthest from the center. These outlying areas were more desirable places to live, partly because they were newer and partly because, with rapid technological advance, they incorporated the benefits of improved technology. Consider, for example, the changes in kinds of residential lighting. The earliest structures in many of our cities were illuminated by the kerosene lamp. With advances in technology, the kerosene lamp gave way to gas illumination, which in turn was displaced by electric lighting, with wiring originally pulled through gas light fixtures. This improved illumination was in turn outmoded by superior electric lighting installed independently of gas fixtures. Moreover, homes so illuminated were generally improved in other respects such as in plumbing, appliances, and picture windows.

It has been noted that the tempo of United States urban and metropolitan growth was an exceedingly rapid one. Our cities grew not structure by structure but by subdivision, neighborhood, and community. To draw upon Chicago again as an illustration, it may be recalled that that city was first reported in a census of the United States in 1840, at which time it had a population of 4,470. Two decades later, in 1860, Chicago was a city of over 100,000; by 1870, a city of over 250,000; by 1880, a city of over half a million; and by 1890, Chicago

[6] Donald J. Bogue, *The Population of the United States* (Glencoe, Illinois: Free Press, 1959), p. 785.

contained more than 1 million inhabitants. Chicago became a city of over a million within a period of fifty years!

Partly as the result of technological advances but partly too because of explosive rates of growth requiring tremendous additions to the city's physical plant, the inner and older zones of our cities became obsolescent and, eventually, blighted and decayed. Our urban plant decayed as it had developed, at fabulous rates, not structure by structure but by entire neighborhoods at a time.

The processes by which city neighborhoods developed, flourished, became obsolescent, and decayed tended to follow uniform patterns throughout the land. The histories of the inner and older areas of our cities have been, on the whole, remarkably uniform. Present inner and older areas were, at their origin, outlying suburbs containing the residences of the fashionably elite. With the continued growth of the city they became, more and more, inner zones, and followed similar patterns of changes in their residential occupancy. They housed first the middle class, then workingmen's families and finally, in many cases, they were turned over to rooming houses and slums. The present inner zones of our cities and metropolitan areas had a natural history of continuous decline in occupancy, from higher to lower income groupings of the population. With the exceedingly rapid growth of our metropolitan areas, the outlying better residential neighborhoods of one generation became the inner, older, and less desirable neighborhoods of the next.

Explosive urban and metropolitan growth, together with the play of market forces, determined both the patterns of land use and the distribution of the population in space. Place of residence in metropolitan areas was determined by social and economic status, with the lower income groups living in the center of the city and the higher income groups toward the periphery (Fig. 2). Rapid growth and the play of market forces produced for the American people the highest mass level of living ever achieved by any nation in the history of man. But they also produced the slum, which became a matter of national and international disgrace and, in recent years, an issue in national politics as well.

As the metropolitan area agglomeration grew in size with twentieth century technology, the size of inner and older zones also increased. Because city boundary lines have tended to remain relatively fixed while metropolitan clumpings of people and economic activities expanded, larger and larger proportions of the total central city land area have become inner and older zones of the entire metropolitan area and have been taken over by lower income groups; and increasing proportions of the higher income groups in the entire metropolitan area have become residents of suburbia.

The urban residential land use patterns which we have inherited will probably be greatly modified during the coming decade by forces which are already at work to change them.

V

Among those forces which must change the patterns of land use in our metropolitan areas are urban renewal programs in central cities, the explosive

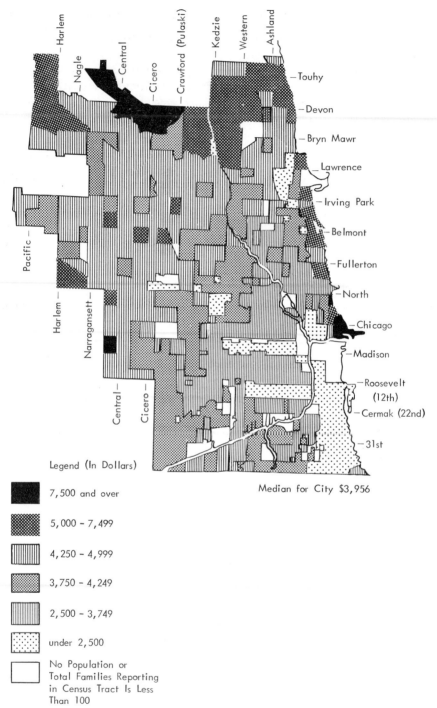

FIGURE 2. Median income for families in Chicago, Illinois, in 1949. (*Source: Chicago Community Inventory*, University of Chicago.)

growth and increasing industrialization of suburban areas, and the discernible tendency for the family to use the metropolitan areas in accordance with the changing requirements of the family cycle.

The urban renewal program is the culmination of a long series of efforts to deal with the problem of urban obsolescence and decay. It is a concerted and systematic attempt on the part of the federal government, in co-operation with city governments, to raze and rebuild the decayed inner core of our central cities, to rehabilitate aging neighborhoods not yet completely decayed, and to conserve the remainder of the residential plant. Thus, its purpose is to alter drastically the natural history of city neighborhoods described above. Urban renewal is an effort, at mid-twentieth century, to clean up the obsolete and decayed parts of the urban plant—the mess produced as a by-product of our remarkable and explosive economic and population growth.

The impact of urban renewal is increasingly visible throughout the land. Urban renewal programs are bulldozing and rebuilding the inner zones of our cities in much the same manner as they grew and decayed—not by individual structures but by entire neighborhoods at a time.[7]

The rate at which urban renewal will proceed will vary with the fortunes of the major political parties and the course of the business cycle. Expenditures for the program are likely to be greater in Democratic than Republican administrations, and in recession or depression than in times of business prosperity. But it may be taken for granted that the urban renewal program has become part of the United States political scene and is here to stay.

As we have seen, our suburban areas are going through the same kind of rapid growth as did central cities during the nineteenth and early twentieth centuries. There is increasing evidence that parts of the suburbs are now faced with the same concomitants of explosively rapid growth—rapid obsolescence and decay.

A factor contributing to the residential downgrading of suburban areas is the decentralization of industry. Industry, like population, is decentralizing within some metropolitan areas because the central city is filled up for many industrial purposes.[8] Industrial concentrations in suburbia are accompanied by housing developments designed for relatively low income workers. Such realty developments have, on the whole, not maintained the standards of housing which have characterized suburban areas in the past—in fact, a good part of what is being built in suburbia, "urban sprawl," is virtually slum even before the concrete is dry.[9] Many of the newer developments have inadequate provisions

---

[7] *Urban Redevelopment: Problems and Practices*, ed. Coleman Woodbury; also *The Future of Cities and Urban Redevelopment* (Chicago: University of Chicago, 1953); Julia Abrahamson, *A Neighborhood Finds Itself* (New York: Harper, 1959).

[8] For analysis of suburbanization of industry see E. M. Kitagawa and D. M. Bogue, *Suburbanization of Manufacturing Activity Within Standard Metropolitan Areas* (Oxford, Ohio: Scripps Foundation, 1955).

[9] The Editors of *Fortune, The Exploding Metropolis* (New York: Doubleday, 1958), Chap. 5.

for drainage, sanitation, and water supply, not to mention recreation, educational facilities, and transportation facilities. Some suburban developments have been deliberately located to escape central city or other municipal zoning and code provisions.

As a consequence of both obsolescence and the new developments in suburbia, newcomers to metropolitan areas are beginning to have available a wider choice than before of cheap and sub-standard housing in which to settle. In-migrants to metropolitan areas are finding ports of entry in suburbia as well as in the inner and older zones of the city, so that suburban areas are no longer developing entirely through the process of radial expansion. A major source for the growth of outlying parts of many metropolitan areas is direct in-migration, rather than radial expansion. Analysis of in-migration to metropolitan rings between 1940 and 1950 shows that of over 7 million net in-migrants to suburbia, about half represented direct migration to the suburbs from places other than the central cities.[10] This process has undoubtedly continued since 1950.

The combination of urban renewal in the inner zones of central cities and blight and urban sprawl in the suburbs is tending to disrupt the pattern of population distribution which has placed the higher income groups farthest out from the center of the city. Should these trends continue, the residential land use pattern in metropolitan areas would be turned inside out, with the newer and more desirable areas located in the rebuilt inner city zones as well as in the most distant parts of suburbia.

Another factor tending to destroy historical and present patterns of residential land use in metropolitan areas is the increasing tendency for the family use of the metropolitan area to change in accordance with its varying requirements during the course of the "family cycle."[11] That is, newly married couples tend both to work and to live in the central city, relatively close to the central business or central manufacturing district which affords them employment. With the coming of children, in keeping with an old American dream, the couple tends to move to outlying areas for fresh air, green grass, and relatively open spaces in which to rear their families. But when the children leave the family for college or marriage, there is a growing tendency for parents with an "empty nest" to gravitate back toward central city residence. In fact, there is some evidence that some such couples are drifting toward high rise, efficiency type accommodations built in urban renewal areas in central cities. Such a reverse movement makes good sense when it is borne in mind that no one is left at home to cut the grass, and that closing a house down is more complicated than leaving an apartment when there is an opportunity to visit Florida or California in the winter, or to baby-sit with grandchildren. The elderly couple without

10 Donald J. Bogue, *Components of Population Change, 1940–1950: . . .* (Oxford, Ohio: Scripps Foundation, 1957), Chap. 3.

11 Paul C. Glick, "The Life Cycle of the Family," *Marriage and Family Living*, XVII, No. 1 (February, 1955); see also Paul C. Glick, *American Families* (New York: John Wiley & Sons, 1957), Chaps. 3, 4, 5.

children constitutes an increasingly important source for the recentralization of central city population.

This type of cyclical use of the metropolitan area is by no means yet the modal one, but considerations which may not be readily apparent strongly suggest that the pattern is there. In 1890, for example, when the last child left the family for marriage, the average wife in the United States had become a widow. By 1950, as the result of decreased age at marriage, decreased birth rate, increased concentration of child bearing under age 30, and decreased death rate accompanied by increased longevity, this was no longer the situation. By 1950, when the last child left home for marriage the average wife still had a husband, and the couple had the prospect of an additional fourteen years of life together. The difference between zero years of marital existence after the children had left home in 1890, and an average of fourteen such years in 1950,[12] is translatable into literally millions and millions of husband-and-wife years of life together without children in the later years. In the aggregate, this change in less than two human generations has created a demand for a new type of housing and land use which will inevitably affect residential land use patterns.

Finally, any consideration of the modification of land use patterns and the structure of our metropolitan areas must include reference to emergent "megalopolis."[13] Tremendous growth of the kind in prospect necessarily means the spilling of population into the open country areas of our metropolitan ring— into exurbia and interurbia. It means that inter-metropolitan area space will be inundated and metropolitan areas, therefore, will tend to coalesce.

The merging of metropolitan areas into "megalopolis" is already in evidence. On the Northeastern seaboard, for example, the area from Boston to Washington constitutes perhaps the farthest advanced and largest of our emergent megalopolises, one that might be termed "Atlantic-opolis" (Fig. 3). In the Middle West several megalopolises are in evidence. One, stretching from Milwaukee to Chicago to South Bend, may form the anchor of a future "Lake Michigan-opolis." Another from Chicago to Peoria to St. Louis may constitute a "Seaway-opolis." Detroit, Toledo, and Cincinnatti offer still another possibility as "Erie-opolis." Moreover, it may be noted that the Chicago-Detroit areas could be linked into a super "Great Lake-opolis," which might also include the area from Toledo to Cleveland to Pittsburgh.

On the West Coast a "Pacific-opolis" is emerging from San Francisco to Sacramento to the North and West, and from San Francisco to Fresno to Los Angeles to San Diego to the South. In the North Pacific areas "Puget-opolis" is visible in the developments from Everett, Seattle, and Tacoma in Washington,

---

12 *Ibid.*, p. 68.

13 The term "megalopolis" was proposed by Jean Gottmann, *Virginia at Mid-Century* (New York: Henry Holt & Co., 1955), pp. 41, 174, 472–79. Other terms to designate essentially the same phenomenon include "connurbation" Patrick Geddes, *Cities in Evolution* (London: 1915), p. 168; "metropolitan region" (series of eight articles reprinted from *New York Times*, January 27 to February 3, 1957); "strip cities" (*U.S. News & World Report*, April 5, 1957. See Fig. 17).

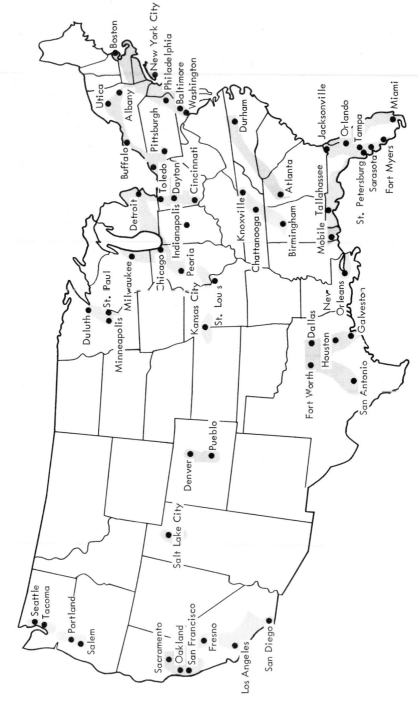

FIGURE 3. The "strip cities" of the future. (*Reprinted from U.S. News & World Report, an independent weekly news magazine published at Washington. Copyright 1958 United States News Publishing Corporation.*)

down through Portland and Salem in Oregon. Other such developments are visible in at least potential outline form as follows:

Jacksonville to Orlando to Miami on the Eastern Coast of Florida; and Jacksonville to Orlando to Ft. Myers on the Western Coast—a potential "Florid-opolis";

Buffalo to Utica to Albany as a "Canal-opolis" linking with "Atlantic-opolis";

Knoxville to Chattanooga to Birmingham as "South Appalachian-opolis";

Denver to Pueblo as a "Rocky-opolis";

Salt Lake City and surrounding area as "Salt Lake-opolis";

Dallas to Houston to Galveston to Forth Worth to San Antonio as a saddle-shaped "Texas-opolis";

Durham to Atlanta as "Piedmont-opolis";

New Orleans to Mobile to Tallahassee as "Gulf-opolis."

With the interplay of the forces described we may be entering a new cycle of development in metropolitan area residential land use patterns—a cycle undoubtedly accelerated by rapid growth. It is almost certain that the present residential stratification of population by social and economic status will change in the metropolitan area in the future. It may be anticipated that there will be both good and bad neighborhoods in the inner and older zones of the city, throughout the city, and throughout the suburbs. Whether a neighborhood will be good or bad will depend much less on the accident of its history, its proximity to the point of origin of the city, and the play of the market mechanism, than on various forms of government interventionism—on city planning, urban renewal and related programs, zoning, codes, and the changing requirements of the population itself as evidenced by rapidly changing age structure, family formation, and changes in the family cycle. We can expect the overflowing population to inundate exurbia and interurbia, and to produce new forms of metropolitan structure in emergent megalopolis.

VI

Urban and metropolitan areas in the United States have been peopled largely by flows of population from the outside. Up to World War I these included a relatively large volume of immigration in addition to internal migratory flows from rural and especially rural-farm areas. Since World War I, and particularly since World War II, internal migratory streams have been the predominant source of "outside" population.

The nation as a whole was, like the urban areas, peopled in large measure through immigration from abroad. Between 1820 and 1960 about 42 million immigrants that the federal government managed to count came to the United States.[14] They came in large waves during the nineteenth and early twentieth centuries. In mid-nineteenth century, streams of Irish and German immigrants

[14] Bureau of the Census, *Statistical Abstract of the United States* (1959), p. 23.

followed the potato famine and economic difficulties in Ireland and the abortive revolutionary attempt of 1848 in Germany. Toward the end of the nineteenth century, crop failures and general economic depression set in motion relatively large volumes of Scandinavian immigrants. During the early part of the twentieth century, sources of immigration to the United States shifted from Northern and Western to Southern and Eastern Europe—to Russians and Poles, including the Jewish groups, to Italians, Greeks, and other peoples from Eastern European nations, who left their homelands for the new opportunities beckoning in the rapidly developing United States.

The processes by which newcomers to urban and metropolitan areas made their entry, achieved a place of residence, and found a niche in the economy

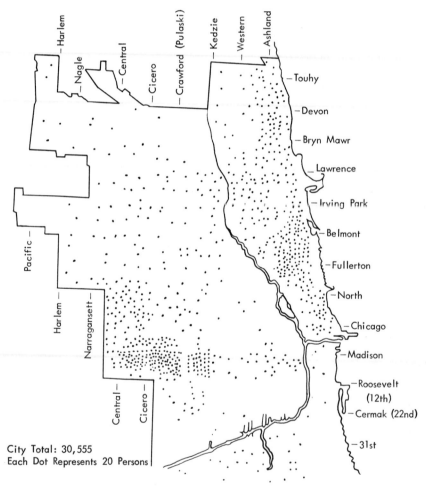

FIGURE 4. Irish foreign born; Chicago, Illinois, 1950. (*Source: Chicago Community Inventory, University of Chicago.*)

and status in the social order, were strikingly uniform. Adapting themselves to the land use patterns described above, the newcomers almost invariably found their ports of entry in the inner, older, and less desirable zones of the city. They worked at the most menial and poorest paid occupations. They were the lowest in social status in the community.

Each wave of newcomers was greeted in the same fashion by those who had preceded them and who had already settled in the community—that is, by attitudes ranging from suspicion and distrust to outright hostility, prejudice, and discriminatory practices. Each group of newcomers was awarded some pithy designation implying inferior status. During the nineteenth century, for example, the new arrivals were greeted as "krautheads," "micks," and "dumb swedes." During the twentieth century we admitted "polacks," "sheenies," "wops," "bohunks," and the like. There were no mass exceptions to this rule.

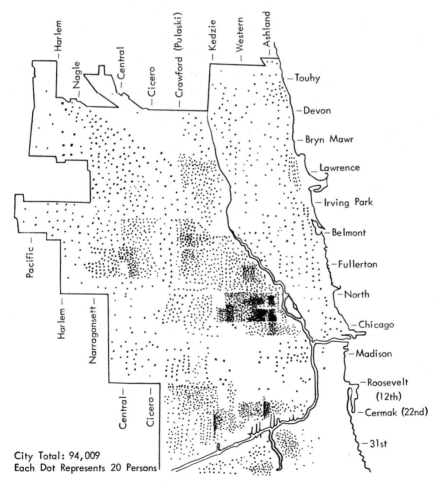

FIGURE 5. Polish foreign born; Chicago, Illinois, 1950. (*Source: Chicago Community Inventory, University of Chicago.*)

With the passage of time, each wave of newcomers climbed the socio-economic ladder as measured by place of residence, education, occupation, income, and general acceptability. It is a striking fact that even today there is a high correlation between the place of residence of immigrant stock and the length of time they have lived in the community. The censuses of the United States reveal a pattern which undoubtedly will be evident for some time to come (Figs. 4 and 5). The longer the immigrant group has been in the community, the farther out from the center of the city is their median location point and the more dispersed or "integrated" is their residential pattern. The shorter the time the immigrant group has been in the community, the closer to the center of the city is their average location point and the more concentrated or "segregated" tends to be their residential distribution. Moreover, the longer the length of residence of the group, the higher tends to be its economic status as measured by type of occupation pursued and income and its social status as measured by educational achievement, broader access to the social and cultural life of the community, and increased general acceptability.[15]

It is not an over-generalization to state that segregated living in the decayed and blighted areas of the city, menial occupation and low income, hostility, prejudice, and discriminatory practices have not been reserved for any one or two minority newcomer groups in the history of this nation. On the contrary, they have been democratically available to all new arrivals without regard to race, religion, or origin.

The processes by which waves of immigrants entered into the American scene are popularly known as "Americanization." To the sociologist and anthropologist they are the processes of acculturation—accommodation and assimilation. Although the "melting pot" theme has probably been overstated in the sense that many of our immigrant groups continue to retain their national, cultural, linguistic, or religious identification, it is clear that the relatively open and competitive social and economic order in the United States has, on the whole, afforded opportunity for successive waves of immigrants to achieve varying degrees of integration into the economic, social, and political orders.

It is not generally recognized that the rapidity of our population growth and relative youth of this nation make the United States one of the more heterogeneous nations on the face of the earth, one which, in large measure, has yet to achieve unification or integration. As recently as 1950, for example, over a fifth of the population of the United States was either foreign-born or native of foreign or mixed parentage; and over a tenth were of nonwhite race.[16] That is, only two-thirds of the population of the United States, as recently as 1950, was

---

[15] Oscar Handlin, *The Uprooted* (Boston: Little, Brown & Co., 1951), and *The Newcomers* (Cambridge, Mass.: Harvard University Press, 1959); O. D. and Beverly Duncan, *The Negro Population of Chicago* (Chicago: University of Chicago Press, 1957); Stanley Lieberson and O. D. Duncan, "Ethnic Segregation and Assimilation," *American Journal of Sociology*, 64 (January, 1959), pp. 364–74; Karl E. Taeuber, "Residential Segregation of Urban Non-Whites" (Ph.D. dissertation, Harvard University, 1960); Stanley Lieberson, "Comparative Segregation and Assimilation of Ethnic Groups" (Ph.D. dissertation, University of Chicago, 1960).

[16] United States Bureau of the Census, *op. cit.* (1959), p. 28.

native white of native parents. As recently as 1900, little more than half of the population of the United States was native white. Moreover, as recently as 1950, in four of our five larger cities, native white population of native parentage constituted less than half of the total. In New York in 1950, only 34 per cent of the population was native white of native parentage; in Chicago, only 41 per cent; in Philadelphia, only 46 per cent; and in Detroit, only 42 per cent. Los Angeles was the only city among the five largest in the United States in which the native white population of native parentage was greater than half, and even there it was only 55 per cent. The first generation in which virtually all the people of the United States share a common nativity is yet to come.

The most recent newcomers to urban and metropolitan United States are in-migrants rather than immigrants. The visible Negro and less visible rural white, especially Southern rural white, in-migrant has replaced the waves of immigrants as a major source of new metropolitan manpower. These in-migrants are, of course, supplemented by flows of Puerto Ricans and Mexicans. Let us focus on the Negro in-migrant to urban and metropolitan areas, for whom the census data permit some analysis.

For purposes of perspective, it is well to note the historical internal distribution of Negroes. The Census of 1860 reported that 92 per cent of all Negroes in the country lived in the South. A half-century later the Census of 1910 disclosed that the concentration of Negroes in the South had decreased by only 3 percentage points, that is, it had declined to 89 per cent.

The first large internal migratory movement of Negroes began during World War I. These migratory streams were the product of a number of forces, chief of which was undoubtedly the need for labor to man industries, and especially war industries in the North, as the United States served as the arsenal for the Allied Powers. Successful U-Boat warfare almost swept Allied shipping from the high seas, and by thus greatly restricting immigration created economic opportunity for the Negro. Moreover, the changing economy in the South was beginning to free the Negro from the soil.

The passage of the Immigration Exclusion Acts during the 1920's greatly curtailed the flow of immigrants. Despite special provisions to admit refugee groups from time to time, immigration has since been a relatively negligible source of growth of United States population. The continuation of internal migratory movements of Negroes from the rural South to urban areas in the North and West, and also to urban places in the South, took the place of the streams of immigrants that could no longer come to man the expanding urban and industrial economy. The exodus of Negroes from the rural South, dampened during the depression thirties, was greatly accelerated by the manpower requirements of World War II. By 1950 only 68 per cent of the Negroes in the United States were left in the South, and by 1960 only about 60 per cent.

Continuation of the present trend could produce a break-even point in the distribution of the Negro between the North and the South by 1970.[17] That is,

[17] Projections by Population Research and Training Center, University of Chicago, for Commission on Race and Housing. On file.

it is possible that by 1970 there will be as many Negroes in the North and West as remain in the South.

Streams of Negro migrants not only moved from the South to the North and West, but also from predominantly rural to predominantly urban areas. In 1910, only 27 per cent of the Negroes in this nation lived in urban places as defined by the Census, that is in places having 2,500 or more persons. By 1950, about 60 per cent of the Negro population was urban, and by 1960 the proportion of Negroes living in cities approximated two-thirds. The trend could easily make this about three-fourths by 1970.[18]

In 1950, over 90 per cent of the Negroes in the North and in the West, and about 48 per cent of the Negroes in the South, lived in urban places. By 1950, nonwhite population in metropolitan areas numbered 8.3 million. This number reflected a fourfold increase since the beginning of the century and an increase of over two-fifths (44.3 per cent) between 1940 and 1950.[19] Thus the Negro, in a little more than a human generation and a half, has been drawn from rural existence under relatively primitive conditions in the South to urbanism as a way of life. Many of the frictions and problems of adjustment in inter-group relations which create hardships both for the Negro in-migrant and the communities of origin and destination may be viewed as products of the exceedingly high rates of population growth and rapid changes in population distribution.

In streaming to metropolitan areas, the in-migrant Negro has generally found the same port of entry as preceding waves of white immigrants. His area of first settlement has been the inner, older, and blighted zones of the metropolitan area,[20] although it should be noted that, because of the increasing industrialization of suburbia, the Negro is also finding industrial areas in suburbia a port of entry to the metropolitan area.[21] Analysis of population movement within metropolitan areas shows the older resident white population following the traditional pattern by moving outward as the latest newcomer, the Negro, enters. This is the pattern of radial expansion described above, but a new development is that in the postwar period the pattern has meant that white populations moved outward beyond the limits of the city as the Negro entered. Thus, the Negro became an increasingly larger proportion of the central city population. By reason of the relatively fixed city boundaries and the process of radial expansion, central city population is becoming decreasingly white and increasingly Negro.

Between 1940 and 1950, as my colleague Professor Bogue has shown, a net total of 6 million persons migrated to Standard Metropolitan Areas. Of this number 4.4 million were white, and 1.6 million nonwhite, migrants. Of the 1.6 million nonwhite migrants, 1.3 million entered central cities and a little over 300,000 the metropolitan rings. The net migration of 4.4 million white persons to Standard Metropolitan Areas, however, was made up of a net in-migration of

[18] *Ibid.*

[19] Conrad and Irene Taeuber, *The Changing Population of the United States* (New York: John Wiley and Sons, 1958), p. 140; Bogue, *op. cit.* (1959), p. 149.

[20] Duncan and Duncan, *op. cit.*, Chap. 5.

[21] Bogue, *op. cit.* (1957), p. 111.

6.9 million white persons to suburbia, and a net out-migration of 2.5 million white persons from central cities.[22] This process has undoubtedly continued during the fifties and may well persist for some time to come.

The Negro faces much the same problems as did white immigrants before him in adjusting to urbanism as a way of life. The process is scarcely one that can be called "Americanization," for the Negro has been an American longer than the average white person in this country. But it is comparable to the situation faced by the immigrant in that the problem of the Negro is also one of acculturation—in his case, transition from a primitive folk culture to urbanism and metropolitanism as a way of life.

Will the Negro follow the patterns observed in the adjustment of white immigrants? In the main, it is still too early to say. Most of the Negroes in metropolitan areas have been there for less than one generation. Less than two human generations have passed since the heavy waves of Negro migrants entered urban and metropolitan places during the course of World War I. From what scanty evidence there is available, however, it would seem that in a number of respects the Negro in-migrant is following the same pathways as the white immigrant.[23] The Negro, like the white immigrant before him, is moving outward from the center of the city through the process of radial expansion. He is achieving higher education. He is climbing the occupational and income ladder.

Up to this point in the transition, however, the adjustment of the Negro in-migrant to life in urban and metropolitan areas differs in at least two important respects from that of the white immigrant who preceded him. First, although he is moving outward toward the periphery of the city and is already knocking at the doors of suburbia, he is finding more rather than less segregation.[24] He is moving outward, but he is doing so in a concentrated stream rather than in a dispersed, integrated fashion. It is also clear that because of segregation practices the Negro is not moving upward as rapidly as did the white immigrant in the social scale or general social acceptability. These differences, undoubtedly, are in large part attributable to the continued greater visibility of the Negro as compared with his white immigrant predecessor.

[22] *Ibid.*, p. 37.
[23] Duncan and Duncan, *op. cit.*, Chap. 4.
[24] Lieberson, *op. cit.*; Karl Taeuber, *op. cit.*

The Urbanization of the World

KINGSLEY DAVIS

Urban phenomena attract sociological attention primarily for four reasons. First, such phenomena are relatively recent in human history. Compared to most other aspects of society—e.g., language, religion, stratification, or the

Reprinted from the *American Journal of Sociology*, 60 (March, 1955), pp. 429–437, by permission of the author and the publisher.

family—cities appeared only yesterday, and urbanization, meaning that a sizable proportion of the population lives in cities, has developed only in the last few moments of man's existence. Second, urbanism represents a revolutionary change in the whole pattern of social life. Itself a product of basic economic and technological developments, it tends in turn, once it comes into being, to affect every aspect of existence. It exercises its pervasive influence not only within the urban milieu strictly defined but also in the rural hinterland. The third source of sociological interest in cities is the fact that, once established, they tend to be centers of power and influence throughout the whole society, no matter how agricultural and rural it may be. Finally, the process of urbanization is still occurring; many of the problems associated with it are unsolved; and, consequently, its future direction and potentialities are still a matter of uncertainty. This paper examines the . . . present rate of progress of urbanization in the world. . . .

THE WORLD TREND FROM 1800 TO 1950[1]

Urbanization has, in fact, gone ahead much faster and reached proportions far greater during the last century and a half than at any previous time in world history. The tremendous growth in world trade during this period has enabled the urban population to draw its sustenance from an ever wider area. Indeed, it can truly be said that the hinterland of today's cities is the entire world. Contemporary Britain, Holland, and Japan, for example, could not maintain their urban population solely from their own territory. The number of rural inhabitants required to maintain one urban inhabitant is still great—greater than one would imagine from the rural-urban ratio *within* each of the highly urbanized countries. The reason is that much of agriculture around the world is still technologically and economically backward. Yet there can be no doubt that, whether for particular countries or for the entire globe, the ratio of urban dwellers to those who grow their food has risen remarkably. This is shown by the fact that the proportion of people living in cities in 1950 is higher than that found in any particular country prior to modern times and many times higher than that formerly characterizing the earth as a whole.

The rapidity of urbanization in recent times can be seen by looking at the most urbanized country, England. In 1801, although London had already reached nearly the million mark (865,000), England and Wales had less than 10 per cent of their population in cities of 100,000 or more. By 1901 no less than 35 per cent of the population of England and Wales was living in cities of 100,000 or more, and 58 per cent was living in cities of 20,000 or more. By 1951 these two proportions had risen to 38.4 and 69.3 per cent, respectively.

Britain was in the van of urban development. A degree of urbanization equal to that she had attained in 1801 was not achieved by any other country until

[1] The writer acknowledges with pleasure the collaboration of Mrs. Hilda Hertz Golden in the statistical work on which this and succeeding sections are based. Such work has been done as part of a continuing program of comparative urban research in the population division of the Bureau of Applied Social Research, Columbia University.

after 1850. Thereafter the British rate of urbanization began slowly to decline, whereas that of most other countries continued at a high level. By assembling available data and preparing estimates where data were lacking, we have arrived at figures on urbanization in the world as a whole, beginning with 1800, the earliest date for which anything like a reasonable estimate can be obtained. The percentage of the world's population found living in cities is as shown in Table 1. It can be seen that the proportion has tended to do a bit better than

TABLE 1. PERCENTAGE OF WORLD'S
POPULATION LIVING IN CITIES

	Cities of 20,000 or More	Cities of 100,000 or More
1800	2.4	1.7
1850	4.3	2.3
1900	9.2	5.5
1950	20.9	13.1

double itself each half-century and that by 1950 the world as a whole was considerably more urbanized than Britain was in 1800. As everyone knows, the earth's total population has grown at an extremely rapid rate since 1800, reaching 2.4 billion by 1950. But the urban population has grown much faster. In 1800 there were about 15.6 million people living in cities of 100,000 or more. By 1950 it was 313.7 million, more than twenty times the earlier figure. Much of this increase has obviously come from rural-urban migration, clearly the most massive migration in modern times.

In 1800 there were apparently less than 50 cities with 100,000 or more inhabitants. This was less than the number in the million class today and less than the number of 100,000- plus cities currently found in many single countries. By 1950 there were close to 900 cities of 100,000 or more people, which is more than the number of towns and cities of 5,000 or more in 1800.

As yet there is no indication of a slackening of the rate of urbanization in the world as a whole. If the present rate should continue, more than a fourth of the earth's people will be living in cities of 100,000 or more in the year 2,000, and more than half in the year 2050. For places of 20,000 or more, the proportions at the two dates would be something like 45 per cent and 90 per cent. Whether such figures prove too low or too high, they nevertheless suggest that the human species is moving rapidly in the direction of an almost exclusively urban existence. We have used the proportion of the population in cities of 20,000 and 100,000 or more as a convenient index of differences and changes in degree of urbanization. Places of less than 20,000 also fit a demographic definition of "urban." When, therefore, more than a third of the population of a country lives in cities of the 100,000 class (38.4 per cent in England and Wales in 1951), the country can be described as almost completely urbanized (81 per cent being designated as "urban" in the English case in 1951). We thus have today what can be called "urbanized societies," nations in which the great majority of inhabitants live in cities. The prospect is that, as time goes on, a greater and greater proportion of humanity will be members of such societies.

The question may be raised as to how such an extreme degree of world urbanization will prove possible. Who will grow the food and fibers necessary for the enormous urban population? The answer is that agriculture may prove to be an archaic mode of production. Already, one of the great factors giving rise to urbanization is the rather late and as yet very incomplete industrialization of agriculture. As farming becomes increasingly mechanized and rationalized, fewer people are needed on the land. On the average, the more urbanized a country, the lower is its rural density.[2] If, in addition to industrialized agriculture, food and fiber come to be increasingly produced by manufacturing processes using materials that utilize the sun's energy more efficiently than plants do, there is no technological reason why nearly all of mankind could not live in conurbations of large size.

THE REGIONAL PATTERN OF URBANIZATION

The highest levels of urbanization are found today in northwestern Europe and in those new regions where northwest Europeans have settled and extended their industrial civilization. The figures are as shown in Table 2.[3] Oceania is the

TABLE 2.   PERCENTAGE OF WORLD'S POPULATION LIVING IN
CITIES, BY REGIONS

	In Cities of 20,000 Plus	In Cities of 100,000 Plus
World	21	13
Oceania	47	41
North America (Canada and U.S.A.)	42	29
Europe (except U.S.S.R.)	35	21
U.S.S.R.	31	18
South America	26	18
Middle America and Caribbean	21	12
Asia (except U.S.S.R.)	13	8
Africa	9	5

most urbanized of the world's major regions, because Australia and New Zealand are its principal components. North America is next, if it is defined as including only Canada and the United States. The regions least urbanized are those least affected by northwest European culture, namely, Asia and Africa.

[2] See Kingsley Davis and Hilda Hertz, "Urbanization and the Development of Pre-industrial Areas," *Economic Development and Cultural Change*, III (October, 1954), 6–26. See also the writer's paper, "Population and the Further Spread of Industrial Society," *Proceedings of the American Philosophical Society*, XCV (February, 1951), 10–13.

[3] From Kingsley Davis and Hilda Hertz, "The World Distribution of Urbanization," *Bulletin of the International Statistical Institute*, XXXIII, Part IV, 230.

The figures for world regions are less valuable for purposes of analysis than are those for individual countries. The latter show clearly that urbanization has tended to reach its highest point wherever economic productivity has been greatest—that is, where the economy is industrialized and rationalized. This explains why urbanization is so closely associated with northwest Europeans and their culture, since they were mainly responsible for the industrial revolution. Of the fifteen most urbanized countries in the world, all but one, Japan, are European in culture, and all but four derive that culture from the northwest or central part of Europe.

The rate of urbanization in the older industrial countries, however, is slowing down. During the twenty years from 1870 to 1890 Germany's proportion in large cities more than doubled; it nearly doubled again from 1890 to 1910; but from 1910 to 1940 the increase was only 36 per cent. In Sweden the gain slowed down noticeably after 1920. In England and Wales the most rapid urbanization occurred between 1811 and 1851. Contrary to popular belief, the fastest rate in the United States occurred between 1861 and 1891. Since, as we noted earlier, there has been no slowing-down of urbanization in the world as a whole, it must be that, as the more established industrial countries have slackened, the less-developed countries have exhibited a faster rate. In fact, such historical evidence as we have for underdeveloped areas seems to show that their rates of urbanization have been rising in recent decades. This has been the case in Egypt, where the rate is higher after 1920 than before; in India, where the fastest urbanization has occurred since 1941; in Mexico, where the speed-up began in 1921; and in Greece, where the fastest period ran from 1900 to 1930. Asia, for example, had only 22 per cent of the world's city population in 1900 but 34 per cent of it in 1950, and Africa had 1.5 per cent in 1900 but 3.2 per cent at the later date.

With respect to urbanization, then, the gap between the industrial and the preindustrial nations is beginning to diminish. The less-developed parts of the world will eventually, it seems, begin in their turn to move gradually toward a saturation point. As the degree of urbanization rises, it of course becomes impossible for the rate of gain to continue. The growth in the urban proportion is made possible by the movement of people from rural areas to the cities. As the rural population becomes a progressively smaller percentage of the total, the cities no longer can draw on a noncity population of any size. Yet in no country can it be said that the process of urbanization is yet finished. Although there have been short periods in recent times in England, the United States, and Japan when the city population increased at a slightly slower rate than the rural, these were mere interludes in the ongoing but ever slower progress of urban concentration. . . .

Power in Local Communities

WILLIAM SPINRAD

Since Floyd Hunter published his study of "Regional City" about a decade ago, many social scientists have devoted their attention to the study of community power.[1] Whatever comments we will make on some of the specific material, we would initially like to welcome this trend in the allocation of the professional resources of the social science fraternity. Particularly in the area of community research, this had been a relatively neglected subject, with the conspicuous exception of the Lynd's monumental study of Middletown.[2] The detailed cataloguing of the status structure was too often the dominant, in fact sometimes the only, theme. Longing for a simple stratification model in which everyone fits, more or less, into an obviously assignable place, the students of American communities tended to avoid the more complicated task of striving to learn "who got things done," why and how. It was, therefore, especially pleasing to read that in the old New England city of New Haven very few of the "social notables," the members of status-exclusive clubs, had any crucial role in the community decision-making process under review.[3]

The efforts at community power analysis have been many, the findings plentiful, the interpretations challenging. But, despite several suggestive attempts, thorough systematization is still wanting; the relation between the "power variable" and the entire community social structure is barely sketched. Let this preliminary appraisal not be misconstrued. The critique which follows is prefaced not only with praise for a worthwhile direction of social scientific inquiry but an appreciation of the valuable material that already exists. It is offered as a modest set of directions for future work in the area.

Several recently published volumes provide a springboard for an excursion into the field. An elaborate compendium of existing data on "public leadership" by Bell, Hill, and Wright offers little assistance to those who seek a comprehensive organization of ideas on the subject.[4] Marshalling a vast array of information, it initially classifies the methods by which leadership is located. The categories listed are: formal position, reputation, degree of social participation, opinion leadership, and role in specific decisions or events. The probability that each type will be drawn from particular demographic groups—sex, age, race, nationality, religion, social class, etc.—is assessed on the basis of reported

Reprinted from *Social Problems*, 12 (Winter, 1965), pp. 335–356, by permission of the author and the Society for the Study of Social Problems.

[1] Floyd Hunter, *Community Power Structure: A Study of Decision Makers*, Chapel Hill: The University of North Carolina Press, 1953.

[2] Robert S. Lynd and Helen M. Lynd, *Middletown in Transition*, New York: Harcourt, Brace, 1937.

[3] Robert Dahl, *Who Governs? Democracy and Power in an American City*, New Haven and London: Yale University Press, 1961, pp. 63–69.

[4] Wendell Bell, Charles J. Hill, Charles R. Wright, *Public Leadership*, San Francisco: Chandler Publishing Co., 1961.

investigations. Finally, the authors present the various findings on public attitudes towards leadership and motivations for leadership. As a catalogue of source material, the book can serve a useful purpose. But no attempt is made to organize or interpret the information. There are thus no summary statements, no attempts to develop models, no formulated clues to assist further discussions about community power. And these are precisely what are needed.

This brief consideration of the volume includes one additional caution. In its formulations, "public leadership" becomes a gross, diffuse concept. The "opinion leader," for instance, can hardly be equated with the other categories. Directed towards locating interpersonal communication networks, one general conclusion from opinion leadership research is that many, many people influence some others on some questions.[5] Such inquiries, valuable in their own sphere, scarcely provide any insight into community "power."

A meaningful organization of the field would be a posing of the major contending analyses. This, in essence, is the function of a symposium entitled *Power and Democracy in America*.[6] Despite its rather grandiose title and the variety of subjects considered by the major contributors and the editors, the core of the book is the debate between two students of community power, Delbert Miller and Robert Dahl. Utilizing their own researches and other relevant material, the two scholars generally represent and expound the two opposite sides of the methodological and analytical conflict that has characterized recent community power discussion. Miller favors the "reputational" form of investigation and finds a pyramidal, quasi-monolithic structure dominated by a "business elite" more or less typical. He is thus quite in accord with the findings of Hunter's original study. Dahl, utilizing "event analysis," searches for evidence of specific decision makers on particular issues, and concludes that a relatively pluralistic power structure is more prevalent. Of course, the divergencies are more complex and detailed, but these are the summary statements around which the discussion evolves.

The reputational technique, which has, with many variations, become fairly widespread in use, seeks to get knowledgeable informants to select, from a list of leading figures in community organizations and institutional areas, those whom they considered most powerful in "getting things done." Those chosen were then interviewed to learn about the personal and social relations among them, and which people they would themselves solicit if they wanted something adopted or achieved. Reviewing many studies with this research emphasis, including his own "Pacific City," Miller's conclusions are, essentially, the following:[7]

---

[5] See Elihu Katz, "The Two-Step Flow of Communication: An Up-To-Date Report on an Hypothesis," *Public Opinion Quarterly*, 21 (Spring, 1957), pp. 61–78.

[6] *Power and Democracy in America*, edited by William V. D'Antonio and Howard J. Ehrlich, Notre Dame, Indiana: University of Notre Dame Press, 1961.

[7] Actually, the major bulwarks for his thesis are his own and Hunter's research, plus a series of inquiries by Charles Loomis and his associates in Southwestern United States for which no published citations are given. The other references offered actually reveal much more complex patterns. See *Ibid.*, pp. 38–71.

1. Businessmen are overrepresented among "key influentials" and dominate community policy-making in most communities.[8]

2. Local governments are weak power centers. The elected officials are mostly small businessmen, local lawyers, and professional politicians. Policy on important questions is formulated by organized interests groups under the influence of the economic dominants. City councils merely respond to their pressures.

3. Representatives of labor, education, religious, and "cultural" groups are rarely key influentials, are underrepresented in city councils.

4. In vivid contrast, Miller reports his investigations of "English City," like "Pacific City" a seaport community of about 500,000 population. Businessmen constitute only a minority of the "key influentials." Labor is significantly represented. There is also an appreciable number from educational, religious, welfare, and "status" leaderships. Furthermore, the city council is the major arena of community decision making, the party organizations the directing groups.

Noting differences between "Regional City" and "Pacific City," Miller does not insist that the power pattern is identical in all American communities. In fact, he develops a typology of possible structures which will be later considered. But the modal type is clearly sketched, particularly in contrast with the findings of his British study.

Dahl's counter propositions are based primarily on his study of New Haven, summarized in the symposium and more fully elaborated in his book *Who Governs?*[9] The power structure of New Haven is seen as relatively pluralistic or, to use his terminology, one of "dispersed inequalities," a metamorphosis from earlier days of oligarchal dominance by "aristocratic patricians" and "entrepreneurs" successively. This is initially indicated in the change in political leadership with the rise of the "ex plebians" from various ethnic groups, often with proletarian backgrounds. The attention is, however, more to the examination of decision-leadership in three issue areas—political nominations, public education, and urban redevelopment, which Dahl insists are both representative and salient. The method in such "event analysis" is typically one of chronological narration of who did what, when, and what effect it had, in this instance supplemented by a more precise systematic tabulation of the kinds of people who held formal positions in the organizations concerned with the above issues and of those who initiated or vetoed significant decisions.

The refutation of the business dominance thesis is quite explicit. Some two hundred "economic notables" were located. Within the issue-areas studied, a significant number occupied formal positions only in connection with urban redevelopment (about fifty), of which seven were actually considered decision leaders. None were formally involved in public education, a handful in political parties.

Even within the area of urban redevelopment, the decision-making role of businessmen was considered minor. Their contributions came largely through

[8] *Ibid.*, p. 61.
[9] Dahl, *op. cit.*

their participation in the "Citizens Action Committee," organized by the Mayor with the objective of legitimizing decisions and providing an arena in which objections to the program could be anticipated and avoided. Neither the Committee, nor individual businessmen or business groups, were responsible for many crucial decisions. Dahl believes that they could, if vigorously in opposition, have blocked proposals, but the political officials, led by the Mayor, prevented such contingencies by a "capacity for judging with considerable precision what the existing beliefs and the commitments of the men on the CAC would compel them to agree to if a proposal were presented in the proper way, time, and place." [10] In general, business groups possess many "resources," but they are also limited by many power "liabilities," so that they simply appeared as "one of the groups out of which individuals sporadically emerge to influence the policies and acts of city officials." [11] "Like other groups in the community, from the Negroes on Dixwell Avenue to teachers in the public school, sometimes the Notables have their way and sometimes they do not." [12]

In the decision areas studied, the "inequalities" are not so widely "dispersed." Only a few people make the key decisions in each issue area, but they achieve their hegemony by accepting the indirect influence of larger groups. Nominations are generally determined by a few party leaders, but with attention to the wishes of their followers within the party organizations, especially sub-leaders and representatives of ethnic groups. Most important redevelopment decisions were made by the Mayor and appropriate staff officials, with full sensitivity to the need for getting support from business and other groups. Major public education policy was directed by the Mayor and his appointees on the Board of Education; superintendents, principals, and teachers organizations played some part, but mostly to mobilize support for public education. A few public and party officials thus constituted the directing leadership, each in his own province, with the office and personality of the dynamic Mayor, Richard Lee, supplying the unifying force. We have advisedly called the leading group a "directing" rather than a "dominating" oligarchy. It apparently got its way less from authority or influence, in the communication sense, than from the ability to please others, particularly potentially opposing groups. In fact, the political leaders favored the existence of organized groups as a means of legitimatizing their decisions and mobilizing support, as well as providing an arena where various sentiments could be expressed and somewhat satisfied. The Citizens Action Committee in the urban redevelopment field was one such example. Similarly, school principals and the Board of Education utilized PTAs "to head off or settle conflicts between parents and the school system." [13]

Dahl does not maintain that the New Haven pattern he describes is the only one possible or existent. Like Miller, he offers a model of power types which

[10] *Ibid.*, p. 137.
[11] *Ibid.*, p. 72.
[12] *Ibid.*, p. 75.
[13] *Ibid.*, p. 156.

will be later discussed. But the New Haven analysis provides the basic elements around which most of the varied forms are structured.

The dispute between the two major contending approaches to American community power is thus, more or less, joined. Partly methodological, it is, at least initially, a disagreement between a business-elite dominance thesis and an acceptance of a relative pluralism. It is also a disagreement about the role of local government and political leadership. Dahl believes that mayors and their staff have increasingly become the initiators and organizers of important community decisions. Miller insists that the political leaders are uncertain about themselves and wait for the cues of others, while businessmen have a clearly defined image "and thus act with more assertion."[14]

A third recent volume further helps locate the principal disputes on the subject. Edward Banfield's *Political Influence*, utilizing event analysis, narrates, with a detailed chronology, how decisions involving six very specific communtity problems were arrived at or, in most cases, blocked or compromised.[15] In all cases, there was a divided opinion around significant forces and individuals. The actual list of issues should be of some interest: proposals for extending a particular hospital's facilities, reorganization of welfare administration, a state subsidy for the Chicago Transit Authority, a plan for a vast business center, the creation of a large Chicago branch of the University of Illinois, the building of an extensive Exhibition Hall. At the time of publication, only the last had been achieved. The welfare reorganization plans had produced a compromise; in all other cases, the contending elements had forced a general stalemate.

Banfield's accounts are in the nature of the best type of scholarly journalistic history. They contain extensive details, but little systematic treatment. However, his interpretations are organized around several summary ideas. Initially, he does not discount the possibility of business dominance. In essence, he believes that the resources of the leading Chicago businessmen, representing the top officials of leading national corporations and prominent regional commercial and banking institutions, offer an apparently unlimited power potential. Yet, he insists that, in his investigations, the "richest men in Chicago are conspicuous by their absence."[16] In fact, "big businessmen are criticized less for interfering in public affairs than for 'failing to assume their civic responsibilities.'"[17]

Businessmen do not dominate community decisions because of lack of unity, lack of interest, and because of the "costs" of intervening on any issue, including the encouragement of counter pressures. Their vital interests are not at stake and they are relatively satisfied with what is done. When their interests are more aroused, either because of some visible economic stake or because of personal predilections, particular business organizations may become heavily involved and be very influential. For instance, the disputed Exhibition Hall was built because it was a pet project of Colonel Robert McCormack and his

[14] D'Antonio and Ehrlich, *op. cit.*, p. 136.
[15] Edward C. Banfield, *Political Influence*, New York: The Free Press of Glencoe, 1961.
[16] *Ibid.*, p. 288.
[17] *Ibid.*, p. 287.

successors on the Chicago *Tribune*. But, usually businessmen are only casually concerned or on all sides of most of the questions studied.

Typically, the most influential people in the community-decision making in Chicago are: "the managers of large organizations, the maintenance of which is at stake, a few 'civic leaders' whose judgment, negotiating skill, and disinterestedness are unusual and above all, the chief elected officials." [18] The organizations referred to are specified as those supported by "customers" rather than "members." [19] They may be profit-making businesses, public agencies which give free services, or public and semi-public agencies which sell services. In most cases, the involved organizations are public and the executives are civil servants, though Banfield describes them as "fighting politicians" rather than "bureaucrats." [20]

However, the most influential leaders in this megalopolis, as in the medium-sized city of New Haven, are the elected political officials, especially the Mayor. Banfield is thus on the side of Dahl against Miller. But, the leadership of Mayor Richard Daley, so frequently bracketed with Mayor Lee of New Haven as one of the "strong" mayors of our times, appears to be less forceful. Though both chief executive and official leader of the powerful Democratic machine, he is faced with many limitations on the exercise of power, even within the political realm. He needs the co-operation of other elected officials, "irregulars" within his own party, elected officials of the other party (especially the Republican Governor in the period under study). He may be, and in this study actually was, blocked by the courts. Voters may veto proposals, as on a bond referendum, and, of course, the possibility of electoral opposition in the next election must always be considered. Above all the Mayor and his associates, like anyone who seeks to wield power in specific situations, has limited resources of "working capital." These cannot be "used up" for every challenge that arises.

Like the business dominants, Banfield seems to consider the political leaders as potentially omnipotent when they go "all out" on any question. But this would require depleting their limited working capital. They have to contend with other power groups besides those mentioned—national government in some cases, businessmen, other strong community elements that may be affected or aroused. They are, therefore, in practice, slow to take up issues and seek compromises. The initiative on most questions thus comes from the maintenance and enhancement needs of the type of formal organization listed. Other organizations may then support, oppose, or strive for modification. The following are some examples: A hospital tries to expand. Another hospital, for its own reasons, opposes. The *Tribune* wants an Exhibition Hall, the owners of another Hall oppose. The state, city, and county Welfare Departments have varying positions on reorganization plans. Attempts are made to line up different elements of the "public" on each side. The political leaders may then adjudicate or support one side or the other, but rarely with all their resources. . . .

[18] *Ibid.*, p. 288.
[19] *Ibid.*, p. 265.
[20] *Ibid.*, p. 266.

POWER POSITION OF BUSINESS AND LOCAL GOVERNMENT

Although many groups thus can and do exercise power in American communities, the major contentions are, quite appropriately about the two major institutional groups, business and local government. The foundations of their respective power positions are accordingly appraised in line with the previous formulations.

Business. Banfield offers this conjecture about possible behavior of leading Chicago businessmen: "In some future case—one in which their vital interests are at stake—they may issue the orders necessary to set in motion the lower echelons of the alleged influence hierarchy."[21] Whatever the results of such an effort, this would imply a crucially divisive issue in the community, a quasi "revolutionary" conflict in which some aspect of legitimacy is debated. None of this appears in the literature. Business power within its own institutional area is hardly an issue in contemporary American communities. Beyond this, the following emerges from the literature.

The most important resources of businessmen are obviously the possession of money—their own and of others whose money can be utilized—and status. For many who postulate business elite dominance, these are the only factors involved, for there is the casual assumption that, in American society, wealth, status, and power are automatically correlated. Additionally, there is the generally accepted legitimacy of business values and the expertise of businessmen. Material interest in the city compels concern about many decisions. There is frequently close internal communications among businessmen.

But the inherent limitations to their exercise of power are also evident, as already suggested. The legitimacy of businessmen and their values is not accepted in all areas of community life and by all people.[22] Conflict of interest and opinion among businessmen is as evident as cohesion. Communication may not be as easy as assumed, especially through their far-flung organizations.[23] The process of formal decision-making on an issue is not always readily available, and potentially divisive decisions, within business organizations or in the community, are avoided. Public relations may be more important than power wielding for its own sake. There is little desire for political activity by corporation officials unless pushed by the companies' desire for a proper public image.

Businessmen expect public officials to handle the political problems and, unless seriously dissatisfied with what is done, will rarely intervene with any vigor. When economic interests are involved, they may participate, but often as supporters and legitimizers of the outspoken proponents. Their role in political affairs may be more extensive when local government is weak or when intervention does not brook serious opposition. In essence, they would then be responding to a "power vacuum," even though it is one of long standing. Their "citizen" activity may tend to be in civic, service, and philanthropic organizations, where objectives are clear, methods "clean," and controversy minimal,

21 Banfield, *Political Influence, op. cit.*, p. 288.
22 See Dahl in D'Antonio and Ehrlich, *op. cit.*, p. 109.
23 Banfield, *op. cit.*, pp. 295–296.

and the thorny arena of political conflict avoided. The exceptions, to repeat, are situations when *direct economic interests are involved.* Small local businessmen and professional people may be more involved in political affairs, particularly in smaller communities, because of more direct material interest, status strivings, or greater value concerns about the community.

Local Government. The basis for the power position of local government can be sketched more briefly. Despite the growing nationalization of government and politics and the checks that automatically follow, municipal government power has grown within the following context: the necessary functions of the government in solving complex contemporary problems and the accompanying role of professionals; a popularly supported plebeian-based political organization, typically with some ties to labor organizations and ethnic groups; a formal political structure which accents the power potential of the mayor and "partisan" organizations and elections. Traditional political machines are typical, though often diminished in power and appeal, but they are rarely involved in major policy decisions. Relative lack of power of political leaders and their staff professionals is correlated with the comparative absence of the above and the power of business groups, because of specific community configurations and historical antecedents, including the dominant position of local-based business and the slowness of change.

THE POWER STRUCTURE OF AMERICAN COMMUNITIES

All that has been said tends to substantiate a pluralistic interpretation of American community power. People try to exercise power when a particular decision is salient and/or required. This obviously means that different groups in the community will be more involved in different kinds of decisions. Many groups possess appropriate resources, internal decision-making mechanisms, access to those who make the necessary formal decisions, widely accepted legitimacy and values, means for communicating to and mobilizing large publics. The investigation of power then becomes a study of discrete decision-making processes, with many sectors of the population revealing varying degrees of impact on different type decisions.[24]

But summary statements about American community power should go beyond such casual nominalism, as they must transcend facile monolithism. Some decisions are obviously more salient to the community than others. Power motivation, formal decision-making potential, resources, access, communication facilities may be widespread, but there are significant differences. To use the abused cliche, some are more equal than others. The two important dominant groups remain businessmen, of varying types, and local government officials. The pattern of American community power observed is mostly a matter of the

[24] A political science text on the government of New York City thus concludes simply by listing six power groups in the city who, among others, appear to be important decision-makers in particular areas. See Wallace S. Sayre and Herbert Kaufman, *Governing New York City*, New York: Russell Sage Foundation, 1960.

respective positions of these two groups and their relation with the residual "all other groups."

Despite their disagreement about the prevailing power picture, Miller and Dahl offer models of possible power structure which are not too dissimilar.[25] Both allow for completely pluralistic patterns, with either particular spheres of influence for specific groups or open struggles by relatively equal groups on the same issues. To Miller, these are subordinate aspects in most American communities. To Dahl, they exist but are less likely possibilities than a system of comparative pluralism with *coordination by the political leadership* in different ways in different communities, a variant not specifically indicated by Miller. Finally both accept the possibility of domination by an economic elite, but Dahl generally relegates such situations to the past while Miller insists that this pattern, with all its variations, is most common in the United States today.

A more composite replica of these typologies is that of Rossi, with his simple division into "monoliths" and "polyliths."[26] The former is typically business elite dominant. In a polylith, local government is the province of the political leaders, backed by strong parties and working class associations.[27] The rest of his formulation is in accord with our previous discussion. Civic associations and community chests are in the hands of the leaders of business and staff professionals. A polylith is associated with strong political parties, based upon class political attitudes, frequently with ethnic concomitants. In response, economic leaders (and others), may advocate changes in government structure (nonpartisan elections) to thwart some of the power of political parties. Absentee corporation officials will tend to set themselves off from purely local political concerns. In monoliths, conflicts tend to take on the character of minor revolts, like the revolutionary postures of the powerless in authoritarian countries.

All this can be restated in terms of what has already been spelled out. Business elite dominance appears most characteristic of communities when the dominant businessmen are most motivated to participate in community decisions (company towns, established commercial aristocracies, etc.) and/or when there are fewer rival power centers. The polylith is characterized by both the leadership of government officials and relative pluralism. Decision-making is widespread among many groups, depending upon motivation, resources, and the other listed ingredients. Businessmen are an important part of the power picture but only as part of the above formula. In fact, a large section avoids the arena of political decisions, except when very pressing, because of the efforts demanded and risks inherent, and concentrates on the private areas of community decision-making, such as civic associations and philanthropic activities, where there is little opposition in power or ideology. The political leaders are the necessary

---

[25] D'Antonio and Ehrlich, *op. cit.*, pp. 62–70; Dahl, *op. cit.*, pp. 184–189.

[26] Peter H. Rossi, "Theory and Method in the Study of Power in the Local Community," paper presented at meetings of American Sociological Association, New York, August, 1960, pp. 24–43.

[27] A good example is provided in the description of Lorain, Ohio, by James B. McKee, "Status and Power in the Industrial Community," *American Journal of Sociology*, 58 (January, 1953), pp. 364–370.

coordinators in such a complex pattern and their power rests on the fairly strong power position of many groups—especially political parties, trade unions, ethnic groups, staff professionals, etc.—and the importance of governmental decisions today.

To complete our review, one additional presentation must be described. Political Scientist Robert Salisbury states that what others would consider polylithic structures are, in most cases, evidence of a "new convergence."[28] A new power triumvirate has arisen to solve the vital problems of the contemporary city. Its elements have already been sufficiently identified: the business interests directly dependent on the condition of the city, particularly the downtown area; the professionals, technicians, experts engaged in city programs; the mayor, generally secure in his tenure. What Salisbury emphasizes is that this constitutes a coordinate power group; the mayor is the most influential, but he appears to be only the first among equals.

The leadership convergence directs most mayor decisions, particularly those that involve allocation of scarce resources; some of these, like redevelopment and traffic control, can determine the future of the city. The rest of the population—other organized groups, other politicians, and unorganized publics—are part of the process in three ways: they must be "sold" on certain issues especially if referenda are in order; their interests and needs must be somewhat satisfied and/or anticipated; some demands must be responded to, such as race relations. Salisbury, however, believes that the importance of the last process can be exaggerated. Specifically, he insists that Banfield's selection of issues tends to magnify the initiative of the groups outside the "convergence." The more vital questions should, with few exceptions such as race relations, reveal the initiating, as well as decision-making position, of the triumvirate.

Salisbury's analysis can thus supply the basis for the concluding statements of this essay. Power over community decisions remains a matter of motivation, resources, mechanisms of decision-making, mobilization of resources, etc. On many, many decisions, various groups may initiate and win out, as in Banfield's account and in some of the descriptions of Dahl and others. Current disputes about race relations offer a fitting example where this more pluralistic interpretation, including both the ideas of spheres of influence and competing pressures around a common issue, may be readily applicable. But on the most salient community issues a directing leadership can be observed. In some communities, for the reasons outlined, the decision leaders have been, and may still be, particular business interests. In most of them, a new pattern has emerged, a polylithic structure in which business groups and local government each lead in their own domains. But the urgent problems of the post World War II era in most large cities have brought some business groups into the same decision area as the local government and the ever growing crop of experts. The extent to which the businessmen are involved may vary, as in the different accounts of the role of businessmen in urban renewal in different cities.

[28] Robert Salisbury, "Urban Politics: The Now Convergence of Power," paper delivered at meetings of American Political Science Association, New York, September, 1963.

Does the rest of the population, organized and unorganized, become merely an audience called on occasionally to affirm and applaud these "big decisions?" Salisbury may have overstated his case. Many groups may initiate, veto, modify, pressure in all decision areas, in accord with the ingredients frequently listed. But those who are part of the new power convergence cannot be circumvented. In some manner, they have the responsibilities and will generally have to assume a decision-making role in all major decisions.

To return to the original debate, whatever evidence is available tends to support Dahl's emphasis against Miller's. Most American communities reveal a relatively pluralistic power structure. On some community-relevant questions, power may be widely dispersed. On the most salient questions, many groups may have an effect on what is decided, but the directing leadership comes from some combination of particular business groups, local government, and, in recent developments, professionals and experts. Communities differ and communities change in the power relations among these elements. A suggestive hypothesis holds that the tendency has been towards their coordination into a uniquely composite decision-making collectively.[29]

[29] One type of community does not seem to fit any model described—the ever growing residential suburb. Perhaps, the reason is that it does not constitute a genuine "community."

ORGANIZATION

A Contemporary View of Industrial Concentration

GARDINER C. MEANS

Chairman Hart and members of the committee, I appreciate this opportunity to testify before your committee. I want to congratulate you on your decision to take a new and fresh look at corporate concentration. And particularly I urge that you make this investigation without any preconceived attitude for or against big business. Bigness in business can serve the public interest or run counter to the public interest depending largely on the public policies which condition its activity. Bigness in business creates problems of economic policy which do not arise with small business. I believe these problems should be the focus of your attention.

Economic concentration is a subject in which I have done much pioneering work. More than 30 years ago I made the first statistical measurements of the long-term trend of concentration. The results of this measurement were presented in "The Modern Corporation and Private Property" which I authored jointly with Adolf Berle.[1] I continued this analysis of overall trends when I was with the National Resources Committee which published the findings in "The Structure of the American Economy."[2] There we published—also for the first time—what have come to be called "concentration ratios" for the various industries based on the reports to the Bureau of the Census.

This morning my testimony will continue this exploration. It will start with a discussion of concentration for the American economy as a whole, it will then focus on concentration in manufacturing which is your committee's most immediate concern; and finally it will discuss the importance of concentration and the problems of policy it engenders.

CONCENTRATION IN THE ECONOMY AS A WHOLE

Let me take you back a century to the economic conditions which prevailed just before the Civil War. Then there was little concentration. Two-thirds of the labor force was engaged in agriculture where the family farm was the usual form of organization and flexible farm prices were determined by the interaction of a considerable number of buyers and sellers in the market. There were no

Reprinted from U.S. Senate, Committee on the Judiciary, Subcommittee on Antitrust and Monopoly, Hearings, July 1, 1964 (Washington, U.S. Government Printing Office, 1964).
[1] Adolf A. Berle, Jr., and Gardiner C. Means, The Macmillan Co., New York, 1933.
[2] National Resources Committee, Washington, 1939.

telephones or electric power companies then and the railroads were just beginning to be consolidated. In 1853 the New York Central was formed by consolidating the 10 short sections of railway, mostly end-to-end, which spanned the 300-mile distance between Albany and Buffalo. At that time, according to Professor Ripley, a railroad ". . . 100 miles in length constituted the maximum for efficient operation."[3] And little railroad mileage had been built beyond the Mississippi.

Likewise, with manufacturing, most production was in small local plants or in small shops. The clothing industry was just coming out of the home with the invention of the sewing machine. The shoe industry was just being brought into factories and shoes were still made by handsewing or by pegging. American ironmasters had only just shifted from the old method of hammering out bar iron in a forge fired by charcoal to the newer methods of rolling. The Bessemer steel furnace, invented in 1856, had not yet been put into practical operation and the open-hearth furnace was still to be developed.

At that time, ours was indeed an economy of small-scale enterprise. For practical purposes there was little concentration. For theoretical purposes even such concentration as existed, could be disregarded. National economic policy could be decided on the basis of a body of economic theory which assumed that all production was carried on under conditions of classical competition; that is, competition in which no producer or consumer had significant pricing power; one in which the laws of supply and demand determined prices; and one in which most prices could not be administered and such administered prices as existed were not significant.

The next 70 years saw a complete change in the character of our economy. Mass production and big corporate enterprises took over much of manufacturing; the railroads were consolidated into a few great systems; public utility empires and the big telephone system developed; and, even in merchandising, the big corporation played a part.

By 1929, the economy of this country had become one in which the big modern corporation was the oustanding characteristic. Only a fifth of the labor force was engaged in agriculture. Railroads, public utilities, over 90 per cent of manufacturing, and much of merchandising was conducted by corporations. In the year 1929, the 200 largest corporations legally controlled 48 percent of the assets of all nonfinancial corporations, that is, of all corporations other than banks, insurance companies, and similar financial companies. If we focus on land, buildings, and equipment—the instruments of physical production—the 200 largest corporations had legal control of 58 percent of the net capital assets reported by all non-financial corporations. Thus, by 1929, the dominantly small-enterprise economy which prevailed in 1860 had been largely replaced by one in which the huge corporation was the most characteristic feature.

[3] William Z. Ripley, "Railroads," Longmans, Green & Co., New York, 1915, p. 456. The largest railroad in 1860 was the recently created Illinois Central Railroad with a total of 700 miles of track.

I emphasize 1929 for three reasons:

First, it is a prosperous year for which we have unusually reliable estimates of corporate concentration.

Second, at that time economic policy was still dominated by the 19th century economic theories which applied only to an economy of small-scale enterprise and flexible prices. In 1929, those theories were still taught as gospel in the universities. There was no other body of economic theory for guiding the operation of a free enterprise system.

My third reason for emphasizing 1929 is that it saw the beginning of the great depression which brought a clear rejection by Government of 19th century economic theory as the basis for overall economic policy.

Since 1929, there have been forces working both against and for greater concentration in the American economy as a whole. In the 1930's, legislation against holding companies was passed and many of the big utility systems were broken up or forced to reorganize; further concentration in railroading was kept to a minimum; and the automobile, bus, and truck took business away from the railroads so that, today, transportation, as a whole, is probably less concentrated than in 1929; in manufacturing, there was greater resistance to mergers among big companies than prevailed in the 1920's; and a larger proportion of national effort has gone into producing services; such as health and recreation which tend to be less concentrated activities. All of these tend to reduce or limit concentration.

On the other hand, there have been developments which have tended to increase the degree of concentration. Today, less than 7 percent of the gainfully employed are engaged in agriculture as compared with 20 percent in 1929; manufacturing is more concentrated than it was in 1929; the chain supermarket and other chainstores have increased in relative importance.

Without making a major study, it would be difficult to say just how concentration for the economy, as a whole, compares today with concentration in 1929. The main source of data for the economy, as a whole, is that derived from corporate income tax returns. But the income tax compilations made public by the Bureau of Internal Revenue give a very incomplete picture of concentration. This is because many companies legally controlled by the big corporations file separate tax returns and are thus treated by the Bureau as independent companies. The importance of this for estimates of concentration is shown by the fact that in 1960, while nonfinancial corporations distributed $13.7 billion in dividends, they received $1.4 billion of dividends distributed by domestic corporations or more than a tenth as much as they paid out. Also the large corporations with a quarter of a billion assets or more received two-thirds of these dividends and three-quarters of the dividends from foreign corporations. An important part of these dividends are from subsidiaries or legally controlled companies which are not consolidated in the returns filed for income tax purposes. Just how much difference the complete consolidation would make is very difficult to tell. But that it would make a big difference was indicated in the

1929 study in which we were able to go back of the published data and take account of the unconsolidated subsidiaries. I am sure this would still be true.

I have tried to make an estimate of the proportion of corporate assets legally controlled by the 200 largest corporations comparable to that we made for 1929. The results are too crude to be worth publishing but they suggest that if a careful study were made based on the tax returns in the Bureau files—and I strongly recommend this be done—it would show the 200 corporations legally controlled somewhat more than the 58 percent of the net capital assets controlled by the 200 that were largest in 1929.[4] However, the most that I can say with reasonable certainty is that concentration for the economy as a whole is not significantly less than it was in 1929.

What is more important for national economic policy is the fact that both in 1929 and today the atomistic economy around which 19th century economic theory was built has ceased to exist. Policy must deal with an economy in which big corporations and inflexible administered prices play a major role. How this affects economic policy, I will discuss after I have examined concentration in the more limited field of manufacturing.*

CONCENTRATION IN MANUFACTURING

Though manufacturing employs less than a quarter of the gainfully employed persons in this country, it is the field in which unregulated competition has been, *par excellence*, the instrument relied on to convert the actions of self-seeking individuals into actions which serve the public interest. It is the field with which this committee is most immediately and quite properly concerned. What has been the trend of concentration in manufacturing?

I have already pointed out that, in 1860, most of manufacturing was carried on in small-scale unincorporated enterprises. In the major industrial center of Pittsburgh with 17 foundries, 21 rolling mills, 76 glass factories, and 47 other manufactures, not a single manufacturing enterprise was incorporated. The only industry in which the modern type of corporation played an important role was the cotton textile industry. The big integrated cotton mills of Lowell, Lawrence, and some other New England towns were incorporated with characteristics that today look quite modern. Indeed, they were known throughout New England as "the corporations."[5] But apart from these cotton mills,

---

[4] The BIR compilations show net capital assets of $240.3 billion for all nonfinancial corporations in 1960 and $139.2 billion reported by 267 nonfinancial corporations or 58 percent of the total. Since consolidation was allowed only if 80 percent or more of a subsidiary's stock was controlled by the parent and not all allowable consolidations were made, many legally controlled companies were not consolidated. This 58-percent figure, therefore, substantially under-represents the proportion of the net capital assets legally controlled by the 267 largest and a significant number of the latter are likely to be legally controlled by others in the group. It seems almost certain that a complete consolidation would show the largest 200 nonfinancial corporations with more than 58 percent of the net capital assets of all nonfinancial corporations. BIR data do not allow even a rough approximation to a complete consolidation.

[5] The Modern Corporation and Private Property, *op. cit.*, pp. 11 and 12.

* [The material referred to is not included—Editor.]

big corporate business was almost nonexistent in manufacturing before the Civil War. Altogether it is doubtful if as much as 6 or 8 percent of manufacturing activity at that time was carried on by corporations and a much smaller proportion by what could be called in these days big corporations.

Between the Civil War and the turn of the century, there was a great increase in corporate manufacturing so that by 1900, close to two-thirds of manufacturing output was produced by corporations.[6]

Also toward the end of the century there was the first great merger movement culminating in the formation of the United States Steel Corp. as a merger of mergers in 1901. The pattern of mergers in this period is shown in Figure 1 which indicates the number of mergers reported in the Commercial and Financial

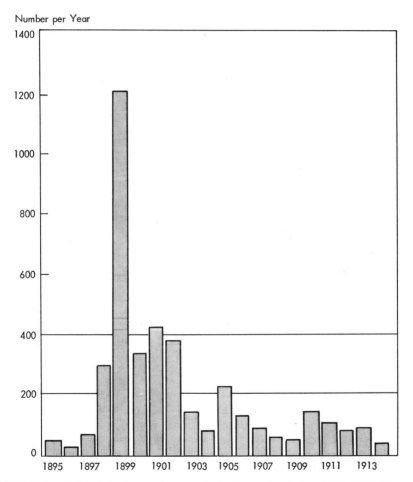

Number per Year

FIGURE 1. Recorded mergers in manufacturing and mining, 1895–1914. (*Source: Nelson*, Merger Movements in American Industry, *Chap. III, App. B.*)

[6] Historical Statistics of the United States, Bureau of the Census, p. 413.

Chronicle year by year from 1895 to 1914. It does not include all the mergers but presumably includes all the important mergers.

As you can see, there was a great burst of mergers from 1898 to 1902. All of this led to a great increase in manufacturing concentration even though a third of manufacturing output was still produced by unincorporated enterprises.

A very sharp peak in 1899, a heavy volume of mergers in 1900, 1901, and 1902, and then a fall off.

But the drive for monopoly created a strong public reaction. When Theodore Roosevelt became President in 1901, he was responsible for vigorous enforcement of the Sherman Act. The *Northern Securities* decision by the Supreme Court in 1904 outlawed the holding company as a device for achieving monopoly and other cases were brought which led to the breakup of the Standard Oil monopoly and the Tobacco Trust. Also some of the early combinations proved to be less successful than had been expected. As Fig. 1 shows, the wave of mergers came to an end as the goal of monopoly was clearly established as illegal. Between 1902 and the First World War, reported mergers averaged only a hundred a year. Whether there was an actual decline in manufacturing concentration in this period or a very slow growth is far from clear.

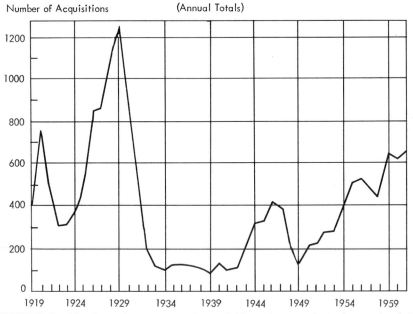

FIGURE 2. Number of mergers and acquisitions in manufacturing and mining, 1919–1961. (*Sources: 1919–1939, Temporary National Economic Committee, Monograph No. 27. 1940–1961, Federal Trade Commission.*)

A second merger movement occurred after World War I, culminated in 1929, and was followed after the great depression by a quiescent period under a second President Roosevelt. This pattern of mergers is shown in Figure 2.

In this second merger movement, the aim of combination appears to have been quite different from that in the first. Particular big companies sought to strengthen their organization by acquiring companies which supplied raw materials or used their products or carried on similar—but not identical—types of manufacturing. Instead of monopoly-seeking horizontal merging we had vertical merging to obtain efficiencies in production and the merging of related products to obtain economies in management and merchandising.

Since World War II, there has been a renewal of the merging process but not on the scale of the earlier monopoly movement. The pattern of this third period also is indicated in Fig. 2 and includes all types of merging. These figures come from the Federal Trade Commission and are more comprehensive in their coverage than those covered by the first chart, but probably fail to include a significant number of small mergers. However, their inclusion would not change the general pattern though they would alter the actual number of mergers in particular years.

It is fair to assume that the greatest increases in manufacturing concentration have come in the three periods of greatest mergering. But increased concentration can also come from internal growth either through the reinvestment of earnings or from the sale of new securities provided, of course, that the growth from these sources is more rapid for larger companies than for smaller companies. In a 6-year period in the 1920's more than fourth-fifths of the growth of large companies came from internal growth and only a fifth from mergers.[7] Presumably the present day concentration has come partly from mergers and partly from more rapid internal growth.

What has been the actual trend of manufacturing concentration and how far has concentration progressed?

Clearly a peak in the rate of concentration was reached just after 1900. It would be nice if we had reliable concentration data for that period but we don't. Certainly some lines of manufacturing such as steel were more concentrated at the turn of the century than they are today and some product lines such as cotton textiles are more concentrated today. But this is not the issue when we are considering concentration for manufacturing as a whole since mergers have been to a much greater extent either vertical or conglomerate and their effect on concentration is not fully reflected in separate product or narrow industry figures. Much careful research will be needed before we can determine the relative change in manufacturing concentration since 1900. And in this connection it is important to remember that, in 1900, only about two-thirds of manufacturing was carried on by corporations while today, 95 percent is corporate.[8]

The most reliable figures we have on concentration in manufacturing are those reported in the study made by the National Resources Committee for 1929. Among the 200 largest corporations in that year, the Resources Committee report included 82 manufacturing corporations. It included the Western Electric

[7] The Modern Corporation and Private Property, *op. cit.*, p. 43.
[8] U.S. Bureau of Census, Historical Statistics of the United States, Washington, 1960, p. 413.

Co. along with the assets of its parent, the American Telephone & Telegraph Co., and it presented unconsolidated data for 107 large industrial corporations for 1935. From these data I have derived two concentration estimates for the 100 largest manufacturing corporations in 1929. According to these figures, 100 large companies in 1929 had legal control of approximately 40 percent of the total assets of all manufacturing corporations and 44 percent of their net capital assets.[9]

| | [Dollar amounts in millions] | | | |
	Total Consolidated assets	Ratio to all manufac- turing (percent)	Net capital assets	Ratio to all manufac- turing (percent)
82 largest (excluding Western Electric)	23,641	37.0	11,803	41.4
Western Electric	309	.5	70	.2
17 next largest	1,350	2.1	605	2.1
100 largest manufacturing corporations	25,300	39.6	12,478	43.7
All manufacturing corpora- tions (including Western Electric)	63,955	100.0	28,531	100.0

SOURCE: For 82 largest, "The Structure of the American Economy," *op. cit.*, p. 285. For Western Electric, Moody's Manual. For total consolidated assets of 17 next largest, the partially consolidated figures given in the Structure of the American Economy, pp. 274–275— complete consolidation might increase the figures slightly. For net capital assets of 17 next largest, the ratio of net capital assets to total assets for all corporations (44.8 percent), was applied to the total assets of the 17 next largest. For all manufacturing corporations, "The Structure of the American Economy," p. 285 plus Western Electric.

Let me explain just what these figures mean. The figures for legal control by the 100 largest mean that these companies either own the assets directly or control them through owning or controlling more than 50 per cent of the stock of the corporations that do own the assets.[10]

By restricting the figures to legal control, the practical degree of concentration tends to be somewhat understated, partly because the figures exclude joint ventures in which each of two or more of the big companies owns 50 percent or less of a smaller company but in combination have legal control and partly because practical or working control of one company can often be exercised with a holding of stock which is not sufficient to give legal control.

The figures for "total assets" include total current assets such as inventories, accounts receivable, and government securities and the fixed assets such as land, buildings and equipment after depreciation and depletion but exclude the

[9] Estimate for 100 largest manufacturing corporations in 1929.

[10] Where 2 or more of the 100 largest corporations have a combined stock holdings of more than 50 percent in another corporation which would otherwise be included in the 100 largest, its assets are combined with the assets of the 100 largest as if it were legally controlled by 1 of them.

estimated holdings of securities of other corporations. The latter are excluded since they represent, in large degree, double counting. This still leaves some duplication in the figures due to intercorporate debt between parent and subsidiary but complete consolidation would probably not affect the concentration percentages significantly.

The figures for net capital assets include only the net property—the land, buildings, and equipment less depreciation and depletion. They constitute the instruments of production and provide the material basis for corporate power. A corporation is not industrially powerful because it has a large amount of bills receivable. It is not industrially powerful because it has large inventories. It is not industrially powerful because it has large holdings of government securities. Its industrial power must rest on its control of factories or natural resources. For this reason, the 44 percent of net capital assets legally controlled by the 100 largest manufacturing corporations in 1929 would appear to be a more significant figure of concentration than the 40 percent of total assets held by the 100 largest. It has the added advantage that the figures for net capital assets do not involve any double counting.

Whether we consider total assets or net capital assets, the 40 percent or more controlled by the largest 100 corporations indicates that a very considerable degree of concentration existed in manufacturing in 1929.

What has happened since 1929? We have no figures for manufacturing concentration which are as reliable as those for 1929. However, I have attempted to make estimates for concentration in 1962 as nearly comparable with the 1929 figures as published data will allow. Because these estimates are less reliable, I want to indicate just how they were made.

The big problem in making such estimates arises from incomplete consolidation in the published figures of the large corporations. A few, like Standard Oil of New Jersey, publish balance sheets in which they consolidate the assets of all corporations in which they control more than 50 per cent of the voting stock. More often corporations consolidate only those subsidiaries in which they have a 95 to 100 percent stock interest, reporting the stocks of corporations over which they have legal control by a smaller percent as "investments in subsidiaries" or in the larger category of "other noncurrent assets." As a result, the assets over which they have legal control exceed the assets reported in their balance sheets to the extent to that the assets of controlled companies exceed the value of their stocks on the books of the controlling company. To get a clear picture of concentration, it is necessary to approximate a more complete consolidation. In making the study for 1929 back in the 1930's, I and a small staff were sworn into the Bureau of Internal Revenue and had direct access to the actual tax returns of corporations. We selected what appeared to be the biggest 200 companies and then for all other corporations with 14 million assets or more and for a sample of still smaller companies, several thousand companies in total, we searched the standard reference books to discover all cases in which more than 50 percent of the stock was controlled by one of the big companies.

While we undoubtedly missed some subsidiaries, we probably picked up most of the important ones. The exact methods and the detailed results were set forth in a 20-page appendix to the structure report.[11]

Today much more information is publicly available than in 1929 but it would still be necessary to go into the detailed information in the hands of Government to make an estimate as reliable as that which we made in 1929. For my present estimates I have done the best I could with the information that has been made public. In table 1, I list what appear to be the 100 largest manufacturing corporations in 1962, giving their total assets, including investments, and their net

TABLE 1.   ONE HUNDRED LARGEST MANUFACTURING COMPANIES BY ASSET SIZE, 1962
[IN MILLIONS]

Asset Rank	Company	Total Assets	Net Capital Assets
1	Standard Oil (New Jersey)	$11,487.7	$6,875.7
2	General Motors	10,239.5	2,884.1
3	Ford Motor	5,416.5	2,140.2
4	United States Steel	5,059.7	2,820.1
5	Gulf Oil	4,243.6	2,458.7
6	Texaco	4,165.8	2,551.7
7	Socony Mobil Oil	4,136.5	2,253.1
8	Standard Oil (California)	3,353.1	2,273.5
9	Standard Oil (Indiana)	3,108.9	2,172.3
10	E. I. DuPont	3,095.7	984.7
11	General Electric[a]	3,047.6	712.9
12	Bethlehem Steel	2,212.2	978.9
13	International Business Machines	2,112.3	960.4
14	Shell Oil	1,989.1	1,281.4
15	Western Electric[a]	1,970.1	888.0
16	Union Carbide	1,791.7	958.5
17	Phillips Petroleum	1,735.3	1,084.0
18	Getty Oil Companies[b]	1,591.7	1,093.1
19	Westinghouse Electric[a]	1,547.6	367.8
20	International Harvester	1,527.2	424.5
21	Chrysler Corp.	1,525.0	398.9
22	Sinclair Oil	1,515.3	961.0
23	Cities Service	1,505.8	882.3
24	Aluminium Co. of America	1,377.8	821.1
25	Monsanto Chemical	1,324.9	769.9
26	Continental Oil	1,241.1	752.2
27	Goodyear Tire & Rubber	1,286.3	422.8
28	Anaconda	1,163.8	704.3
29	Republic Steel	1,131.6	644.7
30	Eastman Kodak	1,102.6	367.8
31	Radio Corp. of America[a]	1,091.9	264.4
32	Procter & Gamble	1,090.4	414.4
33	Reynolds Tobacco	1,080.7	145.6
34	International Paper	1,038.0	583.9
35	Allied Chemical	1,022.4	678.0
36	Dow Chemical	1,021.5	577.9
37	Reynolds Metals	1,002.1	565.5

[11] *Op. cit.*, app. 11, pp. 277–297.

TABLE 1. (CONTINUED)
ONE HUNDRED LARGEST MANUFACTURING COMPANIES BY ASSET SIZE, 1962
[IN MILLIONS]

Asset Rank	Company	Total Assets	Net Capital Assets
38	Armco Steel	995.0	464.4
39	Boeing[a]	964.0	114.9
40	American Can	958.7	524.8
41	International Telegraph & Telephone (manufacturing)[d]	950.8	206.2
42	Firestone Tire & Rubber	931.0	302.9
43	Sperry Rand[a]	914.1	251.2
44	Atlantic Refining	908.3	664.9
45	National Steel	902.5	564.4
46	Olin Mathieson	878.3	398.2
47	Lockheed Aircraft[a]	857.4	94.3
48	Inland Steel	853.8	490.9
49	Sun Oil	844.7	549.2
50	American Tobacco	839.5	65.2
51	Kennecott Copper	831.0	434.1
52	Jones & Laughlin	829.8	540.6
53	Continental Can	806.8	486.4
54	Union Oil of California	796.9	502.1
55	National Dairy Products	774.3	326.6
56	Youngstown Sheet & Tube	772.7	376.0
57	Brunswick	768.3	59.0
58	North American Aviation[a]	765.9	106.7
59	Kaiser Industries[e]	761.6	355.1
60	W. R. Grace	722.2	326.7
61	General Dynamics	696.2	170.8
62	American Cynamid	695.9	311.6
63	U.S. Rubber	686.1	202.9
64	United Aircraft[a]	670.9	134.9
65	Burlington Industries	667.2	252.7
66	Singer Manufacturing Co.	648.0	88.4
67	B. F. Goodrich	647.7	218.4
68	John Deere	643.2	119.7
69	Pure Oil	642.5	432.7
70	National Distillers & Chemical	642.4	216.6
71	Weyerhaeuser	639.9	409.0
72	Caterpillar Tractor	638.0	260.0
73	Pittsburgh Plate Glass	637.7	308.7
74	Crown Zellerbach	621.6	368.3
75	Marathon Oil	610.8	422.2
76	General Foods	602.3	193.2
77	Swift & Company	593.4	242.7
78	Sunray DX Oil	592.9	408.5
79	St. Regis Paper	585.2	284.6
80	Minnesota Mining & Manufacturing	573.3	217.3
81	Martin-Marietta[a]	566.3	241.4
82	General Telephone & Electronics (manufacturing)[f]	548.1	157.4
83	Owens-Illinois Glass	529.2	255.6
84	Allis-Chalmers[a]	517.4	129.1
85	Corn Products	503.6	204.1
86	Borden	502.7	208.7
87	General Tire & Rubber	502.4	137.0
88	Seagrams (United States)	488.7	81.2

TABLE 1 (Continued)
One Hundred Largest Manufacturing Companies by Asset Size, 1962
[In Millions]

Asset Rank	Company	Total Assets	Net Capital Assets
89	American Smelting & Refining	477.1	148.5
90	Georgia Pacific	477.0	167.3
91	Borg-Warner	469.0	131.9
92	Schenley Industries	461.4	39.4
93	Celanese	456.4	182.8
94	National Cash Register	452.6	123.8
95	Coca-Cola	452.0	145.1
96	General American Transportation	450.3	341.0
97	Phelps Dodge	445.9	143.1
98	Kimberly-Clark	443.7	237.7
99	National Lead	438.6	145.2
100	Armour	436.1	145.4
	Total, 100 largest	136,234.3	62,951.2
	Add jointly controlled big corporations:		
	Kaiser Aluminum & Chemical[g]	729.6	491.0
	Richfield Oil[h]	404.6	294.9
	Adjusted total, 100 largest	137,368.5	63,737.1
	All manufacturing[c]	291,222.0	114,589.0
	Ratio (in percent)	47.2	55.6

[a] Assets reported in Moody's Industrials, with adjustment for reported progress payments on government contracts (credited by company as a deduction from inventory value). Procedure follows FTC/SEC reporting practice.

[b] Consolidated assets (less equities of each company in the others) of Getty Oil Co., Mission Corp., Mission Development Co., Tidewater Oil Co., and Skelly Oil Co.

[c] Revised figure for total assets and net capital assets supplied by the Federal Trade Commission.

[d] I. T. & T. assets, excluding telecommunications, derived from company's 1962 Annual Report. Company reports breakdown based on net current assets (i.e., current assets less current liabilities). Consolidated current liabilities have been prorated between manufacturing and telecommunication on the following bases: bank loans and long-term debt maturing within 1 year, on the basis of the ratio between net property in manufacturing and that in telecommunications; accounts payable, on the basis of the ratio between manufacturing and telecommunications inventories; accured taxes, on the basis of the ratio between manufacturing and telecommunications net incomes.

[e] Kaiser Industries and Kaiser Steel (79.3 percent of voting stock, Dec. 31, 1962, held by Kaiser Industries) consolidated.

[f] General Telephone & Electronics Co., assets of manufacturing subsidiaries only, as reported in company prospectus for debenture issue, dated Mar. 1, 1963.

[g] More than 50 percent of Kaiser Aluminum & Chemical Co. voting stock held by 2 other firms among the 100 largest: Kaiser Industries (42.2 percent) and Kennecott Copper Co. (12.6 percent). Book values of Kaiser and Kennecott holdings subtracted from total assets of firm.

[h] More than 50 percent of Richfield Oil Corp. voting stock held by 2 firms among the 100 largest: Sinclair (30.2 percent) and Cities Service Co. (31.0 percent). Book values of Sinclair and Cities Service holdings subtracted from total assets of firm.

Source: "Moody's Industrial Manual." As reported in Moody's except as footnoted. Total assets includes tax anticipation securities, following the FTC/SEC practice.

TABLE 2. ESTIMATED ASSETS OF 100 LARGEST AND ALL MANUFACTURING CORPORATIONS AFTER CONSOLIDATION OF LEGALLY CONTROLLED COMPANIES

100 Largest Corporations	Total Assets	Net Capital Assets
Assets partly consolidated (from table 1)	$137.3	$63.7
Estimated investments in other corporations[a]	6.5	
Assets exclusive of investments in other corporations	130.8	63.7
Estimated investments in legally controlled corporations not consolidated in published balance sheets ($6,500,000,000 × 43 percent)[b]	2.8	
Estimated investments in legally controlled domestic corporations not consolidated in published balance sheets as carried on corporate books ($2,800,000,000 × 40 percent)[c]	1.1	
Estimated equity represented by investments in unconsolidated domestic subsidiaries ($1,100,000,000 × 3 percent)[d]	3.3	
Estimated total equity of unconsolidated domestic subsidiaries ($3,300,000,000 ÷ 80 percent)[e]	4.2	
Estimated total assets of legally controlled domestic corporations not consolidated in published balance sheets ($4,200,000 × 163 percent) ($6,800,000,000 × ratio of $63,700,000,000 to $130,800,000,000)[f]	6.8	3.3[7]
Assets of 100 largest corporations including unconsolidated domestic subsidiaries	137.6	67.0
All manufacturing corporations:		
Assets consolidated (from table 1)	291.0	114.6
Estimated investments in other corporations[h]	10.2	
Assets exclusive of investments in other corporations	280.8	114.6
Ratio of consolidated assets of 100 largest to all manufacturing corporations (in percent)	49.0	58.4

ᵃ Compiled from "Moody's Manuals."

ᵇ Estimate based on a sample of 30 of the 100 largest corporations covering half their combined assets and reporting investments in legally controlled subsidiaries. The ratio of investments in subsidiaries to total investments (43 percent) was applied to the total investments of $6,500,000,000.

ᶜ Assumes 40 percent of estimated investments in legally controlled but unconsolidated subsidiaries is in domestic subsidiaries.

ᵈ Estimate based on a sample of 9 large companies which report both the value of their investments in unconsolidated subsidiaries as carried on their books and the equity or market value of these investments. For 3, the average ratio of equity to value of investments as carried in the books was 3.11 to 1; for 5, the average market value to value on the books was 3.33 to 1. In the above estimate, the equity interest was assumed to be 3 times the value of the investments as carried on the books.

ᵉ Assumes average of 80 percent of equity interest in unconsolidated subsidiaries is controlled by parent (directly or indirectly).

ᶠ Estimate derived by applying the ratio (163 percent) of total assets to stockholders' equity for all manufacturing corporations with assets under $250,000,000 as reported for December 1962 in "Quarterly Financial Report," *op. cit.*, 4th quarter 1963, pp. 28–32 to estimated equity in unconsolidated domestic subsidiaries.

ᵍ Applies same ratio of net capital assets to assets exclusive of stock holdings for subsidiaries as for partens (48 percent).

ʰ Includes the $6,500,000,000 of investments by the 100 largest corporations in other corporations and, for the investments of smaller corporations in other corporations, assumed such investments bore the same relation to assets exclusive of, such investments that investments by the 100 largest corporations in corporations other than those legally controlled bore to their consolidated assets exclusive of such investments.

capital assets. Except where footnotes are attached, the figures given are those filed with the Securities and Exchange Commission and, for total assets, are identical with those published in the Fortune magazine list of 500 largest American corporations. Table 2 adjusts the total assets and property of these 100 companies for intercorporate stockholding and compares the result with the adjusted assets of all manufacturing corporations to give ratios of concentration comparable to those for 1929.

On this basis I estimate that the 100 largest manufacturing corporations in 1962 controlled at least 49 percent of the assets of all manufacturing corporations (excluding stocks in other corporations) and 58 percent of the net capital assets—the net land, buildings, and equipment—of all manufacturing corporations.

These estimates, though less reliable than those for 1929, suggest that there has been a very considerable increase in concentration in manufacturing as a whole in the last 33 years. The difference is shown in Fig. 3 which compares the estimates for the 2 years.

Proportion of Assets
of all Manufacturing Corporations
Legally Controlled by the 100 Largest
Manufaturing Corporations

Total Assets Less Stocks of Other Corporations

1929   40%

1962   49%

Net Capital Assets

1929   44%

1962   58%

FIGURE 3.   Increase in manufacturing concentration measured by assets, 1929–1962. (*Source Text: and Table 2.*)

The top panel shows the increase in the proportion of total assets held by the 100 largest from 40 to 49 percent, the area in black. The lower panel shows the corresponding increase for net capital assets from 44 to 58 percent. This is a very sizable increase in concentration since 1929.

Just when this increase in concentration took place is debatable. There is little question that there was a considerable increase in concentration from 1929 to 1933 as business activity declined in the great depression. How much of this was a temporary depression effect which would be reversed with recovery and how much it was a part of the longrun trend in manufacturing concentration is not clear. Certainly some of it was reversible. The net capital assets of the big companies declined only 6 percent in that period while the net capital assets of smaller companies declined 24 percent. Some of this was the result of big companies acquiring the assets of smaller companies. But to a greater extent it reflected the simple closing down of many smaller companies which would be reopened or replaced in the period of recovery. In measuring trends in concentration as in measuring trends in so many other economic factors, I believe the only valid comparisons are between years which are reasonably comparable in the rate of business activity.

The question of whether—and the extent to which—events during and after World War II contributed to this overall increase is a subject on which I am not commenting here but I hope that this question will be examined by the subcommittee during the course of these hearings. What I can testify to is that manufacturing concentration, whether measured by total assets or by net capital assets, has increased greatly since 1929 and that, without taking account of joint ventures or companies controlled through less than a majority ownership, somewhere in the close vicinity of 58 percent of the net capital assets of manufacturing are controlled by 100 companies. This concentration, along with concentration in other aspects of the economy, presents a set of problems in economic policy which need more intense attention. . . .

The Growth of Bureaucracy

REINHARD BENDIX

. . . Historically, the clearest index of bureaucratization is the over-all increase in the number of salaried employees. While it is clear that bureaucratization in this sense is a characteristic trend in all industrialized countries, it is noteworthy that there exist marked differences between them. A very general, quantitative measure of this trend may be obtained, at any rate, for a recent period by comparing the number of administrative (or salaried) employees with the number of production workers in the manufacturing industries of several countries. In Table 1 figures are given for the United States, France, Great Britain, Germany, and Sweden in selected years.

For each country an A/P ratio has been added, which indicates the number of administrative employees as a per cent of the number of production employees. This ratio is a useful measure of the composition of employees in industrial enterprises in each of the several years, and it is instructive to observe the striking differences between countries (Fig. 1). While the A/P ratio has increased in all of them, that increase has been most marked in the United States and Sweden, while it has been more moderate in Great Britain and Germany. In the case of France, it is noteworthy that in the early years of the twentieth

From *Work and Authority in Industry* by Reinhard Bendix. Copyright © 1956, by John Wiley and Sons, Inc. Reprinted by permission of John Wiley and Sons, Inc.

TABLE 1. Number of Administrative and Production
Employees in Industry for Selected Countries and Selected
Years*

Year	(A) Administrative Employees†	(P) Production Employees	A/P
	I. United States		
1899	348,000	4,496,000	7.7%
1909	750,000	6,256,000	12.0
1923	1,280,000	8,187,000	15.6
1929	1,496,000	8,361,000	17.9
1937	1,518,000	8,553,000	17.7
1947	2,578,000	11,916,000	21.6
	II. France		
1901	425,000	3,609,000	11.8
1906	392,000	3,772,000	10.4
1921	671,000	4,650,000	14.7
1926	699,000	5,458,000	12.8
1931	762,000	5,496,000	13.9
1936	635,000	4,355,000	14.6
	III. Great Britain		
1907	408,000	4,755,000	8.6
1924	627,000	4,708,000	13.0
1930	589,000	4,286,000	13.7
1935	676,000	4,482,000	15.0
1948	1,126,000	5,651,000	20.0
	IV. Germany‡		
1895	266,000	5,530,000	4.8
1907	606,000	7,922,000	7.6
1925	1,122,000	9,463,000	11.9
1933	802,000	5,718,000	14.0
	V. Sweden		
1915	25,000	374,000	6.6
1920	37,000	417,000	8.9
1925	34,000	392,000	8.7
1930	45,000	455,000	9.9
1935	54,000	471,000	11.5
1940	76,000	555,000	13.7
1945	111,000	639,000	17.3
1950	140,000	663,000	21.0

* Figures in this table have been obtained from the follow-
ing sources:
United States: Recomputed from Seymour Melman,
"The Rise of Administrative Overhead in the Manufacturing
Industries of the United States, 1899–1947," *Oxford Economic
Papers* (1951), Vol. III, p. 66.
France: Ministère du Travail et de la Prévoyance Sociale,
Résultats du Recensement Général de la Population 1906, Vol. I,
2nd section, p. 187, Table IV (for 1901 and 1906); *ibid.*, (1927),
Vol. XLVII, pp. 11, 13 (for 1921). Sous-secretariat d'état et
d'Economie Nationale, Bureau de la Statistique Générale,
Recensement Général de la Population (1931), Vol. I, 3rd
section, p. 95 (data for 1926), p. 94 (data for 1931); Institut

National de la Statistique et des Etudes Economiques, Statistique Générale de la France, *Annuaire Statistique* (1946), Vol. LVI, pp. 17, 19 (for 1936).

Great Britain: Seymour Melman, *Dynamics of Industrial Productivity* (Chapter 11, Table 1), unpublished manuscript, by permission of the author.

Germany: Statistik des Deutschen Reichs, Berlin, 1937, Vol. 466; Table 7, p. 194.

Sweden: Fritz Croner, *Die Angestellten in der Modernen Gesellschaft* (Frankfurt: Humboldt Verlag, 1954), pp. 120–21.

Great care has been taken to make the figures for each country internally consistent and to make them as comparable as possible for all five countries. Success in this respect, however, can only be proximate, and it is best to think of comparisons among several countries in terms of orders of magnitude and over-all trends.

† The figures for administrative employees *exclude* owners and top executives.

‡ The German and French series were not extended beyond the 1930's because the more recent figures cannot be put on a basis comparable with the earlier figures. Taken independently, however, the more recent data also show an increasing bureaucratization.

century the level of bureaucratization of French industry (as measured by this index) was considerably higher than in any of the other countries. During subsequent years, however, the French index remained at roughly the same level, while the corresponding index of the other countries increased markedly, though at different rates. . . .

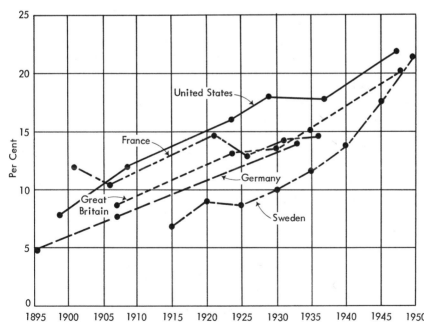

FIGURE 1. Ratios of administrative and production employees for five countries in selected years.

Ownership and Control in the 200 Largest Nonfinancial Corporations, 1929 and 1963

ROBERT J. LARNER

In 1932, Adolf Berle and Gardiner Means published their classic study, *The Modern Corporation and Private Property*, a major thesis of which was that "Ownership of wealth without appreciable control and control of wealth without appreciable ownership appear to be the logical outcome of corporate development" [4, p. 69]. Since then, the existence of management control among giant corporations and its increasing extent over time have been generally accepted in the literature as part of the "conventional wisdom" [2, pp. 70–74] [3, p. 30] [5] [7] [13, p. 53]. Yet, with the exception of the 1939 study which the Securities and Exchange Commission prepared for the Temporary National Economic Committee [18], no attempt seems to have been made to determine the extent of management control in the years since the Berle and Means study.

This article attempts to measure systematically the extent to which management control actually exists among the 200 largest nonfinancial corporations in the first half of the 1960's. The article is divided into two parts: the first part describes the method followed in the study, and the second summarizes the results of the study and compares them with the findings of the 1929 Berle and Means study.

I. THE METHOD OF THIS STUDY

To assure as direct a comparison as possible between the 1929 and the 1963 findings, this paper will follow very closely the definitions, procedures, and classifications used in the Berle and Means study. Since direction over the activities of a corporation is legally and theoretically exercised by its board of directors, Berle and Means defined control as the ". . . actual power to select the board of directors (or its majority)" [4, p. 69]. Although the power to control and the actual exercise of that power can conceivably reside in different individuals, there are nevertheless cogent reasons for accepting Berle and Means's definition of control. First, even if the owner of a majority or substantial minority of a corporation's voting stock were to surrender control to the management, he would still retain the legal power to vote an unsatisfactory board of directors out of office, and even such a dormant power can be a strong influence. Secondly, to prevent biased results which are solely dependent on arbitrary judgements, it seems wise to use objective criteria which are easily observed and capable of precise measurement in determining the type of corporate control.

Berle and Means distinguished between "ultimate control" and "immediate control." This distinction occurred where one corporation controlled another

Reprinted from the *American Economic Review*, 56 (September, 1956), pp. 777–787, by permission of the author and the publisher.

through a dominant minority stock interest.[1] In this case, the controlled corporation was always classified as immediately controlled by either minority or joint-minority interests. If the controlling corporation itself was management-controlled, then the controlled corporation was also classified as ultimately controlled by management. If the controlling corporation was not management-controlled, then the controlled corporation was said to be ultimately controlled through pyramiding. The present study also uses this distinction.

Following Berle and Means, our list of the 200 largest nonfinancial corporations is composed of firms primarily engaged in manufacturing, mining, merchandising, transportation, and electric, gas, and pipeline utilities. Banks, insurance companies, and investment companies are excluded. Size is measured in terms of book assets, a procedure which overstates the size of the transportation and utility companies relative to the size of firms in other industries. The use of sales to measure size, however, would introduce an equally serious opposite bias.[2] Moreover, since Berle and Means, the SEC study [18], and R. A. Gordon [6] all used assets to measure size, this paper will follow the same procedure to maintain comparability.[3]

Berle and Means classified the firms in their study according to the following five types of corporate control: (1) privately owned, (2) controlled through the ownership of a majority of the voting stock, (3) controlled through the ownership of a dominant minority of the voting stock, (4) controlled by means of a legal device,[4] and (5) management-controlled.[5] This study uses the same categories.

A firm is considered to be privately owned if an individual, a family, or a group of business associates holds 80 per cent or more of its voting stock. For majority ownership, the individual, family, or group of business associates must own between 50 and 80 per cent of the voting stock. In the Berle and Means study, stock ownership of between 20 and 50 per cent was generally necessary for minority control, although in several specific instances a smaller holding was

---

[1] In the Berle and Means study, a corporation which was majority-controlled by another corporation was classified as a subsidiary of the latter and was disregarded, except where an important element of pyramiding entered in. The present study follows the same procedure, except where the controlling corporation is a smaller firm not included among the "200 largest." In this case the controlled corporation is retained as if it were an independent company: e.g. Hughes' Tool Co. is ignored and TWA is treated as majority-controlled. If the controlling corporation is a foreign firm, no attempt is made to determine if the foreign firm is management-controlled, and the controlled corporation is assigned either to ultimate minority control or to ultimate control through pyramiding. This is the same procedure which Berle and Means followed.

[2] Perhaps the best measure of size is value added, since it compares the value of the factors of production controlled by each firm [1], but data on value added by firm are not generally available.

[3] The names and assets of the 200 largest nonfinancial corporations in 1963 appear in the appendix to this article, which may be obtained from the author on request. Requests can be addressed in care of the Department of Economics, University of Wisconsin, Madison, Wisconsin 53706.

[4] Berle and Means recognized four kinds of legal devices by which corporate control might be obtained: (1) pyramiding, (2) nonvoting common stock, (3) stock with disproportionate voting power, and (4) the voting trust. Only the first and the fourth devices are found today.

[5] For a more detailed description of these five categories and of the criteria for each, see Chapter 5 in *The Modern Corporation and Private Property* [4].

credited with the power of control. In view of the greater size of the 200 largest nonfinancial corporations in 1963 and the wider dispersion of their stock, this lower limit to minority control seems too high. In the present study a firm is classified as immediately controlled by minority stock ownership if 10 per cent or more of its voting stock is held by an individual, family, corporation, or group of business associates.[6]

Berle and Means assigned corporations in which no base of control in stock ownership could be found to management control on the belief that no group of stockholders would be able under ordinary circumstances to muster enough votes to challenge the rule of management. This study follows the same procedure.[7]

When all of the above criteria are applied to the 1963 data, it is generally not difficult to distinguish management control from the other types of control, but several errors or distortions occur when ownership control is further broken down into privately owned, majority-controlled, and minority-controlled corporations, and those controlled through a legal device.[8]

II. SUMMARY AND COMPARISON OF THE RESULTS

Each of the 200 largest nonfinancial corporations in 1963 is listed in the appendix,* together with its size and rank in assets, its type of control, immediate and ultimate, in both 1963 and 1929, and the source and basis of its classification in 1963.[9]

[6] In two cases, this rule has been disregarded. The Transcontinental Gas Pipe Line Company is classified as management-controlled even though the Stone & Webster Company holds of record an 11 per cent stock interest, since the latter is not represented on Transcontinental's board of directors. On the other hand, May Department Stores Company is classified as minority-controlled even though the May family has only a 3.9 percent stock interest, since members of the May family hold the offices of chairman, vice-chairman, and president, and occupy five seats on the board of directors.

[7] In addition, Berle and Means found 16 companies to be controlled jointly, either by two or more minority interests or by a minority interest and management. In the latter case, they divided the corporation into two "half companies," each possessing one-half of the assets of the original company. One of these "half companies" was then classified as management-controlled and the other as minority-controlled. This joint minority-management control category is not used in the present study.

[8] Following the Berle and Means definitions, the author classified Tidewater Oil, Shell Oil, and the Coca-Cola Company as ultimately controlled by pyramiding because of their peculiar organizational structures, even though the evidence suggests that Tidewater and Shell are effectively majority-controlled and Coca-Cola effectively management-controlled. The Berle and Means definitions were followed exactly in order to keep the two studies as comparable as possible. Similarly, although Trans World Airlines is classified as majority-controlled, an equally convincing argument might be made for classifying it as controlled by a legal device, since Howard Hughes's 78 percent stock interest (through the Hughes Tool Company) in TWA was, at least temporarily, being held in trust by a group of insurance companies and banks in 1963. Hughes's stock was sold to the general public in May, 1966. The TWA management was reported to be "anxious that no one should gain effective control—which might be done with as little as 10 percent of the stock" [19, p. 145].

[9] The principal sources used in determining type of corporate control were the definitive proxy statements filed with the SEC by all of the 200 corporations, the annual reports filed with the Interstate Commerce Commission by each railroad, and the annual reports filed with the Federal Power Commission by the utilities which it regulates. A more complete description of these sources and references to other sources used can be found in the appendix.

* [The material referred to is not included—Editor]

TABLE 1. SUMMARY ACCORDING TO THE TYPE OF ULTIMATE CONTROL OF THE 200 LARGEST NONFINANCIAL CORPORATIONS, 1963 AND 1929

Part 1: Number of Corporations

Type of Control	Number of Corporations				Proportion of Companies by Industrial Groups			
	Total	Industrials	Public Utilities	Transportation Cos.	Total	Industrials	Public Utilities	Transportation Cos.
1963					%	%	%	%
Private ownership	0	0	0	0	0	0	0	0
Majority ownership	5	3	1	1	2.5	3	2	4
Minority control	18	18	0	0	9	15	0	0
Legal device	8	5	0	3	4	4	0	13
Management control	169	91	58	20	84.5	78	98	83
	200	117	59	24	100	100	100	100
1929								
Private ownership	12	8	2	2	6	8	4	5
Majority ownership	10	6	3	1	5	6	6	2
Minority control	46½	34½	7½	4½	23	32	14	11
Legal device	41	14½	19	7½	21	14	36	18
Management control	88½	43	19½	26	44	40	38	62
In receivership	2	—	1	1	1	0	2	2
Total	200	106	52	42	100	100	100	100

SOURCES: 1963—Appendix (see footnote 3); 1929—Berle and Means, *The Modern Corporation and Private Property* [4, p. 115].

463

TABLE 1—*Continued*
Part 2: Assets of Corporations

	Assets (In Millions of Dollars)				Proportion of Assets by Industrial Groups			
Type of Control	Total	Industrials	Public Utilities	Transportation Cos.	Total	Industrials	Public Utilities	Transportation Cos.
1963					%	%	%	%
Private ownership	0	0	0	0	0	0	0	0
Majority ownership	3,307	2,098	697	512	1	1	1	2
Minority control	28,248	28,248	0	0	11	19	0	0
Legal device	8,765	4,959	0	3,806	3	3	0	15
Management control	224,377	117,732	85,300	21,345	85	77	99	83
Total	264,697	153,037	85,997	25,663	100	100	100	100
1929								
Private ownership	3,366	2,869	221	276	4	9	1	1
Majority ownership	1,542	779	480	283	2	3	2	1
Minority control	11,223	9,258	1,261	704	14	31	5	3
Legal device	17,565	4,307	9,406	3,852	22	14	37	15
Management control	47,108	13,142	14,291	19,675	58	43	55	79
In receivership	269	0	108	161	—*	0	—*	1
Total	81,073	30,355	25,767	24,951	100	100	100	100

* Less than 1 per cent.
SOURCES: 1963—Appendix (see footnote 3); 1929—Berle and Means, *The Modern Corporation and Private Property* [4, p. 115].

TABLE 2. SUMMARY ACCORDING TO THE TYPE OF IMMEDIATE CONTROL OF THE 200 LARGEST NONFINANCIAL CORPORATIONS, 1963 AND 1929

Part 1: 1963

Type of Control	Total		Industrials		Public Utilities		Transportation Cos.		Distribution of Total	
	Number of Companies	Assets ($000,000)	Number of Companies	Assets ($000,000)	Number of Companies	Assets ($000,000)	Number of Companies	Assets ($000,000)	By Company	By Assets
Private ownership	0	0	0	0	0	0	0	0	0%	0%
Majority ownership	9	8,387	5	5,218	2	1,480	2	1,689	4	3
Minority control	28	37,252	23	31,641	0	0	5	5,611	14	14
Legal device	0	0	0	0	0	0	0	0	0	0
Management control	160	216,818	87	114,792	57	84,517	16	17,509	80	82
Joint minority control*	3	2,240	2	1,386	0	0	1	854	2	1
Total	200	264,697	117	153,037	59	85,997	24	25,663	100	100

* Includes corporations jointly controlled by two or more minority interests.
SOURCE: Appendix (see footnote 3).

465

TABLE 2 (Continued)

Part 2: 1929

Type of Control	Total		Industrials		Public Utilities		Transportation Cos.		Distribution of Total	
	Number of Companies	Assets ($000,000)	Number of Companies	Assets ($000,000)	Number of Companies	Assets ($000,000)	Number of Companies	Assets ($000,000)	By Company	By Assets
Private ownership	12	3,367	8	2,870	2	221	2	276	6%	4%
Majority ownership	10	1,542	6	779	3	480	1	283	5	2
Minority control	73	25,593	38	11,179	22	10,105	13	4,309	36.5	32
Legal device	21	9,232	10	2,260	10	5,372	1	1,600	10.5	12
Management control	65	35,802	41	12,736	10	8,040	14	15,026	32.5	44
Joint control*	16	5,164	3	532	4	1,441	9	3,191	8	6
Special situations	3	374	0	0	1	108	2	266	1.5	—
Total	200	81,074	106	30,356	52	25,767	42	24,951	100	100

* Includes corporations jointly controlled by two or more minority interests or jointly controlled by a minority interest and management.
SOURCE: Berle and Means, *The Modern Corporation and Private Property* [4, p. 116].

Tables 1 and 2 provide a summary of the type of control, by number of corporations and by assets in 1963 and 1929, for the 200 corporations as a whole and for each of the three major industrial groups (industrials, public utilities, and transportation companies). A significant finding of this study is that management control[10] has substantially increased among the 200 largest nonfinancial corporations since 1929. As Table 1 illustrates, 44 per cent of the 200 largest nonfinancial corporations in 1929 and 58 per cent of their assets were management-controlled. In 1963, however, 84.5 per cent of the "200 largest" of that year and 85 per cent of their assets were so controlled. Management control increased substantially within each of the three industrial groups and became the overwhelmingly predominant type of control within each group.

As shown in Table 1, private ownership had *completely disappeared* among the 200 largest nonfinancial corporations by 1963. Of the 12 privately owned firms on the 1929 list, six had dropped out of the "200 largest" by 1963. Of the remainder, one (A & P) was majority-controlled, four (Alcoa, Ford, Gulf Oil, and National Steel) were minority-controlled, and one (Jones & Laughlin) was apparently management-controlled. Only five companies (A & P, Duke Power Co., Kaiser Industries, Sun Oil, and TWA) were found to be majority-controlled in 1963, and in the case of TWA actual control was, at least temporarily, in the hands of trustees.

Only 18 firms were found to be controlled by minority stockholders in 1963, roughly a third of the $46\frac{1}{2}$ firms which Berle and Means classified as minority-controlled in 1929. Control through legal devices decreased even more sharply—from 41 in 1929 to 8 in 1963. On the other hand, the number of management-controlled firms almost doubled, from $88\frac{1}{2}$ in 1929 to 169 in 1963.

Five companies on the 1963 list which are classified as management-controlled appear to be controlled, or at least very strongly influenced, by a single family within their management. Yet these families owned only a very small fraction of the outstanding voting stock. The five companies and their controlling families are: IBM (Watson), Inland Steel (Block), Weyerhaeuser (Weyerhaeuser), Federated Department Stores (Lazarus), and J. P. Stevens (Stevens). Federated Department Stores is the best illustration of this. In 1963 its chairman of the board, its president, and five of its 19 directors were members of the Lazarus family, even though the combined stock interest of the entire family was only 1.32 per cent. Since the present basis of control by these families appears to be their strategic position in management and the traditional identification of the corporation with the family rather than any appreciable amount of stock ownership, these companies are classified as management-controlled.

Management control was distributed rather evenly among the three industrial groups in 1963. Its highest incidence was among the utilities where it accounted for all but one of the 59 firms. Yet the public utilities had the lowest incidence of management-controlled firms in 1929 (38 per cent). This drastic change can

---

10 "Management control" without qualification should be understood to mean *ultimate* control by management. The same applies, *mutatis mutandis*, to the other types of corporate control.

be explained by the "death sentence" provision of the Public Utility Holding Company Act of 1935, which proscribes pyramiding beyond the second degree among public utility holding companies. Management control was the predominant type of control for the industrials and the transportation companies as well, accounting for 78 per cent of the former and 83 per cent of the latter.

A significant difference between 1963 and 1929 is that the proportion of the 200 largest nonfinancial corporations that were management-controlled in the later year was about the same as the proportion of assets so controlled, while in 1929 the proportion of assets that were management-controlled was a good deal larger than the proportion of companies so controlled. This indicates that management control, which was concentrated among the larger firms on the 1929 list, has since reached down to relatively smaller (though absolutely larger) firms than it touched in 1929 and has become rather evenly distributed among the "200 largest." This contrast is illustrated by Table 3, which divides the

TABLE 3. "200 LARGEST" DIVIDED BY RANK INTO 5 GROUPS AND NUMBER OF MANAGEMENT-CONTROLLED FIRMS IN EACH GROUP

	Number of Management-Controlled Firms	
Firms Ranking	*1963*	*1929*
1 through 40	34	27
41 through 80	33	21
81 through 120	32	$15\frac{1}{2}$
121 through 160	37	$15\frac{1}{2}$
161 through 200	33	$9\frac{1}{4}$
Total	169	$88\frac{1}{2}$

SOURCE: Appendix (see footnote 3).

"200 largest" of each year by rank into five groups of 40 firms each and lists the number of management-controlled firms in each group.

This evidence suggests that a firm may reach a size so great that, with a few exceptions, its control is beyond the financial means of any individual or group. This point appears to have been reached only by the larger firms on the 1929 list, but by all of the firms on the 1963 list. The smallest corporation among the top 200 in 1963 had assets of 423 million current dollars or, deflating by the GNP deflator, 204 million 1929 dollars. A corporation of this size would have ranked 111th on the Berle and Means list. Of the 110 firms which would have ranked ahead of it, 55 per cent were management-controlled, compared with only 31 per cent of the remaining 90 firms. Moreover, many of the remaining 45 per cent of the top 110 firms in 1929 were either public utilities controlled by a kind of pyramiding which is now illegal or industrial firms still owned and controlled by their founder.

The present study may classify some firms incorrectly because of the limited information available to outsiders about the control of the 200 largest nonfinancial corporations. Generally, such errors would involve failure to locate an existing center of ownership (especially minority) control, so that the company is mistakenly classified as management-controlled. This would result, of course, in our overstating the extent of management control in 1963. Berle and Means, however, would seem to be in greater danger of overstating the extent of management control because of the less authoritative and less systematic sources of data upon which they had to rely and because of the larger minimum stock-holding which they required as sufficient evidence of minority control. It follows that, even though the findings of the present study may overstate somewhat the *extent* of management control in 1963, they are also likely to understate the *change* in the extent of management control from 1929 to 1963 when compared with the findings of the Berle and Means study.

In summary, it would appear that Berle and Means in 1929 were observing a "managerial revolution" in process. Now, 30 years later, that revolution seems close to completion, at least within the range of the 200 largest nonfinancial corporations.

References

1. M. A. ADELMAN, "The Measurement of Industrial Concentration," *Rev. Econ. Stat.* Nov. 1951, *33*, 269–96; reprinted in R. B. Heflebower and G. W. Stocking, eds., *Readings in Industrial Organization and Public Policy*, Homewood 1958, pp. 3–45.
2. A. A. BERLE, *Power Without Property*. New York 1959.
3. ———, *The 20th Century Capitalist Revolution*. New York 1954.
4. ——— and G. C. MEANS, *The Modern Corporation and Private Property*. New York 1932.
5. ———, *et al.*, "Symposium on the Impact of the Corporation on Classical Economic Theory," *Quart. Jour. Econ.*, Feb. 1965, *79*, 1–51.
6. R. A. GORDON, *Business Leadership in the Large Corporation*. Washington 1945.
7. R. J. MONSEN, JR. and A. DOWNS, "A Theory of Large Managerial Firms," *Jour. Pol. Econ.*, June 1965, *73*, 221–36.
8. *Moody's Industrial Manual, 1964*. New York 1964.
9. *Moody's Public Utility Manual, 1964*. New York 1964.
10. *Moody's Transportation Manual, 1964*. New York 1964.
11. M. J. PECK, *Competition in the Aluminum Industry, 1945–1958*. Cambridge, Mass. 1961.
12. T. K. QUINN, *Giant Business: Threat to Democracy*. New York 1953.
13. E. V. ROSTOW, "To Whom and for What Ends Is Corporate Management Responsible?", in E. S. Mason, ed., *The Corporation in Modern Society*, Cambridge, Mass. 1959, pp. 46–71.
14. Standard and Poor's, *Standard Listed Stock Reports*. Ephrata, Pa.
15. R. B. TENNANT, *The American Cigarette Industry*. New Haven 1950.
16. "*Fortune's* Directory of the 500 Largest Industrial Corporations," *Fortune*, July 1964, *70*, 179–98.
17. "*Fortune's* Directory: Part II," *Fortune*, Aug. 1964, *70*, 151–62.
18. TEMPORARY NATIONAL ECONOMIC COMMITTEE, *Distribution of Ownership in the 200 Largest Nonfinancial Corporations*, "Monograph No. 29." Washington 1940.
19. "What's behind the Big TWA Sale?," *Business Week*, April 16, 1966, 145–50.

COLLECTIVE BEHAVIOR

Poverty and Political Movements

MAURICE PINARD

It is the hypothesis of this paper that the poor, though they may come to form an important element in political movements and even may come to be disproportionately represented in them, are not their first recruits. If political movements are understandably often not successful among the rich because they are economically satisfied, it seems that at first they are not successful among the poor because, paradoxically, they are too dissatisfied. In short, we suggest that the poorer segments of the population are not the first joiners, but late joiners of mass movements. We are not of course the first to suggest this, though there is little sound empirical evidence on this question. The purpose of this paper is to present such evidence and to try to interpret it. Though the bulk of our data is derived from a survey done to study the rise of the Social Credit party in Quebec federal politics in 1962,[1] we shall also test some of the propositions with other data on this movement,[2] as well as with data on other movements.

That misery is not a sufficient condition for protest action has been suggested by many. Trotsky, for instance, wrote: "In reality, the mere existence of privations is not enough to cause an insurrection; if it were, the masses would always

Reprinted from *Social Problems*, 15 (Fall, 1967), pp. 250–263, by permission of the author and the publisher, The Society for the Scientific Study of Social Problems.

[1] The Social Credit party is a populist, right-wing movement which has been a strong force in Western Canadian politics since the thirties (the party is currently in power in two Canadian provinces, Alberta and British Columbia), but which made a strong inroad in Quebec politics in the 1962 Federal election, when it obtained 26 percent of the votes (as compared to less than 1 percent in the previous election) and one-third of the seats. For a general background on the movement's early success and on its philosophy, see John A. Irving, *The Social Credit Movement in Alberta*, Toronto: University of Toronto Press, 1959; C. B. Macpherson, *Democracy in Alberta: Social Credit and the Party System*, Toronto: University of Toronto Press, 2nd ed., 1962.

[2] The survey data are from a multi-stage stratified cluster sample of 998 Quebec residents nineteen years of age and over. The results presented in the paper are usually based on a lower N. This is generally due (except when otherwise indicated) to the fact that about 14 percent reported not to have voted and that another 22 percent either refused to reveal their vote or did not remember. This last percentage may appear to be high, but seems to be a general feature of Canadian voting studies. Whenever possible, the survey analysis has been replicated with aggregate voting and census statistics. Nowhere has this study yielded conflicting results when using these two types of data. (The larger study as well as the sample design will be fully reported in *The Rise of a Third Party*, near completion). See also Maurice Pinard, "One-Party Dominance and Third Parties," *Canadian Journal of Economics and Political Science*, 33 (1962), pp. 358–373.

be in revolt." [3] Closer to us in time, Key wrote: "A factor of great significance in the setting off of political movements is an abrupt change for the worse in the status of one group relative to that of other groups in society. The economics of politics is by no means solely a matter of the poor against the rich; the rich and the poor may live together peaceably for decades, each accepting its status quietly." [4] Similarly, Bell, discounting the importance of mass society in the rise of extremist movements, wrote: "It is not poverty *per se* that leads people to revolt; poverty most often induces fatalism and despair, and a reliance, embodied in ritual and superstitious practices, on supernatural help. *Social tensions are an expression of unfulfilled expectations.*" [5] And Turner and Killian argued that "frustration by itself is never a guarantee of receptivity to movements. Long-continued frustration characteristically leads to hopelessness which mitigates against participation in the promotion of any reform. Frustration from *recent* losses or the experience of *improving* conditions is more likely to make receptive individuals than long-continued frustration." [6] Lipset commented in *Agrarian Socialism*: "It is possible to adjust to a continuously low income and standard of living, as do many farmers in the Maritime Provinces. . . . But it is the 'boom and bust' character of wheat production that unhinges life's plans." [7] Finally, the proposition we have hypothesized seems to hold true in all forms of non-routine politics, including revolutions, as already implied in Trotsky's statement. Davies claimed that "revolutions ordinarily do not occur when a society is generally impoverished—when, as de Tocqueville put it, evils that seem inevitable are patiently endured . . . because the physical and mental energies of people are totally employed in the process of merely staying alive. . . . Enduring poverty makes for concern with one's solitary self or solitary family at best and resignation or mute despair at worst." [8]

Let us try to document this general proposition by showing that the poor were relatively weak supporters of Social Credit in Quebec in 1962, and that the poor generally have not been the early joiners of other political movements, whether of the right or of the left.

THE POOR AND SOCIAL CREDIT

If poverty is defined as a net income of less than $3,500 a year, [9] the survey data clearly indicate that the poor were not the strongest supporters of the new

[3] Quoted by Crane Brinton, *The Anatomy of Revolution*, New York: Vintage Books, 1960, p. 34.

[4] V. O. Key, Jr., *Politics, Parties, and Pressure Groups*, New York: Thomas Y. Crowell Company, 4th ed., 1958, p. 28.

[5] Daniel Bell, *The End of Ideology*, New York: Collier Books, revised edition, 1962, p. 31. Italics in original.

[6] Ralph H. Turner and Lewis M. Killian, *Collective Behavior*, Englewood Cliffs: Prentice-Hall, 1957, p. 432. Italics in original.

[7] S. M. Lipset, *Agrarian Socialism*, Berkeley and Los Angeles: University of California Press, 1950, p. 29. Lipset also developed the same theme in his *Political Man*, Garden City: Doubleday, 1960, p. 63.

[8] James C. Davies, "Toward a Theory of Revolution," *American Sociological Review*, 27 (1962) p. 7. See also Wm. Bruce Cameron, *Modern Social Movements*, New York: Random

TABLE 1. VOTE IN 1962 BY INCOME AND EMPLOYMENT

	Income Groups*		
	Low	Middle	High
Vote 1962:	No Unemployment in the Family		
Social Credit**	16%	27%	11%
Progressive Conservative	40	29	25
Liberal	44	42	61
N.D.P.	1	2	3
N=	(140)	(176)	(150)
	Some Unemployment in the Family		
Social Credit	36%	32%	21%
Progressive Conservative	27	28	45
Liberal	32	38	34
N.D.P.	4	2	0
N=	(69)	(50)	(29)

* Low Income: a yearly net income of less than $3,500; middle income: between $3,500 and $5,000; high income: $5,000 or more. In the above, as in other tables to be presented, in order to increase the case base and to make income comparable, those who refused to give their income are classified according to the rent or property value of their home, and farmers are always classified according to the size of their farms.

** Comparing Social Credit against all others, the probability that this curvilinear relationship could have resulted from chance is smaller than .001. This test follows A. E. Maxwell, *Analysing Qualitative Data* (London: Methuen, 1961), ch. 4, pp. 63–69.

movement (Table 1). The relationship is clearly curvilinear in the group of those whose families were not hit by unemployment. Those above the poverty level, not those who live in poverty, were the first joiners in the Social Credit upsurge in Quebec. Notice, however, that this does not hold among those whose family had at least one person unemployed.[10] This would suggest that unemployment—

House, 1966, pp. 39–40; W. G. Runciman, *Relative Deprivation and Social Justice*, Berkeley and Los Angeles: University of California Press, 1966.

[9] The Conference on Economic Progress has stated, on the basis of studies by the U.S. Department of Labor, that families in the U.S.A. with an income below $4,000 "live in poverty," while those with an income between $4,000 and $5,999 "live in deprivation." See Conference on Economic Progress, *Poverty and Deprivation in the United States: The Plight of Two-Fifths of a Nation*, Washington, 1962, esp. Ch. 3. It is interesting to note that the main break in the data is at a net income of $3,500, which is close to the above definition for the poverty level.

[10] In his analysis of Gallup poll data, Alford reports that "the emerging Social Credit party took over the votes of the poorer Quebeckers." This divergent finding may be due to the loose definition of socioeconomic status (interviewers' rating from A to D) and/or to the fact that he does not control for immediate strains in the respondents' families as we do. Robert R. Alford, "The Social Basis of Political Cleavage in 1962," in John Meisel, ed., *Papers on the 1962 Election*, Toronto: University of Toronto Press, 1964, pp. 219–220. However, using aggregate data, Irvine reports a finding similar to ours (see below, Table 3). W. P. Irvine, "An Analysis of Voting Shifts in Quebec," in John Meisel, *ibid.*, pp. 131–132.

and very likely any sudden economic reversal—is a sufficient condition to stir the low income people out of their low tendency to protest and make them one of the groups (if not the group) most likely to support a new movement. Short of a very severe crisis, however, the poor will refrain from participation.

The hypothesis can also be documented in a different way for a subgroup in the population. Among farmers, if we consider the size of their farm as an indicator of their wealth, we find that those with medium-size farms were the most likely to have voted Social Credit: 50 percent of those with farms ranging from seventy to one hundred and eighty acres supported the new movement (N = 22). Among those who possessed larger farms (one hundred and eighty to four hundred acres, and four hundred acres or more), the support was relatively smaller: 26 and 18 percent of these, respectively, voted Social Credit (N = 19 and 17 respectively). But those with very small farms (less than seventy acres) were barely more favorable than the latter—only 25 percent of them voted Social Credit (N = 20).

The relationships observed at the individual level also obtain with aggregate data, which provide independent tests of the hypothesis. If we consider the economic level of the electoral districts, we find the same curvilinear relationship as for the individual data. It can be seen in Table 2 that the support for the new

TABLE 2. PERCENT VOTING SOCIAL CREDIT IN ELECTORAL DISTRICTS BY AVERAGE TOTAL FAMILY INCOME

	Average Total Family Income (Male Heads)*		
% *Social Credit Vote:*	*Low*	*Middle*	*High*
40% or more**	18%	59%	36%
20% to 40%	46	29	27
Less than 20%	36	12	36
N (Districts) =	(11)	(17)	(22)

* Low: less than $4,000; Middle: $4,000 to $4,750; High: more than $4,750. Calculated from D.B.S., *1961 Census of Canada*, Vol. IV, Bulletin 4. 1–6, Table F.6. As previously, rough adjustments had to be made between the Census counties and the electoral districts. The districts from Montreal (21) and Quebec cities (4) are excluded, since adjustments cannot be made. The data are not available for smaller units.

** Considering the districts with a Social Credit vote of 40 percent or more against others, the probability that the curvilinear relationship results from chance is smaller than .05.

movement came disproportionately from the districts of middle income, while the poorer districts gave much weaker support.

If the proportion of commerical farms, rather than the average family income, is taken as an indicator of the wealth of a district, similar results are obtained. While we find that 81 percent of the rural districts with a moderate proportion of commercial farms gave a vote of 30 percent or more to Social Credit, the corresponding figures for the districts with a small and a large proportion of commercial farms are only 58 and 38 percent respectively.[11] The poorer as well as the richer districts resisted the Social Credit party drive.

It may be worth mentioning at this point that while curvilinear relationships are found when, as above, indices of *poverty* in a district are used, other parts of our study revealed positive and linear relationships between *economic reverses* in a district and the proportion Social Credit. If poverty prevents one from joining a new movement, changes for the worse in one's economic conditions do not.

An obvious objection could be raised against our interpretation of these data. One could say that Social Credit is a conservative party, or more properly, a party with populist appeals based on an ideology of the right.[12] It therefore

TABLE 3. PERCENT VOTING SOCIAL CREDIT BY
OCCUPATIONAL GROUPS AND
CLASS IDENTIFICATION

| | Self-Identification on Class Position | |
	Middle-Class*	Working-Class
Occupational Groups:	% Social Credit	
Non-manual	7 (124)	20 (70)
Manual	19 (100)	28 (227)
Farmers	20 (25)	39 (46)

* a_1 (average effect of class identification) $= .137$; one-tailed p. $< .001$. a_2 (effect of class identification for workers) $= .09$; one-tailed $p = .03$. (This measure of effects and the significance test follow James S. Coleman, *Introduction to Mathematical Sociology*, New York: The Free Press, 1964, Ch. 6, pp. 189–201, pp. 205–207.)

failed to recruit the most disinherited strata of the population and instead attracted middle-class support. In other words, the party's support would reflect the party's ideology.

[11] N = 16, 12, and 21 respectively. Proportion of commercial farms—small: less than 55%; moderate: 55% to 69%; large: 70% or more. Calculated from D.B.S., 1961 Census of Canada, *Agriculture: Number and Areas of Farms*, Bulletin SA-1. As previously, rough adjustments had to be made between the census counties and the electoral districts. The districts from Montreal (21) and Quebec (4) cities, and the district of Longueuil are all excluded since they are completely urban. If we break the dependent variable as in Table 2, we get similar results, though the relationship is weaker.

[12] Very much like Father Coughlin's movement in the United States during the thirties. See S. M. Lipset, "Three Decades of the Radical Right: Coughlinites, McCarthyites, and Birchers," in Daniel Bell, ed., *The Radical Right*, Garden City: Anchor Books, 1964, pp. 374–446, esp. pp. 374–391.

We do not, however, think that this objection is correct. First of all, the concept of "middle-class support" would have to be substantially extended to cover the present instance. In occupational terms, the party got the bulk of its support from the working class and the farmer, and not from the middle class. Moreover, the data demonstrate that the party was particularly successful among workers who identified with the working class and not among those who identified with the middle class (Table 3). Indeed, in all three occupational groups—non-manual, manual, and farmer—the party got disproportionate support from those who identified with the working class.[13] We also found that it got disproportionate support among the unionized segments of the working class. One cannot, therefore, interpret the greater support of the middle-income group as resulting from a middle-class ideology.

Another set of facts also stands contrary to the objection. The phenomenon we observed in the case of Social Credit in Quebec has also been observed for other political movements with *both* leftist and rightist ideologies.

THE POOR IN OTHER MOVEMENTS

Lipset has observed, in his study of the socialist C.C.F. party in Saskatchewan, that the doubling of rural backing for the party between 1934 and 1944 did not reflect an extension of support from "extremely poor farmers" to more conservative "middle-class agrarians," but "the exact opposite": "C.C.F. supporters in 1934 came from the groups in the rural population which had the highest social and economic status. The party's vote was highest in prosperous farm areas where land-tax assessment was high and tenancy was low," while "in the election of 1944 the party made most of its electoral gains from the low-status groups, the poorer and non-Anglo-Saxon farmers."[14]

Lipset also presents some data showing that in the 1934 election, the C.C.F. vote in Regina was lower in areas populated predominantly with unskilled workers (20%) than in those populated predominantly with skilled workers (33%), while middle-class areas were also low (19%). Notice that in 1944, the relationship became linear, the corresponding figures being 62, 61, and 32 percent respectively.[15] This last relationship will be discussed below.

If we consider the Poujadist movement in France during the fifties—a movement that has many similarities with Social Credit—the same type of curvilinear relationship is found. Hoffman observed that richer departments of France—as measured by per capita production and per capita income—did not offer strong support to Poujadist candidates. But he was puzzled by the fact that the relationship was weaker at the other end of the continuum, and concluded: "If it is

---

[13] The relationship is maintained if only those without unemployment in the family are considered.

[14] S. M. Lipset, *Agrarian Socialism, op. cit.*, pp. 163–165. This would seem to indicate that the relationship between wealth and C.C.F. support was first positive, then negative, but not curvilinear. However, some of the empirical data he presents show clearly a curvilinear relationship in the first period, as will be presently indicated.

[15] See *ibid.*, p. 168, Table 18.

certain that Poujadism has but little succeeded in penetrating departments with a high per capita production or income, it cannot on the contrary be said that it has particularly well succeeded in the least productive and poorer departments."[16]

A reanalysis of Hoffman's data for the 1956 French election yielded the results presented in Table 4. A curvilinear relationship similar to that observed

TABLE 4. PERCENT VOTING POUJADIST IN FRENCH
DEPARTMENTS BY PER CAPITA INCOME*

| | *Index of Per Capita Income*** | | |
	Low	*Middle*	*High*
% Poujadist Vote:			
13% or more***	29	41	4
10% to 12%	24	30	21
Less than 10%	48	30	75
N (Departments) =	(21)	(37)	(24)

* Recalculated from S. Hoffman, *op. cit.*, Annex X, pp. 205–208.
** Index of per capita income: Low: less than 75; Middle: 75 to 94; High: 95 or more (France = 100). Eight departments without Poujadist lists are excluded.
*** Considering the departments with a Poujadist vote of 13 per cent or more against others, the relationship is curvilinear with a p. < .02.

in the Quebec data is apparent—the relatively poorer departments were more resistant to Poujade's movement than those of moderate wealth.

It is interesting to note that in his analysis of one department, Leleu has commented that "it is peculiar to observe that the poorest regions are not those which brought more votes to the U.F.F. (Poujade). The extreme poverty of the South-East region of the department has been the least permeable to Poujadism. And it is precisely in the most disinherited canton of the department that the U.F.F. obtained its weakest rural percentage of the votes."[17] Then the author went on to show that in that department as a whole—as in Quebec—the Poujadist success was attributable to an economic crisis (here in the textile industry and in agriculture).[18]

If we consider Goldwater as the representative of a right-wing conservative movement, it is also noteworthy that Goldwater adherents (those who, regardless of party preference, selected Goldwater, among many Republicans, as the Republican nominee) were not predominantly white-collar workers, but farmers. Further, "there appears to be a tendency for Goldwater support to peak at the

[16] S. Hoffman, *Le Mouvement Poujade*, Paris: A. Colin, 1956, pp. 194 ff., p. 196 (My translation).
[17] Claude Leleu, "La géographie des partis dans L'Isère," in Maurice Duverger, *et al.*, *Les élections du 2 janvier 1956*, Paris: A. Colin, 1957, pp. 393 ff. (My translation.)
[18] *Ibid.*, p. 394.

$3,000 to $4,999 income bracket" among both white-collar and blue-collar people in all regions.[19] Both poorer and richer people were less likely to support him.[20]

The same curvilinear relationship was observed in a study of the Freedom Ride movement in Baltimore. Though the participants were almost all middle-class (96%), when they were classified by an extended North-Hatt scale of status the data showed that those of middle status were more likely to have joined the movement a year or more ago (36%) than those of lower status (27%) or of higher status (27%).[21] It is well known that the support of lower-class Negroes for desegregation movements has been conspicuously low. The processes discussed here can certainly account for much of this phenomenon.

This varied array of data strongly document the proposition that the poorer segments of the population are not the supporters of new movements. The generality of the finding is all the more impressive when one considers that it was found in quite different contexts. . . .

Additional Readings

COMMUNITY

KINGSLEY DAVIS, "The Urbanization of the Human Population," *Scientific American,* 213 (September, 1965), pp. 41–53.

KINGSLEY DAVIS and ANA CASIS, "Urbanization in Latin America," *The Milbank Memorial Fund Quarterly*, 24 (April, 1946), pp. 186–207.

ROBERT M. LILLIBRIDGE, "Urban Size: An Assessment," *Land Economics*, 28 (November, 1952), pp. 341–352.

T. LYNN SMITH, "Urbanization in Latin America," *International Journal of Comparative Sociology*, 4 (1963), pp. 227–242.

[19] Irving Crespi, "The Structural Basis for Right-Wing Conservatism: The Goldwater Case," *Public Opinion Quarterly*, 24 (Winter, 1965–1966), pp. 523–543, esp. pp. 529, 533.

[20] There are indications that a similar curvilinear relationship existed insofar as the support for McCarthy in the United States is concerned. A recomputation of some of Polsby's data suggests that its strongest support came at some middle points of the stratification continuum: its supporters were relatively fewer in the lower social-economic grouping as well as in the highest educational grouping. Moreover, after reporting inconsistent findings, Lipset concluded that "perhaps the higher-income people within lower occupational and educational strata were precisely those who were most drawn to [McCarthy]." If we are correct, both Polsby's and Lipset's findings and interpretations would have to be reassessed. See Nelson W. Polsby, "Toward an Explanation of McCarthyism," in Nelson W. Polsby *et al.*, *Politics and Social Life*, Boston: Houghton Mifflin, 1963, pp. 809–824; S. M. Lipset, "Three Decades of the Radical Right: Coughlinites, McCarthyites, and Birchers (1962)" in Daniel Bell, ed., *The Radical Right, op. cit.*, pp. 373–446, p. 402.

[21] Maurice Pinard, Jerome Kirk, and Donald Von Eschen, "The Growth of the Sit-In Movement: Some Processes," mimeo, 1967.

ORGANIZATION

BERNARD BARBER, "Participation and Mass Apathy in Associations," in Alvin W. Gouldner (ed.), *Studies in Leadership* (New York: Harper & Row, Inc., 1950), pp. 477–504.

MURRAY HAUSKNECHT, *The Joiners* (New York: The Bedminster Press, 1962).

CARL KAYSEN, "The Corporation: How Much Power? What Scope?" in Edward S. Mason (ed.), *Corporation in Modern Society* (Cambridge, Mass.: Harvard University Press, 1960), pp. 85–105.

CHARLES R. WRIGHT and HERBERT H. HYMAN, "Voluntary Association Memberships of American Adults: Evidence from National Sample Surveys," *American Sociological Review*, 23 (June, 1958), pp. 284–294.

COLLECTIVE BEHAVIOR

SEYMOUR M. LIPSET, "Three Decades of the Radical Right: Coughlinites, McCarthyites, and Birchers," in Daniel Bell (ed.) *The Radical Right*, (Garden City, N.Y.: Doubleday & Company, 1963), pp. 313–377.

PART IV

Population and Ecology

Introduction

Part IV, "Population and Ecology," contains two sections, "Population" and "Ecology." As in Part III, a single introduction will serve for both sections.

POPULATION. The first selection, Hauser's "Population Growth in the United States," reports a number of apparent contradictions. For example, despite the relatively high growth rate for the nation between 1950 and 1960, over half of the counties showed a *population* loss. Or again, Americans in 1960 were on the average younger than in 1950; however, they were also older than in 1950 as measured by the proportion of individuals sixty-five years old and older. Still again, average family size increased, but average size of household decreased.[1]

The selection by Dorn, "World Population Growth: An International Dilemma," reports information relevant to the "population explosion" in the world and in its major regions. It took between 50,000 and 100,000 years for the world population to reach one quarter of a billion, the estimated number of people at the beginning of the Christian era. In 1950 the world population was slightly over 3 billion, a twelve-fold increase since the beginning of the Christian era. For the major regions of the world, the birth rates in the countries of Africa, Asia, Middle America, and South America average nearly 40 per 1,000. In the rest of the world—Europe, North America, Oceania, and the Soviet Union—the birth rate averages about 20 to 25 per 1,000. The death rate in the former regions, although still definitely higher, is rapidly approaching the death rate in the latter regions. The result of these differences in birth rates and death rates is that the highest rates of natural increase in population are found in the regions with the highest birth rates.

[1] The information that Hauser presents about "Population Composition" is also relevant to the discussion of "Kinship" in Part II, "The Social Structure of the Group"; the information about "Population Composition" is also relevant to discussions of "minorities" ("racial and ethnic relations").

Dorn's information lends substance to the idea of a "population explosion." For a somewhat different perspective on world population growth, the reader is referred to a recent article by Bogue.[2]

Fertility and *mortality* are two processes basic to the study of population; the next two selections summarize factual information about these basic processes. Freedman, in his "American Studies of Family Planning and Fertility: A Review of Major Trends and Issues," emphasizes eight major findings. First, there has been a long-run decline in fertility. Second, before World War II, there was a negative relationship between fertility and class: the higher the class, the lower the fertility.[3] The negative relationship between fertility and class has been one of the classic findings in population research. Third, fertility is higher in rural than in urban areas. This finding has also been one of the classics of population research. Fourth, there has recently been a contraction of almost all the standard fertility differentials—education, occupation, income, and residence. This means that the classic relationship between fertility and class is declining. Fifth, there is a high degree of consensus on a moderate-sized family of two to four children. Despite the "baby boom" since the end of World War II, there has been no return to the large family of five or more children. Sixth, contraception is used almost universally by couples of the childbearing age to limit the size of their families. Seventh, wives who work have lower fertility than wives who do not work. This finding is significant because an increasing proportion of wives are working. Eighth, Catholics have higher fertility than non-Catholics.[4] The eighth finding is especially interesting, because it has been widely believed that religious differences of all kinds would vanish as the United States increasingly became more industrialized and urbanized.

The selection by Dorn, "Differential Mortality," unlike the previous selection by Freedman, is based on comparative data. Dorn suggests that males, nonwhites, urban residents, unskilled laborers, and the unmarried generally have higher death rates than females, whites, rural residents, professional employees, and the married.[5]

ECOLOGY. The final two selections present information about *mobility*; mobility, fertility, and mortality constitute the three basic processes studied in population and ecology. In "Internal Migration and Residential Mobility," Bogue reports information about mobility in the United States and in the most mobile segments of the population. It is generally believed that the United States has a high amount of mobility. Bogue basically agrees with this belief; he indicates, for example, that during the course of a single year, between 19 and 22 per cent of the nation's inhabitants move from one house or apartment to another. Bogue also indicates that men, nonwhites, residents of rural-nonfarm areas, the young, the more educated, and unemployed individuals generally are more mobile than women, whites, residents of urban or rural-farm areas, the old, the less educated, and employed individuals.[6]

[2] Donald J. Bogue, "The End of the Population Explosion," *The Public Interest*, 7 (Spring, 1967), pp. 11–20.

[3] In this instance, class is measured by any of three measures: occupation, education, and income.

[4] There is no inconsistency between this finding and the previous assertion that Baptists have higher fertility than Catholics. (This latter assertion comes from Bogue's "Religious Affiliation," in the section on "Religion" in Part II, "The Social Structure of the Group.") When Catholic fertility—which is relatively high—is compared to non-Catholic fertility, the non-Catholics include high fertility groups—such as Baptists—and low fertility groups—such as Jews, Presbyterians, and Episcopalians. The inclusion of low fertility groups among non-Catholics results in higher fertility for Catholics than non-Catholics.

[5] The selections by Freedman and Dorn have material which is relevant to most of the sections in the first three parts of the anthology.

[6] Bogue also has mobility differences by occupation and income. The occupational differences are too complex to summarize briefly and the income differences are not supported by much data.

It is generally believed that there is a high degree of residential segregation between whites and Negroes within the cities of the United States. The information summarized by Taeuber, in "Negro Residential Segregation: Trends and Measurement," agrees with this general belief. As Taeuber states: ". . . Whether a city is in the North, South, or West; whether it is a large metropolitan center or a suburb; whether it is a coastal resort town, a rapidly growing industrial center, or a declining mining town; whether nonwhites constitute forty per cent of the population or less than one per cent; in every case white and Negro residences are highly segregated from each other. . . ." In this instance, systematic information, rather than disproving a general belief—which is so often the case—confirms the belief.

POPULATION

Population Growth in the United States

PHILIP M. HAUSER

POPULATION SIZE[1]

. . . On April 1, 1960 the population of the United States was 179.3 million persons (excluding members of the Armed Forces abroad). Thus, between 1950 and 1960 inhabitants of the nation increased by some 28 million or 18.5 per cent. This absolute increase was half again greater than the increase of 19 million between 1940 and 1950—the largest previous intercensal increase. The percentage gain was the second largest the nation has experienced during this century, being exceeded only by the 21.0 per cent increase between 1900 and 1910 (Table 1).[2] The decennial rate of population growth declined between 1900 and 1940, falling to the record low of 7.2 per cent during the depression 1930's. It increased to 14.5 per cent during the war-time 1940's and continued its upward climb in the 1950's.

The upsurge in national growth since 1940 began with the rise of marriage and birth rates accompanying economic recovery and war-time full employment. It was accelerated by the great marriage and baby booms following demobilization in 1946. The marriage rate in 1946 reached a peak of 16.4 marriages per 1,000 population, or 121 per 1,000 unmarried females. At the bottom of the depression in 1932, the comparable marriage rates were but 7.9 and 56, respectively. The birth rate between 1946 and 1960 hovered close to 25 (births per 1,000 persons per year), as contrasted with the low of 18.4 in 1932 and 1936. During the 1950's the nation gained about 41 million babies and nearly 3 million net immigrants (immigrants minus emigrants). This gain was offset, of course,

Reprinted from *Population Review*, 6 (July, 1962), pp. 49–61, by permission of the author and the publisher.

[1] The summary of the U.S. 1960 Census results available at the time of this writing were drawn from the *1960 Census of Population, Advance Reports* issued by the U.S. Bureau of the Census as the statistics became available. These data will be incorporated into the 1960 Census volumes. To facilitate reading specific references to these ephemeral sources are omitted. An outline of the U.S. 1960 Census publications may be obtained by writing to the Director, U.S. Bureau of the Census, Washington 25 DC.

[2] The historical census data drawn largely from U.S. Bureau of the Census, *Historical Statistics of the United States to 1957*, Washington, D.C., U.S. Government Printing Office, 1960. Historical data are also available, and have been drawn upon in: Taeuber, Conrad and Irene, *The Changing Population of the United States*, New York, John Wiley and Sons, 1958; and Bogue, Donald J., *The Population of the United States*, Glencoes, Illinois, The Free Press, 1960.

TABLE 1. POPULATION OF THE UNITED STATES, 1900 TO
1960

| Year | Populations (thousands) | Increase over Preceding Census | |
		Number (thousands)	Per Cent
1960	179,323	27,997	18.5
1950	151,326ᵃ	19,028	14.5
1940	131,669	8,894	7.2
1930	122,775	17,064	16.1
1920	105,711	13,738	14.9
1910	91,972	15,978	21.0
1900	75,995	–	–

[a] Includes Alaska and Hawaii.
SOURCE: U.S. Bureau of the Census. See footnotes 1 and 2.

by over 15 million deaths to produce the net total population increase of 28 million.

The average annual percentage population increase between 1950 and 1960, about 1.8 per cent, was about the same in the U.S. as the average increase for the world as a whole. The U.S. rate of increase, however, was the results of a birth rate and a death rate far below the world average. Mortality had fallen to such a low level, 9.4 deaths for 1,000 persons in 1959, that even though the post-war boom birth rate at about 25 births per 1,000 persons was less than half of the U.S. birth rate in 1800, it was high enough to produce relatively great growth. Should the birth rate be sustained, it would produce a population of 214 millions by the 1970 Census and 260 millions by 1980.[3] By 2000 it could produce a U.S. population of 380 million; and by 2050, a date which some persons now alive will live to see, about 1 billion Americans![4]

POPULATION DISTRIBUTION

The national population increase was not evenly distributed geographically. Of the four census regions the West experienced the most rapid increase during the 1950's, a pattern this region has shown since it first appeared in a census in 1850. Between 1950 and 1960, the population growth of the West, at 39 per cent, was more than twice that of the nation as a whole. Each of the other regions— the South, the North Central and the Northeast—had increases below the

[3] Bureau of the Census, U.S. Department of Commerce, "Illustrative Projections of the Population of the United States, by Age and Sex, 1960 to 1980,"*Current Population Reports* (Series P-25, No. 187). Nov. 10, 1958.

[4] Projections for 2000 and 2050 from: Division of The Actuary, Social Security Administration, U.S. Department of Health, Education and Welfare, *Illustrative United States Population Projections*, Washington, U.S. Government Printing Office, 1957.

national average. The South and the North Central regions both increased at about 16 per cent; the Northeast showed an increase of only 13 per cent for the decade.

Despite the relatively rapid growth of the West, it remained the smallest of the four regions. However, it rose from 13 to 16 per cent of the total population of the nation during the decade, and experienced the largest absolute increase—almost 7.9 million persons. The absolute increase of the South, the most populous region, was not far behind, almost 7.8 million. The North Central region increased by 7.2 million. The Northeast registered the smallest absolute gain, 5.2 million.

The extent to which the population of the nation is being redistributed as the result of differential rates of growth becomes even more evident by states. Over 60 per cent of the national increase was accounted for by 8 states, each of which gained over a million persons between 1950 and 1960. California alone gained over 5 million inhabitants; Florida over 2 million; Texas, Ohio and New York over 1.7 million each; and Michigan, Illinois and New Jersey gained between 1 and 1.5 million persons each. Eight additional states experienced increases of 500,000 to 1 million persons. Hence, 16 states with the most rapid growth accounted for 22 million of the 28 million increase in total population, that is, for almost four-fifths of the total national increase.

At the other extreme, despite the population boom for the nation, three states—Arkansas, Mississippi and West Virginia—and the District of Columbia actually posted population decreases for the decade. The losses in Arkansas and Mississippi were a continuation of declines which set in during the 1940's. Two other states which lost population in the 1940's, North Dakota and Oklahoma, reversed the pattern and showed some increase in the 1950's.

Natural increase, the excess of births over deaths, was the predominant factor in national increase during the decade. For the individual states, however, and particularly for those with the highest rates of gain, migration rather than natural increase was the primary factor. California and Florida, for example, combining favorable climate with rapid economic growth have attracted large numbers of migrants. In contrast, West Virginia, Arkansas and Mississippi, with declining economies, lost sizeable numbers of their inhabitants to other states.

Differential County Growth. The unevenness of population change within the nation is even more strikingly shown by differential growth patterns among counties. There were some 3,107 counties (and independent cities) in the country as a whole. Despite the relatively large national increase over half of the counties, 1,578, actually lost population during the 1950's. Every state in the Union except Connecticut and Delaware contained some counties which lost population. Even the states with the largest rates of population increase, Florida, Nevada and Arizona, had population decreases in about a fifth of their counties. And even in California which experienced an increase of over 5 million persons, 7 of the 58 counties registered population decline. In the West, the region with the greatest population increase 156, or about 38 per cent of the 416 counties, showed population decline. In the South and in the North Central regions, about 58 per cent and 52 per cent, respectively, of the counties lost population. Surprisingly, the Northeast region, which showed the smallest regional growth rate, also had the smallest proportion of counties with actual population losses, that is 25 per cent.

In general, the states in which the largest proportion of counties lost population were either predominantly farm or rural states, contained large expanses of farm or rural territory, or sizable economically depressed areas, that is, areas with a shrinking economic base by reason of the exhaustion of natural resources or an increasingly unfavorable competitive position in the national economy. Declines in county population were largely the result of the out-migration of rural farm population or of the residents of economically depressed areas.

POPULATION CONCENTRATION

The population density of the United States (persons per square mile) has about doubled since 1900, increasing at each census with the increase in the size of the population. In 1950 there were 50.7 persons per square mile in the nation. In 1960 U.S. population density had declined to 50.5 persons per square mile. The explanation of this apparent contradiction is a simple one. Alaska and Hawaii became states during the 1950's, adding considerably more in the way of territory than people. Had these new states been in the Union in 1950, national population density would have been 42.6 persons per square mile. Population density of the United States in 1960 was still somewhat below that of the world average of about 55 persons per square mile.

Densities varied considerably within the nation. The most densely populated state, Rhode Island with 812 persons per square mile, had a density little below the most densely populated nation on the globe—the Netherlands with over 890 persons per square mile. On the other hand, Alaska, with only 1 person for each $2\frac{1}{2}$ square miles, had a density well below that of the nations with lowest density—Canada with a density of 4, Australia with a density of 3, and Libya with a density of 2. . . .

POPULATION COMPOSITION

Differences in rates of population growth were evident also among the sub-groupings of the population considered by sex, age, color or race, and household composition (Table 2).

The nation in 1960 had a larger female than male population, a situation which began during the 1940's. The 1950 Census was the first in which women outnumbered men, the sex ratio being 99 men for every 100 women. In 1960, the sex ratio had declined further to 97 men for every 100 women. The decline in the relative number of males reflects the greater longevity of women as well as the decrease in the importance of immigrations which tended to be predominantly male.

For the first time in the history of the United States, the average (median) age of the population declined between censuses. In 1950 the median age was

TABLE 2. Sex, Age, Race, and Marital Status for
United States: 1960 and 1950

Item	1960 (thousands)	1950ᵃ (thousands)	Per Cent Increase, 1950 to 1960
Total Population	179,323	151,326	18.5
Sex:			
Male	88,331	75,187	17.5
Female	90,992	76,139	19.5
Age:			
Under 5	20,321	16,243	25.1
5 to 9	18,692	13,262	40.9
10 to 14	16,773	11,167	50.2
15 to 19	13,219	10,671	23.9
20 to 24	10,801	11,549	− 6.5
25 to 29	10,869	12,306	− 11.7
30 to 34	11,949	11,572	3.3
35 to 39	12,481	11,294	10.5
40 to 44	11,600	10,241	13.3
45 to 49	10,879	9,102	19.5
50 to 54	9,606	8,296	15.8
55 to 59	8,430	7,253	16.2
60 to 64	7,142	6,074	17.6
65 and over	16,560	12,295	34.7
Median age	29.5	30.2	−
Race:			
White	158,832	135,150	17.5
Non-white	20,491	16,176	26.7
Marital Status:			
Single	27,793	25,976	7.0
Married	85,166	74,696	14.0
Widowed	10,165	9,021	12.7
Divorced	3,152	2,457	28.3

ᵃ Includes Alaska and Hawaii.
Source: U.S. Bureau of the Census. See footnote 1.

30.2 years, culminating a process of aging recorded in each of the censuses of
the United States. Unlike the individual person, however, a population can
grow younger as well as older. In 1960 the median age of the population of the
United States was 29.5 years—that is, the average American had grown .7 of a
year younger between 1950 and 1960. This decline in median age reflects, of
course, mainly the impact of the baby boom which greatly increased the proportion of younger persons in the nation. Even with this decline, however, the
average American was still considerably older than his counterpart in 1800,
who was some 16 years old.

Average age is but one measurement of the aging of the population. Another
measurement is given by the changing proportion of senior citizens, those

65 years of age and over. By this index the population of the United States continued to age between 1950 and 1960. During the decade persons 65 years of age and over increased by about 35 per cent, a growth rate almost twice that of the nation as a whole. The growth rate of the population under 18 years of age, however, was even greater, about 37 per cent, which, of course, accounts for the decrease in the median age. The population, therefore, grew both younger and older during the 1950's as measured by the increases in the proportion of the young and the old, respectively. Curiously enough the population of intermediate ages, 18 to 64 years, increased by only 7.2 per cent, a rate well below one-half that of the national average. Moreover, the age group 20–29 years, reflecting the low depression birth rate of the 1930's, actually declined between 1950 and 1960.

Some appreciation of the tremendous pressure placed upon the country's schools during the 1950's is afforded by the fact that youngsters roughly of elementary age, 5 to 14 years old, increased by some 45 per cent during the decade, from 24.4 to 35.4 million. Those of approximately high school age, 15 to 19 years old, increased by over 23 per cent, from 10.7 to 13.2 million.

The non-white population of the United States continued to increase more rapidly than the white, a trend begun in 1920 after a long-time reverse pattern. Between 1950 and 1960 the non-white population increased by about 26.7 per cent as compared with the white increase of 17.5 per cent. The Negro population, which made up almost 93 per cent of the non-white, increased by 25.4 per cent during the decade. Thus the Negro population, totalling about 18.9 million in 1960 made up 10.5 per cent of the total as compared with 10.0 per cent in 1950.

The 1960 Census also recorded the continuing redistribution of Negroes within the nation. In 1960, 40 per cent of the Negro population was in the North and the West, 34 per cent in the former and 6 per cent in the latter; whereas 60 per cent of the Negroes resided in the South. In 1950, 68 per cent of the Negroes were still in the South and only 32 per cent in the North and West, 28 per cent in the former and about 4 per cent in the latter. The extent of the redistribution of the Negro population is appreciated when it is recalled that, as recently as 1910, over 90 per cent of the Negroes were still in the South, a proportion which had not changed appreciably since the Census of 1860 ante-dating the Civil War. Despite the decreased proportion of the Negroes in the South, however, the absolute number of Negroes in that region continued to increase, from 10.2 to about 11.3 millions, or by about 11 per cent. The redistribution of Negro population is largely in the form of migration from the South and from rural areas to the North and to metropolitan areas.

The 1960 Census statistics, available to date, also throw some light on changes in the marital status (Table 2) and in the living arrangements of the American people. (Table 3).

The post-war boom in marriage continued to be reflected in the relatively large proportion of persons 14 years of age and over who were married. About two-thirds of the population 14 years of age and over were married in 1960 as in 1950. The changes in marital composition were influenced, of course, by the

TABLE 3. Population by Household Relationship, for the United
States: 1960 and 1950.

(1950 Data Based Partly on Sample)

Household Relationship	1960 (thousands)	1950 (thousands)	Per Cent Increase, 1950 to 1960
Total	179,323	150,845	18.9
In households	174,373	145,116	20.2
Head of household	53,021	42,394	25.1
Head of primary family	44,670	37,758[a]	18.3
Primary individual	8,351	4,636[a]	80.1
Wife of head	39,210	33,378	17.5
Child under 18 of head	59,582	42,255	41.0
Other relative of head	19,592	23,020	−14.9
Non-relative of head	2,968	4,069	−27.1
In group quarters	4,950	5,729	−13.6
Inmate of institution	1,916	1,574	21.8
Other	3,034	4,155	−27.0
Population per household	3.29	3.42	−

[a] Includes estimates for Alaska and Hawaii.
Source: U.S. Bureau of the Census. See footnote 1.

changes in age distribution discussed above. During the decade persons 14 years of age and over in the nation increased by 12.6 per cent. Married persons, however, increased by twice the rate of single persons, 14 per cent as compared with 7 per cent. Divorced persons increased by twice the rate of married persons, 28 per cent. The widowed increased by 12.7 per cent.

The number of households, as in all previous censuses of the U.S., increased more rapidly than did the population, by 25 per cent as compared with 18.5 per cent. There were 53.0 million households in 1960, compared with 42.3 million in 1950.

The greater growth rate of households than of population results from the decreased number of persons per household—reflecting the continuation of the transition from the "large" or three generation, to the "small" or two generation household. That is, adult children whether married or single are tending increasingly to live apart from their parents or their in-laws.

Thus, the average size of household in keeping with the long-time trend, decreased from 3.42 persons per household in 1950 to 3.29 persons in 1960. This decline occurred in spite of the increase in family size, reflecting the increased birth rate during the decade. The family consists of two or more persons living together related by blood, marriage, or adoption; whereas the household includes all persons who occupy a house, an apartment or other group of rooms or a room which constitutes a housing unit. Between 1950 and 1960 the average size of family increased from 3.54 persons to 3.68 persons.

Persons living in households also increased more rapidly than did total population, by 20.2 per cent. While heads of households increased by 25 per cent household heads who were heads of "primary families"—that is, heads living with one or more persons related to him by blood, marriage or adoption—increased by only 18.3 per cent to reach a total of 44.7 million; whereas heads who were "primary individuals"—persons living alone or with non-related persons—increased by 80 per cent to reach a total of 8.4 million in 1960. Hence, household heads who were also heads of families grew at about the same rate as did total population. The greater growth rate of households than of population was entirely attributable, therefore, to the greater increase in households comprising single persons or non-related groups of persons. This change in living arrangements undoubtedly follows from increased income which enables a larger proportion of the population to live apart from their families.

The changing character of the living arrangements of the American people is further attested to by differential rates of growth of other household members. Wives of heads for example, increased by 17.5 per cent between 1950 and 1960. Children of the head under 18, however, increased by 41 per cent. On the other hand, "other relatives" of the head decreased by 14.9 per cent during the decade; and non-relatives of heads decreased by 27.1 per cent. Thus, changes in the living arrangements of the population seem to indicate greater "togetherness" in the sense that more persons are living in households; and less "relatedness" in the sense that fewer relatives other than the wives and children of heads are found in households.

The population living in group quarters decreased by 13.6 per cent during the decade. These are the persons living in institutions; or in arrangements of five or more unrelated persons, as in lodging houses, military and other types of barracks, college dormitories, fraternity and sorority houses, hospitals, homes for nurses, convents, monasteries, ships, etc. Inmates of institutions increased by 21.8 per cent during the decade to reach a total of 1.9 million. This increase, however, was more than offset by persons living in other types of group quarters, who declined to 27 per cent from 4.2 to 3.0 million during the decade. . . .

World Population Growth: An International Dilemma

HAROLD F. DORN

During all but the most recent years of the centuries of his existence man must have lived, reproduced, and died as other animals do. His increase in number was governed by the three great regulators of the increase of all species of plants and animals—predators, disease, and starvation—or, in terms more applicable to human populations—war, pestilence, and famine. One of the most significant developments for the future of mankind during the first half of the twentieth century has been his increasing ability to control pestilence and famine. Although

Reprinted from *Science*, 135 (January 26, 1962), pp. 283–290, by permission of the publisher.

he has not freed himself entirely from the force of these two regulators of population increase, he has gained sufficient control of them so that they no longer effectively govern his increase in number.

Simultaneously he has developed methods of increasing the effectiveness of war as a regulator of population increase, to the extent that he almost certainly could quickly wipe out a large proportion, if not all, of the human race. At the same time he has learned how to separate sexual gratification from reproduction by means of contraception and telegenesis (that is, reproduction by artificial insemination, particularly with spermatozoa preserved for relatively long periods of time), so that he can regulate population increase by voluntary control of fertility. Truly it can be said that man has the knowledge and the power to direct, at least in part, the course of his evolution.

This newly gained knowledge and power has not freed man from the inexorable effect of the biological laws that govern all living organisms. The evolutionary process has endowed most species with a reproductive potential that, unchecked, would overpopulate the entire globe within a few generations. It has been estimated that the tapeworm, *Taenia*, may lay 120,000 eggs per day; an adult cod can lay as many as 4 million eggs per year; a frog may produce 10,000 eggs per spawning. Human ovaries are thought to contain approximately 200,000 ova at puberty, while a single ejaculation of human semen may contain 200 million spermatozoa.

This excessive reproductive potential is kept in check for species other than man by interspecies competition in the struggle for existence, by disease, and by limitation of the available food supply. The fact that man has learned how to control, to a large extent, the operation of these biological checks upon unrestrained increase in number has not freed him from the necessity of substituting for them less harsh but equally effective checks. The demonstration of his ability to do this cannot be long delayed.

Only fragmentary data are available to indicate the past rate of growth of the population of the world. Even today, the number of inhabitants is known only approximately. Regular census of populations did not exist prior to 1800, although registers were maintained for small population groups prior to that time. As late as a century ago, around 1860, only about one-fifth of the estimated population of the world was covered by a census enumeration once in a 10-year period.[1] The commonly accepted estimates of the population of the world prior to 1800 are only informed guesses. Nevertheless, it is possible to piece together a consistent series of estimates of the world's population during the past two centuries, supplemented by a few rough guesses of the number of persons alive at selected earlier periods. The most generally accepted estimates are presented in Fig. 1.

These reveal a spectacular spurt during recent decades in the increase of the world's population that must be unparalleled during the preceding millennia of human existence. Furthermore, the rate of increase shows no sign of diminishing (Table 1). The period of time required for the population of the world to

[1] *Demographic Yearbook* (United Nations, New York, 1955), p. 1.

TABLE 1. THE NUMBER OF YEARS REQUIRED TO
DOUBLE THE POPULATION OF THE WORLD. [FROM
UNITED NATIONS DATA (9, 14)]

Year (A.D.)	Population (billions)	Number of Years to Double
1	0.25 (?)	1,650 (?)
1650	0.50	200
1850	1.1	80
1930	2.0	45
1975	4.0	35
2010	8.0*	?

* A projection of United Nations estimates.

double has sharply decreased during the past three centuries and now is about 35 years.

Only a very rough approximation can be made of the length of time required for the population of the world to reach one-quarter of a billion persons, the

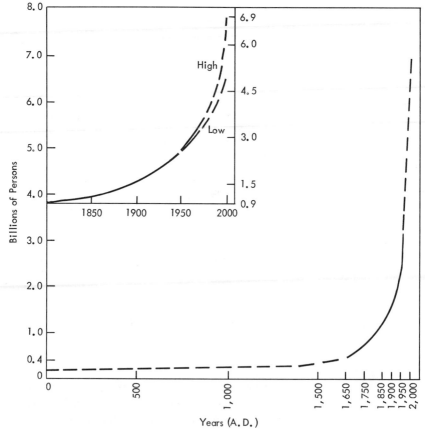

FIGURE 1. Estimated population of the world, A.D. 1 to A.D. 2000.

estimated number at the beginning of the Christian era. The present subgroups of *Homo sapiens* may have existed for as long as 100,000 years. The exact date is not necessary, since for present purposes the evidence is sufficient to indicate that probably 50,000 to 100,000 years were required for *Homo sapiens* to increase in number until he reached a global total of one-quarter of a billion persons. This number was reached approximately 2,000 years ago.

By 1620, the year the Pilgrims landed on Plymouth Rock, the population of the world had doubled in number. Two hundred years later, shortly before the Civil War, another 500 million persons had been added. Since that time, additional half billions of persons have been added during increasingly shorter intervals of time. The sixth half billion, just added, required slightly less than 11 years, as compared to 200 years for the second half billion. The present rate of growth implies that only 6 to 7 years will be required to add the eighth half billion to the world's population. The change in rate of growth just described has taken place since the first settlers came to New England. . . .

DECLINE IN MORTALITY

The major cause of the recent spurt in population increase is a world-wide decline in mortality. Although the birth rate increased in some countries—for example, the United States—during and after World War II, such increases have not been sufficiently widespread to account for more than a small part of the increase in the total population of the world. Moreover, the increase in population prior to World War II occurred in spite of a widespread decline in the birth rate among persons of European origin.

Accurate statistics do not exist, but the best available estimates suggest that the expectation of life at birth in Greece, Rome, Egypt, and the Eastern Mediterranean region probably did not exceed 30 years at the beginning of the Christian era. By 1900 it had increased to about 40 to 50 years in North America and in most countries of northwestern Europe. At present, it has reached 68 to 70 years in many of these countries.

By 1940, only a small minority of the world's population had achieved an expectation of life at birth comparable to that of the population of North America and northwest Europe. Most of the population of the world had an expectation of life no greater than that which prevailed in western Europe during the Middle Ages. Within the past two decades, the possibility of achieving a 20th-century death rate has been opened to these masses of the world's population. An indication of the result can be seen from the data in Fig. 2.

In 1940, the death rate in Mexico was similar to that in England and Wales nearly 100 years earlier. It decreased as much during the following decade as did the death rate in England and Wales during the 50-year period from 1850 to 1900.

In 1946–47 the death rate of the Moslem population of Algeria was higher than that of the population of Sweden in the period 1771–80, the earliest date for which reliable mortality statistics are available for an entire nation. During

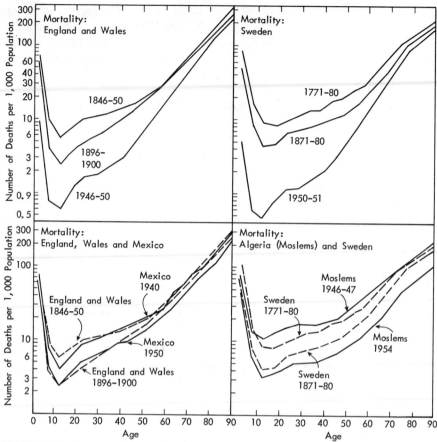

FIGURE 2. Age-specific death rates per 1000 per year for Sweden, England and Wales, Mexico, and the Moslem population of Algeria for various time periods from 1771 to 1954.

the following 8 years, the drop in the death rate in Algeria considerably exceeded that in Sweden during the century from 1771 to 1871.[2]

The precipitous decline in mortality in Mexico and in the Moslem population of Algeria is illustrative of what has taken place during the past 15 years in Latin America, Africa, and Asia, where nearly three out of every four persons in the world now live. Throughout most of this area the birth rate has changed very little, remaining near a level of 40 per 1,000 per year, as can be seen from Fig. 3, which shows the birth rate, death rate, and rate of natural increase for selected countries.

Even in countries such as Puerto Rico and Japan where the birth rate has declined substantially, the rate of natural increase has changed very little, owing to the sharp decrease in mortality. A more typical situation is represented by

[2] Although registration of deaths among the Moslem population of Algeria is incomplete, it is believed that the general impression conveyed by Fig. 2 is essentially correct.

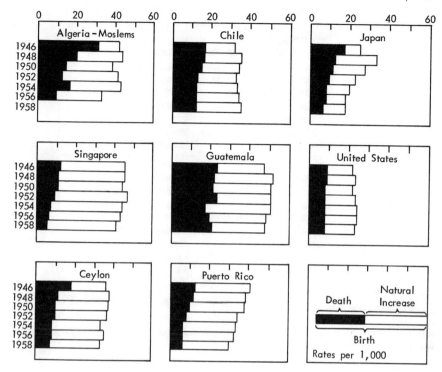

FIGURE 3. Birth rate, death rate, and rate of natural increase per 1000 for selected countries for the period 1946–58.

Singapore, Ceylon, Guatemala, and Chile, where the crude rate of natural increase has risen. There has been a general tendency for death rates to decline universally and for high birth rates to remain high, with the result that those countries with the highest rates of increase are experiencing an acceleration in their rates of growth.

REGIONAL LEVELS

The absolute level of fertility and mortality and the effect of changes in them upon the increase of population in different regions of the world can be only approximately indicated. The United Nations estimates that only about 33 percent of the deaths and 42 percent of the births that occur in the world are registered.[3] The percentage registered ranges from about 8 to 10 percent in tropical and southern Africa and Eastern Asia to 98 to 100 percent in North America and Europe. Nevertheless, the statistical staff of the United Nations, by a judicious combination of the available fragmentary data, has been able to prepare estimates of fertility and mortality for different regions of the world that are generally accepted as a reasonably correct representation of the actual but

[3] *Demographic Yearbook* (United Nations, New York, 1956), p. 14.

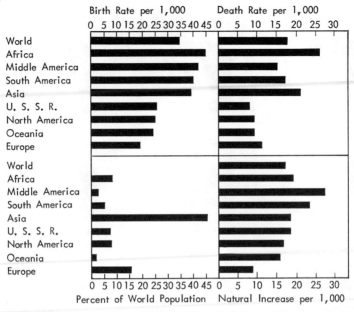

FIGURE 4. Percentage of the 1958 world population, birth rate, death rate, and rate of natural increase, per 1000, for the period 1954–58 for various regions of the world.

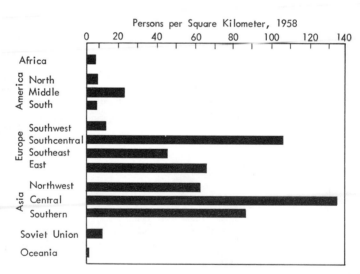

FIGURE 5. Number of persons per square kilometer in various regions of the world in 1958.

unknown figures. The estimated birth rate, death rate, and crude rate of natural increase (the birth rate minus the death rate) for eight regions of the world for the period 1954–58 are shown in Fig. 4.

The birth rates of the countries of Africa, Asia, Middle America, and South America average nearly 40 per 1000 and probably are as high as they were 500 to 1000 years ago. In the rest of the world—Europe, North America, Oceania, and the Soviet Union—the birth rate is slightly more than half as high, or about 20 to 25 per 1000. The death rate for the former regions, although still definitely higher, is rapidly approaching that for people of European origin, with the result that the highest rates of natural increase are found in the regions with the highest birth rates. The most rapid rate of population growth at present is taking place in Middle and South America, where the population will double about every 26 years if the present rate continues.

These regional differences in fertility and mortality are intensifying the existing imbalance of population with land area and natural resources. No matter how this imbalance is measured, that it exists is readily apparent. Two rather crude measures are presented in Figs. 4 and 5, which show the percentage distribution of the world's population living in each region and the number of persons per square kilometer.

An important effect of the decline in mortality rates often is overlooked—namely, the increase in effective fertility. An estimated 97 out of every 100 newborn white females subject to the mortality rates prevailing in the United States during 1950 would survive to age 20, slightly past the beginning of the usual childbearing age, and 91 would survive to the end of the childbearing period

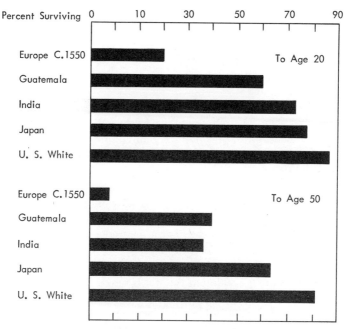

FIGURE 6.   Percentage of newborn females who would survive to the end of the reproductive period according to mortality rates in Europe around A.D. 1500 and in selected countries around 1950.

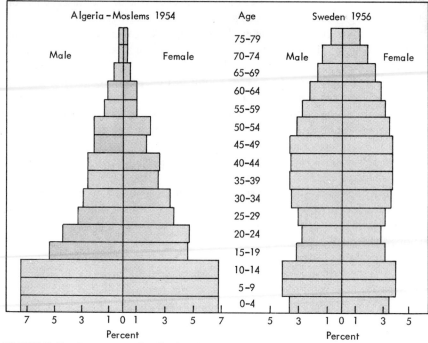

FIGURE 7. Percentage distribution by age of the population of Sweden in 1956 and the Moslem population of Algeria in 1954.

(Fig. 6). These estimates are more than 3 and 11 times, respectively, the corresponding estimated proportions for white females that survived to these ages about four centuries ago.

In contrast, about 70 per cent of the newborn females in Guatemala would survive to age 20, and only half would live to the end of the childbearing period if subject to the death rates prevailing in that country in 1950. If the death rate in Guatemala should fall to the level of that in the United States in 1950—a realistic possibility—the number of newborn females who would survive to the beginning of the childbearing period would increase by 36 percent; the number surviving to the end of the childbearing period would increase by 85 percent. A corresponding decrease in the birth rate would be required to prevent this increase in survivorship from resulting in a rapid acceleration in the existing rate of population growth, which already is excessive. In other words, this decrease in the death rate would require a decrease in the birth rate of more than 40 percent merely to maintain the status quo.

As can be seen from Fig. 3, the birth rate in countries with high fertility has shown little or no tendency to decrease in recent years. Japan is the exception. There, the birth rate dropped by 46 percent from 1948 to 1958—an amount more than enough to counterbalance the decrease in the death rate, with the result that there was a decrease in the absolute number of births. As yet there is very little evidence that other countries with a correspondingly high birth rate are likely to duplicate this in the near future.

Another effect of a rapid rate of natural increase is demonstrated by Fig. 7. About 43 percent of the Moslem population of Algeria is under 15 years of age; the corresponding percentage in Sweden is 24, or slightly more than half this number. Percentages in the neighborhood of 40 percent are characteristic of the populations of the countries of Africa, Latin America, and Asia.

This high proportion of young people constitutes a huge fertility potentia for 30 years into the future that can be counterbalanced only by a sharp decline in the birth rate, gives rise to serious educational problems, and causes a heavy drain on the capital formation that is necessary to improve the level of living of the entire population. A graphic illustration of this may be found in the recently published 5-year plan for India for 1961–66, which estimates that it will be necessary to provide educational facilities and teachers for 20 million additional children during this 5-year period.[4]

HISTORICAL PATTERN IN WESTERN EUROPE

Some persons, although agreeing that the current rate of increase of the majority of the world's population cannot continue indefinitely without giving rise to grave political, social, and economic problems, point out that a similar situation existed in northwestern and central Europe during the 18th and 19th centuries. Increasing industrialization and urbanization, coupled with a rising standard of living, led to a decline in the birth rate, with a consequent drop in the rate of increase of the population. Why should not the rest of the world follow this pattern?

There is small likelihood that the two-thirds of the world's population which has not yet passed through the demographic revolution from high fertility and mortality rates to low fertility and mortality rates can repeat the history of western European peoples prior to the development of serious political and economic problems. A brief review of the circumstances that led to the virtual domination of the world at the end of the 19th century by persons of European origin will indicate some of the reasons for this opinion.

Around A.D. 1500 the population of Europe probably did not exceed 100 million persons (perhaps 15 to 20 percent of the population of the world) and occupied about 7 percent of the land area of the earth. Four hundred years later, around 1900, the descendants of this population numbered nearly 550 million, constituted about one-third of the world's population, and occupied or controlled five-sixths of the land area of the world. They had seized and peopled two great continents, North and South America, and one smaller continent, Australia, with its adjacent islands; had partially peopled and entirely controlled a third great continent, Africa; and dominated southern Asia and the neighboring islands.

[4] New York *Times* (5 Aug. 1961).

The English-, French-, and Spanish-speaking peoples were the leaders in this expansion, with lesser roles being played by the Dutch and Portuguese. The Belgians and Germans participated only toward the end of this period of expansion. Among these, the English-speaking people held the dominant position at the end of the era, around 1900.

The number of English-speaking persons around 1500, at the start of this period of expansion, is not known, but it probably did not exceed 4 or 5 million. By 1900 these people numbered about 129 million and occupied and controlled one-third of the land area of the earth and, with the non-English-speaking inhabitants of this territory, made up some 30 percent of the population of the world.

This period was characterized by an unprecedented increase in population, a several-fold expansion of the land base for this population, and a hitherto undreamed of multiplication of capital in the form of precious metals, goods, and commodities. Most important of all, the augmentation in capital and usable land took place more rapidly than the growth in population.

A situation equally favorable for a rapid improvement in the level of living associated with a sharp increase in population does not appear likely to arise for the people who now inhabit Latin America, Africa, and Asia. The last great frontier of the world has been closed. Although there are many thinly populated areas in the world, their existence is testimony to the fact that, until now, these have been regarded as undesirable living places. The expansion of population to the remaining open areas would require large expenditures of capital for irrigation, drainage, transportation facilities, control of insects and parasites, and other purposes—capital that the rapidly increasing populations which will need these areas do not possess.

In addition, this land is not freely available for settlement. The entire land surface of the world is crisscrossed by national boundaries. International migration now is controlled by political considerations; for the majority of the population of the world, migration, both in and out of a country, is restricted.

The horn of plenty, formerly filled with free natural resources, has been emptied. No rapid accumulation of capital in the form of precious metals, goods, and commodities, such as characterized the great 400-year boom enjoyed by the peoples of western-European origin, is possible for the people of Africa, Asia, and Latin America.

Last, but not least, is the sheer arithmetic of the current increase in population. The number of persons in the world is so large that even a small rate of natural increase will result in an almost astronomical increment over a period of time of infinitesimal duration compared to the duration of the past history of the human race. As was pointed out above, continuation of the present rate of increase would result in a population of 50 billion persons in another 150 years. A population of this magnitude is so foreign to our experience that it is difficult to comprehend its implications.

Just as Thomas Malthus, at the end of the 18th century, could not foresee the effect upon the peoples of western Europe of the exploration of the last great frontier of this earth, so we today cannot clearly foresee the final effect of an unprecedented rapid increase of population within closed frontiers. What seems to be least uncertain in a future full of uncertainty is that the demographic history of the next 400 years will not be like that of the past 400 years.

WORLD PROBLEM

The results of human reproduction are no longer solely the concern of the two individuals involved, or of the larger family, or even of the nation of which they are citizens. A stage has been reached in the demographic development of the world when the rate of human reproduction in any part of the globe may directly or indirectly affect the health and welfare of the rest of the human race. It is in this sense that there is a world population problem.

One or two illustrations may make this point more clear. During the past decade, six out of every ten persons added to the population of the world live in Asia; another two out of every ten live in Latin America and Africa. It seems inevitable that the breaking up of the world domination by northwest Europeans and their descendants, which already is well advanced, will continue, and that the center of power and influence will shift toward the demographic center of the world.

The present distribution of population increase enhances the existing imbalance between the distribution of the world's population and the distribution of wealth, available and utilized resources, and the use of nonhuman energy. Probably for the first time in human history there is a universal aspiration for a rapid improvement in the standard of living and a growing impatience with conditions that appear to stand in the way of its attainment. Millions of persons in Asia, Africa, and Latin America now are aware of the standard of living enjoyed by Europeans and North Americans. They are demanding the opportunity to attain the same standard, and they resist the idea that they must be permanently content with less.

A continuation of the present high rate of human multiplication will act as a brake on the already painfully slow improvement in the level of living, thus increasing political unrest and possibly bringing about eventual changes in government. As recent events have graphically demonstrated, such political changes may greatly affect the welfare of even the wealthiest nations.

The capital and technological skills that many of the nations of Africa, Asia, and Latin America require to produce enough food for a rapidly growing population and simultaneously to perceptibly raise per capita income exceed their existing national resources and ability. An immediate supply of capital in the amounts required is available only from the wealthier nations. The principle of public support for social welfare plans is now widely accepted in national affairs. The desirability of extending this principle to the international level for the primary purpose of supporting the economic development of the less advanced nations has not yet been generally accepted by the wealthier and more advanced countries. Even if this principle should be accepted, it is not as yet clear how long the wealthier nations would be willing to support the uncontrolled breeding of the populations receiving this assistance. The general acceptance of a foreign-aid program of the extent required by the countries with a rapidly growing population will only postpone for a few decades the inevitable reckoning with the results of uncontrolled human multiplication.

The future may witness a dramatic increase in man's ability to control his environment, provided he rapidly develops cultural substitutes for those harsh but effective governors of his high reproductive potential—disease and famine— that he has so recently learned to control. Man has been able to modify or control many natural phenomena, but he has not yet discovered how to evade the consequences of biological laws. No species has ever been able to multiply without limit. There are two biological checks upon a rapid increase in number— a high mortality and a low fertility. Unlike other biological organisms, man can choose which of these checks shall be applied, but one of them must be. Whether man can use his scientific knowledge to guide his future evolution more wisely than the blind forces of nature, only the future can reveal. The answer will not be long postponed.

American Studies of Family Planning and Fertility:

A Review of Major Trends and Issues

RONALD FREEDMAN

On balance we probably know more about the fertility and family planning of the American population than about that of any other country in the world. While this accumulation of information is impressive, the gaps in knowledge are large. Our large-scale field surveys have been much more successful in measuring and describing the variations in fertility and family planning than in finding the causes of these variations. Both the GAF and Princeton Studies[1] are adding significantly to our descriptive knowledge. In addition the Princeton Study is making especially notable contributions to measurement techniques for studying various aspects of reproductive behavior. But we do not yet have many principles or theories about causal factors sufficiently well established to permit their application with assurance in other countries. This is not to minimize the

From *Research in Family Planning* by Clyde V. Kiser (ed.) Copyright © 1962, by Princeton University Press. Reprinted by permission of the Princeton University Press.

[1] The references for the Princeton Study, the Indianapolis Study, and the Growth of American Families Study are found in the preceding papers by Kiser, Westoff, and Campbell.* In addition, some of my comments are based on materials in *Family Growth in Metropolitan America* (Princeton: Princeton University Press, 1961), by Westoff, Potter, Sagi, and Mishler.

* [The material referred to is not included—Editor.]

great value of what has been done. The significant findings are sufficiently numerous to make my assignment of summarizing the main trends very difficult, if not presumptuous. Necessarily, I shall confine myself to a limited number of ideas and methodological developments which are central tendencies or which are especially significant, in my view.

STUDIES BASED ON OFFICIAL GOVERNMENT DATA

As in other countries, studies based on official government reports have been important in developing our knowledge of American fertility and—by inference—of family planning. Special field studies . . . have been unusually extensive and intensive in the United States, but they have much of their meaning in amplifying and interpreting the trends developed from official data which are more massive and regular, if limited in the variables treated.

Despite some serious limitations, there are unusually rich resources for fertility research in our decennial censuses, the interim Current Population Surveys, and the birth registration statistics. Many excellent studies are based on these data. I call attention to two of special importance: the continuing series of studies of cohort fertility by P. L. Whelpton and his colleagues[2] and *The Fertility of American Women*[3] by Grabill, Kiser, and Whelpton, which provides an admirable summary of the long-run trends as well as the early post-war developments.

For the prewar period, the studies based on official statistics have documented a series of changes roughly similar to those of other countries in the process of industrialization:

(1) There is the long-run secular decline in fertility associated with our transformation to an urban industrial nation. Deviations from this secular trend are strongly correlated with cyclical economic changes both in the cohort analyses and in a series of time series analyses—the most recent by Dudley Kirk.[4] Both the secular decline and the cyclical variations are—by inference—evidence for the spread of family limitation practices, but we have almost no historical trend data bearing directly on family planning practices.

(2) There is considerable evidence for the prewar period of a negative correlation of fertility and social status as measured by occupation, education, or

[2] See especially Whelpton, P. K.: *Cohort Fertility: Native White Women in the United States* (Princeton: Princeton University Press, 1954), and Whelpton, P. K., and Campbell, Arthur A.: *Fertility Tables for Birth Cohorts of American Women.* U.S. National Office of Vital Statistics, Special Reports, Vol. 51, No. 1, January 29, 1960.

[3] Grabill, Wilson H.; Kiser, Clyde V.; and Whelpton, Pascal K.: *The Fertility of American Women* (New York: John Wiley and Sons, 1958).

[4] Kirk, Dudley, and Nortman, Dorothy L.: "Business and Babies: The Influence of the Business Cycle on Birth Rates," *Proceedings of the Social Statistics Section, American Statistical Association,* December 1958, pp. 151–160. For earlier studies see: Galbraith, Virginia L., and Thomas, Dorothy S.: "Birth Rates and the Inter-war Business Cycles," *Journal of the American Statistical Association,* Vol. 36, No. 216, December 1941, pp. 465–476; and Ogburn, William F., and Thomas, Dorothy S.: "The Influence of the Business Cycle on Certain Social Conditions," *Quarterly Publications of the American Statistical Association,* Vol. 18, 1922, pp. 324–340.

income.[5] That such fertility differentials were linked with differentials in contraceptive practice is again mainly a plausible inference for the national population, although we have supporting evidence for such limited populations as that of the Indianapolis Study. There was some evidence of a positive correlation with fertility at the upper end of the status scale long before the war.

(3) The higher fertility of the rural population—and especially the farm sector—has been well documented for a long time. Recent analyses[6] have added the important conclusion that the long-run secular decline occurred simultaneously in both the rural and urban sectors and was not primarily a direct consequence of the transfer of population between the sectors. Changes in the rural sector, although undoubtedly linked to changes in the urban sector, accounted for a large part of the long-run decline. Probably changes in the rural sector were produced by its involvement in a specialized market economy centered in the city. It suggests that the farmer need not go to the city to become urbanized. In various ways the city can come to him. This may be significant for progress for the newly industrializing countries.

(4) According to the cohort fertility studies particular cohorts have responded to changing social and economic circumstances by variations in the age at marriage and the spacing of children independently of the variations in completed family size. Again, by inference, this is evidence for family planning practice. However, we have only crude general ideas about the particular historical variables producing these shifts in fertility.

In the postwar period the studies based on the official statistics have helped to define and to describe the continuing baby boom which has been more or less distinctive of the Western countries outside of Europe.

The official statistics have also documented for period rates an important contraction of almost all the standard traditional fertility differentials—by education, occupation, income, or residence.[7] They do not indicate the elimination of these differentials—only a trend for their contraction involving a reduction of the variability of family size both within and between major strata. There appears to be an emerging consensus on family size throughout the population.

We can see now from the official statistics to 1958 that the baby boom has had four major components: first, in the early stages, a making up of babies postponed in the depression; second, a shift in the timing of marriages and births to earlier stages independently of the changes in completed family size; third, a significant increase in the proportion marrying; and fourth, an apparent shift from small to moderate size for completed families among the married. There has been a remarkable decrease in childlessness to levels below what was formerly considered to be the physiological minimum for complete sterility. The increase

[5] Grabill, Kiser, and Whelpton, *op. cit.*

[6] Okun, Bernard: "Trends in Birth Rates in the United States Since 1870." *The Johns Hopkins University Studies in Historical and Political Science*, Series LXXVI, No. 1, 1958; also Grabill, Kiser, and Whelpton, pp. 16–19.

[7] Grabill, Kiser, and Whelpton, *op. cit.*

in average family size is still almost entirely a result of more births of the first to fourth orders.[8]

So far as we can tell at present, the demographers were right in their early insistence that the baby boom was not an indication of a return to a large family system. All of the changes are consistent with the view that the postwar American family model involves the early creation by almost all adults of their own families with at least some children; but not too many—a moderate number indicated by the range of two to four.

We must admit, I think, that in the early stages of the baby boom demographers were inclined to view the whole development as a temporary deviation from the long-run secular decline. In part, this resulted from the fact that there was little in the official statistics to signal the basic change that was occurring, until it was far advanced. Demographers, along with many other social scientists, tended to assume that fertility would return to former low levels without appreciation of the shifts in family size that were occurring. If such special field studies as Growth of American Families had been available at that time, or if we had annual national time series for expected and desired family size, such changes might be caught at an earlier point and studied in relation to other historical series.[9]

I think the failure to appreciate earlier that aspect of the baby boom which did involve larger families also resulted from a theoretical bias demographers shared with sociologists. This was the view that urbanization with its accompanying specialization and high rate of mobility inevitably would lead to a growth of secularism and rationality, to the declining influence of such traditional forces as religious faith, to a shattering of traditional family ties and other primary group influences, to a growth of individualism, and to the attachment of the individual to large, impersonal, and rational organizations. The functions of the family were seen as becoming dispersed among specialized institutions, and children were seen as an impediment to participation in the larger organizations from which the rewards of the urban society came. The dominant view among both demographers and sociologists was that as all of the population becomes closely involved in an urban society, family planning would become universal and the size of families planned would continue to decline. A logical extension of the basic premises of this model made it appear that the family would continue to decline in importance among the major institutions. Some of us still are inclined to view childbearing as a rather irrational act. The costs of

---

[8] For example, the cohort reaching age 30–34 in 1958 had 710 births per thousand more than the cohort reaching this age in 1942. Ninety-two percent of this increase resulted from more births of the first to fourth orders and 80 per cent from more births of the first to third orders. Only 8 per cent of the increase is attributable to births beyond the fourth order while 21 per cent is attributable to larger numbers of first births. A similar result is obtained by comparing the cohort reaching age 35–39 in 1958 with the cohort reaching this age in 1946 (the latter cohort having the lowest cumulative fertility to age 35–39 recorded in the United States). These data are from Whelpton and Campbell, *op. cit.*

[9] Dr. Philip Hauser has stressed the desirability of time series studies in several earlier Milbank Round Table meetings.

bearing children are emphasized without a balancing assessment of the continuing positive functions of the family and of children in a modern society.

A continuing revision of the older view of urban society since the war gives more weight to the persistence of religious and other traditional allegiances. There is growing emphasis on the persistence and even resurgence of the family and other primary groups as the channels through which the larger bureaucratic organizations reach the individual, in large measure. Urbanization and industrialization are seen as leading to the reorganization of society in new forms rather than to inevitable disorganization and mass anomy. This basic shift in the sociological orientation toward urbanism in the United States is important in interpreting both the official statiscs and the special field studies such as those just reported us.

Before turning from the official statistics to the special field studies I want to stress an important limitation of the latter—they give us very little about marriage itself. For this we rely on the official statistics. In fact, neither the field studies nor the official statistics cover a number of the important intermediate variables which Davis and Blake[10] have outlined as standing between the structure of the society and fertility itself.

SPECIAL STUDIES

The special field studies have many objectives and their findings are too diverse for any succinct summary. I shall try to deal with some of their leading findings only as they bear on four broad questions:

(1) Does what appears from the official statistics to be an emerging consensus on a moderate size family have support in the value system of the population? Can we use these survey data on values to anticipate the change to a new fertility pattern while it is in process?

(2) Is the widespread adoption of a moderate size family pattern supported by effective family limitation practices of a particular kind? Here we are looking for direct evidence to support the inferences about contraception from the official statistics.

(3) Given an apparent consensus on a range of two to four children, can we explain the variations within this range by reference to a combination of social and psychological variables?

(4) Can we explain the existence of the range itself? For example, why is the consensus and the performance at a higher level now than during the 30's and why is it higher here than in the European countries?

THE CONSENSUS IN VALUES

The GAF and Princeton Studies as well as others on a smaller scale[11] indicate a remarkable consensus in the American population on a moderate size

[10] Davis, Kingsley, and Blake, Judith: "Social Structure and Fertility: An Analytic Framework." *Economic Development and Cultural Change*, Vol. 4, No. 3, April 1956.

[11] Similar results for the national United States population were obtained in 1954 in an unpublished Survey Research Center Study based on 500 couples with questions only on

family of two to four children, whether the measure of values used is desired, ideal, or expected number of children. As Dr. Westoff has indicated, 90 per cent of the two parity women in the Princeton Study desire two, three, or four children. The GAF Study covering a wider range of parities and backgrounds shows a similar consensus with respect to desires and ideals. As to the number of children actually expected the GAF Study indicates that many of the variations found are due to involuntary factors: fecundity impairments among those with fewer than two children and involuntary excess fertility for those with five or more children.

The studies also indicate that the consensus on a moderate size family exists in all the major strata of the population. If expectations and desires of the younger cohorts are realized the contraction of differences noted in the official statistics for incomplete families will apply also to completed families. It is likely that these analyses based on attitudes and values exaggerate the contraction that will occur because they fail to take into account the likelihood that over the whole childbearing period the lower social strata will be least effective in limiting family size to the desired range. This will have the effect of increasing differentially low status fertility rates late in the childbearing period. The value statements in the Princeton Study especially may underestimate eventual fertility differentials because all of its subjects are at the bottom end of the desired range. Many of them don't know yet just how ineffective their family planning will be. In any case, the Princeton Study asks about desired rather than expected number of children, and the GAF Study indicates that there is a discrepancy between what is wanted and what is expected. No doubt differentials in completed family size will be greater than the differentials in values, but there is little doubt that the value data do support the inference from current official statistics of a marked contraction in the differentials.

The extensive use of data on such attitudes as expectations, plans, or desires in the recent American studies—as well as in other countries—raises important methodological issues. Can such statements be used to predict the future fertility for incompleted cohorts? It can be argued that in a society in which the use of contraception is almost universal the plans and expectations of the married couples will guide their behavior more or less closely so that fertility of each cohort is predictable and the cumulation of cohort predictions will give a value for the total population. Unfortunately, the situation is more complex than this simple model suggests.

First, it seems unlikely that the prediction of completed family size for specific individual couples based on their desires and expectations at an early point in marriage will be very successful. The remarkable 20-year longitudinal

expected and ideal family size. The Detroit Area Study has periodically collected data on family size and ideals for the Detroit Metropolitan Area. See Freedman, Ronald; and Sharp, Harry: "Correlates of Values About Ideal Family Size in the Detroit Metropolitan Area." *Population Studies*, July 1954, Vol. 8, No. 1, pp. 35–45; Freedman, Ronald; Goldberg, David; and Sharp, Harry: "Ideals About Family Size in the Detroit Metropolitan Area." Milbank Memorial Fund *Quarterly*, 1954, Vol. 33, No. 2, pp. 187–197. Goldberg, David: "The Fertility of Two Generation Urbanites." *Population Studies*, Vol. XII, No. 3, March 1959.

study by Kelly and others[12] produced a rather low correlation for individuals between their desires just before marriage and their actual performance after 20 years. It may be, as the Princeton Study assumes, that greater success can be achieved in making predictions for couples who have had some experience in married life and who state their desires at a similar stage in the family life cycle. But difficulty in predicting fertility from individual value statements should not be too surprising. Even if we assume that there exists during a given generation a stable social norm about the right number of children (e.g. two–four) many variations within that range are to be expected. The large complex of forces in varied permutations for individual couples during the long childbearing period certainly will lead many couples to revise their expectations and desires upward or downward within the acceptable range. In a stable social situation we might expect such changes to balance each other in their effects on the total distribution of family size. This supposes a range of acceptable variation for each cultural epoch so that only minor sanctions are attached to variations within the range but significant sanctions do operate outside the range. For example, in the contemporary American situation this would mean that two, three, or four are all acceptable numbers of children and are not socially defined as very different, but being childless or with an only child or having a large family does carry negative consequences. A recent study by Goldberg and others[13] in Detroit indicates that in the recent economic recession a significant number of couples did change their expectations as to a family size up or down but the net change for all the couples was almost zero. Even in the 20-year Kelly Study the final average number of children closely approximated the average desires 20 years earlier.

While predictions for the distributions of cohorts or other groups probably will be more successful than predictions for individuals, it is unlikely that social norms will be so stable as to be unaffected by social and economic changes occurring in the several decades of reproductive life. How much change there is and under what circumstances are important topics for further research. The Princeton Study will shortly give us better information on the short-run stability of desires for a particular parity. The new GAF Study will test the utility of the expectation data for the entire childbearing population over a five year period. Neither can give definitive assessments of the utility of the attitudinal data. What is needed is a time series on an annual basis for the national population of expected and desired number of children. Such a series along with data on actual fertility can then be related to a variety of other series on other basic social and economic data as well as to unique historical events as they occur. Such time series will have maximum value if there are simultaneous intensive

[12] Westoff, Charles F.; Mishler, Elliot G.; and Kelly, E. Lowell: "Preferences in Size of Family and Eventual Fertility Twenty Years After." *American Journal of Sociology*, Vol. LXII, No. 5, March 1957, pp. 491–497. Westoff, Charles F.; Sagi, Philip; and Kelly, E. Lowell: "Fertility Through Twenty Years of Marriage: A Study in Predictive Possibilities." *American Sociological Review*, Vol. 23, October 1958, pp. 549–556.

[13] Goldberg, David; Sharp, Harry; and Freedman, Ronald: "The Stability and Reliability of Expected Family Size Data." Milbank Memorial Fund *Quarterly*, October 1959, Vol. 37, No. 4, pp. 369–385.

longitudinal studies to establish how net changes are produced by a balance of different kinds of individual changes. It is quite likely that we shall have to learn how to adjust or discount data on expectations or desires on the basis of what we can learn from such time series analyses as well as data on fecundity impairments and contraceptive effectiveness. In the longitudinal study of Kelly's data social and psychological factors were more accurate than the couple's stated desires in predicting individual fertility. The social scientist eventually may be able to predict a couple's fertility better than the couple can, but it is likely that the attitudes and values of the couple and the groups to which it belongs will enter the calculation.

THE USE OF CONTRACEPTION

The Princeton and GAF Studies have demonstrated that contraception is used almost universally by fecund couples in the United States to make their desires for a moderate size family a reality. Building on the Indianapolis Study these new studies give us the most comprehensive description ever available of a nation's family planning activity. This information will be relevant for many research and policy questions.

While the practice of contraception at some stages of the reproductive process is virtually universal, it is very far from a rational model of the effective use of modern contraceptives to carefully plan and space all births. The Indianapolis Study and both the recent major studies show that a rather large proportion of all pregnancies are "accidents" or otherwise unplanned. Among the large number of couples who do not begin to use contraception before their first conception, a significant number do not want their first pregnancy as soon as possible. Many use methods they consider unreliable. Far from being rational planners many do not seriously think about contraception until the pressure of a growing family brings the problem to their attention. There are even significant sectors at the bottom of the social structure in which a majority of the families can be described as very ineffective in family planning. Lee Rainwater's interesting exploratory study[14] of lower working class families has documented this very dramatically. The evidence about communication and consensus between husbands and wives also does not strongly support the image of the American family as a highly rational, effective, joint planning unit.

Despite the fact that the rational model does not fit well, the patterns of family planning followed are successful in enabling most couples to have the number of children they want. The contraceptive practice—imperfect though it may be for individuals—is successful for the society in reducing fertility far below its physiological potential. This confirms what we already know from English data: average family size can be reduced to very low levels in a large modern society with far less than the most rational use of the modern contraceptive methods.

[14] Rainwater, Lee: *And the Poor Get Children* (Chicago: Quadrangles Books, 1960).

FACTORS EXPLAINING VARIATIONS IN FERTILITY AND FAMILY PLANNING

While the great majority of Americans are having small or moderate size families, there remains a considerable variability within and around the range of consensus even after we have taken into account the families that are smaller or larger than desired. A central objective in American studies has been to explain this variation or at least to find its correlates. Overall, we have not been conspicuously successful—as Dr. Kiser has indicated. Only a small amount of the variance was explained in the Indianapolis Study and most of the explanation finally achieved was attributable to socio-economic status. Despite heroic efforts, the Princeton Study has not yet been able to account for the major part of the variance, although it may come closer to this objective when the data from its follow-up interviews are analyzed.

Socio-Economic Status. In the postwar studies, unlike the Indianapolis Study, correlations with socio-economic status measures are non-existent or very modest. In fact, all of the traditional differentials with respect to education, occupation, income, and rural-urban origin are destined to disappear or to contract sharply, if current desires and expectations are realized in action. The contraction of these differentials is somewhat less pronounced in the GAF Study than in the Princeton Study, because the representation of a wider range of parities and backgrounds permits the less effective fertility control of the lower status and rural sectors to widen the differentials somewhat. In the GAF Study education appears to be more important than income, occupation, or rural background. It accounts for most of the correlation between these other variables and family planning, for example. This may be an important clue to what is fundamental in the complex we call socio-economic status.

The apparent contraction of the traditional differentials is certainly a development of major importance. This is a major finding, even if it doesn't help to explain the variation remaining. While we do not have any definitive explanation for the contraction of status or rural-urban differentials there are several plausible theories:

(1) Contraceptive practice has spread through all strata of the population, thus diminishing the role of differential contraceptive practice as a basis for differential fertility. Our evidence here is mainly the present widespread use of contraception in all major population strata. The existence of greater contraceptive differentials at an earlier period is mainly an inference from the fertility patterns.

(2) There is evidence that the higher fertility of the lower status groups in the past may have been largely a function of their recent rural origin. Goldberg found this to be the case for women of completed fertility in Detroit. In the Detroit data as well as in a reanalysis of Indianapolis data [15] he found that the

---

[15] Goldberg, David: "The Fertility of Two Generation Urbanites." *Population Studies*, Vol. 12, No. 3, March 1959, pp. 214–222; and "Another Look at the Indianapolis Fertility Data." The Milbank Memorial Fund *Quarterly*, Vol. 28, No. 1, January 1960, pp. 23–36.

traditional inverse relation of status and fertility was most characteristic of the couples with a farm background and least characteristic of the couples with an urban background. Eliminating the effect of both ineffective fertility planning and farm background produced a significant—if modest—positive correlation between fertility and measures of economic status. Few Americans in the younger generation will have been reared on farms, so this rural basis for fertility differentials will cease to be important.

(3) More speculative is the theory that the change is related to the fact that class differences are becoming blurred in the United States as the working class takes on many middle class characteristics.[16] Without time for development, I only can suggest here the idea that the functions of children and of the family are becoming more similar in different major social strata. If this is true, then it is reasonable to expect a contraction of fertility differentials, since family size in the various strata should depend on the functions in those strata of children and of the family in relation to other institutions.

The Economic Factor. The specifically economic status measures deserve special attention. It has seemed plausible to many scholars that the couple's economic position should be positively rather than negatively correlated with fertility once effective contraception is widespread in all economic strata. The argument has been stated in various ways but in essence it involves the following assumptions: (1) that under conditions of a specialized urban society children play similar roles in the families at various economic levels. In particular, children cease to have a differential economic value either as laborers in family enterprises or as safeguards for old age security; (2) under these conditions children become only consumer goods; they yield direct emotional satisfactions to their parents which must compete with satisfactions derived from other consumer goods; (3) since children are expensive, couples of higher economic status can afford more children and are under less pressure to choose between children and other consumer durables. Better economic status should also permit the parents to overcome more easily some of the negative aspects of childrearing by paying for more household help. This line of argument leads to the conclusion that economic status should be positively correlated with fertility once the disturbing effects of differential contraceptive practice and of anachronistic farm backgrounds are eliminated from the social situation.

There is another possibility suggested by Becker.[17] Higher economic status may also lead to "better quality" children rather than to a larger number of children. The parents may invest more in each child rather than having a larger number. In the purchase of automobiles economic status is more closely correlated with the price of the car purchased than with the number. A similar situation may exist with respect to children.

[16] Mayer, Kurt: "Fertility Changes and Population Forecasts in the United States." *Social Research*, Vol. 26, No. 3, Autumn 1959, pp. 347–366.

[17] Becker, Gary: "An Economic Analysis of Fertility," a paper in *Demographic and Economic Change in Developed Countries*, A conference of the Universities–National Bureau Committee for Economic Research (Princeton: Princeton University Press, 1960), pp. 209–231.

The empirical evidence relevant to the economic variable is rather contradictory. The Indianapolis Study did find a small positive correlation between economic status and fertility for completely planned families, and this correlation was increased when the influence of rural background was eliminated. A series of studies—the latest by Kirk—have found that period fertility rates are strongly correlated to variations of the business cycle from secular trends. These variations in fertility are mainly a result of variations in the marriage rate and of the lower order births. But such variation may simply result from changes in the timing of vital events without any necessary effect on completed fertility or long-run fertility trends. Kirk points out that the secular trend of fertility bears no significant relation to the secular trend of business conditions.

In an interesting, unpublished, and still preliminary analysis, Arthur Campbell of the Scripps Foundation constructs a weighted economic index for the whole childbearing period of each of a series of completed cohorts. He finds no consistent relation between the economic index and the completed fertility for the cohort.

Neither the Princeton Study nor GAF has found any consistent significant relation between various measures of economic status or attitudes and fertility or fertility planning. However, in both studies more refined analyses are still in process.

The finding of no correlation in the recent studies instead of the expected positive correlation may indicate simply that we have been passing through a necessary transition from the former negative correlation to a future positive correlation. It may also be that the postwar cohorts need to proceed farther into the childbearing period before differences positively associated with economic status will appear. Since most people are having at least two children now differences are more likely to develop only after all strata have passed together through the early parities and the real differentials will develop only in the later half of the childbearing period.

It is also possible, however, that there really is no significant positive relationship. While children may be consumer's goods, whether higher income will lead to consuming more of them depends on the elasticity of demand for them. A case can be made for the theory that this demand, like that for salt, is rather inelastic. Under present conditions, everybody must have at least a few children but nobody wants very many.

Wife's Labor Force Participation. One characteristic that continues to be associated with differential fertility is the wife's status as a worker. Official statistics have documented lower fertility for working wives for some time. In the Indianapolis Study the wife's work history was one of the very few variables fairly strongly correlated with planning status and fertility even when socioeconomic status was controlled. In the GAF Study both fertility to date and total expected fertility decrease with the increasing length of the wife's work experience and this relationship persists when fecundity and a variety of socioeconomic factors are controlled.[18] The GAF Study shows that part—but only

[18] Ridley, Jeanne Clare: "Number of Children Expected in Relation to Non-Familial Activities of the Wife." Milbank Memorial Fund *Quarterly*, July 1959, Vol. 37, No. 3, pp. 277–296.

part—of the relationship is a function of fecundity impairments. Many wives work because fecundity impairments prevent them from having many children, thus creating an opportunity for work. It is also true, however, that even when only the fecund wives are considered, a long work history for the wife is associated with lower fertility and more effective fertility planning. These results are supported in general by the Princeton Study findings, although the authors attach less importance to them than I would.

These findings are important for several reasons: (1) the proportion of working wives is increasing steadily in the United States despite the baby boom; (2) the wife's work experience is an excellent index—but only one—of the extent to which this central family figure is seriously affected by the competing influences of non-familial institutions and activities. It seems plausible that such extra-familial activity will change the division of labor within the family and between the family and other institutions. These changes in turn are likely to have an impact on the functions of children in the family. In an analysis of the Indianapolis data Pratt and Whelpton[19] found that not only the wife's work history but also a crude measure of other extra-familial involvements was associated with better family planning and lower fertility—even after allowance for the effect of socio-economic status. This probably is an especially promising area for further research. We must know more about the conditions under which wives work or engage in other extra-familial activities and how these activities affect the organization of family life and family growth.

Religious Differentials. One of the striking findings of the postwar American studies is the persistent importance of religious differentials, and in particular the higher fertility and the lesser use of appliance contraceptives by Catholics. The distinctive Catholic pattern apparently is not a result of low social or educational status or of recent urbanization. In fact it is most distinctive among the well educated urban group.

These findings are striking, because most American demographers have until recently assumed, I think, that religious differentials represented a cultural lag which would disappear with increasing education and urbanization. This was part of the erroneous view of urban life mentioned earlier—a view that urbanism would eventually and inevitably secularize all relationships and destroy the power of such traditional institutions as the Church. This view is contradicted not only by the fertility data but also by evidence on the persistence of Catholic-Protestant differences in the United States in a variety of other behavioral areas.[20] European sociologists and demographers who are more accustomed to the "persistence of ethnic and religious differentials for generations under presumably secularizing urban conditions might have been less inclined than Americans to discount prematurely the influence of religious institutions. While

[19] Pratt, Lois, and Whelpton, P. K.: "Attitudes Toward Restriction of Personal Freedom in Relation to Fertility Planning and Fertility." Milbank Memorial Fund *Quarterly*, Vol. 33, No. 1, January 1955, pp. 63–111.
[20] Extensively documented in Lenski, Gerhard: *The Religious Factor* (Garden City, N.Y.: Doubleday, 1961).

these religious differentials are clear and marked we certainly do not yet understand their origin or meaning. In particular we need to know more on a comparative basis as to why Catholic institutions appear to affect reproductive patterns much more in some countries than in others. What is distinctive about Catholic institutions in such countries as the United States and the Netherlands, for example, as compared with other countries? The persistence of religious differences under urbanized conditions is relevant for the doubts that some have expressed that urbanization in underdeveloped areas necessarily will have only secularizing effects.

Social-Psychological Factors. The search for social-psychological and strictly psychological factors to explain variations in current fertility has not yet been successful. In retrospect, the failure of the strictly psychological variables in the Indianapolis Study to predict fertility was ascribed by critics as well as by the authors themselves to poor conceptualization or poor measurement. The Princeton Study has not yet been much more successful in this area although the authors worked with newer psychological measurements and with commandably thorough pretests and analyses.

On a more social psychological level and as a central concern, the Princeton Study has investigated very thoroughly the hypothesis that social mobility is associated with more effective family planning and lower fertility. The already reported finding of essentially no relationship has been supported in at least three other studies,[21] and there is even some evidence for the United States of a modest positive correlation of mobility with fertility rather than the hypothesized negative relationship.

In retrospect—and it is easy to second guess—I suggest that the original hypothesis of a negative correlation is linked to the erroneous view of urban society mentioned earlier. It assumes that the mobile family is one of many individualistic units which rationally restrict family commitments and costs in order to compete successfully in an impersonal and highly individualistic market. Such a model may be applicable to the transitional stage when an urban society is developing indigenous institutions and drawing large masses of immigrants from rural areas. In this situation large numbers of people are unaccustomed to urban institutions and without established precedents or rules to guide their careers. But in the contemporary American scene large numbers have been socialized as indigenous urbanites to expect social change. Change and mobility are an established part of the social structure. The large bureaucratic enterprises in which more and more people work institutionalize mobility. People learn to expect and plan for change within reasonable limits as part of the routine of life. As Boggs has suggested in interpreting his interesting study,

[21] Yellin, Seymour: "Social Mobility and Familism," Ph.D. dissertation in Sociology, Northwestern University, 1955; Brooks, Hugh E., and Henry, Franklin J.: "An Empirical Study of the Relationships of Catholic Practice and Occupational Mobility to Fertility," Milbank Memorial Fund *Quarterly*, July 1958, Vol. 36, No. 3, pp. 222–281; Boggs, Stephen T.: "Family Size and Social Mobility in a California Suburb," *Eugenics Quarterly*, December 1957, Vol. 4, No. 4, pp. 208–213.

the young urban American husband is accustomed to change and expects to be able to make the adjustment it requires while his family is growing.

As I have suggested elsewhere,[22] it is precisely in such a highly mobile and specialized urban society that the nuclear family has the unique function of serving the individual as the only continuing primary group which he can carry with him in his travels in space and society and which selects and integrates for him the specialized stimuli and services of a complex society. It may be a positive functional necessity rather than a negative cost in a society of institutionalized mobility.

EXPLAINING VARIATIONS IN THE SOCIAL NORMS ABOUT REPRODUCTION

In my opinion the most significant problem for fertility research in the United States now may be why the social norm is for two to four children rather than why particular individuals prefer one instead of another number within this generally acceptable range. A similar question is why a social norm condemning contraception has been transformed to one of approval and the practice of contraception almost as a matter of course.

It appears likely that the difficulty we are having in predicting variations among individual couples in fertility may result partly from the fact that most of the variation is in a narrow range within which the significance of the differentials is not great. In any case, providing that the whole distribution is reasonably stable, which particular individuals have a somewhat larger and which a somewhat smaller number of children may be interesting but not really important for many demographic and social problems. The more significant social problem may be what changes the nature of the distribution rather than why some people are at one point rather than another on the distribution.

Such questions probably can only be answered by more general comparative and historical studies.[23] Neither American nor other demographers really have given much serious systematic study to these problems, although the quantitative data for comparative and historical studies are probably better in demography than in most other social science fields. For the United States we do have business cycle studies mentioned already. The work in cohort analysis is providing us with excellent data about the range of some of the dependent variables but we have little systematic analyses of the factors affecting the cohort variations.

For the historical and comparative questions I am raising, a single major cross-section survey may only provide some of the descriptive parameters for a single case in the analysis—a society or a stratum at a particular period in history. The independent variables may be derived from the survey but they may have to be characteristics of the society or the stratum rather than of an individual. A series of such studies in different times and places supplemented by the

[22] Social Values About Family Size in the United States," *International Population Conference* (Vienna: 1959), pp. 173–183.

[23] Mayer, Kurt: *op. cit.* also makes a case for the importance of historical and comparative analyses.

mounting volume of comparable international demographic statistics will be necessary to provide data for comparative analysis. This is not to denigrate the value of the individual surveys. They help us to understand a particular time and place. Probably, they are indispensable as the units in a larger sample of studies, but they are not the only source of significant data.

Certainly factors related to individual variations in a cross-section sample may also be the causes of major historical changes. But this may not necessarily be the case. We very well may find that factors which are related to differences in fertility and family planning as between societies do not explain differences within the society. This may be true for income variations, for example. We still need to learn how cross-section data can best be related to historical series.

The long-run secular decline in fertility in the West and the development of family planning usually is explained as a consequence of basic changes in the functions of the family and of children in relation to new institutions and principles of social organization. This seems to me to be an eminently reasonable frame of reference if not scientifically demonstrable. I see the broad task of comparative demography as seeking the variations in the functions of the family and of children which can explain the variations in social norms and practices about family planning and fertility. I doubt that we can ever really understand the current American demographic situation except in the perspective of such a comparative and historical approach. Without the comparative frame of reference we are trying to accomplish the impossible task of generalizing from the unique case.

Differential Mortality

HAROLD F. DORN

... Just as the levels of mortality vary from one nation to another, or vary over time for a given nation, so also do they vary widely among different population groups within a nation. Part of this variation is related to the biological characteristics of a population, namely, age, sex, and ethnic or racial origin; the remainder is related to social and environmental factors like marital status, occupation, social class, size of community, and place of residence. In practice, it is not possible to disentangle the effect of biological from social and environmental factors since the mortality rates at a given moment for a specific population result from the composite effect of these two groups of factors.

... Perhaps the most universal mortality differential with respect to both time and place is that by sex. The first national mortality table computed by Wargentin for Sweden from deaths during the period 1755–63 showed a higher average death rate for men than for women. In England and Wales a corresponding sex differential has existed since the first national mortality rates were computed for the period 1841–45.

In some population groups where the general mortality level is high, the death rates during late adolescence and early adult life have been higher for females than for males owing in large part to excess mortality from tuberculosis and childbearing. As the general level of mortality has decreased, the higher mortality rates for females have dropped more rapidly; today in most countries having relatively low mortality rates those for males are greater than the rates for females throughout the entire span of life.

The sex differential in mortality has slowly widened as death rates have dropped. The life table for the original registration states of the United States for 1900–1902 showed an expectation of life at birth of 48.2 years for white males and 51.1 years for white females. By 1953 the difference had widened to 6.1 years, the figures being 66.8 and 72.9 years, respectively. Undoubtedly, part of the higher mortality among men arises from their greater exposure to occupational and industrial hazards and from differences in manner of living between males and females. The available evidence suggests, though, that much of the sex difference is biological in origin. It has been observed among deaths *in utero* and continues throughout the remainder of the life span with minor exceptions.

The evidence for a biological basis for racial or ethnic differentials is less convincing. In general, the death rate for the white population is the lowest, that for the yellow population is intermediate, and that for the black population is the highest. But this relative standing appears to reflect social, economic, and environmental rather than biological differences. The decline of the mortality rate in Japan to a level comparable to that of western Europe and North America rather clearly demonstrates the absence of any general racial biological traits affecting mortality. It is true that there is some evidence for differences in racial susceptibility to specific diseases, but the extent to which these differences have their origin in biological traits, in contrast to environmental conditions, remains undetermined.

Additional evidence that observed racial differences in mortality reflect social and environmental rather than biological factors is provided by the experience of Negroes in the United States. In 1953, although the expectation of life at birth was definitely lower for non-whites than for whites, it had risen to 59.7 years for non-white males and to 64.4 years for non-white females. Only crude estimates of the level of mortality exist for the Negro population of Africa, but it seems unlikely that the expectation of life at birth is much above that of western Europe during the Middle Ages, or about thirty to thirty-five years. Yet the Negroes of North America and of Africa are of the same racial origin.

Of the social and environmental factors related to mortality, the most is known about geographic and rural-urban differentials. Within all countries marked variations in death rates are found from one region to another. In the United States during 1950, after adjusting for differences in the age composition of the population, a relative difference of about 40 per cent existed between the highest and lowest rates for the forty-eight states. Corresponding geographic variation is found in European countries (United Nations, Population Division, Department of Social Affairs, 1953).

The magnitude of geographic differentials in death rates has decreased as the level of mortality has fallen. The differentials undoubtedly arise from variation in the degree of urbanism, in economic status, in the availability and utilization of medical and health services and facilities, and other social factors. Few studies attempting to account for observed geographic differentials have been made. More than a century ago William Farr proposed that the healthiest districts be identified and used as a measuring rod for improving health conditions in other areas, but this idea has not been extensively followed up.

It is not surprising that the early writers on mortality devoted considerable attention to urban-rural differentials. The filthy and unsanitary condition of most cities makes them fertile breeding grounds for infectious and communicable diseases. Until about 1800, burials were more frequent than christenings during most years; therefore the population of large cities was maintained only by migration from rural areas. At least one-sixth of the population of London is estimated to have perished during the last great epidemic of plague during 1664–65 (Buer, 1926). As late as 1750 the death rate in London is thought to have been between 40 and 50 per 1,000 population.

When discussing urban-rural differentials in mortality, one must differentiate between the contrast among countries and that within a single country. Agricultural populations usually have a shorter average length of life than the populations of highly industrialized nations, but within a given country the rural population historically has experienced lower death rates than the urban population. Advances in medicine, public health, and sanitation combined with the concentration of hospital and medical facilities in cities have resulted in a remarkable improvement in the health of urban populations; today the rural-urban differential in mortality that has been so marked in the past has sharply diminished and in some instances has disappeared.

A thorough analysis of this problem has never been made in the United States. Because of the failure to allocate deaths to place of residence and because of differences in the definition of urban population used in the compilation of population and vital statistics, mortality statistics prior to 1940 are unsatisfactory for the analysis of the variation in death rates by size of community. At the present time, lack of information concerning the amount of misclassification of place of residence in mortality statistics makes uncertain the interpretation of observed differences between urban and rural areas.

A young man's choice of an occupation is perhaps the most important decision affecting his future length of life. The work a man does, the conditions under which this work is done, and the wages received largely determine where he lives, the food he eats, the medical care he receives, and his habits and ways of life. Those who choose a profession or a white-collar job can expect to live longer than those who choose manual labor. Those who become miners or sandstone grinders have a relatively short expectation of future lifetime.

Most of what we know today concerning the relationship of occupation and social class to mortality has come from the decennial studies of occupational mortality in England and Wales, initiated by William Farr in 1851 and continued since then by the General Register Office of England and Wales. Only fragmentary data are available from other countries. Investigations of the special health hazards of specific occupations have been conducted in countries with large industrial populations, but these fall outside the scope of this discussion.

In England and Wales, mortality rates in general are lowest for the professional classes and highest for unskilled laborers. The same general rank order has been found in other countries with comparable statistics. There is some evidence of a narrowing of social class differentials in mortality during recent years (Logan, 1954). Except for occupations with special health hazards, most of the variation in mortality rates by occupational groups probably results from the general living conditions and manner of life of workers in these occupations rather than from the direct effects of the occupations themselves (Stocks, 1938). To test this hypothesis, the Registrar General of England and Wales (1938) compared the social class differentials in mortality of wives with that of their husbands by assigning each married woman the social class of her husband. Not only did wives show the same gradient in mortality by social class as their husbands, but, in addition, the range in death rates was greater for women than for men. Corresponding data are not available for other countries, but there is no reason to doubt the applicability of these findings to the populations of most of the countries of Europe and North America.

Married persons generally have lower age-specific death rates than unmarried. The differentials usually are larger for men than for women. In population groups with a relatively high maternal mortality rate the death rate of young married women sometimes is higher than that of single women. The differentials by marital status undoubtedly arise in part from a selection of healthy persons for marriage and in part from differences in the habits and living conditions of the married and unmarried.

ECOLOGY

Internal Migration and Residential Mobility

DONALD J. BOGUE

HOW INTERNALLY MOBILE IS THE POPULATION OF THE UNITED STATES?

Few, if any, populations in the world are so mobile, on a routine basis, as the residents of the United States. During the course of a single year, between 19 and 22 per cent of the nation's inhabitants move from one house or apartment to another, and about 5 to 7 per cent of them move from one county to another in the process of changing their residence. Not more than 2 or 3 per cent of the adult population has spent its entire life in one house or apartment, and perhaps not more than 10 to 15 per cent live their entire lives within the same county. The present chapter undertakes to show that this residential flux is not simply a whimsical or aimless wandering, but that it has a definite pattern and is intimately related to the structuring of the population and to social change and adjustment. Because of the fundamental role it plays in population change and redistribution, residential mobility is a topic worthy of widespread study.

Migration is a tradition in the United States. Beginning on the Atlantic seaboard, the colonists settled the land by a process of westward migration that lasted for more than three centuries. Throughout our entire national history, as a part of the growing-up process, young men and women have asked themselves seriously whether or not they could better their fortunes by moving to some other place and by "striking out on their own" among strangers—often with no personal resources except ambition and courage. The legend of great statesmen, scholars, and businessmen beginning their careers by coming to a big city almost penniless has been reenacted by American youngsters many millions of times, all over the country. The fact that such a large share of the population are children of immigrants may also be connected with this propensity to be "on the move."

Population students divide all residential mobility into two parts: (a) *local moving*, or the changing of residence from one part of a community to another, and (b) *migration*, or the changing of residence from one community to another. For the sake of greater ease in collecting statistics concerning mobility, it has become customary to define as a migrant any person who changes his residence from one county to another, and as a local mover any person who changes residence within the same county. Both of these types of residential mobility are significant and worthy of attention. Migration usually involves the complete severance of a person's economic and social ties with the community he leaves, and requires that he adjust to a new job, a new set of community institutions, and a new group of people. Also, migration can change the size or the composition of a particular population rather quickly. Such changes can result from a mass exodus of people, a mass invasion of people, or a large-scale selective interchange of people with other areas. For these reasons and for other reasons elaborated below, migration tends to receive more popular, as well as more scientific, attention than local moving. Nevertheless, local moving can change the internal distribution of population within a community, and can cause particular neighborhoods to undergo rather dramatic changes within a comparatively short time. For this reason, local moving is coming to the fore as a subject considered worthy of more intensive research.

Table 1 reports the mobility status of the civilian population from 1935 to 1958, as measured by censuses and special surveys. By comparing the place of residence at the time of enumeration with the place of residence at some specified

TABLE 1. MOBILITY STATUS OF THE CIVILIAN POPULATION FROM 1935 TO 1958 (CIVILIAN POPULATION INCLUDES MEMBERS OF THE ARMED FORCES LIVING OFF POST AND WITH THEIR FAMILIES ON POST)

| | | Per Cent of the Population Alive at Beginning of Interval | | | | Per Cent Migrants Are of All Mobile Population |
| | Length of Migration Interval (*years*) | Non-mobile | | Mobile | | |
Migration Interval			Total[a]	Local Movers	Migrants[a]	
April, 1935 to April, 1940[b]	5	62.0[c]	38.0[c]	24.6[c]	13.4	35[c]
April, 1940 to April, 1947	7	42.5	57.5	36.2	21.3	37
April, 1947 to April, 1948	1	79.8	20.2	13.6	6.7	33
April, 1948 to April, 1949	1	80.8	19.1	13.0	6.1	32
March, 1949 to March, 1950	1	80.9	19.0	13.1	5.9	31
April, 1950 to April, 1951	1	78.8	21.2	13.9	7.3	34
April, 1951 to April, 1952	1	79.7	20.2	13.2	7.0	35
April, 1952 to April, 1953	1	79.4	20.6	13.5	7.1	34
April, 1953 to April, 1954	1	80.7	19.2	12.2	7.0	36
April, 1954 to April, 1955	1	79.6	20.5	13.3	7.2	35
March, 1955 to March, 1956	1	79.0	21.0	13.7	7.3	36
April, 1956 to April, 1957	1	80.1	19.4	13.1	6.2	32
March, 1957 to March, 1958	1	79.7	49.8	13.1	6.7	30

[a] Includes persons abroad at the beginning of the migration interval who entered the continental United States during the interval.

[b] Includes military population.

[c] Estimated from ratio of migrants to total population for later years. Migration for 1935–40 included an estimated 1,500,000 persons who moved between a city of 100,000 or more and the balance of the county combining the city. If an adjustment were made to remove these "quasi-county" migrants, it would lower all rates for 1935–40 by about 9 or 10 per cent.

SOURCE: U.S. Bureau of the Census, *Current Population Reports*, Series P-20, Nos. 14, 61, 73, 82, and 86.

earlier date, it is possible to determine what percentage of the population are migrants (living in a different county), what percentage are local movers (living in a different house in the same county), and what share are nonmobile (living in the same house). This table shows that the percentages cited in the second sentence of this chapter have been valid with respect to each year's migration experience between 1947 and 1958. Because the migration interval (the span of time over which movement is measured) varied in length before 1947, the data concerning the period 1935 to 1947 are only roughly comparable with the data for the period 1947 to 1958; during the latter period, annual surveys covered movement which had occurred within the past year. Therefore, it cannot be determined whether the annual rates prevailing from 1947 to 1958 are about the same as the average rate has been for the past 20 or 30 years, or whether they are inflated as a result of postwar adjustment and economic prosperity. Certainly these annual rates from 1947 to 1958 are higher than the estimated average annual rates for the 1935 to 1940 period and the 1940 to 1947 period, which were obtained by dividing the rate for each period by the number of years the period covers (these earlier enumerations were for a longer interval of time, and the fact that they show lower average annual rates is undoubtedly due, at least in part, to circular migration and to problems of response).

The mobility rates for each year are large enough to indicate that, over a period of a very few years, a large proportion of the population changed residence one or more times. This conclusion is confirmed by the data for 1935 to 1940 and for 1940 to 1947. More than one-half of the population changed residence between 1940 and 1947, and during this period more than one-fifth of the population were migrants (changing county as well as residence). This was not a typical period, since it included wartime movements; but the rates which prevailed from April, 1947, to March, 1958, would have made possible a turnover of the total population at twice the extent indicated in Table 1. A very high proportion of the population does change its place of residence in the course of a lifetime, as was demonstrated by a recent census report that "nine out of every ten persons 1 year old and over in the United States in April, 1952, had moved at least once in their lifetime." This same report found that less than 2 per cent of the population 25 years of age and over had always lived in the same house.[1]

The year-to-year fluctuations in the rate of total mobility, the rate of local moving, and the rate of migration, as shown by the eleven-year series of annual rates, have been surprisingly small, even though the largest of these fluctuations are statistically significant. The low rates for the year 1953 to 1954 appear to reflect a decrease in business activity. Local moving (which is sensitive to the volume of residential construction) tends to have greater year-to-year fluctuations than migration has.

To summarize: The frequently-made statement that the population of the United States is a fluid one appears to be justified by the facts. However, it is

[1] Current Population Reports, Series P-20, No. 47, September, 1953.

local moving more than long-distance migration which gives it this character. Although the present rates of residential mobility are not high enough to indicate that every person is moving or migrating every year, they are so high that the annual volume of movement and migration involves many millions of persons. Over a period of only a few years, mobility involves a majority of the population; over a period of a lifetime, it involves almost everybody.

WHICH SEGMENTS OF THE POPULATION ARE MOST MOBILE?

Census surveys taken in recent years have provided data about the total residential mobility of the population, classified according to several characteristics.[2]

Sex Differences. During almost every interval between 1940 and 1958, men appear to have been more mobile with respect to residence than women, but the difference in rates between the sexes is very small (Table 2). This difference has consisted largely of a tendency for males to be slightly more migratory than females. There is very little evidence that either sex, at the local level, has been a great deal more mobile than the other. During the period 1935 to 1958 the migration rates for males have been about 3 per cent higher than for females, whereas over the period 1940 to 1958 the rates of local movement for the sexes were almost identical. The year-to-year fluctuations in mobility rates tended to affect each sex in the same way and by about the same amount.

Color Differences. Total residential mobility for the nonwhite population has been somewhat higher than for the white population, during ten of the eleven mobility periods between 1940 and 1958 for which mobility data were collected by color. This difference is an average of two different patterns, however. The nonwhite population, on the average, was about 3 or 4 percentage points more mobile locally (within the same county) than the white population. On the other hand, the white population averaged about 2 percentage points higher with respect to migration than the nonwhite population between 1935 and 1958. This latter difference has not been found by all surveys, however. During the years from 1940 to 1947 the non-white population is reported to have been slightly more migratory than the white, a tendency which was especially marked with respect to interstate, as contrasted with intrastate, migration. World War II seems to have provided an unusually strong stimulus to out-migration on the part of Negroes from the South. To summarize: Under most circumstances, the nonwhite population tends to be less migratory than the white, but to be somewhat more mobile locally than the white population.

Urban-rural Differences. All but one of the surveys taken to date show that the rural-nonfarm population has been residentially more mobile than either the urban or the rural-farm population. (It must be kept in mind that the

---

[2] Several of the characteristics discussed in this section are the subjects of later chapters. [The material referred to is not included—Editor.] They will be discussed here only insofar as they are associated with mobility, and the mobility aspects of these topics are omitted in the later chapters.

TABLE 2. PER CENT OF THE CIVILIAN POPULATION CLASSIFIED AS RESIDENTIALLY MOBILE BY COLOR, SEX, AND TYPE OF MOBILITY: 1940 TO 1958
(CIVILIAN POPULATION INCLUDES MEMBERS OF THE ARMED FORCES LIVING OFF POST AND WITH THEIR FAMILIES ON POST)

Per Cent of Population Alive at the Beginning of the Interval

| Type of Mobility and Mobility Interval | Sex | | | Color | | | | | |
| | | | | White | | | Nonwhite | | |
	Both Sexes	Male	Female	Both Sexes	Male	Female	Both Sexes	Male	Female
All Residential Mobility									
April, 1940 to April, 1947	57.0	57.3	56.7	56.8	–	–	58.7	–	–
April, 1947 to April, 1948[a]	19.9	20.1	19.7	–	–	–	–	–	–
April, 1948 to April, 1949	18.8	18.9	18.6	18.9	18.9	18.8	18.3	19.1	17.6
March, 1949 to March, 1950	18.7	19.0	18.5	18.6	18.8	18.4	19.9	20.3	19.5
April, 1950 to April, 1951	21.0	21.3	20.7	20.9	21.2	20.6	21.7	22.3	21.2
April, 1951 to April, 1952	19.8	20.0	19.7	19.8	19.8	19.7	20.5	21.3	19.8
April, 1952 to April, 1953	20.1	20.1	20.1	19.1	19.2	18.9	27.9	27.4	28.3
April, 1953 to April, 1954	18.6	18.8	18.5	18.3	18.6	18.2	20.8	21.1	20.6
April, 1954 to April, 1955	19.9	20.1	19.6	19.5	19.8	19.3	22.4	22.8	22.0
March, 1955 to March, 1956	20.5	20.6	20.4	20.0	20.1	19.9	24.8	25.0	24.6
April, 1956 to April, 1957	19.4	19.6	19.1	19.0	19.2	18.9	22.2	23.1	21.4
March, 1957 to March, 1958	19.8	20.3	19.4	19.2	19.7	18.7	25.1	25.2	24.9
Local Movers									
April, 1940 to April, 1947	36.2	36.6	35.9	36.1	–	–	36.9	–	–
April, 1947 to April, 1948[a]	13.6	13.6	13.5	–	–	–	–	–	–
April, 1948 to April, 1949	13.0	12.9	13.1	13.0	12.8	13.1	13.6	13.9	13.3
March, 1949 to March, 1950	13.1	13.1	13.1	12.9	12.9	12.9	15.2	15.4	15.1
April, 1950 to April, 1951	13.2	14.1	13.8	13.7	13.9	13.5	16.1	16.3	16.0
April, 1951 to April, 1952	13.2	13.2	13.2	13.0	12.9	13.0	15.5	16.2	14.8
April, 1952 to April, 1953	13.5	13.5	13.6	12.4	12.4	12.4	21.7	21.2	22.2
April, 1953 to April, 1954	12.2	12.3	12.1	11.8	11.9	11.7	16.0	16.3	15.8
April, 1954 to April, 1955	13.3	13.4	13.2	12.7	12.9	12.6	18.0	18.2	17.8
March, 1955 to March, 1956	13.7	13.6	13.9	13.0	12.9	13.1	19.9	19.9	19.9
April, 1956 to April, 1957	13.1	13.3	13.0	12.5	12.7	12.4	17.8	18.3	17.4
March, 1957 to March, 1958	13.1	13.3	13.0	12.3	12.5	12.1	19.8	19.3	20.2
Migrants[b]									
April, 1935 to April, 1940[c]	13.1	13.3	12.9	13.5	–	–	9.5	–	–
April, 1940 to April, 1947	20.8	20.7	20.8	20.7	–	–	21.8	–	–
April, 1947 to April, 1948[a]	6.4	6.5	6.2	–	–	–	–	–	–
April, 1948 to April, 1949	5.8	6.0	5.5	5.9	6.1	5.7	4.7	5.2	4.3
March, 1949 to March, 1950	5.6	5.9	5.4	5.7	5.9	5.5	4.7	4.9	4.4
April, 1950 to April, 1951	7.1	7.2	6.9	7.2	7.3	7.1	5.6	6.0	5.2
April, 1951 to April, 1952	6.6	6.8	6.5	6.8	7.0	6.6	5.1	5.1	5.0
April, 1952 to April, 1953	6.6	6.7	6.5	6.7	6.8	6.6	6.2	6.2	6.1
April, 1953 to April, 1954	6.4	6.5	6.3	6.6	6.7	6.5	4.8	4.8	4.8
April, 1954 to April, 1955	6.6	6.7	6.4	6.8	7.0	6.7	4.4	4.6	4.2
March, 1955 to March, 1956	6.8	7.0	6.5	7.0	7.2	6.8	4.9	5.1	4.7
April, 1956 to April, 1957	6.2	6.3	6.2	6.5	6.5	6.4	4.4	4.8	4.0
March, 1957 to March, 1958	6.7	7.0	6.4	6.9	7.2	6.6	5.3	5.9	4.7

[a] Data by color not available.
[b] Excludes persons abroad at the beginning of the migration interval who entered the continental United States during the interval.
[c] Includes military population.
SOURCE: U.S. Bureau of the Census, *Current Population Reports*, Series P-20, Nos. 14, 36, 49, 61, and 73.

urban-rural classification of Table 3 applies to residence at the end of the migration interval, and that the rates in the table are rates of in-migration, not of out-migration, to urban and rural areas.) This differential seems to reflect the growth of suburbs and the building up of more dense settlements in the vicinity

TABLE 3. PER CENT OF THE CIVILIAN POPULATION CLASSIFIED AS RESIDENTIALLY MOBILE, BY URBAN-RURAL RESIDENCE AT DESTINATION AND TYPE OF MOBILITY: 1940 TO 1958

Type of Mobility and Mobility Interval	Per Cent of Population Alive at Beginning of the Interval			
		Type of Residence at Destination		
	Total	Urban	Rural Non-Farm	Rural Farm
All Residential Mobility				
April, 1940 to April, 1947	57.0	56.4	62.9	52.1
April, 1947 to April, 1948	19.9	18.3	24.0	20.1
April, 1948 to April, 1949	18.8	17.8	22.2	18.2
March, 1949 to March, 1950	18.7	18.5	21.4	16.2
April, 1950 to April, 1951	21.0	21.3	23.7	16.0
April, 1951 to April, 1952	19.8	20.5	19.7	17.0
April, 1952 to April, 1953	20.1	20.7	22.9	13.3
April, 1953 to April, 1954	18.6	18.6	20.9	14.9
April, 1954 to April, 1955	19.9	20.2	22.1	14.5
March, 1955 to March, 1956	20.5	20.5	23.8	14.3
April, 1956 to April, 1957	19.4	19.4	21.7	13.9
March, 1957 to March, 1958	19.8	19.7	22.8	14.4
Local Movers				
April, 1940 to April, 1947	36.2	36.7	37.4	33.3
April, 1947 to April, 1948	13.6	12.7	16.1	13.1
April, 1948 to April, 1949	13.0	12.7	15.3	11.5
March, 1949 to March, 1950	13.1	13.3	13.8	11.6
April, 1950 to April, 1951	13.9	14.7	14.8	9.4
April, 1951 to April, 1952	13.2	14.2	12.0	10.5
April, 1952 to April, 1953	13.5	14.4	14.2	8.4
April, 1953 to April, 1954	12.2	12.5	12.7	10.2
April, 1954 to April, 1955	13.3	13.9	14.0	9.5
March, 1955 to March, 1956	13.7	14.2	14.7	9.7
April, 1956 to April, 1957	13.1	13.7	13.7	9.1
March, 1957 to March, 1958	13.1	13.8	13.7	8.6
Migrants[a]				
April, 1935 to April, 1940[b]	13.1	11.9	18.5	11.3
April, 1940 to April, 1947	20.8	19.7	25.5	18.8
April, 1947 to April, 1948	6.4	5.6	7.9	7.0
April, 1948 to April, 1949	5.8	5.1	6.9	6.7
March, 1949 to March, 1950	5.6	5.2	7.6	4.6
April, 1950 to April, 1951	7.1	6.5	8.9	6.6
April, 1951 to April, 1952	6.6	6.3	7.8	6.5
April, 1952 to April, 1953	6.6	6.3	8.7	5.0
April, 1953 to April, 1954	6.4	6.1	8.3	4.7
April, 1954 to April, 1955	6.6	6.3	8.2	5.0
March, 1955 to March, 1956	6.8	6.3	9.1	4.6
April, 1956 to April, 1957	6.2	5.8	8.0	4.8
March, 1957 to March, 1958	6.7	5.9	9.1	5.8

[a] Excludes persons abroad at the beginning of the migration interval who entered the continental United States during the interval.

[b] Includes military population.

SOURCE: U.S. Bureau of the Census, *Current Population Reports*, Series P-20, Nos. 14, 22, 28, 36, 47, 49, 57, 61, 73, 82, 86, and tabulations of the Bureau of the Census.

of metropolises, rather than a flow of population to open country, villages, or hamlets. As new subdivisions are created in suburban areas, they attract a flow of families from the central city. Such subdivisions tend to be classed as rural-nonfarm rather than urban.

TABLE 4. PER CENT OF THE CIVILIAN POPULATION CLASSIFIED AS RESIDENTIALLY MOBILE, BY AGE, AND TYPE OF MOBILITY: 1940 TO 1958
(CIVILIAN POPULATION INCLUDES MEMBERS OF THE ARMED FORCES LIVING OFF POST AND WITH THEIR FAMILIES ON POST)

Type of Mobility and Mobility Interval	Total all Ages	Per Cent of Population Alive at the Beginning of the Interval								
		Age (years)								
		Under 14	14 to 17	18 and 19	20 to 24	25 to 29	30 to 34	35 to 44	45 to 64	65 and Over
All Residential Mobility										
April, 1940 to April, 1947	57.0	63.2a	53.2	56.3	67.3	74.2		59.8	42.5	38.0
April, 1947 to April, 1948	19.9	20.6	16.0	27.1	34.9	27.4		17.6	12.0	11.5
April, 1948 to April, 1949	18.8	20.1	14.7	26.6	35.0	26.0		16.4	10.9	9.6
March, 1949 to March, 1950	18.7	20.5	16.6	23.3	34.0	25.9		16.5	10.8	9.4
April, 1950 to April, 1951	21.0	23.0	17.6	29.8	37.7	33.6	25.5	18.3	12.4	9.7
April, 1951 to April, 1952	19.8	22.0	16.9	28.5	37.8	31.6	24.2	17.1	11.3	8.9
April, 1952 to April, 1953	20.1	22.7	17.0	28.2	40.5	33.4	23.9	18.2	10.5	8.8
April, 1953 to April, 1954	18.6	20.4	14.9	25.5	38.1	30.5	22.7	15.5	11.3	9.6
April, 1954 to April, 1955	19.9	21.8	16.4	28.9	41.8	31.3	23.6	16.3	12.3	9.8
March, 1955 to March, 1956	21.0	22.8	18.1	29.8	47.6	33.8	25.5	17.7	12.3	10.0
April, 1956 to April, 1957	19.4	21.7	16.4	26.9	41.2	32.0	23.2	16.5	10.8	9.2
March, 1957 to March, 1958	19.8	21.9	15.6	28.7	42.6	34.6	23.2	16.6	11.5	9.7
Local Movers										
April, 1940 to April, 1947	36.2	41.5a	35.5	35.0	39.6	44.6		37.5	28.8	26.1
April, 1947 to April, 1948	13.6	14.1	10.7	18.0	22.3	18.8		11.9	8.7	7.8
April, 1948 to April, 1949	13.0	13.9	10.3	17.2	24.4	17.6		11.6	7.8	6.7
March, 1949 to March, 1950	13.1	14.6	11.5	15.4	22.9	17.4		12.0	7.8	7.2
April, 1950 to April, 1951	13.9	15.0	12.6	18.2	24.1	21.0	16.4	12.9	8.6	7.3
April, 1951 to April, 1952	13.2	14.4	11.5	17.2	24.0	19.9	15.6	11.9	8.3	6.9
April, 1952 to April, 1953	13.5	15.1	12.3	17.0	23.5	22.3	16.1	13.1	7.3	6.6
April, 1953 to April, 1954	12.2	13.7	10.2	15.0	22.3	19.5	14.9	10.4	8.0	6.3
April, 1954 to April, 1955	13.3	14.9	11.2	17.9	26.1	20.2	15.7	11.0	8.7	6.8
March, 1955 to March, 1956	13.7	15.4	12.2	18.7	26.5	21.9	16.0	11.5	8.6	7.2
April, 1956 to April, 1957	13.1	14.9	11.6	16.0	26.2	20.9	15.4	11.5	7.8	6.4
March, 1957 to March, 1958	13.1	14.6	10.6	17.6	26.8	21.7	15.7	11.0	8.0	7.0
Migrantsa										
April, 1935 to April, 1940b	13.1	12.5c	10.5	13.6	18.4	19.0		13.6	9.1	6.9
April, 1940 to April, 1947	20.8	21.7d	17.7	21.3	27.7	29.6		22.3	13.7	11.9
April, 1947 to April, 1948	6.4	6.5	5.3	9.1	12.6	8.6		5.7	3.3	3.7
April, 1948 to April, 1949	5.8	6.2	4.4	9.4	10.6	8.4		4.8	3.1	2.9
March, 1949 to March, 1950	5.6	5.9	5.1	7.9	11.1	8.5		4.5	3.0	2.2
April, 1950 to April, 1951	7.1	8.0	5.0	11.6	13.6	12.5	9.0	5.4	3.8	2.4
April, 1951 to April, 1952	6.6	7.6	5.4	11.3	13.8	11.7	8.6	5.2	3.1	2.0
April, 1952 to April, 1953	6.6	7.6	4.7	11.2	17.0	11.1	7.8	5.2	3.2	2.2
April, 1953 to April, 1954	6.4	6.7	4.7	10.5	15.8	11.0	7.8	5.1	3.3	3.3
April, 1954 to April, 1955	6.6	6.9	5.3	11.0	15.7	11.1	7.9	5.3	3.6	3.0
March, 1955 to March, 1956	7.3	7.4	5.9	11.1	21.1	11.9	9.5	6.2	3.7	2.8
April, 1956 to April, 1957	6.2	6.8	4.8	10.9	15.0	11.0	7.8	5.0	3.1	2.8
March, 1957 to March, 1958	6.7	7.3	5.0	11.1	15.8	12.9	7.5	5.6	3.5	2.7

a Excludes persons abroad at the beginning of the migration interval who entered the continental United States during the interval.
b Includes military population.
c 5 to 13 years.
d 7 to 13 years.
SOURCE: U.S. Bureau of the Census, Current Population Reports, Series P-20, Nos. 14, 22, 28, 36, 39, 47, 49, 61, 73, 82, and 86.

Rates of movement to rural-farm residences and to urban residences were about equal during the 1940's, in terms of both local mobility and migration. This does not necessarily imply that rural-farm and urban populations were making the same *net* gains or losses in population, however. It merely indicates that the people residing in rural-farm homes were tending to change residence about as frequently as those living in urban areas. A high proportion of this rural-farm mobility consists of short-distance moves from one farm to another.

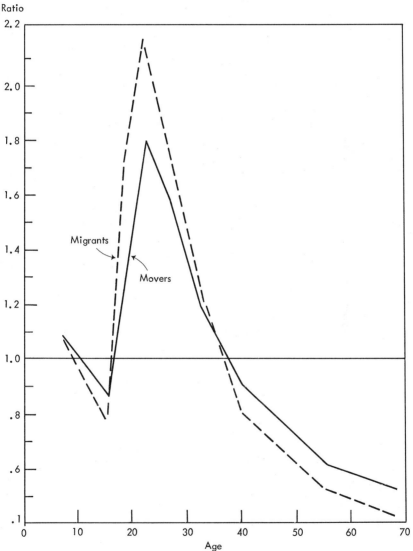

FIGURE 1. Ratio of migration and local mover rates for each age group to the average rate for all ages, United States: 1947 to 1955.

Since 1949, the rural-farm population has tended to be less mobile than it was in the 1940's, and less mobile (both with respect to local moving and migration) than the urban population. As the farm population has continued to shrink, the rural-farm areas have declined in the rate at which they attract migrants.

Age Differences. Persons in their late teens, their twenties, and their early thirties are more mobile than the general population. Persons who are 14 to 17 years old, and those who are 35 years old and over, tend to be less mobile than average. The validity of these statements has been documented frequently. It is not generally recognized, however, that local mobility also has a higher rate among persons at the young adult ages, and that it varies with age according to much the same pattern as migration. Table 4 and Figure 1 show that several of the recent mobility tabulations of the census reveal this same pattern. *Thus, all residential mobility is primarily a phenomenon of late adolescence and early maturity.* The high degree of mobility prevailing among the young adult population is a fundamental aspect of population dynamics. Each year, 35 to 40 per cent of that part of the population which is aged 20 to 24 changes residence, and about 14 to 16 per cent of this change is migratory. By way of contrast, 7 per cent or less of the population aged 65 years and over changes residence within a year, and only about 3 per cent or less become migrants. The higher-than-average mobility of children under 14 years of age is evidently due to the movement, both local and migratory, of their parents. The age pattern of mobility is understandable in view of the fact that 18 years is the median age for graduating from high school and, thus, for either going to college or seeking work, that the median age of marriage falls in the interval 20 to 24, and that the gradual transitions from smaller-to-larger living quarters and from the status of renter to home owner are made by a great many families while the adult members are between the ages of 25 and 35. Most marriages involve a change of residence for two people, and the arrival of a second or third child may require a family comprising four or five persons to change residence. Note that migration is a much larger proportion of all mobility between the ages of 18 and 29 than at other ages.

The two types of mobility do not have identical age patterns, however. The child population and the older adult population tend to exhibit rates of local mobility that are nearer the average for all ages than are the migration rates of these two age groups.

Educational Differences. Information concerning the educational attainment of each mobility group is presented for only two periods, 1935 to 1940 and 1940 to 1947 (Table 5). There is a considerable variation between age groups with respect to the level of educational attainment. Because older people had fewer opportunities in their youth to obtain a secondary education than did the generations following them, the population at the older ages has a lower average attainment than the young adult population. Inasmuch as mobility status varies sharply with age, some control over the age factor should be a part of any examination of mobility differences between educational groups. Such a control may consist of presenting the data separately for each age group. Table 5 shows

TABLE 5. PERCENT OF THE CIVILIAN POPULATION 25 TO 34 YEARS OF AGE CLASSED AS RESIDENTIALLY MOBILE, BY YEARS OF SCHOOL COMPLETED AND TYPE OF MOBILITY: 1940 TO 1947 AND 1935 TO 1940

		Years of School Completed				
		Grade School		High School		
Type of Mobility and Mobility Interval	Total 25 to 34 Years of Age	Not Rptd. and Less than 7 Yrs	7 and 8 Years	1 to 3 Years	4 Years	College 1 Year or More
April, 1940 to April, 1947						
Total mobility	74.2	83.2	72.1	73.1	74.9	77.7
Local movers	44.6	46.0	50.3	46.2	45.2	32.1
Migrants	29.6	27.2	21.8	26.9	29.7	45.6
April, 1935 to April, 1940						
Migrants	19.0	13.8	14.4	17.8	21.3	33.0

SOURCE: U.S. Bureau of the Census, *Current Population Reports*, Series P-20, No. 14, Table 9, and Sixteenth Census, *Social Characteristics of Migrants*, Table 7.

data for the age groups 25 to 34 years of age only. The relationships which are shown to exist through study of the data concerning this group are roughly representative of the relationships which characterize mobility and education for most of the other age groups.

Although the most mobile segment of the population appears to be the portion with above-average educational attainment, no one educational segment is a great deal more mobile than the others on the basis of total mobility. However, the pattern for local moving differs in detail from the pattern associated with migration. The rates for local moving are highest at the center and the lower end of the educational-attainment scale, and lowest at the upper end. The reverse is true for migration; by far the highest rates of migration are those for groups with some college training, and the lowest rates are for those with no more than grade school education. Migration exhibited a similar pattern between 1935 and 1940. Thus, it seems that rates of local moving are much higher among those segments of the population with average or below average educational attainment, whereas rates of migration are higher among those with above-average educational attainment.

Differences in Labor Force Status and Employment Status. Even though the labor force participation pattern is quite different for men and for women, the mobility patterns of both sexes in the various employment statuses are quite similar. Among both men and women, one of the most mobile segments of the population since 1940 has been that part which is unemployed. (See Table 6.) One of the least mobile segments has been that part which is not in the labor force. Both of these differences undoubtedly reflect, at least in part, the unique age composition of that portion of the population which is seeking work, and of that portion which is not in the labor force. The unemployed population, at any given moment, consists in part of young people seeking their first job or

TABLE 6. PER CENT OF THE CIVILIAN POPULATION CLASSIFIED AS RESIDENTIALLY MOBILE, BY SEX AND LABOR FORCE STATUS: 1940 TO 1958
(CIVILIAN POPULATION INCLUDES MEMBERS OF THE ARMED FORCES LIVING OFF POST AND WITH THEIR FAMILIES ON POST)

Type of Mobility and Mobility Interval	Male					Female				
	14 yrs. Old and Over	Labor Force			Not in Labor Force	14 Yrs. Old and Total	Labor Force			Not in Labor Force
		Total	Employed	Unemployed			Total	Employed	Unemployed	
All residential mobility										
April, 1940 to April, 1947	56.5	58.2	57.9	59.9	48.6	55.7	56.7	56.4	65.8	55.3
April, 1947 to April, 1948	20.0	20.7	19.8	29.0	16.9	19.3	20.4	20.0	31.2	18.8
April, 1948 to April, 1949	18.8	19.4	18.7	24.1	16.3	18.1	18.4	17.6	33.1	18.0
March, 1949 to March, 1950	18.5	18.9	17.9	25.0	16.8	17.9	18.7	18.1	27.8	17.6
April, 1950 to April, 1951	20.3	21.0	20.9	25.7	16.9	19.9	21.4	21.0	32.2	19.2
April, 1951 to April, 1952	19.2	20.3	20.2	23.3	14.4	18.9	19.7	19.5	28.4	18.5
April, 1952 to April, 1953	19.4	20.7	20.4	31.2	13.8	19.0	20.2	19.9	34.3	18.5
April, 1953 to April, 1954	18.2	19.4	18.3	27.6	13.0	17.9	19.1	18.4	30.1	17.3
April, 1954 to April, 1955	19.4	20.2	19.3	23.7	16.4	18.9	19.3	18.7	33.7	18.6
March, 1955 to March, 1956	20.0	21.1	19.9	33.2	15.3	19.6	20.2	19.6	34.4	19.2
April, 1956 to April, 1957	19.0	19.9	19.0	29.7	15.4	–	–	–	–	–
March, 1957 to March, 1958	19.7	20.6	18.8	31.7	16.1	–	–	–	–	–
Local movers										
April, 1940 to April, 1947	35.8	37.2	37.4	34.9	29.6	35.1	35.3	35.2	37.0	35.0
April, 1947 to April, 1948	13.5	14.3	14.0	16.9	10.0	13.2	14.8	14.6	19.5	12.5
April, 1948 to April, 1949	12.8	13.6	13.3	15.3	9.1	12.8	13.7	13.3	21.3	12.4
March, 1949 to March, 1950	12.6	13.4	12.9	17.4	9.3	12.7	13.9	13.6	17.6	12.2
April, 1950 to April, 1951	13.6	14.3	14.3	15.9	10.7	13.4	15.1	14.8	21.0	12.6
April, 1951 to April, 1952	12.7	13.8	13.7	14.5	8.0	12.8	14.2	14.2	14.5	12.2
April, 1952 to April, 1953	12.9	13.9	13.8	18.7	8.3	12.9	14.7	14.6	20.1	12.1
April, 1953 to April, 1954	11.9	12.8	12.5	14.9	7.8	11.6	13.4	13.0	20.1	10.7
April, 1954 to April, 1955	12.8	13.7	13.4	13.5	9.2	12.6	14.0	13.6	22.0	11.9

TABLE 6—Continued

March, 1955 to March, 1956	13.0	13.8	13.3	19.4	9.9	13.2	14.3	14.0	21.4	12.7
April, 1956 to April, 1957	12.7	13.5	13.1	19.3	9.7	—	—	—	—	—
March, 1957 to March, 1958	12.7	13.5	12.7	20.0	9.7	—	—	—	—	—
Migrants										
April, 1935 to April, 1940[a]	13.3	13.7	14.0	11.9	11.7	12.9	13.8	14.3	10.8	12.6
April, 1940 to April, 1947	20.7	21.0	20.5	25.0	19.0	20.6	21.4	21.2	28.8	20.3
April, 1947 to April, 1948	6.5	6.4	5.8	12.1	6.9	6.1	5.6	5.4	11.7	6.3
April, 1948 to April, 1949	6.0	5.8	5.4	8.8	7.2	5.3	4.7	4.3	11.8	5.6
March, 1949 to March, 1950	5.9	5.5	5.0	7.6	7.5	5.2	4.8	4.5	10.2	5.4
April, 1950 to April, 1951	6.6	6.7	6.6	9.8	6.2	6.5	6.3	6.1	11.2	6.6
April, 1951 to April, 1952	6.5	6.6	6.5	8.8	6.4	6.0	5.5	5.2	13.8	6.3
April, 1952 to April, 1953	6.5	6.7	6.6	12.5	5.5	6.1	5.5	5.3	14.2	6.4
April, 1953 to April, 1954	6.3	6.6	5.7	12.5	5.2	6.3	5.7	5.4	10.0	6.6
April, 1954 to April, 1955	6.6	6.5	5.9	10.2	7.2	6.3	5.3	5.0	11.7	6.7
March, 1955 to March, 1956	7.0	7.4	6.6	13.8	5.4	6.3	5.9	5.6	13.0	6.5
April, 1956 to April, 1957	6.2	6.4	5.9	10.4	5.7	—	—	—	—	—
March, 1957 to March, 1958	7.0	7.1	6.1	11.7	6.4	—	—	—	—	—

[a] Rates are based upon populations that include "Migration Status Not Reported."

SOURCE: U.S. Bureau of the Census, *Current Population Reports*, Series P-20, Nos. 14, 36, 39, 47, 49, 57, 61, 82, and 86; Series P-50, Nos. 10 and 20; and Sixteenth Census, *Economic Characteristics of Migrants*, 1935–40, Table 1.

TABLE 7. PER CENT OF THE CIVILIAN MALE POPULATION CLASSIFIED AS RESIDENTIALLY MOBILE, BY MAJOR OCCUPATION GROUP AND TYPE OF MOBILITY: 1940 TO 1956

(CIVILIAN POPULATION INCLUDES MEMBERS OF THE ARMED FORCES LIVING OFF POST AND WITH THEIR FAMILIES ON POST)

Type of Mobility and Mobility Interval	Total Employed Males	Major Occupation Group of the Employed Male								
		Professional, Technical, and Kindred Workers	Farmers and Farm Managers	Managers, Officials and Proprietors, except Farm	Clerical, Sales, and Kindred Workers	Craftsmen, Foremen, and Kindred Workers	Operatives and Kindred Workers	Service Workers	Farm Laborers, and Foremen	Laborers, except Farm and Mine
All Residential Mobility										
April, 1940 to April, 1947	57.9	64.1	46.3	56.8	58.4	59.3	61.8	57.7	55.7	59.9
April, 1947 to April, 1948	19.8	21.6	14.9	17.3	19.0	19.9	21.5	17.6	26.8	23.5
April, 1948 to April, 1949	18.7	22.0	11.7	14.4	20.6	16.8	21.8	17.5	25.8	23.1
March, 1949 to March, 1950	17.9	22.7	10.9	14.9	18.4	17.0	20.4	19.0	21.8	21.2
April, 1950 to April, 1951	21.0	22.5	11.8	17.7	21.0	21.7	23.8	18.6	26.3	24.7
April, 1951 to April, 1952[a]	–	–	–	–	–	–	–	–	–	–
April, 1952 to April, 1953[a]	–	–	–	–	–	–	–	–	–	–
April, 1953 to April, 1954[a]	–	–	–	–	–	–	–	–	–	–
April, 1954 to April, 1955[a]	–	–	–	–	–	–	–	–	–	–
March, 1955 to March, 1956[b]	16.6	16.9	8.0	15.1	14.8	15.3	19.7	17.2	26.9	17.5
Local Mover										
April, 1940 to April, 1947	37.4	31.7	31.1	35.1	38.9	38.6	41.8	38.8	34.2	38.6
April, 1947 to April, 1948	14.0	11.6	10.6	12.6	14.2	14.6	15.6	12.2	15.4	17.0
April, 1948 to April, 1949	13.3	12.1	7.8	10.4	14.6	12.6	16.7	12.8	16.1	16.5
March, 1949 to March, 1950	12.9	13.6	7.5	10.0	13.0	12.8	16.0	13.4	14.3	16.0
April, 1950 to April, 1951	14.3	12.6	7.1	13.3	14.4	14.5	16.7	14.2	12.4	18.5
April, 1951 to April, 1952[a]	–	–	–	–	–	–	–	–	–	–
April, 1952 to April, 1953[a]	–	–	–	–	–	–	–	–	–	–

TABLE 7—Continued

April, 1953 to April, 1954ᵃ	—	—	—	—	—	—	—	—	—	—
April, 1954 to April, 1955ᵃ	—	—	—	—	—	—	—	—	—	—
March, 1955 to March, 1956ᵇ	11.2	10.4	5.6	9.5	10.7	10.2	14.1	13.3	13.4	12.2
Migrants										
April, 1935 to April, 1940ᶜ	14.0	25.4	8.2	15.4	15.8	13.4	12.6	17.9	16.0	12.0
April, 1940 to April, 1947	20.5	32.4	15.2	21.7	19.5	20.7	20.0	18.9	21.5	21.3
April, 1947 to April, 1948	5.8	10.0	4.3	4.7	4.8	5.3	5.9	5.4	11.4	6.5
April, 1948 to April, 1949	5.4	9.9	3.9	4.0	6.0	4.2	5.1	4.7	9.7	6.6
March, 1949 to March, 1950	5.0	9.1	3.4	4.9	5.4	4.2	4.4	5.6	7.5	5.2
April, 1950 to April, 1951	6.7	9.9	4.6	4.3	6.5	7.2	7.1	4.5	13.9	6.2
April, 1951 to April, 1952ᵃ	—	—	—	—	—	—	—	—	—	—
April, 1952 to April, 1953ᵃ	—	—	—	—	—	—	—	—	—	—
April, 1953 to April, 1954ᵃ	—	—	—	—	—	—	—	—	—	—
April, 1954 to April, 1955ᵃ	—	—	—	—	—	—	—	—	—	—
March, 1955 to March, 1956ᵇ	5.4	6.5	2.4	5.5	4.2	5.2	5.5	4.0	13.4	5.2

ᵃ Information not tabulated.

ᵇ Information based upon males 20 to 64 years of age employed in March, 1956, who worked in 1955, by occupation group of longest job held in 1955. Data for clerical workers does not include sales workers.

ᶜ Rates are based upon populations that include "Migration Status Not Reported."

SOURCE: U.S. Bureau of the Census, *Current Population Reports*, Series P-20, Nos. 14, 36, 39, and 73; Series P-50, Nos. 10 and 20, and Sixteenth Census, *Economic Characteristics of Migrants*, 1935–40, Table 5.

transferring from a part-time to a full-time job. Persons who are not in the labor force are largely students, persons who are in ill health, housewives, and persons who have retired. Note that in Table 6 unemployed women are shown to be consistently more spatially mobile than unemployed men (the period 1935 to 1954 is an exception to this pattern). This difference could be a reflection of the fact that a higher proportion of the female than of the male labor force is concentrated in the younger ages, where mobility rates are highest. In general, employed persons have not tended to be exceptionally mobile, either locally or as migrants. Since employment status and labor force status are determined as of the *end* of the mobility interval, and no indication is given as to what these statuses were at the beginning of the interval, no decisive statement can be made either about the effect of mobility on employment status or the effect of employment status on migration. Scattered evidence does indicate that an above-average proportion of unemployed persons are in-migrants, in comparison with the general population, even after the factor of age is controlled. This may be due in part to the fact that some migrants had arrived so recently that they had not yet found a job when they were enumerated. During the period 1947 to 1958, unemployed persons of both sexes had higher rates of migration, as well as higher rates of local moving, than employed persons. This was a reversal of the situation prevailing in the 1935 to 1940 period, when the unemployed were comparatively less migratory. Those persons who are not in the labor force have also shown a surprisingly high degree of migration in recent years, in comparison with earlier years. The differences between the two periods may be accounted for in part by differences in the length of the time intervals, but it is also reasonable to assume that the unfavorable economic conditions between 1935 and 1940 may have discouraged jobless persons from migrating.

Occupational Differences. Men and women are so unlike in their occupational composition, and so unlike with respect to their mobility in the several occupational groups, that the mobility of each occupational group is analyzed separately for each sex. Statistics concerning the mobility of employed workers in each occupational group are available for six intervals, covering the years 1940 to 1951 and 1955 to 1956. Table 7 presents the rates for male workers and Table 8 presents those for female workers.

(a) *Males:* One of the most mobile segments of the employed male population is that portion whose members are in professional or semiprofessional occupations. Since 1940, laborers (both farm and nonfarm) and operatives have also shown above-average mobility. The above-average mobility of operatives and of nonfarm laborers is due to a higher rate of local movement. Farm laborers are one of the most migratory of all occupational groups. The least mobile occupational group (with respect to both local mobility and migration) is comprised of farmers and farm managers. Proprietors, managers, and officials also tend to have below-average mobility, as an occupational group.

As was found to be true of educational-attainment groups, occupational groups also vary with respect to kind of mobility. Operatives, service workers, and laborers consistently have had higher rates of moving than the general

TABLE 8. PER CENT OF THE CIVILIAN FEMALE POPULATION CLASSIFIED AS RESIDENTIALLY MOBILE, BY MAJOR OCCUPATION GROUP AND TYPE OF MOBILITY: 1940 TO 1955 (CIVILIAN POPULATION INCLUDES MEMBERS OF THE ARMED FORCES LIVING OFF POST AND WITH THEIR FAMILIES ON POST)

Type of Mobility and Mobility Interval	Total Employed Females	Major Occupation Group of the Employed Female									
		Professional, Technical, Kindred Workers	Farmers and Farm Managers	Managers, Officials, Proprietors, Exc. Farm	Clerical, Sales, and Kindred Workers	Craftsmen, Foremen, and Kindred Workers	Operatives and Kindred Workers	Private Household Workers	Service Workers	Farm Laborers and Foremen	Laborers, except Farm and Mine
All Residential Mobility											
April, 1940 to April, 1947	56.4	57.0	36.3	54.9	55.6	52.2	56.7	59.1	62.5	47.6	56.4
April, 1947 to April, 1948	20.0	21.7	14.2	17.0	19.9	9.2	19.0	–	23.4	15.5	–
April, 1948 to April, 1949	17.6	21.8	6.3	13.3	16.9	12.1	14.8	–	23.6	8.8	–
March, 1949 to March, 1950	18.1	18.3	5.5	14.2	19.1	10.3	17.4	21.0	19.7	11.4	–
April, 1950 to April, 1951	21.4	25.0	18.3	17.3	21.5	20.0	19.4	–	27.0	13.0	–
April, 1951 to April, 1952a	–	–	–	–	–	–	–	–	–	–	–
April, 1952 to April, 1953a	–	–	–	–	–	–	–	–	–	–	–
April, 1953 to April, 1954a	–	–	–	–	–	–	–	–	–	–	–
April, 1954 to April, 1955a	–	–	–	–	–	–	–	–	–	–	–
Local Movers											
April, 1940 to April, 1947	35.2	24.8	25.7	35.0	34.8	37.1	38.6	39.1	38.6	30.6	29.5
April, 1947 to April, 1948	14.6	11.2	10.6	11.9	15.0	5.4	15.6	–	16.6	11.4	16.5
April, 1948 to April, 1949	13.3	13.6	4.2	9.5	12.8	9.7	12.6	–	17.8	6.2	–
March, 1949 to March, 1950	13.6	12.2	4.4	11.0	14.9	8.1	14.0	15.7	14.0	8.0	–
April, 1950 to April, 1951	15.1	15.3	6.7	11.4	15.0	13.6	15.8	–	17.8	8.8	–
April, 1951 to April, 1952a	–	–	–	–	–	–	–	–	–	–	–
April, 1952 to April, 1953a	–	–	–	–	–	–	–	–	–	–	–
April, 1953 to April, 1954a	–	–	–	–	–	–	–	–	–	–	–
April, 1954 to April, 1955a	–	–	–	–	–	–	–	–	–	–	–
Migrants											
April, 1935 to April, 1940b	14.3	23.9	5.7	12.9	11.8	8.9	7.8	17.9	18.1	9.9	11.0
April, 1940 to April, 1947	21.2	32.2	10.6	19.9	20.8	15.1	18.1	20.0	23.9	17.0	26.9
April, 1947 to April, 1948	5.4	10.5	3.6	5.1	4.9	3.8	3.4	–	6.8	4.1	–
April, 1948 to April, 1949	4.3	8.2	2.1	3.8	4.1	2.4	2.2	–	5.8	2.6	–
March, 1949 to March, 1950	4.5	6.1	1.1	3.2	4.2	2.2	2.4	–	5.7	3.4	–
April, 1950 to April, 1951	6.3	9.7	11.5	5.9	6.5	6.4	3.6	5.3	9.2	4.2	–
April, 1951 to April, 1952a	–	–	–	–	–	–	–	–	–	–	–
April, 1952 to April, 1953a	–	–	–	–	–	–	–	–	–	–	–
April, 1953 to April, 1954a	–	–	–	–	–	–	–	–	–	–	–
April, 1954 to April, 1955a	–	–	–	–	–	–	–	–	–	–	–

a Information not tabulated.

b Rates are based upon populations that include "Migration Status Not Reported."

SOURCE: U.S. Bureau of the Census, *Current Population Reports*, Series P-20, Nos. 14, 36, 39; Series P-50, Nos. 10 and 20, and Sixteenth Census, *Economic Characteristics of Migrants, 1935–40*, Table 5.

population. Professional, proprietary, and managerial occupations, on the other hand, have had lower-than-average rates of moving. Clerical workers, and craftsmen and foremen, have shown about average local mobility. In summary, the high total mobility of the professional group results from a high rate of migration. The high mobility of the laborer group derives from moderately high rates of both moving and migration. Farm operators and farm managers have low rates with respect to both types of mobility. Clerical workers and craftsmen have about average rates for both types of mobility. Operatives have lower-than-average rates of migration, but higher-than-average rates of local movement.

These inter-occupational differences are probably, in part, a reflection of the differences in the average age of members of the particular occupational groups involved. The pattern of differences probably varies also with changing economic conditions. For example, laborers were much less migratory during the period 1935 to 1940, in comparison with the other occupation groups, than they were in the period 1940 to 1950.

(b) *Females:* Among women workers, there has been a higher proportion of mobility in the service and the professional occupations than in the other occupations. Female service workers have been both more migratory and more locally mobile than has the employed female population generally. Professional female workers, like professional male workers, have been much more migratory but considerably less locally mobile than the employed population as a whole. Women craft and operative workers tend to have about average local mobility, but low rates of migration. Apparently, the women who are employed in these latter types of work are recruited locally, or else do not move a great distance

TABLE 9. MEDIAN INCOME OF THE CIVILIAN LABOR FORCE, BY MOBILITY STATUS, AGE, AND SEX FOR THE UNITED STATES: MARCH, 1949 TO MARCH, 1950

Sex and Type of Mobility	Median Income, by Age			
	All Ages[1]	14 to 24 Years	25 to 44 Years	45 to 64 Years
Male, total	$2,536	$1,334	$2,864	$2,685
Nonmobile	2,578	1,240	2,900	2,732
Local mover	2,456	1,809	2,762	2,393
Migrant	2,071	1,343	2,621	1,813
Female, total	$1,467	$1,191	$1,650	$1,483
Nonmobile	1,505	1,239	1,676	1,511
Local mover	1,417	1,240	1,646	1,231
Migrant	947	831	1,176	(2)

[1] Includes civilian labor force of all ages, including those 65 years of age and over.
[2] No data reported.
SOURCE: U.S. Bureau of the Census, *Current Population Reports*, Series P-20, No. 36, Table 9.

to take these kinds of jobs. Female workers in clerical occupations tend to have average mobility, both locally and as migrants.

Income Differences. As yet, only scanty data are available concerning the incomes received by mobile and nonmobile persons. The evidence presented in Table 9, based on a single survey, leads to the hypothesis that among adult workers 25 years of age and over, the median income of mobile workers is smaller than the income of nonmobile workers. This seemed to be the case among both the male and the female workers. Migrants had a smaller median income than movers, and movers, in turn, had a smaller median income than the nonmobile population. Thus, these data suggest that an inverse relationship may exist between degree of mobility and average size of income. Much of this difference could be accounted for by the younger average age of migrants (incomes are lower among younger workers), but since this relationship persists within each of two broad age groups, 20 to 44 years and 45 to 64 years, the difference is probably not due solely to the different age compositions of the various income groups. However, this need not force one to conclude that moving or migration has the effect of reducing income. It should be kept in mind that the migration-interval and the earnings-interval both refer to the same span of time—the year preceding enumeration. The mobile person may lose his job and then move, or he may move because of low earnings. Both the loss of income and the movement may be indirect consequences of unemployment. In addition, if moving requires a person to be off work, it can act to reduce his income. On the other hand, these data do not give any evidence that movement acts to increase earnings, at least within the year of the move. Whether movement eventually tends to increase earnings cannot be determined by means of these data.

Differences in Marital Status. Data concerning differences in mobility according to marital status categories, with a necessary control on age, have been published in two Current Population Surveys. Evidence for two age classes, summarized in Table 10, indicates that unmarried persons tended to be less residentially mobile than married, widowed, or divorced persons. Divorced persons were found to be more mobile than widowed persons, and widowed persons more mobile than married persons. The direction of cause and effect cannot be determined here in all cases. The act of marrying involves mobility for at least one member of each couple. On the other hand, it is possible that purchasing a home, moving to a larger house or apartment, or moving to the suburbs may cause married persons to be more locally mobile, age-for-age, than single persons. On the other hand, it is also possible that persons who have migrated as unmarried persons tend to marry at an earlier age than nonmigrants.[3] *Summary:* There is great variation within the population in degree of mobility—both local movement and migration. There are variations associated with sex, color, age, educational attainment, employment status, occupation, income, and

[3] The Current Population Survey Report, Series P-20, No. 82, also contains data for the year 1956–57; these data indicate patterns very similar to those discussed here for the year 1948. The 1948 data are given because they report more detail both for age and for marital status.

TABLE 10. Percent of the Civilian Population Classified as Residentially Mobile, by Type of Mobility and Marital Status, for Two Age Groups: 1948

Age Period and Type of Mobility	Total	Single	Married	Widowed	Divorced
			Marital Status		
1947 to 1948					
25–34 years old					
Total mobility	27.4	14.9	30.0	21.8	32.1
Movers	18.8	8.7	20.9	12.3	21.0
Migrants	8.6	6.2	9.1	9.5	11.1
35–44 years old					
Total mobility	17.6	15.3	17.3	22.8	31.3
Movers	11.9	8.9	11.9	15.5	21.0
Migrants	5.7	6.4	5.4	7.3	10.3

Source: U.S. Bureau of the Census, *Current Population Reports*, Series P-20, No. 22.

marital status. These differences tend to be patterned, and to persist year after year. Differential local mobility is not always identical with differential migration mobility, either in pattern or intensity. In many instances, local movement seems to be a poor man's substitute for migration. Persons toward the lower end of the socio-economic scale seem to move locally under certain circumstances which would cause persons higher in the socio-economic scale to migrate. . . .

Trends in Negro Residential Segregation

KARL TAEUBER

Residential segregation of whites and nonwhites effects their separation in schools, hospitals, libraries, parks, stores, and other institutions without legal or direct discrimination. Reviewing these interrelations, Myrdal noted that "residential segregation is basic in a mechanical sense."[1]

The differentiation of residential areas according to the skin color or racial designation of the occupants is but one particular form of the differentiation and segregation of urban land uses. It is necessary to distinguish carefully between this perspective and the more customary approaches in the race relations literature. To oversimplify somewhat, the distinction is between the behavioral processes involved in the allocation of residences on a racially segregated basis,

Reprinted from *Social Problems*, 12 (Summer, 1964), pp. 42–50, by permission of its authors and the publisher, the Society for the Study of Social Problems.

[1] Gunnar Myrdal, *An American Dilemma*, New York: Harper and Brothers, 1944, Vol. I, p. 618.

and the spatially segregated distribution of residences resulting from these behaviors. This paper focuses on the degree to which whites and nonwhites were residentially segregated from each other in a number of cities at several points in time. Like other studies which have attempted to measure residential segregation, segregation is viewed in terms of quantifiable results rather than in terms of the social, psychological, and economic forces producing the observed pattern. . . .

FINDINGS

Indexes of residential segregation between whites and nonwhites have been computed for 109 cities for which the basic data were available for 1940, 1950, and 1960, and which at the beginning of the period, in 1940, contained more than 1,000 nonwhite occupied dwelling units. One basic fact stands out in examination of the computed index values: There is pronounced residential segregation between whites and nonwhites in all cities with sizable Negro populations. The indexes range in value from 60.1 to 98.0 for all three years.* In each year, between one-fourth and one-half of these 109 cities had index values above 90.0, and more than three-fourths had values above 80.0. It can be shown that these values are far higher than could occur by chance under a null hypothesis of no relationship between race and residence. More significantly, indexes for white-nonwhite segregation are far higher than similar indexes for various immigrant groups against native whites,[2] or for various occupational groups against each other.[3] Racial residential segregation is clearly more pronounced than class or ethnic residential segregation, and it is a universal feature of American urban society.

The research strategy for this analysis is comparative, and derives from the focus on racial residential segregation as one aspect of differential urban land use. Two basic questions are posed: What accounts for the variation between cities in the degree of residential segregation at any given point in time? What accounts for the variation between cities in the direction and magnitude of changes over time in the degree of residential segregation?

Average segregation index values for various groupings of cities for 1940 and 1960, along with the average changes in index values, during each of the two intercensal periods, are presented in Table 1. The top row of this table summarizes the average performance for the entire set of cities. At the start of the period, the average value was 85.2, a very high level. During the 1940's the average value increased by 2.0 points; during the 1950's declines wiped out many of the earlier increases, leaving the average in 1960 only a fraction higher than 20 years before.

* [The material describing the construction of the index is not included—Editor.]

[2] Otis Dudley Duncan and Stanley Lieberson, "Ethnic Segregation and Assimilation," *American Journal of Sociology*, LXIV (January, 1959), pp. 364–374.

[3] Otis Dudley Duncan and Beverly Duncan, "Residential Distribution and Occupational Stratification," *American Journal of Sociology*," LX (March, 1955), pp. 493–503.

TABLE 1. Average Values of Indexes of Residential Segregation for Cities Grouped by Region, Percentage Nonwhite, and City Size, 1940 and 1960, and Changes, 1940–1950 and 1950–1960

City Grouping	Number of Cities	Average Values of Indexes			
		1940	Change 1940–50	Change 1950–60	1960
All cities[a]	109	85.2	+2.0	−1.2	86.1
Region					
Northeast	25	83.2	+0.4	−4.7	78.9
North Central	29	88.4	+1.5	−1.5	88.4[a]
West	10	82.7	+0.3	−6.5	76.4
South	45	85.0	+3.7	+2.2	90.7
S. Atlantic	22	87.0	+1.9	+1.9	90.6
E. S. Central	9	85.0	+3.2	+3.1	91.2
W. S. Central	14	81.7	+6.8	+2.0	90.5
Percentage nonwhite, 1940					
1.2— 4.2	22	84.8	+0.4	−4.4	80.8
4.4— 8.0	22	84.6	+1.3	−3.9	81.9
8.2—12.9	22	84.8	+1.9	−1.9	84.8
14.4—27.5	22	86.4	+3.6	+1.0	91.1
28.5—48.6	21	85.5	+3.1	+3.4	92.0
City size (in thousands), 1940					
46— 69	22	83.8	+2.5	+0.6	86.8
71— 111	22	83.7	+2.8	−0.9	85.6
112— 178	22	86.6	+1.7	−2.2	86.1
193— 368	22	84.9	+2.7	−1.1	86.5
385—7,455	21	87.2	+0.5	−2.4	85.3

Interrelationships[b]

Region	Size	Percent Nonwhite		1940	Change 1940–50	Change 1950–60	1960
North	Small	Low	20	82.9	+0.6	−4.6	78.9
North	Small	High	8	86.9	+2.2	−2.0	87.1
North	Large	Low	29	86.3	+0.8	−3.6	83.4
North	Large	High	7	87.7	+1.1	−2.2	86.6
South	Small	Low	3	80.8	+2.6	+1.7	85.2
South	Small	High	26	84.9	+3.7	+2.2	90.8
South	Large	Low	2	82.0	+6.5	+0.2	88.6
South	Large	High	14	86.1	+3.4	+2.5	91.9

[a] All cities for which census block data are available for 1940, 1950, and 1960, and which in 1940 contained more than 1,000 nonwhite households.

[b] Size as of 1940; small, less than 150,000; large, above 150,000. Percentage nonwhite as of 1940; low, less than 10.0 per cent; high, 10.0 per cent or above.

Region. Trends in the size, social status, and composition of Negro urban populations differ between North, South, and West. Regional groupings thus provide a logical starting point for the analysis of inter-city variations in residential segregation. Using the four census regions, in 1940 the North Central cities had, on the average, a greater degree of residential segregation between whites and nonwhites than the other three regions, whose average index values were similar to one another. Within the South, however, there was geographic differentiation, with cities along the Atlantic coast tending to have higher index values than cities farther west, particularly those in Texas.

The changes between 1940 and 1960 altered the rank order and increased the differences between the regions. The average for the western cities declined during each decade, so that by 1960 cities in the West had the lowest average segregation index values. The large numbers of Chinese, Japanese, Filipinos, and Indians in the nonwhite populations of some western cities together with the very rapid rates of growth of Negro population probably contribute to the differentiation of the West from the other regions. Cities in the Northeast had very slight increases during the 1940's, and sizable average declines during the 1950's, so that by 1960 northeastern cities had the second lowest average values. North Central cities, which started out at higher levels, had larger increases during the 1940's and smaller decreases during the 1950's than either the Northeast or the West, and in 1960 the region was only a little below its 1940 position. However, it was no longer the top-ranking region, for the South had larger increases than the other regions during the 1940's, and was the only region to register average increases during the 1950's. By 1960, residential segregation was more pronounced in southern cities than in those of any other region. Within the South, those cities which had been lowest had the largest gains during the 20 year period, so that there was little geographic variation within the South in 1960.

Percentage Nonwhite. An extensive literature on prejudice and discrimination suggests the relevance of the "visibility" of a group to the perceived threat it arouses.[4] Regardless of specific behavioral mechanisms, there is ample reason to expect the relative size of a minority population to be related to its social position. In 1940, nonwhites comprised small percentages of the population in most western and northern cities and much larger percentages in most southern cities.

The relationship between percentage nonwhite in 1940 and average segregation index value, shown in Table 1, is slight, but systematic changes during the two intercensal periods produced a clear-cut pattern by 1960. During the 1940's the cities with the lowest percentages nonwhite registered the smallest increases in index values, and during the 1950's these cities registered the largest decreases. By 1960 there was a direct relationship between the two variables, so that the higher the percentage nonwhite, the higher the degree of residential segregation. Percentage nonwhite in 1940, however, is closely related to region. If the classification is made as of 1960, when many northern cities had large percentages of nonwhites in their populations, the association between percentage nonwhite and the degree of residential segregation is negligible.

City Size. It is sometimes assumed that the spatial differentiation of urban areas increases with city size[5] and, in particular, that Negroes are more rigidly segregated in the largest cities. As of 1940, however, city size appeared to have

[4] Gordon W. Allport, *The Nature of Prejudice*, Cambridge, Mass. Addison-Wesley, 1954.
[5] Amos H. Hawley, *Human Ecology*, New York: The Ronald Press, 1950, pp. 122–123.

an inverse relationship with the level of residential segregation. Changes during the two intercensal periods were not systematic, and by 1960 there was little variation in segregation by city size.

Interrelationships. Region, percentage nonwhite, and city size are not independent of each other, but are badly confounded. The bottom panel of Table 1 presents an abbreviated cross-classification of these three variables. Region stands out as the most significant factor with respect to the changes. Percentage nonwhite retains significance: Within most of the region and size groupings, cities with the lower percentages nonwhite have the lower average segregation index values, and the smaller increases or larger decreases over time. Within region and percentage nonwhite groupings, there remains a small positive relationship between city size and segregation index values, but there is no systematic variation in the changes over time.

DISCUSSION

Substantively, the most interesting finding of this research is the universally high degree of residential segregation between whites and Negroes within the cities of the United States. Whether a city is in the North, South, or West; whether it is a large metropolitan center or a suburb; whether it is a coastal resort town, a rapidly growing industrial center, or a declining mining town; whether nonwhites constitute forty per cent of the population or less than one per cent; in every case white and Negro residences are highly segregated from each other. There is no need for cities to vie with each other for the title of "most segregated city"; there is room at the top for all of them! . . .

Additional Readings

POPULATION

DONALD J. BOGUE, "Population Growth in the United States," in Philip M. Hauser (ed.), *The Population Dilemma* (Englewood Cliffs, N.J.: Prentice-Hall, Inc., 1963), pp. 70–93.

KINGSLEY DAVIS, "Population," *Scientific American*, 209 (September, 1963), pp. 62–71.

PHILIP M. HAUSER, "The Census of 1960," *Scientific American*, 205 (July, 1961), pp. 39–45.

PHILIP M. HAUSER, "More from the Census of 1960," *Scientific American*, 207 (October, 1962), pp. 30–37.

PHILIP M. HAUSER, *Population Perspectives* (New Brunswick, N.J.: Rutgers University Press, 1960), pp. 3–63.

CARMEN A. MIRÓ, "The Population of Twentieth Century Latin America," in J. Mayone Stycos and Jorge Arias (eds.), *Population Dilemma in Latin America* (Washington, D.C.: Potomac Book, Inc., 1966), pp. 1–10.

IRENE B. TAEUBER, "Population Growth in Underdeveloped Areas," in Philip M. Hauser (ed.), *The Population Dilemma* (Englewood Cliffs, N.J.: Prentice-Hall, Inc., 1963), pp. 29–45.

ECOLOGY

IRWIN KATZ, "Review of Evidence Relating to Effects of Desegregation on the Intellectual Performance of Negroes," *American Psychologist*, 19 (June, 1964), pp. 381–399.

CHARLES C. MOSKOS, Jr., "Racial Integration in the Armed Forces," *American Journal of Sociology*, 72 (September, 1966), pp. 132–148.

ERNEST RUBIN, "The Demography of Immigration to the United States," *The Annals: The American Academy of Political and Social Science*, 367 (September, 1966), pp. 15–22.